7.44 - B+T 1-67 (Kauffman)

Fisher Ames

FEDERALIST AND STATESMAN

1758-1808

*The Institute of Early American History and Culture
is sponsored jointly by the College of William and Mary
and Colonial Williamsburg, Incorporated.*

Winner of the Institute Manuscript Award

Fisher Ames

FEDERALIST AND STATESMAN
1758-1808

by WINFRED E. A. BERNHARD

Published for
the INSTITUTE OF EARLY AMERICAN HISTORY AND CULTURE
at Williamsburg, Virginia
by THE UNIVERSITY OF NORTH CAROLINA PRESS · *Chapel Hill*

To Betty

*Whose perceptiveness and understanding
have made this book possible*

Preface

This first full length biography of Fisher Ames grew out of my discovery that a leading Federalist statesman had been historically neglected. A representative from Massachusetts, Ames gained a national reputation during Washington's presidency as an exceptionally able legislator and as the most brilliant orator in Congress. In promoting Federalist policies in the House, he plunged into controversy, becoming the principal rival of James Madison. Forced to cut short his public career because of chronic illness, Ames continued to be an articulate spokesman for his party in the remaining years of his life. He retained his influence among Federalists largely through the force of his personality and through his polemical writings. Following his death, Ames the orator remained unchallenged, while Ames the arch Federalist was the object of vehement approval or criticism. With the demise of the party, his image became obscure. Few but historians recalled that he had existed.

In general, those who interpreted Ames from a positive point of view for nineteenth-century journals, praised him indiscriminately. The opposition was equally unrestrained in condemning him. Henry Adams, perpetuating his family's hostility to the extreme Federalists, analyzed Ames as one whose "best political writing was saturated with the despair of the tomb to which his wasting body was condemned." In the twentieth century, Vernon Parrington, surveying the American mind, elaborated the theme of a pessimistic politician who was antithetical to the main stream of the nation's development. His mordant essay on Ames did not go beyond delineating him as a prejudiced Jeremiah whose greatest pleasure was to belabor democracy and to predict the triumph of the unthinking mob. Not until Samuel Eliot Morison characterized Fisher Ames as keenly intelligent, colorful, and witty, albeit inflexible, did he begin to seem human. In spite of this broader view of the orator, the Adams interpretation has lingered in the minds of historians.

The picture of Ames as one of the most depressed members of the party, which first became unpopular with and then anathema to the majority, has obviously discouraged a comprehensive study of him. Furthermore, his congressional career was abbreviated and one of his greatest gifts was in the realm of oratory, where a man, his audience, and the milieu are inevitably ephemeral. Even though his speeches and remarks in debate have been preserved, the authentic moments of delivery have passed and with them some of the drama of reality. A scarcity of personal letters and papers has also militated against thorough historical investigation.

Few prominent men of the early national period have been quoted more frequently than has Fisher Ames. His astringent comments on national affairs, taken out of context, have become at times the sum total of the public's knowledge of the man. To analyze him merely on the basis of his political position is to over-simplify a complex personality. In this biography, I have intentionally avoided regarding Ames as a stereotype. I have tried to deal with him as an individual, one whose contribution to the new government should neither be expanded nor negated. It has been my purpose to discover the nature of his role in American history.

In writing the book, I have been helped in significant ways by certain historians and friends. While at Columbia University, Professor Dumas Malone stimulated my interest in Federalist and Jeffersonian America. His guidance and criticism when the manuscript was in its formative stages were of great value to me. Professor Richard B. Morris of Columbia University not only gave me the benefit of his expert advice at crucial points, but also showed an enthusiasm for this study which influenced me to complete it.

The Director of the Massachusetts Historical Society, Dr. Stephen T. Riley, was especially helpful and drew my attention to various collections among the Society's wealth of manuscripts. Mrs. Edward S. Baker and Miss Marion Conant graciously made the holdings of the Dedham Historical Society available, often keeping the library open beyond regular hours to facilitate my work. Professor Donald Gillin of Duke University and Professor Glenn E. Tinder of Lake Forest College read portions of the manuscript and aided me with critical evaluations. In their editorial capacities, Lester J. Cappon, James Morton Smith, and Robert J. Taylor of the Institute of Early American History and Culture generously gave of their time and effort during the process of preparing the book for the press.

Of the many librarians who furthered my research by ferreting out material, those at Duke University Library, the Goodell Library of the University of Massachusetts, and the Amherst College Library gave me substantial assistance. Jones Library in Amherst provided me with a study room for which I am grateful. The Ames project was completed under a grant from the Research Council of the University of Massachusetts. In typing the final manuscript, Mrs. Charles Holden rendered real service both through her cooperation and her precision.

For permission to quote from original manuscripts, I would like to acknowledge my obligation to the directors and officials of the following depositories: the Adams Manuscript Trust, the American Antiquarian Society, the American Philosophical Society, the Boston Public Library, Columbia University, the Connecticut Historical Society, the Dedham Historical Society, Harvard University, Marietta College, the Massachusetts Historical Society, the Pierpont Morgan Library, the New-York Historical Society, the New York Public Library, the New York Society Library, the New York State Library, the University of North Carolina Library, the Historical Society of Pennsylvania, and the University of Virginia. I am indebted to the Honorable Henry Cabot Lodge for his permission to reproduce the portrait of Fisher Ames by Gilbert Stuart which is in the Henry Cabot Lodge Collection.

I deeply appreciate the encouragement which my parents, Senta H. Bernhard and the late Hermann R. L. Bernhard gave me in undertaking this study. For the continuing interest shown by Mary C. and Edward Kromer, I am particularly grateful. Finally, this book could not go to press without an acknowledgment of the fact that my small daughter, Elizabeth, has often encouraged me by her omnipresence.

Winfred E. A. Bernhard

Amherst, Massachusetts
March 1965

Table of Contents

List of Illustrations

Fisher Ames

FEDERALIST AND STATESMAN
1758-1808

Chapter I

Fisher Ames: Inheritance and Childhood

In midsummer of 1770 Fisher Ames rode from his native Dedham, Massachusetts, to Cambridge in order to appear before the President and tutors of Harvard College. He was only twelve years of age; but he was applying for admission to the freshman class. The decision to go to college was only partly his own. His forceful mother was aware that he was precocious and had made up her mind that he should follow his older brothers to Harvard. Through her efforts he had secured a sound early education which included a thorough knowledge of Latin and an understanding of the world of antiquity and classical literature. The Reverend Jason Haven, the Congregational minister at Dedham, had often guided his studies and now believed that his student was fully prepared for college. With a facile mind and intellectual ambition, young Ames was ready to compete in the academic milieu of Harvard.[1]

Fisher Ames was a member of a family long settled in New England. His paternal ancestors had come from the charming English town of Bruton, situated in the undulating countryside of eastern Somerset near the headwaters of the Brue River. They were of the yeoman class, living in an agricultural and weaving region where the inhabitants cherished a history dating from the Norman Conquest. In the mid 1630's, William

---

1. *Boston Evening Post*, June 18, 1770; J. T. Kirkland, "Memoir of the Life of Fisher Ames" in Seth Ames, ed., *Works of Fisher Ames*, 2 vols. (Boston, 1854), I, 4; "A Memoir of the Late Honorable Fisher Ames," *The Diocesan Register and New England Calendar for ... 1812* (Dedham, 1811), 238.

and John, sons of John and Cyprian Ames, emigrated to New England, each establishing his home in settlements south of Boston. The older brother, William, born in Bruton in 1605, was to be the great-great-grandfather of Fisher Ames. Although John had no descendants, he played an important role in the family destiny.[2]

The brothers' departure from strongly royalist Bruton in a period of increasing controversy to settle in Puritan and Separatist communities may have reflected their political and religious outlook. There is some indication, however, that John may have been forced to flee from Bruton for other reasons. Several years after he settled in Plymouth Colony, rumors circulated that he had "come out of England for stealeing of a calf." At the General Court of March 13, 1645, Thomas Hayward made a formal deposition that James Torey had stated "it was so commonly reported in the shipp that they came ouer together in." Hayward further testified that Torey had "made no question but he could prove what he had sayd." Yet when John Ames brought a complaint against Torey in an action of slander before the General Court, the defendant pleaded that he did not have witnesses ready, and the case was postponed. Since the records contain no further reference to the suit, it was evidently dropped. At least the unconfirmed reports did not stand in John's way when on October 20, 1645, he married Elizabeth Hayward, apparently the sister of his accuser.[3]

After his arrival in New England, William settled in Braintree in southeastern Massachusetts Bay Colony, where he became an iron worker and farmer. In this community he rose to a respected position and was named freeman in 1647. He and his wife, Hannah, reared a family of five daughters and one son, John. Upon his death on January 11, 1654, William's entire estate, valued at £45 11s, was left to his wife as administratrix in behalf of herself and the children. It consisted of a house and among other items, "2 Young Cattle, 3 Swine, 1 Bible, Tubbs, 1 Pot and hangers, 1 Anvill," and "1 Cubbard and a pail." [4]

2. Fisher Ames, *A Bit of Ames Genealogy* (n.p., 1898), 3; Ellis Ames, *Ames Genealogical Chart* (Canton, Mass., 1851); Winthrop Ames, *The Ames Family of Easton, Massachusetts* (privately printed, 1938), 2-3, 16, 201-3; Alden Ames, *The History of the Family of Ames* (privately printed, 1957), 1; Douglas L. Hayward, *The Registers of Bruton, County Somerset, 1554-1680* (London, 1908), 6, 12; W.B.T., "Some Account of Dr. Nathaniel Ames and His Family," *New England Historical and Genealogical Register*, 16 (1862), 255. In the Bruton, Somerset, Parish Church there is a memorial window in honor of the brothers; Basil H. Lloyd-Orwell to the author, Winchester, Eng., Mar. 29, 1958.
3. Winthrop Ames, *Ames Family*, 12, 202-3; Nathaniel Shurtleff, ed., *Records of the Colony of New Plymouth in New England*, 12 vols. (Boston, 1855-61), II, 80, 168, VII, 39; Nahum Mitchell, *History of the Early Settlement of Bridgewater ...Massachusetts* (Bridgewater, Mass., 1897), 98, 181.
4. Nathaniel Shurtleff, ed., *Records of the Governor and Company of the Massachusetts Bay*, 5 vols. (Boston, 1853-54), II, 295; Lucius R. Paige, ed., "List of Freemen," *New Eng. Hist. and Geneal. Register*, 3 (1849), 191, 637; "Inventory

Having no children of their own, Elizabeth and John Ames took a particular interest in their nephew, John, who was left fatherless in his seventh year. They had first lived in the coastal community of Duxbury, but in 1656 they settled in Bridgewater, where John was an original proprietor. This frontier "plantation" of Plymouth Colony subsequently became the home of several generations of the Ames family. John achieved a measure of local prominence as a landholder and town official, serving at various times as constable and surveyor of highways, and on one occasion being entrusted with the duty of raising the minister's salary "by all loving persuasions and legal means." [5]

When young John reached maturity, his uncle granted him thirty acres of upland and a piece of meadow land from his own holdings, a first step in the ultimate transfer of all of his property to his nephew. Sarah Willis, a daughter of Deacon John Willis, gave the younger Ames another reason to remain in Bridgewater. They were married early in the 1670's and John quickly established himself as a farmer, taking as active a part as his uncle in community affairs. During the crucial period of King Philip's War in 1675, when imminent Indian attacks convinced the inhabitants that "God hath now begun to pour out ... the cup of trembling," John Ames II was one of the most active defenders of Bridgewater. In an encounter with the Indians, he distinguished himself by saving his companions from capture by the enemy.[6]

Among the eight children of Sarah and John Ames was Nathaniel, born in 1677. A worker in the local mill and an iron master, Nathaniel must have served in the militia, for he became known to townspeople as Captain Ames. When he was twenty-five he married Susanna Haward, whose grandfather, John Haward, had been an original settler of Bridgewater. Susanna and Nathaniel's first child, the father of Fisher Ames, was born on July 22, 1708, and was christened Nathaniel.[7]

---

of the Goods of William Ames, dec.," Fisher Ames Papers, Dedham Historical Society, Dedham, Mass.; Samuel A. Bates, ed., *Records of the Town of Braintree, 1643-1793* (Randolph, Mass., 1886), 637; William B. Trask, ed., "Abstracts From the Earliest Wills on Record in the County of Suffolk, Massachusetts," *New Eng. Hist. and Geneal. Register,* 9 (1855), 142.

5. Mitchell, *History of Bridgewater,* 10-11, 65; Shurtleff, *Records of New Plymouth,* II, 168, III, 48, 101, 136, IV, 183, V, 36, 58.

6. Winthrop Ames, *Ames Family,* 42; Mitchell, *History of Bridgewater,* 62; the Rev. James Keith to Gov. Thomas Hinckeley, Apr. 17, 1676, *ibid.,* 38; Nahum Mitchell, "A Description of Bridgewater, 1818," Massachusetts Historical Society, *Collections,* 2d Ser., 7 (1826), 157. For the causes of King Philip's War and the military events, see Douglas E. Leach, *Flintlock and Tomahawk: New England in King Philip's War* (New York, 1958), and Herbert L. Osgood, *The American Colonies in the 17th Century,* 3 vols. (N.Y., 1904-7), I, 520-78.

7. The name was spelled Haward until the end of the 17th century; thereafter it became Howard. Mitchell, *History of Bridgewater,* 98, 99, 197, 409; Winthrop Ames, *Ames Family,* 203; Josiah Edson, "Memorandum Book," Bridgewater, N.Y.,

In spite of the limitations of education in a rural community, Nathaniel II developed wide interests under the influence of a father who stimulated his intellectual curiosity. When Nathaniel I died in 1736, his son wrote an ode, reflecting his deep respect for his father:

> I, in his arms from Evening Dews preserv'd.
> The wandering Glories overhead observ'd.
>
> . . . .
>
> When puzzled, I could unto him repair,
> Who knew the Heav'ns as if he had dwelt there:
>
> . . . .
>
> Bear the Deceas'd upon thy Wings, O, Fame
> Among th' *Astronomers* give him a Name:
> For if *Pythagoras* believ'd had been,
> Men might have thought great *Newton's* soul in him.[8]

The legacy of the early members of the Ames family in New England was modest in material goods, but cultivation of the mind became part of the heritage. Seventeen-year-old Nathaniel II found a medium for his intellectual interests when in 1725, he first compiled an almanac. With the assistance and encouragement of his father, he launched an enterprise which eventually made him known throughout New England.[9] In computing some of the essential information on the position of planets and the expected times of eclipses, he revealed sound astronomical knowledge, considerable mathematical ability, and a flair for making his publication absorbing. Before his almanac was printed, he had had some fears about the public reaction and expressed a hope in the preface that it would not fall victim "to the dangerous and sharp Teeth of envious Detractors." [10] Pleased with the popularity of the initial issue, Ames prepared another almanac the next year and continued to present one annually for thirty-seven years thereafter. While

---

Public Library; List of purchases of Nathaniel Ames in Shepard Fisk Account Book, 1726, Jonathan Ames Papers, Massachusetts Historical Society, Boston, Mass. Nathaniel and Susanna Ames were the parents of six children: Nathaniel b. 1708, Susanna b. 1711, Seth b. 1713, Sarah b. 1716, Ann, and Mary.

8. Mitchell, *History of Bridgewater*, 98; Nathaniel Ames, Jr., *An Astronomical Diary, or, an Almanack for the Year of Our Lord Christ 1737*, quoted in Samuel Briggs, *The Essays, Humor, and Poems of Nathaniel Ames* (Cleveland, 1891), 109-10.

9. Nathaniel Ames, Jr., "To the Reader," *An Astronomical Diary, or, an Almanack for the Year of Our Lord Christ 1726 . . .* (Boston, 1726); hereafter cited as Ames, *Almanack*. The title page is reproduced in Briggs, *Essays of Nathaniel Ames*, 46. A complete set of Ames's almanacs is in the Dedham Hist. Soc.

10. Ames, *Almanack for 1726*, in Briggs, *Essays of Nathaniel Ames*, 50.

it yielded only a modest income, the venture brought the author a re-markably wide reputation. For many years Ames's *Astronomical Diary and Almanack* appeared concurrently with Benjamin Franklin's well-known *Poor Richard's Almanack*, though it was first published several years earlier. Like his contemporary Franklin, Ames brought new ideas to the average man in the colonies. A tasty *pot pourri* of humorous sayings, prognostications, and practical information, his publication reached an estimated circulation of 60,000 copies yearly.[11]

Nathaniel Ames was also fascinated by medicine, absorbing what-ever he could on the subject. His interests were not merely youthful ones to be discarded along the road to maturity. Throughout his life he enthusiastically observed scientific developments. Although he was largely self-educated in both astronomy and medicine, these sciences became important elements in his professional existence.

Shortly after the publication of his first almanac, sometime between 1726 and 1728, Ames decided to leave his native Bridgewater and move to the more promising village of Dedham, ten miles from Boston on the roads to Hartford and Providence. An early settlement of Massachu-setts Bay Colony, Dedham enjoyed the distinction of being one of the communities where the town meeting had initially developed. Situated on the Charles River, it was rich in woods and pastures, with flourish-ing apple orchards, and meadows lying fragrant in summer heat. The meeting house, with its cupola and weather vane rising above the sur-rounding wooden dwellings, was a focal point in the village. On week-days the sounds of the church bell drifted through Dedham at noon and at nine in the evening, and on Sundays at the time of religious services.[12]

Nathaniel Ames quickly entered into the community life of Dedham, taking up farming and making a success of his almanac. These activities were not enough to occupy fully a man of vitality nor to fill his pock-etbook. Once settled, he began to practice medicine, and by the 1730's

11. Ames's *Almanack* appeared yearly until 1775 when it was discontinued by his son, Nathaniel, Jr.; Isaiah Thomas, *The History of Printing in America*, 2 vols. (Albany, 1874), I, 126. Ames's *Almanack* was the first imprint in the colony of New Hampshire in 1757; Douglas C. McMurtrie, "The Beginnings of Printing in New Hampshire," *The Library, A Quarterly Review of Bibliography, Trans-actions of the Bibliographical Society*, 2d Ser., 15 (London, 1935), 341. For an appreciation of Ames as an almanac writer, see Moses C. Tyler, *A History of American Literature*, 2 vols. (N.Y., 1879), II, 122, and N. W. Lively, "Notes of New England Almanacs," *New England Quarterly*, 8 (1935), 264-77.

12. Nathaniel was in Bridgewater in Oct. 1726; Briggs, *Essays of Nathaniel Ames*, 48. In 1728 Ames was in Dedham from where he subscribed to Thomas Prince, *A Chronological History of New England* (Boston, 1728); "Subscribers to Prince's Chronology," *New Eng. Hist. and Geneal. Register*, 6 (1852), 189; Frank Smith, *A History of Dedham, Massachusetts* (Dedham, 1936), 34, 50, 52.

he had become a justice of the peace and a village lawyer as well. While his almanac business flourished early, it was considerably longer before his medical practice was important. In 1741 he noted philosophically at the end of his account book, "exceeding Healthy, but Little Practice for the year ... but be thankfull for that." [13] The duties of a country lawyer, consisting principally of humdrum cases, were as varied as those of a country doctor. Nathaniel Ames's accounts reveal that most of the legal cases he handled were actions for damages involving small sums of money or trivial issues. Rarely was there a term of the inferior court from 1740 on in which an action was not entered under his name, and in a decade he was attorney for the plaintiff in sixteen cases.[14]

Soon after his twenty-seventh birthday, in 1735, Nathaniel married Mary Fisher, the third daughter of Hannah and Joshua Fisher, Jr., of Dedham. Mary's father had been the proprietor of the Fisher Tavern, which had become her responsibility upon his death in 1730. Following their marriage, she and Nathaniel resided at the tavern, where they shared the management of the property and Nathaniel supervised the remodeling of the structure. The couple had been married a brief two years when Mary Ames died on November 11, 1737, after the birth of their first child, Fisher. Before a year had passed the infant died, and Nathaniel had lost his family.[15] Coming shortly after the death of his father, whom he highly revered, these new tragedies were especially hard to bear, leading Nathaniel to express his grief in verse:

> My muse with Grief has dimn'd her Virgin Sight,
> And's loth to sing of Phoebus or his Light;
> To've sung my Spouse and only Son's Decease
> Her Song had been perhaps a finish'd Piece,
> Because the Thot's that roll within her Mind,
> Are unto Death and Tragedies inclin'd:
> Why droops thy Wing? Uplift thy mournful Head,
> Heaven's Glories View; leave poreing o're the Dead.[16]

Three years elapsed before Nathaniel remarried. His second wife, Deborah Fisher, distantly related to Mary, turned seventeen on the

13. Nathaniel Ames, "Diary of Accounts," Nathaniel Ames Papers, Dedham Hist. Soc.

14. Nathaniel Ames, "Lists of Actions," *ibid.*

15. Don G. Hill, *The Record of Births, Marriages, Deaths, and Intentions of Marriage in the Town of Dedham, 1635-1845*, 5 vols. (Dedham, 1886-99), I, 62, 64, 65; Philip A. Fisher, "The Fisher Family," *Dedham Historical Register*, 4 (1893), 65; Erastus Worthington, *The History of Dedham* (Boston, 1827), 92; Briggs, *Essays of Nathaniel Ames*, 23.

16. Ames, *Almanack for 1739*, in Briggs, *Essays of Nathaniel Ames*, 126.

day of her wedding, October 30, 1740. A small, erect young woman, she was a descendant of a vigorous and enterprising family, closely connected with the early settlement of Dedham. Her great-grandfather, Daniel Fisher, had represented the town for twenty-two years in the General Court, had served in the Court of Assistants, and had been a captain of the militia as well. In the Restoration period his sympathies had been with the opponents of the Royalists, and according to family tradition, he had aided two of the fleeing regicide judges involved in the trial of King Charles I. This resistance to royal authority was carried on by Deborah's grandfather when, during the Glorious Revolution of 1689, he seized Governor Edmund Andros by the coat collar and forced his resignation.[17]

Throughout the early years of his second marriage, Nathaniel was involved in litigation over the estate of his first wife, a protracted process which revealed a contentious and aggressive side of his character. Joshua Fisher, Jr., Mary's father, had devised the Fisher Tavern and some real estate to his daughter, subject to his widow's life interest in the property. When Hannah Fisher died in December 1744, Nathaniel insisted on claiming Mary's inheritance. He successfully petitioned Josiah Willard, Judge of Probate, to designate him the legal owner of the property.[18] But Ames was blocked in his attempt to take over the inn and lands by appeals of the Fisher family. Hannah and Benjamin Gay, Mary's sister and brother-in-law, further complicated the situation by actually moving into the tavern.[19] In the course of the legal dispute which followed, Nathaniel "commenced and prosecuted" a plea of ejectment against Benjamin Gay in the Inferior Court of Common Pleas in October 1746. Eventually the case came before the Superior Court of Judicature, where it was decided in favor of Gay.[20] Ames was assessed the "cost of Courts," *35s 6d.* Fully convinced that he had been dealt

17. Hill, *Dedham Records*, I, 68; Worthington, *History of Dedham*, 92; Fisher, "Fisher Family," *Dedham Hist. Register*, 4 (1893), 17; John G. Palfrey, *History of New England During the Stuart Dynasty*, 5 vols. (Boston, 1858-90), III, 580-87.
18. Fisher, "Fisher Family," *Dedham Hist. Register*, 4 (1893), 65; Petition of Nathaniel Ames to the Hon. Josiah Willard, Judge of Probate for Suffolk County, n.d., Nathaniel Ames Papers, Dedham Hist. Soc.
19. Benjamin Gay v. Nathaniel Ames, Vol. 384, No. 61478, Court Files, Suffolk County, Clerk of the Court, Supreme Judicial Court of the Commonwealth of Massachusetts, Boston, Mass. See also John Simpson, Appellant v. Nathaniel Ames, Appellee, Feb. 1745, Vol. 385, No. 61556, Mar. 1745/6, Vol. 385, No. 61633, *ibid.*
20. Appeal of Nathaniel Ames to his Excellency William Shirley, n.d., Probate-Appellate, Vol. 797, No. 129, 880, *ibid.* See also Minute Book, Aug. 1749, Suffolk County, for particulars of the case of Nathaniel Ames v. Benjamin Gay continued from August term, 1748. The full facts in the inheritance case, and the damage suit of Ames v. Gay in 1746, as well as Ames's appeal to reverse the judgment, are given in Superior Court of Judicature, 1747-50, 268-69, *ibid.*

with unfairly, Nathaniel filed a plea for a review of his suit in the Superior Court in August, 1748.

In his effort to reverse the previous decision and to recover the costs, Ames based his claims on the inheritance laws of the Province of Massachusetts rather than on English common law. In a tone almost truculent he presented a well-reasoned legal argument, an elaborate analysis claiming that the estate of Mary descended to their son at her death, and that by the Massachusetts law governing the distribution of estates of intestates, the property went to the nearest kin rather than reverting to the heirs of the widow of Joshua. "If you will take weake Arguments for Demonstration," he addressed both the judges and jury, "and be led by ... Shaddows instead of truth ... then you may Give the Case against me." After several postponements the justices of the Court reached a decision that " 'tis Considered by the Court that the former Judgm't be reversed and that the plaintif recover possession of the premises demanded and cost of Courts taxed at £16 15s 7d." [21]

Nathaniel celebrated his legal victory by composing a stanza for his almanac entitled "On a Judgment of Court Obtain'd after a long Law-Suit," in which he castigated the lawyer for the defense "who puzzl'd Right and Justify'd the Wrong." The dissent of two judges in the case still rankled Ames, who proceeded to lampoon the august Court with a sign showing the erring justices seated with their backs turned to a tome labeled "Province Laws." When it was erected in Dedham, the affronted justices ordered the sheriff to bring it to court. A hasty ride home from Boston enabled Nathaniel to hide the sign before he was again embroiled in legal matters.[22]

With a clear title to the inn, Nathaniel "began to keep tavern" as sole owner on January 25, 1750.[23] Joshua Fisher, the great-grandfather of Ames's first wife, had established the tavern a century earlier to furnish liquid refreshment for Dedham settlers as well as travelers. In his day, the place of primary interest was "the great room," with enormous low beams, a smooth oaken floor, and a massive hearth where a fire roared on cold winter days. Here thirsty customers could draw up

21. Nathaniel Ames, "Defense to the Inheritance of Fisher Ames. Prepared for the Superior Court on a Review," Nathaniel Ames Papers, Dedham Hist. Soc.; Superior Court of Judicature, 1747-50, 268-69, Court Files, Suffolk County, Clerk of the Court, Supreme Judicial Court of the Commonwealth of Massachusetts. Also see Richard B. Morris, *Studies in the History of American Law* (N.Y., 1930), 76-78, 111-19, and Julius Goebel, "King's Law and Local Custom in Seventeenth Century New England," *Columbia Law Review*, 31 (1931), 416 ff.

22. Ames, *Almanack for 1750*, in Briggs, *Essay of Nathaniel Ames*, 25, 215; Worthington, *History of Dedham*, 92.

23. John F. Whiting, ed., "Diary of John Whiting of Dedham, Mass., 1743-1784," *New Eng. Hist. and Geneal. Register*, 63 (1909), 186.

stools and chairs to catch the warmth. In all seasons the inn had been a symbol of hospitality in Dedham. Its facilities had been greatly improved by the alterations made soon after Ames's first marriage. The almanac now served as a means of encouraging people to lodge at the tavern, and Nathaniel Ames in 1751 printed an advertisement which urged travelers on the "great Post Road south west from Boston" to stop "at the sign of the Sun." [24]

The permanent acquisition of the inn marked the beginning of a new period in Dr. Ames's life, bringing him interesting personal contacts and increasing his income appreciably. Travelers such as the Earl of Loudoun, the commander in chief of the British forces in America, and Benjamin Franklin stopped at the tavern. Nathaniel added to its traditional reputation, for he was a convivial host, providing his guests the spice of good conversation to accompany the excellent food and drink. To the inhabitants of Dedham there was nothing incongruous about a physician and lawyer having a tavern; he did not lose the esteem of his neighbors. When four new pews were added to the First Church "for eight Gentlemen of this Town," one of them was designated for the Ames family.[25]

The Reverend Mr. Haven was concerned that Nathaniel did not occupy the pew more often, and furthermore, it seemed to him that Dr. Ames's religious convictions as a member of the Congregational church were not at all what they should have been. Exhorting Ames to give more attention to "seek[ing] the Advancement of Your Spiritual Health and Prosperity," Jason Haven attempted to win back his neighbor to participation in the church. It grieved him in particular that Dr. Ames, who was "so well acquainted with Religion in Theory, should in so many Instances fall short of acting up to the Character of a true Christian." He felt that Ames had been engrossed in a multiplicity of businesses which would "crowd out the Exercises of Religion," and he detected that his parishioner was too much inclined to skepticism about the church. The Reverend Mr. Haven had more specific admonitions

24. Smith, *History of Dedham*, 166-67.
25. Entries of Mar. 11, 1758, Oct. 12, 1763, Sarah B. Baker, ed., "Extracts From the Diary of Dr. Nathaniel Ames," *Dedham Hist. Register*, 1 (1890), 11, 26. The diary, begun by Nathaniel, Jr., in 1758 and continued until 1821, has been partially published without annotation in *ibid.*, 1-15 (1890-1904). See also Charles Warren, *Jacobin and Junto, or Early American Politics as Viewed in the Diary of Dr. Nathaniel Ames, 1758-1822* (Cambridge, 1931). Nathaniel Ames, Sr., by 1753, was a substantial property holder in Dedham. The "Single Tax Rate for 1753" indicates his property was rated at £24/0 real estate, and £46/0 personal estate. Only three of the 139 names listed had higher valuations. Nathaniel Ames Papers, Dedham Hist. Soc. See also Whiting, ed., "Diary of John Whiting," *New Eng. Hist. and Geneal. Register*, 63 (1909), 187.

in mind which he could no longer restrain. Nathaniel frequently was
not careful "to suppress those Sallies of Passion and Anger" resulting
in "rash and unadvised . . . Language," and his minister felt impelled to
warn him, "O, Sir, gaurd especially against the amusing hurrying scenes
of the World which are so fatal to Religion." [26]

Nathaniel had become so much a son of the Enlightenment that he
could not accept the typically orthodox views of his minister and, in
fact, rejected interpretations based on revelation and a literal view of
the Bible. The more deeply he probed, the more thoroughly he became
convinced that God could best be comprehended by man through
reason. "The true System of the Universe . . . being understood," he
wrote, "will exalt our Ideas and excite our highest Admiration of the
magnificent Works of God." [27] Year after year, he reiterated the theme
in his almanacs, endeavoring to bring to the attention of the public the
wonders of the natural world as a basis for rational religion and spreading to the common man knowledge about scientific discoveries. Nathaniel Ames was important as a disseminator and popularizer of new
ideas, but his brief writings are of particular interest as they reveal his
intellectual viewpoint.

True Newtonian that he was, Ames never doubted the existence of
God, discovering proofs in the physical laws governing the universe.
When he was still in his early twenties he wrote:

> Stupendous Atheistical Nonsense!
> That Atoms floating in a Space Immense.
> Should by the jumbling hand of Chance be hurl'd
> Into that order which compos'd the World!
> Or if the Concave of the vast Expance,
> Was by the senseless Hand of giddy Chance.
> . . . .
> Almighty Power doth over all preside.
> And Providence the smallest Atoms guide,
> And every Atom of this mighty Frame,
> (By him Created) out of Nothing came.[28]

Ames's profound admiration for the English physicist is evident in numerous passages in his almanacs. In an article on the force of gravity,

26. The Reverend Jason Haven to Nathaniel Ames, Sr., Dedham, July 17, 1759,
Nathaniel Ames Papers, Dedham Hist. Soc.; also published in Milton Byrd, ed.,
"Nathaniel Ames and His Minister," *William and Mary Quarterly*, 3d Ser., 14
(1957), 595.

27. Ames, "The Solar System," *Almanack for 1759*, in Briggs, *Essays of Nathaniel
Ames*, 295; Chester E. Jorgenson, "The New Science in the Almanacs of Ames and
Franklin," *New England Qtly.*, 8 (1935), 556.

28. Ames, *Almanack for 1731*, in Briggs, *Essays of Nathaniel Ames*, 72-73.

he asked emphatically, *"Who* before the Great Sir *Isaac Newton* did behold the Wisdom of the Creator, in that he has bestowed on Matter such a property as that every Particle thereof throughout the Creation, has a tendency towards every other Particle?" [29]

By numerous explanations of observable phenomena Nathaniel Ames carried on his appointed task of making the scientist's world intelligible. Through the years he discussed the discoveries in astronomy, presenting Newton's laws of motion, writing about Kepler's calculations on the elliptical orbits of planets, or defending the Copernican hypothesis by asserting that the earth's rotation was "not Repugnant to Sacred Scriptures." Frequently his enthusiasm for his subject gave his almanac almost the appearance of a handbook of astronomy with short essays on planets, stars, and comets. Several of them, especially his article on the destruction of the solar system and another on the nature of the solar system, introduced his readers to new concepts of time and the age of the earth.[30] In a long poem entitled "An Essay Upon the Microscope" Ames turned to a favorite theme, the wonder of creation. To Nathaniel the biological world, revealed by the microscope, was as amazing as the astronomical, and he asserted:

> These Massy Globes their Maker's Skill display,
> But the Minutest Creatures do their part,
> The groveling Worm that under Foot is trod
> And smallest Mite proclaim a GOD.[31]

Ames the physician was convinced that a basic knowledge of hygiene was essential, especially for the lower classes, and he often sought to educate the public on the necessity of healthful living. "Since this Sheet enters the solitary Dwellings of the Poor . . . where the studied Ingenuity of the Learned Writer never comes," he wrote, "if these brief Hints do good, it will rejoice the Heart of your humble Servant." [32] In his later almanacs, Dr. Ames recommended fresh air, exercise, and a well-balanced diet of meat and fresh foods. He also suggested that as a means of reducing infant mortality, mothers should nurse their own babies instead of relying on wet nurses. In addition, he was a staunch

29. Ames, *Almanack for 1740*, in Briggs, *Essays of Nathaniel Ames*, 140.

30. Ames, *Almanack for 1734*, in *ibid.*, 86-87, 92; *Almanack for 1740, ibid.*, 140; *Almanack for 1750, ibid.*, 221; *Almanack for 1737, ibid.*, 113-14; *Almanack for 1759, ibid.*, 295-98.

31. Ames, *Almanack for 1741*, in *ibid.*, 147. This is the earliest known example of an ode in irregular verse in America. W. P. Trent, J. Erskine, C. Van Doren, *et al.*, eds., *The Cambridge History of American Literature*, 3 vols. (N.Y., 1931), I, 161.

32. Ames, *Almanack for 1754*, in Briggs, *Essays of Nathaniel Ames*, 249.

supporter of inoculation against smallpox.[33] Clearly, his views were progressive and independent.

Ames had an unquenchable sense of humor, which he revealed in witty comments scattered throughout his almanac. His humor was often obvious, but he largely avoided the ribald jests of his contemporaries. At times his amusing statements concealed bits of wisdom. He admonished his readers to "Live temperate and defy the Physician," or advised them that "If you fall into Misfortunes, creep thro' those Bushes which have the least Briars." He also liked to write such maxims as, "All Men are by Nature equal, But differ greatly in the sequel." [34] Nathaniel, who relished an interchange of barbed wit, kept up a lively debate in verse with some Boston vintners over the best recipe for making currant wine, ending his reply,

> Yet Vint'ners the Victory is thine,
> Your Art (I own) by far exceedeth mine,
> For you can make your *Cyder* into *Wine*.[35]

To a man with such *joie de vivre* and ambition as Ames had, writing a yearly almanac was hardly a chore when it gave him the welcome opportunity of sharing his interests with a large public. Preparing his pamphlet, ministering to the health and legal affairs of his neighbors, and entertaining a lively company at his tavern gave zest to his life and occupied much of his time.

In the years following his marriage to Deborah Fisher, Nathaniel's responsibilities had grown. A first child, Nathaniel, arrived on October 9, 1741; Seth was born the next year, Deborah in 1747, and William in 1755. Nathaniel Ames was in his fiftieth year when in the spring of 1758, his wife gave birth to their last child, Fisher.[36] At the time, rural

33. Ames, "A Page for the Ladies," *Almanack for 1762*, in *ibid.*, 328-32; "An Essay upon Regimen," *Almanack for 1754*, *ibid.*, 253-54. See also the article on diet and exercise, *Almanack for 1755*, *ibid.*, 259-61, and "Of the Small-pox," *Almanack for 1761*, *ibid.*, 320-22.

34. Ames, *Almanack for 1761*, in *ibid.*, 319. *Almanack for 1758*, *ibid.*, 282. Also see Ames, *Almanack for 1762*, *ibid.*, 327. Among his many witticisms were such as "December: This cold uncomfortable Weather, Makes Jack and Jill lie close Together," *Almanack for 1749*, *ibid.*, 212. Ames commented about a Harvard commencement, "Much money sunk, Much liquor drunk," *Almanack for 1764*, *ibid.*, 351.

35. *Almanack for 1762*, *ibid.*, 324, also printed in the *Boston Evening Post*, Nov. 30, 1761.

36. Hill, *Dedham Records*, I, 72, 76, 88, 94; Mitchell, *History of Bridgewater*, 100; Herman Mann, *Historical Annals of Dedham* (Dedham, 1847), 88; "Some Account of Dr. Nathaniel Ames...," *New Eng. Hist. and Geneal. Register*, 16 (1862), 255.

Dedham was swarming with soldiers, temporarily encamped there as a result of the French and Indian War. A local resident, John Whiting, recorded the fact that one thousand Highland soldiers were in town on April 9, and he also noted the only other event of importance, "Mrs. Ames Brought to Bed with her Son Fisher the Same day." According to the town records of Dedham, Fisher Ames was born at half past nine in the morning. His baptism, duly noted in the documents of the First Church, took place a week later.[37]

With a large family to support, Dr. Ames persisted in his efforts to provide enough income. His tavern was frequently crowded with thirsty customers, as soldiers passed through Dedham on their way to Canada or Cape Breton. Nathaniel's medical practice increased, especially when such ailments as the "Mezels [were] thick about." He was also actively engaged in farming and, in November 1758, built a barn, which he immediately filled with two hundred bushels of corn, as his winter's supply.[38] Adequate support for his children was not Dr. Ames's sole concern; their education was important to him as well. Although it would be a financial strain, he and Deborah had decided that they wanted their sons to attend Harvard College. Nathaniel, Jr., had, in fact, entered there the year before Fisher Ames was born. In 1758 young Nathaniel was struggling to master "Ware's Logic," fighting with the sophomores, and being punished for "carrying on much Deviltry" with his friends. During this period, Seth was studying in preparation for Harvard. The Ames household was a place of activity, especially when Nat returned from Cambridge at vacation time or brought some of his classmates for a winter "frolic."[39]

Dr. Ames was always close to his children, and his relationship to them is reflected in a letter which he wrote to young Nathaniel in March 1758: "My child...as for all your Wants? Mine nor yours will not be supply'd in this World, but you may Name what Presses the hardest....I am now Collecting Money to pay My Rents and Excise have sent you 20/- old tenr. to keep your Purse from being as Empty as a Poets. be Docile be Humble, be Good Natured to all about

37. Whiting, ed., "Diary of John Whiting," *New Eng. Hist. and Geneal. Register,* 63 (1909), 189; Hill, *Dedham Records,* I, 94, II, 63. The verses in Ames's *Almanack for 1757* and the *Almanack for 1758* in Briggs, *Essays of Nathaniel Ames,* 274, 281-82, indicate the concern of Nathaniel Ames, Sr., about the miltary situation. One of the best essays by Nathaniel is "A THOUGHT upon the past, present, and future State of NORTH AMERICA." See the *Almanack for 1758,* in *ibid.,* 284-86.

38. Whiting, ed., "Diary of John Whiting," *New Eng. Hist. and Geneal. Register,* 63 (1909), 190.

39. Diary of Nathaniel Ames, Mar. 14, 18, 20, 30, Apr. 3, 20, 1758, Nathaniel Ames Papers, Dedham Hist. Soc.

you and into a tender and Honest Heart may you Receive the Grace of God." [40]

When a "distemper" or smallpox epidemic threatened Boston and the surrounding areas in the winter of 1764, the Ameses were fearful that the disease might spread to their family. Nathaniel Ames, therefore, immediately took steps to protect their sons from contagion by sending them to Dr. Thomas Mather's hospital in Boston for inoculation, which induced a mild case of the disease in order to develop an immunity to it. He was full of praise for the process, asserting that it was "the greatest thing ever achieved in the Art of Medicine to disarm so dreadfull a Distemper of all its terrors and dangers," and he was profoundly grateful to Dr. Mather, "as the Instrument for Carrying my Sons so far through the Small-Pox, so they may return with Safety." [41]

Early in July 1764, Dr. Ames himself became sick with a "billious Disorder" which developed into a "nervous fever." Suddenly this vigorous man who had been the mainstay of his family lay stricken. The symptoms of his illness were alarming, and Nathaniel, Jr., hastily rode to Boston, then to Watertown, for physicians who could help. Two doctors responded, "pronouncing my Father almost irrecoverable," as Nathaniel sorrowfully wrote. The children were called up to see their father as he lay ill. For a day he seemed to rally, giving even one of the attending doctors a slight hope. On the morning of the eleventh, however, Dr. Nathaniel Ames died at the age of fifty-six. Nathaniel, Jr., recorded in his diary, "Six o'clock A.M. my Father's noble and generous Soul took her flight into the Region of Spirits." His last thoughts had been concerned with his litigation, and he had turned to his son saying, "Natty, Natty, is it not very hard that I cannot have one Trial?" [42]

Since Nathaniel Ames, Jr., was the eldest son, he was the logical administrator of his father's estate. Closely resembling Dr. Ames in temperament, he had worked with him since graduating from Harvard in 1761, and under his tutelage, had already begun to practice "the Art of

40. Nathaniel Ames to Nathaniel Ames, Jr., Dedham, Mar. 31, 1758, Julius H. Tuttle, "The Two Nathaniel Ameses," Colonial Society of Massachusetts, *Transactions*, 19 (1917), 260-62.

41. Nathaniel Ames to Dr. [Thomas] Mather, Dedham, Mar. 26, Apr. 5, 1764, Briggs, *Essays of Nathaniel Ames*, 26; John Boyle, "Journal of Occurrences in Boston, 1759-1788," *New Eng. Hist. and Geneal. Register*, 84 (1930), 165, for a comparison of deaths from the natural disease and from inoculation. The records do not mention that Deborah Ames, Nathaniel's daughter, was inoculated.

42. Entries of July 5, 6, 7, 8, 11, 13, 1764, Baker, ed., "Diary of Dr. Nathaniel Ames," *Dedham Hist. Register*, 2 (1891), 25-26. See also the *Boston Evening Post*, July 16, 1764. A legal case in which Ames was a plaintiff had been dismissed by the Court in 1763. Samuel Quincy to Nathaniel Ames, Boston, July 16, 1763, Nathaniel Ames Papers, Dedham Hist. Soc.

Physick." Now he endeavored to protect the family interests by continuing the publication of the almanac and by carrying on the medical practice of Nathaniel, Sr.[43] These efforts proved to be taxing to the young Nathaniel, who was both headstrong and temperamental, and he soon disagreed with his determined mother over vexatious details.

Dr. Ames left £406 6s in personal property and £1561 4s 7d in real estate, but numerous small debts totaling more than £1000 had to be paid to various creditors and were only partially offset by £202 collected from his debtors. In his attempt to continue his father's work, Nathaniel, Jr., had to contend with several unscrupulous competitors, one of whom produced a counterfeit copy of Ames's *Astronomical Diary and Almanack,* and others who tried to take over Dr. Ames's medical practice.[44]

Members of the Fisher family soon threatened to renew litigation over the Fisher inheritance. Nathaniel, Jr., wisely decided to engage two prominent lawyers in Boston to defend his family's right to the tavern, and the furor quickly subsided. The tavern served as a substantial source of income for Deborah Ames and her children, but she clashed with Nathaniel when he left the supervision of it to her while he immersed himself in calculations for the next almanac. He felt that her dissatisfaction was unfair, and in a fit of exasperation he exploded that he had been forced to break off his work, "by the importunity of my Mother to settle the Estate...I [will be] deprived of the only means of getting a living in this World wherefore I pray God to take my Soul into the next scene of Being." [45] For many years the final settlement of the estate was a source of recurring disharmony in the Ames family.

Although Nathaniel, Sr., died when Fisher Ames was only six years old, he obviously influenced the development of his son's mind and

43. Entries of June 19, 30, July 15, 16, 18, 1761, concerning Nathaniel's graduation, and Aug. 1761, Baker, ed., "Diary of Dr. Nathaniel Ames," *Dedham Hist. Register,* 1 (1890), 144-45. Dr. Ames, Sr., had an apprentice, James Gerauld, with whom he had an indenture "to teach [him] the art, mystery, and science of a Physician," at the same time Nathaniel, Jr., was learning medicine. Indenture, Sept. 13, 1760, Nathaniel Ames Papers, Dedham Hist. Soc.
44. Estate of Nathaniel Ames, Nathaniel Ames Papers, Dedham Hist. Soc. Mrs. Ames requested authority to sell real estate and was granted permission to sell land to amount of £579 4s 8d. Entries of Apr. 5, Aug. 9, 1769, Baker, ed., "Diary of Dr. Nathaniel Ames," *Dedham Hist. Register,* 2 (1891), 150; Petition of Deborah Ames to the Governor, His Majesty's Council, and the House of Representatives, Dedham, Jan. 26, 1767, Nathaniel Ames Papers, Dedham Hist. Soc. Nathaniel Ames, Jr., *Almanack for 1766,* in Briggs, *Essays of Nathaniel Ames,* 372; entry of Sept. 3, 1764, Baker, ed., "Diary of Dr. Nathaniel Ames," *Dedham Hist. Register,* 2 (1891), 27.
45. Entries of Aug. 3, 17, 1764, Sept. 4, 1766, in Baker, ed., "Diary of Dr. Nathaniel Ames," *Dedham Hist. Register,* 2 (1891), 26-27, 96.

personality. As he matured, Fisher revealed unusual intellectual gifts,
a facility for self-expression, and even a sense of humor, which could
be seen in varying degrees in the make-up of Dr. Ames. Fisher's boy-
hood was spent in the midst of exciting events growing out of the
political strife of the 1760's. In living at the Ames Tavern, he was at
one of the hubs of community life. Distinguished visitors, express
riders, and soldiers returning from the French and Indian War frequently stopped there for refreshment and brought news of the outer
world. The mood of the townspeople at the end of the war was one
of jubilation over the British victory, but this mood soon turned to
uneasiness and even dismay when the British government imposed new
taxes and stringent regulations on the colonies in 1764.[46] Vigorously
opposing the measures, the people of Dedham expressed their anger
by instructing their delegates to the General Court to stand resolutely
against any execution of the Stamp Act. The crisis in 1765 so agitated
Ames's brother, Nathaniel, that he became an ardent champion of colonial liberties and joined friends in the local Sons of Liberty. When the
"glorious news" of the total repeal of the Act reached Dedham on
May 17, 1766, the villagers were elated. Subsequently, Nathaniel Ames
was instrumental in helping to erect a "Pillar of Liberty" to William
Pitt for his efforts in securing the repeal.[47]

During these years Fisher Ames was too young to participate with
Nathaniel and Seth in the "Sociable Club," which they had started, or
in dances and husking bees. He could, however, enjoy evenings at
home, where they performed with friends such plays as "The Orphan."
Family life was also enlivened when a visiting minister or other guest
came to dinner.[48]

Fisher Ames's formal schooling began at the age of six. Dedham
prided itself on its school system, but basic education was at times a
haphazard affair, since teaching was often entrusted to inexperienced
young college students and recent graduates of Harvard and Yale.
Usually these teachers had little insight into the educational needs of
the individual children, and frequently they remained for only a few

46. Entries of Aug. 11, 1760, Mar. 12, 14, Aug. 15, Sept. 8, 10, 18, 1761, Jan. 22,
Apr. 6, 10, July 5, Nov. 18, 25, 1762, Jan. 20, Mar. 10, Sept. 24, Oct. 12, 1763, June
18, 1764, *ibid.,* 1 (1890), 112, 114, 145, 146, 147, 148; 2 (1891), 25, 26.
47. Smith, *History of Dedham,* 167, 435, 437; entries of Apr. 30, May 17, July
22, 1766, Baker, ed., "Diary of Dr. Nathaniel Ames," *Dedham Hist. Register,* 2
(1891), 60, 96; Whiting, ed., "Diary of John Whiting," *New Eng. Hist. and Geneal.
Register,* 63 (1909), 264. Worthington, *History of Dedham,* 64; Erastus Worthington, "The Pillar of Liberty," *Proceedings at the Celebration of the Two Hundred
and Fiftieth Anniversary of the Town of Dedham* (Dedham, 1888), 170-77.
48. Entries of Nov. 13, Dec. 8, 1765, Mar. 21, 28, Apr. 11, 1766, Baker, ed.,
"Diary of Dr. Nathaniel Ames," *Dedham Hist. Register,* 2 (1891), 27, 59, 60.

months before accepting more attractive openings in their professions of the ministry or law. Both Nathaniel and Seth Ames had done such a stint of teaching. Fisher attended public school at intervals, but when the caliber of the teaching fell below par, it was the Reverend Jason Haven who took charge of his education. Mrs. Ames, believing as she did that her youngest son had an unusual mind, hoped that his academic training would enable him to become a lawyer. After completing his early studies in six years, Fisher Ames prepared to leave his family in 1770 to seek admission to Harvard.[49]

49. "A Memoir of the Late Honorable Fisher Ames," *The Diocesan Register*, 238; Kirkland in Ames, *Works of Ames*, I, 4. On the Rev. Jason Haven, see Smith, *History of Dedham*, 75-77, and Carlos Slafter, "The Schools and Teachers of Dedham," *Dedham Hist. Register*, 3 (1892), 176. Manasseh Cutler, teaching in Dedham's South Parish in 1766, found conditions difficult. He wrote in his diary, "extremely cold—no wood at the schoolhouse—studied Dr. Bates on the Immortality of the Soul." William P. and Julia P. Cutler, *Life, Journals and Correspondence of Rev. Manasseh Cutler*, 2 vols. (Cincinnati, 1888), I, 10.

Chapter II

Harvard and the Revolutionary Years

As the youthful Fisher Ames approached Cambridge he rode through farmland and crossed the meandering Charles River, which looked quite different near Dedham. Low-lying salt meadows and muddy tidal flats replaced the familiar wooded embankments and grassy fields along the upper course of the river. The town itself also contrasted with Ames's native community. The rows of neat clapboard houses, the numerous streets converging on the Square, the high-spired First Parish Church, the county courthouse, and the cluster of red brick buildings of Harvard all gave Cambridge a more imposing aspect.[1] Fisher Ames's trip marked the beginning of a new formative phase of his life, one which was to open intellectual vistas and to prepare him thoroughly for his later public career as a lawyer and political figure.

The "Business of Examination" had brought him to Harvard shortly after the annual commencement exercises, along with other young men who hoped to gain admission to the college. Ames appeared before an examining group consisting of President Samuel Locke and the two tutors who conducted both the written and oral parts of the examination. Admission requirements, most recently revised in 1767, emphasized a good knowledge of the classics. "No one shall be admitted," the

1. *Boston Evening Post,* June 18, 1770; Henry Pelham, comp., *A Plan of Boston in New England with Its Environs* (1777); A. Hamilton, Jr., comp., *An Accurate Map of the Country Round Boston in New England* (London, 1776). Description of Cambridge from Model of Harvard College in the 1770's, Widener Library, Harvard University.

regulations stipulated, "unless he can translate Greek and Latin authors in common use such as Tully, Virgil, Xenophon, understand the Rules of Grammar, can write Latin correctly, and hath a good moral character." In testing a candidate the president questioned him about grammar and logic, then gave him a Latin essay to write and a passage in Horace or Virgil to translate. Members of the entrance board, impressed by Ames's quickness and accuracy of mind, "pronounced him a youth of uncommon attainments and bright promise." [2]

Before Ames was officially admitted to the class of 1774, he had to be familiar with the college laws. Since there were no printed copies, it meant laborious copying of a variety of rules concerning attendance at classes and precepts on such topics as "Of a Religious and Virtuous Life." He also had to get a certificate from the steward indicating that he had paid 30 shillings, the fees for the first quarter of the college year. Every freshman had to post a bond, signed by his parent, pledging payment of all bills from the steward, the butler, and the glazier, on penalty of forfeiting £40. When all was completed, President Locke signed the order, "Admittatur in Collegium Harvardinium," accepting Fisher Ames. [3]

Harvard College at this time consisted of an attractive group of four buildings and a small chapel. In the nine years since Nathaniel's graduation, the college had not expanded in enrollment significantly, but a new residence for students, Hollis Hall, had been built. A disastrous fire in midwinter of 1764 had burned out the entire interior of Harvard Hall, but through the aid of donations from individuals and from the provincial government, the library and scientific equipment it had housed were replaced. By 1766 the building itself had been rebuilt, once again becoming a center of college activities with its dining hall and chapel, ornamented with two brass chandeliers. Opposite Harvard Hall was Massachusetts Hall, used as a dormitory, and farther in the Yard, Stoughton and Hollis Halls. To the east, through the trees of an orchard, were the residences of the president and of the faculty, facing Braintree Street. Half hidden by Harvard Hall and the four stories of Stoughton was the diminutive Holden Chapel, once used for daily devotions and now used as a lecture hall. Although the buildings were

2. Samuel Eliot Morison, *Three Centuries of Harvard: 1636-1936* (Cambridge, 1937), 103-4; Kirkland in Ames, *Works of Ames*, I, 4; "The Laws of Harvard College [1767]," chap. 1: "Of Admission into the College," Harvard College Records, Pt. III, Col. Soc. of Mass., *Collections*, 31 (1935), 347-48.
3. "The Laws of Harvard College [1767]," Col. Soc. of Mass., *Collections*, 31 (1935), 348-50; William C. Lane, "Manuscript Laws of Harvard College," Col. Soc. of Mass., *Transactions*, 25 (1923), 252.

fine examples of Georgian architecture, little had been done to give them an attractive setting; the Yard in these years served as a place for student games.[4]

Late in August 1770, after the four-week summer vacation had ended, Ames returned to Cambridge to begin his college education. A month before, the whole class had been admitted and assigned to Joseph Willard, one of the tutors, but not until classes started did the entering freshmen assemble as a group. With one exception Ames's classmates came from Massachusetts, mostly from small towns and villages scattered throughout the Province. There were some boys from the upper levels of New England society, but there also were many from the less influential and affluent groups—sons of hard-working farmers, country ministers, and tradesmen. In 1770 most of the students were between sixteen and eighteen, a few were twenty, and, as in previous years, the average age of the freshman class was seventeen. Only one student, Sam Jennison, was younger than Ames, having entered college before his twelfth birthday.[5]

Soon after registering at the butler's office, Fisher Ames was absorbed in college life, but as he and his classmates quickly discovered, the position of a freshman was lowly indeed. The ancient system of petty servitude remained unchanged, emphasizing the inferiority of the new students in relation to upperclassmen and graduates. Sophomores herded together the members of Ames's class in the "large chamber" of Harvard Hall to warn them about the severe penalties which would befall them if they did not implicitly obey student and college customs. All freshmen had to carry out errands for any of the upperclassmen and at the behest of their lordly superiors frequently scurried to and fro between the library, the butlery, and neighborhood taverns and shops. Restrictions on boyish behavior were numerous; the older students were insistent that the members of the entering class stand upright and walk bareheaded in the Yard. Fisher Ames found that prompt attendance at chapel was requisite, and that he could not risk even the comfort of leaning on the pews without evoking the wrath of his superiors.

4. "Description of Harvard Buildings," *Massachusetts Magazine* (June, 1790), reprinted in *Harvard Graduates' Magazine*, 15 (1907), 774. Morison, *Three Centuries of Harvard*, 95-98. John Mayhew to Thomas Hollis, Apr. 8, 1766, Eliot-Mayhew-Hollis Correspondence, Bancroft Transcripts, N.Y. Public Library, New York, N.Y. The letter concerns the Hollis donation of books and scientific equipment. "Boyle's Journal of Occurrences in Boston, 1759-1778," *New Eng. Hist. and Geneal. Register*, 84 (1930), 163-65.

5. Faculty Records, III, 170, Harvard Archives, Harvard Univ. John L. Sibley, ed., *Catalogus Senatus Academici Collegii Harvardiani* ... (Cambridge, Mass., 1880), 33.

Fortunately for him, the practice of having the freshmen mow and rake-in the president's hay had recently been abandoned.[6]

The educational influences to which Ames was exposed were largely traditional ones based on a thorough training in the classics, logic, and metaphysics. During a long tenure in office, between 1737 and 1769, President Edward Holyoke effected some marked improvements in the curriculum which were showing results by the time Ames entered college. Holyoke had increased the emphasis on English oratory and had started a revival of elocution, instituting a program of public speeches and debates by the students. Science was now gaining in importance, and the first outstanding scholar in this field at Harvard, Professor John Winthrop, regularly gave a series of "experimental lectures in Natural Science." Modern language study, although encouraged, had not been integrated into the course of study. One of the most significant improvements was having each tutor teach a specific subject rather than having him teach all courses to a class assigned to him. In addition to the specialty, he was still expected to give instruction in the elements of English grammar, speech, and rhetoric. These innovations tended to revivify education at Harvard in the eighteenth century.[7]

As in the past, the classics constituted the core of the freshman curriculum. Ames's class had barely become settled in the new routine of college life when each member was provided with a Hebrew grammar, and teaching in the fundamentals of the language began. Intensive study in Latin and Greek started with assignments chosen from classical writers, among them Virgil, Sallust, Cicero, Homer, and Xenophon. English was an integral part of the program, and students were required to take elocution, rhetoric, and grammar. During the first year some time was also devoted to mathematics, logic, and geography. In the balance of the college program such courses as ethics, metaphysics, natural philosophy, and astronomy offset the great emphasis on the ancient languages.[8]

6. College Records, II, 335, Board of Overseers, Records, III, 56, Harvard Archives; Morison, *Three Centuries of Harvard*, 105-6; entry of July 1, 1758, Baker, ed., "Diary of Dr. Nathaniel Ames," *Dedham Hist. Register*, 1 (1890), 13. See also Diary of John Page, June 28, 1758, Harvard Archives.

7. Board of Overseers, Records, III, 19, Harvard Archives; Morison, *Three Centuries of Harvard*, 83, 90, 92; Josiah Quincy, *The History of Harvard University*, 2 vols. (Cambridge, 1840), II, 123-24, 217-23; "The Laws of Harvard College [1767]," Col. Soc. of Mass., *Collections*, 31 (1935), 351; Leonard W. Labaree, *Conservatism in Early American History* (N.Y., 1948), 92-101; Clinton L. Rossiter, *Seedtime of the Republic: the Origin of the American Tradition of Political Liberty* (N.Y., 1953), 120.

8. Faculty Records, III (Sept. 1770), Harvard Archives. "The Laws of Harvard College [1767]," Col. Soc. of Mass., *Collections*, 31 (1935), 351. Morison, *Three Centuries of Harvard*, 89 ff.; Franklin B. Dexter, *Extracts from the Itineraries of*

Although there had been a definite improvement by the 1770's in the requirements of the various courses, the students rebelled in 1774 against being forced to study more Greek when they preferred Latin. On occasion, Ames himself was critical of assignments. He found that Webb's *Beauties of Poetry* palled as he wrote down extracts on the structure of English verse, and that the author was singularly unimaginative in his choice of illustrative passages. After copying two lines:

> To those whom fevers burn the piercing smell
> Of vigorous wine is grievous death and Hell,

he added a comment that "the reading of such execrable stuff is worse than the effect of wine in a fever." [9]

The library in Harvard Hall with its carefully chosen collection held many works which were far more appealing than the compulsory texts, and Fisher Ames frequently borrowed books to read in his room. In August 1772 he read a volume of the *Arabian Nights' Entertainment*, but when classes were well under way again in the autumn he confined himself largely to history, taking out both volumes of Anderson's *History of France*, Harris's *Voyages*, and the *History of England* by Smollet. At various times he charged out volumes of Shakespeare's works and also read Dryden, as well as Spenser's *Faerie Queen*. For almost a month he kept out Quintilian's famous work on rhetoric, *Institutio Oratoria* (*The Training of an Orator*), then turned to Phalaris's *Epistles*, later reading Lucan's *Pharsalia*. Ames and many of his classmates made heavy demands on Rollins's *Ancient History*, Home's *On Criticism*, and Fordyce's *Moral Philosophy*, very likely required reading for various courses. But the folio volume of Thévenot's *Travels*, Franklin's *Letters*, or Wildman's *On Bees* were certainly read for the sake of enjoyment.[10]

For Ames the routine of learning was fundamentally the same as it had been for others during most of the eighteenth century; students were expected to spend long hours working intensively. Fisher's day at the college began at six in the morning, when the bell tolled for morning prayers, but it was a common practice to risk a fine of 4*d* in order to have an extra bit of sleep or to have breakfast in the warm comfort of one's room. Frequently the boys did not go to compulsory prayers

---

Ezra Stiles (New Haven, 1916), 397. Stiles described the course of study as of 1787. A list of books used in Harvard during the Revolution is given in Col. Soc. of Mass., *Transactions*, 20 (1918), 150.

9. Diary of Samuel Chandler, Feb. 16, 1774, Harvard Archives. Daniel Webb, *Remarks on the Beauties of Poetry* (London, 1762). Extracts from Webb in Fisher Ames's hand, Gratz Collection, Historical Society of Pennsylvania, Philadelphia, Pa.

10. Library Charging List, Class of 1774, Harvard Archives.

and on flimsy pretexts avoided lectures or recitations. In his sophomore year Ames was punished once, paying the trifling fine of 1*d;* but the next year as a junior sophister he paid many petty fines imposed by the administration for infractions of the rules, and in each quarter, with one exception, from September 1772 until his graduation in 1774 he incurred several shillings in fines.[11]

After four hours of morning classes, dinner at noon and a recreation period with games of bats and balls were a welcome relief. Study hours continued the rest of the afternoon and evening except for prayers late in the day. Yet there were numerous diversions for the students. Youthful diaries kept by a few Harvard undergraduates during this period give the impression that the boys often had a good time in spite of administration restrictions. In Fisher Ames's time treks out to Fresh Pond for skating in winter were a popular pastime, and there was no decline in enthusiasm for the traditional sport of hunting in the fields around the college. In spite of the regulations against keeping firearms, students frequently went gunning for robins. It was also a long established custom to make cider or cherry punch and to drink wine when it was available. Drinking was often the source of merriment and mischief, for the boys would have a "high-go," breaking the windows of unpopular tutors or having a fight with another class.[12]

In December 1773, the faculty and students were shocked by the sudden resignation of President Locke. They would have been even more shocked had they known the reason; it was not generally known at the time that an affair with his housemaid had forced his resignation and retirement to the country. The Reverend Samuel Langdon, whose greatest attribute seems to have been his patriotism, was his successor.[13]

The resignation of the president heightened the excitement in Cambridge. At no time during the era of the American Revolution was Harvard a sheltered academic retreat, but during the early 1770's the influence of the tensions between Massachusetts and Great Britain was

11. Morison, *Three Centuries of Harvard,* 116-17; Diary of Sam Chandler, Mar. 13, 17, 1773, Quarter Bill Book, 1770, Harvard Archives. The Quarter Bill Book reveals that Ames paid £3 5s 10d for "commons and sizings" or board during the first quarter, June 14 to Sept. 13, 1771, 4s study rent, 10s tuition, 1s 3d for repairs, 9d for the library, and 1s 6d special levy for the Hancock Professorship.

12. Morison, *Three Centuries of Harvard,* 110, 114-16; for student activities in the late 18th century, see Baker, ed., "Diary of Dr. Nathaniel Ames," *Dedham Hist. Register,* I, 9-16, 49-52, 111-14; Diary of Sam Chandler, Harvard Archives; Moses Adams to Ameriah Frost, May 17, 1768, Chamberlain Collection, Boston Public Library, Boston, Mass. Adams remarked about a college custom, "I have some sollid comfort for now and then I shute A ROBIN altho' I do not do it allways at noontime."

13. Morison, *Three Centuries of Harvard,* 100; Franklin B. Dexter, ed., *The Literary Diary of Ezra Stiles,* 3 vols. (N.Y., 1901), I, 461.

almost impossible to escape. The year before Ames entered college, Harvard had suddenly become the center of political activity when the General Court convened there. Governor Bernard, harassed by the legislature's demands to remove the military forces stationed in Boston, denied his authority to do so. Believing that the General Court could not legally function outside of Boston without the consent of its members, he peremptorily adjourned the assembly to Cambridge. Undaunted by the Governor's clever move, the hostile legislators invaded the halls of the college and proceeded to transact the colony's business.[14]

Initially the members of the Harvard Corporation, cognizant of emergency circumstances, did not resist this disruption of academic life. But when it became evident that the Court might continue indefinitely to meet in Cambridge, the Corporation protested to Lieutenant Governor Thomas Hutchinson that after all, Harvard "had been instituted for the sole purpose of the education of youth, and the property of it given for this important end." The Lieutenant Governor endeavored to conciliate the administration by formally requesting thereafter the use of space for specific purposes. Harvard Corporation was mollified by his adroit courtesy and allowed the legislature to continue holding its sessions at the college until 1772.[15]

To the student, ever alert for new activity, the presence of the General Court and many of the popular leaders was electrifying after the dull routine of college life. When James Otis made an impassioned speech to the House of Representatives in June 1769, as many students as could wedge into the room eagerly listened to his stirring words. Aware of his youthful audience, he took advantage of the occasion to recite the grievances of the colonists—the limitations of their rights, the imposition of a standing army in Boston, the false accusations to which they had been subjected. He appealed to his listeners' patriotism and hinted that they might soon have to prove their loyalty by action.

How greatly the boys were carried away by the stimulus of politics-in-the-making, Andrew Eliot, one of the members of the Corporation, revealed. In a letter to Thomas Hollis, Harvard's friend and benefactor in London, he wrote, "The young gentlemen are already taken up with politics. They have caught the spirit of the times. Their declamations

14. Thomas Hutchinson, *The History of the Colony and Province of Massachusetts Bay,* ed. Lawrence S. Mayo, 3 vols. (Cambridge, 1936), III, 171-73; William Tudor, *The Life of James Otis of Massachusetts* (Boston, 1823), 354; Palfrey, *History of New England,* V, 400-401.

15. Quincy, *History of Harvard,* II, 148, 151; Thomas Hollis to the Rev. Dr. Eliot, Palmal, June 2, 1770, Thomas Hollis Papers, Mass. Hist. Soc. Hollis commented, "A more likely means for burning down the College a second time and thereby checking the growth of learning and all ingenious action could not be devised than that of holding there again the General Court."

and forensic disputes breathe the spirit of liberty . . . but they have . . . been wrought up to such a pitch of enthusiasm, that it has been difficult for their tutors to keep them within due bounds." [16]

For several years the administration had endeavored to promote public oratory by offering increased instruction in speaking techniques. With legislators actually debating at Harvard, oratorical competition spread among the students. Tutors were encouraged to have the boys "read a suitable portion before the rest of the class out of some celebrated English author," and the president arranged public performances for the better orators to promote a "free and easy, as well as animated way of speaking." When the Board of Overseers attended an exhibition of the students in the spring of 1773, they were very favorably impressed; they expressed the hope that these students would become "ornaments to the college and blessings to their Country." [17]

Under the leadership of Samuel Phillips, some of the more eager students organized the Speaking Club in the autumn of 1770. A year later Ames and his friends formed an equally secret organization of student orators, the Mercurian Club. When the members of the original group learned of a similar club, they proposed an amalgamation, which was effected by March 1773. Greatly strengthened in membership, the club met once a week at "Mr. Reed's," where each student spoke twice a month. The secrecy of the group was due more to a penchant for exclusiveness than to any need to hide their actions from the college authorities; yet for many years members always abbreviated the name of the club whenever they wrote to their friends.[18]

In solemn meetings the members listened to one of their number speak on a dramatic subject, critically observing his style. At the end of the speech, the "remarker," a post held by Ames in 1774, pointed out "the propriety or impropriety of the Pronunciation and Gesture of the Speakers." Each orator was expected to observe the club's rules not to address the group without rising and only to declaim on a subject approved before the meeting began. Prompt attendance was required. On one occasion Ames was fined 4d for being late; indeed, he was evidently not as attentive to his duties as he should have been. He was appointed to a committee, but soon afterwards the club "voted to punish Ames for negligence." [19]

16. Tudor, *Life of Otis*, 355-56. Andrew Eliot to Thomas Hollis, n.p., n.d., quoted in Quincy, *History of Harvard*, II, 163.
17. Board of Overseers, Records, III, 56, 60, Harvard Archives.
18. "Catalogue of the Members of the Patriotic Association of Harvard University, From the Time of its Foundation, September, 1770," Speaking Club Records, I, 35, 55, 58, Harvard Archives; Morison, *Three Centuries of Harvard*, 138-40.
19. Speaking Club Records, Orders, I, 54, 59, Harvard Archives.

Many of the young speakers turned to the great classical orations, but current political topics were even more fascinating to them. On May 4, 1773, Fisher Ames presented an extract from Benjamin Church's stirring speech delivered the previous March on the third anniversary of the Boston Massacre. In choosing this material, Ames was obviously in sympathy with the speaker's revolutionary mood. After recapitulating the usurpations of the Crown, Dr. Church had asked his audience, "When will the locust leave the land?" Recalling the Massacre, he declared that "the wan tenants of the grave still shriek for vengeance," and that "the whole soul clamours for arms and is on fire to attack the brutal banditti." [20]

In his last two years at Harvard, Ames spoke twelve times before his colleagues in the society, and on two of the occasions he again turned to political themes. Developing his own ideas, he gave "An address to the People of England"; in his last performance in May 1774, he chose "Erskine's harangue to the Crown." With a flair for the dramatic, he presented Cicero's eloquent defense of Titus Annius Milo, and at another meeting he selected a speech of Galgaeus from Tacitus. Even as an under-age college student, not yet seventeen, Ames impressed his audience by the force and excellence of his speeches.[21]

A distinction which came to Fisher Ames at Harvard was his selection on two occasions as "scholar of the house" in Stoughton Hall, where he lived. In his senior year, he was one of several students chosen to show their oratorical abilities at the semi-annual meeting of the Overseers. A classmate of Ames's, Sam Chandler, recorded that, on May 3, 1774, "it cleared away fair in the afternoon ... the Exhibitioners performed ... Clark spoke a Latin Oration ... Litchfield and Wittman spoke an English Dialogue ... then concluded with an oration by Ames." [22] Fisher thoroughly enjoyed his efforts at public speaking. The experience of belonging to an organization such as the Speaking Club was stimulating to a lively young mind.

As Fisher Ames's college life drew to a close the Board of Overseers

20. *Ibid.*, 89. Dr. Benjamin Church, *An Oration Delivered March Fifth, 1773. At the Request of the Inhabitants of the Town of Boston; To Commemorate the Bloody Tragedy of the Fifth of March 1770* (Boston, 1773), 18-19.
21. Ames's speeches were on the following dates: Mar. 16, May 4, 25, June 29, July 13, Sept. 7, 21, Nov. 30, 1773, Mar. 1, two speeches, Mar. 29, May 31, 1774, Speaking Club Records, I, 87, 89-95, Harvard Archives; Kirkland in Ames, *Works of Ames*, I, 5.
22. College Records, 1750-78 (Copy of College Book, No. 7), 356, 371, Board of Overseers, Records, III, 31, 72, Faculty Records, VIII, Mar. 27, 1774, Diary of Sam Chandler, May 3, 1774, Harvard Archives; Kirkland in Ames, *Works of Ames*, I, 4-5.

announced that "considering the present dark aspect of our public affairs," there would be no formal commencement exercises. Within the college itself there were as yet only a few clashes between patriots and loyal adherents to the Crown, and no major upheaval took place during the spring and summer of 1774. Nevertheless, the administration was aware of public sentiment and was sensitive to the feeling of gloom which pervaded the Province. It would not do to encourage the carnival spirit of gaiety and levity, traditional at the annual commencement, when Bostonians had just received news of two of Parliament's Coercive Acts stringently regulating the administration of justice and the government of Massachusetts as partial punishment for the Boston Tea Party. Now by decree of the Overseers, the gala day of the Province was canceled, and the class of 1774 had to make the best of the new austerity. On July 20, after the president had transmitted to the Board of Overseers the names of the students meeting the requirements for graduation, Bachelor of Arts degrees were conferred on them by a general diploma.[23]

Ames received his degree just as the Revolution began, and the colonial era ended. Fortunately he completed his college course before war disrupted academic life and education in Cambridge. Tory sympathizers left precipitously, some ardent young patriots eagerly joined the armed forces after Lexington, and Harvard was forced into a hegira when American troops took over the college buildings. Only by moving to Concord, Massachusetts, could the college continue to function.[24]

Harvard had offered Fisher Ames a vital stimulus for both intellectual and political development. Coming from a home where there was great sympathy with the evolving patriotic cause, Ames had moved into a world where the academic and the political had temporarily become inseparable. In such a climate, he had been encouraged to think, to reason concisely, and to present ideas cogently. This training proved to be of inestimable value when he became a lawyer and a legislator. His rapid rise to political prominence and his recognition as an exceptional orator were to a large extent the rewards of the intensive study

23. Board of Overseers, Records, III, 73-74 (June, July, 1774), Harvard Archives; Morison, *Three Centuries of Harvard*, 119 ff; entries of July 15-18, 1761, Baker, ed., "Diary of Dr. Nathaniel Ames," *Dedham Hist. Register*, 1 (1890), 144. The *Boston Gazette*, July 26, 1773, reported on the numerous "salutatory Orations" and "forensic Disputes." Occasional critics opposed the "comic Buffoonery" accompanying the solemn ceremonies. See A. Croswell, *Brief Remarks on the Satyrical Drollery at Cambridge Last Commencement Day* (Boston, 1771). The *Boston Gazette*, July 25, 1774, dated the commencement July 20 and printed a copy of the Latin diploma.

24. Morison, *Three Centuries of Harvard*, 149-50; see also George R. Minot to S. Minot, Concord, Feb. 28, 1776, Sedgwick (Minot) Papers, Mass. Hist. Soc. Minot, later a close friend of Ames's, was a student while Harvard was in Concord.

of his college years. In his choice of subjects in the Speaking Club, he identified himself with those who were vehement in their condemnation of British policies in the colonies. He was clearly an ally of the patriots. For Ames, this alliance proved to be a first step toward Federalism. He emerged from Harvard with scholarly understanding and the intellectual vigor necessary to bring him at a later time into the First Congress.

A swift succession of events in the critical summer of 1774 heralded an oncoming storm and made Ames's immediate future uncertain. At sixteen with very limited means and without important contacts, he turned again to his parental home in Dedham. He was not, however, returning to quite the same surroundings he had known so intimately as a child, since there were changes at home which deeply affected his sensitive nature.

While Fisher was still in college, his mother had remarried, after eight years of widowhood. In February 1772, John Whiting had noted her marriage in his diary, "Richard Woodard [Woodward] married to the Widow Ames—after a Long and Clost Siege, he took her." Nathaniel Ames also made a pointed comment in his own diary, "Dick Woodward cuts a flash Bridegroom." Woodward, a forceful, aggressive person, quickly antagonized the family and soon had several clashes with the emotionally vulnerable Nathaniel. During a disagreement growing out of Woodward's interference with Mrs. Ames's inheritance, Woodward struck Nathaniel with a saw, and Nathaniel obtained a warrant for his arrest and had him bound to good behavior.[25]

Fisher Ames felt distressed by his family's problems. His own clashes with Woodward had been allayed while he was in college, but conflicts soon developed upon his return to Dedham. Seething with anger at Woodward's abusiveness and his claims to parental authority, Ames denounced his stepfather's mistreatment of the family. In a blistering letter to Woodward, Ames asked, "When personal abuse, not only scandalous but open is offered, when Injustice triumphs...and destroys the pleasures of life by cutting off the fountain of its support, to what quarter shall the injured and insulted Orphan fly for protection?"[26]

Woodward had assumed the management of the family inn and had replaced the familiar tavern sign of the "Rising Sun" with one display-

25. Diary of John Whiting, Feb. 23, 1772, Whiting, ed., "Diary of John Whiting," *New Eng. Hist. and Geneal. Register*, 63 (1909), 186; entries of Mar. 1, 1772, May 9, 12, 1773, Baker, ed., "Diary of Dr. Nathaniel Ames," *Dedham Historical Register*, 3 (1892), 23, 71; Diary of Jason Haven, May 12, 1773, American Antiquarian Society, Worcester, Mass.
26. Fisher Ames to Richard Woodward, July 28, 1775, Fisher Ames Papers, Dedham Hist. Soc.

ing a law book. The tavern itself now became known to many as Woodward's Tavern. Fisher was both hurt and aggravated by Richard Woodward's appropriation of the estate his father had left his mother. Ames openly accused his stepfather of taking nearly $1,000 for his own use and that of his children by a former marriage. "I have often heard you say you married her for her money," Fisher wrote bitterly, "and the public can witness that you left her without the necessities of life." [27] Rejecting any submission to his stepfather, he declared his freedom from Woodward's control. In spite of Ames's outspoken criticisms, he did not cut himself off from his family, but when in Dedham remained, as far as the records indicate, in his mother's home.

Fisher Ames's older brothers, Nathaniel and Seth, had established their independence. After graduating from Harvard, Seth had begun practicing medicine in Amherst, New Hampshire, and his visits to Dedham were infrequent. Although not yet married, Nathaniel had built his own house in 1771 and was living not far from the Ames home. William, on the other hand, was trying a variety of jobs as an apprentice clerk, and Deborah, the only sister, was at home during these years. [28]

Dedham at the outbreak of the Revolutionary War was not the placid colonial village it had once been. The people were drawn into the drama which was unfolding and by their actions in the town meeting and on the militia training field showed that in general they had already committed themselves to the patriot side. By the autumn of 1774, the town favored unequivocally an inter-colonial meeting to assert the rights of the colonies and through its Committee of Correspondence supported the plan of a county convention to meet at Woodward's Tavern. The town then chose five delegates, Nathaniel Ames noting tersely in his diary on September 6, 1774, that the "county convention [was] held here." This laconic notice fails to reveal the radical nature of the meeting. [29] At Dedham the delegates discussed

27. *Ibid.*; Smith, *History of Dedham*, 167-68.
28. Herman Mann, *Historical Annals of Dedham* (Dedham, 1847), 88; Diary of Jason Haven, Oct. 21, 1772, Amer. Antiq. Soc. Haven mentions a visit of Seth's to his home. Entries of June 25, Aug. 10, Sept. 7, 1771, Sept. 23, 1773, Feb. 28, 1775, Baker, ed., "Diary of Dr. Nathaniel Ames," *Dedham Hist. Register*, 3 (1892), 22, 71, 129.
29. Don G. Hill, "The Record of a New England Town from the Passage of the Stamp Act to the Declaration of Independence," *National Magazine*, 16 (1892), 160-74. Dedham Committee of Correspondence to the Boston Committee of Correspondence, Jan., 1773, Boston Committee of Correspondence Papers, Bancroft Collection, N.Y. Pub. Lib.; Dedham Town Records, 1773-84, VIII, Town Clerk's Office, Dedham, Mass.; N. Patten to ? , Roxbury, August 18, 1774, Chamberlain Collection, Boston Pub. Lib. At a meeting in Jan. 1774, Richard Woodward was chosen a member of a committee to cooperate with other towns toward a redress

suggestions presented by Dr. Joseph Warren that no obedience be paid
to the Coercive Acts and that military preparations be made against
the possibility of British attack. Later at a second meeting in Milton,
the Dedham declarations, which virtually advocated armed resistance
to England, were adopted, given the name of Suffolk Resolves, and
hurriedly sent to the Continental Congress in Philadelphia.[30]

Alarms that the British troops were on the march spread through the
country towns and villages, and late in 1774, it seemed as though war
could not be far off. Frequent musters of the militia kept the atmosphere tense. In 1775 the news of the skirmish at Lexington instantly
aroused Dedham to dispatch contingents of militiamen to Lexington
and soon after to raise 120 additional minutemen. On June 17, barely
two-and-a-half weeks later, Fisher Ames was among the 122 men of
Captain Aaron Guild's company who marched toward Boston "upon
the alarm of Bunker Hill Fight." Accompanying Ames were Ebenezer
Battle, Jr., a friend and former schoolmate of his, and Cato, the faithful
family servant. Only seventeen of the Dedham soldiers actually took
part in the battle, while the others, including Ames, remained on duty
for two days. The detachment was then released and returned home,
where each man received 8s pay for his service.[31]

For a time, military dangers were negligible, but the inhabitants of
Dedham were menaced by a succession of epidemics which reached
dangerous proportions. In August 1775 "mortal dysentery" swept the
town shortly after large numbers of soldiers had been encamped close
by. Fisher Ames very fortunately escaped, but the disease brought
death to several neighbors. The next summer there was an outbreak of
the dreaded smallpox, which in the words of John Adams became "the
King of Terrors to America this year." In Dedham, Dr. Nathaniel
Ames commenced inoculating his patients. Among them was Fisher
Ames, who though he may have been treated against the smallpox in

---

of grievances. Entry of Sept. 6, 1774, Baker, ed., "Diary of Dr. Nathaniel Ames,"
Dedham Hist. Register, 3 (1892), 72.

30. Edmund C. Burnett, *The Continental Congress* (N.Y., 1941), 42. Burnett
described the Suffolk Resolves as "a small bomb, loaded with political explosives
which was touched off in the assembled Congress." John C. Miller, *Sam Adams*
(Boston, 1936), 323. John C. Miller, *Origins of the American Revolution* (Boston,
1943), 384, 389. The Resolves are printed in Worthington C. Ford, ed., *Journals of
the Continental Congress*, 34 vols. (Washington, 1904-37), I, 32-39.

31. Entries of June 22, July 14, Sept. 1, 4, 6, 9, Nov. 3, 16, 22, 1774, Apr. 19, 20,
22, 23, June 1, 16, 17, 1775, Baker, ed., "Diary of Dr. Nathaniel Ames," *Dedham
Hist. Register*, 3 (1892), 72, 73, 129, 130. Worthington, *History of Dedham*, 47;
Mann, *Annuals of Dedham*, 34; Smith, *History of Dedham*, 447, 461; Cato presumably was a Negro, though from the infrequent references to him, it is not
possible to determine conclusively that he was a slave.

his childhood, now underwent the somewhat risky injection of the diluted virus as a protective measure.[32]

Between 1774 and 1777 Fisher "kept school" intermittently, teaching briefly in Roxbury, not far from Dedham, and at the Governor Dummer Academy near Newburyport, Massachusetts. At intervals he took over the duties of running the family farm, but he continued to pursue his scholarly interests through omnivorous reading and further study in prose and poetry, as well as history. He was especially drawn to the Greek and Roman writers and could quote dramatically the most brilliant passages from works of Virgil. In English poetry, the flowing language of Shakespeare and Milton appealed to Ames, and he committed segments of their writings to memory. In this period of almost indiscriminate reading, he obviously increased his ability to utilize written and spoken English. He also acquired rich sources of material upon which his retentive mind could draw for the images and allusions characteristic of his vivid prose.[33] Three years after graduation, Ames received a Master of Arts degree from Harvard College. The granting of a "second degree" was virtually an automatic procedure which involved no additional academic work, merely the payment of a special fee. Ames's plans for the future gradually crystallized, and encouraged by his mother's wish that he become a lawyer, he began studying law on his own in 1777. The following year he sought the guidance of William Tudor, a prominent young attorney of Boston.[34]

The late 1770's brought sorrow and distress to the Ames family. Seth Ames, who had enlisted as a surgeon's mate in the fall of 1775, had returned home after his tour of duty at the Roxbury encampment with an illness diagnosed as consumption. According to one source his respiratory ailment was intensified by a "boundless indulgence in snuff." Dr. Ames could do nothing for his brother, and it was hard for those closest to him to watch him fail. On December 31, 1777, he was unable

32. Entries of Aug. 23, 29, 1775, July 11, 1776, Baker, ed., "Diary of Dr. Nathaniel Ames," *Dedham Hist. Register*, 3 (1892), 130-32. John Adams to John Warren, July 24, 1776, Charles F. Adams, ed., *Familiar Letters of John Adams and his Wife Abigail Adams During the Revolution* (N.Y., 1876), 204-5. Hannah Winthrop to Mercy Otis Warren, n.p., n.d., quoted in Alice Brown, *Mercy Warren* (Boston, 1899), 129.

33. "Memorial of Fisher Ames," *Boston Monthly Magazine*, 1 (1826), 410-11; Kirkland in Ames, *Works of Ames*, I, 7-8; "Field Day at Dummer Academy," Essex Institute *Historical Collections*, 19 (1882), 197; entry of Feb. 22, 1775, Baker, ed., "Diary of Dr. Nathaniel Ames," *Dedham Hist. Register*, 3 (1892), 129; Diary of Jason Haven, Feb. 24, 1775, Amer. Antiq. Soc.; "Fisher Ames," *Port Folio*, 3d Ser., 1 (1813), 8.

34. Board of Overseers, Records, III, 112 (July 14, 1777), Harvard Archives; William C. Lane, "Letters of Nathaniel Appleton," Col. Soc. of Mass., *Transactions*, 8 (1904), 315.

to speak, and a day later he died, just a few weeks before his thirty-fifth birthday. Shortly after Seth's death, Fisher took over the administration of his estate.[35] Meanwhile, another tragedy was in the making for the Ames family. Fisher's brother William had left his clerk's job to go to sea. Sometime in 1777 he embarked on a voyage and was never heard from again. After two years of fruitless waiting, the Ameses concluded that he was dead and Nathaniel appraised his clothes and took over his effects.[36]

In March 1778, there was once again a call for volunteers in Dedham, and Fisher Ames enlisted in Captain Abel Richards' company, which was sent to man the old entrenchments at Roxbury, guarding the land approaches to Boston. After a period of fifteen days' service, the soldiers returned home to catch up on chores and resume their usual activities. This military duty proved to be Ames's final service in the war.[37]

Even though Massachusetts was no longer the main scene of military activity, the hardships and privations continued during the remaining years of the Revolution. A rampant inflation, the product of a chronic shortage of goods and excessive printing of paper money by the state, brought about financial chaos. In its efforts to cope with the economic strains, the government of Massachusetts found itself in an inextricable position. Unable to stem the flood of Continental paper money and forced to continue to emit its own bills of credit and treasurer's certificates in large quantity, the state's only recourse was to attempt to control prices and wages.[38] From 1776 on, public demand for relief from constantly increasing prices dinned about the ears of the General Court with the consequence that the state encouraged a succession of interstate, as well as local, conventions to arouse public support for limiting prices. When the value of paper money declined precipitously in the spring of 1779, the Boston Committee of Correspondence called a convention to meet at Concord to establish a new scale of legal prices

35. Mann, *Annals of Dedham*, 88; W. Winthrop Papers, Harvard Archives, contains a brief obituary note stating that Seth Ames "had long been in declining health." Secretary of the Commonwealth, ed., *Massachusetts Soldiers and Sailors in the Revolutionary War*, 17 vols. (Boston, 1896-1908), I, 222; entry of Dec. 31, 1777, Baker, ed., "Diary of Dr. Nathaniel Ames," *Dedham Hist. Register*, 3 (1892), 186. In 1805 Fisher Ames and his wife named their sixth child after Seth.

36. Entry of Aug. 16, 1779, Baker, ed., "Diary of Dr. Nathaniel Ames," *Dedham Hist. Register*, 4 (1893), 65.

37. Secretary of the Commonwealth, ed., *Massachusetts Soldiers and Sailors*, I, 217.

38. Ralph V. Harlow, "Economic Conditions in Massachusetts During the American Revolution," Col. Soc. of Mass., *Transactions*, 20 (1918), 166. Harlow states that Massachusetts emitted £500,042 in bills of credit and £656,000 in treasurer's certificates.

on essential commodities. Dedham responded by sending delegations to both the session in July and in October.[39]

Members of the first session of the Concord Convention recommended new wage and price ceilings which the towns were to enforce. The Dedham Town Meeting unanimously accepted the proceedings of the Convention and appointed Ames to a committee to enforce the restrictions, as well as to regulate the prices of articles which had not been listed by the group at Concord. On this same occasion, Fisher Ames was chosen one of the two representatives of the town for the second session of the Convention to be held at Concord.[40] The committee of enforcement then prepared its supplementary table of prices, setting limits on hides, shoes, flax, and hay. Carpenters were to receive a maximum of $8 per day; wood was priced at $24 per cord; and blacksmiths were not to charge more than $11 for shoeing horses nor $22 for oxen.[41]

During the second session in Concord in early October, Ames and his fellow delegates had to revise the price scale again, especially with respect to food, since the value of money had continued to fall. In the debate over the new arrangement, Ames spoke emphatically against the whole concept of restrictions. He was convinced that employing the power of the state to establish the value of commodities was false, as prices resulted from agreement and consent between buyer and seller and could not be arbitrarily determined. The embarrassment of

39. Richard B. Morris, *Government and Labor in Early America* (N.Y., 1946), 92-135; Harlow, "Economic Conditions in Massachusetts," Col. Soc. of Mass., *Transactions,* 20 (1918), 168, 182. See also Richard B. Morris, "Labor and Mercantilism in the Revolutionary Era," in Morris, ed., *The Era of the American Revolution,* (N.Y., 1939), 94-103; Andrew McFarland Davis, "The Limitation of Prices in Massachusetts, 1776-1779," Col. Soc. of Mass., *Transactions,* 10 (1905), 119-34; Kenneth Scott, "Price Control in New England During the Revolution," *New Eng. Qtly.,* 19 (1946), 453-73; Oscar and Mary Handlin, "Revolutionary Economic Policy in Massachusetts," *Wm. and Mary Qtly.,* 3d Ser., 4 (1947), 3-26; Dedham Town Meeting, July 29, 1779, Dedham Town Records, 1773-84, VIII, Town Clerk's Office, Dedham.

40. *Proceedings of the Convention Held at Concord, July 14, 1779* (Boston, 1779), Broadside, Chamberlain Collection, Boston Pub. Lib.; *Proceedings of the Convention Begun and Held at Concord . . . on the Sixth Day of October, A.D. 1779* (Boston, 1779). See also Printed Circular Letter of Thomas Walley, Boston, July 21, 1779, *Copy of the Proceedings of the Convention at Concord, on the 14th Instant,* Broadside, Mass. Hist. Soc.; Dedham Town Meeting, Aug. 4, 1779, Dedham Town Records, 1773-84, VIII, Town Clerk's Office, Dedham.

41. *Ibid.* An indication of the sharp rise in prices is given in the Diary of Nathaniel Ames. Material for a coat cost $4 per yard in June 1773, $8 per yard in Dec. 1776. Ames paid $100 rent for one lot of land in Apr. 1779 and $450 for the same lot in June 1780. A hand-vise cost 18d silver or $160 paper money. "Colliflower" seed cost $15 for 36 grains. Baker, ed., "Diary of Dr. Nathaniel Ames," *Dedham Hist. Register,* 4 (1893), 25, 67.

a depreciating currency, he stated, was inevitable and could be met only with patience and fortitude. Ames did not persuade the Convention to adopt his views. In fact, somewhat prematurely, the president of the Convention asserted that the resolutions adopted at Concord immediately re-established public faith in the monetary system. Before a month had passed, however, the regulations were already being violated in Boston. Local efforts to end inflation were certain to fail as long as there was a shortage of goods and excessive quantities of money continued to circulate. In spite of its questionable success, the meeting was an important one for Fisher Ames, since it gave him his first experience in public affairs.[42]

42. Kirkland in Ames, *Works of Ames,* I, 8. Speech of Walter Spooner, Oct. 12, 1779, quoted in Davis, "Limitation of Prices," Col. Soc. of Mass., *Transactions,* 10 (1905), 131.

Chapter III

From Law to Politics

When Fisher Ames returned from Concord in mid-October 1779, he resumed his legal studies, which had now become the chief focus of his life. Several more years of systematic study under William Tudor lay ahead, and during this period, Ames acquired a thorough knowledge of law. As a fledgling lawyer, he was exposed to the political and economic philosophy of the rising businessmen with whom he soon allied himself. Once engaged in law, he was but a short step from politics; but not until he had taken this step did Ames find his métier.

When Ames began his work under Tudor's supervision, he asked permission to continue studying in Dedham. It was unusual for a law student to study on his own, since candidates for the legal profession were expected to serve an apprenticeship in the office of a practicing lawyer. Tudor presented Ames's case on July 21, 1778, to the members of the Suffolk County Bar Association with the plea that his protégé "might be considered as a student with him from last April, and that he might be permitted to prosecute his studies at Dedham." [1] The lawyers attending the meeting maintained that it was a bad precedent, but postponed a final decision. Not until December 1779 did the Bar Association finally admit Ames as a regular student of the law. After discussing the request again, they agreed that he should be regarded as a student from January 1, 1779, an exception from the rules which they were

1. George Dexter, ed., "Record Book of the Suffolk Bar, 1770-1805," Mass. Hist. Soc., *Proceedings*, 19 (1882), 153.

willing to allow because of "some particular circumstances in his favor." If he continued, henceforth, to study in Mr. Tudor's office, he could present himself to be examined by the members of the bar "in the practical business of the profession" in January 1782.[2]

The members of the bar wanted Ames to participate in the day-to-day routine of a lawyer's office. Although he had steeped himself in the theoretical aspects of law through his private studies, it was essential for him before his admittance to the bar to have the practical experience which close association with Tudor could provide. At a time when only the leading members of the profession had extensive collections of law books, Ames would thus have access to his mentor's law library and manuscript notes of cases decided by the Massachusetts courts.[3] In applying to "read law" with William Tudor, Fisher Ames had chosen an attorney of the highest professional standards, one who was sympathetic to the individual needs of his students. Eight years older than Ames, Tudor had himself received legal training under John Adams, then the leading lawyer of Massachusetts. During the revolutionary crisis, Tudor strongly supported the cause of liberty, but his philosophic outlook was tempered with a moderation which led him to criticize freely the extremes of the most ardent patriots. "In this town," he had commented to his friend Theophilus Parsons in 1773, "the noble cause is made too much a party matter, whilst our patriotic declaimers are so illiberal as to deny any man, who dissents from their measures, either common sense or honesty."[4] He went on to quote Voltaire's view that the true philosopher is most pleased with moderate governments. Tudor's complete support of the Revolution is substantiated, however, by the fact that he became Judge Advocate General in the Continental forces for a period of three years. In 1778 he resigned to return to his legal career and reopen his law office in Boston. It was then that Ames contacted him with the intent of beginning his formal law study. Fisher Ames found his relationship with Tudor a satisfying one and almost a decade after the completion of his legal course, was still corresponding with his distinguished teacher. As a guide to the

2. *Ibid.*
3. *Ibid.;* Charles Warren, *A History of the American Bar* (Boston, 1911), 160-61, 165-67, 178. An advertisement in the *Essex Gazette*, Dec. 1774, of lawbooks for sale is quoted in Emory Washburn, *Sketches of the Judicial History of Massachusetts, From 1630 to the Revolution in 1775* (Boston, 1840), 197; see also Paul M. Hamlin, *Legal Education in Colonial New York* (N.Y., 1939), 73-94.
4. Entries of Aug. 10, 11, 1769, in L. H. Butterfield, ed., *Diary and Autobiography of John Adams,* 4 vols. (Cambridge, Mass., 1961), I, 338-39. William Tudor to Theophilus Parsons, Boston, May 7, 1773, "Memoir of Hon. William Tudor," Mass. Hist. Soc., *Collections,* 2d Ser., 8 (1819), 287.

intricacies of the law, Tudor had obviously left the imprint of his conservative attitude upon his pupil.[5]

Despite its informality, legal training such as Ames experienced was by no means a haphazard affair. By the time he started studying law, the profession had successfully established, through the Bar Association, educational requirements and a definite term of study as prerequisites for admission to practice before a court. The swarm of unlearned, self-made lawyers, who to the dismay of John Adams had overrun the Massachusetts courts in the 1760's, had been eliminated by the more rigid standards. After this legal reformation, long years of probation became the rule, and not even the disruption of the court system during the Revolution altered the requirement. Following three years of preliminary study, Ames might expect to be admitted to practice as an attorney before the court of common pleas. Two years later he would be allowed to plead causes before the august judges of the Superior Court of Judicature, and after two further years of practice he would qualify as a barrister or counselor.[6]

Like most budding lawyers in the eighteenth century, Ames had to devote himself to diligent study of standard legal works. To overcome the complexities of common law, he had to master both Coke's *Commentary Upon Littleton* and Blackstone's *Commentaries on the Laws of England*. While common law was of primary importance, a student was expected to be well versed in natural and civil law as well. This meant more than a cursory acquaintance with such works as Pufendorf's *De Jure Naturae et Gentium* [*On the Law of Nature and of Nations*], Hugo Grotius's *De Jure Belli ac Pacis* [*Concerning the Law of War and Peace*], and Vattel's *Droit des Gens* [*Law of Nations*].[7] The general outline of training was fairly consistent, but the additional works each student mastered varied largely with the inclination of the individual teacher. Since there were no prescribed courses of study,

5. Tudor to Parsons, May 7, 1773, "Memoir of Tudor," Mass. Hist. Soc., *Collections*, 2d Ser., 8 (1819), 293.

6. Regulation of attorneys in Massachusetts began in 1701. Dexter, "Record Book of the Suffolk Bar," Mass. Hist. Soc., *Proceedings*, 19 (1882), 143; H. R. Bailey, *Attorneys and Their Admission to the Bar* (Boston, 1907), 21. Entry of July 28, 1766, Butterfield, ed., *Diary of John Adams*, I, 316-17.

7. Sir Edward Coke, *The First Part of the Institutes of the Laws of England: or A Commentary Upon Littleton*. The most recent edition during Ames's student days was that of E. and R. Nutt, London, 1783. Jeremiah Gridley advised John Adams in 1758: "In the study of law, the common law ... deserves your first and last attention, and he has conquered all the difficulties of this law who is master of the Institutes." Entry of Oct. 25, 1758, Butterfield, ed., *Diary of John Adams*, I, 54; Warren, *American Bar*, 170-77. Sir William Blackstone, *Commentaries On The Laws of England* (Oxford, 1765-69).

lawyers occasionally would draw up lists of suggested readings. Among
the works frequently used were Wood's *Institutes of the Common Law
of England,* Bohun's *Introduction to the Study and Practice of the
Laws of England,* and Sir Michael Foster's *Discourse upon a Few
Branches of the Crown Law.*[8]

After entering Tudor's office, Ames formed a close and lasting
friendship with fellow apprentice George Richards Minot, the youngest son of a Boston merchant. Minot had completed his A.B. degree at
Harvard in 1778, in spite of his doubts about the value of his studies
during the period when the college had been temporarily located at
Concord. Following graduation, he began to study law with William
Tudor, and it was then that Minot and Ames, only months apart in age,
found mutual interests both in law and in politics. With an inquiring
and versatile mind, Minot responded to Ames's lively nature and found
that he was stimulated in his own endeavors by the "flame which
burned so intensely in the imagination of his companion." [9]

Ames's professional training was completed sooner than had been
expected. In the autumn of 1781, just as the fighting in the Revolution
was drawing to a close, he prepared for the final examination. On
October 9, members of the Bar Association gathered for a business
meeting in Tudor's office and considered Ames's case. In spite of their
former decision about the term of his studies, they now felt that he
should be recommended to the court of common pleas. They were
aware that he had studied on his own before entering upon a supervised
program, and that he could rightfully be regarded as having been a
student "for four years and upwards." His steady application had undermined his health, making relaxation from all work imperative. They
then voted unanimously to recommend him, "in consideration of his
cheerfully offering himself to an examination, and his moral, political,
and literary character standing in the fairest point of view." At the next
meeting of the court, Ames was sworn in after taking the oath of an
attorney.[10]

8. Warren, *American Bar,* 170-77; for a typical course of legal study in the
1780's, see the entries of Oct. 3 and Dec. 12, 1787, in Charles F. Adams, ed., *Life
in a New England Town, 1787-1788: the Diary of John Quincy Adams* (Boston,
1903), 43, 69, 74, 107-8.

9. Dexter, "Record Book of the Suffolk Bar," Mass. Hist. Soc., *Proceedings,* 19
(1882), 154; "Character of the Hon. George Richards Minot, Esq.," Mass. Hist.
Soc., *Collections,* 8 (1802), 86-109; George R. Minot to Stephen Minot, Concord,
Feb. 28, 1776, Sedgwick (Minot) Papers, Mass. Hist. Soc.; James S. Loring, *The
Hundred Boston Orators* (Boston, 1853), 147.

10. Dexter, "Record Book of the Suffolk Bar," Mass. Hist. Soc., *Proceedings,*
19 (1882), 155. Washburn, *Judicial History of Massachusetts,* 201-2, gives the names
of members of the bar, both attorneys and barristers, in 1775, many of whom were
still practicing after the Revolution.

Even before he was admitted to practice, Ames had planned to establish himself in Dedham. In October, he made an agreement with Nathaniel to rent the "South East lower room" in his house for a law office. Fisher was to furnish the lumber and nails and to pay for the carpentry while Nathaniel stipulated that he would reimburse Fisher for his expenditures "so far as the same shall be valuable to me . . . after his tenancy." On November 7, Fisher opened his office, and it was not long before he presented several cases before the court of common pleas.[11]

Soon after he had commenced practice, Ames had an action of trespass to consider, and he found that all his reading and training did not suffice to guide him. It was a knotty problem, causing him to turn to his friend Minot for advice about the technicalities of the situation. With all the assuredness of a veteran lawyer, Minot answered Ames's note, suggesting authorities who offered the best precedents for the case. "As to the action of trespass lying in the case you have put there is an authority in Strange 1239, The Mayor of Northampton v. Ward, quoted in Bacon thus 'An action of trespass lies for erecting a stall in a public market, for notwithstanding every man has a common right to the liberty of selling in such market, no man can erect a stall in the soil of another without his permission.' which I think is a case very similar to yours and seems to warrant this kind of action. Rufus and myself both think it may be managed as a private nuisance. You are the best judge of the expediency of the mode."[12]

In April 1782, five months after he was admitted to the bar, Ames had four cases entered in the docket for the April term of the court of common pleas, and in the January term, 1783, he had seven. In most of the cases, involving the recovery of goods, debts, or unpaid promissory notes, Ames was attorney for the plaintiff. The sums involved were never large, usually between £7 and £60, and reflected the propensity of individuals to take to court cases which might have been settled without costly litigation. In a case involving the default of £2 payment on a promissory note of £8, the costs to the plaintiff, including Ames's fee of 4s 6d were £1 11s 6d.[13]

11. Agreement Between Fisher Ames and Nathaniel Ames, Dedham, Oct. 31, 1781, Fisher Ames Papers, Dedham Hist. Soc.; entry of Nov. 7, 1781, Baker, ed., "Diary of Dr. Nathaniel Ames," *Dedham Hist. Register,* 4 (1893), 68.

12. George R. Minot to Fisher Ames, Boston, Dec. 1, 1781, Fisher Ames Papers, Dedham Hist. Soc. "Rufus" was Rufus G. Amory.

13. List of Cases, New Entries for Apr. Term, 1782, Vol. 534, No. 94038, Court Files, Suffolk County, Clerk of the Court, Supreme Judicial Court. Ames was attorney for the plaintiff in the following cases, Jan. term, 1783: Tyler v. Fisher, and Tyler v. Bullard (recovery of goods); Richardson v. Richardson (debts); Cunningham v. Vinal, Farmington v. Houghton, and Farmington v. Richardson

One of the more interesting cases, involving wartime debts, came before the court in June 1782. As attorney for James and Eliakim Morse, Ames was trying to recover a debt of £61 4s from the town of Medfield. During the war, militia officers and selectmen had been authorized to obtain a loan on the credit of the town to procure soldiers for service in the Continental Army. They borrowed money from James Morse and hired various individuals for military service. The plaintiffs, through Ames, contended that the inhabitants of Medfield had thereby benefited and "that by reasons of the premises, the inhabitants were liable and obliged to pay ... the sum on demand." Since the town had never paid, the plaintiffs claimed £50 damages. On behalf of the defendants, James Sullivan entered the plea that there never had been an agreement. The case was continued to the October term and finally the jury found "that the defendant did promise as set forth in the writ." [14] With true Yankee frugality, they assessed the damages at £7 10s. Ames had won his case, but the nominal award left him no alternative except to appeal the decision. A jury in the May term of the Supreme Judicial Court in 1783 reconsidered the matter and awarded the Morses a total of £17 16s 8d against the town of Medfield.[15]

On occasion Ames himself was the plaintiff. In a suit against John Fuller of Needham, a yeoman, Ames recovered judgment for £20 damages and costs. Fuller appealed the decision, but failed to argue the appeal. Thereupon Ames requested the court to assess further penalties with additional damages. The court finally affirmed the judgment, adding 2s damages and £3 15s 8d more in costs.[16]

Ames's family played an important part in his life at this time. From the extant records it appears that much of Fisher's legal activity consisted of collecting payments on notes or transmitting sums of money for his clients. His sister, Deborah, aided him by taking over his transactions when he was in Boston. In turn, he assisted with affairs at home. The Ames household became more peaceful when before the end of the Revolution, Richard Woodward left his wife and moved to New Haven, Connecticut. After his peremptory departure, Deborah Ames Woodward, once again called Mrs. Ames, was forced to assume responsibility for the tavern. Fisher helped his mother keep it open, even taking out a license as innkeeper in his own name. Meantime, he con-

(promissory notes), Vol. 534, No. 94078, *ibid.;* Davis v. Gleason, Vol. 536, No. 94781, *ibid.* See also Vol. 536, No. 94725, for the writs of the July and Oct. terms, 1783, *ibid.*

14. Morse v. Town of Medfield, Vol. 534, No. 93943 and No. 94265, *ibid.*
15. Medfield v. Morse et al., Vol. dated 1783, 6, *ibid.*
16. Ames v. Fuller, Vol. dated 1784, 216, and Ames v. Gay, Oct. 1783, Vol. 534, *ibid.*

tinued to work the fields adjoining the inn property, just as Nathaniel did with his own land. While Ames probably did little of the physical labor himself, he developed an interest in horticulture which later became one of his chief avocations.[17]

Before the end of his three-year term in the lower court system, Ames was recommended for admission to practice before the Supreme Judicial Court. In February 1784, a prominent lawyer, John Lowell, suggested the names of three young colleagues and friends, Ames, Minot, and Rufus G. Amory, to the Supreme Court and requested that they be allowed to practice. Seven months elapsed before Ames was presented to the court, and on a motion of the attorney general, took both the attorney's oath and the oath of allegiance to the state, in which he swore loyalty to the Commonwealth and renounced any attachment to the king of Great Britain. George Minot wrote in a notebook on September 8, 1784: "This day I was admitted to the Attorneys oath at the Supreme Judicial Court as were also Mr. R. G. Amory and Mr. F. Ames. I am the junior of the three." [18]

Ames soon found a secure place among his fellow lawyers, who thoroughly respected him for the unusual abilities he had brought to the practice of law. Not only did he reveal a profound knowledge of general principles, but he displayed exceptional qualities as a speaker whenever he argued a case before the court. "Good judges have declared that few young men who came to the bar at this period knew so much of precedent or elementary principles as Ames." [19] Although he was an exceptional speaker, his sensitivity at times impinged on his legal objectiveness. His standards of professional ethics made him avoid any semblance of trickery, and evidence of it in his own client would upset him. "The hesitation or tergiversation of a witness would disturb him through a whole cause and the moment he felt his side of the question was wrong his good genius deserted him." [20] He could not depend

17. Fisher Ames, note and receipt, June 11, 1784, Washburn Collection, VI, Mass. Hist. Soc.; Fisher Ames to Debby Ames, Boston, July 25, 1783, Fisher Ames Papers, Dedham Hist. Soc.; List of Fisher Ames's Purchases, Jonathan Avery Account Book, 1784-1827, Dedham Hist. Soc. Fisher Ames to Debby Ames, Boston, Apr. 29, 1784, Miscellaneous Manuscript Collection, N.Y. Pub. Lib.; Mann, *Annals of Dedham*, 90; "Names of Persons Licensed in County of Suffolk 1782," Vol. 534, No. 94043, Court Files, Suffolk County, Clerk of the Court, Supreme Judicial Court.
18. Vol. dated 1784, 39, 223, Court Files, Suffolk County, Clerk of the Court, Supreme Judicial Court; Dexter, "Record Book of the Suffolk Bar," Mass. Hist. Soc., *Proceedings*, 19 (1882), 157-58. Fisher Ames, Oath of Allegiance, n.d., Chamberlain Collection, Boston Pub. Lib.; George R. Minot, Notebook Fragment, Box 1, Sedgwick (Minot) Papers, Mass. Hist. Soc.
19. William Sullivan, *Familiar Letters on Public Characters* (Boston, 1834), 58-59.
20. "Memorial of Fisher Ames," *Boston Monthly Magazine*, 1 (1825), 411.

merely on his great command of language and his knowledge of law
to support him in presenting a case in court. Other lawyers like James
Sullivan and Theophilus Parsons seem to have made greater impressions
on juries than Ames. Sullivan, for example, had a great gift for sensing
the psychology of juries and adapting his presentation to their standards with solid, unornamented reasoning, while Ames frequently resorted to a more scintillating and figurative approach.[21]

The Dedham lawyer did not take all the nuances of his legal cases
seriously, however, for he could often see humor in them. Once when
a court had decided a case in his favor, and the opposing counsel continued to argue on various points, Ames said, "The gentleman puts me
in mind of an old hen which persists in setting after her eggs are taken
away." [22] On another occasion, after spending an unpleasant day in the
court presided over by Judge Robert Treat Paine, who was both deaf
and irascible, Ames asserted that he would not go into court again
without carrying "a bludgeon in one hand and a speaking trumpet in
the other." [23]

An attorney's life was not entirely devoted to drawing up writs or
arguing cases. Whenever Ames went into Boston and looked up his
friends at William Tudor's office, a lively discussion on law or politics
took place. Then, too, there were occasions when the members of the
bar invited the judges of the Supreme Court to dine. Usually these dinners were somewhat solemn evenings, but were important to young
lawyers eager to widen the circle of their professional acquaintances
and in turn to become more widely known. The meetings centered
around professional matters, but at least on one evening, the gentlemen
of the bar had a merry time. Eleven members, among them Ames and
William Tudor, assembled "at Mr. Marston's" for their quarterly meeting and enjoyed both the dinner and each other's company. The secretary added a note to the record of the meeting: "This was a very social
meeting, and several points of practice (not proper for matter of record) were liberally discussed and very amicably adjusted and agreed
upon." [24]

By 1785 Ames had risen to modest heights as a lawyer. Although he

21. Samuel L. Knapp, *Biographical Sketches of Eminent Lawyers, Statesmen, and Men of Letters* (Boston, 1821), 301.
22. Theophilus Parsons, *Memoir of Theophilus Parsons, Chief Justice of the Supreme Judicial Court of Massachusetts with Notices of Some of his Contemporaries* (Boston, 1859), 171.
23. *Ibid.*, 212-13.
24. Dexter, "Record Book of the Suffolk Bar," Mass. Hist. Soc., *Proceedings*, 19 (1882), 159-60. Fisher Ames and other members of the Boston bar presented the Judges of the Supreme Judicial Court with judicial robes on Oct. 4, 1783, R. T. Paine Papers, IV, Mass. Hist. Soc.

did not have the extensive business of a John Lowell or a James Sullivan, he was far from being a country attorney in a small community. Judging from the records of the Supreme Judicial Court, he had a fair number of cases in comparison with those attorneys practicing directly in Boston.[25] Among the cases which Ames handled, there occasionally would be one of more than routine meaning. In 1786 he undertook the task of trying to recover a debt owed to the Reverend William Clark, formerly of Dedham, then an exile living in London. Clark was attempting to reclaim a sum of £214, a debt Nathaniel Smith and others had secured by a bond in 1770. More because of former friendship with Clark than from business considerations, Ames agreed to undertake the lawsuit. He vividly remembered how the Reverend Mr. Clark had been harassed in Dedham for his Tory opinions and Episcopalian faith. Although Clark had been circumspect in avoiding political discussions, his efforts to aid two fleeing loyalists with a letter of recommendation had proved to be his undoing. For this indiscretion he had been condemned as an enemy to his country and brought to trial before the Court of Special Sessions in Boston in June 1777. When he had refused to swear allegiance to the Commonwealth, he had been sentenced to banishment and confined on a prison ship until Nathaniel Ames and several townspeople had intervened in his behalf. Fisher himself had ridden to Boston in June 1778 to help secure Clark's release, and had brought him the pass permitting him to return to his house in Dedham. Subsequently Clark had left Massachusetts and sailed for England.[26]

The passions and antipathies engendered by the war had largely subsided by the mid 1780's, yet enough remained to serve as a stumbling block to the recovery of debts. In the case of "William Clark versus Nathaniel Smith et.al.," both the court of common pleas and the Su-

25. Minute Books, Court Files, Suffolk County, Clerk of the Court, Supreme Judicial Court. Not all of the cases listed indicate the attorney's name. In Feb. 1788, 203 cases were listed, but when the case was defaulted, continued, or the parties reached an agreement, the attorneys' names were not given. J. Lowell had eighteen cases, J. Sullivan, nineteen, W. Tudor, five, Ames, three, T. Parsons, three, and nine other lawyers were listed with one or two cases.

26. William Clark v. Nathaniel Smith *et al.*, Vol. 650, No. 105049, *ibid.* Worthington, *History of Dedham*, 70-71. Smith, *History of Dedham*, 94-95. Copy of letter of William Clark, Dedham, May 21, 1777, Samuel Holten Papers, Library of Congress, Washington, D.C. The petition of Clark to be released was granted by the Governor's Council, Aug. 1777; *The Acts and Resolves, Public and Private of the Province of Massachusetts Bay*, 21 vols. (Boston, 1869-1922), XX, 99. See also the case of Nathaniel Fisher, an uncle of Fisher Ames's, imprisoned in 1781 as a Tory. Both Fisher and Nathaniel Ames signed a petition for his release, Nov. 16, 1781, which was granted by the Council, Vol. 172, No. 66, Massachusetts Archives, Office of the Secretary of the Commonwealth, State House, Boston, Mass.

preme Judicial Court denied the plaintiff's right to reclaim his loan. A
bond, available as evidence, showed that the defendants had paid full
interest to 1776, as well as £52 of the principal, but still owed the
balance of the £214 plus interest for a ten year period. When the Supreme Judicial Court reviewed the case, the defendants entered a plea
to the effect that "the writing Obligatory in the writ" was not theirs.
The Court accepted the plea as "sufficient" and before dismissing the
case, ordered that the defendants be reimbursed for the costs of the
suit, and that Ames, as Clark's attorney, be assessed £10.[27]

By defending the interests of a Tory, Ames did not risk his standing
among his fellow lawyers, nor was he subjected to any personal censure. Yet he was aware of a continuing public dislike for members of
his profession. Originating in an earlier period in Massachusetts when
erudite lawyers were suspect, and when greedy pettifoggers filled the
courts with litigation, the antipathy to attorneys appeared again after
the Revolution. The large number of cases, especially for the recovery
of debts, reflected the malaise of the postwar economy, but in the
popular mind the legal web in which many individuals were caught was
due solely to the "order of lawyers." Animosity toward lawyers was
only one aspect of growing dissatisfaction within the state, which ultimately culminated in Shays' Rebellion.[28]

Eventually, Dedham also joined in a denunciation of rapacious lawyers. At a town meeting in May 1787, the residents declared that they
were "not inattentive to the almost universally prevailing complaints
against the practice of the ... lawyers and many of us ... feel the effects of their unreasonable and extravagant exactions." They instructed
their delegates at the General Court in very forceful terms to introduce
laws to regulate the courts and the "order of lawyer[s] as that we may
have recourse to the Laws and find our security and not our ruin in
them." If restraints were impracticable, they were "to endeavor that
the order of Lawyers be totally abolished." [29]

27. Clark v. Smith, Vol. 650, Court Files, Suffolk County, Clerk of the Court,
Supreme Judicial Court.
28. Washburn, *Judicial History of Massachusetts*, 51-52, 104, 189; Robert J.
Taylor, *Western Massachusetts in the Revolution* (Providence, 1954), 134-35; Lee
N. Newcomer, *Embattled Farmers, A Massachusetts Countryside in the American
Revolution* (N.Y., 1953), 135; George R. Minot, *The History of the Insurrections
in Massachusetts in the Year 1786 and the Rebellion Consequent Thereon*, 2d ed.,
(Boston, 1810), 28-29; Benjamin Austin, *Observations on the Pernicious Practice of
the Law* (Boston, 1819); Caleb Strong to Theodore Sedgwick, June 24, 1786,
Sedgwick Papers, Vol. A, Mass. Hist. Soc.; *Boston Gazette*, Mar. 6, 27, Sept. 30,
1786, Feb. 19, Mar. 19, 1787.
29. Resolutions of the Town Meeting, May 1787, Dedham, quoted in Smith,
History of Dedham, 370.

Such an arraignment of the profession was indicative of the inflamed state of the public mind, brought on by the widespread feeling that there was no justice to be had for the common man when insistent creditors, clever lawyers, and unsympathetic judges were arrayed against him. Everything seemed designed to erect a bulwark for the protection of property rights, while the poor debtor found that his own small property was subject to seizure to satisfy any judgment against him, and that debtor's prison was a serious threat.[30]

During the summer of 1786 an increasing number of the rural inhabitants of the state had grown restive. Added to the resentment against the legal system was a genuine burden of economic troubles, the outgrowth of rigid financial policies on the part of the Commonwealth and the continued fall in agricultural prices. Grievances generated by high taxes, a lack of paper money, strict collection of debts, and frequent foreclosures in bankruptcy cases were mounting by the autumn months.[31] Bands of armed men, led by Daniel Shays and others, acting on the assumption of an inherent right to forceful protest against existing conditions, prevented the meeting of the county courts, especially in Hampshire and Berkshire.[32]

The men of wealth and position in the state became convinced that property rights, as well as political power, were jeopardized and that mob rule might readily supplant law and order. In the view of one conservative the uprising constituted a real danger: "Every man of observation is convinced that the end of government security cannot be attained by the exercise of principles founded on democratic equality. A war is now actually levied on the virtue, property and distinctions of the community." [33] Although the armed dissidents were quickly dispersed during the early winter, Shays' Rebellion acted as a catalyst on the conservative business and political groups within the state. Henceforth, the men of property saw more clearly than before that their objectives of encouragement of commerce, payment of the con-

30. Newcomer, *Embattled Farmers*, 135; Anson E. Morse, *The Federalist Party in Massachusetts to the Year 1800* (Princeton, 1909), 37.

31. Richard B. Morris, "Insurrection in Massachusetts" in Daniel Aaron, ed., *America in Crisis* (N.Y., 1952), 21-49; Robert East, "The Massachusetts Conservative in the Critical Period," in Morris, ed., *Era of the American Revolution*, 354-55. Allan Nevins, *The American States During and After the Revolution, 1775-1789* (N.Y., 1924), 535-37; Morse, *Federalist Party*, 33-35.

32. Taylor, *Western Massachusetts*, 129 ff; Jonathan Smith, "Some Features of Shays' Rebellion," *Wm. and Mary Qtly.*, 3d Ser., 5 (1948), 89-90; Minot, *History of the Insurrections*, 37-49; Henry Jackson to Henry Knox, Boston, Sept. 28, 1786, Knox Papers, XIX, No. 19, Mass. Hist. Soc.; Mercy Otis Warren to Catherine Macauley, n.d., 1786, Mercy Warren Letterbook, Mass. Hist. Soc.

33. Theodore Sedgwick to Rufus King, Boston, June 18, 1787, Charles R. King, ed., *The Life and Correspondence of Rufus King*, 6 vols. (N.Y., 1894-1900), I, 224.

48   *Fisher Ames*

tinental debt, and the protection of property rights could best be
achieved under the aegis of a strong national government controlled
by themselves.[34] It was to this body of prospective nationalists, the
precursors of the Federalists, that Fisher Ames had gravitated during
the turmoil of Shays' uprising. The extent to which he reflected their
views and also gave voice to them became very evident in a series of
political essays which appeared in 1786 and 1787.

On October 12, 1786, the *Independent Chronicle*, a weekly Boston
newspaper, published Ames's first essay, which he had signed with the
pseudonym Lucius Junius Brutus. It was appropriate that the article
appeared in juxtaposition to accounts of the insurrection in western
Massachusetts, as it dealt explicitly with the crisis in the government
of the state. With a few forceful sentences Ames caught the attention
of readers by asserting that "many friends of the government seem to
think it a duty to practise a little well-intended hypocrisy, when con-
versing on the subject of the late commotions in the Commonwealth.
They seem to think it prudent and necessary to conceal from the
people, and even from themselves, the magnitude of the present danger." [35] The writer warned against "pusillanimous councils, and half-
way measures." To him, it was not the occasion to sit idly by while
the state disintegrated. "It is time," he proclaimed, "to . . . rouse the
torpid patriotism of men, who have everything to lose by the subversion of an excellent Constitution." [36]

He took the categorical position that inasmuch as rioting was high
treason, it was wrong to pardon this crime against the state. "No sooner
is the standard of rebellion displayed, than men of desperate principles
and fortunes resort to it; the pillars of government are shaken; the
edifice totters from its centre, the foot of a child may overthrow it; the
hands of giants cannot rebuild it. For if our government should be

34. Minot, *History of the Insurrections*, 81-101; East in Morris, ed., *Era of the
American Revolution*, 350, 388, 390-91; Oscar and Mary Handlin, "Radicals and
Conservatives in Massachusetts After the Revolution," *New Eng. Qtly.*, 17 (1944),
343-55; Stephen Higginson to Henry Knox, Boston, Nov. 25, 1786, Knox Papers,
XIX, No. 58, Mass. Hist. Soc.; Rufus King to Theodore Sedgwick, Oct. 22, 1786,
Sedgwick Papers, Vol. A, Mass. Hist. Soc.; Samuel Lyman to Samuel Breck,
Springfield, Dec. 27, 1786, "Bowdoin and Temple Papers," Mass. Hist. Soc., *Col-
lections*, 7th Ser., 6 (1907), 122-24.
35. *Independent Chronicle* (Boston), Oct. 12, 1786; Ames, *Works of Ames*,
II, 91-97. Nathaniel Ames's opinions regarding Shays' Rebellion contrast sharply
with those of Fisher. "Many oppressions having been practised . . . all property
accumulating . . . into a few people's hands, has occasioned great Tumults, County
Conventions and Petitions to the Legislature . . . the People unsatisfied take to
arms." Entry of Jan. 21, 1787, Baker, ed., "Diary of Dr. Nathaniel Ames,"
Dedham Hist. Register, 5 (1894), 32-33.
36. Ames, *Works of Ames*, II, 92.

destroyed, what but the total destruction of civil society must ensue?" If the public were timid or even moderate toward these criminals, insolence and acts against the state would grow in numbers, and inevitably "national policy" would depend on the worst types of men, bankrupts, sots, and "tavern-haunting politicians." He felt that "such men, actuated by the strongest passions of the heart... will acquire in every society a larger share of influence, than equal property and abilities will give to better citizens." [37] Lenience on the part of the government, Ames argued, would evoke only further challenges from men who were convinced that the state lacked the will to enforce its authority. Many individuals, he acknowledged, "would rebel, rather than be ruined, but they would rather not rebel than be hanged."

An active government, which effectively protected every citizen, was essential to persuade the adherents of democracy that the constitution of the state was worthy of defense. He believed that it was of the utmost importance that government not appease the rioters by acceding to their demands for paper money. Such a resolution of the problem would constitute a confiscation of property, a breach of the compact under which government was formed, and a "legal triumph of treason." How little sympathy Ames had for the aggrieved farmers was revealed when he asked a rhetorical question: "Am I to lose my property, and to be involved in distress, to relieve persons whom I never saw, and who are unworthy of compassion if they accept the dishonest relief?" [38] Graphically Ames bared the consequences of delay. If the state did not take action, the constitution would be extinguished, government dissolved, and the people would then rank "somewhere below the Oneida Indians." He ended with an exhortation to rally behind the government and defend the constitution even if it did fall. "Let us not furnish our enemies with a triumph, nor the dishonored page of history with evidence that it [the constitution] was formed with too much wisdom to be valued, and required too much virtue to be maintained by its members." [39]

This first political essay of Ames's is noteworthy chiefly because it etches sharply his early political tendencies and the outlines of his later political positions. His reaction to Shays' Rebellion was volatile, almost violent; he was convinced that the ship of state was in perilous waters, and that only by giving command to the men of education and wealth was there any hope of safety. Typically he saw things in the strongest contrasts, usually black and white. His later views about the calamitous

37. *Ibid.*, 92-94.
38. *Ibid.*, 94-97.
39. *Ibid.*, 97.

effects of democracy in American politics were clearly foreshadowed
in his early writing. Ames was not by nature vindictive, even when he
tended to be adamantly cocksure of himself, but he felt emphatically
that the insurgents constituted such a threat to the life of the state that
they must be crushed beyond all possibility of revival.

It was apparent to observers at the scene of the disorders in western
Massachusetts that by mid-December 1786, the dangers were largely
past. Yet the implications of the rebellion continued to loom large in
the thought of many who were concerned about the future of government on both a local and a national plane. To Ames there were still
many risks evident in the existing state of affairs. Government was not
yet secure, faction not yet extinguished. Therefore he commenced a
series of three articles on the political aftermath of the rebellion which
were published in the *Independent Chronicle* under the signature of
"Camillus." He felt that the public must be made aware of its erroneous
political views before all the disturbances were forgotten, and, he
hoped, "we may . . . succeed in eradicating the destructive notions
which the seditious have infused into the people." [40]

Ames's first "Camillus" essay demonstrated the continuing weakness
of government and the fertile ground for renewed rebellion. How vain
it was, he argued, to assume that there would not be advocates for
unjust and absurd schemes since the people "have drunk down decep-
tion like water. They will remain as blind, as credulous . . . as ever."
There would be no cessation of "opposition to federal measures, and
the schemes of an abolition of debts and an equal distribution of property . . . will be pursued with unremitting industry, till they involve us
again in general confusion." [41] Again, after raising the specter of anarchy, he asserted that the only remedy was a government based on
system, energy, and honesty, one which would make all the laws irre-
sistibly supreme.

Ames graphically outlined the consequences of the lack of patriotism
and firm government. He foresaw man giving rein to his passions,
growing weary of the liberty bought at such sacrifice and creating a
"chaos of morals and politics." Equally abhorrent was the lack of national pride, so necessary as a cement of political union. Without a
national character, Ames asserted, the people would turn against public
liberty and arraign institutions and fundamental laws of the country.

40. Thomas Dwight to John Lowell, Springfield, Dec. 13, 1786, Miscellaneous
Manuscript Collection, Mass. Hist. Soc.; Morse, *Federalist Party*, 183; John Noble,
"A Few Notes on the Shays Rebellion," Amer. Antiq. Soc., *Proceedings*, 15 (1902),
203; "Camillus," I-III, *Independent Chronicle* (Boston), Mar. 1, 1787; Ames,
Works of Ames, II, 97-108.
41. Ames, *Works of Ames*, II, 99.

In summation, Ames expressed his indignation that the people did not venerate a state government which was so closely connected with the preservation of their rights and privileges.[42]

His next essay, interlaced with sarcastic comments, attacked the proponents of more extreme modes of government, the theorist who advocated complete democracy as well as the ardent monarchist. The enthusiast for perfection, a dreamer in speculation, "had dipped his pencil in the rainbow to portray a picture of national felicity for admiration to gaze at." All the talk of restoring the golden age only resulted in too much freedom and loosening the "sudden passions and ignorant prejudices of their constituents." He then sent a shaft against those who had lost faith in republican principles and had begun to rave about monarchy, "as if we were willing to take from the plough-tail or dram-shop some vociferous committee-man, and to array him in royal purple, with all the splendor of a king of the gypsies ... the presumption is, that our king, whenever Providence in its wrath shall send us one, will be a blockhead or a rascal." [43]

Ames ridiculed the idea of a royal government for Americans, who had recently chosen to be republicans. "We are too poor to maintain, and too proud to acknowledge, a king." The desire for a change in the mode of government was entirely unnecessary. Only when the republic had grown corrupt through time and wealth would posterity have the melancholy task of laying the basis for a new government. "We, who are now upon the stage, bear upon our memories too deep an impression of the miseries of the last revolution to think of attempting another." [44]

The third "Camillus" essay was by far the best Ames had written. Forcefully and directly he focused on the urgent need to strengthen the government of the Confederation. In discussing this necessity, Fisher Ames reflected upon the consequences of Shays' Rebellion and upon existing and imminent dangers. "The combustibles are collected; the mine is prepared; the smallest spark may again produce an explosion," he declared. Such a crisis in the affairs of government very obviously arose from the lack of power, "from the relaxation and almost annihilation of our federal government; from the feeble ... temporizing ... character of our own State ... from the perversion of principles among the people." This path led only to anarchy. The alternative—vigorous exertion of lawful authority—would lead to power and pros-

---

42. *Ibid.*, 100-101.
43. *Ibid.*, 102-4. On the interest in monarchism see Louise Dunbar, *A Study of Monarchical Tendencies in the United States, 1776-1801* (Urbana, 1922), 1-164.
44. Ames, *Works of Ames*, II, 104.

perity. Ames disavowed any interest in despotism. What was vital for
the future was "a well-digested, liberal, permanent system of policy"
which "must be supported, in spite of faction, against every thing but
amendment." [45]

Ames was not specific in his recommendations for reinforcement of
the government. His primary goal was to make men cognizant of the
need for change, rather than to analyze details of the change. He believed that this was a time of rising interest in affairs of state, and that
if the opportune moment for bolstering the government were not
seized, ruin would be inevitable. "If we fall, we fall by our folly, not
our fate, and we shall evince to the astonished world of how small
influence to produce national happiness are the fairest gifts of heaven,
—a healthful climate, a fruitful soil, and inestimable laws,—when they
are conferred upon a frivolous, perverse, and ungrateful generation." [46]

The storm was subsiding, yet a spirit of opposition remained alive.
With the dispersal of the insurgents, overt acts of resistance against the
courts and the government ceased. Instead, attention turned to politics
and the activities of the state government because many representatives,
chosen in the spring election of 1787, were sympathetic to the Shays-
ites. This infusion of new members in the General Court and the return
of the ever-popular John Hancock to replace Governor James Bowdoin presaged continuing concern with issues which had not been resolved by the recent uprising. Men of conservative political beliefs were
certain that the "dregs and the scum of mankind" would continue their
attacks on existing governmental institutions and on property holders.
More and more they were convinced, following Shays' Rebellion, that
the proper course of action was to support a movement to strengthen
the national government, as Ames had suggested.[47]

While the problems of the nation were being considered at the Constitutional Convention in Philadelphia during the spring and summer of
1787, Fisher Ames was faced with difficulties in his personal life. His

45. *Ibid.*, 106-7.
46. *Ibid.*, 108. Stephen Higginson to Henry Knox, Nov. 12, 1786, Henry Knox
to Stephen Higginson, Jan. 28, 1787, Higginson to Knox, Jan. 20, Feb. 8, 1787,
Knox Papers, XIX, Nos. 50, 142, 130, 157, Mass. Hist. Soc. James Madison to
George Washington, Feb. 21, 1787, Edmund C. Burnett, ed., *Letters of Members
of the Continental Congress, 1774-1788*, 8 vols. (Washington, 1921-38), VIII, 546.
47. Entry of Mar. 21, 1787, Fitch E. Oliver, ed., *The Diary of William Pynchon
of Salem* (Boston, 1890), 273; Barnabas Bidwell to David Daggett, Tyringham,
June 16, 1787, Franklin B. Dexter, ed., "Selections From the Letters Received by
David Daggett, 1786-1802," Amer. Antiq. Soc., *Proceedings*, 4 (1887), 368;
Theodore Sedgwick to Nathan Dane, July 5, 1787, Sedgwick Papers, II, Mass.
Hist. Soc.; Political Journal of George R. Minot, Sedgwick (Minot) Papers,
Mass. Hist. Soc. Benjamin Lincoln to George Thatcher, May 9, 1787, Thatcher
Papers, Chamberlain Collection, Boston Pub. Lib.

brother, Nathaniel, having served as administrator of their father's estate since 1764, had never divided the inheritance according to the will
of the elder Nathaniel. Innumerable pleas and reminders had not persuaded Dr. Ames to reach an agreement on the issue with his sister,
Deborah, and with Fisher. After a lapse of twenty-three years, it was
now imperative, Fisher insisted, for Nathaniel to settle the accounts
and all matters pertaining to the estate. With determination, Fisher
Ames wrote to his brother, calling attention to his proposal to buy
Nathaniel's share of the land or to have his own legally set apart. "A
Brother would have preferd the first," he asserted, "a *stranger* wd. have
acceded to the second. . . . But all have been refused. . . . This morning
was appointed to give me information. . . . When I applied . . . [you]
refused to let me know for your want of temper and want of sincerity,
you assigned a reason which was antiquated more than twenty years
ago—that you did not incline to be hurried." [48]

Nathaniel responded with asperity. "Squire Ames, I embrace the first
moment of leisure, tho not in the humor of writing, but barely from
civility to notice your letter of today." He denied Fisher's accusations,
insisting that he was willing to sell his rights "for what uninterested
persons judge reasonable," and in concluding his note, revealed a basic
feeling for his brother by saying "with embers of affection, hard to
be totally extinguished, [I] subscribe myself, with humble civility,
N. A." [49] By May 3 the differences had been settled and a legal agreement made between the brothers. Fisher was to deliver "valid Releases"
signed by himself, his mother, and sister with respect to Nathaniel, Jr.'s
administration of the estate. In addition, he was to convey a small tract
of land to Nathaniel and to pay off a note for "the sum of One Hundred and Twenty Pounds" which Nathaniel owed. In return Nathaniel
stipulated that he would deliver to Fisher "all his right interest and title
in the Dower or Thirds assigned out the Estate of the late Doct Nath.
Ames." [50] Before the agreement was signed, Nathaniel became suspicious of Fisher's actions and motives, as his brother had drawn up the
document to include only a release covering demands on Nathaniel's
personal estate and not on his real estate. Dr. Ames, therefore, peremptorily demanded a new release.[51]

Fisher, by this time, was thoroughly irritated and replied that "if the
Agreement is not performed, such Damage will be demanded . . . as will
make me amends for the breach of it." Then, at some length, he pointed

48. Fisher Ames to Doctor Ames, Apr. 19, 1787 (copy), Fisher Ames Papers,
Dedham Hist. Soc.
49. Nathaniel Ames to Squire Ames, Apr. 1787, *ibid.*
50. "Memorandum of an Agreement made this 3d of May 1787," *ibid.*
51. Nathaniel Ames to Fisher Ames, Saturday Afternoon, May 19, 1787, *ibid.*

out the "infinite anxiety . . . the disgrace, perplexity and expense" which
he had endured because of the controversy. These injuries were only
a part of the problem. The property, Fisher said, was in a poor state
with the result that "Great and immediate expenses are necessary to
prevent great losses." [52] In every respect Ames felt that he was entitled
to damages because he had undertaken the care of his mother and
sister while Nathaniel had never contributed "a farthing" to their support. On June 8, 1787, the two brothers reached a final agreement on
their father's estate. Nathaniel noted in his diary: "Settled with Heirs
of my Father, Released my Right to F. Ames for $500 and strip of
land." [53]

52. Fisher Ames to Doctor Ames, n.d., *ibid*.
53. Entry of June 8, 1787, Baker, ed., "Diary of Dr. Nathaniel Ames," *Dedham
Hist. Register*, 5 (1894), 33.

Chapter IV

A Taste of Politics

Fisher Ames's political career was launched by the unique document which was prepared at the Constitutional Convention in Philadelphia and presented to the public in September 1787. Less than a year passed between his participation as a delegate in the Massachusetts Ratifying Convention and his election to the House of Representatives of the first federal Congress, but in that period he gained much experience in public service.

As soon as the first copies of the proposed Constitution reached Boston on September 25, 1787, one Boston newspaper after another published the text. Within little more than a week the document was widely known throughout the state. It outlined a government which Ames, with his firm conviction that strong central authority was essential, could genuinely endorse. Mercy Otis Warren, an astute observer of the contemporary scene, remarked that "almost everyone whom I have yet seen reads with attention, folds the page with solemnity and silently wraps up his opinion within his own breast as if afraid of interrupting the calm expectation that has pervaded all ranks for several months past." [1]

Soon the public plunged into controversy. The Constitution, requiring ratification by conventions of nine out of thirteen states, had been

1. Samuel B. Harding, *The Contest Over the Ratification of the Federal Constitution in the State of Massachusetts* (*Harvard Historical Studies*, 3 [N.Y., 1896]), 15; Mercy Otis Warren to Catherine Macaulay, Sept. 28, 1787, Mercy Warren Letterbook, No. 24, Mass. Hist. Soc.

transmitted by the Philadelphia Convention to the Congress of the Confederation. This body then referred it to the various state legislatures. In the Massachusetts House of Representatives there was a spirited debate on the whole question of calling a convention. Several members insisted on a direct public vote on the Constitution in town meetings, but on October 25 the General Court reached an agreement that each town would choose as many delegates to the Ratifying Convention as it had representatives in the General Court. In contrast to Boston, where there was a vigorous campaign to elect advocates of the Constitution, Dedham very quietly called a town meeting on Monday, December 10, 1787, and selected "the Reverend Mr. Thomas Thacher and Fisher Ames, Esq." to represent the town. The freeholders then chose Ames as moderator of the meeting for a discussion of purely local matters.[2]

Initially the supporters of the Constitution had been in high spirits and were confident that there would be little opposition to ratification. James Sullivan was in an optimistic frame of mind when he wrote, "Our people expect so much happiness from the doings of the Convention that they stand ready to adopt anything which may be offered." [3] In western Massachusetts, however, Theodore Sedgwick found considerable hostility to a new constitution, especially among former insurgents, and suggested that "the subject must be managed with great care and caution." [4] When Elbridge Gerry, after his return from the Philadelphia Convention, vigorously expressed his objections to the new Constitution in a letter to the General Court, it became clear that ratification would not be easily accomplished. The conservative nationalists, now becoming known as the Federalists, were incensed at this attack on a constitution which incorporated to a large extent their views on government. One of them, Henry Jackson, exploded that Gerry had "damn'd himself in the mind of every liberal, judicious and Federal Man . . . damn him—everything . . . had the most favourable appearances . . . previous to this." [5] Hostility to the new framework of government

2. Harding, *Ratification in Massachusetts*, 46-47; Letter of the Governor to the Legislature, in the *Independent Chronicle* (Boston), Oct. 25, 1787; Theodore Sedgwick to Henry Van Schaack, Oct. 28, 1787, Sedgwick Papers, III, Mass. Hist. Soc.; Dedham Town Records, 1784-93, IX, 89, Town Clerk's Office, Dedham; "Constitutional Convention," Vol. 278, Mass. Archives, Office of the Secretary of the Commonwealth, State House.
3. James Sullivan to Rufus King, Boston, Sept. 23, 1787, King, *Life of King*, I, 259.
4. Sedgwick to Van Schaack, Oct. 28, 1787, Sedgwick Papers, III, Mass. Hist. Soc.
5. Elbridge Gerry to the Senate and House of Representatives of Massachusetts, N.Y., Oct. 18, 1787, in James T. Austin, *The Life of Elbridge Gerry*, 2 vols. (Boston, 1827-29), II, 42-45; Henry Jackson to "Harry" [Henry Knox], Boston,

increased when Antifederal critics began to publish incisive analyses of the Constitution, pointing out its lack of a protective bill of rights and revealing the threat of national powers to the position of state governments. For several months a heated discussion over the merits of the Constitution raged in Massachusetts, and the expression of public opinion in newspapers and pamphlets foreshadowed a sharp debate within the Convention. At the end of December, one ardent Federalist objectively summed up the situation. He thought that there was almost an equal chance of ratification of the document in Massachusetts. "It will have substantial friends here," he observed, "but not . . . a great many very zealous admirers, I doubt whether it has monarchy enough in it for some . . . or democracy enough for others." [6]

When Fisher Ames met with the delegates in the State House in Boston on Wednesday, January 9, 280 were present, many of whom had been instructed by their towns to vote specifically for or against the Constitution. From the outset of the Convention the Federalists knew how hard it would be to overcome the critics and win the adherence of the uncommitted delegates. They were counting heavily on Nathaniel Gorham, Rufus King, and Caleb Strong, who had been members of the Federal Convention, to enlighten the Ratifying Convention by interpreting the different sections of the Constitution. Other leaders of the formidable Federalist group were Theophilus Parsons, renowned for his legal acumen, Theodore Sedgwick, a man of powerful conservative views, Judge Increase Sumner, and Judge Francis Dana. Yet several of the younger delegates, Fisher Ames, George Cabot, and Christopher Gore, who had recently arrived on the political scene, were to make

Nov. 5, 1787, Chamberlain Papers, Boston Pub. Lib.; Jackson to Henry Knox, Boston, Nov. 11, 1787, Knox Papers, XXI, No. 47, Mass. Hist. Soc. Charles Warren, "Elbridge Gerry, James Warren, Mercy Warren and the Ratification of the Federal Constitution in Massachusetts," Mass. Hist. Soc., *Proceedings*, 2d Ser., 64 (1931), 148.

6. Harding, *Ratification in Massachusetts*, 32, 59; Nathan Dane to Henry Knox, Boston, Dec. 27, 1787, Knox Papers, XXI, No. 88, Mass. Hist. Soc. For examples of Antifederalist arguments, see the *Boston Gazette*, Nov. 12, "A Federalist" and "One of the Common People," Dec. 3, 1787; *Massachusetts Centinel* (Boston), Oct. 6, 1787, *American Herald* (Boston), Sept. 30, Oct. 8, 15, 29, Nov. 12, 26, Dec. 3, 10, 1787. Cecilia M. Kenyon, "Men of Little Faith: the Anti-Federalists on the Nature of Representative Government," *Wm. and Mary Qtly.*, 3d Ser., 12 (1955), 4-44; Jackson T. Main, *The Antifederalists, Critics of the Constitution, 1781-1788* (Chapel Hill, 1961), 121-26; Paul L. Ford, ed., *Pamphlets on the Constitution of the United States . . . 1787-1788* (Brooklyn, 1888); Paul L. Ford, ed., *Essays on the Constitution of the United States . . . 1787-1788* (Brooklyn, 1892). For the private opinions of several New England Antifederalists, see Thomas B. Wait to George Thatcher, Portland, Jan. 8, 1788, Nathaniel Barrell to Thatcher, Boston, Jan. 15, 1788, Silas Lee to Thatcher, Biddeford, Jan. 23, 1788, in William F. Goodwin, ed., "The Thatcher Papers," *Historical Magazine*, 2d Ser., 6 (1869), 255-71.

a real contribution to the ultimate Federalist victory. Henry Jackson, one of the more outspoken conservatives, wrote to his friend Henry Knox about the Convention. "It is astonishing to see the weight of respect, integrity, property and ability on the side of the proposed Constitution and on the other side, the characters that oppose it—my God the contrast—Harry it is too much to think of." [7]

While tardy delegates were still arriving, the Convention began its work, the members devoting the first few days to the process of organization as well as to preliminary sparring. By Friday, January 11, 316 members were present out of a total of 364 elected delegates, far more than the usual size of the annual General Court. In the view of one person, "Little else, among us is thought or talked of but the new Constitution, . . . it is feared the greater part of the Convention were chosen rather for their hands than their heads—they move but slowly, which Doubtless is owing to their Number . . . too many to do anything with Order or propriety." [8]

After the Convention voted that the members "shall enter into a free conversation on the several parts" of the Constitution, the delegates began to discuss it, section by section. They had progressed only to the second paragraph of the first section, when Antifederalists expressed serious concern about the long term of office representatives in Congress would have. Accustomed only to the annual elections within the state, many individuals felt that tyranny lurked in any system not providing for frequent elections. Sedgwick attempted to explain the advantages of a two-year term for representatives in a national government, but Dr. John Taylor, a strong Antifederalist from Worcester County, countered his argument by reminding his colleagues that annual elections had always been "considered as the safeguards of the liberties of the people." [9] Samuel Adams agreed and in his determination

7. Henry Jackson to Henry Knox, Boston, Jan. 20, 1788, Knox Papers, XXI, No. 143, Mass. Hist. Soc. Harding, *Ratification in Massachusetts*, 60-61. Forrest McDonald, *We the People, The Economic Origins of the Constitution* (Chicago, 1958), 182-202. McDonald presents a detailed analysis of the individual delegates, listing their occupations and holdings of public securities.

8. List of returns from the various towns, "A Journal of a Convention of Delegates," in B. K. Peirce and C. Hale, eds., *Debates and Proceedings in the Convention of the Commonwealth of Massachusetts Held in the Year 1788* (Boston, 1856), 31-43; Samuel P. Savage to George Thatcher, Weston, Jan. 11, 1788, Goodwin, ed., "Thatcher Papers," *Historical Magazine*, 2d Ser., 6 (1869), 264.

9. "Journal of a Convention" in Peirce and Hale, eds., *Debates in the Convention*, 55; the detailed discussion in the Convention was a significant factor in winning over the support of the Rev. Isaac Backus to the Constitution. See his comments in the Diary of Isaac Backus, 11 (1783-89), 77-80, John Hay Library, Brown University, Providence, R.I.; Jonathan Elliot, ed., *The Debates in the Several State Conventions on the Adoption of the Federal Constitution*, 5 vols. (Philadelphia, 1836-59), II, 4-5.

to embarrass the Federalists, pressed for an explanation for the change from annual to biennial elections.

Fisher Ames rose to answer him with a speech which turned the attention of leading Federalists to him. He disarmed the opponents momentarily by candidly admitting that he, too, considered frequent elections "one of the first securities for popular liberty." Even though the term of office should be long enough to enable the representative to understand the public interest, he felt that it must be sufficiently limited to ensure fidelity to the will of the constituents. He went on to reject pure democracies as paltry creations, subject to faction and violence. Representative governments were much superior, he maintained, for the people retained their power, and "they . . . become the true sovereigns of the country when they delegate that power, which they cannot use themselves, to their trustees." He disagreed that a representative form meant any significant loss of freedom. "The liberty of one depends not so much on the removal of all restraint from him, as on the due restraint upon the liberties of others. Without such restraint, there can be no liberty. Liberty is so far from being endangered or destroyed by this, that it is extended and secured." [10] Ames felt that "this article with all its supposed defects, is in favor of liberty." As a part of the Constitution it was not subject to repeal by law and was a barrier against "ambitious encroachments, too high and too strong to be passed." [11] Biennial elections were a necessity in a large country such as the United States might become, extending perhaps from New Brunswick to Lake Superior, and including some fifty million people. He then reached the heart of his argument, the theme of the incompatibility of unchecked democracy and good government.

Adroitly connecting biennial elections with effective administration, he asserted that both were essential to liberty. It was through factions and the uncontrolled impulses of the public that popular governments were destroyed, not by the threat of a powerful aristocracy. "The people when they lose their liberties are cheated out of them," he contended. Factions could be manipulated to acquire power, and the momentary impulse of the public too easily became law. "A democracy is a volcano," Ames declared, "which conceals the fiery materials of its own destruction. These will produce an eruption, and carry desolation in their way." People meant to do right, he averred, and would do so if given time for reflection. Biennial elections were therefore a protection against the clamor of the moment and would be an assurance that the "sober second thought of the people" would actually prevail. Ames

10. Elliot, ed., *Debates*, II, 6-9.
11. *Ibid.*

ended his speech by turning to Samuel Adams and answering his question with an inquiry of his own. "What reason can be given ... if annual elections are good, biennial elections are not better?" [12]

Adams very obviously wanted to drop the matter for, according to one reporter, "he only made inquiry for information and ... had heard sufficient to satisfy himself of its propriety." [13] His failure to take the lead in the assault against the Constitution perturbed the Antifederalists and elated the Federalists, who marked Ames's victory over Adams as one of the initial turning points for their side. Although the speech subdued Adams, it did not immediately resolve the question of biennial elections. For the remainder of the day there was an animated debate, but all the earnest reasoning of King, Gore, and others could not overcome Antifederalist fears that "congress might perpetuate themselves and so reign emperors over us." [14]

Before the first week of the Convention was over, some Federalists reflected discouragement in reports to James Madison. Upon receipt of the news, the Virginian wrote Washington that "the intelligence from Massachusetts begins to be very ominous to the Constitution ... and there was very great reason to fear that the voice of that State would be in the negative." [15] Nathaniel Gorham, on the scene in the Convention, admitted "the prospects [are] not very good" as "numbers are at present against us and the opposition leaders say they are sure of the victory." Then he added a more optimistic note: "If they succeed in opposition to such a phalanx of sensible men and good speakers as are in this assembly, it will be very extraordinary. We know all is at stake and work accordingly." [16]

When the Convention took up the structure of the Senate, the Antifederalists once again showed a deep distrust of granting power, especially for a six-year term, as senators would forget their dependence on the people in that length of time. Ames instantly rejected the argument that senators should be chosen annually so the public could better control them. Nor would he give any credence to the idea that the new

12. *Ibid.*, 10-11. See reference to Ames's statement in the *American Herald* (Boston), Jan. 21, 1788. Ames's speech on biennial elections was printed in *The American Museum or Repository of Ancient and Modern Fugitive Pieces*, 3 (1788), 358-62. Elliot, ed., *Debates*, II, 11; Harding, *Ratification in Massachusetts*, 67-68. See criticisms of "Ezra," *Massachusetts Centinel* (Boston), Jan. 23, 1788.

13. Elliot, ed., *Debates*, II, 11.

14. Miller, *Sam Adams*, 380; Elliot, ed., *Debates*, II, 21.

15. James Madison to George Washington, N.Y., Jan. 20, 1788, Gaillard Hunt, ed., *The Writings of James Madison*, 9 vols. (N.Y., 1900-1910), V, 85.

16. Nathaniel Gorham to Henry Knox, Jan. 16, 1788, Knox Papers, XXI, No. 110, Mass. Hist. Soc.

plan would result in a consolidation of states since they were integral
to a federal system. The senators, representing the "sovereignty of the
states," were similar to ambassadors, and in order to carry out their
functions, needed a long tenure of office. "If they were chosen yearly,"
he asked, "how could they perform their trust?" If senators were
brought more under popular control, they would become representatives of individuals and encroach on the functions of the other house.
If chosen by the people at large, they would not represent the states
but the people, and the federal features of the Constitution would be
totally obliterated. Turning the argument of the Antifederalists against
them, he asserted that changing the Senate would deprive the states of
a means of defense against encroachments of the federal government.
"Too much provision cannot be made against a consolidation," he
said.[17] Although the statement may have been a tactical one, it seems
to have reflected real conviction on Ames's part. Had it come from
any of the determined nationalists like Knox, it would have seemed
insincere.

King followed Ames with a more detailed account of the Senate,
emphasizing that public opinion would always act as a check upon the
senators. Dr. Taylor punctured his argument by stressing that there
were more adequate checks under the Articles of Confederation with its
annual elections, provision for rotation, and the right of recalling delegates. On Monday, January 21, Ames continued his analysis of the
powers of the federal legislature. Much had been made of the assumption that the two houses of Congress would attempt to perpetuate
themselves in office, but he felt that the critics had overlooked the
fundamental need to trust the general government. "If we can trust our
own legislature," he asked, "can we trust the legislature of other States
rather than Congress? This section is not a trap, but a security for the
liberties of the people, and [was] introduced to guard them." [18] Ames
acknowledged quite candidly that initially he had had some doubts
about the powers and functions of the Senate. Had these doubts not
been removed, he asserted, he would have felt obliged to vote against
the Constitution.

Even the persuasive reasoning of Ames and other advocates of the
Constitution did not reduce the adamant opposition of the Antifederalists, who refused to be convinced that the new government would not
jeopardize the principles for which they had striven during the Revo-

17. Elliot, ed., *Debates*, II, 45-46.
18. *Ibid.*, 48-49; "Judge Parson Minutes," Peirce and Hale, eds., *Debates in the Convention*, 308.

lution. As early as January 20 Rufus King hinted to Horatio Gates that the Federalists were devising new tactics to overcome the objections of their opponents. "Perhaps we shall adopt and recommend to the Delegates ... certain alterations," he suggested.[19]

The idea of amendments to the Constitution had been discussed since the first days of the Convention. Now that the obstinacy of some Antifederalists had been revealed, the Federalists were turning in earnest to the possibility of winning over the more moderate of their adversaries. John Avery, Secretary of the Commonwealth, one of the first to mention the advantages of amendments, expressed the opinion "that if the most sanguine among them who are for adopting the proposed Constitution as it now stands would discover a conciliating disposition and give way a little to those who are for adopting it with amendments, I dare say they would be very united. ... That amendments should be made seems to be the prevailing opinion." [20]

There was some indication that the Antifederalists were beginning to weary of the elaborate dissection of the Constitution, when Samuel Mason moved to reconsider the discussion by paragraphs and "leave the subject at large open for consideration." [21] Some of the Antifederalists wanted to end the Convention, while for their part, many of the Federalists were tiring of the recurring obstacles which blocked a successful conclusion. "The Federal speakers," wrote Jeremy Belknap, "are obliged to combat them with the same arguments over and over again. ... They [the Antifederalists] *will* not be convinced, they *will* not be silenced." [22]

Ames felt the time had come for a direct appeal to the patriotism of the members. In a short speech on Friday, January 25, he exhorted those of the delegates "who stood forth in 1775 to stand forth now, to throw aside all interested and party views, to have one purse and one heart for the whole." He stated emphatically that "as it was necessary then so was it necessary now, to unite,—or die we must." Continuing in the same vein, he said, "If this Constitution will destroy the liberties of the country, we should reject it, but such is the ruin if we reject it,

19. Elliot, ed., *Debates*, II, 60; Rufus King to Horatio Gates, Boston, Jan. 20, 1788, Emmet Collection, N.Y. Pub. Lib.; Rufus King to James Madison, Boston, Jan. 20, 1788, King, *Life of King*, I, 314; Harding, *Ratification in Massachusetts*, 82-83.

20. John Avery to George Thatcher, Jan. 19, 1788, Goodwin, ed., "Thatcher Papers," *Historical Magazine*, 2d Ser., 6 (1869), 265.

21. Elliot, ed., *Debates*, II, 94.

22. Jeremy Belknap to Ebenezer Hazard, Boston, Jan. 25, 1788, "The Belknap Papers," Mass. Hist. Soc., *Collections*, 5th Ser., 3 (1877), 9; Miller, *Sam Adams*, 381; Harding, *Ratification in Massachusetts*, 83; Henry Jackson to Henry Knox, Boston, Jan. 23, 1788, Knox Papers, XXI, No. 116, Mass. Hist. Soc.

we ought to be sure our liberties are in danger before we [do]. Our liberties cannot be preserved without union." [23]

By calling on the patriots of 1775, Ames unwittingly opened the way for a sharp rejoinder from Amos Singletary, who said that "he had been one of them," and that "if anybody had proposed such a constitution as this in that day, it would have been thrown away at once." Then he heaped strictures on the educated men in the Convention. "These lawyers and men of learning, and moneyed men, that talk so finely, and gloss over matters so smoothly, to make us poor illiterate people swallow down the pill, expect to get into Congress themselves . . . and get all the power . . . in their own hands, and then they will swallow up all of us little folks." [24]

One supporter of the new constitution outside of the Convention believed that the "masterly speeches of . . . Dana, Parsons, King, [and] Ames . . . would add a Lustre to any Parliment in Europe." Joseph Crocker, who thus extolled the Federalist speakers, was convinced that "the Constitution will be adopted and that the opposers will soon sink into their primitive Nothing." [25] Leading Federalists at the meetings were less confident and during the last week of January expressed doubt concerning the outcome. Their expectations for a favorable result hinged more and more on their plan to win the support of enough Antifederalist votes by advocating certain amendments to the Constitution. In a caucus the Federalists proposed a bargain to Governor Hancock, who was neutral about the Constitution. The Federalists suspected that he did not wish to risk his political future by committing himself until the opportune time. Because of his great prestige throughout the state, they asked him to present the compromise proposals to the members of the Convention as his original idea.[26] In return, he was to receive the support of the Massachusetts Federalists in the forthcom-

23. "Judge Parson Minutes," Peirce and Hale, eds., *Debates in the Convention*, 317; Elliot, ed., *Debates*, II, 101.

24. Elliot, ed., *Debates*, II, 102.

25. Joseph Crocker to George Thatcher, Jan. 26, 1788, Thatcher Papers, Chamberlain Collection, Boston Pub. Lib.; John Forbes to John Quincy Adams, Jan. 19, 1788, Adams, ed., *Diary of John Quincy Adams*, 86.

26. Rufus King to James Madison, Boston, Jan. 27, 1788, King, ed., *Life of King*, I, 317; Nathaniel Gorham to Henry Knox, Boston, Jan. 30, 1788, Knox Papers, XXI, No. 124, Mass. Hist. Soc.; Belknap to Hazard, Jan. 25, 1788, "The Belknap Papers," Mass. Hist. Soc., *Collections*, 5th Ser., 3 (1877), 11. The authorship of the proposed amendments is discussed in Jeremy Belknap to Ebenezer Hazard, Boston, Feb. 3, 1788, *ibid.*, 15. Political Journal of George R. Minot, Sedgwick (Minot) Papers, Mass. Hist. Soc.; Harding, *Ratification in Massachusetts*, 84-86. Austin, *Life of Gerry*, 75; Herbert S. Allan, *John Hancock, Patriot in Purple* (N.Y., 1948), 329-30; Eben F. Stone, "Parsons and the Constitutional Convention of 1788," Essex Institute *Hist. Collections*, 35 (1899), 81-102.

ing election for the governorship. They also agreed to promote him for the presidency. The bargain was too tempting for Hancock to resist.[27]

A motion, made by Theophilus Parsons, to ratify the Constitution was already on the floor when the Governor appeared before the delegates. Making dramatic use of a recent illness, Hancock was carried into the crowded hall, and in an important speech, allied himself with the advocates of the Constitution. Expressing his conviction that ratification was essential, he presented nine amendments which protected state powers and ensured certain civil rights. To the astonishment of the Antifederalists, Samuel Adams, too, now warmly approved the Constitution. He praised Hancock's proposals and suggested that the Convention formally consider them. In the last days of the meeting, a committee approved the amendments which were to be recommended but not made a condition of ratification. Until the final vote, the opposing sides appeared to be very evenly balanced, but the Federalists had gained necessary support by their strategic move. Within the Convention, the appeal of the conciliatory propositions was beginning to have an effect, and it was at this crucial point that Fisher Ames made his concluding speech.[28]

In defending the Constitution he remarked that almost everyone who had been against it was now willing to accept it with the recommended changes. He acknowledged that some of the former opponents had been very candid in discussing their altered stand, but he found some objections to Governor Hancock's plan still unanswered. Critics maintained that the Convention had the power only to ratify or to reject, and consequently no authority to advocate amendments. Others, he stated, contended that "the very propositions imply the Constitution is not perfect" and argued that it should be rejected. "Have we no right to propose amendments?" he asked. The assembly of delegates was the most representative the state had known; therefore if this Convention did not have the power to reflect the wishes of the public, he questioned how they could be determined. Ames quickly showed the implausibility of the argument that the document was too imperfect to

27. Rufus King to Henry Knox, Boston, Feb. 1, 1788, King, *Life of King,* I, 319; King to Knox, Boston, Jan. 27, 1788, Nathaniel Gorham to Knox, Boston, Jan. 30, 1788, Knox Papers, XXI, No. 121, 124, Mass. Hist. Soc. Gorham wrote, "We cannot gain the question without some recommendatory amendments—with them I presume we shall have a small majority."
28. Allan, *John Hancock,* 330. Harding, *Ratification in Massachusetts,* 95-98. Elliot, ed., *Debates,* II, 122-24. Belknap to Hazard, Feb. 3, 1788, "The Belknap Papers," Mass. Hist. Soc., *Collections,* 5th Ser., 3 (1877), 15. Nathaniel Gorham to Henry Knox, Charlestown, Feb. 3, 1788, Henry Jackson to Knox, Boston, Feb. 3, 1788, Knox Papers, XXI, No. 129, 131, Mass. Hist. Soc.

adopt. "Do they expect to find that perfection in government which they well know is not to be found in nature?" he queried. The Constitution was good, he continued, "and yet the amendments may be good, for they are not repugnant" to it. No government in the past, as far as he knew, had had so excellent a framework. "If we adopt it," Ames proclaimed, "we shall demonstrate to the sneering world, who deride liberty because they have lost it, that the principles of our government are as free as the spirit of our people." [29]

Continuing to interlace his speech with rhetorical questions, Ames attempted to prove that rejection of the Constitution would be illogical and disastrous. If this document were not accepted and another were presented in two or three years, why should anyone expect greater unanimity? "If we reject, we are exposed to the risk of having no constitution, of being torn with factions, and at last divided into distinct confederacies." Everything which the people held precious would be jeopardized by such a course of action, the orator insisted. If assent to the life-giving Constitution were withheld, the country would inevitably wither away just as a girdled tree, deprived of its sap, lost its leaves and branches and finally was torn down by a gale. In conclusion, Ames suggested that although the state government was "a beautiful structure," it could not resist anarchic inundation unless it were protected. "The Union is the dike to fence out the flood. That dike is broken . . . if we do not repair it . . . we shall be buried in one common destruction." [30]

At last, after twenty-five days of deliberation, the Convention was ready to vote on ratification. On Wednesday afternoon, February 6, the Constitution was adopted by a slim majority of nineteen votes. In the eyes of the Federalists it was very fortunate that the ratification was not made conditional on the incorporation of amendments; these were merely proposed to the forthcoming federal Congress. No sooner was the vote counted than several jubilant Federalists hurriedly wrote notes informing their friends of the good news. Henry Jackson reflected the excitement of the moment. "Huzza! Huzza! the grand question was put this afternoon. . . . I attend in the Gallery from 9 o'clock in the morning . . . and eat my dinner there . . . Gingerbread and Cheese. . . . The Gallery remained full the whole time of the adjournment from 1 to 3 o'clock, such was the anxiety of the minds of the people. . . . State Street was crowded with thousands." [31]

29. Elliot, ed., *Debates*, II, 154-55.
30. *Ibid.*, 156, 158-59.
31. Harding, *Ratification in Massachusetts*, 99-100; Morse, *Federalist Party*, 50-53. The final vote was 187 for the Constitution, 168 against, with 9 members absent; Henry Jackson to Henry Knox, Boston, Feb. 6, 1788, Knox Papers, XXI,

Before the Convention adjourned several of the leading Antifederalists expressed their acquiescence in the will of the majority and vowed they would support the Constitution "so that we may all live in peace." The last day of the meeting was given over to final business matters and the formality of proclaiming the ratification. A harmonious mood prevailed and the members voted to proceed to the State House to "take an affectionate leave of each other." In keeping with the new spirit of unity, votes of thanks to the president and vice president were passed, and Fisher Ames was chosen with four other members to convey the sentiments of the Convention to Governor Hancock and William Cushing.[32]

As this historic gathering formally ended, the members and the populace united in a joyous celebration. The whole Convention, with the shouts and hurrahs of the crowd ringing in their ears, adjourned to take part in a "decent repast, prepared in the Senate Chamber." Wine and spirits were evidently abundant, and the reports of the gathering were written in glowing words. "In mutual congratulations and testimonials of satisfaction, all party ideas were done away, and such a spirit of joy, union, and urbanity diffused, [which] must be attended with the most happy consequences through the Commonwealth."[33] Newspapers, so recently full of the most partisan articles, now added to the expressions of jubilation and conciliation. Referring to the sixth of February, the *Independent Chronicle* commented in verse:

> Hail the Day and Mark it well
> Then old Anarch's kingdom fell,
> Then our dawning Glory shone
> Mark it, Freemen, 'tis our own.[34]

Fisher Ames had come to the Convention at twenty-nine with little more than a local reputation as a gifted young lawyer, and almost from the beginning of the proceedings had drawn the attention of all upon him by his superb oratorical abilities. His speeches in support of the Constitution increased the respect of the Federalists for him, making

---

No. 135, Mass. Hist. Soc.; Christopher Gore to George Thatcher, Boston, Feb. 6, 1788, Goodwin, ed., "Thatcher Papers," *Historical Magazine*, 2d Ser., 6 (1869), 269.

32. Elliot, ed., *Debates*, II, 181-83; "Journal of the Convention," Peirce and Hale, eds., *Debates in the Convention*, 92-93. The statement of the vote of thanks to William Cushing, the Vice President of the Convention, is in the Cushing Papers, Mass. Hist. Soc.

33. *Massachusetts Centinel* (Boston), Feb. 9, 1788.

34. *Independent Chronicle* (Boston), Feb. 7, 1788; Harding, *Ratification in Massachusetts*, 106-7.

them aware of his potential in the field of politics, and he was now linked with Rufus King, Theophilus Parsons, and Judge Francis Dana, as one of the leading figures at the Convention.[35] More than his other experiences, this participation in the Convention was a determining point in his life. Once he had fully sensed the allure of politics, he never wholeheartedly returned to the legal profession.

As a consequence of Ames's growing prominence, the townspeople of Dedham on May 12, 1788, elected him as one of their two representatives to the General Court. Aside from personal and local considerations, his election was indicative of a political trend away from Antifederalism. Since their victory in the ratification contest, the Federalists had derived political advantage from their connection, tenuous as it was, with the Hancock faction. Overcoming a measure of reluctance, Federalists aided Hancock in winning the governorship. But General Benjamin Lincoln, their candidate for lieutenant governor, did not receive reciprocal support. Ultimately he was chosen by the Federalist-controlled Senate, as none of the candidates for lieutenant governor had won a majority in the election. Despite the attempt of the Antifederalists to discredit their political rivals by condemning them as aristocrats, the Federalists were able to control the Senate and obtain a House in which at least two-thirds of the members were supporters of the Constitution. When newly elected members of the House met at the opening of the session on May 28, the *Massachusetts Centinel* commented that "old Massachusetts will be blessed with wise, prudent, and federal Rulers for the coming year." [36]

Although Fisher Ames was one of the new members, the setting for the meeting of the General Court was familiar enough to him. Whenever he had had any business in the Supreme Judicial Court or the court of common pleas, he had walked up the hill at the head of State Street to the large brick building with its Doric pillars. Now this was to be

35. See Ralph V. Harlow in *DAB* s.v. "Dana, Francis" and Claude H. Feuss in *ibid.*, s.v. "King, Rufus"; W. P. Cresson, *Francis Dana, A Puritan Diplomat at the Court of Catherine the Great* (N.Y., 1930).

36. Dedham Town Records, 1784-93, IX, 98-100, Town Clerk's Office, Dedham; Henry Jackson to Henry Knox, Boston, Mar. 10, 1788, Jackson to Knox, Boston, Apr. 20, 1788, Knox Papers, XXI, No. 165, XXII, No. 19, Mass. Hist. Soc.; Christopher Gore to Rufus King, Mar. 2, 1788, King, *Life of King*, I, 323; Samuel Savage to George Thatcher, Mar. 7, 1788, Thatcher Papers, Chamberlain Collection, Boston Pub. Lib.; Theodore Sedgwick to Henry Van Schaack, Boston, May 29, 1788, Sedgwick Papers, III, Mass. Hist. Soc.; Political Journal of George R. Minot, Feb. 27, 1788, Sedgwick (Minot) Papers, Mass. Hist. Soc.; "Diary of John Quincy Adams," Mass. Hist. Soc., *Proceedings*, 2d Ser., 16 (1903), 404; *Massachusetts Centinel* (Boston), Apr. 12, 16, 26, May 28, 31, 1788; *American Herald* (Boston), Mar. 13, 20, May 1, 1788; *Independent Chronicle* (Boston), Apr. 18, 1788.

the scene for his widening civic and political experience.³⁷ On the first
day of the session, the ninety-six new members were sworn in and after
the Reverend Mr. Parsons had presented a "spirited sermon," the General Court began its annual work. Among Ames's associates in the
House were Theodore Sedgwick, who was now chosen Speaker, and
George R. Minot, who became Clerk of the House for the year.³⁸

A wide variety of public bills came before the legislators immediately
following the usual flurry of private petitions. Within a month Ames
gave his attention to several issues in which his legal training stood him
in good stead. He was engaged in revising the statute of limitation and
actions, working on the means of quieting executors of solvent estates,
and arranging the division of certain townships within the state. The
pressure of public business meant of necessity a neglect of private affairs, and Ames requested and was granted a leave of absence early in
June. It was a short respite from the General Court, as he was on hand
again on June 10 to cast his vote in favor of a bill for lowering the
wages of members of the legislature. He likewise was active in bringing
in a bill to remit all fines which had been imposed on the insurgents of
1786, but this did not mean that Ames had a new-found sympathy for
the participants in Shays' Rebellion. He had merely been one of several
designated by the Speaker to attend to this placating measure. Just before the legislature adjourned its first session on June 20, Ames with
several other representatives and senators was delegated to present an
address of welcome to John Adams, who was returning home after
many years of diplomatic efforts in Europe.³⁹

When the General Court resumed its work on October 29, it was
quickly confronted with intricate problems relating to the approaching
federal election. A committee consisting of nine legislators from the
two houses proposed that the presidential electors be chosen by joint
ballot of the state representatives and senators, that the state be divided
into eight districts for electing members of Congress, and that each
branch of the state legislature should have the power to veto the appointment of any federal senator by the other branch. On November 6
the report of the Committee on Federal Elections came before the entire House, and Ames, Parsons, and several other members engaged in

37. "From the Geographical Gazeteer of 1785," *American Magazine*, 1 (1788),
689.
38. *Massachusetts Centinel* (Boston), May 31, 1788; see also, Journal of the House
of Representatives for 1788, Mass. Archives, Office of the Secretary of the Commonwealth, State House.
39. Journal of the House of Representatives, May 30, June 3, 10, 12, 1788, Mass.
Archives; *Massachusetts Centinel* (Boston), June 11, 21, 1788; William Prescott to
Nathan Dane, Beverly, June 29, 1788, Nathan Dane Papers, Lib. Cong.

a learned and animated debate on the constitutionality of legislative selection of electors. A spirited controversy also developed on regulating the election of representatives, with many members arguing that the candidates in each district must be residents therein. Eventually, this idea prevailed and by a vote of 89 to 72 was incorporated in the Election Law. Ames took an active part in the debates, his name being mentioned fairly frequently in newspaper reports of the General Court proceedings, but only rarely was the substance of his observations and speeches given.[40]

Early in November, Ames was appointed to a committee to determine measures necessary to carry into effect the laws prohibiting the importation of various articles. At the same time he was chosen one of five members of the House to draw up impeachment proceedings and to manage the case of the Commonwealth against Sheriff Greenleaf of Worcester County, who was accused of misconduct, maladministration, and wrongfully detaining public money for his own use. The prosecution, under the lead of Theophilus Parsons, presented a well-knit case and confounded the defense, which despite an address of nearly six hours, was not able to counter the damaging evidence. Parsons summed up the case for the state, and after Greenleaf was pronounced guilty, Ames addressed the Senate, demanding that the sheriff be removed from office.[41]

During the summer and autumn of 1788, when the approaching federal elections were never far out of mind among those with political interests, Ames came before the public eye, and confidence in his abilities increased. By midsummer the campaign got under way with preliminary maneuvering for position. As it developed, Ames's political destiny was affected by the recently approved law which required that a federal representative be a resident of the district in which he was elected. This law brought Rufus King's political career to an end in Massachusetts, and in so doing gave Ames an opportunity to move into the national scene. To his friends, Rufus King was the logical person to be selected for the Senate or the House of Representatives, as a reward for his distinguished public service in the past. Yet King's long absences from Massachusetts and his marriage and residence in New York created a barrier to winning public support. In early August, Christopher Gore wrote to King, urging him to take up residence in

40. *Massachusetts Centinel* (Boston), June 21, Nov. 5, 8, 22, 1788. The General Court was prorogued until the 1st Wednesday in September; and then until Oct. 28. Samuel A. Otis to Nathan Dane, Oct. 29, 1788, Nathan Dane Papers, Lib. Cong.
41. *Massachusetts Centinel* (Boston), Nov. 5, 8, 12, 15, 19, 1788. The newspaper remarked that "the proceedings on the part of the Managers have been marked with openness, candour and liberality."

Boston again. "Your friends are very desirous of your being in the admin. of the new Govt.; but are anxious as to your election, unless you are really an inhabitant of Massachusetts. . . . The Candidates in this County are Jarvis, Otis, Dawes and Heath. I think Dawes the most likely to succeed . . . unless there is a probability of our having you for the Representative of Suffolk." [42] King was reluctant to re-establish himself in Boston, but because of the importunities of his friends he took steps to purchase a house in Cambridge. Even so it was too late to counteract the insinuations of his political adversaries.

Among the Federalists John Lowell, Thomas Dawes, and Samuel A. Otis were the favored candidates; yet Gore continued to encourage King to remain in the running as late as the end of November. Early in December, Lowell, Dawes, and Charles Jarvis withdrew from the contest leaving Samuel Otis as the leading choice for the representative of Suffolk district.[43] Eliminating some of the candidates helped the Federalists only slightly, as they were unable to concentrate all their efforts behind one particular person. They were more than a little concerned when their old adversary, Samuel Adams, entered the contest with support from partisans of Governor Hancock. There was obvious need to find a new political figure, and on December 4 the name of Fisher Ames was presented to the voters of Suffolk County.[44]

Federalists did not expect Ames to win against such a veteran politician as Adams, but they hoped he would succeed in unifying the vote. The theme of unity was stressed in one election announcement soliciting votes for Ames. "As Fisher Ames, Esq. is the person whom it is certain the Federal Electors of Suffolk . . . out of town, will vote for it is hoped, that all in Town who wish to unite in a federal character— altho intended to give their votes for Mr. King, Mr. Otis, Mr. Adams . . . will now give their vote for Mr. Ames. Freemen! Federalists! on your unanimity depends the SALVATION OF OUR COUNTRY." [45] Edward H. Robbins informed his friend Theodore Sedgwick about the

42. Morse, *Federalist Party*, 61; *Massachusetts Centinel* (Boston), July 23, 1788, Aug. 27, 30, Sept. 3, 6, 20, 1788; *Independent Chronicle* (Boston), Oct. 9, Nov. 6, Dec. 4, 1788. *The Herald of Freedom* (Boston), Oct. 30, 1788, advocated the choice of "competent Commercial Characters" to represent Massachusetts. Christopher Gore to Rufus King, Boston, Aug. 10 and Nov. 26, 1788, Henry Knox to King, Boston, Aug. 17, 1788, King, *Life of King*, I, 341, 347, 342; Christopher Gore to Theodore Sedgwick, Boston, Aug. 31, 1788, Sedgwick Papers, Vol. A, Mass. Hist. Soc.; *Massachusetts Centinel* (Boston), Dec. 3, 1788.

43. *Massachusetts Centinel* (Boston), Dec. 3, 1788; *Independent Chronicle* (Boston), Dec. 4, 1788.

44. *Independent Chronicle* (Boston), Dec. 4, 1788. The newspaper reported that "in this and the neighbouring towns, FISHER AMES, Esq., who is a gentleman of acknowledged abilities, and unimpeachable integrity, is much talked of as a representative for the district of Suffolk"; Miller, *Sam Adams*, 385.

45. *Herald of Freedom* (Boston), Dec. 15, 1788.

progress of electioneering and wrote, "S. Adams has all his myrmidons to support him, and they are numerous. Otis, a considerable party—we are pressing brother Ames and shall make some figure, at least prevent a choice." [46] Gore, likewise, felt that the votes would be scattered. "Suffolk will . . . be much divided. Adams, Otis, Ames and Heath and James Bowdoin Jr. will probably be voted for; and it is probable that at the first meeting no choice will be made; tho' many fear that S. Adams will be elected. A week hence we shall know more of this matter; at present we are in a very sorry condition." [47]

With increasing intensity as election day neared, the Federalists drummed on the theme that it was necessary to elect good men to office to put the new Constitution into operation. The *Massachusetts Centinel* republished a letter of "Publius" which reiterated the need to elect advocates of "a firm efficient federal Government; men who are fully possessed of a thorough knowledge of the principles of the New System . . . on such alone we can rationally place any confidence." [48] Even the *Herald of Freedom*, formerly leaning toward Antifederalism, expressed the opinion that "tis the operation of the federal government alone to which we must turn our eyes and expectations; that alone . . . opens any . . . prospect upon us. . . . Elect such FEDERAL CHARACTERS for the new government as will be competent to [do] justice to TRADE AND COMMERCE." [49]

On the day before the election there were more specific reminders to the "Freemen" as well as to the "Federal Mechanicks" to vote for Ames. "Will they elect a man of at least suspected federalism . . . ? No surely the Electors of Suffolk will shun the dire consequences of mean duplicity and avoid the effects of an almost heretical obstinacy" by voting for Fisher Ames, "who has given *full evidence* through *every stage* of the business of his being heartily engaged in the cause." [50] In rhapsodic terms a news writer reminded people how, during the debates in the Convention, "the words of that truly independent, learned and ingenious Federalist . . . dropped upon you as the rain upon the thirsty ground and how 'his speech distilled like the dew.' " [51]

On Thursday, December 18, the polls in the towns of Suffolk district

46. Edward H. Robbins to Theodore Sedgwick, Dec. 14, 1788, Sedgwick Papers, Vol. A, Mass. Hist. Soc.

47. Christopher Gore to Rufus King, Boston, Dec. 14, 1788, King, *Life of King,* I, 347.

48. *Massachusetts Centinel* (Boston), Dec. 13, 1788.

49. *Herald of Freedom* (Boston), Dec. 15, 1788.

50. *Massachusetts Centinel* (Boston), Dec. 17, 1788.

51. *Ibid.* The electioneering articles in favor of Samuel Adams were numerous in the *Independent Chronicle* (Boston), Dec. 11, 18, 1788. "Some of us know Fisher Ames, Esq. as a *pretty speaker,* but the World knows the Hon. Samuel Adams as a PATRIOT and STATESMAN," *ibid.,* Dec. 18, 1788.

were opened at 10 A.M. to receive the votes of the legally qualified
inhabitants. In Boston, the town meeting assembled at Faneuil Hall,
in the heart of Adams's bailiwick, and after a prayer by the Reverend
Mr. Freeman, proceeded to vote. When the votes of the Boston citizens
were tallied, Ames had won 445 votes to Adams's 439. The tabulation
proceeded at an extremely slow pace as each town in the district sent in
its returns. Ames led from the start, but the large number of scattered
votes for other candidates decreased the total which he, as well as
Adams, might have received. By January 3, 1789, Ames had been credited with 818 votes, just eleven more than a majority; and he was conclusively declared the winner on January 7. In Dedham itself, he had
received twenty votes, while his opponent got only eight.[52]

As early as December 21 eager Federalists, scanning the returns, predicted that Ames would win. Christopher Gore, who had tried so hard
to further the candidacy of his friend Rufus King, wrote him in detail
about the outcome of the election. "The election in Suffolk is clearly
for Ames..., who is strictly federal, an honorable man and in the
estimation of his friends wants nothing but age and experience to render him a very able supporter of his country's rights. I ought to say in
justice to Ames that he was very desirous that Mr. K shou'd be elected
...and...did use all his influence till he was convinc'd that it would
not avail." [53]

At the height of the election campaign, and even after his victory,
Fisher Ames was subjected to criticism and disparaging remarks in the
Boston newspapers. A writer using the pseudonym of "Traveller" remarked in the *Gazette* of December 29 that Ames was merely the son
of an almanac writer, had little professional standing as a lawyer, and
worst of all, had never been beyond the borders of Massachusetts.
Several friends immediately rose to Ames's defense. "Candidus" countered this gratuitous attack with an assertion that Ames proved himself
a politician in the Convention, where spectators witnessed his honesty
and independence. As to his political views, they had been highly

52. Miller, *Sam Adams*, 387; Record Commission, Report, "Boston Town
Records 1784 to 1796," *Records Relating to the Early History of Boston*, XXXI
(Boston, 1903), 183; Dedham Town Records, 1784-93, IX, 107, Town Clerk's
Office, Dedham; Federal Election Returns, Mass. Archives, Office of the Secretary
of the Commonwealth, State House; *Massachusetts Centinel* (Boston), Dec. 27,
1788, Jan. 3, 7, 1789. There were 9,417 polls in Suffolk District; 1,613 votes were
cast or 17.1 per cent of the total polls. A total of 274 votes were cast for 13 other
candidates, indicating the lack of rigid party lines.
53. Christopher Gore to Rufus King, Boston, Dec. 21, 1788, Rufus King Papers,
Box 3, No. 61, New-York Historical Society, New York, N.Y., published in King,
Life of King, I, 348. Henry Jackson to Henry Knox, Boston, Dec. 21, 1788, Knox
Papers, XXIII, No. 43, Mass. Hist. Soc.

spoken of by Benjamin Rush and George Washington "and Dr. Ramsay has copied his sentiments in a publick Oration delivered before the citizens of Charleston." In the *Herald of Freedom* "North End" attacked the Antifederalists for "raising a hue and cry that the liberties will be swallowed up and republicanism soon be extinct.... Now these mighty advocates for equality ... are ... against a man because his father was an Almanack-maker." [54]

Ames had allied himself unequivocally with the Federalist group, which was accused of constituting an "aristocratical junto." Early in 1789 when the General Court took up the question of a salary for the lieutenant governor, it was apparent that the strength of the Federalists was precarious. The salary problem had grown out of a disagreement between Governor Hancock and Lieutenant Governor Benjamin Lincoln. For political reasons Hancock had withheld from Lincoln the traditional captaincy of a Boston harbor post, Castle William. Normally the income from this sinecure was granted to the incumbent lieutenant governor in lieu of a salary. Under the existing circumstances, Lincoln realized no income from his office. [55]

Confronted with the gradual disintegration of the recent political alliance with Governor Hancock, the Federalists sought to rally the support of all their political adherents. Ames recognized that they could ill afford the prolonged absence of their Ajax, Theophilus Parsons, and wrote to him, urging an immediate return to his duties in the legislature. "Surely the last session did not inspire you with so much esteem for the present assembly as to induce you to think it safe to leave us alone," he commented. [56]

Ames and several colleagues were appointed to form a committee to consider the salary issue. When this committee presented its report, proposing an annual salary of £300 for the lieutenant governor, Ames defended the recommendation. According to one reporter in the Boston *Massachusetts Centinel*, he made "two short but eloquent ... speeches [which] arrested the attention of a full house and a crowded gallery." [57] Despite his efforts, the lieutenant governor's salary was set at only £160 when a vote was taken on January 23, 1789, in the lower house.

54. *Boston Gazette*, Dec. 29, 1788; *Massachusetts Centinel* (Boston), Dec. 31, 1788; *Herald of Freedom* (Boston), Jan. 1, 1789.
55. Political Journal of George R. Minot, Jan., 1789, Sedgwick (Minot) Papers, Mass. Hist. Soc.; *Massachusetts Centinel* (Boston), Nov. 15, 1788, Jan. 17, 21, 1789.
56. The separation between Hancock and the Federalists grew with the Governor's dwindling chances for the Presidency. Miller, *Sam Adams*, 385. Morse, *Federalist Party*, 214. Ames to Theophilus Parsons, Boston, Jan. 8, 1788 [1789], Parsons, *Memoir of Parsons*, 462. The year given, 1788, is incorrect.
57. *Massachusetts Centinel* (Boston), Jan. 17, 1789.

From the early part of January until mid-February, Ames was incessantly active, attending to the business of the General Court and his legal work, while preparing to leave for the first meeting of the federal Congress. During a brief visit at home in Dedham, he wrote to Thomas Dwight, who had returned to Springfield, Massachusetts, to practice law after serving in the General Court. A Harvard College graduate, Dwight was a contemporary of Ames and destined to be a lifelong friend. In his letter, Ames indicated that he very much wanted to visit him, as well as other friends in Springfield, and he found delays vexing.

> I doubt my right of teazing you with my ill-humors. You will see how many reasons are superadded, by my election to Congress, to keep me busy here. Previous to the sitting of the General Court, I was absent from my office, without intermission . . . about eight weeks. . . . The next week the choice of Electors in the General Court and the Court of Common Pleas made a slave of me.
>
> Ever since I have been running away from the Court-house to the State-house. . . . Add to this, I am about to leave and renounce this world and go to New York and must so far settle my worldly affairs as to be in a degree prepared for my future state (a state of terror and uncertainty to me) by the end of February. . . . For in spite of obstacles, seeming not to be surmounted, I indulge a hope of seeing you next week. For if that prospect should fail me, I shall despair of making my best bow in Springfield till I see it on my way to New York.

In closing his letter, Ames added two significant lines: "You are in heaven or very near it. Do not forget your frail friends, who are still in a state of probation." [58] Undoubtedly this reference was to Dwight's developing friendship with Hannah, one of the four daughters of a distinguished Springfield resident, Colonel John Worthington.

It was only after the General Court had ended its session on February 17 that Ames was able to make arrangements to leave for Congress. He set out for New York with two other representatives, Elbridge Gerry and George Leonard. At Springfield, Senator Caleb Strong joined the group.[59] The coach did not tarry long there, but Ames may just have had time enough for that promised visit with Thomas Dwight.

58. Benjamin W. Dwight, *The History of the Descendants of John Dwight of Dedham, Massachusetts,* 2 vols., (N.Y., 1874), II, 829; Mason A. Green, *Springfield, 1636-1886, History of Town and City* (Springfield, 1888), 309-11; Ames to Thomas Dwight, Dedham, Jan. 18, 1789, Gratz Collection, Case 1, Box 28, Hist. Soc. of Pa.

59. *Herald of Freedom* (Boston), Feb. 24, 1789. The *Massachusetts Centinel* (Boston), Jan. 28, 1789, published an address to the newly elected representatives expressing confidence that they would carry out the new system of government. *Ibid.,* Feb. 26, 1789.

Even more important, he probably saw Hannah Worthington's sister, Frances, a young lady whose charm and intelligence appealed to him.

Once in New York, Representative Ames had a few days to orient himself before the meeting of Congress on March 4. Along with several members from Massachusetts he took lodgings at 15 Great Dock Street in Mrs. Dunscomb's boarding house. After he was settled in his new quarters, Ames presented himself at the home of John Jay to deliver a letter to Mrs. Jay from her friend Abigail Adams. Mrs. Adams had written, "This letter will be delivered to you by Mr. Ames ... a young Gentleman of an amiable character and very good abilities. He was so good as to offer to take charge of any letters I might have for New York." [60] This was Fisher Ames's first introduction into the society of the new capital of the nation. His political introduction to Congress was to follow during the next few weeks.

60. Thomas E. V. Smith, *The City of New York in the Year of Washington's Inauguration* (N.Y., 1889), 30; *The New York Directory and Register for the Year 1789* (N.Y., 1789). Abigail Adams to Mrs. John Jay, Feb. 20, 1789, H. P. Johnston, ed., *The Correspondence and Public Papers of John Jay*, 4 vols. (N.Y., 1890-93), III, 364-65.

Chapter V

The Congressional Drama Begins

Amid the din of pealing church bells, Fisher Ames left his lodgings on the morning of March 4 and strode toward Federal Hall. Earlier that day gunners at the Battery had fired a salute of eleven guns to proclaim the opening of Congress and the start of a new era. New York City was in a festive mood, with flags decorating every building. Crowds of people filled the streets, and according to one reporter, "marks of evident satisfaction were visibly imprinted on every countenance." The meetings of both houses of Congress had been set for eleven o'clock, and as the hour approached members began to gather in the newly renovated hall.[1]

There Ames met a handful of congressmen, a few of whom he already knew from the Convention and the General Court. The Massachusetts delegation was on hand; it included not only Elbridge Gerry, George Leonard, and Caleb Strong, but also George Thatcher, who represented the district of Maine, a part of the Commonwealth of Massachusetts. Others he knew by reputation or had made their acquaintance since his arrival. Senators Oliver Ellsworth and William S. Johnson, two of Connecticut's delegates to the Constitutional Convention, were there, as well as Jeremiah Wadsworth and Jonathan Trumbull. Six members from Pennsylvania had arrived, including the renowned Robert Morris, the two Muhlenbergs, Thomas Hartley, and William Maclay. From the states to the south of the Potomac, only one senator,

1. *Massachusetts Centinel* (Boston), Mar. 14, 1789; *Maryland Journal and Baltimore Advertiser*, Mar. 13, 1789.

William Few of Georgia, had put in an appearance, and Alexander White was Virginia's sole representative. The difficulties of travel and, in a few cases, sheer procrastination had kept the rest of the elected members from attending the opening of Congress.[2]

At eleven o'clock Ames and twelve other representatives took their seats in a makeshift room; although carpenters had been busy with hammer and saw for months, the representatives' chamber was not yet complete. More disappointing was the fact that there was no quorum, and the House adjourned until the next day. The Senate, too, was unable to commence its work, and a brief hour after the opening of the first session, the renewed firing of guns and ringing of bells signaled the adjournment. Yet the cheering and noise outdoors could not cloak the fact that the structure of the government was as incomplete as Federal Hall itself.[3]

Only a trickle of members came to New York during March, never enough to form a quorum for business. Ames kept a close watch on the situation, tallying the numbers and writing his friends to tell them of the current strength. Even after James Madison, Richard Bland Lee, and John Page swelled the Virginia delegation in mid-March, he was not reassured. "Many seem to be confident that both Houses will be formed this week," he reported. "However, I do not expect it so soon. I hope business will be transacted with more alacrity than this delay indicates." [4] Ten days later, on March 25, the House was still four short of the necessary thirty and he was perturbed at the continuing inactivity. It seemed as though "the languor of the old Confederation was transfused into the members of the new Congress." This indeterminate situation was unsettling. "The old Congress still continues to meet, and it seems doubtful whether the old government is dead or the new one alive." Increasingly apprehensive, he maintained that "we lose £1000 a day revenue. We lose credit, spirit, everything. The public will forget the government before it is born." He burst out vehemently, "God deliver us speedily from this puzzling state, or prepare my will, if it subsists much longer, for I am in a fever to think of it." [5]

2. Joseph Gales, ed., *The Debates and Proceedings in the Congress of the United States ... Compiled From Authentic Materials ...*, 42 vols. (Washington, 1834-56), I, 100. Hereafter cited as *Annals*.

3. Smith, *New York in 1789*, 43-44. George Thatcher to Nathan Dane, Oct. 2, 1788, Burnett, ed., *Letters of Members of the Continental Congress*, VIII, 802. *Massachusetts Centinel* (Boston), Mar. 14, 1789. *Annals*, I, 100, Mar. 4, 1789.

4. Ames to ?, N.Y., Mar. 15, 1789, Boston Public Library. For Madison's expectations about Congress, see James Madison to Edmund Randolph, Mar. 1, 1789, Madison Papers, XI, Lib. Cong.

5. Ames to George R. Minot, N.Y., Mar. 25, 1789, Ames, *Works of Ames*, I, 32; Alexander White to Gen. Adam Stephen, N.Y., Mar. 24, 1789, Adam Stephen

On April 1, the House at last had a quorum and could begin to function. Ames sent the gratifying news to William Tudor and expressed his own satisfaction that many members strongly supported the federal government. In his view, the primary need of the country was a "right and temperate administration of government. . . . The feds," he acutely observed, "have too much faith in its *good* and the anti's too much forecast of its *ill* tendencies. Both will be baulked probably." [6]

Ames quickly evaluated his new associates as "sober, solid, old-charter folks, as we often say." There were few geniuses, but the competence of the group in general impressed him. These were not people to inspire awe or to terrify him by their superior capabilities, as he at first surmised. Instead, they were men of firm habits, well versed in government, and devoid of any penchant for intrigue. He felt decidedly more at ease in their presence than he expected, and his self-assurance rose as he was given more responsibility. [7]

On April 13 he was appointed to the standing committee on elections. Later the same month, he was one of three members chosen by the House to meet Vice President John Adams and accompany him on his arrival in New York to the house of John Jay on lower Broadway. Preparation for the inauguration of George Washington increased his duties. When a joint committee of both houses was created to determine the time and place for the inaugural, he was asked to serve on it. The delegation from the House, including Egbert Benson and Daniel Carroll as well as Ames, worked closely with the Senate's delegation in making the necessary arrangements. It was this committee which suggested that Washington take the oath in the outer gallery of Federal Hall in full view of the populace, rather than in the representatives' chamber. [8]

General Washington was given an enthusiastic reception when he arrived in New York on April 23. To William Tudor, Ames wrote, "When I saw Washington, I felt very strong emotions. I believe that no man *ever* had so fair a claim to veneration as he. Next Thursday he is to be received in form by the two houses, and to take the oath in

---

Papers, Lib. Cong. Benjamin Goodhue to Elias H. Derby, N.Y., Apr. 5, 1789, "Letter of Honorable Benjamin Goodhue, Member of Congress," Essex Institute *Hist. Collections,* 1 (1859), 111; George A. Boyd, *Elias Boudinot, Patriot and Statesman, 1740-1821* (Princeton, 1952), 155-56.

6. Ames to William Tudor, N.Y., Apr. 1, 1789, "Memoir of Tudor," Mass. Hist. Soc., *Collections,* 2d Ser., 8 (1819), 316. On prospective legislation of Congress, see James Madison to Edmund Pendleton, N.Y., Apr. 8, 1789, Madison Papers, XI, Lib. Cong.

7. Ames to Minot, N.Y., Apr. 4, 1789, Ames, *Works of Ames,* I, 32-33.

8. *Annals,* I, 128, 157, 200, 208, 216, Apr. 13, 16, 24-25, 27, 1789.

public. This will impede business a good deal till it shall be over."[9] The only flaw in the welcome for Washington, he reported, was a violent rain which washed out the evening illumination.

On the long-awaited inaugural day, the House of Representatives assembled in mid-morning, in order to hold a brief meeting before adjourning for their joint session with the Senate. Unexpectedly there was confusion and delay in the Senate chamber when the Speaker of the House and a full complement of representatives, including Ames, appeared. The Senate was engrossed in a debate on a minor matter in a committee report, and the senators who were speaking were so reluctant to yield that they ignored repeated reminders of the presence of the representatives. Even Senators Richard H. Lee, Ralph Izard, and Tristram Dalton, members of the joint committee on arrangements, were slow to withdraw from the scene. Ames and his colleagues in the House finally got the laggard senators to join them, and the escort group set out belatedly for Cherry Street to bring the President-elect back to Federal Hall.[10]

It was 12:30 P.M. before the stately procession of the President, congressmen, and soldiers commenced. Ames followed behind the President's coach and throughout the day was often close enough to Washington to have a unique opportunity to observe him. On entering the Hall, the committee conducted Washington to the Senate chamber, where Vice President Adams ceremoniously welcomed him and after a brief hesitation, informed him that all was in readiness. Then on the balcony in full view of the public, Chancellor Robert R. Livingston administered the oath of office, and after the prolonged cheering subsided, Washington delivered his presidential address.[11]

Ames vividly recreated the momentous event for his friends. Washington, he related, "addressed the two Houses in the Senate chamber. It was a very touching scene, and quite of the solemn kind. His aspect grave, almost to sadness; his modesty, actually shaking; his voice deep, a little tremulous, and so low as to call for close attention; added to the series of objects presented to the mind, and overwhelming it, pro-

9. Ames to Tudor, N.Y., Apr. 25-26, 1789, "Memoir of Tudor," Mass. Hist. Soc., *Collections*, 2d Ser., 8 (1819), 318; J. Blakeley to Noah Webster, N.Y., Apr. 8, 1789, Noah Webster Papers, N.Y. Pub. Lib.

10. Charles A. Beard, ed., *The Journal of William Maclay* (N.Y., 1927), 8. Douglas Freeman, *George Washington, A Biography*, 7 vols. (N.Y., 1948-57), VI, 189; Smith, *New York in 1789*, 40 ff; R. B. Lee to Col. Levin Powell, N.Y., Apr. 30, 1789, Levin Powell Papers, Lib. Cong.

11. Freeman, *Washington*, VI, 188-96; Smith, *New York in 1789*, 40; Tristram Dalton to M. Hodge, N.Y., May 2, 1789, Eben F. Stone, "Sketch of Tristram Dalton," Essex Institute *Hist. Collections*, 25 (1888), 25.

duced emotions of the most affecting kind upon the members. I, Pil-
garlic, sat entranced." Ames continued, "It seemed to me an allegory
in which virtue was personified, and addressing those whom she would
make her votaries. Her power over the heart was never greater, and the
illustration of her doctrine by her own example was never more perfect." [12]

When Washington had completed his brief address, he accompanied
the members of Congress and other dignitaries to St. Paul's Chapel,
where a divine service brought the ceremonies to a close. Here, Ames,
who sat in the same pew with Washington, was struck anew by his
appearance. "Time has made havoc upon his face," he commented.
"That, and many other circumstances not to be reasoned about, con-
spire to keep up the awe which I brought with me." [13] To another
acquaintance he wrote in a similar, though more restrained fashion:
"I saw and listened to Washington with as much emotion as you have
supposed." Again he alluded to his sensation of an allegorical vision,
which he felt overwhelmed his mind with limitless reflections. "The
crowd was great," he reported, "but not a stupid one—each expressing
as much admiration and joy as a painter would have on his canvas. The
modesty, benevolence, and dignity of the President cannot be described," he concluded. "Your own feeling heart must finish the picture." [14] Throughout his life, Ames's admiration for Washington never
waned.

Even before the inauguration, the House of Representatives had
begun working on the urgent matter of providing a revenue for the
nation, debating James Madison's plan to raise money through tariff
and tonnage duties. Basing his ideas on his experience in the Congress
of the Confederation, Madison proposed a system which he believed
would remedy "the deficiency in our Treasury" and enable the nation
"in its first act, to revive those principles of honor and honesty that
have too long lain dormant" by paying its obligations.[15] In order to
permit the government to tax the springtime imports from Europe, the
Virginian recommended establishing a temporary rather than a permanent system at this juncture. His plan had the attraction of brevity
and simplicity; it would include the revenue tariff of 1783, as well as
a tax on all shipping entering the country. Specific duties would be set

12. Ames to Minot, N.Y., May 3, 1789, Ames, *Works of Ames*, I, 34.
13. *Ibid.*
14. Ames to Nathaniel Bishop, N.Y., May 1789, Crofts Autograph Collection,
Boston Pub. Lib.
15. *Annals*, I, 107, Apr. 9, 1789. Irving Brant, *James Madison: Father of the
Constitution, 1787-1800* (Indianapolis, 1950), 246; R. B. Lee to Col. Levin Powell,
N.Y., Apr. 13, 1789, Levin Powell Papers, Lib. Cong.

for rum, liquor, molasses, wines, teas, pepper, sugar, cocoa, and coffee. Duties on all other imports would be *ad valorem*. Madison's primary purpose was to raise revenue to operate the government and provide for the national debt, rather than to protect native industries. He felt, however, that a tax on foreign shipping offered the struggling nation an opportunity to increase its bargaining powers by exerting pressure on nations not having commercial treaties with the United States.

Reflecting on Madison's economic views, Ames concluded that he had come under the influence of Adam Smith's *Wealth of Nations*. The principles of the work seemed sound, but Ames felt that they had to be applied cautiously to America since there was a much greater need to encourage commerce and manufacturing in the United States than in England. He suspected, however, that Madison's desire to use discrimination as an economic weapon was actually related to his attachment for the French. While the Massachusetts representative recognized that his state would be affected by any decision on tariff rates, he did not enter into the early debates on the merits of Madison's plan.[16]

During his first days in Congress, Ames's attention centered on James Madison. He was continually intrigued by his colleague's personality, and he persisted in trying to assess his motives and character until he felt he had taken the measure of him. Ames was impressed with Madison's abilities; he was "a man of sense, reading ... and integrity"; yet from the beginning the Massachusetts representative was not attracted to him. He was "very much Frenchified in his politics," Ames thought, and was not bold in action. "He is not a little of a Virginian ... but is afraid of their State politics, and of his popularity there, more than I think he should be." [17] Still Ames considered him the "first man" in the House, placing him among such leading public figures as President Washington, Chancellor Robert Livingston, and Alexander Hamilton.

In Ames's opinion James Madison was not an impressive speaker; he was too cool, too reflective, too grave, lacking in pleasantries and warmth of heart. The southerner spoke slowly, stating his principles and unfolding his reasons clearly and simply. His approach to oratory was not based on reason alone, however, for he would desert it in an effort to move his listeners by reminding them about consistency, precedents, or pride in the House of Representatives. Ames seemed to feel that Madison's speeches lacked fire and that they were pedantic and theoretical rather than practical.[18]

When George Minot chided him for his severity toward his fellow

16. Ames to Minot, N.Y., May 29, 1789, Ames, *Works of Ames*, I, 49.
17. Ames to Minot, May 3, 1789, *ibid.*, 35.
18. Ames to Minot, N. Y., May 18, 1789, *ibid.*, 42.

representative, Ames responded in a surprised tone, "But did I express any contempt for Madison? Upon my word, I do not recollect a word of it, and there is not in my heart a symptom of its having ever been there." Although he admitted that his impatience with many of Madison's ideas had probably led him to seem excessively bitter, he denied any intent to reflect upon the basic worth of the man. Madison had a masterful knowledge of public affairs and a devotion to public service. "Upon the whole, he is an useful, respectable, worthy man. . . . He will continue to be a very influential man in our country." [19]

Ames would have liked to find an ideal legislator whom he could admire wholeheartedly, but his hero would not be James Madison. Both congressmen were devoted supporters of the Constitution; both advocated a strong central government with a national revenue system; yet they differed widely on details of legislation that would effect their goals. Despite his southern orientation, Madison attempted to avoid a sectional viewpoint and to put the general concerns of the Union first. He persistently maintained that the impost must be based on mutual concession and not on local or state interest. Ames also favored a national emphasis, yet strongly upheld tariff and tonnage duties beneficial to his region. He very genuinely believed that the welfare of the country as a whole was dependent on shipping and commerce; therefore, federal policies must encourage the New England economy.[20]

In the debates over the proposed tariff bill, the tug of sectional interests became apparent. Thomas Fitzsimmons, a representative from Pennsylvania, countered Madison's plan with proposals to establish a permanent system based on the protective principles of his state's tariff of 1785. Thomas T. Tucker of South Carolina expressed southern opposition to any protective duties and at the same time attacked possible tonnage duties which would bear hardest on the southern states, dependent as they were on foreign shipping. Within a few days it became evident that Madison's tariff resolutions could not gain enough support for passage. Madison himself attributed the collapse of his plan to the "apparent impracticability of reaping the spring harvest from importations." [21] On April 11, Elias Boudinot of New Jersey presented a motion for the appointment of a committee to prepare an interim tariff

19. Ames to Minot, May 29, 1789, *ibid.*, 47, 49.
20. *Annals*, I, 116, Apr. 9, 1789; Brant, *Madison, Father of the Constitution*, 247.
21. James Madison to Edmund Randolph, N.Y., Apr. 12, 1789, Madison Papers, XI, Lib. Cong.; *Annals*, I, 110, 122, Apr. 9, 11, 1789. For the origins of protectionist ideas in the U.S., see Malcom R. Eiselen, *The Rise of Pennsylvania Protectionism* (Phila., 1932), 10-25; William Hill, "Protective Purposes of the Tariff Act of 1789," *Journal of Political Economy*, 2 (1893), 54-76; William Hill, "The First Stages of the Tariff Policy of the United States," American Economic Association, *Publications*, 8 (1893), 107-30.

bill. When the motion failed, the House, meeting as a committee of the whole, began hammering out a permanent tariff with specific duties on enumerated articles.

How forcefully Ames and his fellow representatives from Massachusetts felt about their particular interests became evident when the committee considered the duty on imported molasses, the essential raw material of the Massachusetts rum industry. As an alternative to an unpopular excise tax on domestically distilled rum, Madison proposed levying an eight-cent duty per gallon on molasses. A tax at this rate, he hoped, would give domestic distillers of rum a competitive advantage over importers of rum. New Englanders promptly resisted with a barrage of arguments. Benjamin Goodhue of Salem explained that a high tax would bear disproportionately on his state of Massachusetts and compared it to the odious pre-Revolutionary British tax on molasses. George Thatcher warned against undue haste in establishing an impost system and emphasized that molasses, a staple in the diet of the poor, should only be taxed at an extremely low duty.[22]

Fisher Ames chose this moment to make his first speech in the House. He pointedly challenged the eight-cent duty, asserting that his colleagues could not hesitate to reject a charge which was so unfair. Until such time in the future when people no longer drank spirits, it was better to encourage domestic manufacture, give useful employment, and maintain a basis for foreign trade. He explained that common varieties of fish, impossible to sell elsewhere, were exchanged in the West Indies for molasses which was then shipped back to New England distilleries. The fisheries, shipping, and distilleries were important elements in American foreign trade and had a direct bearing on the welfare of the nation. Ames then reached the climax of his speech: "Let me ask if it is wise . . . to take measures subversive of your very existence? For I do contend, that the very existence of the eastern states depends upon the encouragement of their navigation and fishery, which receive a deadly wound by an excessive impost on the article before us." [23]

Ames's speech evoked a rejoinder from Thomas Fitzsimmons, who tried to show that even if a duty bore hard on one area, it should be considered in light of its effect on the nation. He rejected the argument

22. *Annals*, I, 137-38, Apr. 14, 1789; Lawrence S. Mayo in *DAB* s.v. "Goodhue, Benjamin"; Robert E. Moody in *DAB* s.v. "Thatcher, George."
23. *Annals*, I, 138, 140, 142, Apr. 14, 1789; J. Avery to George Thatcher, Apr. 22, 1789, Thatcher Papers, Chamberlain Collection, Boston Pub. Lib. Avery commented, "Mr. Ames's Idea of the matter is perfectly just . . . as the importation of Molasses . . . is such an important branch in the eastern States . . . to lay a high duty will tend . . . to impoverish us."

that an eight-cent duty per gallon on molasses would ruin an important segment of the economy, contending that the tax would be passed on to the ultimate consumer. In reply to the Pennsylvanian, Ames argued that the tax imposed on molasses, and thus indirectly on domestic rum, was disproportionately high in comparison to the duty levied on imported rum. A desirable goal, he stated, would be a duty on molasses which did not injure the rum industry. The high rate proposed by others would, in his estimation, damage public morality since it would precipitate evasion of the law and encourage smuggling.

Gradually Ames's insistence and dramatic emphasis on the baneful consequences of a tax on molasses swayed the members of the committee of the whole. Madison's efforts to carry through the eight-cent rate failed, but a proposal of New York's John Laurance for a six-cent rate was approved. Though the molasses duty was amicably settled for the moment, the Massachusetts congressmen repeatedly returned to the theme of lower duties in ensuing debates. As far as Ames and his colleagues were concerned, the issue was far from concluded.[24]

Shaping the impost bill proceeded slowly, especially as local considerations had to be balanced with the national interest. In a jocular frame of mind Ames wrote about activities in the House, "We are busy in contriving an act to get your money. I fear that by straining duties too high, we shall find that you have tied hard knots in the purse strings. We hear something of the murmurs of local and state prejudices, but the general wish seems to be to favor the agriculture, trade, and arts of the country by moderate duties on foreign ships and goods."[25] During a period of two weeks the representatives devoted most of their time to debating the terms of the tariff bill. Not until April 21 did the committee of the whole finally complete its report. As Thomas Fitzsimmons explained in a letter to Dr. Benjamin Rush, "it has so intirely occupyed us that little else has been thot of"; but in spite of the difficulties of adjusting differing opinions and interests, he, as well as other members, emphasized that there was general harmony within the House.[26]

This accommodating spirit was severely tested when the representatives took up the report. The opponents of high duties now demanded substantial reductions in the proposed rates. Elias Boudinot of New

24. *Annals,* I, 143, Apr. 14, 1789.
25. Ames to Samuel Henshaw, N.Y., Apr. 22, 1789, Personal Papers, Lib. Cong.; for eastern and southern views on the tariff, see James Madison to Edmund Pendleton, N.Y., Apr. 19, 1789, Madison Papers, XI, Lib. Cong.
26. Thomas Fitzsimmons to Dr. Benjamin Rush, N.Y., Apr. 20, 1789, Gratz Collection, Hist. Soc. of Pa.; Lee to Powell, Apr. 13, 1789, Levin Powell Papers, Lib. Cong.

Jersey, an advocate of a tariff for revenue only, insisted that articles were taxed so highly that revenue could not be collected. Madison, however, defended the proposed duties as essential to provide revenue for the new government. Momentarily Thomas Fitzsimmons allied with him, but only with the objective of retaining the hard-won protection for manufactures.[27]

The Massachusetts delegation, under strong pressure from the rum distillers and other constituents, resumed the fight for a lower rate on molasses. One voter wrote to George Thatcher admonishing him, "I have just heard that you have laid a duty on molasses, for heaven sake what motive, what inducement could you have for that for it is the meat and drink of this state ... for God's sake don't destroy the labors of the diligent." [28] Ames and his colleagues, Goodhue, Gerry, Thatcher, and Jeremiah Wadsworth of Connecticut, presented a solid phalanx of opposition to the duty. Senator Maclay of Pennsylvania, listening in on the debates, commented sharply, "The partiality of the New England members to [molasses] was now manifest. All from their quarter was a universal cry against it." [29] Goodhue drummed on the connection between the molasses trade and the fisheries; Gerry contended that the commercial states should not pay more taxes than others; and Wadsworth emphasized the maritime trade's close interrelationship with and dependence on the molasses trade. George Thatcher, carried away by the heat of the debate, reminded southerners that they would no more like an impost on Negro slaves than New Englanders would on molasses. Ignoring Thatcher's pointed remarks, Madison endeavored to show with precise logic that the domestic distilling industry would not be unduly injured by the tax.[30]

Once more Ames attempted to cope with the Virginian's arguments. "I appeal, Mr. Speaker, with confidence, to the justice of this House," he began, "though I am far from being convinced that any liberality has been shown in fixing the duty on molasses." [31] Using all the techniques of oratory at his command, he tried to sway his fellow representatives. Candidly he asserted that the Constitution was dictated by the needs of commerce. If the duty defeated the primary objects of government,

27. *Annals*, I, 200-204, Apr. 24, 1789. Fitzsimmons to Rush, Apr. 20, 1789, Gratz Collection, Hist. Soc. of Pa.
28. I. Tucker to George Thatcher, Apr. 26, 1789, Thatcher Papers, Chamberlain Collection, Boston Pub. Lib.; Christopher Gore to Rufus King, Boston, Apr. 25, 1789, Rufus King Papers, Box 3, No. 76, N.-Y. Hist. Soc.; *Gazette of the United States* (N.Y.), Apr. 23, 1789. The *Boston Gazette*, Apr. 27, 1789, commented that "the high flying ones ... grumble on account of the impost on Molasses."
29. Entry of Apr. 27, 1789, Beard, ed., *Journal of Maclay*, 4.
30. *Annals*, I, 217, 219-20, 223-24, 227-28, Apr. 27, 28, 1789.
31. *Ibid.*, 230, Apr. 28, 1789.

such as the advancement of commerce or the promotion of the general welfare, he was convinced the representatives would abandon it. Lashing out at Madison, he insisted that a low duty on molasses would not sacrifice "the interest of three million of people to the establishment of a few New England distilleries." Ames defended his own position as being in the national interest, not merely in the interest of his region. In answer to the argument that a high duty on molasses might reduce rum consumption, he contended that it was futile to attempt to reform public habits and morals. "We are not to consider ourselves while here, as at church or school," he proclaimed, "to listen to the harangues of speculative piety; we are to talk of the political interests committed to our charge." In a derisive manner, he asserted that if anyone thought a law would change the taste of people, he must have "more romantic notions of legislative influence than experience justifies." [32] He then drew a picture of languishing fisheries and of the declining trade of New England, which would be utterly ruined by the duty. Molasses was such a necessity for the poor in his section that to deprive them of it by an oppressive tax would lead them to detest the national government. There was every reason, therefore, to persist in opposition to the measure, and he hoped the House would limit the duty to one cent a gallon.

Immediately Madison replied heatedly to Ames. Why, he wanted to know, was there more apprehension for one part of the Union than another? "Are the Northern people made of finer clay? Do they respire a clearer air? . . . are they the chosen few? Are all others to be oppressed . . . and they . . . take their course easy and unrestrained? No. I trust the general government will equally affect all." Only by impartial acts could this be done, he concluded emphatically. [33] Ames apologized to Madison for having injured his feelings. He had no intention, he insisted, of drawing an unfair comparison between Massachusetts and the South. Yet he would not retract his remarks about the detrimental effect of the duty. Persistent as Ames and his Massachusetts colleagues were, when the vote was finally taken, they could not persuade the House to reduce the rates. [34]

This setback was only temporary, as Ames assuredly would have further opportunities to argue his cause before the impost became law. Pride in his efforts was mingled with concern because the New York newspapers had not published his speech accurately. "My friend, listen," he hurriedly wrote to Minot, "Fenno published the speeches. *Inter nos* I suppose Goodhue and Gerry wrote theirs, and gave to him.

32. *Ibid.*, 232, Apr. 28, 1789.
33. *Ibid.*, 236, Apr. 28, 1789.
34. *Ibid.*

Mine is not flattered by the publication." Perhaps Minot could have it published anonymously or under his name in the Boston papers. He would let his friends decide whether the speech "will tend to create invidious observations against me, or be a prudent thing." [35]

After turning briefly to other business matters, the House on May 6 read the impost bill a second time and then referred it to a committee of the whole House. In the course of renewed debate on the tariff rates, Ames was often on his feet arguing, admonishing, pleading. On May 9 he took up a favorite theme that excessive duties were offensive to a large number of people and that such duties would be impossible to collect. Only if the general level of duties were moderate would the public acquiesce in them and the government be assured of a revenue. "How much better is this," he asserted, "than holding out temptations for men to enrich themselves and beggar your treasury, to trample on your laws, and despise the Government itself." [36] Madison, obviously unimpressed by Ames's dramatization of the issue, dismissed his argument with the implication that the Massachusetts representative did not have "a right understanding of this subject." Now was the time, according to Madison, when as much money as possible should be realized from the impost; but if there were a widespread lowering of duties, the needs of the government could not be supplied.

Ames soon rose in the House to suggest that if the government needed additional revenue, it should resort to other taxes and excises rather than to "overloading" the tariff.[37] The idea of using an excise as a supplement to the tariff seemed to Ames like a logical solution for a difficult problem. "The southern people dread it . . . ," he explained to his friends. "They are afraid for their whiskey. Madison will oppose this, and it will be a work of labor and some responsibility." Still, Ames thought an excise could be a valuable source of revenue for the government.[38] By dint of persistent argument the Massachusetts representatives won a concession for their cause when on May 12 the House reduced the molasses duty an additional penny, to five cents per gallon. "Another molasses battle has been fought," Ames related to George Minot. "Like modern victories, it was incomplete, but we got off one cent." [39]

With molasses safely out of the way, the tariff bill moved forward

35. Ames to Minot, May 3, 1789, Ames, *Works of Ames*, I, 35. John Fenno was the editor of the *Gazette of the United States*.
36. *Annals*, I, 276, 308, 312, May 6, 9, 1789.
37. *Ibid.*, 312, 321-24, May 9, 1789.
38. *Ibid.*, 323-24; Ames to Minot, N.Y., May 14, 1789, Ames, *Works of Ames*, I, 37.
39. Ames to Minot, May 14, 1789, Ames, *Works of Ames*, I, 37; *Annals*, I, 349, May 12, 1789. Gerry's political vacillations are discussed in Samuel Eliot Morison, "Elbridge Gerry, Gentleman Democrat," *New Eng. Qtly.*, 2 (1929), 6-33.

to completion, yet it continued to engender controversy. When Madison proposed an amendment to limit the duration of the act, Ames immediately rejected the move. It was an astonishing attempt, in Ames's eyes, to put through a fundamental change in the bill just before the final vote on it. "I opposed it instanter," he excitedly related to his Boston friends. "He supported it by reasons which I despise. It was, he said, anti-republican to grant a perpetual revenue, unappropriated; it was unwise to part with the power ... and it would be ... unprecedented to establish a perpetual tax." [40] By a vote of forty-one to eight on May 16, the House decided to accept a limitation of seven years for the impost. On the same day the bill at last passed the House and was sent to the Senate.

During the course of the debates on the tariff, Thomas Fitzsimmons had become irritated at the long, drawn-out controversy over molasses. In particular he was disturbed by the "tenacity of the Massachusetts people who have shown a littleness injurious to their reputation." He continued his remarks to Benjamin Rush, "They have (to carry a point of 1st or 2d rate on Molasses) used arguments unworthy of their national character and extremely so of the respectability of their own. The Old Ideas of State interest and state politicks keep strong hold of too many of the present representatives." [41]

Ames was conscious of Fitzsimmons' antagonism toward New Englanders throughout the debates. Offended by his attitude, he described the Pennsylvania representative to Minot as an uncivil and artful person who glared while speaking. In one sentence, filled with more indignation than charity, Ames epitomized Fitzsimmons' character: "He is one of those people, whose face, manner, and sentiments concur to produce caution, if not apprehension and disgust." [42]

Almost as complex an issue as the impost was that of tonnage duties. As a part of his revenue system, Madison initially suggested an overall policy on tonnage, but left the decision of specific rates to the representatives. His plan was to differentiate between American vessels, ships

40. *Annals*, I, 358, 366-68, May 15, 1789; Ames to Minot, N.Y., May 16, 1789, Ames, *Works of Ames*, I, 39-40. Southern opinion with respect to New England economic interests is brought out in William Grayson to Patrick Henry, N.Y., June 12, 1789, Lyon G. Tyler, ed., *The Letters and Times of the Tylers*, 3 vols. (Richmond, 1884-96), I, 165-69.

41. Thomas Fitzsimmons to Benjamin Rush, N.Y., May, n.d., 1789, Gratz Collection, Hist. Soc. of Pa. A letter from H. Williams to James Madison, Suffolk, Va., May 19, 1789, Madison Papers, XI, Lib. Cong., indicates that in Baltimore and Norfolk there was dissatisfaction with the six-cent molasses duty.

42. Ames to Minot, May 18, 1789, Ames, *Works of Ames*, I, 41-42; Beard, ed., *Journal of Maclay*, 28-29; see Asa E. Martin in *DAB* s.v. "Fitzsimmons, Thomas." Fitzsimmons spelled his family name variously.

of nations having treaties with the United States, and those of all other nations. Countries which had made reciprocal commercial agreements with the government would be favored by lower tonnage duties. Those like Britain, which restricted American shipping, would be placed at a disadvantage by higher rates. Madison hoped that discriminatory duties would bring about changes in the policies of foreign nations toward American commerce. Clearly directed against Britain, the plan was so shaped that other nations such as France would gain a part of the Anglo-American trade.[43]

Representatives from South Carolina, Aedanus Burke, Thomas T. Tucker, and William L. Smith, were alarmed at the implications of discrimination and voiced criticism of high tonnage duties which would add excessively to the cost of exporting southern agricultural products. When Benjamin Goodhue made a motion to tax ships of nations in alliance at sixty cents per ton, he met immediate opposition from the southerners, who foresaw that taxes would be even greater for nations without alliances. Unable to gain support, Goodhue withdrew his proposal. After further discussion the committee of the whole recommended a thirty-cent rate for treaty nations and subsequently, a rate of fifty cents per ton for nations not in treaty.[44]

As a means of aiding the growth of domestic shipping, Ames favored taxing foreign ships at a higher level than American vessels; yet he was definitely against Madison's larger concept of using tonnage duties as a commercial weapon. Fundamentally he wanted to establish moderate duties which would be sufficient to encourage shipbuilding and also would place American ships in an advantageous position in the highly competitive Atlantic trade. Therefore he could not agree with the southern critics of high rates that a further reduction on foreign ships would be desirable. When James Jackson presented a motion to reduce duties on ships of allied nations from thirty to twenty cents, Ames rose in the House. He insisted that the low duty suggested by the Georgian would be completely inadequate as an encouragement for "indispensably necessary" American shipping. Only a higher rate, but without Madison's discriminatory measures, would promote domestic shipping and place it at least on a par with foreign shipping. Ames assured his audience that even if the various sections in the nation had differing

43. *Annals*, I, 107, 187-89, 253, Apr. 9, 21, May 4, 1789; for Virginian opinion about the tonnage duty, see H. Williams to James Madison, Suffolk, Va., May 19, 1789, Madison Papers, XI, Lib. Cong.; Lee to Powell, Apr. 13, 1789, Levin Powell Papers, Lib. Cong.; A. A. Giesecke, *American Commercial Legislation Before 1789* (N.Y., 1910), 123-48; Vernon G. Setser, *The Commercial Reciprocity Policy of the United States, 1774-1829* (Phila., 1937), 99-109.
44. *Annals*, I, 184, 196, 199, Apr. 21, 1789.

economic interests, they did not necessarily have diametrically opposed ones. "I believe," he said, "the individual interest of each part is compatible with the general interest. . . . On this principle our existence as a nation depends." [45] In light of Britain's commercial preponderance and the precarious situation of New England shipping, he considered the thirty-cent rate on ships of treaty nations a bare minimum.

Jackson stated that he would go so far as to support drastic restrictions against foreign ships if the South could actually "see the American ships" Ames had said would be built. In a conciliatory way, the Massachusetts representative responded that he did not wish to exclude foreigners; he did, however, hope that American navigation would greatly increase in a shorter period of time than some representatives seemed to anticipate. As the debate continued, Madison endeavored to draw together disparate views by suggesting the adoption of a temporary rate for vessels of allies at twenty-five cents and a permanent rate at sixty cents per ton. Ames promptly objected to this scheme. With Jackson's motion on the floor, Madison's suggestion did not become a formal proposal. Adroitly, the defenders of higher tonnage duty combatted the southern onslaught and on May 6 succeeded in defeating the motion to reduce the duty on allied vessels to twenty cents per ton. The House then voted to accept the original recommendation of the committee of the whole and to levy thirty cents per ton for nations having commercial agreements.[46]

Neither Ames nor the other members of the Massachusetts delegation were as tenacious about retaining the committee's proposal of a fifty-cent tonnage duty on ships belonging to non-treaty nations. Influenced by the close commercial ties of their section with Britain, some of the New Englanders felt that the discriminatory policy might antagonize their best customer. Consequently when Madison made another compromise motion to lower the duty to forty cents until 1791 and then to increase it to seventy-five cents, Ames was willing to accept the proposal. He would not, however, capitulate to the policy of discrimination. Upon the failure of Madison's motion, the House voted to accept the committee's recommendation on tonnage for nations not in treaty.[47]

The tonnage bill which was forwarded to the Senate now dealt with tonnage duties apart from the tariff. It specified that ships of nations with treaties be taxed at thirty cents per ton and all other vessels at

45. *Ibid.*, 261-66, May 5, 1789. A petition from Boston shipbuilders was printed in the *Pennsylvania Packet and Daily Advertiser* (Phila.), May 21, 1789; *Boston Gazette*, May 11, 1789.
46. *Annals*, I, 266-67, 270, 293-94, 302, May 5, 7, 1789.
47. *Ibid.*, 293-94, 302, May 7, 1789. *Journal of the House of Representatives of of the United States* (Washington, 1826), I, 30.

fifty cents. Both American built and foreign built vessels which were wholly owned by Americans were taxed at the rate of six cents per ton.[48] Silent in the last stages of the important debate on tonnage, Ames voted against the final bill. To Minot, he insisted that he could not support the discrimination policy even if a higher duty for nations without alliances would give New England shipping a commercial advantage. He maintained that discrimination was a scheme for "favoring the French and restricting the English," and that it would result in a commercial war with Britain. Ames was disgruntled because many of his New England colleagues, although in basic agreement with him, voted in favor of the bill simply because it would benefit their region's shipping. "Is that a just principle of action," Ames fumed. "It is little and mean, as well as unwise and unsafe to discriminate. I wish I may never sacrifice national principles to local interests." [49]

In mid-May the upper house took up the impost bill and three weeks later the tonnage bill. With determination the senators proceeded to revise both bills, reducing the molasses duty to four cents and striking out the discriminatory tonnage clauses. Ames reacted jubilantly, "I feel as Enceladus would if Etna was removed." He was especially gratified that "the Senate, God bless them, as if designated by Providence to keep rash and frolicsome brats out of the fire," had abolished discrimination.[50]

When the Senate returned each of the bills to the lower house, disagreement over the amendments and rivalry with the upper chamber delayed final acceptance of the measures. Madison made a spirited attempt to restore his pet idea of discrimination, but was unable to prevent ultimate acceptance of the Senate's amendment. Committees from each legislative house ironed out the differences over the bills. The tariff bill became law on July 4; the tonnage bill on July 20. By the terms of the impost act numerous articles were taxed at specific rates, the rates in many cases obviously protecting American producers of goods from foreign competition. Most important to Ames and the New England contingent in the House was the fact that the molasses duty had been reduced again to two and a half cents. In its final form, the tonnage act levied a duty of six cents per ton on American owned

48. *Annals*, I, 302, May 7, 1789.
49. Ames to Minot, May 16, 1789, Ames, *Works of Ames*, I, 38-39; Madison's views on tonnage discrimination are given in *Annals*, I, 268-69. Ames remarked, "I am now unable to account for Madison's passionate attachment to the discrimination.... He is very much devoted to the French, it is said." Ames to Minot, May 29, 1789, Ames, *Works of Ames*, I, 48.
50. Ames to Minot, N.Y., May 27, 1789, Ames, *Works of Ames*, I, 45-46; Tristram Dalton to M. Hodge, N.Y., May 30, 1789, Stone, "Sketch of Dalton," Essex Institute *Hist. Collections*, 25 (1888), 23.

vessels whether American or foreign built. Ships built in the United
States but owned by foreigners were taxed thirty cents per ton, and
all other ships fifty cents per ton. American ships that engaged in trade
along the coast or in fishing were specifically exempted from tonnage
duties. Further advantage was given Americans by the provision that
foreign vessels in the coastal carrying trade had to pay fifty cents per
ton duty.[51]

The debates over revenue gave Fisher Ames an early opportunity in
Congress to prove his competence as an orator. At thirty-one years of
age, he had discovered a stimulating and abrasive medium in which to
communicate his ideas. Ames quickly captured the attention of visitors
to the gallery of the House when he rose to speak. His erect, well-
proportioned figure, his handsome mouth, blue eyes, and powdered
hair accentuated his poise, and produced a lasting impression on those
who heard him debate. With his head slightly raised and his chin thrust
out, Ames would begin speaking in an unassuming manner. His
speeches were well thought out, clever, honest, and unusually full of
substance; never were they verbal froth aimed to delight an audience.
To prove his points, he used a technique of exaggeration which made
his oratory compelling.[52]

After hearing Ames speak, Thomas Lowther commented in a letter
to Judge James Iredell, "The members all appear to be very able men,
particularly a Mr. Ames, from Massachusetts, who, notwithstanding, he
is a very young man delivers his sentiments with the greatest ease and
propriety, and in the most elegant language of any man in the House."
Years later, John Randolph of Roanoke, reminiscing about the high
points of an early visit to New York, recalled that he had attended
Washington's "coronation," and had also heard both Ames and Madison
when they initially appeared in the House.[53]

In debate Ames made a conscious effort to maintain his aplomb.
Rarely did he lose his self-command and resort to asperities, although
in the heat of discussion his passionate convictions were hard to sup-

51. *Annals*, I, 43-44, 46-48, 533, 574, 608, 614, 632, 635, 639, 643, May 29, June 2,
11, 17-19, 23-25, 27, 29, July 1, 2, 1789. Richard Peters, ed., *The Public Statutes at
Large of the United States of America*, I (Boston, 1848), 24-28. The two acts were
entitled "An Act for laying a Duty on Goods, Wares, and Merchandizes imported
into the United States," and "An Act imposing Duties on Tonnage."
52. William Sullivan, *The Public Men of the Revolution, Including Events from
the Peace of 1783 to the Peace of 1815. In a Series of Letters*, ed. John T. S.
Sullivan (Phila., 1847), 59.
53. Thomas Lowther to Judge James Iredell, N.Y., May 9, 1789, Griffith J.
McRee, ed., *Life and Correspondence of James Iredell, One of the Associate
Justices of the Supreme Court of the United States*, 2 vols. (N.Y., 1857-58), II, 258.
John Randolph to Tudor Randolph, Dec. 13, 1813, William Cabell Bruce, *John
Randolph of Roanoke, 1773-1833*, 2 vols. (N.Y., 1922), I, 74.

press. They found their vent in some sarcastic phrases, sharp-pointed thrusts intended to disarm but not to offend an opponent. As he said of himself after one interchange with Madison, "You may be assured that I was not betrayed into any warmth in the argument.... There are certain bounds which my zeal arrives at, almost instantly. The habit of being in public assemblies has imposed sufficient restraint on my mind, and I seldom pass those bounds.... I am sensible that the excess of that zeal would very much lessen me." [54]

With his friends, however, Ames freely revealed his emotional reactions. On an occasion when George Minot remarked about his despondent frame of mind, Ames observed that the weather had turned pleasant, and he had entirely forgotten this mood. Yet he acknowledged that he often felt things very intensely, and consequently expressed himself that way. "With a warm heart, and an hot head, I often dupe my friends and myself." [55]

Politically, Ames wanted to rise above a narrowly local viewpoint and to hew out national policies which would guarantee a lasting government. He did not regard his nationalism as incompatible with a loyalty to New England since he could not conceive of the success of any government which neglected the interests of his region. Of first importance to him, however, was the necessity for Congress to bolster the nation, untried, lacking in revenue, and subject to the constant rivalry of the states. Far from being a Hercules, this government, in his opinion, "might come off second best in the struggle with the serpent." The economic security of the nation hinged on the revenue. "No revenue, no government," according to Ames. Without stability, the passion for government could vanish in a few years, factions could spring up, and states predominate once again. As Congress plunged into debate, Ames exclaimed, "I am sick of fluctuating counsels, of governing by expedients, let us have stability and system." [56]

The establishment of the revenue system was encouraging to Ames; he regretted, however, that a time limitation on the tariff bill left future revenue "to the caprice of ... antifederalism." Congressional progress was slow and he began to doubt the ability of the legislature to resolve some of the issues confronting it. With his experience in the Ratifying Convention and the General Court vividly in mind, he looked at popu-

54. Ames to Minot, May 29, 1789, Ames, *Works of Ames,* I, 48; Ames wrote in superscript, "This letter is a piece of egotism. You may read as little as you think fit."

55. Ames to Minot, May 27, 1789, *ibid.,* 44.

56. Ames to Tudor, Apr. 25, 1789, "Memoir of Tudor," Mass. Hist. Soc., *Collections,* 2d Ser., 8 (1819), 318; Ames to Minot, May 16, 1789, Ames, *Works of Ames,* I, 40.

lar assemblies with a critical eye. He was inclined to see in all of them, "the same refining, quiddling scepticism" comparable to "our General Court nicety." Most disturbing was the attitude of some congressmen who revealed "yawning listlessness . . . in regard to the great objects of the government." [57] He disliked their responsiveness to popular arguments; he resented their state prejudices; and he deprecated their punctiliousness over trifles and formalities. Ames had come to Congress with the enthusiasm and the lingering high ideals of youth. Now he had to readjust his outlook. No longer tenable were his ideas of "demi-gods and Roman senators" in Congress. On cool reflection, it appeared that the majority would never be as he supposed. "If a few understand the business," he mused, "and have . . . the confidence of those who do not, it is better than for all to be such knowing ones . . ." else there would be a constant struggle to dominate and there would be little cohesive force.[58] More and more as his political values became fixed Ames moved in the direction of a small group of a ruling elite, which in his view ought to carry the burdens and provide the leadership for the nation.

57. Ames to Minot, Apr. 4, May 16, 27, 1789, Ames, *Works of Ames*, I, 32, 40, 44.
58. Ames to Minot, May 27, 1789, *ibid.*, 45.

Chapter VI

A Rising Federalist

Federal Hall continued to stir with activity throughout the summer of 1789. The House took up in succession such questions as the executive power, the ratio of congressional representation, and the jurisdiction of the federal courts. Fisher Ames, adhering to his conviction that only if the government were vigorous and centralized could it survive, supported extension of the national authority.

Though Ames spent much of his time either at Federal Hall or at his lodgings in Great Dock Street, he could observe in strolling about New York that the capital was recovering from the Revolution and growing with the government. A city of some 29,000 people, its buildings were largely English in architectural style, though many gabled Dutch houses recalled an earlier day. Broadway was a particularly imposing street, wide, paved, and bordered by walks of brick. In addition to some places of business along this thoroughfare, there were scattered residences, surrounded by attractive gardens. Near the north end of the street were the almshouse, the jail, and the criminal prison, the Bridewell; not far to the west of these buildings lay the college, originally chartered by the king and now known as Columbia. In process of construction on lower Broadway, Trinity Church would have a 200-foot spire, higher by twenty-five feet than any other spire in the city. Its graveyard still contained many white wooden markers with letters in black, placed there during the Revolution when stone was not available. By day the harbor city was a scene of animation. At night its commotion subsided, and some New Yorkers could be seen on the long summer evenings sitting in their old-fashioned "Dutch stoops at the doors." The atmosphere was both cosmopolitan and provincial.[1]

The business and ceremonies of the new government added color to the burgeoning city. At times Ames's congressional work was interrupted by official functions or by private gatherings. On one occasion he traveled out of the city to dine and spend the evening with Vice President and Mrs. Adams at their handsome country home, Richmond Hill. Of a more informal nature was such an event as breakfast at "Mrs. Loring's" with George Partridge, J. Williams, and a visitor from Plymouth, Massachusetts, Samuel Davis. When George Cabot and other close friends made trips to New York, Ames seized the opportunity to visit with them.[2]

Swept along by his responsibilities as a representative, Ames nevertheless anxiously awaited a congressional recess. More than anything else he wanted to get away from New York to visit in Springfield. It was evident that Frances Worthington was increasingly on his mind. He even mused about marriage and Thomas Dwight's progress in that direction. George Minot encouraged his friend to follow Dwight's example, but Ames commented, "I never think of that fascinating subject without trying to unbewitch myself by the school-boy trash about one who 'all the bread and cheese he got, he laid upon a shelf,' and when the quantity was sufficient... he got a wife." He did not feel, he confided to Minot, that he was in a land of bread and cheese. "I know not what I am here for. I was satisfied with my former condition, and was looking forward to a better. Now my future state seems to be receding. Is this enigmatical?"[3]

The uncertainty about his future was accentuated by his enforced stay in New York and the infrequent news he got of the Worthington household. Indirectly he heard that one of the Worthington sisters was not well, and he was eager for more specific information. He understood that it was not "Miss Fanny," but he assured Dwight, "I should be unhappy to know that sorrow of any kind has entered that house. Be so kind as to write me upon the subject."[4]

1. Samuel Davis, "Journal of a Tour to Connecticut—Autumn of 1789," Mass. Hist. Soc., *Proceedings*, 11 (1871), 21-23; Sidney I. Pomerantz, *New York, An American City, 1783-1808, A Study in Urban Life* (N.Y., 1938), 147, 161, 163, 199-201, 226-31; Smith, *New York in 1789*, 6-7, 24-26.
2. Ames to George R. Minot, N.Y., Sept. 3, May 31, 1789, Ames, *Works of Ames*, I, 70, 51; Ames to Thomas Dwight, N.Y., June 11, 1789, Fisher Ames Papers, Dedham Hist. Soc.; Davis, "Journal of a Tour," Mass. Hist. Soc., *Proceedings*, 11 (1871), 22; Ames to Gen. S. B. Webb, Aug. 1789, Webb Family Papers, Yale University.
3. Ames to Minot, May 27, 1789, Ames, *Works of Ames*, I, 46.
4. Ames to Dwight, June 11, 1789, Fisher Ames Papers, Dedham Hist. Soc.

Before the first session came to an end, Ames became very con-
science-stricken over his long absence from Springfield and was determined to explain the difficult situation to Thomas Dwight, hoping his
friend would give him good advice. He could conceive that Frances
might take exception to his incessant work. If she did, he reasoned, "it
is either because the delicate sensibility of her own mind is wounded
by the least appearance of injury or because she may think my conduct
has some such appearance to the world." [5] He could only enter a plea
of necessity and question whether the basis of his security was solid.
Since Frances was not greatly interested in politics, it was most difficult
to explain in his letters that his attendance and vote in Congress were
essential. If Dwight thought that he should appear, he would take the
stage immediately, though to ask for leave, he ruefully admitted, "will
expose me to more rallying and banter than a face not absolutely plated
could well stand." He would risk everything rather than cause Frances
uneasy moments. "I am not such a blockhead as to be willing to lie
under displeasure a day, in the hope of future vindication." [6] Dwight
in all probability responded to his entreaties, reassuring him that his
cause was not irrevocably lost, for Ames stayed on in New York.

Although the Massachusetts representative was growing restive over
legislative progress, Congress continued to absorb his attention. When
the lower house turned to the establishment of the executive departments, pronounced differences flared up over the constitutional power
of the executive to remove his appointees from office. On May 19 Madison proposed to the committee of the whole on the State of the Union
that three executive departments, to be called the Departments of Foreign Affairs, Treasury, and War, should be created. A clause in his
motion to the effect that a department head was "to be removable by
the President" quickly evoked controversy. As there were no provisions in the Constitution regarding the removal of officials except by
impeachment proceedings, members of the House expressed a variety
of interpretations of this knotty issue. In the ensuing discussions, Madison distinguished four doctrines regarding the removal power: it might
be determined by legislative act; it was only to be exercised through
impeachment; it was "incident to the power of appointment" and
therefore shared by the Senate and the President; and finally it was part
of the executive power not specifically taken away from the President. [7]

5. Ames to Dwight, N.Y., Aug. 4, 1789, *ibid.*
6. *Ibid.*
7. *Annals*, I, 385, May 19, 1789; James Madison to Edmund Pendleton, N.Y.,
June 21, 1789, Madison to Edmund Randolph, N.Y., June 17, 1789, Madison Papers,
XI, Lib. Cong.; James Hart, *The American Presidency in Action, 1789* (N.Y.,
1948), 155-248; Edward S. Corwin, *The President's Removal Power Under the*

On the removal question, Fisher Ames and James Madison were basically in agreement. Both wanted to establish the President's right to have sole administrative control over his appointees. Both were determined not to permit the Senate to gain strength at the expense of the executive by sharing in the removal of officials. Madison reasoned that above all the separation of executive and legislative powers should be maintained. The executive power, as he interpreted it, was granted to the President alone "in like manner as the legislative is vested in Congress." Ames held that "the meddling of the Senate in appointments is one of the least defensible parts of the Constitution. I would not extend their power any further." [8]

Not until June 16 did Ames actually enter the discussions on the power of removal. Just as in the tariff debate he avoided taking an active part until the issues were clearly defined. To Minot he had admitted at an earlier phase in the discussion, "I have scarcely opened my mouth in the House these ten days, and if my restraining grace should hold out against the temptations I am exposed to, my judgment will lead me to decline any part in the tedious frivolity of the daily business." [9] He was far too much interested in the significant constitutional issue, however, to continue as a bystander, and his convictions were too pronounced to suppress them.

In his first speech on the question of retaining Madison's clause, Ames responded to remarks made by William Loughton Smith. The Massachusetts representative attempted to establish beyond cavil the exclusive right of the President to dismiss executive officers and at the same time supported the theory that the President derived this power from the Constitution. The distribution of power in the Constitution was designed to protect the people. Under this system all executive power had been granted to the President, and obviously he must have the right to exercise his power in the choice, control, and dismissal of his assistants. Ames pointed out that no office was a permanent estate nor was it established for the benefit of an individual. In the course of events, there would be a variety of reasons for removing officials. The Constitution outlined impeachment for officials guilty of high crimes and misdemeanors. But was impeachment "the only mode of removal," as William Loughton Smith maintained? Ames rejected this interpreta-

---

Constitution (*National Municipal League Monograph Series* [N.Y., 1927]). Charles C. Thach, *The Creation of the Presidency, 1775-1789* (Baltimore, 1922).

8. Ames to Minot, May 31, May 19, 1789, Ames, *Works of Ames*, I, 52, 43; James Madison to Edmund Randolph, N.Y., May 31, 1789, Madison Papers, XI, Lib. Cong.; *Annals*, I, 387, 394-95, May 19, 1789.

9. Ames to Minot, May 29, 1789, Ames, *Works of Ames*, I, 49-50.

tion, contending that impeachment proceedings could be too drastic on the one hand and too slow on the other to be considered a practical means of removal in many cases. What of removal for infractions of law which were not criminal? Who then could remove an official? Logically the right to remove lay in the executive's sphere. Since "the leading principle in every free Government" and "a prominent feature in this" was the separation of legislative and executive powers, the Senate could not claim to share in the removal power.[10]

Ames acknowledged that the Constitution did not specifically grant the power of removal to the President, but pointed out that it also did not grant the power jointly to the President and the Senate. Under the existing circumstances he suggested that it was incumbent upon Congress to confirm the President's dismissal power in order that he would be guaranteed full freedom to control his assistants. This action, Ames indicated, would not mean Congress was granting legislative power to the executive. Even if Madison's clause for the exclusive presidential power were struck out, the legislature still would not have the power nor could Congress keep the President from exercising it. In conclusion, Ames said that if there were a question of the legality of congressional action on the power of removal "the judiciary will revise our decision." [11]

Two days later Ames brought together, in summary, the numerous arguments which had been presented to prove that the executive had the exclusive power of removal. It was highly probable from the tenor of the Constitution, he reasoned, that this power was in the President's hands. While the Constitution was not explicit, it implied that the executive should have the removal power. The only powers withheld from the President had been specified; otherwise, all executive powers were his. Denial of the President's right to remove officials, Ames contended, might lead to the destruction of his "responsibility—the great security which this constitution holds out to the people of America." [12] To unite the Senate and the President in the exercise of the removal power could lay the foundation of a tyranny. If either the executive or the legislature dominated over the other a despotism would result. Congress must, therefore, act so that it retained "the limits of each authority" in the issue under debate. If the Senate were to share in executive powers, intrigue, faction, and usurpation would be promoted.

10. *Annals*, I, 492-94, June 16, 1789; George C. Rogers, Jr., *Evolution of a Federalist, William Loughton Smith of Charleston* (Columbia, S.C., 1962), 172.
11. *Annals*, I, 494-96, June 16, 1789; Ames to Minot, May 31, 1789, Ames, *Works of Ames*, I, 51-52; Madison to Randolph, May 31, 1789, Madison Papers, XI, Lib. Cong.
12. *Annals*, I, 561, June 18, 1789.

Dramatically Ames reached the climax of his speech: "Sir, it is infusing poison into the constitution; it is an impure and unchaste connexion ... it is tempting the Senate with forbidden fruit.... Far from being champions for liberty, they will become conspirators against it." [13] The clause in Madison's motion, he stated, was entirely in keeping with the principles of the Constitution; therefore, he intended supporting it.

By a vote of thirty-four to twenty the committee of the whole decided to retain the power-of-removal clause in Madison's motion. It then referred its recommendations on the creation of a Department of Foreign Affairs to the House, where the bill was further debated. Egbert Benson proposed two amendments designed to remove any implication of a legislative grant of power and at the same time, to make the President's removal power inviolate. Ames approved the move, voting in favor of both changes, and ultimately he was among the twenty-nine members who passed the bill on June 24.[14]

For the benefit of his Boston friends, Ames later explained the complexities of Benson's maneuver. The New York representative had attempted to prevent any subsequent withdrawal of the President's power by the legislature. An explicit declaration by Congress, Ames was certain, "would be a construction of the Constitution, and not liable to future encroachments." Since he continued to have some reservations about basing the President's authority solely on implied powers, he readily accepted his colleague's proposal. "I feel perfectly satisfied," he commented to Minot, "with the President's right to exercise the power, either by the Constitution or the authority of an act. The arguments in favor of the former fall short of full proof, but in my mind they greatly preponderate." [15] The resolution of the problem pleased Ames.

Nevertheless, certain aspects of the recent debates disturbed him, since he was convinced that in the opposition to a forceful executive there were overtones of a spirit which should not be fostered. He felt that a blow had been struck at one of the indispensable powers of government, but luckily, it had been parried. The attack reflected the attitudes of some members who were constantly alarmed at the growth

13. *Ibid.*, 562-64, June 18, 1789.
14. *Ibid.*, 599-608, 614, June 22-24, 1789; F. A. Muhlenberg to Richard Peters, N.Y., June 18, 1789, Richard Peters Papers, IX, Hist. Soc. of Pa. In reference to the debates, Muhlenberg commented, "The Antis now begin to discover themselves and they are on this Occasion bringing their whole force to a point"; Thomas Hartley to Jasper Yeates, N.Y., June 19, 1789, Jasper Yeates Papers, Hist. Soc. of Pa.
15. Ames to Minot, N.Y., June 23, 1789, Ames, *Works of Ames*, I, 55-56.

of a centralized authority. "They are for watching and checking power," he commented sardonically. "They see evils in embryo; are terrified with possibilities." Ames fundamentally mistrusted men who advocated limited executive power, men who held that their position stemmed from a concern for freedom. "I am commonly opposed to those who modestly assume the rank of champions of liberty and make a very patriotic noise about the people," he avowed. "It is the stale artifice which has duped the world a thousand times, and yet though detected, it is still successful." [16]

He insisted that he was not averse to the spirit of liberty; on the contrary he had an inherent pride in it, for it was the "true title of our people to distinction above others." In his opinion, however, strong laws would be more effective in preserving liberty than shallow oratory. "The men of information and property who are stigmatized as aristocrats," he commented to William Tudor, "appear to me more solicitous to secure liberty than the loudest champions of democracy. They not only wish to enjoy, but to perpetuate liberty, by giving energy enough to government to preserve its own being, when endangered by tumult and faction." [17]

In general, the men with whom Ames so heartily disagreed were the "Antis" or Antifederalists. This somewhat amorphous group usually championed legislative supremacy and saw in every effort to strengthen the executive or to establish a permanent revenue system, a subversion of their ideal of good government. Ames observed that the Antifederalists lacked strength, but that at times "violent republicans" and representatives with local sympathies allied with them over particular issues, creating a stronger element. For his own part, Ames had become identified with those congressmen who had previously supported the adoption of the Constitution and had considered themselves Federalists ever since the ratification controversy. These men were now bent on establishing a government on a firm centralized base. While he recognized that political diversity was developing in the House, Ames looked upon the Federalists as men who were committed to building an indestructible government, not as men of faction.[18] Despite his uneasiness about opposition to Federalism, Ames balanced his pessimism with some

16. Ames to Minot, N.Y., July 8-9, 1789, Ames to Minot, June 23, 1789, *ibid.*, I, 64, 56.

17. Ames to William Tudor, N.Y., July 12, 1789, "Memoir of Tudor," Mass. Hist. Soc., *Collections*, 2d Ser., 8 (1819), 318-19.

18. Ames to Minot, June 23, July 8-9, 1789, Ames, *Works of Ames*, I, 56, 61-62, 64; Ames to Tudor, July 12, "Memoir of Tudor," Mass. Hist. Soc., *Collections*, 2d Ser., 8 (1819), 319.

optimism. Initially he had felt that his adversaries had been artful in the recent debate, but on further reflection he became less judgmental and decided that they had not been. "There is no intrigue," he insisted, "little asperity in debate, or personal bitterness out of the House." [19] Still, he could not look upon Congress as a Roman Senate.

Another problem before the House related to the establishment of the Treasury Department. In May, at an early stage of discussion on the proposed Treasury bill, several representatives expressed serious reservations about appointing a single Secretary of the Treasury. Elbridge Gerry advocated reviving the Revolutionary War treasury board system, but was unable to win adoption of his proposal. The continuing fear that a Secretary of the Treasury might arrogate dangerous powers to himself was apparent late in June when the House continued its work on the Treasury bill. Both John Page of Virginia and Thomas Tucker of South Carolina protested strongly against a clause in the proposed measure which stipulated that the Secretary was to "digest and report plans" to the House on financial matters. During the course of the debate Page vehemently asserted that he could never accept such interference on the part of an executive officer in the affairs of the legislature. To him, granting the Secretary the right to propose financial legislation before the House was tantamount to setting up a dictatorship.[20]

Initially Ames had considered the debate "puerile" and had scornfully observed that "the champions of liberty drew their swords, talked blank verse about the treasury influence... [and] violation of the privileges of the House." But the views propounded by Tucker and Page, as well as his own desire to develop an organic connection between the Treasury and the House, led him into active participation in the discussion.[21] Rejecting Page's arguments, Ames maintained that the possibilities of improper outside influences on Congress were exaggerated. There was a very real advantage in having a close liaison between the Treasury and Congress as the House could base financial legislation on sound information provided directly by the Secretary. Financial matters were both "abstruse and dry" for most congressmen; consequently, Ames contended that the aid of the Secretary was indispensable. The head of the Treasury in his judgment must have large powers and the assurance of sufficient tenure in office to enable him to cope with the "deep, dark, and dreary chaos" of the nation's finances.

19. Ames to Minot, July 9, 1789, Ames, *Works of Ames*, I, 64.
20. *Annals*, I, 615-18, June 25, 1789; Hart, *American Presidency*, 223-26; Wilfred E. Binkley, *President and Congress* (N.Y., 1947), 30-31.
21. Ames to Minot, June 23-25, 1789, Ames, *Works of Ames*, I, 56.

He hoped, therefore, that the clause permitting the Secretary to report his plans to the House would be retained as it would provide the necessary "sunshine" in financial matters.[22]

Through the concerted efforts of Ames, Madison, John Laurance of New York, and Theodore Sedgwick of Massachusetts, the attempt to strike out the clause under consideration was defeated. Fitzsimmons, however, proposed a compromise motion changing the wording of the clause from "digest and report" to "digest and prepare." The committee of the whole accepted this change by a great majority and preserved the basic idea of having the Secretary of the Treasury communicate information to the House. In Ames's opinion the representatives who did not wish to give the Treasury head enough power to deal directly with the House had gravely miscalculated their support. "They persevered so long and furiously that they lost all strength, and were left in a very small minority," he observed.[23] On July 2, within a few days after the committee reported the completed Treasury bill, the House passed it without a major debate. The Senate, however, amended the House bill, but did not alter the provisions governing the relationship of the Secretary to the House of Representatives. After differing over the amendments, the two houses at last reached an agreement, and on August 28 the House sent to the Senate an enrolled bill establishing the Treasury Department. A few days later on September 2, the President signed the bill.[24]

During the course of the summer it seemed to Ames that Congress was protracting its business excessively. Many bills remained in the House in various stages of completion; others were stalled while differences over the House and Senate versions were resolved. Fortunately the public had excused the "slow trot" of Congress and had commended the legislators for their "wisdom and prudent caution"; yet the Massachusetts congressman was anxious to complete the basic legislation of the session. He did not place the blame for the situation on the members as individuals, since they attended the daily five-hour sessions punctually, were diligent in their work, and showed little evidence of intrigue and cunning. The long discussions on the floor of the House

22. *Annals*, I, 619-20, June 25, 1789.
23. *Ibid.*, 639, 643, July 1, 2, 1789. Ames to Minot, June 23-25, 1789, Ames, *Works of Ames*, I, 56. Brant, *Madison, Father of the Constitution*, 261. Broadus Mitchell, *Alexander Hamilton*, Vol. II: *The National Adventure, 1788-1804* (N.Y., 1962), 15-20. Leonard D. White, *The Federalists: A Study in Administrative History* (N.Y., 1956), 67-68.
24. Mitchell, *Hamilton*, II, 21; White, *Federalists*, 118; *Annals*, I, 75, 643, Aug. 28, July 2, 1789; F. M. Meyer, "A Note on the Origin of the Hamiltonian System," *Wm. and Mary Qtly.*, 3d Ser., 21 (1964), 579-88. Peters, ed., *U.S. Statutes at Large*, I, 65-67.

were one source of delay, leading Ames to remark pungently, "Our House is a kind of Robin Hood society, where everything is debated." The primary difficulty, however, was the frequent resort to a committee of the whole, consisting of nearly fifty representatives. It was "a great, clumsy machine—the hoof of an elephant to the strokes of a mezzotinto." [25] He felt that select committees should be substituted for an unwieldy group not geared to the expeditious shaping of legislation. At the same time he acknowledged that many members, particularly the Virginians, were adamant in their opposition to a change.

Ames's subjective reactions to Congress were often revealed in the analytical letters he wrote to George Minot in Boston. On one occasion Ames even took up his pen while he was "sitting very lazily in the House" during a debate which bored him. His fellow lodgers referred to him as the "Secretary of State" because of his penchant for letter-writing. In May Minot had proposed a weekly exchange of letters in order that Ames might keep the friends in the "Wednesday night club" informed of congressional activities. In agreeing to undertake the assignment, Ames observed with amusement that members of the club were, after all, constituents and that he could not ignore the wishes of constituents. Obviously the group consisted of keenminded professional men much interested in political events and the developing government. The full membership of the club is not known, though apparently George and Clarke Minot, Thomas Dawes, William Smith, Samuel Dexter, and Fisher Ames were among those who belonged.[26]

Of interest to the Boston .club was Ames's position on the question of constitutional amendments. On June 8, James Madison introduced in the House of Representatives various amendments to the Constitution, advocating that they be discussed by a committee of the whole. In taking this step, he was prompted by a sense of duty to honor the recommendations of the state ratifying conventions. At the same time, he was even more concerned with forestalling a move of the Antifederalists to have Congress call a general convention to alter the Constitution.[27]

In the Massachusetts Ratifying Convention Ames himself had made

25. Ames to Dwight, June 11, 1789, Fisher Ames Papers, Dedham Hist. Soc.; Ames to Minot, July 8, 1789, Ames, *Works of Ames*, I, 61; Ames to Tudor, July 12, 1789, "Memoir of Tudor," Mass. Hist. Soc., *Collections*, 2d Ser., 8 (1819), 320. Ralph V. Harlow, *The History of Legislative Methods in the Period Before 1825* (New Haven, 1917), 92-103.

26. Ames to Minot, May 3, 14, 18, 31, 1789, Ames, *Works of Ames*, I, 34-35, 37, 41, 50.

27. *Annals*, I, 440-41, 443-44, 448-59, June 8, 1789; John C. Miller, *The Federalist Era, 1789-1801* (N.Y., 1960), 20-22; Robert A. Rutland, *The Birth of the Bill of Rights, 1776-1791* (Chapel Hill, 1955), 190-206; Edward Dumbauld, *The Bill of Rights* (Norman, Okla., 1957), 30-32.

a vigorous speech endorsing the proposal of Governor Hancock to adopt the Constitution with a recommendation of amendments. On that occasion he had rejected the contention that the delegates had no legal right to take such a course. His support of the amendments seemed to spring from a belief that they were essential to an acceptance of the Constitution rather than from a belief that a "comparatively perfect" document could be improved. Now in June of 1789, he had not altered his basic point of view. Ames was not averse to carrying out the agreement made at the time of ratification, but he considered the amendment issue as a secondary one. He looked dourly on the interjection of a new, controversial issue into the complex business of the first session. In his opinion any digression from the pre-eminent task of passing fundamental legislation was unsound. Privately, he acknowledged that the list of alterations Madison had presented were "the fruit of much labor and research"; yet to him they were indicative of his colleague's diligence in "hunt[ing] up all the grievances and complaints of newspapers, the articles of conventions, and the small talk of their debates." [28]

From the many changes suggested to him, Madison winnowed a series of amendments which incorporated protection of individual liberties, readjustment of the ratio of congressional representation, preservation of the separation of powers, and reservation to the states of powers not delegated by the Constitution. Somewhat flippantly Ames commented about the proposals: "Upon the whole, [they] may do some good towards quieting men, who attend to sounds only, and may get the mover some popularity, which he wishes." He compared the amendments to a medicine which would "stimulate the stomach as little as hasty-pudding." [29]

One of Ames's primary concerns related to the consideration of amendments by the committee of the whole. Such a large committee, he believed, would amount to another constitutional convention. While he favored discussing specific recommendations, he strenuously disagreed with reopening the entire Constitution to analysis. There would be a strong possibility that members attempting to secure "the inestimable rights and liberties they have just snatched from the hand of despotism" would carry matters too far. The consequence would be the introduction of other amendments tearing "the frame of Government into pieces." To avoid this eventuality, Ames moved that the amendments be submitted to a select committee. In his remarks to the

28. Elliot, *Debates*, II, 154-55. Ames to Dwight, June 11, 1789, Ames, *Works of Ames*, I, 53.
29. Ames to Dwight, June 11, 1789, Ames to Minot, N.Y., June 12, 1789, Ames, *Works of Ames*, I, 53, 54; Brant, *Madison, Father of the Constitution*, 264.

House, he commented that the government would suffer while debate on the amendments was protracted. When the House agreed to appoint the select committee, composed of a member from each state, he commented, "I hope much debate will be avoided by this mode, and that the amendments will be more rational, and less *ad populum,* than Madison's. It is necessary to conciliate, and I would have amendments. But they should not be trash, such as would dishonor the Constitution, without pleasing its enemies." [30]

Reflecting on the fact that some states had not joined the Union, Ames wrote to George Minot that congressional action on the amendments might have immediate practical value and encourage North Carolina, Vermont, and Rhode Island to ratify the Constitution. He acknowledged that he was eager to have the foundations of the government deeply laid; consequently he wished "every American [to] think the union so indissoluble and integral, that the corn would not grow, nor the pot boil, if it should be broken." Elaborating on the theme of sound government, Ames added some thoughts to his letter. "I believe," he wrote, "that ignorance is unfavorable to government, and government (and a braced one too) indispensable to freedom." [31]

When the select committee presented its report on the amendments to the House, the lower chamber resolved itself into a committee of the whole. Ames's attention was promptly captured by one of the suggested changes which would have increased congressional representation. The amendment retained the constitutional ratio of one representative for every 30,000 people, but proposed that when there were 100 members in the House, Congress would then regulate the size of the House so that it would never be smaller than 100 nor larger than 175 members. In keeping with his ideas of limiting popular control of government, Ames immediately proposed a motion to whittle down the number of representatives by substituting a new ratio of 1:40,000. He contended that to enlarge the size of the House was unwise, as the public would be dissatisfied with too numerous a representation. Not only would it create an additional financial burden on the Union, but as the number of congressmen increased the quality of the House would inevitably decline.[32]

The drift of his thinking was apparent. In his mind he had the image of a select group of representatives, men of wisdom and great capabili-

30. *Annals,* I, 686-90, July 21, 1789; Ames to Minot, July 9, 23, 1789, Ames, *Works of Ames,* I, 64-65.

31. Ames to Minot, July 23, 1789, Ames, *Works of Ames,* I, 66.

32. Ames to Minot, N.Y., Aug. 12, 1789, Ames, *Works of Ames,* I, 67. *Annals,* I, 747-48, Aug. 14, 1789; Edmund J. James, "The First Apportionment of Federal Representatives in the United States," American Academy of Political and Social Science, *Annals,* 9 (1897), 1-41.

ties, who were devoted to the interests of the nation and would conduct its business on a high level. If the House were enlarged, he foresaw that the ferment of conflicting interests and party spirit would prevail. Frequently enough, he assured his listeners, people had questioned whether the country could remain united, even though it was under the administration of highly able men. What might happen to the country if it fell into different hands? Only by keeping the numbers of representatives from increasing would it be possible to prevent such a calamity.[33]

Without delay, Madison criticized Ames's plan, contending it would result in "momentary advantage" at the expense of the people's wish. Gerry, so often at odds with his fellow representatives from Massachusetts, also objected to his colleague's position and asserted that having few representatives would not give as much security as having many. Replying to Ames's assertion that enlarging the representation would diminish the dignity of the House, he asked whether Ames meant that "we should establish our own importance at the risk of the liberties of America." If so, Gerry added, "it has been of little avail that we successfully opposed the lordly importance of a British Parliament." [34]

Ames quickly responded to this thrust. The House, he declared, would be a more responsible body if it were restricted in size and composed of men "of independent principles, integrity, and eminent abilities." [35] Although his motion was defeated by a considerable majority, Ames was not easily deterred. He proposed to the committee of the whole and later, to the House of Representatives a modification of his idea to establish a ratio of 1:30,000 at the first census, then to increase it to 1:40,000 later on. It was very evident to him that inherent in representative governments was a "constant tendency" to expand the lower house, and he felt impelled to check its influence. After some "desultory conversation" among members on the floor of the House, his idea of a graduated ratio was adopted. In the final House version, the apportioning of representation was established by a ratio of 1:30,000 until there were 100 Congressmen. Thereafter Congress was to regulate the House membership so that there would be a minimum of 100 members, and a ratio of at least 1:40,000 until the House had 200 members. After this number had been reached, the proportion was to be 1:50,000. Eventually the states rejected this particular amendment to the Constitution, leaving the apportionment of representatives entirely to congressional discretion.[36]

In July, a Boston newspaper, the *Herald of Freedom,* had commented

33. *Annals,* I, 749, Aug. 14, 1789.
34. *Ibid.,* 750, Aug. 14, 1789.
35. *Ibid.,* 751-55, Aug. 14, 1789.
36. *Ibid.,* 802, Aug. 21, 1789; Rutland, *Bill of Rights,* 208.

favorably on Ames's national outlook and his freedom from local attachment. When his position on the representation question became
known to his constituents, he was severely taken to task in several
letters to the editor of the *Independent Chronicle.* One critic asked,
"What authority has this gentleman to make so bold . . . an assertion
as that the people are universally satisfied with the present state of representation in Congress?" He further challenged Ames to show how
"he reconciled his conduct with the instructions of the convention . . .
which have inforced the necessity of one Representative for every
30,000 persons." [37] Another writer acknowledged that Ames was held
in esteem because of numerous achievements, but insisted that he explain his stand contradicting the views of the Massachusetts voters.
Replying to these aspersions with dignified but positive statements, one
correspondent in the *Massachusetts Centinel* defended the views Ames
had expressed in the House. It was the unanimous opinion of visitors
to Congress, according to this anonymous writer, that "for abilities,
assiduity . . . and candour, Mr. Ames is not excelled by any person in
the House, and on every subject where the rights of the people, and
the interest of our country have been concerned, his exertions in their
behalf have been unceasing." [38] Ames weathered the strictures on his
political conduct, which quickly died out, but it was reassuring to have
friends at home who watched the vagaries of public sentiment and
were alert to protect his political interests.

Several members of the House introduced new amendments designed
to curb the powers of Congress. Ames resisted all such moves as dangerous encroachments on the federal government which would enhance
the position of rival state legislatures. When Thomas Tucker of South
Carolina proposed guaranteeing the right of the people "to instruct
their Representatives," Ames recognized that such instructions would
be channeled through the state legislatures, inevitably making the
federal representatives dependent on "the dictates of another body." [39]
He consequently voted against Tucker's amendment, which was defeated by a vote of 41 to 10. Immediately afterward Ames took steps
to block additional consideration of the constitutional amendments by

37. *Herald of Freedom* (Boston), July 28, 1789; *Independent Chronicle* (Boston),
Aug. 27, Sept. 3, 1789. The *Boston Gazette*, Sept. 7, 1789, raised the question
whether "A. gets his 'local and general information' from the great body of the
People or from 'St. Kitts,' alias the 'small party.' "
38. *Independent Chronicle* (Boston), Aug. 27, 1789; *Massachusetts Centinel*
(Boston), Aug. 29, 1789. A defense of Ames is in the *Boston Gazette*, Sept. 7, 14,
1789.
39. *Annals*, I, 772, 776, 778, 797-98, 802, Aug. 15, 21, 1789; Brant, *Madison, Father
of the Constitution*, 273.

the committee of the whole and moved that the House "discharge the committee from further proceeding." He regarded the unrestrained discussions of the committee as a waste of valuable time, and in addition, he raised doubts regarding the validity of deciding on the amendments by a simple majority at the committee stage when a two-thirds vote was necessary in the House. Gerry replied to Ames's motion with an accusation that its purpose was to hinder a full consideration of an important topic. Ames, his colleague from Massachusetts asserted, "proposes to curtail debate, because gentlemen will not swallow the propositions as they stand." [40] Sedgwick came to Ames's defense and seconded his move, but as it did not win support, Ames substituted another motion requiring a two-thirds vote to carry a question in the committee of the whole. This later motion was tabled and did not come to a vote.

The committee proceeded with consideration of the amendments. After its report was presented to the House, the representatives continued to engage in animated debate over the constitutional changes. At one point Gerry rose to support the Antifederalist views of Tucker and proposed an amendment to reserve to the states all powers which were "not expressly delegated by the Constitution" to the general government. The word *expressly*, denying any enlargement of federal powers by implication, perturbed committed Federalists, among them Ames. A motion presented by Roger Sherman of Connecticut to alter the clause by dropping the word *expressly* finally prevailed, and in this form the amendment, later to be designated the Tenth Amendment, was passed. Ames remained alert to moves which could result in the diminution of congressional powers. When Aedanus Burke of South Carolina proposed prohibiting Congress from regulating federal elections of representatives and senators, Ames immediately objected. He maintained that this action would not only alter the intention of the Constitution by depriving Congress of an essential power, but it also would vest "the supreme authority in places where it was never contemplated." [41] After a spirited discussion in which Gerry attempted to rebut Ames's arguments, Burke's proposed amendment was brought to a vote and defeated. A day later the completed amendments were referred to a committee which forwarded them to the Senate.

Early in the session the judicial system had been a frequent topic of conversation among the members of Congress. Ames had considered it, along with the revenue system, a most necessary piece of legislation for the successful operation of the new government. Linking both revenue

40. *Annals*, I, 776, Aug. 15, 1789.
41. *Ibid.*, 797-98, 800, 802, Aug. 21, 1789.

and judiciary together, he commented to William Tudor, "They are the law and the prophets of our government," and forecast that creating the judicial system would be arduous.[42] Even before enough members of Congress had gathered for the necessary quorum, Fisher Ames had discussed a tentative plan for a judiciary with a few fellow congressmen. He sought advice and suggestions from legal associates in Boston, Judge John Lowell, Sr., Judge James Sullivan, Theophilus Parsons, and William Tudor. The extent to which Ames figured in the formulation of the judiciary bill is not certain. Since the measure actually originated in the Senate, he was not officially involved until it came before the House. He watched with interest while a large committee of senators worked doggedly for two months at the task of writing the bill. With a degree of admiration, he commented that this group had "labored with vast perseverance, and [had] taken as full a view of their subject, as I ever knew a committee [to] take." [43] Ames singled out Caleb Strong, Oliver Ellsworth, and William Patterson as the senators who had had the most influence in preparing the draft.

A crucial feature of the judiciary system concerned the limits to be established on the original jurisdiction of the federal circuit and district courts. There had been pressure outside of Congress to give the state courts large jurisdiction in federal issues. When the Senate committee presented the proposed judiciary bill to the Senate, a major disagreement developed between the advocates of limited authority and those insisting on extensive federal jurisdiction. In the committee and on the floor of the Senate, Richard H. Lee of Virginia took the lead in attempting to limit the jurisdiction of the circuit and district courts, leaving the state courts with original jurisdiction on many federal issues. Opposing this position, Oliver Ellsworth of Connecticut took the initiative in an effort to vest in the federal courts the maximum judicial powers granted by the Constitution.[44]

The judiciary bill as it emerged from the Senate on July 17 was a complex measure organizing the Supreme Court and establishing federal circuit and district courts. For the latter courts, the bill prescribed the extent of their jurisdiction, and the legal procedures to be followed. This measure was definitely a compromise between the two extreme views on federal jurisdiction and as such did not win the approval of

42. Ames to Tudor, Apr. 1, 1789, "Memoir of Tudor," Mass. Hist. Soc., *Collections*, 8 (1819), 316.
43. Ames to ?, N.Y., Mar. 15, 1789, Manuscript Collection, Boston Pub. Lib.; Ames to Minot, July 8, 1789, Ames, *Works of Ames*, I, 64.
44. *Annals*, I, 685, July 20, 1789; Charles Warren, "New Light on the History of the Federal Judiciary Act of 1789," *Harvard Law Review*, 37 (1923), 60-67; entry of July 2, 1789, Beard, ed., *Journal of Maclay*, 95.

some leading members of Congress. Senator Maclay of Pennsylvania reacted strongly against it, commenting in his journal, "I can scarce account for my dislike to this bill. I really fear it will be the gun-powder plot of the Constitution, so confused and so obscure it will not fail to give a general alarm." [45] James Madison recognized that the Senate judiciary bill had not resolved many of the problems inherent in establishing a judicial system; yet he still hoped that "fundamental and obnoxious errors" could be avoided before the bill became law. Not until August 24, after the amendments to the Constitution were sent to the Senate, did the House consider the judiciary bill. Just as Ames expected, efforts were made by some representatives to pare down the proposed national judiciary. "It will be attempted to exclude the Federal courts from original jurisdiction and to restrain them to the cognizance of appeals from the State courts," he wrote to Theophilus Parsons, and added, "I think the attempt will fail." [46]

Precisely the same lines of cleavage appeared in the House as in the Senate. Both Tucker of South Carolina and Judge Samuel Livermore of New Hampshire made vigorous attacks on the entire structure of the inferior federal courts and set the tone of the debate in the House. Tucker considered that the state courts were quite able to carry out the duties which the Senate had assigned to the federal circuit and district courts. Livermore, in turn, fearing that a wholly new system of jurisprudence was being set up, made a motion to have the entire clause on inferior federal courts struck out. Establishing an extensive federal judiciary would create a government within a government, he argued. State courts had proven their ability to decide both local and national cases with impartiality. He, therefore, was willing to establish federal courts only for the purpose of handling admiralty cases and hearing appeals at the Supreme Court level.[47]

To refute such opinions Ames spoke out on August 29, attacking Livermore's motion. Since William L. Smith of South Carolina had already discussed the inexpediency and unconstitutionality of the motion, the Massachusetts orator approached the question from another angle. Addressing himself primarily to fellow lawyers in Congress, Ames presented his idea of "the exclusive nature of certain parts of the national judicial power (offences against statutes, and actions on stat-

45. Entry of July 7, 1789, Beard, ed., *Journal of Maclay*, 99.
46. Warren, "Federal Judiciary Act," *Harvard Law Review*, 37 (1923), 114-16; Robert Morris to Richard Peters, N.Y., Aug. 24, 1789, Richard Peters Papers, IX, Hist. Soc. of Pa.; Ames to Theophilus Parsons, N.Y., Aug. 3, 1789, Parsons, *Memoir of Parsons*, 466; James Madison to Thomas Jefferson, N.Y., Aug. 2, 1789, Julian Boyd, ed., *Papers of Thomas Jefferson* (Princeton, 1950–) XV, 324.
47. *Annals*, I, 813-14, 827, Aug. 24, 29, 1789.

utes)." [48] His argument was structured to prove that a federal court system was legally imperative because the judiciary of the individual states did not have authority to consider strictly federal cases. In his opening remarks Ames indicated that without federal courts the government would be weakened and the people defrauded. "A Government that may make but cannot enforce laws, cannot last long, nor do much good," he stated. The proposal to rely on state courts to adjudicate in federal cases was equivalent to "hiring out our judicial power and employing courts not amenable to our laws." [49]

Fundamental to Ames's concept of a federal judiciary was the distinction between the jurisdiction of the courts, namely the legal power to hear and determine a cause, and the rules of decision—that is, the regulations or principles by which a court arrived at a verdict upon a question of law. Jurisdiction was of first importance to the court; without it the court could not legally proceed. Ames suggested that the Constitution did not deprive the state courts of the jurisdiction they previously exercised in a variety of cases, though individuals might now choose to have a case tried before a federal court as an alternative. "But," he queried, "who shall try a crime against a law of the United States, or a new created action? Here jurisdiction is made *de novo*." Clearly such cases should only come before a federal court. The Constitution gave Congress the right to establish a federal system of lower courts and specified that judges should be commissioned and given salaries. Thus, Ames insisted that state judges were not authorized to try cases under exclusive federal jurisdiction since the states could not grant them this power and the federal government had not granted them this power. He questioned the right of Congress to require state judges to serve simultaneously in the capacity of federal judges. State judges were expected to abide by the common law and the law of the state. "The law of the United States is a rule to them, but no authority for them," Ames asserted. In conclusion, he summarized his position: "Offences against statutes of the United States, and actions, the cognizance whereof is created *de novo*, are exclusively of federal jurisdiction; ... no persons should act as judges to try them, except such as may be commissioned agreeably to the constitution; ... for the trial of such offences and causes, tribunals must be created." There was no question in his mind but that admiralty jurisdiction should also fall to the federal judiciary.[50]

48. Ames to Minot, Sept. 3, 1789, Ames, *Works of Ames*, I, 69; *Annals*, I, 837-39, Aug. 29, 1789.
49. *Annals*, I, 837, Aug. 29, 1789.
50. *Ibid.*, 838-39, Aug. 29, 1789.

James Jackson of Georgia, favoring Livermore's motion, rose to challenge Ames's position. He argued that a Supreme Court was sufficient on the federal level to "keep the State Judiciaries within their bounds."[51] In Jackson's opinion, the Constitution and federal laws "surpassed in power" any state laws; therefore, state courts could not ignore the laws of the Union or fail to recognize them. When the vote was taken on Livermore's motion to strike out the clause on inferior federal courts, only eleven members supported it; thirty-one, including Ames, opposed it. As Ames anticipated, the committee of the whole postponed consideration of other aspects of the judiciary bill while the House turned to the controversial issue of the permanent residence of the government. In a letter to George Minot, Ames reported that the bill would probably be enacted "as an experimental law without much debate or amendment, in the confidence that a short experience will make manifest the proper alterations."[52] Between September 8 and 16 the committee of the whole made certain amendments to the Senate bill, none of which vitally altered it. On September 17 the judiciary bill passed the House and was thereupon returned to the Senate for concurrence with the House changes.[53]

Ames had long been anxious to end the session and proposed a resolution, which the House adopted, to adjourn on September 22. In spite of pressure to complete the legislative program, Thomas Scott of Pennsylvania introduced a motion on the question of the permanent residence of the government. When an attempt to table this motion failed, an irritated Ames expressed his indignation that the House would take up such an acrimonious subject at this time. "Instead of infusing life into [the government] . . . we have been altering our Constitution, and are now entering into a lengthy discussion to determine where we shall sit," he commented.[54] But too many interested partisans were maneuvering to gain the coveted prize of the national capital to be dissuaded from plunging into the issue. By the end of August a multitude of intrigues had created unprecedented tension in Congress.

Soon after the first session started, agitation for a decision on a permanent site resulted in *sub rosa* negotiations among representatives of

51. *Ibid.*, 844-45, Aug. 29, 1789.
52. Ames to Minot, Sept. 3, 1789, Ames, *Works of Ames*, I, 69
53. *Annals*, I, 82, Sept. 17, 1789; Peters, ed., *U.S. Statutes at Large*, I, 73-93; Warren, "Federal Judiciary Act," *Harvard Law Review*, 37 (1923), 127-31, indicates that the final Judiciary Act was "a compromise between the extreme Federalist view that the full extent of judicial power . . . should be vested by Congress in the Federal Courts and the view of those who wished all suits to be decided first in State Courts and only on appeal by the Federal Supreme Court."
54. *Annals*, I, 810, 816, 820, Aug. 24, 27, 1789.

the various regions. The undercurrents were not clear, however, so that it was difficult to discern actual alliances. By its very nature the question aroused sectional loyalties in both the House and the Senate with the southerners on the one hand, the New Englanders on another, and men from such states as New York, New Jersey, and Pennsylvania in between. A surprising number of places were suggested as possible sites —Trenton, York, Lancaster, the Potomac, and the Susquehanna. As the residence discussions began in the House, James Madison and William Maclay reflected factional differences in their interpretations of existing conditions. The Virginian, an ardent proponent of the Potomac site, sensed that "some preconcert of a pretty serious nature" was developing and conjectured that there was a coalition between Pennsylvania, New York, and the eastern states.[55] The Pennsylvania senator, in turn, was perpetually suspicious of the motives of his fellow members of Congress and accused the New Englanders of basely deserting the Pennsylvanians in an effort to prevent an alliance between representatives from his state and the southerners.[56]

Initially, after consulting together, the New England congressmen unanimously agreed to support a location along the banks of the Susquehanna River in Pennsylvania. Benjamin Goodhue consequently presented a resolution in the House to establish the permanent seat on the Susquehanna and to have New York remain the temporary capital. Ostensibly the New Englanders were acting on broad principles; actually the underlying idea was to prevent the capital from being moved even farther southward. According to Ames this decision was an attempt to break a movement to unite on Philadelphia for the temporary residence and on the Potomac for the permanent seat. Each group suspected the other of duplicity. Hartley of Pennsylvania, who recognized how precarious the eastern support of the Susquehanna was, succinctly expressed his fears: "If our New England brethren fly the way, we go to pot." [57] At the same time Ames expected a coup of the Pennsylvanians which would permanently establish the government in Philadelphia once it was located there. He felt that matters were so shrouded in secrecy and "in such dark intrigues [that] the real designs of members are nearly impenetrable." [58] Sadly he had to admit that reasoning with them would do no good.

55. James Madison to Alexander White, N.Y., Aug. 24, 1789, Box 1, Madison Papers, N.Y. Pub. Lib. Brant, *Madison, Father of the Constitution*, 276-77.
56. Entry of Aug. 28, 1789, Beard, ed., *Journal of Maclay*, 136.
57. Ames to Minot, N.Y., Sept. 6, 1789, Ames, *Works of Ames*, I, 71. Thomas Hartley to Jasper Yeates, N.Y., Sept. 6, 1789, Yeates Papers, Hist. Soc. of Pa. Hartley noted, "Yesterday the ground was hardly contended for. The passions of our whole body seem to be up and the best of friends are at variance."
58. Ames to Minot, Sept. 3, 1789, Ames, *Works of Ames*, I, 69.

To Madison's growing irritation, Ames and other northern congress-men attempted to undermine the chances of the Potomac site. Sensing how strong the opposition was, Madison wanted to postpone further debate; yet Ames would not let him shift his position so easily, pointing out that previously Madison had insisted on settling the issue. Although Ames had resisted a discussion of the residence question, he was now too concerned about the outcome to be willing to drop it. When fur-ther objections were raised, Madison burst out in anger, "Give me leave now to say, that if a Prophet had risen in . . . [the Virginia Con-vention] and brought the declarations and proceedings of this day into view, that I . . . firmly believe Virginia might not have been a part of the Union at this moment." [59] Again Ames prodded Madison about his inconsistency and retaliated by remarking that the Virginians "seem to think the banks of the Potomac a paradise, and that river an Eu-phrates." By the end of the day tempers were short, and an "infinitely disappointed and chagrined" minority were trying to get a day's delay. "Whose stomachs will conquer, I know not," Ames observed.[60]

When Madison renewed his assertions about the advantages of the Potomac, Ames entered into an altercation with him about the com-parative distances from the Potomac and the Susquehanna to the Ohio. Both Madison and Daniel Carroll of Maryland challenged his calcula-tions that the Potomac-Pittsburgh route to the western territory was longer, but cleverly he quoted Jefferson's *Notes on Virginia* to sub-stantiate his view. On the basis of these careful calculations, he felt that Madison's "ponderous edifice . . . crumbles to powder." [61] Partly on the strength of his speech, the day was saved for the Susquehanna, for immediately afterward, the Virginians were defeated in another at-tempt to get a majority for the Potomac.

"The world will wonder what inflames and busies Congress so much," Ames remarked to Minot during the residence struggle. He proceeded to recapitulate recent congressional activity as he saw it. All representatives and senators south of the Delaware had agreed on Philadelphia as the temporary site with the Potomac as the permanent residence. To counteract this plan, Ames explained, the New England-ers and New Yorkers joined forces in support of New York City for the present capital with the permanent site on the Susquehanna. The Pennsylvanians held the balance of power and, after hesitating, finally decided to support the Susquehanna rather than the Potomac for the permanent capital. Musing on the decision of the Pennsylvanians, Ames

59. *Annals*, I, 873, 882, 890, Sept. 3, 1789.
60. *Ibid.*, 891, Sept. 3, 1789; Ames to Minot, Sept. 3, 1789, Ames, *Works of Ames*, I, 70.
61. *Annals*, I, 904-5, Sept. 4, 1789.

observed, "How they got clear of their allies is none of my business."
As soon as the southerners realized that representatives from New York,
Pennsylvania, and New England had reached agreement, they con-
demned the bargain "with great purity of virtue." [62]

The tension in Congress was graphically described by Representative
Hartley of Pennsylvania: "We have just passed over three remarkable
Days; such Intrigue, such striking Changes I have never been witness to
before," he commented.[63] On September 5 Thomas Fitzsimmons of
Pennsylvania presented a resolution authorizing the appointment of
commissioners to determine a site on the Susquehanna River. This resolution, as well as the one presented by Goodhue, was approved by the
committee of the whole, and then taken up by the House. In the
lengthy debates which followed, nine successive attempts were made to
change the location to the Potomac or at least to the Delaware, but
each was defeated by a slender margin. Ames missed the initial roll call
vote; thereafter, he and the other New England representatives voted
against every proposal to alter the resolutions of the committee. At the
end of the day, the House agreed to establish the permanent seat of
government on the Susquehanna in the near future and to retain New
York as the temporary capital. Along with two other representatives,
Fisher Ames was assigned the duty of preparing the bill. In the midst
of the excitement, he hastily wrote a note to Theodore Sedgwick urging his immediate return to Congress from Stockbridge, Massachusetts.
Several weeks later he told his colleague that "many a fervent wish and
perhaps prayer was uttered for your return—tho' I do not know any
praying folks that took part in the business." [64]

On September 15 the House referred the completed bill to the committee of the whole, where debate on the Susquehanna location was soon
reopened. Shrewd Maryland representatives introduced uncertainties
about the Pennsylvania site by advocating a proviso that no capital
district be established until Maryland and Pennsylvania passed acts to
remove from the Susquehanna River barriers to navigation. After this
proviso was approved, southerners continued their obstructionist tactics in the contest over the bill. Madison rose to question the constitutionality of the clauses providing for a temporary capital. Ames sharply
replied that despite the Virginian's contributions in the Constitutional
Convention, he himself was not willing "to pay implicit deference" to
Madison's analyses of the Constitution. Regardless of the opposition,

62. Ames to Minot, Sept. 6, 1789, Ames, *Works of Ames,* I, 71.
63. Hartley to Yeates, Sept. 6, 1789, Yeates Papers, Hist. Soc. of Pa.
64. *Annals,* I, 915-20, Sept. 7, 1789. Ames to Theodore Sedgwick, N.Y., Sept. 8,
Springfield, Oct. 6, 1789, Sedgwick Papers, Vol. A, Mass. Hist. Soc.

the House on September 22 passed the amended bill by a vote of thirty-one to seventeen and quickly forwarded it to the Senate.[65]

To the dismay of the Susquehanna advocates, the Senate returned the House bill altered so as to substitute the Philadelphia suburb of Germantown as the site of the capital. Behind the change was an adroit move on the part of Senator Robert Morris, in whom Ames had earlier discovered a "discerning selfishness." Morris, who had wanted the capital on the Delaware, feared that the accession of Vermont, Rhode Island, and North Carolina to the Union would forever prevent Pennsylvania from acquiring the permanent capital. "The only danger is a coalition of the Southern and Eastern members," he explained to Richard Peters. "At present they are jealous of each other, their passions are engaged—delay is therefore dangerous to our views." [66] By proposing to New England and New York senators that Congress remain in New York City until 1793, he obtained their support of Germantown for the permanent capital.

Late in September Senator Dalton of Massachusetts speculated that "after spending a little more time . . . and vibrating from one proposed place to another, it is probable they will . . . set down in the neighborhood of Philadelphia." [67] But in the last two days of the first session in the House, swiftly paced parliamentary maneuvers wiped out plans for a permanent capital. In light of Senate resistance, Ames and the northern representatives did not attempt to revive House support for the Susquehanna site. They continued to resist a southern location for the capital and, therefore, rallied in favor of Germantown. When the Potomac advocates attempted to postpone the issue until the next session, they were voted down. Ames related the sequel. "Then I moved to concur [with the Senate amendment on Germantown]. Madison moved that it should lie on the table. I insisted on my motion as prior. Then an adjournment [for the day] was moved. . . . It was a hair breadth business for a vote in five minutes would probably have made it a law except the King's signature." [68]

By the next day Madison had devised another scheme, moving a proviso that the Pennsylvania laws should remain in effect in the capital

65. *Annals*, I, 927, 929, 932, 940, 943-44, 946, Sept. 15, 17, 21, 22, 1789.
66. Ames to Minot, Sept. 3, 1789, Ames, *Works of Ames*, I, 69; Memorandum of a meeting between the delegates of Pennsylvania and those of New York and the eastern states in hand of Rufus King, Rufus King Papers, Box 3, No. 90, N.-Y. Hist. Soc.; Robert Morris to Richard Peters, N.Y., Sept. 13, 1789, Richard Peters Manuscripts, IX, Hist. Soc. of Pa.
67. Tristram Dalton to M. Hodge, Sept. 20, 1789, Stone, "Sketch of Dalton," Essex Institute *Hist. Collections*, 25 (1888), 24.
68. Ames to Sedgwick, Oct. 6, 1789, Sedgwick Papers, Vol. A, Mass. Hist. Soc.; *Annals*, I, 961-62, Sept. 28, 1789.

district until Congress decided otherwise. His motion passed without debate and "many of the gallery folks," Ames remarked, thought that Madison "had taken us in." It was not so, Ames insisted, but rather that the New York representatives had actually decided to support a move which would result in postponing a decision. These men feared that they might lose the temporary capital sooner than had been agreed upon. "Thus the house that Jack built is vanished in smoke," Ames wrote, "for the Lord knows what next session will produce." [69]

With the belated adjournment of Congress on September 29, a notable session came to a close, and Ames at last could resume briefly his life in Massachusetts. These first few months in the House of Representatives had brought him into the center of the stage; it was clear that he would be one of the most effective voices of active Federalism. His deep sincerity and lack of pomposity heightened the impact of his public speeches. His views, often regional, were the result of his intellectual and economic orientation, but did not reflect upon his basic integrity. In the light of his rising importance, it was not surprising that Vice President Adams wrote to William Tudor late in June, "Your pupil Ames makes a very pretty figure, let me congratulate you on his fame." [70]

69. Ames to Sedgwick, Oct. 6, 1789, Sedgwick Papers, Vol. A, Mass. Hist. Soc. The residence bill, as amended by the House, was returned to the Senate where action on it was deferred.

70. John Adams to William Tudor, June 28, 1789, Adams Papers, Microfilm Reel 115, Mass. Hist. Soc.

Chapter VII

Ames and the Funding System

As soon as Congress had adjourned, Ames eagerly set out on the trip to Springfield. Arising very early each day, he rode long hours, often chilled to the bone, hungry, and nodding from lack of sleep. Exhausted by the time he arrived on October 3, he caught a bad cold and fever. But under the stimulus of seeing Frances Worthington and meeting close friends again, he soon recovered. Within a few days he was rekindling his interest in politics by discussing the recent battles in Congress amid a circle of legal acquaintances. He was disappointed at having missed a reunion with Theodore Sedgwick and Senator Caleb Strong, with whom he had wanted to converse about the political situation. In the past months Ames's contacts with Sedgwick had led to a growing friendship between them, and looking ahead to the next session of Congress, he wrote to his friend, "I esteem it an acquisition to the felicity of my life that I am to spend an interesting part of it with you as your associate." [1]

After his pleasant visit in Springfield, Ames returned to Dedham and Boston to take up his law work once more during the interval between meetings of Congress. He arrived just in time to be caught up in the excitement which pervaded Boston as it prepared to welcome President Washington on his eastern tour. As a member of Congress, Fisher Ames was inescapably involved in the ceremonies, and he suggested to Benjamin Goodhue that they join the escort of Washington at Watertown.

1. Ames to Theodore Sedgwick, Springfield, Oct. 6, 1789, Sedgwick Papers, Vol. A, Mass. Hist. Soc.

For several days, as he expressed it, he "dangled after the President" to the point where he was glad when Washington left. Subsequently he wrote to Thomas Dwight about the maneuverings behind the scenes of civic jubilation. Governor Hancock, it seemed, was not at all pleased at the prospect of the President's visit. His vanity, piqued at the thought of taking an inferior position, led him to create an impasse in protocol. As Governor of the Commonwealth, Hancock steadfastly insisted that he would not honor the President by an initial call upon him.[2]

Criticizing Hancock's actions, Ames related that the Governor's gout returned, most opportunely, making it "doubtful whether his humility would be gratified with the sight of his *superior*." Fortunately the Governor's attitude in no way dampened the spirit of the tour. "Everybody, except Hancock and his tools," he was pleased to report, "has been anxious to show more respect . . . than he could find means to express." [3] Hancock, he added, finally visited the President, while his political friends found excuses. Here Ames revealed his deep disdain for the seeker of popular acclaim and for the politician who gained a following by devious tactics. That Washington himself had to resort to subtle pressure on Hancock to honor the President's office, he had no way of knowing; yet he sensed that Washington's popularity had borne down all opposition. Proud of New England, Ames asserted, "The good man has (I think) seen that the zeal for supporting government, and the strength, too, are principally on this side of the Hudson." [4]

Since his return from Congress, Ames admitted he had accomplished little. Now he had to turn to his legal practice and follow the county court sessions. Middlesex Court was already over, but he still could attend the Essex Court in Salem. After stirring experiences in Congress, he was forced to acknowledge, his law work seemed pallid. "Ah, politics!" he remarked, "how have they spoiled me for my profession." He saw how essential it was to decide about his career before he became too devoted to politics and was "crazed with the chase as other [men] have been." Public life, in spite of its appeal, would yield little of permanent value. "Either I must become a mere politician," he ra-

2. *Massachusetts Centinel* (Boston), Oct. 14, 1789; Ames to Benjamin Goodhue, Boston, Oct. 21, 1789, Benjamin Goodhue Manuscripts, New York Society Library, New York; Ames to Thomas Dwight, Boston, Oct. 21 and 30, 1789, Ames, *Works of Ames*, I, 73, 74; Freeman, *Washington*, VI, 241-42.
3. *Ibid.*, 244-45; Christopher Gore to Rufus King, Boston, Dec. 3, 1789, King, *Life of King*, I, 369. *Massachusetts Centinel* (Boston), Oct. 17, 28, 1789; *Independent Chronicle* (Boston), Oct. 29, Nov. 5, 1789. Ames to Dwight, Oct. 21, 30, 1789, Ames, *Works of Ames*, I, 73, 74.
4. Ames to Dwight, Oct. 30, 1789, Ames, *Works of Ames*, I, 74; Allan, *John Hancock*, 343-49.

tionalized, "and think of my profession as a secondary matter, or renounce politics and devote myself to the humble drudgery of earning bread." [5] His deep interest in national affairs, however, was the determinant. After his experience in Congress he could not return to the pleading of minor causes and the routine of a lawyer's existence with wholehearted devotion.

The recess of Congress passed quickly, and by Christmas Ames was again en route to New York. In all likelihood he was able to carry out his intention of breaking the journey with another visit to Springfield, but he did not delay long, for he was present at the opening of the second session on January 4, 1790. The first days were devoted to formalities and preliminary business, which, with the President's address to Congress, seemed to presage a calmer meeting than the first. Ames, as a committee member, had called on the President to arrange the date of his speech and had also been one of a group of congressmen invited to dine with Washington on the same evening. In a confident vein, the President presented his annual message, "the King's speech" as Ames called it, on January 8. Aside from a review of the accomplishments during the previous year, there were only the most guarded expressions of policy and little to guide the lawmakers in terms of the problems they would soon face.[6]

The House itself had already set the theme of the second session the previous September. In response to a petition from Pennsylvania creditors, it had agreed to take up the matter of public finance and requested the Secretary of the Treasury to submit a plan to resolve the financial problems of the government. At that time Fisher Ames had not favored an immediate discussion of the issue, suggesting that "there is an interval between the organization of the government and the ordinary business, in which nothing should be done [by Congress]. We shall return . . . [and] find business prepared by our great officers, and a weight given to national plans, which they have not at present." [7]

Shortly after the Treasury Department was officially set up in September 1789, Washington appointed Alexander Hamilton as the first Secretary of the Treasury. Hamilton came to this important post in the new administration with the high recommendation and warm support of Senator Robert Morris, who himself had been the government's fi-

---

5. Ames to Dwight, Oct. 30, 1789, Ames, *Works of Ames*, I, 74.
6. *Massachusetts Centinel* (Boston), Dec. 26, 1789; *Annals*, I, 969, 1075-76, Jan. 4, 8, 1790. John C. Fitzpatrick, ed., *The Diaries of George Washington*, 4 vols. (Boston and N.Y., 1925), IV, 66, Jan. 7, 1790; Ames to the Rev. J. Freeman, N.Y., Jan. 9, 1790, Houghton Library, Harvard Univ.; Freeman, *Washington*, VI, 249.
7. *Annals*, I, 822-25, 924, 939, Aug. 28, Sept. 10, 21, 1789; Ames to George R. Minot, Sept. 3, 1789, Ames, *Works of Ames*, I, 70; Mitchell, *Hamilton*, 41-43.

nancial expert during the Revolution and the Confederation period. Morris judged Hamilton to be the only person capable of solving the nation's financial problems. During the congressional recess, the Secretary had been deeply engaged in examining numerous fiscal works and in consulting with Madison, William Bingham, and Stephen Higginson in order to prepare his report to the House. This first report on public finances was the object of great anticipation at the opening of Congress, and enough was already known about its general tenor to stir public speculation and to promote the buying up of depreciated government and state securities.[8]

Early in the new session the House discussed how the Secretary of the Treasury should present his report on the public credit. Neither the Treasury Act nor the House resolution requesting the Secretary's report had been explicit on this point. Briefly the members considered the question of procedure. Should the Secretary be required to present his proposals in writing, as Gerry suggested, or should he be allowed to explain his report in person, as Boudinot maintained? Ames continued firm in his conviction that the House should receive financial information directly from its "highest source," the Secretary of the Treasury. But he anticipated that a verbal report could lead to misunderstandings; therefore he urged that all of the Secretary's communications be in writing. Ames had no wish to keep Hamilton from supporting his own projects on the floor of the House; yet he wanted messages from the Secretary to be in the form of permanent state papers. A majority of the representatives favored a move to request written reports, and thus Hamilton lost the opportunity to explain his program before the lower chamber.[9]

In accord with the instructions of the House, Hamilton submitted his report on January 14. Ames, who had only seen it briefly before publication, cautiously expressed the opinion that "it is allowed to be a masterly performance" which has "set curiosity in motion" not only in congressional circles but among the people at large. As he sensed

8. Oliver Wolcott to Oliver Wolcott, Sr., N.Y., Nov. 3, Dec. 2, 21, 1789, George Gibbs, *Memoirs of the Administrations of Washington and John Adams,* 2 vols. (N.Y., 1846), I, 23-24, 26; Thomas Fitzsimmons to Samuel Meredith, Phila., Nov. 30, 1789, Dreer Collection, Hist. Soc. of Pa.; Fitzsimmons wrote: "Every species of public security are advancing in value and the Speculators begin to persuade themselves that their golden dreams are on the point of being realized." Robert Morris to Gouverneur Morris, Phila., Dec. 11, 1789, Gouverneur Morris Papers, No. 911, Columbia University, N.Y.; Introductory Note, "Report on the Public Credit," Harold C. Syrett, ed., *The Papers of Alexander Hamilton* (N.Y. and London, 1961–), VI, 51-65; E. James Ferguson, *The Power of the Purse, A History of American Public Finance,* 1776-1790 (Chapel Hill, 1961), 255-57, 269-70.

9. *Annals,* I, 1080, Jan. 9, 1790. John C. Miller, *Alexander Hamilton, Portrait in Paradox* (N.Y., 1959), 238; Mitchell, *Hamilton,* 43-44.

from a hasty reading of the proposals, the Secretary supported his ideas with skillful, cogent arguments which would have great appeal among businessmen. It was apparent to Ames that a complex plan of this nature was certain to "furnish the fuel for fresh heats" and to result in prolonged debate in Congress. He was convinced that Hamilton's system should not be approved without a thorough discussion. The direction in which Congress moved in this case would "do infinite good or mischief." [10]

The essential task which Hamilton undertook was to reorganize the debts of the United States, amounting to $54,124,464 in 1790, and by establishing a funded debt, to secure the nation's financial credit. Inherent in his program were related goals of expanding the capital of the nation and developing firm economic bonds between men of wealth and the federal government. The Secretary's report also included plans for federal assumption of the debts of the individual states, these debts being estimated at $25,000,000. In elaborate detail he supported his cardinal points that the foreign debts must be paid in full, that in funding there should be no discrimination or distinction made between the original and the present owners of certificates of debts, and that arrears of interest must be paid.[11]

Funding involved the consolidation of the numerous types of certificates of indebtedness issued by the national government during and after the Revolution. In place of these certificates a new loan was to be floated of interest-bearing government bonds. Permanent funds, raised from duties on imports, tonnage, and additional levies on luxury goods, were to ensure interest payments. Since the government could not maintain the contracted 6 per cent interest rate, Hamilton offered creditors new terms reducing the interest to 4 per cent but compensating for the loss with such options as annuities and western lands. The surplus from Post Office operations was designated as a sinking fund to

10. *Annals*, I, 1092, Jan. 14, 1790; Ames to Minot, N.Y., Jan. 13, 1790, Ames, *Works of Ames* I, 72; Ames to William Tudor, N.Y., Jan. 17, 1790, "Memoir of Tudor," Mass. Hist. Soc., *Collections*, 2d Ser., 8 (1819), 320; *Massachusetts Centinel* (Boston), Nov. 11, 1789; Oliver Wolcott, Sr., to Oliver Wolcott, Litchfield, Dec. 23, 1789, Chauncey Goodrich to Oliver Wolcott, Hartford, Jan. 2, 1790, Gibbs, *Memoirs*, I, 33-34; James Madison to Thomas Jefferson, N.Y., Jan. 24, 1790, Madison Papers, XII, Lib. Cong. Madison wrote, "The business of Congress is as yet merely in embryo ... [Hamilton's plan] has scarcely been long enough from the press to be looked over ... it would seem as if doubts were entertained concerning the success of the plan in all its parts."

11. "Report on Public Credit," Syrett, ed., *Papers of Hamilton*, VI, 65-85; Hamilton's plan was published in the *Gazette of the United States* (N.Y.), Jan. 27, 30, 1790, Feb. 3, 6, 13, 17, 24, 27, 1790; Mitchell, *Hamilton*, 47-53. Joseph Dorfman, *The Economic Mind in American Civilization*, 3 vols. (N.Y., 1946-49), I, 412; Benjamin U. Ratchford, *American State Debts* (Durham, 1941), 52.

be used to purchase bonds in the open market and thus reduce the
national debt.[12] On the state debt issue, Hamilton proposed that each
state be charged with funds advanced to it by the United States, as
well as with the amount of its debts to be assumed by the national
government. Each state would be credited with its contributions to the
United States during the war. His plan provided for an assumption of
the state debts as they stood in 1790, but did not include reimbursement
for that portion of debt which an individual state had paid off. Only
after the state debts were assumed by the national government would
a balancing of federal and state accounts be carried out. The Congress
of the Confederation in 1782 had actually authorized a settlement of
accounts between the federal government and the states. Because this
settlement had not yet been effected, many people feared that it would
never take place.[13] The tenor of Hamilton's proposals did not reassure
them.

Rumor had it that the financial report would be debated on January
28. Many of the visitors who crowded the galleries in the representatives' hall were disappointed when Ames earnestly requested a postponement until the members had more time to comprehend the document.
James Jackson, the aggressive representative from Georgia, supported
Ames, but only on the basis that on such an important issue it was
necessary to await instructions from the state legislatures. Once he had
the attention of the members, Jackson began a denunciation of the
rapidly increasing speculation in state and Continental debt certificates.
"Since this report has been read in this House," Jackson thundered,
"a spirit of havoc, speculation, and ruin, has arisen, and been cherished
by people who had an access to the information the report contained,
that would have made a *Hastings* blush." With mounting disgust at the
situation, he added vehemently, "My soul rises indignant at the avaricious and immoral turpitude which so vile a conduct displays." [14] His
emotional outburst was but the forerunner of a mounting storm of
criticism of Hamilton's proposed financial measures, and, as Ames anticipated, the controversy was like a breeze fanning the coals of opposition. To John Marshall likewise, the publication of the program

12. "Report on Public Credit," Syrett, ed., *Papers of Hamilton*, VI, 85-110.
13. *Ibid.*, 81-83, 109-10.
14. *Annals*, I, 1131-32, Jan. 28, 1790; Henry Wynkoop to Dr. Reading Beattie,
N.Y., Jan. 28, 1790, Joseph M. Beatty, ed., "The Letters of Judge Henry Wynkoop,
Representative From Pennsylvania to the First Congress of the United States,"
Pennsylvania Magazine of History and Biography, 38 (1914), 188; Jeremy Belknap
to Ebenezer Hazard, Boston, Jan. 30, 1790, "The Belknap Papers," Mass. Hist. Soc.,
Collections, 5th Ser., 3 (1877), 211. Belknap described the numerous placards ad-
vertising the sale or purchase of public securities in Boston.

"seemed to unchain all those fierce passions which a high respect for government and for those who administered it, had in a great measure maintained." [15]

In New York the financial report had quickly gained public attention and by February had become a universal topic of animated discussion. On the eve of the congressional debate on its provisions, Fisher Ames commented, "Tomorrow we are going to turn financiers—scarce a head in New York that is not ready to burst with a plan." [16] At this point he himself was dubious about the success of the financial system in Congress when he contemplated the antagonism already evident. Ames's position became abundantly clear in the subsequent months. He was convinced that Hamilton's proposals, if approved, would reinforce and make secure the central government. Toward those who disagreed, he was condemnatory, certain that they could not possibly be right-thinking people. Massachusetts citizens would be "mad," he concluded, if in any way they opposed assuming the state debts, which had had such a disastrous effect on industry, had kindled Shays' Rebellion, and would "banish the farmers to the western woods." [17] Ames, himself, regarded an assumption as the *sine qua non* of any financial plan. Until the states and central government ceased to compete for revenue, the income of the national government would not be sufficient to meet its needs.

Within Ames's circle of friends and political supporters, Christopher Gore, Theodore Sedgwick, Thomas Dwight, and Jonathan Jackson all expressed strongly favorable opinions in regard to assumption. Gore hoped that the national government would take over the debts, although he recognized the political implications of such a move. "If attempted," he wrote to Senator Rufus King, "this must be done speedily—that it will tend to a consolidation of the union will presently be foreseen and therefore objected to by State demagogues." [18] Assumption of the Massachusetts debts, in Thomas Dwight's opinion, would

15. John Marshall, *The Life of George Washington*, 5 vols. (Phila., 1804-7), V, 244.

16. *Annals*, I, 1170, Feb. 8, 1790. Ames to William Tudor, N.Y., Feb. 7, 1790, "Memoir of Tudor," Mass. Hist. Soc., *Collections*, 2d Ser., 8 (1819), 321. *Gazette of the United States* (N.Y.), Feb. 3, 1790. The *Gazette* reported, "The subject of the Secretary's Report engrosses the public attention universally: It is the topic in all companies: the principles . . . are perpetually in discussion." Thomas Hartley to Jasper Yeates, N.Y., Jan. 30, 1790, Yeates Papers, Hist. Soc. of Pa.

17. Ames to Tudor, Feb. 7, 1790, "Memoir of Tudor," Mass. Hist. Soc., *Collections*, 2d Ser., 8 (1819), 320-22.

18. Christopher Gore to Rufus King, June 7, 1789, King, *Life of King*, I, 362; Samuel Henshaw to Theodore Sedgwick, June 14, 28, 1789, Nathaniel Gorham to Sedgwick, Jan. 23, 1790, Thomas Dwight to Sedgwick, July 9, 1789, Sedgwick Papers, Vol. A, Mass. Hist. Soc.

ensure the domestic peace of the Commonwealth, since people would
more readily accept the collection of a national excise if it were applied
to the reduction of the state's debt. Sedgwick, in a letter published in
the *Massachusetts Centinel*, emphasized that no other measure would
"so effectually and lastingly cement our union—we should then truly
be one people." [19]

When Ames received a judicious evaluation of Hamilton's report
early in February from Jonathan Jackson, he had confirmation that
Boston businessmen generally acclaimed the document, heralding it as
an ingenious and clever production. Jackson reported that few among
the wealthy investors were concerned about the proffered 4 per cent
interest, but he advised against any further reduction. In his estimation,
the establishment of an excise was equal in importance to the assumption and a "principle hinge upon which will turn the stability of your
government." There were some Bostonians, he knew, who disliked the
report and "would kick at it if they dared." Hamilton himself had
roused some difficulties inasmuch as he had "come Yorkshire over us . . .
by not referring the question to our legislatures." In weighing the
strength of resistance against assumption, Jonathan Jackson reminded
Ames "to distinguish the opinions thrown out by the snarlers and
bawlers in our gazettes and our Assemblies from the Good Sense of
the public at large." [20]

Even though Massachusetts might benefit greatly by the assumption
of her wartime debts, there was actually a sharp cleavage in public opinion within the state over the main features of the Hamiltonian program.
A considerable number of Ames's constituents in the Boston area found
fault with the methods of the proposed financial reorganization. Ardent
champions of state supremacy, many of whom were deeply attached to
Governor Hancock, immediately saw that the absorption of the debts
implied dangerous consolidation of state and national governments. One
Federalist in Boston commented, "Samuel Adams together with a number of our old, *genuine old 75* patriots are much opposed to a transfer

19. Thomas Dwight to Theodore Sedgwick, Springfield, July 9, 1789, Sedgwick
Papers, Vol. A, Mass. Hist. Soc.; letter of Theodore Sedgwick, Stockbridge,
Apr. 6, 1789, printed in the *Massachusetts Centinel* (Boston), May 30, 1789.
20. Jonathan Jackson to Fisher Ames, Boston, Feb. 7, 1790, Sedgwick Papers, II,
Mass. Hist. Soc.; Christopher Gore to Rufus King, Boston, Jan. 24, 1790, King,
Life of King, I, 385-86. Gore maintained that more than 4 per cent had to be
offered to win over Boston investors. *Gazette of the United States* (N.Y.), Jan.
30, Feb. 13, 1790; Stephen Higginson to John Adams, Boston, Mar. 1, 1790, J. F.
Jameson, ed., "Letters of Stephen Higginson, 1783-1804," American Historical
Association, *Annual Report for 1896* (Washington, 1897), I, 773; Samuel Henshaw
to Theodore Sedgwick, Boston, Jan. 30, Feb. 14, 1790, Vol. A, Mass. Hist. Soc.

of our state debt." [21] In addition, investors in western lands, who had contracted to pay for their purchases in depreciated securities, had no desire to see them appreciate to par value. A number of people vehemently criticized Hamilton's system because they feared it would result in oppressive land taxes. Others denounced it as a scheme which would defraud unwary widows and former soldiers, who had been forced to sell their depreciated securities earlier.

On February 8, the day appointed for a consideration of Hamilton's First Report on the Public Credit, Thomas Fitzsimmons of Pennsylvania presented resolutions dealing with specific aspects of the debt. These resolutions were accepted for discussion by the committee. At the outset, the representatives consented to pay in full the foreign holders of Revolutionary securities. Beyond this point, agreement and harmony rapidly declined. Previously disagreement in Congress had been controlled by the spirit of support for the new government. Now, the political philosophies of congressmen collided to such an extent over Hamilton's financial scheme that the development of parties was guaranteed.[22]

In a contentious manner Georgia's James Jackson questioned the whole idea of establishing any permanent national debt. Asserting that every European country which had resorted to a public debt eventually was impoverished, he gloomily forecast the ruin of the United States. Although Jackson's suggestion that the committee rise to terminate the discussion did not win support, his criticism did introduce the matter of scaling down the outstanding debt. As the debate continued, Samuel Livermore of New Hampshire and Thomas Scott of Pennsylvania took the position that the debt was artificially large and that it should be

21. Public interest in the plight of security holders is evident in the Boston press 1788-89, *Independent Chronicle* (Boston), Mar. 6, 1788, May 28, June 11, Aug. 20, Dec. 3, 17, 24, 31, 1789, Jan. 7, Feb. 11, 1790; *Massachusetts Centinel* (Boston), May 30, Nov. 11, Dec. 30, 1789; *Herald of Freedom* (Boston), July 31, 1789; Nathaniel Gorham to Oliver Phelps, June 25, 1789, Phelps and Gorham Papers, Box 17, New York State Library, Albany, N.Y.; Thomas Dawes, Jr., to John Hancock, Jan. 12, 1790, Domestic Letters, XVII, Hancock Papers, Harvard Business School, Boston, Mass.

22. *Annals*, I, 1170, 1178-79, Feb. 8, 1790; Beard, ed., *Journal of Maclay*, 189; Boyd, *Boudinot*, 178; Benjamin Rush to James Madison, Phila., Apr. 10, 1790, Lyman Butterfield, ed., *Letters of Benjamin Rush*, 2 vols. (Princeton, 1951), I, 543. Rush accused Fitzsimmons of becoming "the *midwife* of a system...he reprobated." Theodore Sedgwick to Peter Van Schaack, N.Y., Jan. 7, 1790, Sedgwick Papers, III, Mass. Hist. Soc.; George Washington to the Marquis de Lafayette, Mount Vernon, Jan. 29, 1789, Washington to Gov. Arthur Fenner, N.Y., June 4, 1790, John C. Fitzpatrick, ed., *The Writings of George Washington, 1745-1799*, 39 vols. (Washington, 1931-44), XXX, 184, XXXI, 48; Joseph Charles, *The Origins of the American Party System: Three Essays* (Williamsburg, 1956), 13-20.

carefully re-examined. Such a re-examination, they anticipated, would result in a reduction of the amount. Elias Boudinot and John Laurance protested against any diminution of the debt, but it was left to Fisher Ames to develop their argument and to counteract the potential threat to Hamilton's plan.[23] Without inferring that his colleagues intended to do wrong, the representative from Massachusetts took a lead from Boudinot to emphasize that the debts were public contracts. "The evidences of the debt," he pointed out, "cannot . . . be considered in any other light than as public bonds, for the redemption and payment of which the property and labor of the whole people are pledged. The only just idea is, that when the public contract a debt with an individual, that it becomes personified, and that with respect to this contract, the powers of Government shall never legislate." [24] Unless the government abided by its contracts and also protected private property, the social compact would be ended, Ames was fully convinced. The arguments of Scott, Livermore, and Jackson won but few followers in the House; and after Hartley, Sedgwick, Boudinot, and Gerry had added the weight of their opinions to those of Ames, the representatives turned away from any direct attempt to reduce the total amount of the debt to be funded. The first skirmish had been won by the advocates of Hamilton's plan; yet a more serious challenge to the scheme quickly followed.[25]

This challenge concerned the government's obligation to the original holders of Continental securities. In the years since the Revolution many of the certificates had been bought up with the hope that they would be redeemed at par. Now a sympathetic public, repelled at the evidence of excessive speculation in both state and Continental securities, demanded that justice be done to the first holders who had alienated their claims. Subsequent purchasers, the argument ran, should be entitled only to the sum they had paid for the securities; the original creditors should get the difference between the market price and the full redemption value. In his report to the House, Hamilton had attempted to rebut the arguments for discriminating between original and present owners; still the issue was not easily dismissed and became a disruptive one.[26]

Madison's position on Hamilton's financial plan was anxiously awaited by the members of the House. When Madison broke his silence on

23. *Annals,* I, 1179-82, 1185-93, Feb. 9, 1790; Mitchell, *Hamilton,* 60-61.
24. *Annals,* I, 1193-95, Feb. 9, 1790; Mitchell, *Hamilton,* 62.
25. *Annals,* I, 1195-96, 1198-1212, 1216-1220, Feb. 9, 10, 1790. Scott's attempt to amend Fitzsimmons's second resolution was defeated, Feb. 11, 1790, *ibid.,* 1224.
26. Ferguson, *Power of the Purse,* 293-94; Brant, *Madison, Father of the Constitution,* 304; Jensen, *New Nation,* 390; Mitchell, *Hamilton,* 48-49.

February 11 with a long speech, Hamilton's supporters were dismayed to learn that the Virginian favored a discrimination. His thesis was that original creditors who had sold their certificates were entitled to recompense, as they had received payment for goods and services only in depreciated securities. He regarded the Continental debt as a valid one due in its entirety and insisted, "No logic, no magic . . . can diminish the force of the obligation." In order to avoid injustice both to Revolutionary soldiers and to purchasers who took risks, he proposed a compromise which he then presented to the committee of the whole as a motion. "Let it be a liberal one in favor of the present holders," he urged, "let them have the highest price which has prevailed in the market; and let the residue belong to the original sufferers." [27]

Thomas Hartley wrote enthusiastically that Madison's speech was in "the finest language I almost ever heard." But many persons, he reported, were surprised by his motion which "had more the heat of the Chamber Lamp than generally appears in his productions." [28] Among men who were displeased over Madison's stand was Theodore Sedgwick, who objected to the fact that Madison had reversed the position he took in 1783. Sedgwick wrote, "our embarrassments are encreased by . . . [Madison's] Proposition. . . . To adopt his ideas would be a most violent breach of public faith. . . . It will tend to render inveterate and perpetual parties on this touchy business." [29] Hamilton himself seemed to feel that Madison had broken faith with him, as the two had substantially agreed in conversation on the plan of funding. According to Isaac Bronson, the Secretary considered that Madison had deserted "principles which he was solemnly pledged to defend, yet the tone of . . . [Hamilton's] remarks . . . were more in sorrow than in anger." [30] Madison's motion to effect a discrimination opened wide the gates of political controversy, and in retrospect, it was seen as the parting of the ways with Hamilton.

A few days after Madison presented his ideas, Ames was ready with an answer, honed to a sharp edge. He agreed with the Virginian on

27. *Annals,* I, 1234-36, Feb. 11, 1790; Miller, *Hamilton,* 239-41; entry of Feb. 11, 1790, Beard, ed., *Journal of Maclay,* 194-95; Brant, *Madison, Father of the Constitution,* 293-95.
28. Thomas Hartley to Jasper Yeates, N.Y., Feb. 14, 1790, Yeates Papers, Hist. Soc. of Pa.
29. Theodore Sedgwick to Henry Van Schaack, N.Y., Feb. 13, 1790, Sedgwick Papers, III, Mass. Hist. Soc.
30. Isaac Bronson to James A. Hamilton, Mar. 2, 1834 (not sent), Bronson Papers, Martin Collection, N.Y. Pub. Lib., quoted in Abraham H. Venit, "An Unwritten Federalist History," *New Eng. Qtly.,* 21 (1948), 243; Bronson, a Connecticut Federalist, had frequently been in the Treasury Department on business during 1791-92. Miller, *Hamilton,* 239.

the basic principle that the national debt was a valid obligation, a debt not to be annulled or altered without the mutual consent of the contracting parties. But he insisted that Madison's measure would actually subvert this principle. The Massachusetts Federalist could not accept Madison's interpretation that there was a contractual obligation to pay the difference between the market value and the face value of securities to an original owner who had sold his certificates. Because the owner had freely made a decision to sell, he had lost his claim against the government and had no "residuary right to the debt." [31]

Ames held that Madison preached an "abstract justice" which in fact would result in "a fragment of justice" for some, not all, of the people affected by discrimination. Madison's measure would be unfair to the group of original owners of certificates who did not sell them. "I think it not difficult to show," Ames remarked, "that . . . [Hamilton] proposes better justice to the present original holders than is contained in the motion." [32] Certainly purchasers would be in a more favorable position if the government did not abandon its principles. The former government had taken a stand against discrimination; contracts and purchases had been made on this basis. If the government controlled and disposed of property instead of protecting it, there was "a cheat in the compact." The only solution, Ames insisted, was to handle all valid claims in precisely the same manner and not to "rob on the highway to exercise charity." From every point of view, Madison's motion was inadequate, partial, and impracticable. A program to benefit those who had sold their securities would create discontent, corruption, and endless law suits. Far from ending speculation, discrimination would intensify it, producing a new harvest. "The after-crop," Ames pithily remarked, "will be more abundant than the first cutting." [33] In conclusion he attempted to persuade Madison to abandon his inappropriate proposal.

Senator Maclay, who had listened to the debates in the lower house, left with vivid impressions of the leading Federalists, Ames, Sedgwick, and Laurance, each attempting to make Madison's solution to the funding issue appear ridiculous. After hearing Ames's speech, Maclay called it a "long string of studied sentences" in which the orator used the terms public faith, public credit, honor and justice as frequently as "an Indian would the great Spirit and . . . with less meaning and to as

31. *Annals*, I, 1261, Feb. 16, 1790.
32. *Ibid.*, 1262, Feb. 16, 1790.
33. *Ibid.*, 1264-65, Feb. 16, 1790; *Massachusetts Centinel* (Boston), Mar. 3, 1790. See comments of a "country correspondent" who was "charmed with Mr. Ames's . . . [speech] against discrimination," *Independent Chronicle* (Boston), Mar. 25, 1790.

little purpose." The senator from Pennsylvania reflected that "Hamilton, at the head of the Speculators with all the Courtiers, are on one side. These I call the party who are actuated by Interest. The opposition are governed by Principle, but I fear in the case Interest will outweigh Principle." [34] There was no doubt in his mind where Ames stood. In contrast, one New Englander found that the speech was a notable refutation of Madison's erroneous ideas. "I am extremely pleased," wrote Nathaniel Barrell to Representative George Thatcher, "with the masterly speech of Mr. Ames in answer to Mr. Madison, and tho' I see he might have said more yet . . . there is not a word wanting . . . it is a compleat reply to everything said on that subject and deserves to be written in letters of gold." [35]

With great intensity the debate over discrimination continued, since neither group wished to end it by calling for a vote on the question until the matter was thoroughly canvassed. Public excitement grew over the issue, and eager visitors as well as senators were enticed away from their work by the succession of orators who held forth. Philip Freneau published a few stanzas of verse noting "the Immense Concourse at Federal Hall, in 1790, while the Funding System was in agitation":

> With eager step and wrinkled brow
> The busy sons of care
> (Disgusted with less splendid scenes)
> To Congress Hall repair.
>
> . . . .
>
> Within these walls the doctrines taught
> Are of such vast concern
> That all the world, with one consent
> Here strives to live—and learn.[36]

In the midst of the vigorous debates, ladies suddenly appeared in the galleries, giving the proceedings a social aspect. Ames was instrumental in making the necessary arrangements for them to be admitted to Federal Hall. In conversation with him at a party one evening, Mrs. John Langdon, the wife of the senator from New Hampshire, had revealed

34. Entry of Feb. 15, 1790, Beard, ed., *Journal of Maclay*, 192.
35. Nathaniel Barrell to George Thatcher, York, Maine, Mar. 4, 1790, Jere Hill to George Thatcher, Feb. 24, 1790, Thatcher Papers, Chamberlain Collection, Boston Pub. Lib.
36. Fred L. Pattee, ed., *Poems of Philip Freneau, Poet of the American Revolution*, 3 vols. (Princeton, 1902-7), III, 26-27. The poem was first published in the N.Y. *Daily Advertiser*, Mar. 12, 1790. Entries of Feb. 10-19, 1790, Beard, ed., *Journal of Maclay*, 189-94.

her disappointment in not being able to hear him address the House. Ames immediately responded that he could see no reason why ladies should be excluded from the speeches and debates. Mrs. Langdon, pleased at his reaction, indicated that she would plan to attend if he would notify her of his next speech. During this period, Abigail Adams wrote her sister, Mary Cranch, that she expected to accompany Mrs. Dalton, Mrs. Jay, and Mrs. Cushing on her first visit to hear the debates in the House. She added further that "Mr. Ames from our state and Mr. Sedgwick and Mr. Gerry are all right upon this Question and make a conspicuous figure in the debates." [37]

The debates on discrimination were spun out for a total of seven days, as those representatives who held the floor seemed to explore every nuance of the subject. On Wednesday, February 17, Boudinot spoke for two hours; Madison, the next day, defended discrimination with a speech of equal intensity and length. Critically Maclay noted that Hamilton was "moving heaven and earth in favor of his ... system"; meantime the senator from Pennsylvania himself was endeavoring to brief a colleague in the House with "every argument in my power against Hamilton's report." [38] The lines were sharply drawn; yet the weight of opinion ultimately was against discrimination, for the vote taken on Madison's proposal found only thirteen members in favor and thirty-six opposed. Ames, along with Egbert Benson of New York, Boudinot, Gerry, Laurance, Sedgwick, and William L. Smith, had succeeded in turning back the most concerted attack as yet on the Hamiltonian system. Funding of the domestic debt on the Secretary's terms was now accepted by the committee of the whole House.[39]

In the long run the antagonisms generated by the failure of the

37. Ben. Perley Poore, *Perley's Reminiscences of Sixty Years in the National Metropolis*, 2 vols. (Phila., 1886), I, 77-78; Abigail Adams to Mary Cranch, Richmond Hills, Feb. 20, 1790, Stewart Mitchell, ed., *New Letters of Abigail Adams, 1788-1801* (Boston, 1947), 37-38.

38. Henry Wynkoop to Dr. Reading Beattie, N.Y., Feb. 18, 1790, Beatty, ed., "Letters of Wynkoop," *Pa. Mag. of Hist. and Biog.*, 38 (1914), 189-91; *Annals*, II, 1310-44, Feb. 18-19, 1790; Madison to Edmund Pendleton, N.Y., Mar. 4, 1790, Madison Papers, XII, Lib. Cong.; entries of Feb. 9, 18, 1790, Beard, ed., *Journal of Maclay*, 189, 194.

39. *Annals*, II, 1344, Feb. 22, 1790; Thomas Hartley to Jasper Yeates, N.Y., Feb. 22, 1790, Yeates Papers, Hist. Soc. of Pa.; Brant, *Madison, Father of the Constitution*, 299; Mitchell, *Hamilton*, 67-68. In central and western Massachusetts there was little support for discrimination, Samuel Henshaw to Theodore Sedgwick, Feb. 28, 1790, Thomas Dwight to Theodore Sedgwick, Springfield, Feb. 27, 1790, Sedgwick Papers, Vol. A, Mass. Hist. Soc.; *Connecticut Courant* (Hartford), Feb. 4, 1790; *Gazette of the United States* (N.Y.), Feb. 17, 24, 1790; Matthew McConnell to William Irvine, Phila., Feb. 24, 1790, General William Irvine Papers, X, Hist. Soc. of Pa.

Hamilton group in Congress to protect the interests of the Revolutionary veteran had the effect of stirring public feeling, at least among the common people, against the Federalists. In Boston the opponents of Hamilton condemned the defeat of discrimination and praised Madison effusively for his role in the debates. One newspaper writer proclaimed that "the Old Soldier, whom necessity alone obliged to sell his pay, is happy that it is so great and so good a man who has stepped forth, the champion of publick justice, publick faith, and publick honour." [40] Although Ames was not denounced in his home district, the eminent Philadelphia physician, Benjamin Rush, anonymously sent a scathing bit of verse to the Philadelphia newspapers in which the stand of the Massachusetts representative on discrimination appeared to be both cynical and self-seeking:

> Pay the poor soldier!—He's a sot,
> Cries our grave ruler B-ud-not.
> No pity, *now* from us he claims
> In artful accent, echoes Ames.
> In *war*, to heroes let's be just,
> In *peace*, we'll write their toils in dust;
> A soldier's pay are rags and fame,
> A wooden leg—a deathless name.
> To Specs, both *in* and *out* of Cong.,
> The four and six per cents belong.[41]

Rush was so incensed about the defeat of discrimination that he vehemently expressed his anger to Madison. "The decision upon that great question will leave a stain upon our country which no time nor declamation can ever wipe away.... I feel disposed to wish that my name was blotted out from having contributed a single mite towards the American Revolution. We have effected a deliverance from the national injustice of Great Britain, to be *subjugated* by a mighty act of national injustice by the United States." [42]

Even before the reverberations of the funding issue had subsided, the

40. *Massachusetts Centinel* (Boston), Feb. 24, 27, Mar. 20, 27, 1790; *Boston Gazette* (Boston), Feb. 22, 1790.

41. *Massachusetts Centinel* (Boston), Apr. 7, 1790; Brant, *Madison, Father of the Constitution*, 299; Benjamin Rush to John Adams, January 10, 1811, Butterfield, ed., *Letters of Rush*, II, 1076-77. Rush commented that Boudinot and Ames were so conspicuous among those who profited from assumption that "your friend characterized their speeches in defense of the funding system ... in the following lines: ...," revealing himself as the author of the stanza.

42. Benjamin Rush to James Madison, Phila., Feb. 27, 1790, Madison Papers, XII, Lib. Cong.

Hamiltonians in Congress were pressing forward the assumption of the state debts. From all indications it appeared to Ames that the House would be more closely divided on this question than on funding. In his initial remarks on the issue to the members of the House, he expressed his opinion that if the state debts were not taken over, then it was possible that Congress had no right to fund the federal debt. Hamilton's systematic arrangement could not be broken into its components without destroying its "symmetry" and "efficacy." [43]

As one member of the House after another expressed his views on assumption, it became evident that the Federalists would have to overcome a host of objections. In part the disagreement over assumption stemmed from the conviction of men like Madison, who believed that the methods by which the financial reorganization was to take place were manifestly unjust. Michael J. Stone of Maryland best symbolized the group in Congress who feared that the states would be inevitably reduced to nullities if assumption carried. In a forceful speech, he expressed his conviction that giving the national government control over all the sources of revenue to pay the debts would deprive the states of important powers and inevitably undermine the structure of the Union. It was doubtful in his mind whether a confederation could even exist on this basis. Such a plan threatened to "swallow up the idea of an absolute existence of a State Government." [44] He asked further whether it was legitimate to consider that the states' debts were actually debts of the United States. It was a dangerous proposal for Congress to assume debts without constitutional authority and then to collect taxes "under the general powers" of government.

Manasseh Cutler, former teacher and minister who had turned Ohio land promoter, attended the debates on the financial issues while he was in New York on business. Listening eagerly, Cutler was impressed with the ability and eloquence of the representatives engaged in the argument. At this time Roger Sherman of Connecticut and George Clymer of Pennsylvania endeavored to answer the objections of Stone.

43. Ames to Tudor, N.Y., Feb. 7, 1790, "Memoir of Tudor," Mass. Hist. Soc., *Collections*, 2d Ser., 8 (1819), 322; *Annals*, II, 1358, Feb. 23, 1790; Manasseh Cutler to the Rev. Oliver Everett, N.Y., Feb. 28, 1790, Cutler, *Life of Cutler*, I, 461; Theodore Sedgwick to Pamela Sedgwick, N.Y., Mar. 4, 1790, Sedgwick Papers, II, Box 3, Mass. Hist. Soc.; Albert S. Bolles, *The Financial History of the United States from 1789 to 1860* (N.Y., 1894), 39.
44. Theodore Sedgwick to Henry Van Schaack, N.Y., Jan. 31, 1790, Sedgwick Papers, III, Mass. Hist. Soc.; Madison to Pendleton, Mar. 4, 1790, Madison Papers, XI, Lib. Cong.; *Massachusetts Centinel* (Boston), Mar. 6, 20, 27, Apr. 3, 10, 1790; *Annals*, II, 1359-63, 1374-80, Feb. 23-24, 1790; Dwight to Sedgwick, Feb. 27, 1790, Sedgwick Papers, Vol. A, Mass. Hist. Soc.; Ferguson, *Power of the Purse*, 310-11.

Such loyal Hamiltonians as Benjamin Goodhue, Theodore Sedgwick, and William L. Smith also participated in the discussions, contending that it was far better to have the central government pay the debts than to leave the question of payment to the discretion of the individual states. Even Elbridge Gerry rose to insist that it would be of great advantage to the states to have their debts assumed.[45]

Late in February, Madison, battling Hamilton's system, proposed an amendment to Fitzsimmons' original resolutions. Very conscious of the fact that his state had already substantially reduced her wartime obligations, he wanted to make certain that a settlement of accounts would be correlated with an assumption. Therefore the Virginian moved that the clause providing for an assumption include provisions for "liquidating and crediting to the States, the whole of their expenditures during the war." [46] At the same time he inserted a phrase to guard the interests of those states which, like Virginia, did not have full legal evidence of their expenses. His argument, couched in the language of justice for all states, was shaped by the fear that an assumption on Hamiltonian terms would mean that Virginia would be taxed to pay the interest on the large existing debts of such states as South Carolina and Massachusetts. Madison's motives were clarified in a letter to Edmund Pendleton in which he asserted that "a simple unqualified assumption of the existing debts would bear peculiarly hard on Virginia. . . . If such an assumption were to take place she would pay towards the discharge of the debts, in the proportion of 1/5 and receive back to her creditor Citizens 1/7 or 1/8, whilst Massachusetts would pay not more than 1/7 or 1/8, and receive back not less than 1/5." [47] While Madison was willing to accept assumption on condition that his state was protected, Alexander White of Virginia attempted to thwart the entire plan. Determined not to permit an assumption prior to a settlement of accounts, he moved that assumption be confined to that sum which a state had advanced beyond an equitable proportion of the common, wartime expenses.[48]

Ames plunged into the debate on February 26, defending the principle of assumption, as well as rejecting the ideas implicit in White's motion. Patriots during the war, he said, had made a common cause, sharing dangers and losses. Why then should not the cost of defending

45. Manasseh Cutler to the Rev. Oliver Everett, N.Y., Feb. 24, 1790, Cutler, *Life of Cutler*, I, 458-59; *Annals*, II, 1363-69, Feb. 23-24, 1790.
46. *Annals*, II, 1386-89, Feb. 24, 1790; Ferguson, *Power of the Purse*, 314-15.
47. Madison to Pendleton, Mar. 4, 1790, Madison Papers, XII, Lib. Cong.; Ferguson, *Power of the Purse*, 313-14.
48. *Annals*, II, 1393-94, Feb. 25, 1790; Miller, *Hamilton*, 242; Ferguson, *Power of the Purse*, 315.

liberty be "a common charge?" Even the ammunition used at Bunker Hill was paid for by Massachusetts. "Nothing," Ames asserted, "can more clearly evince the injustice of calling these State debts, than this circumstance." [49]

From every point of view an assumption would be advantageous. Unity of the nation would be enhanced, interference between state and national authorities would be avoided, and the debts actually would be paid, he argued. Far from constituting an "improper and unsafe" use of power, assumption would be a legitimate exercise of Congress's war power. Since the debt was the result of the war, it seemed to him "to be in strict conformity to the spirit, as well as the letter of the constitution, to assume it." [50] If assumption placed dangerous powers in the hands of the national government, these powers would be even more exaggerated in the hands of the states. To rely on the state governments to liquidate the debts was unsound, for many states would do nothing for their creditors until a settlement of accounts took place between the states and the national government. Commenting on White's position, Ames remarked, "We are told, that the accounts are in train of being settled. We are advised to wait that event. But, in the meantime, what is to become of the State creditors?" He questioned whether those states expecting balances in their favor would be willing to pay their creditors. Without an assumption the value of debt certificates would fluctuate, and the states themselves would have to resort to unproductive direct taxes if they attempted to pay the debts. The states thus were far less able to provide for the debts than the United States. Congress had already accepted the idea of paying the states the balances of accounts due to them, he stated in conclusion. "This is virtually an assumption—why should we forbear to do that in the first instance which we are ultimately bound to do?" [51]

Discussion on Alexander White's amendment continued briefly after Ames's speech, but before the meeting adjourned, the committee of the whole defeated it by a majority of fourteen. For the moment, it appeared that the House might accept some form of assumption. The representatives soon turned again to Madison's motion. Anxious to gain additional votes for assumption, the Hamiltonians decided to support the proposal. Surprisingly enough when the measure was brought to a vote on March 1, the representatives unanimously approved it. The accord spurred Madison to suggest another alteration in Fitzsimmons'

49. *Annals*, II, 1417-18, Feb. 26, 1790.
50. *Ibid.*, 1420.
51. *Ibid.*, 1421-22.

resolutions to the effect that "the amount of debts actually paid by any State to its creditors, shall be credited and paid to such State on the same terms as shall be provided in the case of individuals." [52]

Ames reacted quickly to this attempt to include in assumption not only the debts still outstanding, but also those already paid by a state. While he did not want to accuse Madison of trying to block matters, he could not avoid suggesting that the Virginian's new amendment was "grounded on an idea, that the assumption ... will impede the liquidation and adjustment of the accounts." [53] To overcome Madison's concern that the accounts would not be settled, Ames read some resolutions which he planned to submit formally at a later time. Clearly these resolutions were of a conciliatory nature. Under his plan, each state was to be charged with advances made by the United States, as well as the amount of its debt assumed by the national government. At the same time, each state was to be credited with all expenditures of money and supplies made in behalf of the general government during the war. All charges and credits were to be converted to specie value with interest of 6 per cent a year. The settlement between the United States and individual states was to be made under a board of commissioners whose decisions would be final. If the present Congress did not work out a ratio for adjusting the contributions of the various states, the commissioners would have the power to devise such a ratio. Senator Maclay, present in the House during the discussions, commented that "Ames ... read ... a string of resolutions touching the manner in which the States were to bring forward their claims, which I thought alarming." [54] Because Ames's plan was unofficial, the representatives did not enter into a discussion of its merits. Instead they returned to the subject of Madison's latest motion. Ames's suggestions remained neglected for the moment; yet ultimately they formed the basis of several sections of the act providing for assumption.[55]

The Hamiltonians in general, and Ames in particular, could not endorse Madison's newest proposal. The Massachusetts representative insisted that Congress should assume only that part of the Revolutionary debt still outstanding and not, as Madison urged, the entire amount. "It would be making a provision *ex abundanti*," he asserted, and would necessitate paying sums already settled, "to the injury of the real cred-

---

52. *Ibid.*, 1424, 1434, Feb. 26, Mar. 1, 1790.
53. *Ibid.*, 1435, Mar. 1, 1790.
54. *Ibid.*, 1435-36; entry of Mar. 1, 1790, Beard, ed., *Journal of Maclay*, 200.
55. *Annals*, II, 1436, Mar. 1, 1790, and 2357-58. Ames's second and third resolutions were carried out by Sections 1 and 5 of the Act of Aug. 5, 1790; Peters, ed., *U.S. Statutes at Large*, I, 178-79.

itors of the United States." [56] Ames's criticism of Madison's proposition
on grounds of expense was a direct appeal to those who, like Thomas
Hartley, already were appalled at the prospects of the high costs of
assumption. His own propositions, Ames declared, would be more
likely to promote a final settlement. If justice were to be fully carried
out, he mused, the government ought to reimburse the states for all the
money spent during the Revolution. This action would, like Madison's
motion, "make the State Treasuries rich, but it must be by making the
citizens poor." Then, he continued sardonically, "it would indeed be
true, that a public debt is not a public blessing." [57]

An irritated Madison retorted, "The gentleman from Massachusetts
thinks my principle would go to cover all the debts contracted during
the war. I ask what is the intention of the gentleman in favor of assumption? . . . will any gentleman contend that we ought to assume
only unpaid debts? Why shall we not assume the paid also?" [58] Ames
quickly responded with some questions of his own on the operation of
the measure. "Is there a citizen in the United States," he asked, "who
would be grateful to the Government for taxing him, in order to pay
money back to him again?" He could not see that it would benefit the
states or do justice to the creditors. Madison's proposal was such a
complete departure from Hamilton's ideas, Ames bluntly stated, that
if it was adopted, the Secretary of the Treasury could not be held
responsible for the consequences.[59]

Subsequently Ames accused the anti-assumption group of inconsistency. "Gentlemen who contend that we are not able to pay the State
debts in the hands of individuals must have their imagination strangely
warped when they suppose us capable of paying perhaps double the
sum." [60] Madison instantly responded, parrying the thrust, by accusing
Ames himself of being inconsistent, emphasizing that he had not opposed enlarging the national debt by assuming interest charges but now
was arguing that the debt should not be increased. "On what principle
does he act?" the Virginian asked.[61] Emphatically Ames denied the
allegation. He asserted that the states should be repaid for their financial
outlay whether the debt consisted of principal or interest. Because he
firmly believed this, he had supported a change in Madison's amendment, making the inclusion of interest charges requisite. When Madi-

56. *Annals*, II, 1434-44, Mar. 1, 1790; Thomas Hartley to Jasper Yeates, N.Y.,
Feb. 28, 1790, Yeates Papers, Hist. Soc. of Pa.
57. *Annals*, II, 1443, Mar. 1, 1790.
58. *Ibid.;* Madison to Pendleton, Mar. 4, 1790, Madison Papers, XII, Lib. Cong.
59. *Annals*, II, 1443-44.
60. *Ibid.*, 1458.
61. *Ibid.;* Brant, *Madison, Father of the Constitution*, 308-9.

son's altered amendment was brought to a vote, it was defeated. The tactics of the Hamiltonians were obvious. By saddling the Virginian's motion with additions which would increase the expense of assumption, they effectively killed his idea of reimbursing the states for their debts *in toto*. Momentarily the pro-assumption representatives had a majority.[62]

Privately, Ames expressed his reactions to the opposition. To William Tudor he wrote, "——— [Madison] hangs heavy on us. If he is a friend, he is more troublesome than a declared foe. He is so much a Virginian; so afraid that the mob will ... *crucify him;* sees Patrick Henry's shade at his bedside every night; ... he has kept himself wrapt up in a mystery, and starts new objections daily. I hope for a favourable event. But the work goes on heavily and slowly." [63]

In Ames's thinking the Hamiltonian plan had become a necessary component of the new government. The Massachusetts orator now saw Hamilton as one who could synthesize Federalist concepts and incorporate them into a solid financial system. In fighting for such a system, Ames was actually fostering his own theories of superior government rather than simply following a dynamic leader. Whatever the elements in Congress, Ames essentially remained an individualist.

62. *Annals*, II, 1455-58.
63. Ames to Tudor, N.Y., Mar. 3, 1790, "Memoir of Tudor," Mass. Hist. Soc., *Collections*, 2d Ser., 8 (1819), 322. Theodore Sedgwick to Pamela Sedgwick, N.Y., Mar. 4, 1790, Sedgwick Papers, II, Box 3, Mass. Hist. Soc.

Chapter VIII

Resolution with a Bargain

In the midst of the assumption conflict, Fisher Ames found the business of Congress absorbing and yet aggravating. By temperament he wanted action when the solution of a problem appeared obvious to him. But assumption proved to be a complex issue, and only after a dramatic struggle was a decision finally reached. On March 8, Senator Maclay noted in his journal that "this is the important week, and perhaps the important day, when the question will be put on the assumption of the State debts." He added, "I suspect this from the rendezvousing of the crew of the Hamilton galley. It seems all hands are piped to quarters." [1]

Ames relentlessly defended the Hamiltonian system in the House. Convinced as he was that it would be a means of establishing the financial integrity of the government, he drummed on the need for an immediate assumption and on the inseparable nature of state and national debts. According to Manasseh Cutler, Ames's efforts to win support for assumption were not limited to Congress. The visitor from the Ohio frontier maintained that "at this stage of the business . . . the friends to the assumption depend more on management out of doors than within and I believe, firmly, will out-general their opponents." [2]

In the present situation, Ames was motivated, no less than Madison, by a realistic concern for the economic position of his own state, as well as by broad concepts of the nation's future development. The New

1. Beard, ed., *Journal of Maclay*, 202-3.
2. Manasseh Cutler to the Reverend Oliver Everett, N.Y., Feb. 28, 1790, Cutler, *Life of Cutler*, I, 460-61.

Englander was very conscious of the fact that Massachusetts still had outstanding a Revolutionary debt of more than $5,000,000. Fundamental to the economic welfare of the state was the lifting of this chronic financial burden without prolonged delay and uncertainty. Moreover, behind the demand of Massachusetts Federalists for an assumption lay the hope that upon a final balancing of accounts the Commonwealth would be a creditor. Local and national considerations were closely intertwined.[3]

The decision on assumption was postponed temporarily when Thomas Hartley presented on March 8 a committee report on anti-slavery petitions submitted by the Quakers. Dealing with congressional powers in the abolition of slavery, the report elicited a sharp exchange of opinions on the right of Congress to interfere in the local affairs of states. Apparently the digression enabled the pro-assumption congressmen to gain another supporter. With the appearance of Representative John Vining of Delaware, the Hamiltonians were ready to risk the vote. The next day at 2 P.M., after all possible influence had been exhausted to sway votes and after two ailing representatives had been carried into the hall, assumption passed the committee of the whole by thirty-one to twenty-six.[4]

The close division was not reassuring to the Hamiltonians, especially as the expected arrival of the representatives from North Carolina, a state known to be hostile to assumption, might upset the favorable majority once the measure was before the House. Rumors circulated that both New England and South Carolina might "fly off" unless assumption was approved by Congress. The representatives of those states which were in financial difficulties were anxious for immediate action and showed no reticence about imposing on the nation new burdens of taxation to meet the obligations incurred by the measure. Their aggressive stand in the past weeks roused antipathy among many southerners, who in some cases were openly suggesting that it was

3. Ratchford, *American State Debts*, 45; Oscar and Mary F. Handlin, *Commonwealth, A Study of the Role of Government in the American Economy: Massachusetts, 1774-1861* (N.Y. and London, 1947), 36, 52, 64-66. Ratchford states that the debt was $5,226,801 on Nov. 1, 1789. The Handlins state that "by 1786, refinancing and accumulated interest had increased indebtedness to $5,440,000 in specie with as much more owed to the Continental Congress." Morse, *Federalist Party*, 63; Charles J. Bullock, "Historical Sketch of the Finances and Financial Policy of Massachusetts, 1780-1905," Amer. Econ. Assoc., *Publications*, 3d Ser., 8 (1907), 269-90.

4. *Annals*, II, 1463-65, Mar. 8, 1790; Ferguson, *Power of the Purse*, 317-18; Beard, ed., *Journal of Maclay*, 208-9; Thomas Hartley to Jasper Yeates, N.Y., Mar. 9, 1790, Yeates Papers, Hist. Soc. of Pa. Neither the *Annals* nor the *Journal of the House* give the vote on assumption in the committee of the whole.

impractical to preserve a union when Virginia and the eastern states
had such dissimilar interests.[5]

Having dealt with assumption, the committee of the whole methodi-
cally proceeded to the remaining resolutions concerning Hamilton's
system. The representatives became entangled in the intricacies of the
Secretary's various propositions regarding the alternate modes of paying interest to the holders of federal bonds. A major stumbling block
proved to be the provision that the principal was not redeemable.
Several members, among them Madison, were critical of the complex
method of paying the interest; others objected to creating an irredeem-
able and perpetual public debt. James Jackson's attempt to alter the
terms Hamilton suggested for creditors brought Ames into the discussion. In his speech he defended the proposed interest rate and gave a
thorough exposition of the sinking fund.[6]

The Massachusetts Federalist argued that it was unlikely the nation
would be able to pay the holders of government certificates the full
6 per cent interest, originally agreed upon, without imposing oppressive
taxes. Clearly the government had a binding agreement at 6 per cent,
but with the approval of the creditors, a substitute contract could be
beneficial to both parties. Ames held that an assured interest, even
though lower than 6 per cent, would profit the creditors more by increasing the financial security of the government. If the domestic debt
were funded and a sinking fund established, public securities would
tend to remain at a "fixed exchangeable value, and at the highest rate."
Such a state of public credit was both obtainable and logical. It was
the sinking fund which would ultimately protect investors by preventing a decline in security values. In the experience of Great Britain with
a public debt, Ames found ample historical precedent for Hamilton's
plan to change the terms of the contract between creditor and government. Continuing his analysis, he presented the advantages a funded
debt would bring to the nation in comparison with an unfunded one.
"Upon the whole," Ames concluded, "I submit it to the candid judge-
ment of the committee . . . whether a Congress of creditors only could,
with any degree of prudence, provide better for themselves." [7]

In his usual loud voice, Jackson denied the validity of Ames's argu-

5. Thomas Hartley to Jasper Yeates, N.Y., Mar. 14, 1790, Yeates Papers, Hist.
Soc. of Pa.; Beard, ed., *Journal of Maclay*, 209; Edward Carrington to James
Madison, Mar. 27, 1790, Henry Lee to James Madison, Mar. 13, 1790, Madison
Papers, XII, Lib. Cong.; David Stuart to George Washington, Mar. 15, 1790, Wash-
ington to Stuart, N.Y., Mar. 28, 1790, Fitzpatrick, ed., *Writings of Washington*,
XXXI, 28; Miller, *Hamilton*, 243.

6. *Annals*, II, 1467-68, 1471-73, Mar. 9, 10, 11, 1790; Mitchell, *Hamilton*, 73.

7. *Annals*, II, 1476-84, Mar. 11, 1790; Ames spoke further on the same subject on
Saturday, Mar. 13, *ibid.*, 1489-92.

ment. Madison, too, was highly critical, remarking that the contemplated changes "however veiled or varnished by ourselves could not be justified." [8] The rumblings of continued opposition to Hamilton's system were soon submerged in a violent storm which broke in the House. "You will wonder at the slumber which the report of the Secretary has enjoyed for more than a week; and still more at the business which has waked in its stead, the Quaker memorial," Ames wrote to George Minot late in March.[9] On the sixteenth, the House had turned again to the report on the Quaker anti-slavery petitions. Initially, Ames felt that the discussions which followed had the distinct advantage of delaying further consideration of the financial plan in the House since key representatives were out of town. When the dispute dissolved into invective, however, Ames considered it in a different light. Rarely was he so angry as on this occasion. Not only had the southerners condemned the Quakers, but they had attacked the eastern states in addition. The House deserved all the contempt it got, he insisted, because "language low, indecent, and profane has been used . . . wit equally stale and wretched has been attempted; in short, we have sunk below the General Court in the disorderly moment of a bawling nomination of a committee." [10]

He felt that the southern representatives lacked moderation and in this instance were aggressors who took an extreme stand on a sensitive issue because of an election year desire to appear as protectors of slavery. "The southern gentry have been guided by their hot tempers, and stubborn prejudices and pride in regard to southern importance and negro slavery," Ames remarked. He himself remained silent during the quarrel. "Upon the whole," he wrote, "I am ashamed that we have spent so many days in a kind of forensic dispute—a matter of moonshine." He voted against entering the report in the Journal of the House on the grounds that it was "highly exceptionable and imprudent" to express constitutional opinions in the official records of the lower house.[11]

The Quaker memorial created hostility that lingered after the House

8. *Ibid.*, 1484-86, Mar. 11, 1790.
9. Ames to George R. Minot, N.Y., Mar. 23, 1790, Ames, *Works of Ames*, I, 75.
10. Ames to Minot, Mar. 23, 1790, *ibid.*; *Annals*, II, 1500, Mar. 16, 1790; James Madison to Edmund Randolph, N.Y., Mar. 21, 1790, Madison Papers, XII, Lib. Cong. Madison commented, "The stile of . . . [the debates] has been as shamefully indecent, as the matter was evidently misjudged." Henry Wynkoop to Dr. R. Beattie, N.Y., Mar. 25, 1790, Beatty, ed., "Letters of Wynkoop," *Pa. Mag. of Hist. and Biog.*, 38 (1914), 193; William Smith to Gabriel Manigault, N.Y., Mar. 26, 1790, Ulrich B. Phillips, ed., "South Carolina Federalist Correspondence, 1789-1797," *American Historical Review*, 14 (1909), 778; Thomas E. Drake, *Quakers and Slavery in America* (New Haven, 1950), 103-6.
11. Ames to Minot, Mar. 23, 1790, Ames, *Works of Ames*, I, 75-76; *Annals*, II, 1523, Mar. 23, 1790.

returned to the financial program. Another New England congressman, Jonathan Trumbull of Connecticut, also reacted negatively to the interruption. "The whole of the past week has been wasted with the Quakers and the Negroes. . . . We shall not finish it [Quaker memorial] till Tuesday next, in the mean time all discussion of the Secretary's Report is at a stand." [12] Madison likewise regarded the recent controversy as "shamefully indecent," but thought assumption had lost ground in the meantime and would finally be defeated in the House. Ames estimated that there would be only a slim majority on the pro-assumption side, especially as a recently arrived delegate from North Carolina was reputed to be against the Hamiltonian financial program. The national government should be strengthened immediately, Ames insisted, by acting "firmly and justly" and approving the Secretary's program. Only in this manner could the jealousy of state governments be controlled. [13]

After the committee of the whole had completed its work on the Report on Public Credit, its resolutions were taken up by the House on March 29. It was evident on what difficult ground the Hamiltonians stood. By a close margin of three votes they were able to block adoption of a motion, presented by Hugh Williamson of North Carolina, to postpone consideration of the entire report. But when a motion was made to return the fourth resolution, dealing with assumption, to a committee of the whole House, Ames and other supporters of Hamilton were unable to muster the votes to defeat it. Subsequently a majority of representatives voted to return all resolutions which followed the fourth to a committee of the whole for reconsideration. [14]

By early April, the differences within Congress over the Hamiltonian system had created two strongly contending factions. Madison was openly acknowledged as the leader of the representatives hostile to the political and economic views of the Federalists. One interested spectator, Thomas Tillotson, commented that the dispute over assuming the debts had "created a Southern and Eastern party that rages with some degree of virulence. The *Amiable* and *Great* Maddison [is] at the

12. Jonathan Trumbull to Jeremiah Wadsworth, N.Y., Mar. 21, 1790, Jeremiah Wadsworth Papers, Box 140, Connecticut Historical Society, Hartford, Conn.
13. Madison to Randolph, Mar. 21, 1790, Madison Papers, XII, Lib. Cong.; Ames to Minot, Mar. 23, 1790, Ames, *Works of Ames*, I, 77; Theodore Sedgwick to Pamela Sedgwick, N.Y., Mar. 22, 1790, Sedgwick Papers, II, Box 3, Mass. Hist. Soc. Sedgwick explained the difficulties, "we have not only to support our measures, but we have also our party to keep in order." Smith to Manigault, Mar. 26, 1790, Phillips, ed., "South Carolina Federalist Correspondence," *Amer. Hist. Rev.*, 14 (1909), 778; Mitchell, *Hamilton*, 73.
14. *Annals*, II, 1529-31, Mar. 29, 1790; Thomas Hartley to Jasper Yeates, N.Y., Mar. 29, 1790, Yeates Papers, Hist. Soc. of Pa.; Oliver Wolcott to Oliver Wolcott, Sr., N.Y., Mar. 27, 1790, Gibbs, *Memoirs*, I, 43.

head of the former and the leader of the latter fights under cover, if any they have." [15] Senator Maclay, however, did not question the identity of the second leader; he was completely convinced that it was Hamilton himself who directed his "gladiators" in both the House and Senate. Young John Quincy Adams sensed the political outcome of the struggle. "The seeds of two contending factions appear to be plentifully sown. The names Federalist and Antifederalist are no longer expressive of the sentiments which they were so lately supposed to contain, and I expect soon to hear a couple of new names, which will designate the respective friends of the national and particular systems. The people are evidently dividing into these two parties." [16]

As the committee of the whole returned to the problem of assumption, the Hamiltonians were not united in their views of the best course of action. Some of the Pennsylvania delegation were considering a prudent compromise to fund only a part of the debts, while the New Englanders talked about walking out unless assumption were adopted along with the funding. Nevertheless, a number of Hamilton's supporters endeavored to win votes for their pet measure. With consummate skill they worked on the weak and the wavering to assure their adherence, and rumors of undue influence were rampant. According to Benjamin Rush, "nightly visits, promises, compromises, sacrifices, and threats" were commonplace both in New York and Philadelphia.[17] Although Ames was unqualified in his support of Hamilton's system, there is no evidence linking him with some of the highhanded tactics to which Federalists supposedly resorted.

When on April 12, the assumption proposition was brought to a vote for the second time in the committee, it met defeat by a vote of thirty-one to twenty-nine. None of the opponents seemed more elated than Senator Maclay, who gleefully wrote to Benjamin Rush, "Dismay seized the Sect's. group. Speculation wiped her eye and the Mass. men threat-

15. Thomas Tillotson to Horatio Gates, N.Y., Apr. 3, 1790, Horatio Gates Papers, N.Y. Pub. Lib.
16. Entry of Apr. 9, 1790, Beard, ed., *Journal of Maclay*, 229; John Quincy Adams to John Adams, Newburyport, Apr. 5, 1790, Worthington C. Ford, ed., *The Writings of John Quincy Adams*, 7 vols. (N.Y., 1913-17), I, 50; John Adams to John Trumbull, Mar. 9, 1790, Microfilm Reel No. 115, Adams Papers, Mass. Hist. Soc.
17. Theodore Sedgwick to Pamela Sedgwick, N.Y., Mar. 14, Apr. 3, 1790, Sedgwick Papers, II, Box 3, Mass. Hist. Soc.; Thomas Hartley to Jasper Yeates, N.Y., Apr. 11, 1790, Yeates Papers, Hist. Soc. of Pa.; Benjamin Rush to James Madison, Phila., Apr. 10, 1790, Madison Papers, XIII, Lib. Cong.; Rush to John Adams, Phila., Jan. 10, 1801, Butterfield, ed., *Letters of Rush*, II, 1076; Benjamin Goodhue to the Gentlemen of the Insurance Offices, N.Y., Apr. 11, 1790, Benjamin Goodhue Manuscripts, N.Y. Soc. Lib.; entries of Apr. 1, 2, 9, 1790, Beard, ed., *Journal of Maclay*, 223, 229-30.

ened a dissolution of the union." [18] In his journal the Pennsylvania senator described how stunned the Federalists were. "Ames's aspect," he related, "was truly hippocratic—a total change of face and features; he sat torpid as if his faculties had been benumbed." [19]

Both Gerry and Sedgwick were greatly disturbed, each vividly showing the emotional impact of the crisis. Gerry, looking "cadaverous," declared in sentences broken by nervous coughing that the Massachusetts delegates would press the point no further until they received instructions from their state. In contrast, Sedgwick vented his disappointment and anger in vehement criticism of the decision. He alleged that Massachusetts had not been accorded justice, and he accused the victors of pretense and mockery in offering to settle the Revolutionary War accounts apart from an assumption. When John Page of Virginia remonstrated, Sedgwick took his hat and stalked out of the hall.[20]

After this emotional outburst, Thomas Fitzsimmons ventured the heartening opinion that the members of the House might yet reconsider their vote. The Hamiltonians were irritated; still they were unwilling to abandon assumption and favored the creation of a special committee in the hope of reaching an "accommodation." The proposal to create such a committee, presented by Elbridge Gerry, was tabled, while the motion of George Gale of Maryland to resume the work of the committee of the whole was brought to a vote on April 15. A majority of the representatives supported the motion. Ames voted against it because he feared that the committee of the whole, having rejected assumption, might adopt only part of the Secretary's program.[21]

From his vantage point, James Madison observed the tenacity of the pro-assumption men, who quickly marshaled their strength to renew the political battle. "Massachusetts and South Carolina, with their allies of Connecticut and New York," he explained to Henry Lee, "are too zealous to be arrested in their pursuit unless by the force of an adverse majority." To James Monroe, he confided that the eastern members had not abandoned their goal and were determined to counter any provision for the public debt which did not encompass assumption, meanwhile calling attention to the dangers confronting the Union if it were not

18. *Annals*, II, 1577, Apr. 12, 1790; William Maclay to Benjamin Rush, N.Y., Apr. 12, 1790, Benjamin Rush Papers, Bancroft Transcripts, N.Y. Pub. Lib.

19. Entry of Apr. 12, 1790, Beard, ed., *Journal of Maclay*, 231.

20. *Ibid.; Annals*, II, 1578, Apr. 12, 1790; ? to Gen. William Irvine, Apr. 12, 1790, Gen. William Irvine Papers, X, Hist. Soc. of Pa. Satirical comments on the failure of assumption appeared in the *Gazette of the United States* (N.Y.), June 2, 1790, *Connecticut Courant* (Hartford), June 21, 1790; Mitchell, *Hamilton*, 74.

21. Entry of Apr. 12, 1790, Beard, ed., *Journal of Maclay*, 237; *Annals*, II, 1583, Apr. 15, 1790; Henry Wynkoop to R. Beattie, N.Y., Apr. 13, 1790, Beatty, ed., "Letters of Wynkoop," *Pa. Mag. of Hist. and Biog.*, 38 (1914), 193.

accomplished. "We shall risk their prophetic menaces," Madison concluded, "if we should continue to have a majority." [22]

Privately the Virginia representative had admitted that he could see certain good points in the idea of an assumption and felt that with some alterations it would not injure the financial interests of his state. But he was adamant in his resistance to Hamilton's mode of assumption. In a speech on April 22, Madison showed a conciliatory attitude; yet his argument was essentially a denial of the fundamental hypothesis, which Ames had defended, that the debts of the states incurred during the Revolution were actually debts of the national government. To proceed with assumption, committing the United States to add $25,000,000 to its debt without knowing whether this sum could be provided for, was precipitous and would hazard "the public faith in a manner contrary to every idea of prudence." [23]

Madison's verbal blows fell heavily on the hopes of the Hamilton group, who again looked to Ames to answer their chief antagonist with some rousing oratory. Representative Wynkoop of Pennsylvania expected Ames to reply to Madison the next day and take up the subject which "like Sylla and Charybdis [had] Dangers on every Side." [24] Before Ames could respond, he was blocked by a successful move on the part of Fitzsimmons to discharge the committee of the whole from further consideration of assumption. In disgust, Ames explained to Judge John Lowell that there had been "no opportunity . . . given to refute such bold, vague and groundless assertions." The continued reverses intensified his belief that the inability of the House to approve assumption jeopardized the government. "Those who see most clearly into the principles of Government and the human character will most disapprove the non-assumption," he commented.[25]

Still reluctant to consider Madison as a permanent political foe, Ames expressed admiration for the ingenuity of his mind and his extensive

22. James Madison to Henry Lee, N.Y., Apr. 13, 1790, Madison to James Monroe, N.Y., Apr. 17, 1790, Madison Papers, XIII, Lib. Cong.; Elias Boudinot to William Bradford, Apr. 15, 1790, Jane J. Boudinot, *The Life, Public Services, Addresses and Letters of Elias Boudinot, L.L.D.,* 2 vols. (Boston and N.Y., 1896), II, 61; Samuel Johnson to James Iredell, N.Y., Apr. 27, 1790, McRee, *Life of Iredell,* I, 286-87; Alexander White to Horatio Gates, N.Y., Apr. 16, 1790, Horatio Gates Papers, N.Y. Pub. Lib.

23. *Annals,* II, 1595-96, Apr. 22, 1790; Madison to Lee, Apr. 13, 1790, Madison Papers, XIII, Lib. Cong.; Miller, *Hamilton,* 247.

24. Henry Wynkoop to R. Beattie, N.Y., Apr. 22, 1790, Beatty, ed., "Letters of Wynkoop," *Pa. Mag. of Hist. and Biog.,* 38 (1914), 194.

25. *Annals,* II, 1597, Apr. 26, 1790; Ames to Judge John Lowell, N.Y., May 2, 1790, Manuscript Collection, Boston Pub. Lib.; George Cabot to Benjamin Goodhue, Beverly, May 5, 1790, Henry C. Lodge, *The Life and Letters of George Cabot* (Boston, 1877), 37.

learning. He was surprised, nevertheless, at the tone of his rival's latest speech since Madison had been considered a champion of the Constitution for such a long time. Point by point Ames recapitulated for Lowell the Virginian's argument, criticizing his specious reasoning and weak statements. Only Peter Pindar, the English political satirist, he insisted, "ought to answer this argument. It will not bear a serious refutation." [26] The sole result of the speech, Ames was convinced, would be to inflame Virginia even more against assumption.

With the divisive assumption issue shunted aside, the committee of the whole was able to reach agreement on the other provisions for the debt and submitted a report to the House. The outgrowth of this report was a bill to fund the debt, prepared by a committee of representatives and presented to the House early in May. No immediate action was taken, as the lower chamber had turned to other bills and to petitions which required legislative consideration. It was not until May 19 that the House returned to the bill on the public debt and resolved itself into a committee of the whole for discussion of a threadbare subject. In the course of debate, Elbridge Gerry presented a motion to reinstate the rejected assumption. Ames defended his colleague's proposal against swelling protest, reminding the committee that if the bill were adopted in its present form, nothing more would be done on the essential assumption question for the remainder of the session. Boudinot added his plea that the advocates of assumption should be given the opportunity to answer Madison's strictures and to present arguments which might convince a majority. The decision of the committee to return to a discussion of assumption gave Ames the right to reply to Madison's polemical speech of a month earlier.[27]

Although Madison had denied the principle that the state debts were debts of the nation, Ames pointed out that both sides in the assumption argument had admitted that the wartime expenses ought to be the government's "common charge." This admission, Ames contended, was proof that assumption was just. Congress in its resolves had acknowledged that "this war was between this country and Britain, and [was] not a war of particular States." Consequently the expenses should be equally apportioned. Ames had a ready solution—"assume the debts, and settle the accounts"; then the matter would be resolved. Opponents of assumption had contended that the accounts never would be settled.

26. Ames to Lowell, May 2, 1790, Manuscript Collection, Boston Pub. Lib.
27. *Annals*, II, 1599, 1601, 1607, 1610, 1639, 1642, 1645, Apr. 26, 27, 28, May 6, 10, 19, 24, 1790; Ames to Lowell, May 2, 1790, Manuscript Collection, Boston Pub. Lib.; Madison to Monroe, Apr. 17, 1790, Madison Papers, XIII, Lib. Cong.; George Thatcher to N. Wells, N.Y., May 25, 1790, Thatcher Papers, Mass. Hist. Soc.; Mitchell, *Hamilton*, 75-76.

There was no basis whatever for such an idea, for the Congress of the Confederation had agreed to a settlement. Commissioners were already actively at work on the project. "Who would oppose it?" Ames asked. "Not New England!—we wish it.... You ought to believe us when it is so easy to bring us to the test." If the House would take steps, he continued, to hasten the liquidation of accounts, further opposition to assumption of state debts would be eliminated.[28]

Ames then answered the contention that Congress had no authority to provide for debts which were exclusively of state concern. By investigating the Journals of the Continental Congress, Ames had found abundant proof that the requisitions by the Continental government to the states for supplies were not considered "debts against the States." Various resolves on the part of Congress recognized that the United States would bear the expense if the states furnished more than they were requested. "Liberty and independence were procured for the whole," he said. "Why then should not all contribute to the price?"[29]

The Massachusetts representative could not agree with Madison that assumption would be unjust to the states. He discussed at some length the inability of the states to pay their debts when the Constitution had deprived them of the impost. "Let the debts follow the funds," he asserted. Assumption could neither increase nor decrease the power of the government. Obviously it should promote public good, rather than evil, since its objects were "to produce equality of burdens and benefits, an uniform revenue system," and protection for both national and state governments from encroachments by the other. Instead of fearing a consolidation of state governments, the public should fear disunion, for a fragmented government was a feeble one. Adoption of assumption would benefit the Union; rejection would "beggar the Government and bind it in chains."[30]

Representative Henry Wynkoop of Pennsylvania called Ames's speech at this time "the Cream of that Debate." Even though the orator could evoke enthusiastic response from some representatives, he was not able to change the mood of the House with respect to assumption. A motion by George Gale to discharge the committee from further work on the debt bill was accepted, and on June 2, the engrossed bill, without provisions for assumption, passed the House.[31]

28. *Annals*, II, 1655-57, May 25, 1790; Ames's speech was printed in the *Columbian Centinel* (Boston), June 3, 1790.
29. *Annals*, II, 1658-59.
30. *Ibid.*, 1660-68; Mitchell, *Hamilton*, 76.
31. *Annals*, II, 1669, 1675, 1684, May 25, 27, June 2, 1790; Henry Wynkoop to R. Beattie, N.Y., May 27, 1790, Beatty, ed., "Letters of Wynkoop," *Pa. Mag. of Hist. and Biog.*, 38 (1914), 196; the *Boston Gazette*, July 5, 1790, later criticized

After the weeks of incessant labor in the legislature, Ames needed
a respite. A trip to Springfield was out of the question until an adjournment took place, or at least until the business of Congress was somewhat
less crucial, but he did promise Thomas Dwight a visit at the first opportunity. In the meantime he welcomed the chance to join several of
his colleagues on a week-end trip to visit the falls of the Passaic River
in New Jersey. With Sedgwick, Benson, William L. Smith, Nicholas
Low of New York, and others, he set out across the Hudson as soon
as the House adjourned on Friday afternoon, June 11. That evening
after enjoying a pleasant meal, the company reached Hackensack
where they found lodgings at an inn. The charm and freshness of the
countryside in June added to the good spirits of the congenial group.
Even a heavy rain the next day scarcely dampened their enthusiasm.
At the falls they observed the water cascading furiously over the rocks
and into a deep fissure. Sedgwick wrote in detail to his wife: "The
roaring of the water is heard at considerable distance, and adds greatly
to the pleasing horrors which the scene inspires." [32] While Ames remained at the crest of the falls, his friend clambered down over slippery
rocks vainly seeking a better view of the tumbling water. On Sunday
the group rode on to the village of Newark. Then in the evening they
returned to the unsolved problems and uncompleted work of the second
session.

The routine of congressional life for Ames continued to include offi-
cial social functions. In early May, he attended a dinner party given by
President and Mrs. Washington at their residence, Macomb House.
Among the ten guests from Federal Hall were Senator Maclay and
Representatives William L. Smith and Peter Muhlenberg. In one of two
large "public rooms," the guests took their places at a long table with
General and Mrs. Washington sitting opposite each other at the center.
The President and his wife carried on a desultory conversation with
those about them, but did little to dispel the air of solemnity which
characterized their formal entertaining. After a sumptuous feast at
which varied kinds of wine were served, the President drank the health
of each of his guests in turn. Maclay, although never greatly impressed
by dinners of state, left a brief record of this particular gathering.
"Went to dine with the President agreeably to invitation. He seemed

his speech: "Mr. Ames must be considered the American Demosthenes but should
force, decision and plain sense be the criterion, he would fall vastly short of obtaining the palm of eloquence."
32. Ames to Thomas Dwight, N.Y., June 11, 1790, Ames, *Works of Ames*, I, 81;
Theodore Sedgwick to Pamela Sedgwick, N.Y., June 14, 1790, Sedgwick Papers, II,
Box 3, Mass. Hist. Soc.

in more good humor than I ever saw him, though he was so deaf that I believe he heard little of the conversation." [33]

In Congress the prospect of favorable action on assumption during the current session had steadily dwindled. The attempts by Massachusetts members to block funding in the House unless assumption were accepted had been unsuccessful. Even Boston creditors, restive over congressional delays and desiring an immediate assumption, had become critical of their representatives. Ames was disheartened that the House had passed the bill on the public debt without assumption; yet he had not given up hope that the state debts would ultimately be assumed. If Hamilton's system were not enacted in its entirety, the government could not be secure. "Without a firm basis for public credit," Ames said, "I can scarcely expect the government will last long." [34]

Confronted by an immovable, though small, majority against assumption, the Hamiltonians seemed to have reached an impasse. The stalemate, however, was overcome by the Secretary of the Treasury himself. In a letter to James Monroe early in June, James Madison hinted at new developments. "The assumption," he wrote, "is still depending. I do not believe it will take place, but the event may possibly be governed by circumstances not at present fully in view." [35] The defeat of assumption in the House implied that only by extraordinary steps could a change in the balance of votes be secured. Hamilton seized the opportunity to take such steps when the question of the location of the capital was revived. As alliances burgeoned, he engaged in bold political bargaining to win enough support to salvage assumption.[36]

When Thomas Fitzsimmons presented a resolution on May 27 that the next meeting of Congress should be held in Philadelphia, he interjected a new element into the assumption struggle. The efforts of the Pennsylvanians to assure themselves of at least the temporary capital,

33. Entries of Aug. 27, 1789, Jan. 14, May 6, 1790, Beard, ed., *Journal of Maclay*, 134, 172, 251; Freeman, *Washington*, VI, 199-200, 226, 252; Fitzpatrick, ed., *Diaries of Washington*, IV, 128.

34. Ames to Minot, N.Y., May 20, 1790, Ames, *Works of Ames*, I, 78; Christopher Gore to Rufus King, Boston, May 6, 1790, King, *Life of King*, I, 386; Christopher Gore to Andrew Craigie, Apr. 25, 1790, Autograph Collection, VII, Special Collections, Columbia Univ.; Stephen Higginson to Alexander Hamilton, Boston, May 20, 1790, Syrett, ed., *Papers of Hamilton*, VI, 422-26; *Independent Chronicle* (Boston), May 6, 1790; see also Resolution of the Massachusetts General Court, Commonwealth of Massachusetts to the Senators of Massachusetts, June 4, 1790, Miscellaneous Documents Relating to the Establishment of the Government of the United States, Lib. Cong. The resolution supported assumption of state debts.

35. James Madison to James Monroe, N.Y., June 1, 1790, Madison Papers, XIII, Lib. Cong.

36. Miller, *Hamilton*, 247-48; Freeman, *Washington*, VI, 262.

the strong desire of the Virginians for the Potomac, and the determination of the easterners to remain in the convenient location of New
York City created an extremely complex situation in Congress.[37] By
the end of the month, the Pennsylvanians had triumphed by gaining
the approval of the House for the Philadelphia location for the next
session. "You have seen that *we* are sold by the Pennsylvanians, and the
assumption with it," a dismayed Ames wrote to Thomas Dwight.[38] He
was certain that the delegation from Pennsylvania had carried out an
agreement to defeat assumption in return for the temporary residence.
Rumors had been rife two months earlier that the Pennsylvanians, who
held a balance of power, might be willing to sacrifice assumption in
order to gain the temporary capital. Now the plot was unfolding. Ames
himself consistently voted against Philadelphia to "defeat this corrupt
bargain," even though in the first session he had strongly supported
Pennsylvania sites for the permanent residence.[39]

According to Ames, the Senate rejected the House resolution on
Philadelphia, and thus the residence topic was again brought up in the
lower chamber on June 10. Representatives opposing Philadelphia as
the temporary site proceeded to delay progress. Their counterparts in
the Senate also sought to thwart the removal to Philadelphia. At one
point in the discussion, they gained a necessary additional vote by
carrying in Senator William S. Johnson of Connecticut, who was recovering from an illness. Later, the senator was unable to leave his
lodgings because of a rainstorm. Taking advantage of this circumstance,
the pro-Philadelphia representatives attempted to hurry the Fitzsimmons resolution through the House and send it to the Senate before
Johnson could return. Gerry and William L. Smith, however, thwarted
the plot with its ludicrous overtones by conducting a filibuster until
the House adjourned. During these swiftly paced events, the lower
chamber voted in favor of Baltimore, and Philadelphia was struck out
of the resolution.[40]

For the moment Philadelphia was shelved, but Ames recognized how
useless this tempest over the capital was. In disgust at the continuing
intrigue, he commented that he would not oppose Fort Pitt if assumption were certain and Congress could proceed with its task peacefully

37. *Annals*, II, 1676, May 27, 1790; Theodore Sedgwick to Pamela Sedgwick,
N.Y., May 29, 1790, Sedgwick Papers, III, Box 1, Mass. Hist. Soc.; Mitchell,
Hamilton, 76-77. The House turned again to the residence question after it had
agreed with the Senate to consider unfinished business of the last session *de novo*.
38. *Annals*, II, 1681, May 31, 1790; Ames to Dwight, June 11, 1790, Fisher Ames
Papers, Dedham Hist. Soc.
39. Ames to Dwight, June 11, 1790, Fisher Ames Papers, Dedham Hist. Soc.;
Annals, II, 1679-82, 1692, May 31, June 11, 1790; Goodhue to Gentlemen of the Insurance Office, Apr. 11, 1790, Benjamin Goodhue Manuscripts, N.Y. Soc. Lib.
40. Ames to Dwight, June 11, 1790, Fisher Ames Papers, Dedham Hist. Soc.

and quietly. "But this despicable grog-shop contest, whether the taverns of New York or Philadelphia shall get the custom of Congress keeps us in discord," he remarked.[41] If the discussion were broadened to include the permanent residence, Ames suggested, then the pro-assumption group might be the deciding element in the vehement struggle over the Philadelphia and Potomac locations. The Pennsylvanians unfortunately stood in the way.

With constant attention to every shift of power in the House or Senate, the defenders of assumption "fasted, watched, and prayed," industriously exerting themselves in behalf of their cause. Sedgwick toiled unceasingly, and Goodhue swore "as much as a good Christian can" at the intractability of Congress.[42] By June 21 the nucleus of New Englanders and South Carolinians, who had so long championed Hamilton's system, were in the desperate position of having to vote against the ways and means bill which was to provide revenue for funding because they feared that assumption would be ignored once such revenue had been provided. To Maclay it looked as though the easterners were determined that if they could not "milk the cow their own way, they [would] not suffer her to be milked at all." [43]

Hamilton had in the meantime commenced adroit negotiations. Initially he approached the members of the Pennsylvania delegation through his new assistant in the Treasury, Tench Coxe, offering them the permanent residence if Pennsylvania would assure enough votes to pass assumption. After negotiating directly with Senator Robert Morris, Hamilton found his scheme faltering when he himself could not get support among New York congressmen for an immediate relocation of the capital in Philadelphia. Obviously there could be no effective coalition among the northern congressional delegations. Hamilton then began feeling out the Virginians about their price for enough votes to carry assumption in both houses.[44]

During the period when the residence–assumption negotiations were in progress, Ames was concerned about a Pennsylvania–Virginia alliance. If those two states were to combine their political strength to

41. *Ibid.*
42. *Ibid.*
43. Ames to Minot, N.Y., June 23, 1790, Ames, *Works of Ames*, I, 82; *Annals*, II, 1694, June 14, 1790; Elbridge Gerry to James Bowdoin, N.Y., June 25, 1790, Bowdoin-Temple Papers, Mass. Hist. Soc.; William Maclay to Dr. Benjamin Rush, N.Y., Apr. 24, 1790, Rush Papers, Bancroft Transcripts, N.Y. Pub. Lib.; Thomas Hartley to Jasper Yeates, N.Y., June 20, 1790, Yeates Papers, Hist. Soc. of Pa. Hartley stated, "The Eastern People want no funding without Assumption . . . and will of course reduce the ways and means as much as possible."
44. Dumas Malone, *Jefferson and the Rights of Man* (Boston, 1951), 299-303; Miller, *Hamilton*, 248-51. Brant, *Madison, Father of the Constitution*, 313; Mitchell, *Hamilton*, 80-84.

defeat assumption and to acquire the temporary and permanent capitals
as well, he was certain that easterners would be outraged. Perhaps the
strong stand New Englanders had taken in favor of assumption would
prevent the Pennsylvanians, in particular Robert Morris, from going
too far.[45] Admittedly, the debates in the House had not won over
enough votes for assumption; yet Ames did feel more assurance than
before, since the vehement opposition in Congress had been reduced.
Far better for the bill to pass on its own worth, he reasoned, than for
the pro-assumption group to have a bargain on their conscience. While
Ames was well aware of the realities of politics and the frequency of
bargaining and compromise, he had high ideals about appropriate political conduct of congressmen, and a revulsion from anything resembling
a surreptitious agreement. "I confess with shame," he stated, "that the
world ought to despise our public conduct, when it hears intrigue
openly avowed, and sees that great measures are made to depend, not
upon reasons, but upon bargains for little ones.... I repeat it ... with
pleasure, that we have kept clear of it." [46]

Hamilton reached a final agreement with Madison and Jefferson
which guaranteed that in return for sufficient votes to pass the assumption the capital would be at Philadelphia for ten years before moving
permanently to the Potomac. This resolution of the problem was an
especially difficult one for the New Englanders and New Yorkers to
accept. Senator King of New York reacted as had Ames to the terms
of the arrangement. King recorded that he had "remonstrated with
Mr. Secy ... and in a subsequent conversation told him that great and
good schemes ought to succeed on ... [their] own merits and not by
intrigue or the establishment of bad measures." [47] Christopher Gore
was likewise critical of the negotiations and was glad that his friend
Ames had not been drawn into the bargain.[48]

45. Ames to Minot, June 23, 1790, Ames, *Works of Ames*, I, 82; Ames to Dwight,
N.Y., June 27, 1790, Fisher Ames Papers, Dedham Hist. Soc.; Theodore Sedgwick
to Pamela Sedgwick, N.Y., July 4, 1790, Sedgwick Papers, II, Box 3, Mass.
Hist. Soc.
46. Ames to Minot, June 23, 1790, Ames, *Works of Ames*, I, 83.
47. Memorandum to Rufus King, June 30, 1790, King, *Life of King*, I, 385;
Miller, *Hamilton*, 251; Elbridge Gerry to James Monroe, N.Y., June 25, 1790,
W. C. Ford, ed., "Letters of Elbridge Gerry," *New Eng. Hist. and Geneal. Reg.*,
49 (1895), 430.
48. Christopher Gore to Rufus King, Boston, July 11, 13, 1790, King, *Life of
King*, I, 390-91; Thomas Dwight to Theodore Sedgwick, Springfield, July 19, 1790,
Sedgwick Papers, Vol. A, Mass. Hist. Soc. Dwight commented that "if such
jobbing, such shameful jockeying is to be the common mode of carrying private
points in our public councils ... I think we may safely predict a speedy end to our
existence as a nation." Freeman, *Washington*, VI, 263-64; Brant, *Madison, Father
of the Constitution*, 314-16.

There was little indication in Congress that the outcome of the residence issue was being decided behind the scenes. On July 6 the battle broke out with renewed fury on the floor of the House when the residence bill, worked out in the Senate, came before the lower chamber. The bill specified that Philadelphia should serve as the capital for a decade, the permanent capital to be on the Potomac thereafter. Unwilling to accept the southern site, Ames made a last-minute move to substitute Germantown, Pennsylvania, for the Potomac. His proposal was defeated thirty-nine to twenty-two. After making thirteen attempts to alter the bill, the opponents of the Potomac location were unable to whittle down the majority. Ultimately the bill, as it came from the Senate, passed the House by a margin of three votes. The first part of the bargain had been realized. To the last Ames and other members of the Massachusetts delegation voted against the residence bill.[49]

A resolution of the assumption quarrel was yet to come. Ames wanted to believe that "the game is in our hands." But as he considered the attenuated debate going on in the Senate over the bill on the public debt and noted the degree of dissension, he questioned whether the Hamiltonians could possibly achieve victory. "I begin to fear," he commented, "that we are but fifteen years old in politics ... and that it will be at least six years before we become fit for anything but colonies. We want principles, morals, fixed habits, and more firmness against unreasonable clamors." [50]

Late in July, the Senate returned the funding bill to the House with various amendments, one of which encompassed the assumption of state debts. Jackson attempted to renew the assault on this "wicked" measure and orated so loudly that the senators upstairs were forced to close their windows. While Jackson proposed dropping the amendment, several other representatives suggested altering it. Overcoming all objections, the House modified the Senate's amendment before approving assumption by a vote of thirty-four to twenty-eight. Madison clearly had kept his promise to deliver the necessary votes for passage.[51]

49. *Annals*, II, 1716, 1735-37, July 6, 9, 1790. The final vote on the residence bill was 32 yeas, 29 nays. Henry Wynkoop to R. Beattie, N.Y., July 9, 1790, Beatty, ed., "Letters of Wynkoop," *Pa. Mag. of Hist. and Biog.*, 38 (1914), 201-2. Wynkoop commented, "We shall have Yeas and Nays in abundance, tho' the majority is decided and there is not the most distant Prospect of defeating the Bill, yet the Opponents are determined to dispute its Progress in every part." Thomas Hartley to Jasper Yeates, N.Y., July 10, 1790, Emmett Collection, N.Y. Pub. Lib.
50. Ames to Dwight, N.Y., July 11, 1790, Ames, *Works of Ames*, I, 86; Theodore Sedgwick to Pamela Sedgwick, N.Y., July 13, 1790, Sedgwick Papers, II, Box 3, Mass. Hist. Soc.
51. *Annals*, II, 1741-67, July 23-26, 1790; Ames to Dwight, N.Y., July 25, 1790, Ames, *Works of Ames*, I, 87; John Steele to William B. Grove, N.Y., July 27,

Toward the very end of the debate on the public debt question, Ames took an intransigent position. He voted "yea" with the majority on assuming the state debts, but he refused to compromise and accept other amendments proposed by the Senate, feeling that they violated the Secretary's financial plan. In voting against most of the Senate amendments, Ames ironically found himself voting with opponents of the Hamiltonian system. Even Theodore Sedgwick criticized him for his unwillingness to yield in the interest of conciliation.[52]

After the long period of concentration on controversial legislative questions, Ames was eager for the adjournment of Congress. Even in early June he was anxious to go to Springfield, writing to Dwight in a veiled way, "I will not say that I have no other reason for the most impatient desire to see you there. You say 'I have rec'd yours inclosing one of your F's.' I wish I could claim property there." [53] Toward the end of the month, as the pressure of work increased, he remarked more vehemently, "While I am shut up here in this pigsty, smelling the perfumes from wharves and the raking of gutters, I long for the air and company of Springfield." [54] But until there was an assurance that the session was drawing to a close, he could not be free to follow the dictates of his heart.

To his keen disappointment he had already missed the marriage of Frances Worthington's eldest sister Mary to Jonathan Bliss of New Brunswick. Teasing Dwight about his own courtship of Hannah Worthington, Ames jestingly said that his friend would gather the Hesperian fruit ahead of him and make his mouth water. He would have enjoyed wishing the newlyweds bon voyage before they left for New Brunswick, but more especially he wanted to comfort Frances after the separation from her sister. At the latest, he informed Dwight, he would reach Springfield on August 16, and help "our fair friends" in the Worthington home "keep house." [55]

1790, Henry M. Wagstaff, ed., *The Papers of John Steele*, 2 vols. (Raleigh, 1924), I, 74. Steele maintained that "the passage of the bill was effected by a change in the sentiments of General Sumpter, Mr. White, Mr. Carroll, Mr. Lee and Mr. Gale." Mitchell, *Hamilton*, 79; "Vox Populi," *Columbian Centinel* (Boston), July 24, 1790.
52. *Annals*, II, 1769-72, July 29, 1790.
53. Ames to Dwight, June 11, 1790, Fisher Ames Papers, Dedham Hist. Soc.
54. Ames to Dwight, N.Y., June 27, 1790, *ibid.*
55. Ames to Dwight, N.Y., July 18, 1790, *ibid.*; Ames to Dwight, N.Y., Aug. 8, 1790, Ames, *Works of Ames*, I, 88; Dwight to Theodore Sedgwick, Springfield, June 24, 1790, Sedgwick Papers, Vol. A, Mass. Hist. Soc.; Thomas B. Warren, Springfield Families (Springfield, 1934-35), 768, typescript mss., Springfield Public Library, Springfield, Mass. For Bliss's loyalism see Jonathan Bliss to Luke Bliss, London, May 13, 1775, Springfield Pub. Lib.

On August 12 the session ended, and although the newspapers had pointedly criticized the slow proceedings, much had been accomplished. The controversial Report on Public Credit had been hammered into law. Despite Ames's reservations about the final form of the act, it essentially adhered to the Hamiltonian concepts of funding the domestic debt, assuming the state debts, and allocating the financial means to carry the provisions into effect. The elusive and complicated residence matter was settled, if only by compromise. To an extraordinary degree, however, the session had revealed the sharp realities of local economic and political interests.[56]

During this period Ames continued to rise in political stature. Invariably promoting Hamilton's financial theories, he became one of the small coterie of representatives who were instrumental in making the Secretary's system law. Ames was, in fact, obviously at the forefront of this group since he so often served as the spokesman in opposing Madison on the floor of the House. At thirty-two, his prominence in the congressional scene had given him national importance.[57]

56. Peters, ed., *U.S. Statutes at Large*, I, 138-44; Ferguson, *Power of the Purse*, 321-22, 326-43; Freeman, *Washington*, VI, 266-68; Miller, *Hamilton*, 253-54; Davis R. Dewey, *Financial History of the United States* (N.Y., 1903), 94-96; Thomas Dwight to Theodore Sedgwick, Springfield, July 19, 1790, Sedgwick Papers, Vol. A, Mass. Hist. Soc. Dwight expressed fears that "drawing a line between Northern and Southern interests" on all congressional questions would lead to a separation of the nation.

57. "An American," *Columbian Centinel* (Boston), Aug. 7, 1790. The writer remarked, "Gerry! and Ames! we hail thee as the guardians of our country's honour! While time remains we will remember your energy in support of Truth." Criticisms of the Massachusetts representatives and of Congress were in the *Independent Chronicle* (Boston), May 13, 27, July 1, Aug. 5, 19, 26, Sept. 2, 1790; *Boston Gazette*, July 5, 1790; *Salem Gazette*, July 27, 1790.

Chapter IX

Evolution of the National Bank

Congress was over for the present, but the months just ahead were destined to be full of activity for Fisher Ames. The trials of re-election were close at hand and were to be followed by a final session of the First Congress. No issue of the third session absorbed more of Ames's interest than the establishment of a national bank, which he felt was essential to the financial stability of the country. With his basic trust in men who controlled capital, he wanted a further centralization of monetary powers in their hands. Until this was achieved the unity of the nation still remained in jeopardy.

In the late summer of 1790, Ames was surfeited with the congressional scene; yet he had no serious thought of giving up his public career. In some measure of exasperation he wrote to Thomas Dwight, "I despise politics when I think of this office." He would endeavor to forget that he was a candidate for re-election in October and try to ignore being "gibbeted in Edes's newspaper," the *Boston Gazette*, which frequently had been unfavorable to him.[1] For the moment all that counted was seeing Frances Worthington in Springfield and receiving assurances that he still had a place in her heart. After a visit, he would have to face the mundane realities of dabbling in the law and of looking after his property in Dedham, which Nathaniel handled in his absence.[2] In addition he had to consider his political interest, for

1. Ames to Thomas Dwight, Aug. 8, 1790, Ames, *Works of Ames*, I, 88.
2. Nathaniel Ames to Fisher Ames, Oct. 18, 1790, Nathaniel Ames Papers, Dedham Hist. Soc. This receipt for £20 11s listed expenditures for wages, hay, and seed to June 5, 1790.

there were indications that he would confront determined adversaries in the forthcoming election.

"The election campaign is begun," a correspondent wrote from Boston to the New York *Gazette of the United States.* "I expect we shall have snarling enough, A⸺ and G⸺ [Ames and Gerry] have discovered so much independence of mind, that every step will be taken to prevent their re-election," he commented, adding pungently, "You know, some people think it is for the glory of God to serve the devil and perplex Government." [3] The opposition to Ames's re-election was intensified by public insistence on rotation in office, causing the rapid proliferation of candidates for Congress throughout the state. The *Salem Gazette* reprinted a prediction that there might well be 1,200 claimants for the Massachusetts seats in the House.[4]

Ames's challengers in Boston were but two, Benjamin Austin and Thomas Dawes. Austin, a member of a Boston mercantile family, had been a close supporter of Samuel Adams, and as a politician and pamphlet writer, championed the common man and the Whig spirit of the Revolutionary years. By constant attacks on the legal profession, as well as on so-called aristocrats, he became the spokesman of the Boston mob. His writings, under the pseudonym of Honestus, on *Observations on the Pernicious Practice of the Law* won him considerable local acclaim; and for a decade, until the Jay Treaty controversy in 1795-96, he was a thorn in the side of conservative political elements in Boston. In the election of 1790 he was decidedly the more formidable of Ames's rivals.[5]

Thomas Dawes, Jr., only a year older than Ames, had had a variety of political experiences as a member of the state constitutional convention in 1780 and as a delegate to the General Court. While widely known in Boston legal circles, he had not previously run for federal office. Dawes's hopes were largely grounded on the political support of Senator Tristram Dalton, while Austin had the assured backing of Governor Hancock's followers. Samuel Adams and Dr. Charles Jarvis took the lead in trying to undermine Ames's position and according to Gore, "were open, warm, and assiduous in favor of their candidate" [Austin].[6]

3. *Gazette of the United States* (N.Y.), Aug. 10, 1790.
4. *Salem Gazette*, Sept. 14, 1790, quoting from the *Massachusetts Centinel.* Opposition of the "real republicans" or Hancock supporters to the Federalists had been intense since the state election in Apr. 1790; *Independent Chronicle* (Boston), Apr. 9, 1790.
5. [Benjamin Austin], *Observations on the Pernicious Practice of the Law* (Boston, 1786); Samuel E. Morison, in *DAB* s.v. "Austin, Benjamin."
6. John H. Brown, ed., *The Cyclopaedia of American Biographies*, 4 vols. (Boston, 1900), II, 387; Christopher Gore to Rufus King, Boston, Oct. 23, 1790, King, *Life of King*, I, 393.

Attacks on Ames as the representative of Suffolk County began appearing frequently in the *Boston Gazette* and the *Independent Chronicle*. Writers took him to task for having aristocratic inclinations and for not voting according to the best interests of the state. One correspondent asked pointedly why Ames, the "Guardian of our Country's Honor should presume to originate a motion [on representation] contrary to the most positive instructions of the State Convention." The *Centinel*, he added, should answer that question and not "content themselves with blazing away on his *pretty sounding Speeches*." Others asserted Ames's voting record was unsound and contrasted his aristocratic principles with "the genuine principles of republicanism of Gerry." [7]

A clever satirical piece which appeared at this time compared the popular phrases of 1775 and 1790, revealing a fundamental shift in values. "*Vox populi, vox dei*," the phrase of 1775, had been supplanted by "democracy is a vulcano," a phrase taken from an early speech of Ames's. Supposedly, the common man had been forgotten, revolutionary "sons of liberty" who once had been heroes were now considered "state demagogues," and "equality of mankind" had given way to emphasis of the "well-born" on property. Such gibes at the conservative outlook were designed to persuade the public that Ames represented the new element in politics and not the Whig spirit of 1776. [8]

To counter the storm which was brewing against Ames, his political adherents, many of whom were among the well-born and wealthy, began to emphasize his accomplishments in Congress. A correspondent wrote to the *Independent Chronicle* that Ames did not merit "the ungenerous insinuations and electioneering slanders" which had appeared against him. The representative had always favored the interests of Massachusetts and in the assumption issue, "early and late, in and out of the House he . . . endeavored . . . to convince those who were opposed of its justice and policy." His integrity, too, was above question, for he was "not in the least concerned in the funds." [9] Taking the stand that the critics of Ames were ignorant and illiberal, his supporters vigorously refuted the attacks on him, showing that he gave "steady attention to promote the interest of Massachusetts as well as that of the

7. *Boston Gazette*, Aug. 9, Sept. 22, 1790, *Independent Chronicle* (Boston), Sept. 23, 1790.

8. *Independent Chronicle* (Boston), Sept. 2, 1790; John Adams to John Trumbull, N.Y., Mar. 9, 1790, Microfilm Reel No. 115, Adams Papers, Mass. Hist. Soc. Adams commented about the rise of a new political group in the nation, "There is a sett of smart young fellows who took their degrees at College since the revolution in 1774, who are now joined by the old Tories in opposition to the old Whigs."

9. *Independent Chronicle* (Boston), Aug. 19, 1790.

Union." "An American" condemned "faction [which] has excellent lungs and the pens of designing men [which] always run free" and reminded the public that Ames deserved gratitude for his share in achieving assumption. Other newspaper articles from a "Hingham Farmer," "An Elector," and the "Boston Victuallers" stressed that Ames had voted favorably on important legislation.[10]

By the eve of the election there was some indication that the electioneering furor was subsiding and that the desire for a change in representatives was dwindling. On Monday, October 4, the polls opened at ten o'clock in the morning and in the district of Suffolk 2,509 voters cast their ballots. When such biweekly papers as the *Columbian Centinel*, the *Massachusetts Gazette*, and the *Salem Gazette* went to press the next day, they were able to carry the news that Ames had far outdistanced his rivals. The complete Boston count showed 1,203 votes for Ames, 213 for Austin, and 128 for Dawes. By the twelfth, the selectmen of sixteen towns had submitted the returns, giving Ames 1,674 votes. The final total showed 1,850 for him, or 73.7 per cent of the ballots cast.[11]

Highly elated, Gore sent the news off to Rufus King, describing some of the circumstances of the election. "Ames' election in Boston was the highest possible evidence that cou'd be produc'd in favor of the Government," he wrote. In spite of the fact that the supporters of Dawes had resorted to extreme political practices bordering on the unethical, their candidate had lost. "The event showed, in a light truly mortifying," commented Gore with disdain, "the little influence and small effects of dishonorable means. Austin boasts that he had more votes than Dawes, and the latter confesses himself mortified that he was less successful than the former." [12] This election, Thomas Dwight remarked to Theodore Sedgwick, showed more evidence of coolness and dispassionate consideration of the candidates than formerly. Although Ames did not express his own feelings, he was sensitive to the opinions of his fellow men and could only interpret the results as approval by his constituents of his course of action in Congress.[13]

As a result of the election Federalists in Massachusetts had the assur-

10. *Columbian Centinel* (Boston), Aug. 4, Sept. 4, 11, 22, 29, Oct. 2, 1790.
11. *Salem Gazette*, Oct. 5, 1790; "A Remarkable Death, The Freedom of Elections," *Boston Gazette*, Oct. 11, 1790; Abstract of Votes, 1790, Mass. Archives, Office of the Secretary of the Commonwealth, State House. Dedham cast 62 votes for Ames, 5 for Austin, but neighboring Needham gave only 9 for Ames and 16 against him. Paul Goodman, *The Democratic-Republicans of Massachusetts, Politics in a Young Republic* (Cambridge, Mass., 1964), 50.
12. Gore to King, Oct. 23, 1790, King, *Life of King*, I, 393.
13. Thomas Dwight to Theodore Sedgwick, Springfield, Oct. 20, 1790, Sedgwick Papers, Vol. A, Mass. Hist. Soc.

ance that their representatives in the Second Congress would protect their interests. Both Benjamin Goodhue in Essex district and Theodore Sedgwick in Hampshire and Berkshire had amassed large majorities; in Middlesex Elbridge Gerry had won decisively over Nathaniel Gorham, at best only a lukewarm Federalist. Only in Worcester had there been an inconclusive contest between the Antifederal incumbent Jonathan Grout and General Artemas Ward, but in a second election, Ward won. George Thatcher from the District of Maine and Shearjashub Bourne, a political newcomer, completed the delegation from Massachusetts. The opponents of the Federalists, whether followers of Governor Hancock or Antifederalists, had been given a decisive setback, and for nearly a year there was little criticism in Massachusetts of the national administration.[14]

Early in December, Ames was en route to attend the opening of Congress, which had been set for the sixth of the month. Accompanying him on the long journey from Boston to Philadelphia, where the government would be in residence henceforth, were Senator Dalton and Oliver Phelps, a Boston businessman and land speculator. The party arrived in Philadelphia on Sunday, the fifth, wearied by the incessant jouncing of the coach and anxious to refresh themselves at the Indian Queen Tavern. Hardly had the newcomers alighted and taken a cup of tea than thieves broke into a storeroom and stole their trunks. Phelps lost about $20,000 worth of securities entrusted to him and about $10,000 of his own, while Dalton lost clothing and cash. Ames's baggage was not touched, and he jocularly explained that since his name was on the trunk, "the partial rogues took that as a mark, that nothing was to be got by taking it away. But see my good temper," he remarked. "I have not felt angry at the slight." Fortunately the trunks were recovered the next day; in the one belonging to Mr. Phelps the securities, still hidden in a letter, were found.[15]

The constant hubbub at the tavern impelled Ames to seek quieter lodgings, which he found at the home of a Mrs. Sage, where a number of congressmen had rented rooms. Sedgwick, who had been such a companionable fellow-lodger in New York, had not yet arrived from Stockbridge, and Ames was obliged to make arrangements without him. Ames wittily explained to Thomas Dwight that he was taking to heart the accusations of Benjamin Edes's *Boston Gazette* that he kept aristo-

14. Abstract of Votes, 1790, Mass. Archives, Office of the Secretary of the Commonwealth, State House; Morse, *Federalist Party*, 141; Freeman, *Washington*, VI, 286; U.S. Congress, *Biographical Directory of the American Congress, 1774-1961* (Washington, 1961), s.v. "Bourne, Shearjashub."

15. Ames to Dwight, Phila., Dec. 12, 1790, Ames, *Works of Ames*, I, 88-89.

cratic company. "I obey the admonition of my constituent. Instead of Sedgwick, Benson, and other bad company, I now lodge with Gerry, Ashe, Sevier, and Parker. Birds of a feather." [16]

Philadelphia, with its 42,400 inhabitants, was much larger than Boston and appeared to Ames to be "a very magnificent city." But after living in the new capital for three weeks, he remarked sharply that it was "becoming a London in wealth, and more than a London already in arrogance." Philadelphia was more public-spirited than Boston, he conceded, and had superior public institutions. "Here everybody is as forward to promote public objects as a Roman, and perhaps because, like a Roman, he thinks all the rest of the world barbarians." [17]

Congress met in a brick building located only a few rods to the west of Independence Hall at Chestnut and Sixth Streets. The new courthouse for Philadelphia County had been placed at the disposal of Congress, and both branches had adequate room within for their needs. The arrangement of the hall was pleasing, though utilitarian. Immediately beyond the Chestnut Street entrance was a space reserved for visitors, and above, a large gallery which could seat nearly 300 persons. The representatives' seats were placed in semicircular rows facing the Speaker's rostrum, which was at the west side of the room. Behind the rows of chairs was a lobby, and next to the Speaker was a space reserved for the assiduous shorthand notetakers. Natural light from the numerous arched windows and a glass chandelier made the room attractive. Tersely, Ames summed up his reaction to the hall: "Our accommodations to meet etc. are good." [18]

On the second day of the session, there already were enough members for a quorum. President Washington addressed both houses of Congress on December 8, recommending, as Hamilton had suggested to him, the reduction of the federal debt and turning the attention of the legislature to the encouragement of shipping and Indian affairs. While his speech was full of confidence about the state of the nation, it was far

16. Ames to Dwight, Phila., Dec. 23, 1790, *ibid.*, 91. Gerry was from Massachusetts, John Ashe and John Sevier from North Carolina, and Josiah Parker from Virginia.

17. Clement Biddle, *The Philadelphia Directory* (Phila., 1791), ix, 112. Ann Sage's Boarding House was at 105 North Front St., near the Delaware River. Ames to Dwight, Dec. 12, 1790, Ames, *Works of Ames*, I, 89; Ames to William Tudor, Phila., Dec. 30, 1790, "Memoir of Tudor," Mass. Hist. Soc., *Collections*, 2d Ser., 8 (1819), 323.

18. Description based on Blueprint of Committee on Preservation of Historical Monuments of Philadelphia, American Institute of Architects, Independence Hall National Monument; Ames to Dwight, Dec. 12, 1790, Ames, *Works of Ames*, I, 89; Theodore Sedgwick to Pamela Sedgwick, Phila., Jan. 9, 1791, Sedgwick Papers, II, Box 3, Mass. Hist. Soc.; *Gazette of the United States* (Phila.), Dec. 4, 1790.

from inspiring. Ames, Madison, and Tucker, who had been appointed to answer it, quickly prepared an address which contained "some divine molasses," as Ames expressed it. The representative from Massachusetts was far less sanguine than the President appeared to be, fully expecting a resumption of political controversy over financial questions. Anti-federalism still appeared to be rampant in Virginia; consequently Ames expected that there would be strong pressure against an effective excise and anticipated that "any other proper mode of provision for the State debts will rub hard." [19]

In mid-December 1790, Alexander Hamilton submitted to the House of Representatives two reports which contained his further recommendations on the establishment of public credit. The first report dealt with possible ways to increase revenue, and the second discussed the need for a national bank. To hasten the legislative process, the House referred the question of a bank, with several other issues, to the Senate. The representatives, actively working on various items, soon concentrated their attention on the proposed revenue changes. "Like good neighbors, we borrow and lend," Ames commented. Obviously he regarded the division of labor as logical since "the Senate were ousted of the greater part of the business" during the previous session.[20] The upper chamber entrusted the writing of a bank bill to a committee of five senators, including Schuyler of New York and Morris of Pennsylvania, both of whom were closely allied with Hamilton. The situation was promising; still Ames could see no basis for the bland assurances of some congressmen that the bank bill would easily pass both houses. In the light of the existing prejudice against all banks and antagonism from state banks, he foresaw the need to overcome substantial obstacles. By January 2, when the bill was still before the Senate committee, he wrote in a more hopeful vein to Thomas Dwight, "You will expect a little politics from me—the Bank is going on in the Senate. I believe it will pass—tho' I have thought the Conococheague folks would apprehend

19. Ames to Dwight, Dec. 12, 1790, Ames, *Works of Ames*, I, 89; *Annals*, II, 1770-73, 1835, Dec. 8-9, 1790; *Journal of the House*, I, 329; "Notes of Objects for Consideration of the President," Dec. 1, 1790, Syrett, ed., *Papers of Hamilton*, VII, 172-73; Freeman, *Washington*, VI, 287-88; Jacob C. Parsons, ed., *Extracts from the Diary of Jacob Hiltzheimer of Philadelphia, 1765-1798* (Phila., 1893), 167. Hiltzheimer noted that the President and members of Congress "attended a concert in the Lutheran Church."

20. Ames to Tudor, Dec. 30, 1790, "Memoir of Tudor," Mass. Hist. Soc., *Collections*, 2d Ser., 8 (1819), 323; "First Report on the Further Provision Necessary for Establishing Public Credit" and "Second Report on the Further Provision Necessary for Establishing Public Credit (Report on a National Bank)," Syrett, ed., *Papers of Hamilton*, VII, 225-35, 305-42; Charles A. Beard, *Economic Origins of Jeffersonian Democracy* (N.Y., 1915), 152.

that it would anchor the Gov't at Philadelphia and of course look sour at its passage." [21] To the task of drafting a plan for a national bank the Secretary of the Treasury brought his broad knowledge of the Bank of England's operations and of American banking practices. He was convinced that a national bank was a necessity for a vigorous government. As early as the winter of 1779-80, he had formulated a plan which became the basis of his banking proposals in 1790. The suggestions of Gouverneur Morris, William Bingham, Tench Coxe, and Samuel Osgood, men of practical business and financial skill, were useful to him. Hamilton's own service as legal counsel and as a director of the Bank of New York in the 1780's had given him actual experience in banking.[22]

Now, as in 1780, the primary objective of Hamilton was to restore public and expand private credit. A national bank, he contended, would not only establish the nation's finances on an orderly basis, but would result in support of the government by moneyed men. It would increase national productive capital and would aid the United States by creating a source of loans for emergencies. The institution would also facilitate the collection of taxes for the federal government. Hamilton proposed a privately directed bank under congressional charter with a capital of $10,000,000. Four-fifths of the stock would be offered to the public, while the remainder would be owned by the government. The bank would be empowered to issue notes, acceptable by the Treasury for all payments to the United States. It would carry on both the functions of a commercial bank and those of a central bank such as the Bank of England.[23]

Alexander Hamilton's latest financial projects were receiving serious consideration in both the House and Senate. While the senators debated the bank bill, the representatives turned to a new revenue bill which had been quickly prepared by a committee under Sedgwick's guidance.

21. *Annals*, II, 1782; Ames to Tudor, Dec. 30, 1790, "Memoir of Tudor," Mass. Hist. Soc., *Collections*, 2d Ser., 8 (1819), 323; Ames to Dwight, Phila., Jan. 2, 1791, Fisher Ames Papers, Dedham Hist. Soc. "Conococheague," the name of a small tributary to the Potomac, was applied as a nickname to the advocates of the Potomac site for a national capital. Bray Hammond, *Banks and Politics in America from the Revolution to the Civil War* (Princeton, 1957), 115.
22. "Introductory Note on the Report on a National Bank," Hamilton to ?, [Morristown, N.J., Dec. 1779–Mar. 1780], Tench Coxe to A. Hamilton, Phila., Mar. 5, 1790, Syrett, ed., *Papers of Hamilton*, VII, 236-56, VI, 234-51, 290. Coxe enclosed his pamphlet, *Thoughts Concerning the Bank of North America* (Dec. 1786); Broadus Mitchell, *Alexander Hamilton, Youth to Maturity 1755-1788* (N.Y., 1957), 346-55; James O. Wettereau, "Letters From Two Businessmen to Alexander Hamilton on Federal Fiscal Policy, November, 1789," *Journal of Economic and Business History*, 3 (1931), 673, 681-82.
23. Syrett, ed., *Papers of Hamilton*, VII, 334-37; Mitchell, *Alexander Hamilton*, II, 87-93.

In the first of his recent reports to the House, Hamilton had proposed raising an additional revenue of $800,000 annually through further import duties and through excise taxes on domestic goods. For imported spirits, he suggested a scale of duties from eight to fifteen cents more than the previous rates. Such spirits as rum, domestically produced from foreign raw materials, were to be taxed an additional eleven to thirty cents per gallon. Liquors entirely of domestic origin were now to be taxed between nine and twenty-five cents; or instead of this excise, stills producing these liquors were to be taxed sixty cents per gallon of their capacity. The House bill, incorporating Hamilton's ideas, at first evoked little opposition. Ames noted with pleasure the favorable trend. He expected that increased revenue would further bolster public credit, which now stood high. "It denotes health in the body politic," he wrote with conviction.[24]

Yet the new revenue bill did not have a smooth course, as several southern representatives were poised to challenge any increase in excise taxes. James Jackson, still vociferous in his opposition to the Hamiltonian program, condemned all excises as "odious, unequal, unpopular, and oppressive." [25] When the committee of the whole took up the question of imposing duties on domestic liquor, Jackson, Josiah Parker of Virginia, and Hugh Williamson of North Carolina protested strongly against taxes which would weigh heavily on their states. In reply, Ames sought to prevent the committee from dropping the excise in preference to other sources of revenue. He showed that the government had an obligation to obtain permanent funds to pay the interest on the national debt. Even though there might be a temporary surplus in the Treasury, there was no justification, in his estimation, for "not making complete provision" for the necessary revenue.[26]

Ames was relieved when the Federalists marshaled thirty-three votes to defeat Jackson's move to eliminate excise duties on domestic liquor. After the bill was reported in the House, the Massachusetts representative confided to Thomas Dwight that "we shall push it forward as fast as possible." Ames would have agreed with the explanation of his friend Sedgwick that the slow progress of the measure was due to many per-

24. Syrett, ed., *Papers of Hamilton*, VII, 226-28; Ames to Tudor, Dec. 30, 1790, "Memoir of Tudor," Mass. Hist. Soc., *Collections*, 2d Ser., 8 (1819), 322-23; *Annals*, II, 1876, 1885, Dec. 27, 30, 1790; Robert Morris to Gouverneur Morris, Phila., Dec. 31, 1790, William Short to Gouverneur Morris, Amsterdam, Jan. 30, 1791, Gouverneur Morris Papers, Special Collections, Columbia Univ.

25. *Annals*, II, 1890-94, Jan. 5-6, 1791; James Madison to Edmund Pendleton, Phila., Jan. 2, 1791, Madison Papers, XIII, Lib. Cong.; Theodore Sedgwick to Ephraim Williams, Phila., Jan. 20, 1791, Sedgwick Papers, III, Box 1, Mass. Hist. Soc.

26. *Annals*, II, 1893, 1907, Jan. 6, 11, 1791.

sons "from the Southward [who] are constantly hanging on our skirts and embarrassing every important measure of the Government." [27]

Although the proponents of the measure had a secure majority, there continued to be further obstacles to completing the House bill. To overcome some of the objections, Sedgwick proposed an amendment to the provision limiting the salaries of the revenue inspectors to be appointed by the President. Gerry quickly offered a counter-amendment, not only to limit the salaries of the inspectors, but also to obviate the President's right to choose these officials. According to Ames, Gerry orated on "the bugbear of influence gained by the Executive ... because it would empower him to establish offices, in effect, by fixing the pay, and forty other topics, were addressed *ad populum*." [28] Ames impatiently reminded the members of the House that there would barely be time enough in the remaining days of the session to complete the bill. He contended that it was important to give the executive the power to determine the salaries on the basis of the merit of the officials. Since the public supposedly disliked the bill, there was all the more reason to make the compensations for the inspectors large enough to attract "men of prudence and judgment." Despite his arguments, the House deleted the clause on paying the inspectors and ordered a separate bill drawn up regarding this detail.[29]

During the debate Ames did not condemn the moves of his colleagues, Sedgwick and Gerry, but privately he expressed his opinions to Thomas Dwight. "We should have passed the excise bill ... if ... one of our Massachusetts members [Gerry] had not seen anti-republicanism in the clause giving the President power to assign compensation to the inspectors." [30] He was provoked by the group in the House who constantly feared any increase in the powers of the executive. Typically Ames believed that the authentic danger was legislative aggrandizement arising from weak executive power.

The opponents of the revenue bill had been so persistent in amending the measure and in protracting discussion that Ames was not confident of immediate success. Yet in the last week of January the bill was passed by a substantial margin of fourteen votes and was forwarded to the Senate. In the upper house there was a renewed attack on the excise sec-

27. *Ibid.*, 1910, Jan. 11, 1791; Theodore Sedgwick to Ephraim Williams, Phila., Jan. 9, 16, 1791, Sedgwick Papers, III, Box 1, Levi Lincoln to Theodore Sedgwick, Jan. 12, 1791, Sedgwick Papers, Vol. A, Mass. Hist. Soc.; Ames to Dwight, Phila., Jan. 17, 1791, Fisher Ames Papers, Dedham Hist. Soc.
28. *Annals*, II, 1922, Jan. 20, 1791; Ames to Dwight, Phila., Jan. 24, 1791, Ames, *Works of Ames*, I, 93.
29. *Annals*, II, 1922-24, Jan. 20, 1791.
30. Ames to Dwight, Jan. 24, 1791, Ames, *Works of Ames*, I, 92.

tions of the bill which was sufficiently alarming to the Federalists to
bring Hamilton on the scene. Maclay noted that the Secretary had
worked closely with the Senate committee to whom the bill had been
referred in order to shape it to his liking. "Nothing is done without
him," the senator from Pennsylvania commented.[31] If the excise prevailed, he felt that Congress could go home, for it would prove Hamilton's supreme power. On February 12 the measure passed the Senate,
but became entangled in differences between the two chambers which
were not resolved until the end of the month. The controversial act had
even split the Massachusetts delegation. On the final vote in the Senate,
both Caleb Strong and Tristram Dalton, influenced by the opposition
of Boston distillers to the new rates, had voted against it. Their action
contrasted with Ames's pronounced support of the excise and his continued championship of the Hamiltonian program.[32]

While the Senate was struggling over the provisions of the House
excise bill, the representatives, in their turn, had begun to work on the
Senate bank bill. Moving swiftly through the first and second readings
in the House, the bank bill was referred to a committee of the whole.
After a single day of discussion it was returned to the House without
amendment on January 31. Then, when the bill was no longer open to
change, on the third reading, William L. Smith raised a question about
the lack of opportunity to discuss so vital an issue. Although he favored
the bill, Smith moved to return it to the committee, and thereby unleashed an intense debate in the House on the constitutionality of the
proposed bank. Other southerners, hostile to the bank, objected that
they were being tricked and deprived of the right to discuss the principles of the bill by the manner in which it was being pushed through
the House.[33]

Ames was rankled by their reasoning and was less prone to be equitable than Smith. The Hamiltonians had gained ground and he was in no
mood to yield. Answering Madison's appeal to the candor of the House,
he insisted that it was "absurd to go into a Committee of the Whole to

31. *Annals*, II, 1932-33, Jan. 25-27, 1791; *Boston Gazette*, Feb. 7, 14, 1791;
entries of Jan. 28, Feb. 5, 1791, Beard, ed., *Journal of Maclay*, 370, 374.

32. *Journal of the Senate of the United States, 1789-1815* (Washington, 1820), I,
362; Freeman, *Washington*, VI, 293-94; *Journal of the House*, I, 379, 381, 384, 386,
388, 391, Feb. 15, 17, 19, 22, 23, 25, 1791. The terms of the act are given in Peters,
ed., *U.S. Statutes at Large*, I, 199-214; James Madison to James Madison, Sr., Phila.,
Feb. 13, 1791, Madison Papers, XIII, Lib. Cong.; Ames to George R. Minot, Phila.,
Feb. 17, 1791, Ames, *Works of Ames*, I, 96; Oliver Wolcott to Oliver Wolcott,
Sr., Phila., Feb. 12, Mar. 5, 1791, Gibbs, *Memoirs*, I, 62, 63.

33. *Annals*, II, 1924, 1940, Jan. 21, Feb. 1, 1791; *Journal of the House*, I, 367;
Mitchell, *Alexander Hamilton*, II, 94-95; Rogers, *Evolution of a Federalist*, 218-19;
Boston Gazette, Feb. 7, 1791, under a Philadelphia dateline, Jan. 28, reported that
"it is expected the Bank Bill will receive but little opposition."

determine whether the bill is constitutional or not." [34] After the day's meeting was over Ames hastily wrote to Andrew Craigie, a prominent Boston financier, that the opponents of the bank had contended they had permitted the bill to pass the committee stage because of a misunderstanding regarding procedure. "They intreated to be restored freely to what they had lost by surprise," he commented. "This was denied them, 34 to 23. It was the old game of Assumption—voting a Bill a stage backwards." [35]

On February 2, Madison made a powerful speech in which he took a well-reasoned stand against a national bank, arguing that its disadvantages predominated and that it would not be beneficial as a financial institution. Then he introduced the fundamental issue whether Congress had the constitutional power to incorporate a bank. With cool logic he attempted to demolish any bastion behind which the Hamiltonians might stand. Madison considered the specific clauses in the Constitution under which a bank might be created. He held that none of the clauses could serve as a constitutional basis for the bank. To incorporate a bank was, in his view, "a precedent . . . levelling all the barriers which limit the powers of the General Government." [36]

After Madison's two-hour speech, Ames merely acknowledged that his adversary "spoke with his usual ability." He could not say whether the Virginian had swayed the House as a whole. Several days later, in writing to Thomas Dwight, Ames analyzed the speech. Warning his correspondent that it was hard to consider an opponent's arguments impartially, he remarked, "Take my opinion with due allowance;—it is, that his speech was full of casuistry and sophistry." To him it was a dull performance and "very little to the purpose, as no man would pretend to give Congress the power, against a fair construction of the Constitution." [37]

At the beginning of February, Ames came to the conclusion that once the speech-making was over, the bank bill would pass. Without revealing to his friends that he himself contemplated a rebuttal of Madison's argument, he prepared to undermine the position of the anti-bank representatives and allow them no chance to sway the undecided before the final vote. On February 3 he had his opportunity. Deliberately Ames set the tone of his speech by suavely shifting Madison's argument

34. *Annals*, II, 1943, Feb. 1, 1791.
35. Ames to Andrew Craigie, Phila., Feb. 2, 1791, Autograph Collection, Hist. Soc. of Pa.
36. *Annals*, II, 1951, Feb. 2, 1791; Brant, *Madison, Father of the Constitution*, 328-29.
37. Ames to Craigie, Feb. 2, 1791, Autograph Collection, Hist. Soc. of Pa.; Ames to Dwight, Phila., Feb. 7, 1791, Ames, *Works of Ames*, I, 94.

and dispelling any doubts about the usefulness of a bank. If it were a
question of granting power to Congress in order to establish a bank, he
was certain "that this House and all America would assent to the affirmative." [38] Ames moved quickly to an exposition of the Constitution.
Lurking beneath the smoothness of his argumentation were some spines,
sharp as a New England hawthorn's, on which he endeavored to impale
his adversary. Madison had been a member of the Constitutional Convention, and his objections to the constitutionality of the bank bill must
have been of long standing, Ames reminded his colleagues. "Why then,"
he wanted to know, "did he suffer the bill to pass the committee in
silence?" Madison's reasons for condemning the bank bill, Ames implied, had no real basis. Until now, "not a whisper has been heard . . .
against the authority to establish a bank"; yet "the old alarm of public
discontent is sounded in our ears." [39]

In light of the later discussion of the constitutionality of the bank by
Hamilton, Jefferson, and Edmund Randolph in their well-known ad-
visory papers for Washington, it is interesting to trace Ames's analysis
in his only speech on the bank bill. The orator observed that two questions were raised, the one being whether Congress could legitimately
exercise powers not specifically granted by the Constitution yet logically
derived from it, the other being whether these unexpressed powers gave
Congress the authority to establish a bank. Many people, Ames acknowledged, were perpetually afraid that Congress could only be arbitrary in basing legislation on implied powers. In their opinion, Congress
should not be allowed to use any powers but those expressly granted
in the Constitution. The Massachusetts representative held that to restrict Congress at this point and deny it the right to govern by implied
powers would be unrealistic. "A great part of our two years labor is
lost . . . for we have scarcely made a law in which we have not exercised
our discretion with regard to the true intent of the Constitution." [40]
Because it was clearly impossible for the framers of the Constitution to
anticipate all developments, the document contained principles, not a
precise interpretation of all possible legislation. It was left to the congressmen to use their best judgment in applying a principle to a given
question.

Implied power, so frequently used, was obviously not hazardous because of its novelty. Whatever danger it generated came from the uncertainty of the power rather than from its degree. Ames pointed out
that the opponents of the bank bill protested the exercise of unexpressed

38. *Annals*, II, 1953, Feb. 3, 1791; Mitchell, *Alexander Hamilton*, II, 96.
39. *Annals*, II, 1953-54.
40. *Ibid.*, 1954.

power by Congress; yet they did not outline explicit limitations of authority any more than the advocates did. Why should it be assumed in this case that the opposition was on "the safe side?" Actually "not exercising the powers we have may be as pernicious as usurping those we have not." [41]

If the Constitution must be interpreted in the present dispute, criteria for doing so should be established. Since the document did not enumerate in detail all that the government could do, it was logical, in Ames's estimation, to establish specifically what it could not do. A fundamental rule should be "Congress may do what is necessary to the end for which the Constitution was adopted, provided it is not repugnant to the natural rights of man, or to those which they have expressly reserved to themselves, or to the powers which are assigned to the States." [42] According to Ames, the creation of a bank would certainly not violate this interpretation. At a slightly later time Hamilton in his opinion on the constitutionality of the bank expressed a concept similar to that of Ames. "If the *end* be clearly comprehended within any of the specified powers," the Secretary stated, "and if the measure have an obvious relation to that *end*, and is not forbidden by any particular provision of the Constitution, it may be safely deemed to come within the compass of national authority." [43]

Continuing his speech, Ames stressed the supreme importance of a bank to the financial stability of the nation during emergencies. If Congress did not have the power to create a bank, it lacked the resources for self-preservation. He showed by example that implied powers had become an essential part of congressional authority. The legislature, he suggested, had as much right to establish a bank as to regulate the western territory. In the latter instance, Congress had not been granted express power to govern the area, but had assumed the authority either by implication or "from the nature of the case." Now the legislature exercised all governmental power in the western territory. Congress had even created a corporation, for the government of that section was a corporation. "And who will deny that Congress may lawfully establish a bank beyond the Ohio?" [44] He maintained, by analogy, that the government's right to establish a bank was irrefutable.

41. *Ibid.*, 1955.
42. *Ibid.*, 1956.
43. Alexander Hamilton, "Opinion as to the Constitutionality of the Bank of the United States," Feb. 23, 1791, Henry Cabot Lodge, ed., *The Works of Alexander Hamilton*, 12 vols. (N.Y., 1904), III, 445-93; Mitchell, *Alexander Hamilton*, II, 99-104.
44. *Annals*, II, 1957, Feb. 3, 1791. Ames's speech was reprinted in condensed form in the *Columbian Centinel* (Boston), Mar. 9, 1791.

Since the bank was to be incorporated, he next discussed the nature of corporations. Congress had the power to establish a public bank but could it create a private corporation to function in the same manner? Inasmuch as the legislature could exclusively regulate federal property, he indicated that it could also set up a corporation to administer the property. On this basis Congress could establish a bank "with corporate powers" on any federal land. In conclusion he reminded his audience that in adopting the Constitution there was every expectation that "national affairs [would be] under a Federal head," and he warned against attempts to "reason away the whole Constitution." [45]

Among the opponents of the bank, Michael Stone of Maryland attempted to rebut Ames's exposition of implied powers. The arguments of the Massachusetts representative, he maintained, were "hostile to the main principle of our Government, which is only a grant of particular portions of power, implying a negative to all others." [46] William Branch Giles, recently elected to Congress from Virginia, launched his congressional career with a lengthy speech characterizing Ames's reasoning as "an ingenious improvement upon sophistical deduction." [47] Although Fisher Ames was in the House while Giles "preached against the Bank," he was not stirred to make a rejoinder.

The Massachusetts Federalist was far more irritated by a second speech of Madison's, which delayed the final vote another day. Somewhat inconsistently, in view of the length of his own speech, Ames remarked, "Our time is precious, because it is short. We sit impatiently to hear arguments which guide, or at least change, no man's vote." [48] At last, on February 8, the members were satiated with the debate and demanded the main question. Largely by a sectional vote the bank bill passed the House, thirty-nine to twenty. Only three members south of the Potomac voted with the majority. Jonathan Grout, still an Antifederalist at heart, was the lone opponent of the bank from the East. Economic motives doubtless had an important bearing on the vote of individuals, but other factors preclude viewing the outcome as a victory for the economic interests of the security holders over the agrarian capitalism of the South. Ames was one who sensed that part of the southern dissension stemmed from a genuine fear that establishing the Bank of the

45. *Annals*, II, 1959.
46. *Ibid.*, 1979-81, Feb. 5, 1791.
47. *Ibid.*, 1993, Feb. 7, 1791; Dice R. Anderson, *William Branch Giles: A Study in the Politics of Virginia and the Nation from 1790-1830* (Menasha, Wis., 1914), 16.
48. Ames to Dwight, Feb. 7, 1791, Ames to Minot, Feb. 17, 1791, Ames, *Works of Ames*, I, 94-95. Referring to Madison's speech, Ames said, "Many of the minority laughed at the objection deduced from the Constitution."

United States in Philadelphia would center so many interests there that "ten years hence, Congress will be found fast anchored and immovable. This apprehension has an influence on Mr. Madison, the Secretary of State, . . . and perhaps on a still greater man." [49] Washington, to whom Ames obliquely referred, delayed in signing the bill until Hamilton, Jefferson, and Attorney General Randolph had given their opinions on the constitutionality of the bank. On February 25, the President finally added his signature to the document, making it law.[50]

In the remaining days of the session, the House resumed work at an accelerated pace on many of the bills it had postponed during the bank debate. With a crescendo of activity, the House and Senate brought the First Congress to a close on the third of March. After a round of final dinner and breakfast engagements with Tench Coxe, Oliver Ellsworth, and Elbridge Gerry, Ames set out at 9 A.M. on March 3 from Philadelphia for New York en route to Boston. He left just before Congress adjourned, with the assurance that his presence was not urgently needed. Accompanying Ames on the rough stagecoach trip were three congressmen from Massachusetts and young John Quincy Adams, who recorded in his diary that they encountered bad roads, poor fare, and uncomfortably crowded rooms in their three-day journey.[51]

During a brief stop in New York, Ames bought several law books, including the five volumes of Burrow's *Reports,* anticipating that he would need to refresh himself on the niceties of the law if he were to carry out a resolve to practice during the recess of Congress. Midway during the session, when it had been determined that Congress would not meet again until early November 1791, he had confided to Minot, "I shall try to turn out of my head all the politics that have been huddled into it, and to restore the little scraps of law which I once hoped to make a market of." [52] Jocularly he mentioned recent attacks

49. *Annals,* II, 2012, Feb. 8, 1791; Beard, *Economic Origins,* 156-57; Ames to Minot, Feb. 17, 1791, Ames, *Works of Ames,* I, 95-96; Joseph Jones to James Monroe, Jan. 27, 1791, S. Tucker to James Monroe, Williamsburg, Va., Feb. 10, 1791, Monroe Papers, Lib. Cong.; Madison to Pendleton, Feb. 13, 1791, Madison Papers, XIII, Lib. Cong.; Theodore Sedgwick to Ephraim Williams, Phila., Feb. 23, 1791, Sedgwick Papers, III, Box 1, Mass. Hist. Soc. Sedgwick expected the President to veto the Bank bill.

50. Freeman, *Washington,* VI, 291-94. The act establishing the Bank of the United States was entitled "An Act to incorporate the subscribers to the Bank of the United States," Peters, ed., *U.S. Statutes at Large,* I, 191-96. Congress passed a supplementary act regulating the procedure for payment of Bank shares which was approved Mar. 2, 1791, *ibid.,* 196-97.

51. *Annals,* II, 2016-24, 2032, Feb. 15, 17-19, 22, 25, Mar. 3, 1791; Ames to Minot, Feb. 17, 1791, Ames, *Works of Ames,* I, 96; John Q. Adams, Almanac Diary, Mar. 3, 1791, Microfilm Reel No. 19, Adams Papers, Mass. Hist. Soc.

52. Ames to Minot, Feb. 17, 1791, Ames, *Works of Ames,* I, 96; Bill from Samuel Campbell, Mar. 5, 1791, Chamberlain Collection, Boston Pub. Lib. Samuel

on the legal profession by writers in the Boston newspapers and commented that he was quite willing to be abused as long as he could have
his share of the profits.

Since law as a profession had never enthralled Ames, he was not
anxious to take up the details of the petty cases which would constitute
the bread and butter of his work. Yet if he ever expected to be in a
financial position to claim the hand of Frances Worthington, he would
have to plunge in and make the most of his opportunity. Hardly had
he returned to Boston than he set out once more for Philadelphia. The
sudden trip, possibly to transact business for Boston friends, delayed
his return to his practice, but by early May he informed Dwight that
he had opened his law office in Boston's King Street with Joseph Hall
as his new partner. His legal work was neither so overwhelming in
extent nor so pressing that he was forced to ignore public affairs. Ames
was primarily interested in domestic politics; yet he was very conscious
of the impact of the French Revolution on the United States and anxious to hear of the latest happenings. Samuel Breck, an acquaintance of
Ames who had just returned to Boston from Europe in May 1791,
recorded that the representative, "inquired with great eagerness for
French news." [53]

At gatherings in Boston where political conversation flourished,
Ames found congenial surroundings. Though he never made much of
social life, he relished the stimulus of interesting and prominent individuals. He was frequently at the center of a lively discussion, and his
opinions were much sought after by his circle of friends. Josiah Quincy
in his later years still had vivid recollections of such conversations between John Lowell, George Cabot, and Ames in the Quincy household.
As a youth, he had enjoyed "the brilliant conversation of Ames, so full
of imagery, drawing similes to illustrate the topics of his discourse
from everything about him." Quincy remarked that in a long and
varied life he had not heard anything equaling it.[54]

Campbell was the proprietor of the New Book and Stationery Store, No. 44
Hanover Square, corner of the Old-Slip, 1786-92. Burrow's *Reports* refers to Sir
James Burrow, F.R.S., F.A.S., *Report of Cases Adjudged in King's Bench in the
Time of Lord Mansfield beginning Michaelmas Term, 30th Geo. II, and ending
Easter Term, 12th Geo. III*, 4th ed., 5 vols. (London, 1790).

53. Ames to Minot, Feb. 17, 1791, Ames, *Works of Ames*, I, 96. Fisher Ames
had been admitted as Counsellor at the Supreme Court of the United States, Feb.
8, 1790, *Independent Chronicle* (Boston), Feb. 18, 1790; Ames to Dwight, Hartford,
Mar. 27, Boston, May 11, 1791, Fisher Ames Papers, Dedham Hist. Soc.; H. E.
Scudder, ed., *The Recollections of Samuel Breck* (Phila., 1877), 176-77.

54. Josiah Quincy to Charles Lowell, Boston, Mar. 30, 1857, Charles Lowell,
"Letters of Hon. John Lowell and Others," *Historical Magazine*, 1 (1857), 257.
Quincy in 1791 was 19 years old and had been graduated from Harvard in the

Ames was a perceptive observer in the social setting, finding ample cause for quiet amusement or wit. Attending a dinner and a ball given by Governor Hancock for several distinguished visitors, Fisher Ames observed that his host appeared pale and weak after another siege of gout, like "a plant that has grown out of a water bottle." At another dinner party, when the company was far less prominent, Ames concluded that one of his companions was a "precious fool," but had to admit that he had laughed at his absurd comments just the same.[55]

Late in April 1791, Thomas Dwight sent him news that he and Hannah Worthington, Frances's older sister, had been married on the fourteenth of the month. All winter Ames had been twitting Dwight about his forthcoming marriage. On one occasion when a letter was slow in arriving, he asked pointedly, "Are you dead, sick or married? Pray relieve my impatience by a line to let me know." [56] Now, regrets at missing the ceremony were genuine despite his jesting tone. "I should have seen the metamorphosis with curious eyes," he wrote Dwight in a congratulatory letter. "What is it? the changing of a young blade into a sober married man," he mused. He was more conscious than ever of his own single state. He was glad, at least, that in the excitement Dwight had remembered "an old friend who is obliged to abide sometime longer in this miserable bachelor state in which he lives to the halves." [57] At most Ames could look ahead to a long-delayed visit to Springfield after he carried out his plan of accompanying his sister Deborah to the Palmer hills of mid-Massachusetts. Then he could ask Dwight's advice in earnest whether he had best get married. There was no doubt in his mind, however, that he wanted Frances if she would have him.

Immersed again in the multiplicity of activities connected with his legal work, Ames found that he had to give up all thought of leaving until "after the last service" for the coming term of the Supreme Judicial Court. On the first of June he informed Dwight that "by staying here I shall do but little"; still "by going away for ten days, I should lose that." Meanwhile, he requested his friend to support his interest in the Worthington household. "I should regret the loss of my popularity

---

class of 1790. The conversations he referred to probably took place in the early 1790's. Edmund Quincy, *Life of Josiah Quincy* (Boston, 1867); James Walker, "Memoir of Josiah Quincy," Mass. Hist. Soc., *Proceedings*, 9 (1867), 83-156.

55. Ames to Dwight, Boston, May 11, June 4, 1791, Fisher Ames Papers, Dedham Hist. Soc.

56. Ames to Dwight, May 11, 1791, *ibid.;* the *Columbian Centinel* (Boston), Apr. 27, 1791, announced the wedding but no date was given. Warren, Springfield Families, 768, gives the date, Apr. 14, 1791; Ames to Dwight, Phila., Jan. 2, 17, 1791, Fisher Ames Papers, Dedham Hist. Soc.

57. Ames to Dwight, May 11, 1791, Fisher Ames Papers, Dedham Hist. Soc.

there too much to put it at risk. As you are now a married man, I may safely trust my affairs to your management." [58] After two weeks of steady work he could write Dwight that Deborah and he would begin their " 'flaming course' toward Springfield" on the coming Wednesday. Currently he was recovering from the stiffness and fatigue induced by a long and unaccustomed ride on horseback to Dedham under a blazing sun. The scheduled reunion apparently took place at the Worthington home in Springfield, but Ames's legal work forced him to return to his office by July 5.[59]

Back in Boston, he was soon exposed to mutterings of dissatisfaction with Congress or the government. He was perturbed that people could not see the great benefits the new nation, and particularly the Federalists, had brought to them. Commenting on the local occurrences in Boston during the extraordinarily hot and dry summer, which had withered crops, Ames observed with amusement, "I tremble for the pumpkins. A bad crop of that vegetable might impair the credit of the new Gov't and bring murmurs and antifeds into vogue again." [60] For the time being Federalists need have no fears, he was certain, because their political adversaries were quite subdued.

Ames was inevitably preoccupied with affairs of state. When an inquiry reached him from Alexander Hamilton about the Bank of the United States, Ames tried to aid the Secretary of the Treasury as he formulated new fiscal policies. In a succession of letters, Ames showed a clear understanding of the reaction of Boston businessmen to fundamental Bank policies, and he revealed, moreover, the nature of his own relationship to Hamilton. Since allying himself with Hamilton's supporters in Congress, Ames's admiration for the Secretary had increased. Earlier in the summer he had written to an acquaintance in Philadelphia, "I know, I respect, I can almost say, I love our Secretary." [61]

Ames obviously knew Hamilton well enough to jest with him; yet he looked upon him with especial respect. He wrote in one letter, "We have you exhibited here in wax. You see that they are resolved to get money by you in every form." In another he questioned whether a letter which Hamilton had requested him to transmit to Mrs. Mercy Otis Warren might be a love-letter.[62] Ames expressed his opinions in a typically vigorous and unreserved manner. His evaluation of Hamilton,

58. Ames to Dwight, Boston, June 1, 1791, *ibid.*
59. Ames to Dwight, Boston, June 14, July 5, 1791, *ibid.*
60. Ames to Dwight, June 14, 1791, *ibid.*
61. Ames to Dr. McKee, Roxbury, June 10, 1791, *ibid.*
62. Ames to Alexander Hamilton, Boston, Aug. 15, 1791, Oliver Wolcott Papers, X, No. 65, Conn. Hist. Soc.; Ames to Hamilton, Boston, July 31, 1791, Hamilton Papers, XVI, No. 99, Lib. Cong.

Evolution of the National Bank   177

however, led him to the point of flattery. He praised the Secretary's great influence in public affairs, stressing how grateful the Bostonians were for the Bank. "They know who merits the praise of it and they are not loth to bestow it," he stated. Such expressions may simply have reflected Ames's courtesy; but when he wrote, "You are so much, and I so little an actor in this affair that I do not ask your correspondence," he assumed a deferential manner that was not routine with him. Yet he obviously did not regard Hamilton with the same feeling of awe as he did Washington.[63]

From friends in Boston financial circles, Ames gathered that there was great confidence in the prospect of a national bank. Nevertheless, many businessmen objected to the distribution of Bank stock which gave Philadelphians a major control. More than anything, they were disturbed that Thomas Willing, President of the Bank of North America, probably would be elected head of the Bank of the United States. So pliable an individual, it was feared, would fall under the spell of Robert Morris, who would "make a property of this man." Willing's appointment, in Ames's opinion, would create a dissatisfied group in Boston. "An idea that the bank will be hazarded by partiality to men who will make desperate speculations would be a bad one to get currency," he warned, though he indicated he was in no way trying to put pressure on the Secretary.[64]

Since its inception the Bank of the United States had signified to Fisher Ames far more than a useful economic institution in the nation. In his correspondence with Hamilton it was eminently clear that he regarded the political consequences of the Bank's existence of transcendent importance. In his opinion another effective means had been devised by the Secretary of the Treasury to ensure the continued success of the new government and to counteract the rivalry of the states. If the economic powers of the Bank were wisely used, for example by loaning money at 5 per cent, then, he assured Hamilton, it would be possible to "overpower the State banks." Better terms for borrowers, it was evident, would win the national bank the support of the "safer people." The local institutions, favored by state political leaders who would use them to flaunt state sovereignty, had the potential to undermine the Bank. Ames foresaw that they readily might "become dangerous instruments in the hands of State partizans, who may have . . . points

63. Ames to Hamilton, July 31, 1791, Hamilton Papers, XVI, Lib. Cong.; Ames to Hamilton, Aug. 15, 1791, Wolcott Papers, X, No. 65, Conn. Hist. Soc.
64. Ames to Hamilton, July 31, 1791, Hamilton Papers, XVI, Lib. Cong.; Hammond, *Banks and Politics*, 122; Christopher Gore to Rufus King, Boston, June 13, 1791, King, *Life of King*, I, 399; Goodman, *Democratic-Republicans*, 37-42.

to carry." To guard against such developments, there was only one feasible course. "All the influence of the moneyed men ought to be wrapped up in the Union, and in one bank." [65]

It might prove impossible to eliminate the state banks, he reasoned, but an effective means of exerting control over their policies could be developed if the stockholders in the state banks would invest in and establish "sub-banks" connected with the national bank. The result would be the absorption of the capital and a decrease in the business of the state banks. Ames hoped that no "cold water would be thrown upon the plan of sub-banks" even if the dominant Philadelphia investors were unfavorable to the idea. Boston financiers had been very eager to have a branch of the Bank established in their city. Searching for a way to achieve their goal, they hit upon the idea of merging the existing Massachusetts Bank with the Bank of the United States and re-creating it as a branch. The state bank appeared to Ames "ready to give up the ghost," and he found that a substantial number of shareholders were willing to make the change in anticipation of greater future gains. When the news reached him that the Secretary of the Treasury was supporting a totally different plan of partnerships rather than the merger of the state banks into the national institution, he was disconcerted. The Bank of New York, he had heard, was to "reserve a number of their shares for the acceptance of the U.S. Bank so as to create a kind of partnership." Under the circumstances, Ames recognized that the project of the Bostonians was in jeopardy and that the state banks might be perpetuated.[66]

Without doubt there should be no delay in improving the position of the Bank, he argued, but in Boston at least the opinion of business circles was strongly against the latest move of Hamilton. "I know that you are as much an unitarian in politics as I am," Ames reminded Hamilton.[67] Only if the Bank were able to take over "the whole business" would it perform the functions the Federalists had envisioned. Enhancing the status of these local institutions might well undermine the Bank of the United States because they retained the "liberty to issue Bills at pleasure" and could flood the financial markets with their paper. "So cheap an augmentation of capital would enable them to give longer

65. Ames to Hamilton, July 31, 1791, Hamilton Papers, XVI, Lib. Cong.; concerning Hamilton's opposition to branch banks, see Hammond, *Banks and Politics*, 126.

66. Ames to Hamilton, July 31, 1791, Hamilton Papers, XVI, Lib. Cong.; Joseph S. Davis, *Essays in the Earlier History of American Corporations*, 2 vols. (Cambridge, 1917), II, 52; Ames to Hamilton, Boston, Sept. 8, 1791, Wolcott Papers, X, No. 66, Conn. Hist. Soc.

67. Ames to Hamilton, Aug. 15, 1791, Wolcott Papers, X, No. 65, Conn. Hist. Soc.

credit and better terms than heretofore" which might result in excluding the notes of the Bank from circulation. The conclusion Ames drew from his "preaching" was that to foster any union of the two banking systems "would give life, too long life, to those who are ready and willing to die." [68]

In Boston the national-minded among businessmen continued to look forward to the opening of a branch bank with a degree of impatience which Ames could fully share. Friends of his like Christopher Gore, whom he had highly recommended to Hamilton, also opposed the contemplated association between the state-chartered Bank of New York and the national bank. Not until November of 1791 was an acceptable plan for establishing branches worked out; yet even a month later, Ames reported from Congress that there was "talk here about some connection to the State Banks, which tho favor'd by the Secty possibly may not be proposed." The objective, he explained, was to end competition and "to put at risk in the separate Banks no more stock than what the U.S. Bank may possess there—whereas now it is alleged each Branch has unlimited powers to involve the Great Bank and a failure in one wd. produce distrust of all." [69]

The desire of some Boston stockholders in the Bank of the United States to have a more effective voice in its affairs led them to nominate fourteen Bostonians, including Ames, for directorships in the new bank. Some disgruntled stockholders protested publicly in the *Centinel* that the decisions had been made by a self-chosen committee and that balloting had been far from secret. According to Stephen Higginson, Boston speculators maneuvered to get proxies for their election to the main board of directors, chosen in October, on the grounds that only these men could ensure the establishment of a Boston branch. When the election took place on October 21 in Philadelphia, Ames, Cabot, Jonathan Mason, Jr., and Joseph Barrell were the Massachusetts men chosen as directors until the first annual election in January 1792.[70]

The task of the newly elected directors was a strenuous one. Not only did the board consider the business of the main bank and the

68. *Ibid.*
69. Ames to Hamilton, Sept. 8, 1791, *ibid.*, No. 66; Ames to Tudor, Phila., Nov. 24, 1791, "Memoir of Tudor," Mass. Hist. Soc., *Collections*, 2d Ser., 8 (1819), 323-24; Ames to Tudor, Phila., Dec. 31, 1791, F. L. Gay Collection, Mass. Hist. Soc.; Christopher Gore to Rufus King, Boston, Aug. 7, 1791, King, *Life of King*, I, 400-401.
70. "A Stockholder," *Columbian Centinel* (Boston), Sept. 24, 1791; Stephen Higginson to LeRoy, Bayard and Co., Boston, Oct. 8, 1791, Gratz Collection, Hist. Soc. of Pa.; James O. Wettereau, "New Light on the First Bank of the United States," *Pa. Mag. of Hist. and Biog.*, 61 (1937), 276. *Gazette of the United States* (Phila.), Oct. 19, 26, 1791.

granting of discounts on loans at its weekly meetings, but it also had to formulate policies and choose officers for the branch banks which were being established in Boston, New York, Baltimore, and Charleston. In the January election Ames received 3,602 votes for another term of office. The pressures of his congressional activities, however, made him feel that he could not continue on the board in spite of the fact that several of his close friends and colleagues, such as Cabot, King, and William Smith, were on it. In mid-March 1792, he wrote to President Willing of the Bank, "the reasons depending on my attendance on the public business have become even more urgent, and oblige me to renew my request that my place be considered as vacant." [71]

From all indications Ames's decision seems not to have been grounded in any personal conviction that there might be a conflict of interest for a legislator to hold a position in a private institution which had unusually close connections with the government. At this time Ames did not come under public pressure from political opponents to resign from the board of directors, although questions about legislators holding multiple offices had been raised in Massachusetts, creating quite a minor political storm. In the early days of the Bank's history, the presence of congressional members on the board was accepted. Some critics, however, advocated keeping them, as well as speculators and lawyers, at a minimum number. Not until some time after Ames's resignation, when the Treasury Department was under investigation in 1793, did the issue flare up, causing George Cabot to yield to complaints, sell his Bank stock, and resign from the board of directors.[72]

The continuing current of opposition to the Bank and to the entire structure of the Hamiltonian financial system grew appreciably with the rapid surge of speculation in public securities during the summer of 1791. From the end of June until early in August, security prices rose as the rage to buy Bank scrip spread through the business groups

71. Davis, *History of American Corporations*, II, 52; *Gazette of the United States* (Phila.), Nov. 2, 19, 1791; James O. Wettereau, "Branches of the First Bank of the United States," *Journal of Economic History*, 2 (1942), 75; Christopher Gore to Rufus King, Boston, Dec. 25, 1791, Jan. 29, Feb. 1, 1792, King, *Life of King*, I, 403-6; *Columbian Centinel* (Boston), Jan. 18, 1792; *Gazette of the United States* (Phila.), Jan. 7, 1792. A list of directors of the Boston branch is given in the *Columbian Centinel*, Jan. 28, 1792. Ames to Thomas Willing, Phila., Mar. 17, 1792, Etting Collection, Administration, I, Hist. Soc. of Pa.; Ames to Dwight, Phila., Mar. 8, 1792, Ames, *Works of Ames*, I, 115. Ames explained that he had accepted the position with the understanding that he intended to resign when the branch banks had been established.

72. *Boston Gazette*, Feb. 1, 15, 1790. Wettereau, "Branches of the First Bank," *Jour. of Econ. Hist.*, 2 (1942), 77; George Cabot to Alexander Hamilton, Mar. 4, 1793, Lodge, *Letters of Cabot*, 73; Cabot to President of the Bank of the United States, Dec. 23, 1793, Gratz Collection, Hist. Soc. of Pa.

in Philadelphia, New York, and Boston. Those who had no money willingly borrowed from banks at a high rate of interest. Madison spoke out emphatically to Jefferson that the subscriptions to the Bank were "a mere scramble for so much public plunder which will be engrossed by those already loaded with the spoils of individuals . . . of all the shameful circumstances of this business, it is among the greatest to see the members of the legislature who were most active in pushing this job openly grasping its emoluments." [73] As stock prices soared higher in each succeeding week, public alarm grew, and newspaper articles as well as private letters communicated apprehensions that the fragile bubble would burst. Some writers attempted to exert a restraining influence on the plunging speculators, even reminding them in verse that:

> For soon or late so Truth advises
> Things must assume their proper sizes
> And, sure as Death all mortals trips
> Thousands will rue the name of Scrips.[74]

When the inevitable reaction set in, between August 11 and 16, prices fell to a considerably lower though still inflated level. To both Hamilton and Ames the increase in stock values of the preceding months was highly significant, for the government securities had at last risen to par. Ames wrote to the Secretary of the Treasury, "the late rise of paper and bank stock tho' now declining has excited no small share of envy among those who might have made money by it, yet did not." He remarked that the increasing security prices reflected "the solidity of the principle on which you founded your system of finances as it shows the reduction of the rate of interest to be in fact as well as in theory a fair ground of bargain with the creditors." [75] A rising market

73. John B. McMaster, *A History of the People of the United States, from the Revolution to the Civil War*, 8 vols. (N.Y., 1883-1913), II, 39. Davis, *History of American Corporations*, I, 202-8; Miller, *Hamilton*, 268-71; James Madison to Thomas Jefferson, N.Y., July 10, Aug. 4, 8, 1791, Madison Papers, XIV, Lib. Cong.; John Taylor, *An Enquiry into the Principles and Tendency of Certain Public Measures* (Phila., 1794).

74. *Gazette of the United States* (Phila.), Aug. 10, 1791, reprinted in the *Columbian Centinel* (Boston), Aug. 20, 1791. A longer poem, "The Bank Scrip Bubble," appeared in the *Columbian Centinel* (Boston), Aug. 24, 1791. Thomas H. Perkins to J. Stilli, July 15, 1791, Thomas H. Perkins Letter Book, Mass. Hist. Soc.; John Inglis to William Constable, London, Oct. 8, 1791, Constable Letters, 1791, Constable-Pierrepont Papers, N.Y. Pub. Lib.; *Columbian Centinel* (Boston), Aug. 13, 1791, *Boston Gazette*, Aug. 15, Dec. 12, 1791; Henry Lee to James Madison, Aug. 24, 1791, Madison Papers, XIV, Lib. Cong.

75. Ames to Hamilton, Aug. 15, 1791, Wolcott Papers, X, No. 65, Conn. Hist. Soc.; a similar view is in "A Traveller," IV, *Gazette of the United States* (Phila.), Oct. 12, 1791. Davis, *History of American Corporations*, I, 203.

appeared not to hold any dangers for the government in Ames's view, but was evidence that Hamilton's financial plans were vindicated.

Ames's outlook raises the question whether he himself had been involved in purchasing or speculating in government securities or in Bank stock while a member of Congress. In 1793 when the Treasury Department was under fire from the Republicans, Jefferson compiled a list, later included in the "Anas," of those members of Congress who were security holders. Ames was mentioned as one of the nineteen "paper men" who actually held either Bank or other government stock. John Taylor, in his *An Examination of the Late Proceedings in Congress,* listed Ames, Cabot, and Gerry as among the Massachusetts congressmen who probably held Bank stock.[76] Many years later in 1811, Benjamin Rush wrote to John Adams in regard to the establishment of the Hamiltonian financial system and asserted bluntly that the funding system was passed by bribery. Many individuals, according to Rush, "were seduced by certificates previously purchased at 2/6 in the pound. Among these Mr. Boudinot and Mr. Ames were ... conspicuous. ... How many other members of congress were seduced by certificates put into their hands for the purpose of obtaining their votes, I know not." [77]

While the statements of Jefferson and Taylor were not as accusatory as those of Rush, the inference from them was that Ames had profited from legislation which he had helped carry through Congress. Charges of wrongdoing rarely were imputed to him, but in the hotly contested election of 1794 the Republican *Independent Chronicle* accused him of making a fortune by speculation. Ames's political associates refuted these assertions by stating candidly that he had invested profits from his legal work in securities and that "this amounted to about 600 dollars specie laid out in three and six per cents and to the purchase of twelve shares in the Bank at the first price making in all about 1800 dollars, specie." [78] From the financial records now extant it is not possible to determine with accuracy the sources and extent of his personal estate, but there is evidence that he had more capital than this public statement of his holdings revealed.

In December 1791, Ames corresponded with Andrew Craigie in re-

76. "The Anas," Mar. 23, 1793, Paul L. Ford, ed., *The Writings of Thomas Jefferson,* 10 vols. (N.Y., 1892-99), I, 223; John Taylor, *An Examination of the Late Proceedings in Congress, Respecting the Official Conduct of the Secretary of the Treasury* (Richmond, 1793), 26; Beard, *Economic Origins,* 166-67, 203.

77. Benjamin Rush to John Adams, Phila., Jan. 10, 1811, Butterfield, *Letters of Rush,* II, 1076-77.

78. "Plain Truth" and "A Consistent Republican," *Independent Chronicle* (Boston), Oct. 20, 1794, *Columbian Centinel* (Boston), Oct. 22, 1794.

gard to reinvesting his capital. He had a balance of £567 according to a statement Craigie had sent him, and on the basis of his friendship he asked the financier to "*consider* how that balance, and as much of the defer'd stock in yr. hands as you may chuse to add to it may be employ'd to my best profit." Ames was entirely undecided how he should apportion his capital and indicated that Craigie had failed to advise him whether to transfer his twelve shares of Bank stock to 6 per cent stock. It seemed urgent to Ames to make a move immediately as he understood that any transaction would have to be made before December 15.[79]

When Ames had heard nothing from Craigie by the eighth, he wrote more insistently about his business transactions: "I am rather solicitous to have the thing done and done correctly. Pray do the needful—." He was still in a quandary how his property should be invested, but he assured his friend he still had confidence in his willingness to advise him. From the deferred stock in his name he expected $3000 specie, and by adding the £567 as well as an additional sum, he hoped to have between $5000 and $6000 to invest.[80]

The existing records of the Treasury Department only partly reveal Ames's subsequent transactions. In Ledger A of the Loan of 1790, Six Per Cent Stock, preserved among the Old Loan Records of the Treasury Department, there are several entries which indicate that Ames carried out his intention of reorganizing his capital. On December 14, 1791, there was a transaction in Ames's name of $1800 through H. and S. Johnson and Co., Merchants of New York City; and seven months later, on July 11, 1792, another sum of $1800 was entered under the heading "To Pres. & Directors & Co." The last entry probably refers to a transfer of 6 per cent stock to the Bank of the United States.[81]

Ferreting out the investments in securities held by Ames is further complicated by the fact that, on occasion, he acted as attorney and agent for friends in Boston to transfer their stock or collect the interest due them. He himself referred to such a transaction when he wrote to Dr. John Warren that he was sending him "the warrants for placing the note (which I funded for you in my own name on the Treasury Books) to your credit in Mr. Appleton's Office." In the Register of Owners, Loan of 1790, Ames is listed as owner of Certificate 1409 for

79. Ames to Andrew Craigie, Phila., Dec. 2, 1791, N. Paine Papers, Amer. Antiq. Soc.

80. Ames to Craigie, Phila., Dec. 8, 1791, *ibid.*

81. Ledger A, Loan of 1790, 6% Stock (N.Y.), XXII, 80, "Old Loans," Records of the Bureau of the Public Debt, National Archives. Samuel Eliot Morison, "The India Ventures of Fisher Ames, 1794-1804," Amer. Antiq. Soc., *Proceedings*, New Ser., 37 (1927), 14; McMaster, *History of the United States*, II, 37.

$163.71, drawing interest from October 1, 1791.[82] This sum, therefore, might well have been that which Warren entrusted to him.

From the available evidence there is no proof that Ames was engaged in any large-scale speculations in securities during the boom of 1790-92. His investments in comparison with those of his friend Christopher Gore were extremely modest. Whether he purchased depreciated securities through Andrew Craigie while Congress was debating the funding and assumption bills in 1790 is a moot question. Nothing in his correspondence indicates that he was using his position for his private benefit or that of his friends, despite Benjamin Rush's later allegations. To place Ames among the security-holders in Congress is quite correct, but to speculate that Ames's votes in support of Hamiltonian measures were motivated by a desire for personal economic gain would constitute a misunderstanding of the man and his motives.[83]

82. Ames to Dr. John Warren, Phila., Nov. 2, 1791, Ames to Tudor, Dec. 31, 1791, F. L. Gay Collection, Mass. Hist. Soc.; Oliver Everett to Ames, Dorchester, Feb. 21, 1793, Gratz Collection, Hist. Soc. of Pa.; Register of Owners, Loan of 1790 (Mass.), Vol. 1119M, "Old Loans," Records of the Bureau of the Public Debt, National Archives. Ames's name is also in the index to Three Per Cent Domestic Stock, 339, Index to Three Per Cent Stock, Massachusetts Office, 8, Index to Records of Various Loans, Vol. 296A, 296B, 296C, National Archives. The ledgers listing the transactions are missing from the records. Philip D. Largerquist *et al.*, *Preliminary Inventory of the "Old Loans" Records of the Bureau of the Public Debt, No. 52*, National Archives (Washington, 1953), entry No. 141, 32.

83. Register of Owners, Loan of 1790 (Mass.), Vol. 1119M, lists Gore as owning $11,132.85 in 6% stock, and $105,131.35 in 3% stock, "Old Loan" Records, National Archives; Beard, *Economic Origins*, 182. Beard in analyzing the economic interests of Congressmen takes the position that, in general, these men represented their constituents' views rather than their own economic interests *per se*.

Chapter X

The Glow of Faction

Toward the middle of October 1791, Fisher Ames left for Philadelphia to be on hand for the opening of the Second Congress on the
twenty-fourth.[1] This session was to be significant in that the national
party system was crystallizing and issues were largely decided on the
basis of party affiliation. For Ames personally, the coming months
brought to an end his life as a bachelor; before another year had passed
he married Frances Worthington.

The change of pace of the congressional recess had relaxed him, and
he was in a buoyant frame of mind. Upon reaching the temporary
capital, he found a room in the same boarding house with five North
Carolina congressmen. Since rooms were at a premium there was little
chance of keeping the Massachusetts delegation together. Senators
Caleb Strong and George Cabot had taken lodgings near those of Theodore Sedgwick; Shearjashub Bourne was housed "in a hovel by himself"; and Benjamin Goodhue had obtained accommodations "at the
back part of an obscure house." Ames wryly regarded his own position
as that of a peaceable man living socially with the southerners, but he
speculated that their political creeds had better not be compared. In
conversations around the fireside, he had begun proselyting, and it

1. Ames to Thomas Dwight, Phila., Oct. 30, 1791, Ames, *Works of Ames*, I, 99;
the *Gazette of the United States* (Phila.), Oct. 22, 1791, mentions Ames's arrival
within the previous week.

seemed as though he were gaining ground. At least he found that they began "to lick molasses." [2]

Life in a boarding house, despite the proximity of congressional friends, made Ames doubly aware of his basic loneliness. Thomas Dwight's advice that it was time for him to marry coincided completely with his own wishes. In writing to Dwight, he expressed high hopes about the outcome of his courtship of Frances Worthington. "A man's patience holds out the better for seeing the work of his deliverance making a progress," Ames commented. During periods when letters were infrequent, he felt like a banished man who was ignored by those more fortunately married. "You have been sleeping in clover," he teased Dwight. "I do not mean in the barn, neither." [3]

In the opening weeks of the new Congress, Ames observed that politics appeared to be asleep, while the members engaged in a "petite guerre" full of rhetorical froth. Even so, there must be constant vigilance to protect the achievements of the First Congress. He believed that "the first acts [of the previous Congress] were the pillars of the federal edifice. Now we have only to keep the sparks from catching the shavings; we must watch the broom, that it is not set behind the door with fire on it." [4]

It became clear, as the session progressed, that the emerging political parties were now the commanding forces in the House. Spurred by James Madison, the opponents of the Federalist tenets had become increasingly unified in their opposition. The Republicans, as they called themselves by 1792, considered their first task to be the protection of the Constitution as it was conceived, against the plot of the Federalists to alter it and to subvert the principles of republican government. During the winter of 1791-92 some seventeen congressmen, mostly from southern states, voted with Madison on a majority of significant issues. At the same time, from thirteen to fifteen representatives of the total number of sixty-five in the House regularly took the Federalist position. The Republicans and the Federalists were now struggling to secure the support of the third element, which was politically uncommitted.[5]

2. Ames to Dwight, Phila., Nov 22, 1791, Ames, *Works of Ames*, I, 100; Ames to Dwight, Phila., Dec. 12, 1791, Fisher Ames Papers, Dedham Hist. Soc.; Theodore Sedgwick to Pamela Sedgwick, Phila., Nov. 6, 1791, Theodore Sedgwick to Ephraim Williams, Phila., Dec. 4, 1791, Sedgwick Papers, III, Box 1, Mass. Hist. Soc.
3. Ames to Dwight, Phila., Nov. 20, 1791, Fisher Ames Papers, Dedham Hist. Soc.; Ames to Dwight, Oct. 30, 1791, Ames, *Works of Ames*, I, 99.
4. Ames to George R. Minot, Phila., Nov. 30, 1791, Ames to Dwight, Oct. 30, 1791, Ames, *Works of Ames*, I, 103, 100; Ames to William Tudor, Phila., Nov. 24, 1791, "Memoir of Tudor," Mass. Hist. Soc., *Collections*, 2d Ser., 8 (1819), 324.
5. Malone, *Jefferson and the Rights of Man*, 420-77; Brant, *Madison, Father of the Constitution*, 349-55; Miller, *Federalist Era*, 99-102, 108-18; Freeman, *Washing-*

Ames regarded the division within Congress largely as the product of sectional interests, and the southern states as the source of existing discontent. On the basis of his contacts with southern congressmen, both around the fireside and in the heat of debate, he compared regional political attitudes for his circle of friends in Boston. The northern states, equated in his mind with New England, had become far more aware of the need for law and order to protect property since Shays' Rebellion. "The men of sense and property, even a little above the multitude, wish to keep the government in force enough to govern." Essential elements of this society, namely money, credit and trade, as well as the industry of people, interacted beneficially.[6] In contrast to the northern concept of the place of law in government was that of the southerners. Members of the dominant upper class in the South conceived of the law as a device for perpetuating a *status quo*. "At the southward, a few gentlemen govern; the law is their coat of mail; it keeps off the weapons of the foreigners, their creditors, and at the same time it governs the multitude, secures negroes, etc., which is of double use to them." [7] Because they wished to maintain their own economic and social position, a number of southern gentlemen preferred that their primary allegiance should be to their individual states. Ames exempted William Smith and his constituents in Charleston from criticism since they were ardent Federalists with a broader outlook.[8] Initially, many people in the South had supported the federal government, but in Ames's opinion, had reconsidered, inasmuch as it did not provide them with an immediate solution to their particular problems. He scathingly evaluated their present attitude, "A debt-compelling government is no remedy to men who have lands and negroes, and debts and luxury, but neither trade nor credit, ... nor the habits of industry." [9] Adoption of the funding system had sharpened the dissatisfaction of southerners who felt that the taxes they paid were a tribute to the

ton, VI, 305; Charles, *Origins of Party System*, 23-25, 52; Noble E. Cunningham, *The Jeffersonian Republicans: The Formation of Party Organization, 1789-1801* (Chapel Hill, 1957), 3-49, 267-72; Wilfred E. Binkley, *American Political Parties, Their Natural History* (N.Y., 1947), 29-71; Stuart G. Brown, *The First Republicans, Political Philosophy and Public Policy in the Party of Jefferson and Madison* (Syracuse, 1954); William L. Smith, *The Politicks and Views of a Certain Party, Displayed* (n.p., 1792); Massachusettensis (pseud.), *Strictures and Observations on the Executive Department of the United States* (n.p., 1792).

6. Ames to Minot, Nov. 30, 1791, Ames, *Works of Ames*, I, 103.
7. *Ibid.*
8. Ames to Minot, Nov. 30, 1791, *ibid.*, 103; U. B. Phillips, ed., "The South Carolina Federalists," *Amer. Hist. Rev.*, 14 (1909), 529-43, 731-43.
9. Ames to Minot, Nov. 30, 1791, Ames, *Works of Ames*, I, 104; Harry Ammon, "The Formation of the Republican Party in Virginia, 1789-1796," *Journal of Southern History*, 19 (1953), 283-310.

security-holding easterners. Large, strong states like Virginia and the Carolinas were excessively haughty. "The pride of the strong is not soothed by yielding to a stronger," Ames observed. Southern Antifederal leaders, among them Patrick Henry, had "assiduously nursed the embryos of faction," to create a party in opposition to the current administration.

An unobserving public was not aware of this hostility on the part of the South. "Tranquility has smoothed the surface. But . . . faction glows within like a coal-pit." For the time being, as long as Washington lived, Ames thought that the disruptive tendencies would remain under control and might be mitigated by encouraging peace and good laws, both of which would improve the southern economy. But he could not help feeling uneasy about the "immense mass of sour matter . . . fermenting at the southward." [10] Ames was convinced that the eastern and middle states were the locus of the real strength of the Union.

Administration of the government according to southern precepts was an impossibility; therefore, he urged that Federalists uphold a vigorous national government. Federalist principles were simple. "We must have a revenue . . . an excise. . . . The debt must be kept sacred; the rights of property must be held inviolate. We must, to be safe, have some regular force, and an efficient militia." [11] Only by adhering to these goals could there be any assurance of preventing a governmental crisis. He believed that awakening the "Massachusetts parties" to these dangers might create a public united in favor of the Federalist administration. Ames himself was certain that there should be only one sentiment. In Congress the dilatory proceedings of the members made him impatient. Interminable deliberation seemed to exclude any real progress toward essential objectives. "We talk a great deal," he remarked. "Will that atone for doing little?" The legislature would meet his approval only if it recognized its responsibility to enhance federal authority. "Consolidation is a bugbear which scares not only those who are in the dark, as might be expected, but those in the broad daylight." [12] Ames was fearful that political dissension might disrupt the nation before it could achieve its potential greatness. In his mind the emergence of an opposing party was not a natural phase of political evolution, but evidence of a faction dedicated to undermining all the foundations of a stable, well-ordered, and effective government. "Faction in this govern-

10. Ames to Minot, Nov. 30, 1791, Ames to Dwight, Phila., Jan. 23, 1792, Ames, *Works of Ames*, I, 104-5, 110. John Adams made similar observations. See John Adams to John Trumbull, Jan. 23, 1791, Adams, ed., *Works of Adams*, IX, 573.
11. Ames to Minot, Nov. 30, 1791, Ames, *Works of Ames*, I, 105.
12. Ames to William Tudor, Phila., Dec. 31, 1791, F. L. Gay Collection, Mass. Hist. Soc.; Ames to Minot, Phila., Feb. 16, 1792, Ames, *Works of Ames*, I, 112.

ment," he explained, "will always seek reenforcements from State factions, and these will try, by planting their men here, to make this a State government." [13] Devising new theories of ruling or changing the form of the government would not suffice to make people more national-minded, he averred. This could only be accomplished by reforming the habits of political thinking. "Instead of feeling as a Nation, a State is our country. We look with indifference, often with hatred, fear, and aversion, to the other States." [14]

Ames's concern for his own state was not diminished by his concern for the nation's unity. In fact, his participation in the first important debate of the Second Congress revealed again his regional sympathies. At issue was the question of reapportioning the representation in the House on the basis of the returns of the first census. According to the Constitution the number of representatives had been specified for each state, the total being sixty-five members. A proposed amendment to the Constitution, establishing a ratio of one representative to every 30,000 of population until the House membership reached 100, had not as yet been ratified by the states. The lower chamber, therefore, now had the task of determining the ratio of representation. Congressmen debated whether the apportionment should be carried out on the basis of the proposed 1:30,000 or a ratio closer to 1:40,000. Ames continued to think that the House could conduct its business more efficiently with a smaller membership. He disagreed with the majority when the ratio of 1:30,000 was approved by the committee of the whole. When the committee's resolution came before the House, Ames supported an unsuccessful attempt to change the ratio to 1:34,000, and thereby restrict the size of the House. But the ratio of 1:30,000 remained in the bill, which would give Massachusetts fifteen representatives and Virginia twenty-one out of the total. After the House passed the bill on November 24, 1791, the Senate amended it, altering the ratio to one representative to 33,000 people, a change reducing the numbers of representatives in some states. Massachusetts, New York, Pennsylvania, Maryland, and North Carolina lost one representative each, and Virginia lost two, while the other states kept the same number as in the House version.[15]

13. Ames to Minot, Feb. 16, 1792, Ames, *Works of Ames*, I, 113. The use of the term "faction" was typically Hamiltonian; Malone, *Jefferson and the Rights of Man*, 421.

14. Ames to Minot, Feb. 16, 1792, Ames, *Work of Ames*, I, 113; Jeremiah Smith to John Smith, Phila., Apr. 20, 1792, John H. Morison, *Life of Jeremiah Smith* (Boston, 1845), 59. Smith stressed that neither of the two parties, whether the friends or the enemies of the funding system, had the good of the nation in sight.

15. *Annals*, III, 148, 191, Oct. 31, Nov. 15, 1791; Joseph Jones to James Monroe, Dec. 3, 1791, Monroe Papers, Lib. Cong.; Ames to Minot, Phila., Dec. 23, 1791, Ames, *Works of Ames*, I, 108; R. H. Lee to H. Lee, Mar. 25, 1792, James C.

Upon the return of the bill from the Senate, Ames plunged into the discussion with zest, arguing strongly that the House should agree to the Senate amendments. He expressed the opinion that the House version of the bill was unjust, for it proposed giving Virginia twenty-one representatives instead of the nineteen to which the state was actually entitled on the basis of its census. The total population of the states of Vermont, New Hampshire, Rhode Island, Connecticut, New Jersey, and Delaware was considerably greater than that of Virginia; yet under the provisions of the bill, these six states would have a total of only twenty-one representatives, the same number as Virginia. Ames maintained that the distribution of seats was neither equal nor constitutional. As a part of his analysis he brought up the sensitive issue of the means by which an apportionment was to be carried out. The question was whether the ratio of representation should be applied on a state-by-state basis or on a nationwide basis. If the first method were used, Ames indicated that there would be a larger residual fraction of unrepresented people. The obvious and just method was to determine the total number of representatives and then to apportion them according to the constitutional stipulations. Pointedly he remarked, "But this method would not suit the present emergency; for that would give Virginia nineteen members and no more." Convinced that the amendments would make apportionment equitable, Ames insisted on accepting them.[16]

On December 19 the House formally voted to reject the Senate changes. An equally determined upper house stuck to its position with the result that further progress was completely blocked and the measure was dropped. As Ames remarked at the conclusion of the debates, "what did we Yankees do but mount the high horse, and scold in heroics against the disfranchisement of the other States." It had been to no avail, for the House had to begin anew on another representation bill.[17]

Ballagh, ed., *The Letters of Richard Henry Lee*, 2 vols. (N.Y., 1911-14), II, 547. "A Citizen," *Gazette of the United States* (Phila.), Nov. 16, 1791, opposed enlargement of the House beyond 75 members. *Journal of the Senate of the United States of America, Being the First Session of the Second Congress...Begun and Held at the City of Philadelphia October 24, 1791...* (Phila., 1792), 55. In the first session of the Second Congress, three separate bills on apportionment, House Bills Nos. 147, 163, and 179, were debated.

16. Ames to Minot, Dec. 23, 1791, Ames, *Works of Ames*, I, 108; *Annals*, III, 254-55, 274, Dec. 19, 1791. Ames's speech on apportionment was printed in the *Columbian Centinel* (Boston), Mar. 7, 1792; a critical article on the Senate alterations is "Plain Truth," *National Gazette* (Phila.), Dec. 15, 1791.

17. *Annals*, III, 250. The House bill on apportionment is in *ibid.*, 32, the amended Senate bill, 254. *Journal of the Senate*, 60-61, 65-66. Ames to Minot, Dec. 23, 1791, Ames, *Works of Ames*, I, 108.

Weeks elapsed before the lower chamber turned from other urgent matters late in January 1792 to reconsider its own future membership. The second representation bill avoided some of the earlier pitfalls by proposing an interim apportionment for the next five years. It provided for another census which was to become the basis for distribution of the House seats after March 1797. The ratio of representation of 1:30,000 was to be applied to the individual states rather than to the nation as a whole. Ames was still unwilling to accept the principle of a state-by-state computation, and he insisted that the proposed bill would inevitably violate the Constitution. In a House speech he categorically listed ten points to reinforce his argument that the proper construction of the constitutional provisions governing representation would necessitate an apportionment on the basis of the population of the entire nation. He denied the validity of the claim by some that in a ratio of 1:30,000 "the number of Representatives [should be] no more than the multiples of 30,000 in each state." [18] His attack was bound to sharpen political animosities, further convincing the southerners that New Englanders were intransigent and antagonistic. When the bill was brought to a vote in the House, Ames and all other New England representatives present voted against it but were defeated, thirty-four to sixteen.[19]

The new representation bill met further criticism in the Senate before it was amended and returned to the House. Ames was willing to accept the altered bill, as it now gave the New England states a better position in relation to the South, although at the price of enlarging the House of Representatives to 120 members. Under the Senate version Massachusetts would have sixteen representatives out of a total of thirty-five for the five New England states; Virginia would have twenty-one out of the forty-four representatives for the five southern states. At first the House refused to approve the Senate amendments, and even a conference committee could not resolve the differences. But by March 23 the proposed changes had gained enough support to pass the lower chamber by the slim margin of two votes, thirty-one to twenty-nine. With New England forthrightness Abigail Adams commented on the decision, "The old dominion is in a Rage, because they could not ... get more than their share of Representation." [20] In a letter to Edmund Pendleton, James Madison revealed a southerner's reaction to congres-

18. *Annals*, III, 331, 403-14, Jan. 24, Feb. 13, 16, 17, 1792; vote on amendments, *ibid.*, 415-16, Feb. 20.

19. *Ibid.*, 418. The final vote in the House was 34 yeas, 16 nays.

20. *Ibid.*, 101-6, 473-74, 482, Mar. 6, 12, 17, 23, 1792; *Journal of the Senate*, 152-54, 158, 164; *Journal of the House*, I, 544-46. Abigail Adams to Mary Cranch, N.Y., Mar. 29, 1792, Mitchell, *Abigail Adams*, 80.

sional approval of the representation bill, "You were right . . . 'northern cocks are true game,' but have erred in adding 'that they *die* hard on the Representation bill.' Their perseverance gained them final victory." [21]

Neither the New Englanders nor Madison had counted on the reaction of President Washington, who after a period of deliberation returned the bill with his first veto. A series of calculations with his cabinet had led the President to the decision that the measure did not conform either to the constitutional prescriptions on apportionment or to the application of the ratio of representation. Nevertheless, Fisher Ames stuck to his position with respect to the final bill and was not at all persuaded that Washington's stand was a correct one.[22]

The representatives who disagreed with the President's action attempted to pass the bill over his veto. Even though the New England congressmen, with the exception of two members from Connecticut, voted in favor of the move, it was defeated. At last in April a third, revised bill, which had the support of Ames, was accepted by the House and the Senate. When the prolonged struggle was over, Massachusetts had fourteen representatives while her arch-rival Virginia had nineteen.[23]

Another recurring problem which confronted Congress was the relation of the government to the western Indians. In October 1791, at the opening of the session, President Washington had spoken about the happy state of the nation, yet had apprised the members of the worsened situation on the frontier. Somberly he stated that efforts to preserve peace had failed and that expeditions were being carried on to subdue the Miami Indians. Seven weeks later, news of General Arthur St. Clair's overwhelming defeat on the Ohio frontier stunned the capital. Couriers had brought meager details of the disaster to the President on December 8. Subsequent dispatches from St. Clair graphically described the battle and the rout of the regulars and the militia. As soon as Ames learned of the debacle he hurriedly informed Dwight of the furious attack on St. Clair's fourteen hundred men and the loss of over six hundred. Many of those killed had come from New England and their names were very familiar to him. Beyond the personal tragedies was the reality of a serious blow to the nation. The entire western

21. James Madison to Edmund Pendleton, Phila., Mar. 25, 1792, Madison Papers, XV, Lib. Cong.
22. Freeman, *Washington*, VI, 345-47. The veto message is in *Annals*, III, 119. Ames to Dwight, Phila., Apr. 15, 1792, Fisher Ames Papers, Dedham Hist. Soc.
23. *Annals*, III, 541, 548, 1359, Apr. 6, 9, 1792.

frontier was on the brink of savage warfare. Pacification of the western Indians could now be achieved only by a long, expensive war.[24]

Ames was acutely aware of the plight of the western settlers in the Ohio Valley, for several of his former acquaintances in Boston and Dedham had moved to the vicinity of Marietta. Early in 1791 he had reassured General Rufus Putnam that the emigrants to the West were not forgotten. "It was impossible to read your letter giving an account of the attack of the Savages ... at Big Bottom, without feeling a strong sympathy with you under the peculiar distress of your situation." [25] Ames had been a member of a House Committee on Indian Affairs and had grappled with the problem of frontier defense at the time of crisis when General Josiah Harmar, the predecessor of St. Clair, had been defeated by the Indians. From his contacts with men like Manasseh Cutler and Putnam, he had come to the conclusion that only if Congress developed an effective policy of defending the frontier would it be possible to end the threat of an independent West. "Our sun will set when the Union shall be divided," he had commented to General Putnam.[26] It was because of his persistent interest in the fate of the Ohio settlements that he was especially active during the Second Congress in matters of military policy as well as in the affairs of the Ohio Company of Associates.

For weeks after the initial news of St. Clair's defeat was published, the circumstances leading to the catastrophe kept the public aroused. The press responded with detailed accounts of the tragedy and long evaluations of the frontier campaign. Newspapers such as the *Boston Gazette* and the *Independent Chronicle*, always prone to criticize the government's policies, constantly fanned the embers of antipathy with articles condemning the entire war. Concern about the losses led to a

24. *Ibid.;* Freeman, *Washington*, VI, 288-89; William H. Smith, ed., *The Life and Public Services of Arthur St. Clair*, 2 vols. (Cincinnati, 1882), II, 199-205, 216; Ames to Dwight, Phila., Dec. 9, 1791, Ames, *Works of Ames*, I, 107; Freeman, *Washington*, VI, 336; Ames to Dwight, Phila., Dec. 12, 1791, Fisher Ames Papers, Dedham Hist. Soc.; *Columbian Centinel* (Boston), Nov. 19, 1791; *National Gazette* (Phila.), Dec. 12, 15, 1791; *Boston Gazette*, Dec. 19, 26, 1791, Jan. 2, 9, 16, 30, 1792; Christopher Gore to Rufus King, Boston, Dec. 25, 1791, King, *Life of King*, I, 403-4.

25. Ames to General Rufus Putnam, Phila., Feb. 22, 1791, Putnam Papers, I, Stimson Collection, Marietta College Library, Marietta, Ohio.

26. *Annals*, II, 1836, Dec. 9, 1791; Freeman, *Washington*, VI, 288-89; Ames to Putnam, Feb. 22, 1791, Putnam Papers, I, Marietta College Lib.; Thomas Jefferson to James Monroe, Phila., Apr. 17, 1791, Monroe Papers, N.Y. Pub. Lib. Jefferson commented: "Every rag of an Indian depredation will otherwise serve as a ground to raise troops with those who think a standing army and a public debt necessary for the happiness of the U.S."

swelling demand early in 1792 to call to account those responsible for the succession of failures.[27]

While Ames recognized the proneness of individuals to condemn, he insisted that the public attitude was based on erroneous information. It was natural to assuage fears or anger by reproaching the government or its officials, but the charges that the United States had dispossessed the Indians of their land and in other ways had aggravated them were just so many "Canterbury tales" in his opinion. He did agree with some of his Boston constituents who insisted that the nation had no "business . . . with Indian lands." To attribute the war to greed for land or ideas of glory was fallacious. It was important not to lose sight of an elementary fact—the need to defend lives against the hostile tribes. "Any backwardness to protect would produce alienation and resentment among the western settlers. Policy as well as duty require effectual aid to them against the Indians." [28]

Toward the end of January the entire Indian policy of the administration came under the review of the House. Ames supported a plan of enlarging the military forces by adding 5,168 men, even though he realized that carrying on the "confounded war" had damaged the nation's prestige. A report submitted by Secretary Knox to the Senate on military policy toward the Indians had intensified Ames's feeling that frontier defense should be left to regular army troops, stationed in part at a military post on the Miami River. A larger, better trained force of cavalry and infantry would be more effective, Ames believed, than the local militia, which many westerners favored because of their desire to serve as volunteers with government pay.[29] The military bill, when it came before the House, was promptly attacked on the grounds that the war was unjust and that peace could be had at much lower cost. Behind the criticism was a basic distrust of a strong army which might be used to enforce the will of the national government. The proponents of the bill insisted that the force must be raised if only to maintain public

27. Ames to Dwight, Dec. 9, 1791, Ames, *Works of Ames,* I, 107; Henry Tazewell to James Monroe, Feb. 14, 1792, Monroe Papers, Lib. Cong.; *Boston Gazette,* Dec. 26, 1791, Jan. 9, 23, 30, Feb. 13, 27, Mar. 19, 1792; *Independent Chronicle* (Boston), Dec. 29, 1791, Jan. 26, June 7, July 5, 1792. The House began an investigation, Mar. 27, 1792, *Annals,* III, 490 ff; James R. Jacobs, *The Beginnings of the U.S. Army* (Princeton, 1947), 85-103.

28. Ames to John Warren, Phila., Jan. 1, 1792, Warren Papers, Mass. Hist. Soc.; Ames to Dwight, Phila., Jan. 13, 1792, Ames, *Works of Ames,* I, 109; *Boston Gazette,* Jan. 9, 23, 30, Feb. 6, 27, Mar. 5, 1792; a criticism of the congressional report on the Western expedition is in *ibid.,* June 4, 1792. The *Boston Gazette* in its column "Indian Department" gathered much information on the frontier wars. *Columbian Centinel* (Boston), Dec. 17, 19, 21, 24, 28, 1791, Jan. 11, 1792.

29. Ames to Dwight, Jan. 13, 1792, Ames, *Works of Ames,* I, 109-10; Freeman, *Washington,* VI, 340; *Annals,* III, 1046-59.

Fisher Ames in 1804
(see p. xiii)

Dedham, Massachusetts, 1795

respect for the government. Such action was the sole way of obtaining redress against the Indians and of ending the war. On the final vote, Ames assented to an increase in the army, in contrast to the stand of most New England representatives, to whom the Indian war was remote and unnecessary.[30]

The protection and extension of central authority continued to be important to Ames. In February the House wrestled with the task of devising a uniform militia system, and state partisans saw in the bill a threat to state control over the militia. The Massachusetts representative was dubious about the effectiveness of the bill as it stood, but voted with the majority in favor of it as he felt the need to make a beginning even if the legislation turned out to be feeble and poor. The House soon responded to public dissatisfaction over the recent massacre of the western army. On March 27, William Branch Giles of Virginia bluntly proposed that the President initiate an investigation of St. Clair's defeat. When the measure failed, an alternate resolution was accepted, creating a committee of seven members for the purpose of investigating the defeat. Ames was among those who voted against having either the President or the House probe into the disaster. He may have wanted to protect St. Clair from undue censure, but more likely he saw in the proposals a covert attack on the administration.[31]

While Congress considered problems of the frontier, the Ohio Company of Associates was confronted with serious financial difficulties. Seeking to resolve these difficulties, several of the directors, Manasseh Cutler and Rufus Putnam among them, went to Philadelphia as lobbyists. Through close contacts with Ames, Sedgwick, and other New England congressmen, Cutler was able to force a decision by a lethargic House on his petition for relief from the terms of the Company's contract to pay the government for the lands it had been granted. Ames's support seems to have been largely behind the scenes in the House, inasmuch as the matter was handled by a select committee of other members. Reluctant congressmen who were unwilling to lower the purchase price of the land prevented Cutler from achieving his main

30. Ames to Dwight, Jan. 13, 1792, Ames, *Works of Ames*, I, 109; *Annals*, III, 337-55, Jan. 26-Feb. 1, 1792. The vote was 29 yeas, 19 nays. Theodore Sedgwick to Ephraim Williams, Phila., Mar. 8, 1792, Sedgwick Papers, III, Box 1, Mass. Hist. Soc.; Oliver Wolcott to Oliver Wolcott, Sr., Phila., Jan. 30, Feb. 14, 1792, Gibbs, *Memoirs*, I, 72-73.

31. Ames to Dwight, Phila., Feb. 23, 1792, Ames, *Works of Ames*, I, 114; *Annals*, III, 418-24, 435, 493-94, Feb. 21, Mar. 6, 27, 1792. According to the *Boston Gazette*, Apr. 30, 1792, "the principles of that Bill are sufficient to make every freeman jealous of his power." Gen. St. Clair resigned from the army in the summer of 1792. Arthur St. Clair to Winthrop Sargent, Phila., Aug. 27, 1792, Winthrop Sargent Papers, Mass. Hist. Soc.

objective. In the final bill, however, the Ohio Company was granted confirmation of its title and was also given 214,285 acres of land to be paid for in depreciated land warrants. Thus by the action of eastern congressmen it was saved from bankruptcy.[32] In 1800 when settlers in the wilderness to the west of Marietta, Ohio, voted on the name for their new community, they chose *Ames*. Ephraim Cutler wrote to his father, Manasseh, explaining the reasons for the decision. "This name I proposed to the people and they unanimously agreed to it. . . . The able support the Hon. F. Ames gave you and the other directors in settling your business with Congress and his enlightened . . . and truly just ideas respecting the western country and politics in general induced me to fix on the name." [33]

Ames's preoccupation with various national issues did not lessen his interest in Massachusetts maritime problems. The plight of the cod and whale fishermen along the northeastern seaboard had been brought to the attention of Congress, and in response George Cabot introduced a bill in the Senate granting bounties to the fishermen employed in the industry. When Giles assaulted the bill, sent to the House for its concurrence, Ames felt impelled to defend it against the imputations that direct bounties were unconstitutional and unjust because they granted exclusive rights.[34]

The fishermen, Ames proclaimed, had equal rights with other men, and he proceeded to show that they should not pay a duty on materials they used to produce fish for export. The government had consequently allowed them a drawback of the duties, which now was inequitably distributed and insufficient to sustain a lagging industry. In place of the drawback the bill offered a direct subsidy or bounty, which he contended would be both more beneficial for the individual fisherman and far less costly to the government. Cleverly he stirred the audience with an appeal to aid the fishermen of New England, so often in the thick of naval action during the Revolution. He did not answer

32. *Annals*, III, 433, 486, 494-95, 539-40, 558, Mar. 21, 26, 29, Apr. 6, 17, 1792; Cutler and Cutler, *Life of Cutler*, I, 470-77; Manasseh Cutler to Mrs. Cutler, Phila., Mar. 5, 23, 1792, *ibid.*, 482-84, 487; Jonathan Dayton to John Cleves Symmes, Phila., May 6, 1792, Beverley W. Bond, ed., *The Correspondence of John Cleves Symmes, Founder of the Miami Purchase* (N.Y., 1926), 268; Thomas J. Summers, *History of Marietta* (Marietta, Ohio, 1903), 108-11; Rowena Buell, ed., *The Memoirs of Rufus Putnam* (Boston and N.Y., 1903).

33. Ephraim Cutler to Manasseh Cutler, Ames, Ohio, Apr. 25, 1801, Julia P. Cutler, *The Life and Times of Ephraim Cutler* (Cincinnati, 1890), 48.

34. *Annals*, III, 51, 363-65, Dec. 20, 1791, Feb. 3, 1792; *National Gazette* (Phila.), Feb. 6, 1792; Stephen Higginson to George Cabot, n.d., 1792, Lodge, *Letters of Cabot*, 52-53; Samuel E. Morison, *The Maritime History of Massachusetts, 1783-1860* (Boston, 1921), 134-40.

Giles's arguments directly, but defended the measure on the basis of justice to the needy fishermen. In his plea he interwove the idea that bounties would save the fisheries, thereby enhancing the national safety and increasing the national wealth.[35]

Ames's argumentation, combining both incontestable facts and an emotional appeal, was effective, but he did not escape criticism from several members who were determined not to pass legislation in behalf of a special group. With all his emphasis on the nation's welfare, Ames could not entirely gloss over the fact that a regional economic group would be the beneficiary. Madison insisted that the proponents of the bill were reading into the general welfare clause of the Constitution a meaning it never had, and he took exception to Ames's use of the term "bounty," which he maintained could not apply to a direct allowance. Hugh Williamson of North Carolina referred disparagingly to Ames's "very ingenious calculations," and John Page of Virginia likewise expressed his disagreement with the Bostonian's pleas. By a substantial majority the bill passed the House on February 9, 1792, in spite of the objections which were raised. A week later the President signed the bill granting cod fishermen up to $170 annually, depending on the tonnage of their vessels. As a New Englander, Ames wholeheartedly supported the measure one of his best friends had submitted. As a Hamiltonian, he was furthering the concepts recently expressed in the Report on Manufactures to encourage particular economic groups by means of government bounties.[36]

During the course of the Second Congress, Ames became concerned about the efforts of southern representatives to place the Secretary of State next in line of succession if there were vacancies in both the offices of president and vice president. President Washington's serious illness in 1790 had made a decision seem imperative. Although Ames strongly disliked enhancing the power of the legislature at the expense of the executive, he supported a Senate bill proposing the President *pro tempore* of the Senate and the Speaker of the House as successors to the presidency, and opposed a House amendment which substituted the Secretary of State. Ames considered the amendment an effort by the Virginia Republicans to place Jefferson within reach of the presidency. He was pleased when the Senate refused to accept the amendment which had been carried over the objections of the Federalists in the House. Finally the original proposal prevailed. The friends of Jefferson,

35. *Annals*, III, 368-69, Feb. 3, 1792; *National Gazette* (Phila.), Feb. 9, 1792.
36. *Annals*, III, 378, 386, 392, Feb. 3, 6, 7, 1792; Ames to Dwight, Phila., Jan. 30, 1792, Ames, *Works of Ames*, I, 112; Miller, *Federalist Era*, 299; Peters, ed., *U.S. Statutes at Large*, I, 229-32.

he commented, "seemed to think it important to hold him up as King of the Romans. The firmness of the Senate kept him out." [37]

By early March the continuous debating on minor matters had made Ames weary. He felt that too many representatives took a delight in captious criticism and in crying out that every forward move in legislative matters was unconstitutional. Important bills were hindered, and proposals strengthening the government languished. There was an incessant clamor that "this is unconstitutional and that is." Hardly a question had been considered during the session which had not evoked such a protest. Sarcastically Ames remarked, "The fishery bill was unconstitutional; it is unconstitutional to . . . give bounties; to make the militia worth having; order is unconstitutional; credit is tenfold worse." He insisted there were "twenty *antis*, dragons watching the tree of liberty," who were determined to prevent the passage of any legislation which might "rob the tree of its fair fruit." [38]

This obstreperous attitude, which troubled Ames, grew out of the perpetual objection on the part of the supporters of Madison and Jefferson to Hamiltonian financial policies. Early in the session, the House had taken its cue from President Washington's address to Congress and had requested a report from the Secretary of the Treasury on the subscribed and unsubscribed amounts of public debt. In his reply, Hamilton suggested that Congress pass a law assuming the remaining portions of the state debts not provided for by previous legislation. The battle over the debt flared anew, although on a diminished scale compared to the winter and summer of 1790. Prominent Republicans seized the opportunity to resist any extension of the Federalist monetary program.[39]

"The bill respecting the public debt is yet before the House, and how many long speeches Messrs. Giles and Mercer have in them, is not to be known till the time of painful experience," Ames wrote. A complete assumption appeared out of the question for the time being. Part of the sum, perhaps $1,000,000, might be assumed, but "all is doubt and darkness," he warned. Not much time remained in this session as both

37. Ames to Minot, N.Y., May 20, 1790, Ames to Dwight, Feb. 23, 1792, Ames, *Works of Ames*, I, 79, 114; Freeman, *Washington*, VI, 259-61; *Annals*, II, 1860, 1902, Dec. 20, 1790, Jan. 10, 1791, III, 89, 90, 402, 417, Feb. 10, 16, 20, 21, 1792; James Madison to Edmund Pendleton, Phila., Feb. 21, 1792, Madison Papers, XV, Lib. Cong.; Joseph Jones to James Madison, Fredericksburg, Mar. 2, 1792, Worthington C. Ford, ed., "Letters of Joseph Jones to James Madison," Mass. Hist. Soc., *Proceedings*, 2d Ser., 15 (1902), 136-38.
38. Ames to Minot, Phila., Mar. 8, 1792, Ames, *Works of Ames*, I, 114-15.
39. *Annals*, III, 495-98, Mar. 29, 1792; Abigail Adams to Mary Cranch, N.Y., Apr. 20, 1792, Mitchell, *Abigail Adams*, 83; *Independent Chronicle* (Boston), Apr. 26, 1792, quoted from the *American Daily Advertiser* (Phila.); James Madison to Gov. Henry Lee, Phila., Feb. 12, 1792, Madison Papers, XV, Lib. Cong.

Houses had agreed to adjourn on May 5, and the opponents of Hamilton were in no mood to compromise. Ames felt that certain key persons in both the Senate and House had deserted the valiant crew members by leaving early. He criticized his friend Sedgwick severely for leaving to look after his wife Pamela, who was ill. "He has been too fond of pushing home and leaving us to fight without hope and against odds," he contended. Later, when Ames learned of the true nature of Mrs. Sedgwick's illness, he was more understanding. "Your letter fully clears him," Ames acknowledged Dwight's explanation. "Without being a husband, as a man, I can decide that he acted properly." [40]

In the last days of the meeting, the additional assumption failed; yet Ames did not give up hope for ultimate victory, expecting that the issue would rise again like a phoenix in the autumn session. Nevertheless he was satiated with the current meeting and was tired of remaining "in this wrangling Robinhood club." Plodding slowly ahead with the essential business of Congress was all too much like attending school. "Every day renews the round of yesterday," he said, expressing succinctly the monotony of a lack-luster meeting.[41] In spite of his remarks, he had to admit that Congress had passed several worthwhile laws. More might have been achieved in the direction of reducing the public debt had the unwelcome reality of the Indian war not intervened. He was certain that Hamilton, even so, was determined to carry out the debt reduction as soon as it was practicable.

In light of the developments of the past months, Ames was acutely aware that the Republicans constituted a serious threat to Federalism. He felt that even though its leaders posed as "champions of liberty," their real objectives were the acquisition of political power and the control of the government. They were endeavoring to supplant the

40. Ames to Dwight, Apr. 15, 1792, Fisher Ames Papers, Dedham Hist. Soc.; Ames to Dwight, Phila., Apr. 25, 1792, Ames, *Works of Ames*, I, 117; Ames to Minot, Phila., May 3, 1792, *ibid.*, 118; *Annals*, III, 499-513, 516-31, Mar. 30-31, 1792; Theodore Sedgwick to Peter Van Schaack, Phila., Nov. 20, 1791, Henry C. Van Schaack, *The Life of Peter Van Schaack L.L.D., Embracing Selections from his Correspondence and Other Writings During the American Revolution, and his Exile in England* (N.Y., 1842), 435; Ames to Dwight, Phila., May 6, 1792, Fisher Ames Papers, Dedham Hist. Soc.

41. *Annals*, III, 594-97, May 5, 1792; Theodore Foster to Dwight Foster, Phila., Apr. 26, 1792, Dwight Foster Papers, Mass. Hist. Soc. Foster asserted that Jefferson and the "Republicans" were making "a Stalking Horse of the Funding System" to oust Adams and Hamilton from office. Ames to Dwight, Apr. 15, 1792, Fisher Ames Papers, Dedham Hist. Soc.; Ames to Minot, May 3, 1792, Ames, *Works of Ames*, I, 118; the *Independent Chronicle* (Boston), May 3, 1792, quoted the *Salem Gazette*, which criticized Congress for its lengthy session and its "passion for spouting."

group currently in power by every possible means, both through the press and through direct influence in Congress. Thus Ames expected that in the coming election "all the arts of intrigue will be practised." [42]

Ames remained in Philadelphia until Congress had adjourned. Only his deep sense of responsibility kept him attending the daily meetings of the House when he would so much rather have been in Springfield. Often throughout the spring months, his heart was not in his work and he yearned to escape the business of this session, which from the start had held scant appeal for him. In a lighthearted vein he told Thomas Dwight, "What better proof can a man give of his public spirit than my conduct affords. I remain here to drudge on in public business when I know of a much more agreeable way of employing my attentions." [43]

In late April Ames determined that he would delay no longer in proposing marriage to Frances Worthington. His decision was the natural outgrowth of the warm understanding that had developed between them. Clearly he had wanted to achieve some professional and economic security before making Frances his wife. If other factors caused him to prolong his courtship over a period of years, they remain obscure. To Dwight he confided that the fates had long been unkind and he had consequently lost much time already.[44] Enclosed in a long political letter, Ames had sent Dwight an important document "on a particular subject," requesting his good friend's help in arranging a declaration of marriage intentions between Frances and himself. "Know all men," he began in mock legal style, "that I, Fisher Ames of Boston, reposing especial trust and confidence in your friendship, fidelity, and zeal do ordain you ... my ambassador extraordinary and irresistible ...

42. Ames to Minot, May 3, 1792, Ames, *Works of Ames*, I, 119; Oliver Wolcott to Jeremiah Wadsworth, July 22, 1792, Chamberlain Collection, Boston Pub. Lib.; Alexander Hamilton to Col. Edward Carrington, Phila., May 26, 1792, Lodge, ed., *Works of Hamilton*, VIII, 251. Hamilton observed that "it was not till the last session that I became unequivocally convinced ... that Mr. Madison, co-operating with Mr. Jefferson, is at the head of a faction decidedly hostile to me and my administration."

43. Ames to Dwight, Phila., Mar. 26, 1792, Fisher Ames Papers, Dedham Hist. Soc. Signed salary receipts show that Ames attended every day between Jan. 1 and May 4, 1792. For the entire session he received $1,164, assuming uninterrupted attendance between Nov. 10 and Dec. 31, 1791, for which the receipts are missing. He was allowed $108 travel expenses. Autograph Receipts ... by Members of the First Session, 2nd Congress, 1791-92, Conn. Hist. Soc. There are samples of endorsed salary checks of members of Congress in U.S. Legislature, 2nd Congress, U.S. Miscellaneous, Box 1, 1789-96, Lib. Cong. Ames received $450 on Dec. 31, 1792, and $480 on Mar. 2, 1793, for the second session.

44. Ames to Dwight, Phila., Apr. 25, 1792, Fisher Ames Papers, Dedham Hist. Soc.

at the court of a certain fair and sovereign princess . . . to supplicate her to say . . . that the said Fisher Ames is not forever to be kept freezing in absence three hundred miles from her presence—but that he is to be taken into favor." [45] He had already written Frances, anticipating that she would accept him, and that Colonel Worthington would also approve the marriage. Dwight, he expected, would make the matter public in Springfield, while Gore would do the same in Boston.

At last on May 8 he could state positively that the business of Congress was almost finished and that he would not sit a day longer. In the final days of the session the report on St. Clair's defeat had been ordered printed with the objective of keeping political fires aglow and the public in a resentful mood until the next meeting of Congress. Ames, however, was ready to set aside the interminable political struggle and leave for New England. He needed a day "to pick up . . . [his] awls"; then he could head directly for Springfield. Until the long trip was over and he could be there in person, he wanted Dwight to continue as his ambassador at the court.[46]

A month later Ames was deeply involved in negotiating for a house, as he and Frances planned to live in Boston during the congressional recesses. He had long been enthusiastic about the city and was very much pleased to find that there had been numerous civic improvements. Christopher Gore had located a place for him which seemed to be only fair, but Ames had to reconcile himself to it after a futile search for a better dwelling. It was "commodius, at least decent, and in point of prospect . . . superior to most situations in the town." Refurbishing the house for his occupancy was a frustrating task, Ames found. By force of persuasion, he would gain a concession from the landlord on one day only to have him retract it the next. He was constantly "on the trot" to get the house repainted, the rooms repapered, and a woodshed added, but once the workmen were engaged, it did not take long before he reported that "the house is smarting up." [47] If all went according to schedule, he himself would move in by early July and hire two servants to keep house. Ames was anxious to finish his preparations so he could leave for Springfield. Impatiently, he wrote, "I am at home no where and scarcely consider my lodgings as a temporary home." He felt he was a nobody at the moment, but once married there would be some-

45. *Ibid.*
46. Ames to Thomas Dwight, Phila., May 8, 1792, *ibid.*
47. Ames to Tudor, Phila., Nov. 24, 1791, "Memoir of Tudor," Mass. Hist. Soc., *Collections*, 2d Ser., 8 (1819) 323-24; Ames to Dwight, Boston, June 12, 1792, Fisher Ames Papers, Dedham Hist. Soc.; Ames to Minot, Sept. 3, 1789, Ames to Dwight, Boston, June 16, 1792, Ames, *Works of Ames*, I, 69, 119-20.

one in the house to care and provide for; therefore he had to think "respectfully of the doctrine of bread and cheese." [48]

Through marriage, Ames was joining one of the most prominent families in western Massachusetts. Frances's father, John Worthington, had been graduated from Yale before studying law and entering the legal profession at Springfield in 1744. He was a man of cultivation and some brilliance who served as a colonel in the French and Indian War. A multiplicity of business and civic activities enlarged his prestige until he became a powerful political force in Springfield. He was a representative to the Massachusetts General Court during most of the years between 1747 and 1774. As the Revolution approached, he became an exceedingly controversial figure because of his conservative Tory sympathies. When the King appointed him as a Mandamus Councilor, however, he declined the offer and later reluctantly accepted a break with Great Britain. Though this vivid, dogmatic lawyer contributed funds to the army in the Revolution, the specter of his early allegiance followed him most of his life. [49]

In 1759, at the age of forty, Colonel Worthington had married Hannah Hopkins. Of the six children born to this couple, the four daughters, Mary, Hannah, Frances, and Sophia, lived to maturity. Frances, who was born on November 18, 1764, was barely two years of age at the time of her mother's death. When the children were still small, the father married Mary Stoddard, the daughter of Colonel John Stoddard of Northampton. [50] Frances Worthington had rare intellectual and social qualities. Her "fine eyes," graceful figure, and warmth of manner contributed to her charm. In her relationships with others, she revealed both empathy and understanding. Her social ease was contagious, as she perceptively elicited response from those about her. She was an excellent conversationalist, being keen-minded, widely read, and witty. Indeed, she was well suited to be the wife of Fisher Ames. [51]

On July 15, 1792, Ames's long period of waiting came to an end

48. Ames to Dwight, Boston, June 12, 28, 1792, Fisher Ames Papers, Dedham Hist. Soc.

49. See E. Francis Brown, *DAB* s.v. "Worthington, John"; Franklin B. Dexter, *Biographical Sketches of the Graduates of Yale College with Annals of the College History, October, 1701-May, 1745* (N.Y., 1885), 658-59; Warner B. Sturtevant, John Worthington, Typescript, Springfield Pub. Lib.; Thomas D. Howard, "Col. John Worthington," Connecticut Valley Historical Society, *Proceedings,* 4 (1907), 101-7.

50. Dexter, *Biographical Sketches,* 659-60; "Stoddard's Journal," *New Eng. Hist. and Geneal. Register,* 5 (1851), 24-25; Ella May Lewis, *Baptisms, Marriages and Deaths, 1736-1809, First Church, Springfield, Mass.* (Springfield, 1938), 13, 14, 16, 18. The four daughters of Col. and Mrs. Worthington were Mary, b. Mar. 9, 1760, Hannah, b. June 14, 1761, Frances, b. Nov. 18, 1764, Sophia, b. Dec. 8, 1765.

51. Susan I. Lesley, *Recollections of My Mother* (Boston, 1886), 41.

when he and Frances were married. The ceremony took place in the unpretentious Congregational meetinghouse, the First Church of Springfield, where the Reverend Bezaleel Howard served as minister. Two weeks later the Ameses were in Boston, established in their own home. As they had not "fixed a week for setting up" they had not been overwhelmed by visitors. Frances, her husband reported, appeared to be "contented," which he gallantly attributed to her "good temper and good sense." [52] The couple kept in touch with relatives and friends. They hoped that Hannah and Thomas Dwight would come for a visit, and that Colonel and Mrs. Worthington might be induced to stay with them after seeing their daughter, Mary Bliss, and her husband set sail on their return to New Brunswick. Ames clearly had great esteem for his father-in-law and enjoyed increasing rapport with Frances's sisters. "Those who are my connections by marriage were my friends before," he remarked, "but I seem to have gained a new title to their friendship, and I enjoy it with increasing satisfaction." [53] The Ameses had planned a trip to Windsor, Vermont, to see Fisher's sister, but Deborah and her husband came to Boston instead. Together, Fisher and Frances made several trips to Dedham, the first time to spend a Sunday with Fisher's mother, and later to join the First Church in Dedham. It was quite evident from the tone of his letters that both he and Frances were very happy. He was already philosophizing about marriage and had easily persuaded himself that married life was the only happy state of existence. "If I say that my experience has confirmed my faith," he remarked, "the unbelievers will say it is yet too soon for me to depose as a witness." [54]

Even though Ames had increased his responsibilities, he did not think of giving up his public career to settle down in Boston. Before the end of August he was making arrangements to take Frances with him to

52. Warren, Springfield Families, 768; Lewis, *First Church Records, Springfield*, 68; *Independent Chronicle* (Boston), Aug. 2, 1792; Mason A. Green, *Springfield, 1636-1886, History of Town and City* (Springfield, 1888), 259; Henry Morris, *History of the First Church in Springfield* (Springfield, 1875), 34-35; Mason A. Green, *Springfield Memories, Odds and Ends of Anecdote and Early Doings* (Springfield, 1876); Ames to Dwight, Boston, Aug. 6, 1792, Fisher Ames Papers, Dedham Hist. Soc.
53. Ames to Dwight, Boston, Sept. 16, 1792, Miscellaneous Autograph Collection, Pierpont Morgan Library, N.Y.; Jonathan Bliss to John Worthington, St. John, New Brunswick, Nov. 4, 1792, Manuscript Collection, Springfield Pub. Lib.
54. Deborah Ames married the Rev. Samuel Shuttleworth of Windsor, Vermont, in Jan. 1792; *Columbian Centinel* (Boston), Jan. 18, 1792; Mann, *Annals of Dedham*, 90; Ames to Dwight, Aug. 6, 1792, Fisher Ames Papers, Dedham Hist. Soc. Fisher and Frances Ames were admitted on Oct. 19, 1792, Church Records of the First Church of Dedham, Dedham Hist. Soc.

Philadelphia when Congress reopened, and he inquired whether a friend, John Vaughan, could find suitable lodgings for them, preferably apart from French sympathizers.[55] He then turned to his plans for re-election in November. Public interest in the national election developed slowly in Boston, in part because of a virulent smallpox epidemic. There were signs of an approaching political contest, but considering the accelerated tempo of politics during the preceding winter the relative calm was unusual. Ames expected that the mild political weather would soon be replaced by an autumn gale which would shake the next meeting of Congress.[56]

The Federalists did not have a statewide party organization, which meant that Ames had to rely on a favorable press and the backing of prominent local political supporters to win over the voters. His record in Congress as champion of assumption and the revenue system would command the allegiance of many conservative businessmen, and his prominence as an advocate of New England commercial interests would have a further appeal. In a period when personal campaigning and speechmaking were not a part of electioneering, the lustre of his name would give him an advantage in the towns outside of Boston in the First District.[57] Ames was alert to the need of keeping his candidacy before the voters by having his name inserted in the election lists in the newspapers, but he was concerned that the notices were slow to appear. By October the election campaign was progressing, and he had been endorsed for the Suffolk seat by the *Columbian Centinel*. In comparison with the contests of 1788 and 1790, the newspapers made virtually no direct attacks on Ames. On occasion the *Independent Chronicle* even published articles in his behalf. Yet Ames's re-election was not a foregone conclusion. His opponent was his old rival Benjamin Austin, the ever popular member of the Hancock party. Recently chosen as one of the Boston representatives to the General Court, Austin could count on the strong support of the *Boston Gazette*, which eulogized

55. Ames to John Vaughan, Boston, Aug. 25, 1792, Dreer Collection, American Statesmen, Hist. Soc. of Pa.
56. Ames to Dwight, Sept. 16, 1792, Pierpont Morgan Lib.; Ames to Dwight, Boston, Oct. 4, 1792, Ames, *Works of Ames*, I, 120-21; *Columbian Centinel* (Boston), Aug. 8, 25, 1792; *Independent Chronicle* (Boston), Aug. 16, 1792.
57. Binkley, *American Political Parties*, 50; Massachusetts, in the federal election of 1792, was divided into three districts, and Maine into one. In the First District, voters cast ballots for representatives for Suffolk, Middlesex, and Essex counties, one for the district, and one for the state at large, a total of five. The votes cast for the district candidates were so scattered that there had to be run-off elections. *Independent Chronicle* (Boston), Oct. 11, 1792; Cunningham, *Jeffersonian Republicans*, 33-35.

him as a foe of speculation schemes and as a champion of popular liberties.[58]

The Federalists, recognizing the importance of the election, urged the "federal patriotick interest" not to become complacent because of prosperity and to be vigilant against dangers threatening the Union from within. By reprinting Hamilton's attack on Jefferson, first published in the *Gazette of the United States* under the pseudonym of "An American," they implanted the idea in the public mind that Jefferson was the "head of a party whose politics aim at depressing the national authority." [59] Articles in the *Columbian Centinel* carried out the theme by equating opponents of administration measures with those wanting to destroy the Union. Attacking their political enemies, Federalist writers asserted that "the grumbling and implacable Antifeds, thrown to the bottom of the political wheel ... headed by the democratical and jesuitical old De Lisle [Hancock?], and ... the aspiring *patriot* Honestus [Benjamin Austin]—disappointed office seekers—those men will slip no opportunity ... to oppose, embarrass and injure the operations and character of the National Government." [60]

The Republican party was only gradually taking shape in the state of Massachusetts. In process of political metamorphosis, it developed from the group still under the leadership of the arch Antifederalists, John Hancock and Samuel Adams. Local political issues, once the primary concern of the Hancock party, were giving way to matters of national concern. With increasing vigor the Republicans lashed out in the newspapers at Federalist policies and activities. The assumption of state debts, the excise, speculation in securities, and the Indian war were constantly reiterated themes. By the time of the election campaign the critics of the Federalists were also making much of the fact that many members of Congress were lawyers, speculators, or Bank directors. Despite the fact that the Republican organization was rudimentary, it was reinforced by growing party spirit. Republicans in Pennsylvania and the leaders in Virginia were anxious to nurture the seedling which was sprouting in Massachusetts. Benjamin Rush, commenting on the

58. *Boston Gazette*, May 7, June 4, 1792.
59. *Independent Chronicle* (Boston), Sept. 27, Nov. 1, 1792; *Columbian Centinel* (Boston), Aug. 8, Sept. 29, Oct. 6, 17, 20, 24, 31. The *Columbian Centinel* republished Hamilton's "An American" articles, Aug. 22, 25, 1792; John Beckley to James Madison, Phila., Sept. 2, 1792, Madison Papers, N.Y. Pub. Lib. Beckley commented on the articles against Jefferson, "this premeditated attack has been pointed as to time and manner and is now industriously circulated thro' all the Eastern Papers." The *Columbian Centinel* also published "Aristides," a defense of Jefferson, Sept. 19, 1792. Malone, *Jefferson and the Rights of Man*, 469-70.
60. *Columbian Centinel* (Boston), Oct. 17, 1792, quoting from the *Salem Gazette*.

"republican ferment" there, suggested to Aaron Burr in New York, "The Association in Boston augurs well. Do feed it by a letter to Mr. S. Adams." Jefferson, too, was aware of developments to the eastward and predicted very optimistically that "Mr. Ames, the colossus of the monocrats and paper men, will either be left out or hard run." [61]

On November 3 only a small number of voters went to the polls to choose the representatives according to the complicated district formula of voting. The principal contest in the Suffolk district was, according to Nathaniel Cutting, "between Fisher Ames, . . . an accomplished lawyer . . . who has given sufficient proofs of his being a staunch Federalist, and Benjamin Austin, Jr., . . . a Democratic *enragée*, who has long been known as an instigator and patron of faction in this town." [62] Cutting, along with other "staunch friend[s] to the Federal Government" rejoiced when at the closing of the polls, Ames had a majority of forty-one votes in Boston. When all the returns were in Ames had amassed 1,627 votes to Austin's 982 in the entire district. His majority would have been smaller had the voting been confined to Suffolk County alone, but even here a substantial number of votes were against him only in the towns of Needham, Stoughton, and Walpole, outside of Boston.[63]

In a post-mortem of the election the *Boston Gazette* attributed his success to speculators and government officials, who gave him 334 votes. These votes were broken down into various categories: customhouse officers, 35 votes; excise officers, 12; branch bank officers, 22; investors in the funds, 177; the remainder of the votes came from merchants, lawyers, and "a noted idle stroller." Reviewing the election more judiciously, Christopher Gore maintained that rarely had there been so few voters in an important election. "The friends of Government reposed with too great Security on the good sense of the voters," he explained. Even so he was certain that when the official returns were in, Ames would have a large portion of them.[64]

61. William A. Robinson, *Jeffersonian Democracy in New England* (New Haven, 1916), 7-9; Benjamin Rush to Aaron Burr, Phila., Sept. 24, 1792, W. C. Ford, ed., "Some Papers of Aaron Burr," Amer. Antiq. Soc., *Proceedings*, 29 (1919), 97; *Independent Chronicle* (Boston), Oct. 11, 18, 25, 1792; *Boston Gazette*, Oct. 15, 29, 1792; Thomas Jefferson to Thomas Mann Randolph, Phila., Nov. 16, 1792, Ford, *Writings of Jefferson*, VI, 134.

62. Nathaniel Cutting, "Extracts from a Journal of a Gentleman Visiting Boston in 1792," Mass. Hist. Soc., *Proceedings*, 12 (1873), 66.

63. *Ibid.*; *Boston Gazette*, Nov. 5, 1792; *Independent Chronicle* (Boston), Nov. 8, 1792; Abstract of Votes, Mass. Archives, Office of the Secretary of the Commonwealth, State House.

64. *Boston Gazette*, Nov. 5, 1792; Christopher Gore to Rufus King, Boston, Nov. 14, 1792, King, ed., *Life of King*, I, 436; Nathan Dane to Benjamin Goodhue, Nov. 13, 1792, Benjamin Goodhue Manuscripts, N.Y. Soc. Lib. Dane asserted that

Weeks passed before Ames, having returned to Congress, finally learned the results of the contest. During this period he was anxiously awaiting word from Boston. In November a friend from Massachusetts, visiting in Philadelphia, informed him that the *Centinel* had listed the votes for Benjamin Austin at 401 and for Ames himself at 235. On the basis of this information, Ames remarked that he probably would be turned out to graze in the field. "I have been stall-fed here for a long time, and I have not any repugnance to trying my luck at the bar." Subsequently he discovered that the initial election report had been erroneous, and that the block of votes to which his friend referred included only 40 for Austin rather than 401.[65] Fisher Ames's congressional life was not to end precipitously after all.

---

little attention was paid to the election and that not one in ten could tell how the votes went because of the complex voting system.

65. Ames to Minot, Phila., Nov. 19, 1792, Ames, *Works of Ames*, I, 123; Ames to John Lowell, Phila., Dec. 6, 1792, Personal Papers, Lib. Cong.

Chapter XI

Ames in the Party Struggle

The trip southward, late in October 1792, with Frances accompanying Ames, had been far more pleasant for him than any previous one to Congress. Even the jostling carriage and bumpy roads had seemed much less fatiguing, and he thought they had had an "uncommonly favorable" journey. Once settled in Philadelphia he was anxious for the second session to get under way. For several days the representatives marked time until the preliminaries of opening the meeting were completed, leading Ames to say that they were moving with their accustomed slowness. Meanwhile Frances had immediately taken part in the social activities of the capital, especially the "great business of visiting by cards." Affectionately Ames said that she had made far more progress than he had in congressional business.[1]

President Washington's address to the Second Congress was pleasing to Federalists, who probably detected the influence of Alexander Hamilton in the passages devoted to finances. Ames felt that the address would be effective in stopping the dogs from barking at the excise, and he expected that even the "wild woodmen" of the West would be willing to gulp down an increase in taxation. While the outlook for the next months appeared to be moderately favorable for the nation, he was not unduly sanguine, for the Indians were still extremely hostile,

1. Ames to Thomas Dwight, Phila., Nov. 12, 1792, Ames to Dwight, Boston, Oct. 4, 1792, Ames, *Works of Ames*, I, 121-22. Ames said he and Frances would leave on the 19th. *Annals*, III, 669-79, Nov. 5-12, 1792; Freeman, *Washington*, VI, 295. Mitchell, *Abigail Adams*, 75, 77.

and the Spanish were obviously meddling in affairs on the southwestern frontier. Party struggles, he prognosticated, would be as violent as before, if the Federalists renewed the attempt to assume the remainder of the state debts. "It would be a weakness to suppose," Ames remarked, "that we shall not find the opposition revived, as soon as any important measure shall stir the wrathful souls of our fault-finders." [2]

Congressional affairs were put into the shade until the electors met early in December to vote for the president and vice president. Since President Washington, as everyone acknowledged, would be unopposed, the real test of political power lay in the vice-presidential contest. John Adams, who was unpopular because of his aristocratic political principles, was strongly challenged by the Republicans. Overcoming their own ambivalence and Jefferson's reservations about Governor George Clinton, the Republicans finally backed his candidacy in preference to his fellow New Yorker, Aaron Burr. To Ames it seemed wrong to attack John Adams, a man known for his firm political opinions and devotion to the Constitution, while Clinton, a notorious Antifederalist, was praised and given political support. In Ames's view it was aggravating that "a life of virtue and eminent usefulness should be embittered by calumny," but it was the way of politics to be ruthless against any opponent. He hoped New Englanders would awaken to the threat and give Adams "zealous support." [3]

At the time of the congressional election on November 2, Massachusetts voters had chosen a partial list of pro-Adams electors. In filling up the vacancies, the General Court likewise chose staunch advocates of the Vice President, and he was given the entire sixteen electoral votes of the state. "Our Elections are unanimous for the old King [Washing-

2. *Annals*, III, 607-10, Nov. 6, 1792; Freeman, *Washington*, VI, 377-78; Ames to Dwight, Nov. 12, 1792, Ames to George R. Minot, Phila., Nov. 19, 1792, Ames, *Works of Ames*, I, 122, 123; Alexander Hamilton to John Jay, Phila., Sept. 3, 1792, Lodge, ed., *Works of Hamilton*, X, 18; Leland D. Baldwin, *Whiskey Rebels: The Story of a Frontier Uprising* (Pittsburgh, 1939), 76-86. The *Columbian Centinel* (Boston), Sept. 19, 1792, advocated that the President take a strong stand against the insurrection in western Pennsylvania.

3. Ames to John Lowell, Phila., Dec. 6, 1792, Personal Papers, Lib. Cong.; Ames to Minot, Nov. 19, 1792, Ames, *Works of Ames*, I, 123; Malone, *Jefferson and the Rights of Man*, 478-82; Freeman, *Washington*, VI, 378-79; Cunningham, *Jeffersonian Republicans*, 33-49; Rufus King to Jeremiah Wadsworth, N.Y., Sept. 23, 1792, Jeremiah Wadsworth Papers, Vol. 141, Conn. Hist. Soc.; James Madison to Edmund Pendleton, Dec. 6, 1792, J. Nicholson to Madison, Phila., Oct. 3, 1792, Madison Papers, XV, Lib. Cong.; George Cabot to Theophilus Parsons, Beverly, Oct. 3, 1792, Lodge, ed., *Letters of Cabot*, 57; Alexander Hamilton to Charles C. Pinckney, Phila., Oct. 10, 1792, Lodge, ed., *Works of Hamilton*, X, 22; Oliver Wolcott to Oliver Wolcott, Sr., Phila., Oct. 8, 1792, Gibbs, *Memoirs*, I, 80-81; Edward Stanwood, *A History of the Presidency from 1788-1897*, 2 vols. (Boston, 1928), I, 39; Nathan Schachner, *The Founding Fathers* (N.Y., 1954), 226-29.

ton] and his second," wrote David Cobb, a Massachusetts representative. He added, "partie influence has had no effect on the votes of the latter." [4] Other New England states unswervingly gave Adams their votes, ensuring him thirty-eight of the seventy-seven electoral votes that brought him victory over George Clinton.

Viewing the election results in the nation as a whole, Ames was uneasy about Republican gains. He offered advice to friends in Massachusets where several inconclusive contests necessitated run-off elections to be held in January 1793. Exhorting Federalists to be alert, he warned them against any "supine neglect" which might enable the wrong men to win the districts. Only loyal men, "known to be unchangeable tho' ever so much temporizing be used," should be sent to Congress. Ames encouraged Thomas Dwight to run for Congress since he might be chosen "on very fair terms." He acknowledged that his brother-in-law might be reluctant to leave his family and his new distillery business. If he did not want to be a candidate, Ames thought that both Samuel Lyman and Samuel Henshaw were good possibilities. He wanted it clearly understood that he was not trying to dictate the choice of candidates, but "several good watchmen for order . . . in this place" were greatly concerned about the possible outcome of the second elections.[5]

Musing on his own re-election, Ames acknowledged the growth of opposition to his ideas. He noted that the *Chronicle* consistently worked against him and that its criticisms coincided with "the prejudices of the merchants." Clearly he was no friend to "the Jefferson scheme of commerce" and its anti-British emphasis. His sense of duty and his beliefs regarding the commercial position of Massachusetts made it impossible for him not "to act on . . . anti-Jefferson principles," or to discuss openly any of his own political tenets.[6]

Until a warring Europe shifted the focus of American politics to foreign affairs in mid-1793, Congress continued to be primarily concerned with domestic issues. During the current session partisan controversy became so intense that positive legislative achievements tended to be obscured. The Republicans, elated by their progress in the November elections, condemned the Hamiltonian system and once sure of

4. *Independent Chronicle* (Boston), Nov. 22, Dec. 13, 1792; David Cobb to Henry Knox, Boston, Dec. 5, 1792, Knox Papers, XXXIII, Mass. Hist. Soc.; Christopher Gore to Rufus King, Boston, Nov. 11, 1792, King, *Life of King*, I, 436; John Avery to George Thatcher, Boston, Dec. 15, 1792, Chamberlain Collection, Thatcher Papers, Boston Pub. Lib.; Stanwood, *History of the Presidency*, I, 39.
5. Ames to Dwight, Phila., Nov. 29, 1792, Fisher Ames Papers, Dedham Hist. Soc.; Dwight Foster to Theodore Sedgwick, Dec. 24, 1792, Sedgwick to Ephraim Williams, Phila., Jan. 31, 1793, Sedgwick Papers, Vols. B and III, Mass. Hist. Soc.
6. Ames to Lowell, Dec. 6, 1792, Personal Papers, Lib. Cong.

COURT HOUSE, RICKETT'S CIRCUS, AND OELLER'S HOTEL

South East and South West corners of 6th. and Chestnut
Streets in 1797.

Congress Hall, Philadelphia

(see p. xiii)

Fisher Ames in 1792
(*see p. xiii*)

their strength, conducted a vendetta against the Secretary himself.[7] Political antagonism developed immediately after the President's address, when the representatives took up the report of the House committee appointed in the previous session to investigate General St. Clair's defeat. Now that the inquiry had taken place, Ames was anxious to give the executive departments the opportunity to clarify the situation. The report had largely exonerated St. Clair from responsibility for the disaster, but implied that Hamilton and Knox were to blame for their failure to ensure proper means of supplying the army. Ames, therefore, took the stand that there was need for "a thorough investigation" and upheld a resolution to request the heads of the two departments to appear before the House in order to furnish essential information. He felt it was the best way to divert the Republican opponents from establishing a basis for possible impeachment proceedings, presumably against Hamilton. The House, however, rejected the Federalist proposal, and the matter of further investigation was turned over to a select committee. Hamilton and Knox thus were prevented from making an official appearance in the House, to the relief of the Republicans, who feared that they might thereby influence the legislature.[8]

The Republican congressmen, determined to reduce Hamilton's power, returned to their attack by taking exception to resolutions directing the Secretary of the Treasury to report a plan for further redemption of the public debt. Again, they professed to see dire consequences in the separation of powers if the House yielded any financial control. Ames had prepared persuasive answers to their objections, which he presented on November 21. All were eager to hear how he would get around the constitutional argument of the other side.[9]

The Massachusetts Federalist first established the point that neither a committee of the whole nor a select committee had as accurate knowledge of financial matters as the Secretary of the Treasury; thus, it was logical for the House to work closely with Hamilton. Criticizing the frequent resort to constitutional objections, he insisted that the way in which the Republicans were interpreting the Constitution was entirely unwarranted. They could not justifiably maintain that this request of the House to the Secretary was an unconstitutional delegation of power

7. Miller, *Hamilton*, 325-30; Brant, *Madison, Father of the Constitution*, 367-68; Cunningham, *Jeffersonian Republicans*, 50-51.
8. The report was brought up Nov. 7, 1792, *Annals*, III, 672, 679-80, 683, 686-87, 689, Nov. 7, 13, 14, 1792; St. Clair to Sargent, Aug. 27, 1792, Winthrop Sargent Papers, Mass. Hist. Soc. St. Clair emphasized that testimony given during the investigation made the committee less hostile to him.
9. *Annals*, III, 696-708, Nov. 19, 20, 1792.

since requesting advice was not the same as originating a bill. Further, consultation with the head of an executive department did not result in encroachment on congressional authority. He then showed that Congress, by its own acts, had provided for direct reports from department heads. Consequently, there was no valid reason for abandoning this arrangement when there was every need to concentrate financial responsibility in one person. Madison opposed Ames's stand because he was certain that carrying out the Federalist doctrine would leave the House no freedom of decision. In the final vote, the House upheld Ames's position, and the important channel of communication between the Treasury and Congress was preserved.[10]

Ames was not only defending Hamilton against charges that he had had undue influence on legislation, but he was also seeking to strengthen the position of the Secretary of the Treasury. His ultimate goal, not fully elaborated at this time, was to enable the Secretary to initiate legislation directly in Congress much as a finance minister would do. He had no use whatever for the concept of a weak executive department, barred from participation in molding legislation. Several years later when close relations between the Treasury Department and the House were broken, he asserted that the departments were prevented from acting and could not even use a speaking trumpet to be heard. Constantly Ames sought to enlarge the sphere of action of the executive in order to give the government stability, efficiency, and direction. In the latter part of the Second Congress, however, he and his Federalist colleagues were on the defensive and were unable to extend executive powers.[11]

Hostility toward the two bastions of Federalism, the Treasury and the War Departments, continued to gain force through the autumn of 1792 and into the new year. Ames became alarmed at the intransigent spirit of the Republicans, who were attempting, he decided, to block all legislative progress. Their actions in Congress—the protest against the role of the Secretary of the Treasury, the investigation of St. Clair, the attempt to reduce the size of the army—all were evidence of "a spirit of faction, which soon must come to a crisis." When the Republican clamor against the chief officers of the government swelled in volume both in Congress and in the *National Gazette*, Ames was con-

    10. *Ibid.*, 715-18, 722, Nov. 21, 1792.
    11. Ames to Lowell, Dec. 6, 1792, Personal Papers, Lib. Cong. Ames maintained, "There is a mass of prejudice...in favor of doing in an assembly what only one man can do." Ames to Alexander Hamilton, Phila., Jan. 26, 1797, James C. Hamilton, ed., *The Works of Alexander Hamilton, Comprising his Correspondence, and his Political and Official Writings*, 7 vols. (N.Y., 1850-51), VI, 200-201; White, *Federalists*, 75-76, 91-95; Harlow, *History of Legislative Methods*, 149-51.

vinced of their evil intent. Venting his wrath at those who would "immolate" Hamilton and not even spare the President, he drew a harsh picture of his political opponents. They were soured men, suspicious of all, and driven to intemperate lengths by an insatiable quest for office. "In the progress of things, they have, like toads, sucked poison from the earth," and now they were thirsting for vengeance.[12]

To the Hamiltonians, the most urgent task of the session was to complete the assumption of the remaining sums of the state debts. That would be a capstone on the edifice of the funding system and would provide financial relief for Massachusetts and South Carolina as well. Early in November, the Federalists were considering opening loans for the unassumed sums as soon as the final balances between the United States and the individual states were determined. It would be a "provisional assumption of what may be found due to creditor States," Ames explained, but he felt that it would "no doubt effect our purpose . . . in Massachusetts."[13] In the current state of politics, he was convinced that no other form of assumption had a chance.

Federalists had to contend with Madison, Hugh Williamson, and John Mercer who kept up a steady stream of objections and attempted to prevent further discussion of a residual assumption. Mercer accused the Federalists of wanting to burn the books to conceal the fact that not all the states were creditors to the government and that the assumption was superfluous. In turn, Madison tried parliamentary maneuvers to prevent a decision on the matter. Ames took the Republicans to task, contending that postponement of a crucial issue was "such an evasion of justice as might put the country in a flame."[14] All the signs, it seemed to him, revealed that the Republicans were determined to stop any payment of the debts. In a few vivid sentences he sketched the political battle then in progress. "Virginia moves in a solid column," he explained, "and the discipline of the party is as severe as the Prussian. Deserters are not spared. Madison is become a desperate party leader. . . . We are fighting for the assumption of the balances. . . . He opposes, *vi et armis.*"[15] Confronted by a determined opposition, the Federalists were barely able to rescue through the single vote of the Speaker a bill providing for a final assumption. A few days later the bill met defeat

12. Ames to Minot, Phila., Feb. 20, 1793, Ames, *Works of Ames*, I, 128. Newspaper attacks on Hamilton in 1792-93 were especially virulent in the *National Gazette* (Phila.), "Brutus," Sept. 1, "Truth," Oct. 10, "Monitor," Oct. 13, 17, 1792, "An American Farmer," Feb. 13, 23, Mar. 2, 9, 16, 1793, *Independent Chronicle* (Boston), Dec. 27, 1792.
13. Ames to Dwight, Phila., Dec. 5, 1792, Ames, *Works of Ames*, I, 125; Ames to Lowell, Dec. 6, 1792, Personal Papers, Lib. Cong.
14. *Annals*, III, 805, 808, 831-33, 848, Jan. 10, 21, 28, 1793.
15. Ames to Dwight, Phila., Jan. (n.d.), 1793, Ames, *Works of Ames*, I, 127.

in the Senate. Ames was convinced that because of southern obstinacy nothing more could be done about the debts until another Congress met. Twice the prospects of completing the assumption had been shattered by political strife.

Republican sniping at Hamilton had increased to a fusillade late in 1792. With great determination Madison and Jefferson had set out to prove that Hamilton had had a corrupting influence on the government. Sensitive to criticism, Hamilton confided to John Jay that there were "malicious intrigues to stab me in the dark." [16] To accomplish their end of forcing the Secretary of the Treasury to make injurious revelations about his administration of finances, the Republicans in the House repeatedly submitted resolutions requesting detailed information on his fiscal transactions. Striving to pin him down, William Giles, under the tutelage of Jefferson, presented resolutions on February 27, 1793, which were obviously an indictment of the Secretary camouflaged as a request for information. [17]

The Federalists in Congress immediately met the assault head on, rather than give their political adversaries the advantage of accusations unanswered until the next Congress. Ames moved that the resolutions should be discussed, and two days of intense debating followed. Federalist orators girded themselves to defend their political leader, while Republicans leveled their sights at Hamilton and fired charges of maladministration at him, prolonging the meetings of the House far into the night. [18]

Madison, citing sections of the financial acts of Congress, built up the case that Hamilton had diverted and misapplied certain funds borrowed to pay interest due foreign bondholders. This action, he declared, was a direct violation of the laws and of presidential orders. Immediately afterward, Ames refuted the accusations against the Sec-

16. *Annals*, III, 851, Jan. 28, 1793. The Senate rejected the House bill, Feb. 4, *ibid.*, 638-39. Ames to Dwight, Phila., Feb. 6, 1793, Ames, *Works of Ames*, I, 127-28; Alexander Hamilton to John Jay, Phila., Dec. 18, 1792, Hamilton to William Short, Phila., Feb. 5, 1793, Lodge, ed., *Works of Hamilton*, X, 29, 31.

17. *Annals*, III, 895, Feb. 27, 1793. Previous resolutions were presented on Dec. 24, 27, 1792, and Jan. 23, 1793, *ibid.*, 753, 761, 835. There is evidence of Jefferson's collaboration with Giles in drafting the resolutions; Ford, ed., *Writings of Jefferson*, VI, 168-71; Miller, *Hamilton*, 327-32; *National Gazette* (Phila.), "Franklin," Feb. 16, 23, 27, Mar. 2, 16, 1793, "Decius," Feb. 20, 23, 1793; Oliver Wolcott to Oliver Wolcott, Sr., Phila., Feb. 8, 1793, Gibbs, *Memoirs*, I, 85-86; White, *Federalists*, 330-34, 352-53; Dumas Malone, *Jefferson and the Ordeal of Liberty* (Boston, 1962), 14-33.

18. *Annals*, III, 899, Feb. 28, 1793; the debates on the resolutions are given in *ibid.*, 901-5, 907-63, Feb. 28, Mar. 1, 1793. The *National Gazette* (Phila.), Mar. 6, 1793, reported on the evening session of March 1, "At this late hour, about midnight, it was observed, that several members had left the house, being so much fatigued, that they were not able to stay for the yeas and nays."

retary. Hamilton's merging of two separate funds was definitely not an indictable crime. To argue, as Madison did, that the Secretary had broken the laws was entirely groundless. Ames deftly presented his defense, "crowded in a nutshell," and left to others the statistical proof of Hamilton's honesty. Turning his attention to specific charges which Giles had made, Ames countered them by showing that, in the daily business of the Treasury, Hamilton's methods of disbursing funds were legitimate. In his defense, the representative from Massachusetts relied more on the conviction which his eloquence might carry than on a step-by-step citation of evidence which would disprove the accusations. He concluded his "elegant speech," as the reporter of the debates termed it, with an admonition against unsubstantiated charges based merely on suspicion.[19] To many of the representatives it seemed as though Giles's resolutions had not been founded on fact. In the evening session of March 1, one by one his six resolutions were defeated by substantial majorities. In the eyes of his admirers Hamilton was amply vindicated and according to one observer had "come forth like gold."[20]

Congress ended on March 2 with political bitterness barely abating. Shortly before the adjournment Ames commented that he looked around with aversion at the scene and already anticipated his release from Philadelphia. With his mind full of politics he first wanted to sit by the fireside with his friend Dwight and "bode evil like a death watch," while discussing recent events. The session had added conviction to an idea he had that politics was not a rigidly determined branch of science. Its "principles are contested after they are demonstrated and resisted in practice after they are admitted in theory."[21] Logic and reason obviously did not have as much weight in day-to-day politics as Ames inwardly wished.

Although Ames frequently expressed sharp criticism of Congress, he did enjoy the intellectual stimulus of participating in the national legislature. He considered public life hard and the lot of the legislator vexatious; yet he must have exaggerated these difficulties, for he per-

19. *Annals*, III, 936-43, 945-46, Mar. 1, 1793. The *National Gazette* (Phila.), Mar. 23, 1793, mentions remarks made by Ames just prior to the voting on Giles's first resolution, which was negatived 14 to 38, Feb. 28, 1793. These are not recorded in *Annals*, III.

20. *Annals*, III, 955-63, Mar. 1, 1793; *Columbian Centinel* (Boston), Feb. 16, Mar. 13, 1793; Thomas Jefferson to Thomas M. Randolph, Phila., Mar. 3, 1793, Ford, ed., *Writings of Jefferson*, VI, 194-96; [John Taylor], *An Examination of the Late Proceedings in Congress Respecting the Official Conduct of the Secretary of the Treasury* (Phila., 1793); Chauncey Goodrich to Oliver Wolcott, Hartford, Mar. 24, 1793, Oliver Wolcott, Sr., to Oliver Wolcott, Litchfield, Mar. 25, 1793, Gibbs, *Memoirs*, I, 90-91.

21. Ames to Dwight, Phila., Feb. 26, 1793, Autograph Collection, Houghton Library, Harvard Univ.

sistently returned to the scene of political combat. Explaining his emotional response to politics to his brother-in-law, he wrote, "I am habitually a zealot in politics. It is I fancy, constitutional, and so the cure desperate. I burn and freeze, am lethargic, raving, sanguine and despondent, as often as the wind shifts." Ames admitted that there often were aggravations in a political career, but he was certain that the difficulties waked "a curiosity, an active interest in the events and measures which gradually becomes the habit of a Politician's being." He found that "the Society of worthy and distinguished men . . . [was] no mean consolation." [22]

Ames was very much pleased that Frances had come with him to Philadelphia. She was evidently a great social asset, for he remarked that her "conduct and sentiments in this situation" had convinced him that their decision to go to the capital together had been a wise one. Her presence made this period far more agreeable to Ames than any had been while he was a bachelor. Even the day-to-day routine of Congress seemed much less tedious to him. He had hoped that his wife might stay with him until the end of the session, but as she was expecting a baby, it was a desirable time for her to visit her family. Thus, she departed for Springfield in February.[23] When Ames returned to Massachusetts, he had to look for another house, as the one he and Frances had rented was now sold. Since he had never entirely severed his ties with Dedham, it was logical under the existing circumstances to settle there. By June 1 they were established in a rented house which had space enough for both a flower and vegetable garden. It was an interim solution until such time as they could build their own home.

During the summer of 1793, Ames resumed his frequently interrupted law work. His long absences at Congress precluded his developing a large practice in the highly competitive legal circles of Boston, but the opening of a court in newly established Norfolk County was certain to bring more legal activity to Dedham. Ames had to build up his law business again from the foundations. Even his commission as justice of the peace had lapsed, and he jestingly remarked that "unless Mrs. D [his sister-in-law] will use influence at St. James I doubt it's resurrection." [24]

22. Ames to Dwight, Phila., Dec. 31, 1792, Ames, *Works of Ames*, I, 126; Ames to Dwight, Feb. 26, 1793, Autograph Collection, Houghton Library, Harvard Univ.
23. Ames to Dwight, Phila., Dec. 5, 1792, Jan. (n.d.), 1793, Fisher Ames Papers, Dedham Hist. Soc.; Ames to Dwight, Dec. 31, 1792, Ames, *Works of Ames*, I, 126.
24. Ames to Dwight, Oct. 4, 1792, Ames, *Works of Ames*, I, 121; Ames to Dwight, Dedham, June 26, 1793, Fisher Ames Papers, Dedham Hist. Soc. One phase of Ames's law business continued to be the collection of debts. Ames to Edward H. Robbins, Dedham, Nov. 19, 1793, J. M. Robbins Papers, Mass. Hist.

Ames continued to keep his finger on the political pulse as well as he could. He was disturbed to hear that Theodore Sedgwick might be forced to retire because of the continued illness of his wife. To lose a single Federalist would be bad, he maintained, but to lose such "an Ajax as Sedgwick" would be a heavy blow. This was especially true now as the country was becoming more and more stirred over the progress of the French Revolution. Repercussions of the European turmoil were bound to become evident in Congress, and calm periods would be only portents of future storms. "We may be safe," he warned. "We must not hope to be quiet."[25]

A wave of pro-French sentiment engulfed the country during the winter of 1792-93, as many Americans cheered wildly at the overthrow of the monarchy in France. Citizens of Boston had outdone themselves with a massive civic feast, complete with an Ode to Liberty and a thousand-pound roast ox, to celebrate the accomplishments of the French patriots. The more conservative and dispassionate, especially among the Federalists, looked askance at these popular civic activities; but not until news of the execution of Louis XVI reached the United States was there an extensive revulsion against the Revolution. Unlike the old patriots of 1776 or the Republicans, Federalists could not excuse the actions of the French and rebelled against the idea that the Revolution was symbolic of the cause of humanity and freedom. To the horror evoked by the death of the King and the Queen was added the fear that the Jacobin clubs would spread to America and overturn property, religion, and the rule by the wealthy and well-born. None who upheld concepts of law and order, Federalists maintained, could now approve the ideals or the deeds of the revolutionaries. From 1793 onward there was thus added a new ingredient to the political cauldron.[26]

Soc.; Ames to Dwight, Dedham, Sept. 16, 1793, Ames, *Works of Ames*, I, 129-30. Ames joined the Massachusetts Agricultural Society during the summer of 1793 and was also elected a member of the American Academy of Arts and Sciences; Massachusetts Society for Promoting Agriculture, *Laws and Regulations* (Boston, 1793), 16; *Columbian Centinel* (Boston), June 8, 1793.

25. Ames to Dwight, June 26, 1793, Fisher Ames Papers, Dedham Hist. Soc.; Ames to Dwight, Boston, Aug. (n.d.), 1793, Ames, *Works of Ames*, I, 129.

26. Charles D. Hazen, *Contemporary American Opinion of the French Revolution* (Baltimore, 1897), 165-69, 253-55, 266-69. Bostonian reaction to the French Revolution may be traced in the *Columbian Centinel*, which became more and more opposed to the Revolution after Mar. 1793. The *Boston Gazette*, the *Independent Chronicle*, and the *American Apollo* remained ardent champions of the French cause. The Civic Feast in Boston is described in the *Boston Gazette*, Jan. 28, 1793; Morse, *Federalist Party*, 67-71, 89-91; Adams, ed., *Works of Adams*, VI, 223-403. Nathaniel Appleton to Noah Webster, Boston, Jan. 6, 1793, Noah Webster Papers, N.Y. Pub. Lib. Appleton expressed the fear that the "*democratic jacobin spirit*" of France was spreading to the United States.

Until the French influence became evident in American politics Ames did not express vehement opposition to the French Revolution. He was convinced that "France is madder than Bedlam" and thought that she would be ruined between her own domestic folly and external hostility. During the Second Congress in March 1792, he had voted in favor of a resolution praising the King of France for accepting the new French constitution, but he had balked at accepting a second resolution which praised the French as a great people. With strong convictions about the political leadership of an intellectual and wealthy segment of society, Ames could have no intrinsic sympathy with the goals of the French patriots.[27]

The arrival of Citizen Genêt, the firebrand who was the new minister from France, and his triumphal procession northward from Charleston to Philadelphia had intensified the pro-French outbursts as far away as Boston.[28] Ames watched the public reaction critically and was relieved to find that Genêt's star waned very swiftly by midsummer. In part he attributed it to the minister's rudeness, which had provoked many against him. But the President's neutrality proclamation and the favorable responses from various towns had undone the French diplomat. Boston, too, was "less frenchified than it was," and by early autumn very little was being said about a French faction there.[29]

With the public mind in a more tranquil state, Ames thought that people were eager to hear the truth. "Such periods occur rarely and ought not to pass away in vain," he wrote to Alexander Hamilton. It was an ideal time to publish articles setting the public straight about the Republican party. He enclosed one he had written on the inconsistency

27. Ames to Dwight, Oct. 4, 1792, Ames, *Works of Ames,* I, 121; *Annals,* III, 456-57, Mar. 10, 1792. The *Independent Chronicle* (Boston), Mar. 30, 1792, criticized Ames for a "luke warm, spiritless, insipid performance" in regard to his support of the resolution.

28. Hazen, *American Opinion,* 173-79; Morse, *Federalist Party,* 71-74; the case of the French frigate "La Concorde," arriving in Boston where its crew denounced leading citizens as aristocrats, stirred Boston profoundly. *Boston Gazette,* May 27, 1793; *Independent Chronicle* (Boston), May 30, 1793; *Columbian Centinel* (Boston), Aug. 14, 17, 21, 24, 1793; Stephen Higginson to Alexander Hamilton, Boston, July 26, 1793, William L. Smith to Hamilton, Boston, Aug. 23, 1793, Hamilton Papers, XX, Lib. Cong.

29. Ames to Dwight, Boston, Aug. 1793, Ames, *Works of Ames,* I, 129; Ames to Dwight, Dedham, Oct. 11, 1793, Fisher Ames Papers, Dedham Hist. Soc. The *Independent Chronicle* (Boston), strongly defended Genêt during the summer of 1793; Aug. 15, "A Moderate Man," Aug. 22, 26, 29, 1793; *Boston Gazette,* "Seventy-five," Sept. 2, 1793. Malone, *Ordeal of Liberty,* 68-79; Charles M. Thomas, *American Neutrality in 1793: A Study in Cabinet Government* (N.Y., 1931); Christopher Gore to Tobias Lear, Waltham, June 2, July 28, 1793, Christopher Gore Papers, Lib. Cong. Gore indicated that Boston Federalists were pleased with the President's proclamation, which had a calming effect on the populace.

of "our Jacobins," which he felt might be revised and improved by a competent person. He did not hide from Hamilton his concern about political developments and suggested that every effort be made to "disarm the faction who distort the truth." [30]

While Ames took the responsibilities of Congress seriously in this period of international tension, he was reluctant to resume the constant political struggle. There was talk toward the end of August that the President might request Congress to convene as early as November. If this occurred he might have to leave Frances in Dedham shortly before the birth of their baby. She had been well and in high spirits earlier in the summer, but from August on, she had, as her husband commented, "an uncommon share . . . of the disagreeables." Although he did not admit it to Frances, he was quite concerned about her at this time. Early in October he wrote to his Springfield relatives that it was still uncertain when the baby was due. With his wife looking over his shoulder as he wrote, he teasingly mentioned that some women had been "fourteen months in that situation." At last on October 22 the long days of waiting were over. Shortly before 9 A.M., Frances bore a son, whom they soon named John Worthington. The little one, Ames hastily informed the Dwights, was doing very well and, surprisingly, had black hair. "It is needless to tell you how happy this event makes me," he wrote with elation, wishing his brother-in-law the same kind of happiness.[31]

Ames returned alone to the capital in the first days of December 1793. Philadelphia was just recovering from an unprecedented attack of yellow fever which had exacted a heavy toll on the inhabitants. For a time it had seemed as though Congress might have to meet in a neighboring town, leading Ames to remark that public officials considered themselves too important to risk the fever. He had heard so many grim accounts of the epidemic before his arrival that he fully expected the town would look like a battlefield. Fortunately cold autumnal weather had dissipated the fever, and now only the malignancy of politics remained.[32]

30. Ames to Alexander Hamilton, Boston, Aug. 31, 1793, Hamilton Papers, XX, Lib. Cong.; Thomas Jefferson to James Monroe, Phila., June 4, 1793, Monroe Papers, N.Y. Pub. Lib.
31. Ames to Dwight, Dedham, Aug. (n.d.), Sept. 16, Oct. 11, 22, 1793, Fisher Ames Papers, Dedham Hist. Soc. John Worthington Ames was named after his grandfather. All four daughters of Col. Worthington named their first-born sons John Worthington. The youngest daughter, Sophia, married John Williams of Wethersfield, Conn., in 1799.
32. Ames to Minot, Phila., Dec. 6, 1793, Ames, *Works of Ames*, I, 130. Ames lodged at No. 35 Walnut St.; *The Federal Gazette and Philadelphia Daily Advertiser*, Dec. 24, 1793; Ames to Dwight, Oct. 11, 1793, Fisher Ames Papers,

In the company of Dwight Foster, newly elected to Congress from Massachusetts, Ames attended one of the initial meetings of the Third Congress on the morning of December 5. After introducing Foster to various members and listening to the Reverend Ashbel Green give a prayer, Ames presented his credentials and took the oath. Almost immediately he was plunged into the depths of a variety of problems. Until the adjournment at 3 P.M., the House heard a report from the commissioners negotiating with the Indians, another report on the perennial question of settling the wartime accounts between the states and the United States, and a message from the President on foreign affairs.[33]

Amid all of the popular excitement and the machinations of Genêt, Ames sensed that it would be difficult to remain at peace. He was consequently pleased at Washington's "rather tart" message which accompanied the official correspondence with Genêt transmitted to the House. Even though the political horizon looked more promising, Ames was not certain that the weather could be trusted. Within two weeks, the initial harmony evaporated, and he reported, "We begin to have trouble enough of a public nature to engross any mind capable of its impression." A renewed motion to investigate the Treasury Department and a wave of foreign problems presaged grave difficulties for the administration. To one newspaper writer, the correspondence between Jefferson and the British minister, Hammond, which was read to the House of Representatives, was both "interesting and melancholy." [34]

Federalists considered foreign affairs so critical that they insisted on barring the public from the discussions of negotiations with Morocco in regard to the depredations of the Algerine pirates. When Madison made a strong plea against this move, Ames granted that the United States had "a republican and a popular government" but asked if a "republic was to have no secrets." An open discussion under the existing state of affairs, he was certain, would deprive the government of all advantage. He obviously could not agree with the idea which Madison

Dedham Hist. Soc. Ames gave an interesting description of the medical treatments used during the epidemic. John H. Powell, *Bring Out Your Dead: the Great Plague of Yellow Fever in Philadelphia in 1793* (Phila., 1949); Benjamin Rush to Mrs. Rush, Aug. 21, Nov. 11, 1793, Butterfield, ed., *Letters of Rush*, II, 637-745.

33. "Journal of Dwight Foster," Dec. 5, 1793, Amer. Antiq. Soc.

34. Ames to Minot, Dec. 6, 1793, Ames, *Works of Ames*, I, 132; Ames to Dwight, Phila., Dec. 17, 1793, Fisher Ames Papers, Dedham Hist. Soc.; "Journal of Dwight Foster," Dec. 6, 10, 1793, Amer. Antiq. Soc.; *Annals*, IV, 136-37, Dec. 5, 1793; *The Federal Gazette and Philadelphia Daily Advertiser*, Dec. 10, 1793.

had publicized two years earlier that public opinion was the "real sovereign" in every free government.[35]

On January 3, 1794, into a tense and uncertain atmosphere, Madison dropped the explosive proposal that Congress should support a forceful commercial policy with retaliatory legislation on all nations which did not grant the United States favorable commercial treaties. The seven resolutions which the Virginian presented were a product of his collaboration with Jefferson over a period of years and represented an effort to evolve an economic policy which would eliminate the undue restrictions on American commerce and shipping in Europe. To the Republicans, Madison's resolutions were the culmination of repeated attempts since 1789 to pass anti-British commercial legislation. Because of the growing number of British confiscations of American ships under the Orders in Council of June 8, 1793, the Jeffersonians felt there was full justification for such legislation. Federalists, in contrast, placed their dependence on the growth of closer commercial ties with Britain as the only security for American trade. In the opinion of Hamilton, Ames, and other key Federalists, the adoption of Madison's resolutions would be tantamount to declaring war against Britain.[36] With such conflicting ideas about foreign trade, it was not surprising that a political battle of the first magnitude quickly flared up.

Maneuvering for a tactical advantage, Ames requested a week's postponement since this subject "required the most mature deliberation of the House." By January 13, when the discussion of Madison's "Commercial Propositions" began, the Federalists were exceedingly well prepared. After consultation with Hamilton, William L. Smith initiated the attack on Madison's position. So well armed was he with words and statistics provided by the Secretary that Jefferson later commented, "The sophistry is too ... ingenious ... to have been comprehended by Smith, much less devised by him." [37] Arguing skillfully, Smith tried to

35. *The Federal Gazette and Philadelphia Daily Advertiser*, Dec. 27, 1793; Samuel Holten to Theophilus Bradbury, Phila., Jan. 7, 1794, Samuel Holten Papers, Lib. Cong.; *National Gazette* (Phila.), Dec. 19, 1791; Adrienne Koch, *Jefferson and Madison: The Great Collaboration* (N.Y., 1950), 121.

36. *Annals*, IV, 155-56, Jan. 3, 1794; Setser, *Commercial Reciprocity Policy*, 109-17; Miller, *Federalist Era*, 116, 145-46; Oliver Wolcott to Jedidiah Morse, Phila., Dec. 30, 1793, to Oliver Wolcott, Sr., Jan. 2, 1794, and Oliver Wolcott, Sr., to Oliver Wolcott, Litchfield, Jan. 13, 1794, Gibbs, *Memoirs*, I, 125-26; Theodore Sedgwick to Ephraim Williams, Phila., Mar. 3, 1794, Sedgwick Papers, III, Mass. Hist. Soc.; Ames to Christopher Gore, Phila., Jan. 28, 1794, Ames, *Works of Ames*, I, 133; Alexander White to James Madison, Woodville, Va., Feb. 1, 1794, Madison Papers, XVII, Lib. Cong.

37. *Annals*, IV, 158, Jan. 3, 1794; Thomas Jefferson to James Madison, Monticello, Apr. 3, 1794, Ford, ed., *Writings of Jefferson*, VI, 501; Samuel F. Bemis,

prove that the British Isles provided a better market for American goods than France and that Jefferson had overrated commercial regulations as a means of forcing Britain to abandon her Navigation Act. Madison contradicted the Federalist speaker by stressing how effectively Britain excluded competing American shipping.

In answer to the Republicans who harked on the theme of an iniquitous Britain, Ames alluded to their "indefinite declamation" and asked them to point out specific evidence of British discrimination. When he repeated his request a few days later, Representative John Nicholas of Virginia rebuked him by saying that he was "astonished that the gentleman possessed so little American feeling . . . [that] it is necessary to tell . . . [him] of the hostilities of the savages on our frontiers . . . and the commercial advantages wrested from our hands by that mean policy which lets loose the Algerines upon our defenceless merchantmen." [38] After listening to prolonged Republican oratory, Ames commented, "It is all French that is spoken in support of the measure. I like the Yankee dialect better." [39]

Ames refrained from giving his own analysis of the commercial policy until many of his colleagues had expressed their views. In a speech on January 27, he raised the question whether the present resolutions would result in an improvement of trade and navigation. Putting aside any question of their constitutionality, he concentrated on proving that they would not have the desired effect. The only consideration in trade was profit. Consequently it was unwise to attempt to use commerce for political purposes, he averred.[40] Since the nations of the world had long been accustomed to their restrictive navigation systems, Ames rejected the Madison-Jefferson concept that the United States could use pressure to effect a change. "The extravagant despotism of this language accords very ill with our power to give it effect, or with the affectation of zeal for an unlimited freedom of commerce," Ames maintained. Any effort to alter the policy of nations by counteracting foreign restrictions with American restrictions was "ridiculous and inconsistent." [41]

The insinuations made by the Republicans that the English system revealed Britain's hatred for the United States led Ames to assert that "the British market for our exports . . . is better than the French, . . . and for many of our products, the only one." He cited extensive evi-

Jay's Treaty: A Study in Commerce and Diplomacy (N.Y., 1923), 190-91; *Annals*, IV, 209-25, Jan. 14, 1794.
    38. *Annals*, IV, 235, 274, 310-11, Jan. 15, 23, 24, 1794.
    39. Ames to Dwight, Phila., Jan. 17, 1794, Ames, *Works of Ames*, I, 133.
    40. *Annals*, IV, 272-74, 293-310, 328-29, Jan. 23, 24, 27, 1794.
    41. *Ibid.*, 330.

dence to prove his point that American trade with Britain was on an exceptionally good basis with only breadstuffs and whale oil restricted by heavy duties. The United States, he affirmed, had a better position in trade with the British Isles than other countries had. He had to admit that trade from the West Indies was less free, although Britain gave the Americans more preference than the French. "The fervor of transient sentiments" motivating the French was "not better than straw or stubble," he insisted. In contrast the "mutual interest" of Britain and the United States "was no hollow foundation to build on," but "a bottom of rock." [42]

After concluding that American commerce and shipping were in a healthy economic condition, he accused the promoters of closer Franco-American ties of demanding that the United States give up the best market for its exports and also challenge the nation's best customer. These policies appeared to Ames to be quite "inconsistent and strange" coming from those who frequently had advocated that "we should even renounce the sea and devote ourselves to agriculture." The promised advantages of the new commercial policy were ephemeral. Applying the ideas of Madison's resolutions would only aggravate an adverse balance of trade with England and increase the demand for credit. The whole theory of giving protection to trade by prohibiting and restricting it, he declared, was "among the exploded dogmas." Assertions had been made that the United States had the economic power to starve the British West Indies. The hard logic of the facts Ames presented proved that even a total cessation of American trade would neither injure the British nor force them to repeal their Navigation Act. "By voting out the resolutions," Ames concluded his lucid exposition of the Federalist position, "we shall show to our own citizens, and foreign nations, that our prudence has prevailed over our prejudices, that we prefer our interests to our resentments. Let us assert a genuine independence of spirit.... We shall be false to our duty ... as Americans, if we basely descend to a servile dependence on France or Great Britain." [43]

Ames's speech against Madison's "war regulations," as he privately called them, was one of the most effective and successful of his career. Writing to Christopher Gore on the day after his oration, he commented, "I have been delivered, safely, of a speech, which I am glad to have off my hands." With his usual modesty he said that Samuel Dexter, a newly elected Federalist from Massachusetts, had made "a speech much better than mine, which has fixed his reputation in the House

42. *Ibid.*, 331-34.
43. *Ibid.*, 338, 342, 349.

very properly." [44] In no way was Ames ever arrogant about his abilities, nor did he flaunt his own importance.

The storm in the House of Representatives continued at full blast for several days after Ames spoke. None of the members heeded the admonition of Representative Uriah Forrest of Maryland that enough had been said on the topic. Madison held forth on two days, combating the statements Ames and Smith had made. Each new speech made tempers grow shorter. When Federalists tried to precipitate a vote in Madison's absence, there were loud cries of unfair dealing, and Abraham Clark of New Jersey finally asserted that if the members sat any longer on the question they would all be petrified. Madison defended the general principles of his first resolution, which specified that additional duties should be imposed on the manufactured goods of nations lacking commercial treaties with the United States. Ames, on his part, insisted that the Federalists would have nothing to do with the idea of retaliatory levies. As far as he was concerned the initial resolution was "a matter of moonshine, including everything, and concluding nothing." [45] In disparaging tones Ames said that no commercial state approved of Madison's commercial proposals because "the people had too much good sense." The Republicans had command of sufficient votes to pass the first resolution by a majority of five. Then, while Federalists objected vociferously, they postponed further consideration of the others. [46]

For more than a month the commercial issue was suspended in the House; yet the public continued the debate concerning the basic directions of American foreign policy. In Boston the Republican newspapers kept matters alive with frequent criticisms of the role Ames had played in the preceding months, as well as constant articles with an anti-British tone. The *Boston Gazette* condemned all who had not advocated breaking off commercial relations with Britain and later saw distinct evi-

44. Ames to Gore, Jan. 28, 1794, Ames, *Works of Ames*, I, 134; Lucius M. Sargent, *Reminiscences of Samuel Dexter* (Boston, 1857); C. W. Bowen, "Samuel Dexter, Councilor, and His Son. Hon. Samuel Dexter, Secretary of War, and Secretary of the Treasury," Amer. Antiq. Soc., *Proceedings*, New Ser., 35 (1925), 23-37; Jedidiah Morse to Oliver Wolcott, Jr., Charlestown, Feb. 11, 1794, Oliver Wolcott Papers, VIII, Conn. Hist. Soc.; Henry Van Schaack to Theodore Sedgwick, Feb. 22, 1794, Sedgwick Papers, Vol. B, Mass. Hist. Soc. Van Schaack indicated that some merchants were highly critical of Ames and Dexter for their opposition to Madison's resolutions.

45. *Annals*, IV, 355, 366-95, 418, 421, Jan. 28, 29, Feb. 3, 1794; Horatio Gates to James Madison, Mar. 13, 1794, Madison Papers, XVII, Lib. Cong.; Gen. Gates remarked, "I have read...your reply to Messr. Smith, Ames, and Dexter. I am certain there is not a sound Whigg from the River St. Croix to...the St. Mary's that does not Honour and applaud the Speaker."

46. *Annals*, IV, 422, 426, 431, Feb. 3, 4, 5, 1794. The vote to postpone was 51 yeas, 47 nays. Ames voted nay.

dences of cowardice on the part of Congress for favoring trade with England. One writer asserted that the Massachusetts representatives should have supported Madison's resolutions as their constituents would be the ones to benefit from them. He then took Ames to task because he "does not (or will not) see the advantage of our commerce with the French Republic." Another writer found fault with him for making Americans appear the "humble supplicants" to Britain. Referring to Ames's recent speech, this antagonist observed, "It so strongly marks the politics of the man, that however his brilliant . . . eloquence may have dazzled (for a season) his unsuspecting constituents, it now appears evident . . . that he sits in that House for the last time." [47]

The editor of the *Columbian Centinel* was alert to defend the Federalist cause, as well as one of its leading spokesmen. With a tone of righteous indignation the Boston Federalist paper accused its arch rival, the *Independent Chronicle,* of willful misrepresentation of Ames's speech, creating a small tempest by its condemnation of the Republican journal. The *Centinel* was also unsparing in its criticism of Madison, dubbing him the leading "War Hawk" and holding him up to ridicule for resorting frequently to "pitiful shifts." With a sharp thrust at the Virginian, the *Centinel* inquired, "Where did Mr. Maddison, any more than Mr. Ames or Mr. Dexter, acquire his knowledge of commerce? Not surely in the interior of Virginia where no other commerce is transacted than buying and selling of negroes." [48]

Popular resentment against Britain, already stirred by the debates in Congress and rumors of British trouble-making among the Indians, was whipped up to a fury when news of wholesale confiscation of American merchant vessels reached the United States. Under the Orders in Council of July and November 1793, the British had attempted to crush French military and commercial rivalry by depriving France of the benefits of neutral American trade. Large numbers of captured American ships were thereupon confiscated on the grounds that all neutral vessels carrying French-owned cargoes had broken Britain's maritime law. Republicans in the United States made good political use of the mounting public outrage, connecting all the outstanding grievances against Britain with an alleged unwillingness of the administration to take a strong stand on the issue.[49]

47. *Boston Gazette,* Jan. 27, Mar. 17, 1794; *Independent Chronicle* (Boston), Feb. 10, 20, 1794.
48. *Columbian Centinel* (Boston), Feb. 22, Mar. 1, 1794.
49. Bemis, *Jay's Treaty,* 192; Theodore Sedgwick to Ephraim Williams, Mar. 6, 1794, Sedgwick Papers, III, Mass. Hist. Soc. Even Sedgwick was impelled to assert, "Such indeed are the injuries which we have received from Great Britain that I believe I should not much hesitate on going to war, but that we must in that case be allied to France."

In Boston, Charles Jarvis and Benjamin Austin attempted to harangue a town meeting to adopt anti-British resolutions, but the mercantile element remained in command and opposed any measures which might lead to war. Endorsing the actions of their congressmen, several hundred residents signed a statement which was forwarded to Ames and to Senator Cabot. According to John Quincy Adams, who was present at the meeting, "the Jacobins were completely discomfited and will have the mortification to find their intended poison operate as an invigorating cordial." [50]

Public opinion elsewhere was not so readily kept in check. Strongly pro-French citizens in Charleston expressed their antipathy toward the leading Federalists in the commercial debate by exhibiting them in effigy. On a stage set up in front of a hotel, the figures of Fisher Ames and William L. Smith were represented as stretching out their arms to the harlot Britain beneath a gallows, while Benedict Arnold and the Devil hovered in the background. A sign on Ames referred to his supposed fortune of £100,000 in 6 per cent securities, and another proclaimed his confession of his crimes. "From the day on which I first commenced horse jockey," the figure of Ames was made to say, "my *Ames* have been villainy. The cries of the wretched soldier, the widow, and the orphan, whom I have cheated, overwhelm me with despair: I must be eternally damned." [51] In honor of the success of the French army at Toulon the effigies were dismantled. When Ames, however, received a report that he had been burned in effigy, he wryly commented, "The fire, you know, is pleasant, when it is not too near; and I am willing to have it believed that, as I come out of the fire undiminished in weight, I am now all gold. I laugh ... at the silly rage of the burners." [52]

Ames did not similarly laugh off the gravity of Anglo-American relations. He attributed much of the blame for the situation to the Republicans, who were using the commercial issue to cover purely political goals. The consequence of their restrictive policy would be to arouse the English temper. If Congress continued to let their feelings concerning Britain and France determine legislation, war was inevitable. Yet Ames was not blind to the responsibility of the British. Their maritime policy toward the United States could result in a serious clash.

50. Christopher Gore to Rufus King, Boston, Mar. 3, 1794, King, *Life of King,* I, 547; John Quincy Adams to John Adams, Boston, Mar. 2, 1794, Ford, ed., *Writings of John Quincy Adams,* I, 179-80; *Boston Gazette,* Feb. 24, Mar. 3, Mar. 17, 1794; Ames to Christopher Gore, Phila., Mar. 5, 1794, Ames, *Works of Ames,* I, 137. The last letter should be dated Mar. 25, 1794.

51. The *Boston Gazette,* Apr. 14, 1794, reprinted a hand bill from Charleston, S.C., describing the incidents of Mar. 11 and 15; Charles Fraser, *Reminiscences of Charleston* (Charleston, 1854), 39-40, 45.

52. Ames to Gore, Mar. 5 [25], 1794, Ames, *Works of Ames,* I, 138.

"If this should be pushed by the English," he forecast, "it ... [will drive] us to the wall." Unresolved grievances had inflamed the members of Congress, but there was some justification. "John Bull, proud of his strength, angry with our partiality to France, ardent in his contest ... shows less patience and respect for us than he ought to do," he explained.[53] The English gave no indication of turning over the frontier posts to their rightful owners, the Americans, and English seizures of shipping were provoking; but he did not think Britain was deliberately attempting to force the United States into war.

Even if public resentment swirled around him, Ames had no fear of taking a firm stand in Congress for a policy which would secure peace. There was no doubt in his mind that the United States should avoid hostile steps and adhere to its obvious duty. "Peace, peace, to the last day that it can be maintained" was the only course; but if war came, then the onus of it should be placed squarely where it belonged: on the Republican party "as their act and deed." Meanwhile Federalists should avoid aggravating the British and at the same time promote an increase in the nation's military strength. While European powers warred, wasting their manpower and resources, Ames maintained that the United States, in contrast, "might hope by delay, to gain as they lose strength." [54]

Early in March 1794, Alexander Hamilton wrote to President Washington that the critical situation of the country "demand[ed] measures vigorous though prudent." [55] Sedgwick carried out his suggestions by proposing a plan to the House to enlarge the military force and authorize the President to place an embargo on American trade. Ames responded positively to the proposed legislation, giving it his entire support. Madison might assert that Sedgwick's proposals were an attempt to counteract his own and to camouflage an increase of force in the national government; yet the Federalists saw their policy as an essential one.[56]

"The English are absolutely madmen," Ames exploded with annoyance. "They act on almost every point, against their interests and their real wishes." He resented the British minister, George Hammond, who petulantly condemned the United States. His counterpart, Thomas

53. Ames to Gore, Phila., Feb. 25, 1794, *ibid.*, 135; Miller, *Federalist Era*, 140-41.
54. Ames to Gore, Phila., Feb. 25, 1794, Ames, *Works of Ames*, I, 136.
55. Alexander Hamilton to George Washington, Phila., Mar. 8, 1794, Lodge, ed., *Works of Hamilton*, X, 63.
56. *Annals*, IV, 500-501, Mar. 12, 1794; James Madison to Thomas Jefferson, Phila., Mar. 14, 1794, Madison Papers, XVII, Lib. Cong. Madison suggested that "the game behind the curtain ... [was] the old trick of turning every contingency into a resource for accumulating force in the Government." Rufus King to Christopher Gore, Phila., Mar. 10, 1794, Gore to King, Boston, Mar. 15, 1794, King, *Life of King*, I, 550-52; Miller, *Federalist Era*, 150.

Pinckney, the American minister in London, did the cause of peace no good with his pro-French prejudices, Ames was convinced. If the British could have sent a man like Lord Dorchester to the United States, mutual difficulties between the two countries would have subsided. The Massachusetts Federalist, therefore, favored the move then under discussion among Federalist senators to send a special minister to England. Cautioning his friend Gore to keep the news to himself, he revealed that Hamilton was under consideration and asked, rhetorically, "Who but Hamilton would perfectly satisfy all our wishes? . . . He is *ipse agmen*." [57]

The prospect of solving the international crisis by negotiating a special treaty led Ames to suggest that preliminary talks should be undertaken with important Englishmen to indicate to them that British policies were tending to "Frenchify" the Americans. He had a host of ideas which he wished he could disseminate in England to help the envoy, as well as the cause of peace. All his hopes to avoid war now were centered in the success of the mission, which by the middle of April became a reality when the President chose Chief Justice John Jay as envoy in place of Hamilton. The prospect of war was abhorrent to Ames, especially as any major conflict would jeopardize the government and give rise to anarchy. "Our happy country seems to stand in need of little more than peace and good order to secure its prosperity. —I own I dread war by which we can gain nothing and may lose everything as a people," he commented. [58] Ames, therefore, thought that all ambitious plans for military expeditions against Canada should be avoided if war actually came about, and instead reliance should be on privateers. It was obvious from his proposals that he did not trust an armed, aggressive populace and hoped that the nation's warlike emotions could be "drawn off into the cold water" of the high seas. In that way the national government would not be weakened, industrial productivity would be maintained, and a minimum of money spent. [59]

In the House of Representatives almost the entire month of March

57. Ames to Gore, Mar. 5 [25], 26, 1794, Ames, *Works of Ames*, I, 137-40. Federalist discussions concerning the choice of an envoy and the final Senate approval of Jay are recorded in Rufus King's memorandum of the proceedings, King, *Life of King*, I, 517-23; Miller, *Hamilton*, 393-94; Freeman, *Washington*, VII, 159-60.

58. Ames to Gore, Mar. 26, 1794, Ames, *Works of Ames*, I, 140; Ames to Stephen Metcalf, Phila., Apr. 1, 1794, Gratz Collection, Statesmen, Box 28, Hist. Soc. of Pa. Freeman, *Washington*, VII, 164-69. Washington's nomination of Jay was confirmed by the Senate, Apr. 19, 1794, *ibid.*, 167; Frank Monaghan, *John Jay, Defender of Liberty* (N.Y. and Indianapolis, 1935), 364-68; Brant, *Madison, Father of the Constitution*, 397-98; Miller, *Federalist Era*, 153-54.

59. Ames to Gore, Mar. 26, 1794, Ames, *Works of Ames*, I, 140-41.

was given over to problems of defense and foreign policy. When Madison's commercial resolutions came up again for discussion on March 14, Federalist intransigence and the effect of a changing international situation rapidly undermined them. Ames at this time emphasized that a long-range retaliatory program was now entirely inadequate. Defense alone counted; regulation of trade was a trifling matter. The Madisonian resolutions were entirely one-sided, he implied pointedly, adding that "they were built on partiality for one nation—they have French stamped on the very face of them." [60] The opportune moment for retaliatory economic policies had passed, and even Madison had to admit that more effective legislation was essential. In the end his resolutions were pushed aside without a final vote.

Ames prescribed forbearance toward England and vigilance on the part of Federalists against rash acts; yet many members of Congress were not at all prone to curb their anger toward Britain. With little discussion a large majority in the House voted to impose an embargo on all shipping for a period of thirty days. A better policy, he thought, would have been to establish an embargo only against the West Indies. In the heat of the controversy members made extreme statements leading him to remark, "We call the British *our* enemies. I would *do* what is firm, and *say* what is not harsh." [61] To adopt this precept when British policy toward American neutral shipping had been curbed only slightly was indeed difficult. He was not trying to exonerate the British, but he was incensed at the fury of the pro-French Republicans. "This French mania," he pungently said, "is the bane of our politics, the mortal poison that makes our peace so sickly." [62]

With the advent of spring weather, political skies began to clear, and the members of Congress appeared to be less truculent. An attempt of Representative Jonathan Dayton of New Jersey to sequester all debts owed to Britain had been vigorously discussed, then allowed to drop by the wayside. An even more extreme resolution of Abraham Clark to forbid all trade until Britain reimbursed Americans for their losses and evacuated the frontier posts, passed the House, but Federalists found a few shreds of comfort when the Senate rejected it.[63] By early

60. *Annals*, IV, 505, 521, Mar. 14, 1794; Brant, *Madison, Father of the Constitution*, 395. Freeman, *Washington*, VII, 160; Theodore Sedgwick to Ephraim Williams, Phila., Mar. 6, 1794, Sedgwick Papers, III, Box 1, Mass. Hist. Soc.; James Madison to Thomas Jefferson, Phila., Mar. 9, 12, 14, 1794, Madison Papers, XVII, Lib. Cong.
61. *Annals*, IV, 529-30, Mar. 25, 1794; Ames to Gore, Mar. 5 [25], 1794, Ames, *Works of Ames*, I, 138.
62. Ames to Gore, Mar. 26, 1794, Ames, *Works of Ames*, I, 139.
63. *Annals*, IV, 535, Mar. 27, 1794. On the question of sequestration of British debts, see *ibid.*, 535-556, Mar. 27, 28, 1794. Clark's resolution is in *ibid.*, 561, Apr. 7.

May the turbulence over foreign affairs was subsiding. Neither the renewal of the embargo nor an effort to revive Clark's non-intercourse plan received much support in the House. Yet Ames was not convinced that there had been a decisive shift away from the path to war. A majority wanted peace, he was certain, but had been "duped into a support of measures tending to war." [64]

On the domestic front, fiscal problems again gained the attention of the House. The Federalists proposed a variety of new taxes, including stamp duties on the transfer of stocks and shares of the Bank of the United States, a carriage tax, and excises on tobacco and sugar, in lieu of a tax on land.[65] In this discussion, Ames took a leading part in winning enough support to pass the suggested legislation. He reported that during the struggle his side had "banged them as hard as we could, and they have been tamer than formerly." [66] Madison admitted to Jefferson that even though the Republicans had the support of petitions from manufacturers, "all opposition to the new excises . . . was [in] vain." Toward the close of the session Senator John Taylor of Virginia also acknowledged that the Federalists had passed most of their essential legislation, had sent an envoy to England, and, in general, had thwarted Republican plans.[67]

The debates about non-intercourse are in *ibid.*, 566-96, 600-603, Apr. 10, 11, 14, 15, 18, 21, 1794. The House passed an amended version of Clark's resolution, and also passed a bill to suspend the importation of certain goods, but the Senate rejected it. *Ibid.*, 90. George Washington to Tobias Lear, Phila., May 6, 1794, Fitzpatrick, ed., *Writings of Washington*, XXXIII, 356; Theodore Sedgwick to Ephraim Williams, Phila., Apr. 4, 1794, Sedgwick Papers, III, Mass. Hist. Soc.; Edmund Randolph to Gouverneur Morris, Phila., Apr. 29, 1794, Gouverneur Morris Papers, Columbia Univ.

64. *Annals*, IV, 657-58, May 8, 1794. Ames voted against a resolution to continue the embargo which was defeated on May 12; *ibid.*, 683. The non-intercourse resolution was defeated, 21 yeas, 46 nays; *ibid.*, 715-16, May 23, 1794. A bill was passed by the House, May 30, to empower the President to lay an embargo; *ibid.*, 735. Ames to Dwight, Phila., May 6, 1794, Ames, *Works of Ames*, I, 143. Ames remarked about the Republicans, "The desperadoes desire war. . . . Whatever kindles popular passions into fury, gives strength to that faction."

65. *Annals*, IV, 616-73, May 1-10, 1794. Debate on revenue bill, *ibid.*, 697-702, 704-8, 716-20, 723-26, May 16-27, 1794.

66. *Annals*, IV, 617, May 1, 1794. Ames discussed the need for further financial support, advocating a tax on manufactured tobacco; *ibid.*, 622, 625. He was against charging owners of two carriages an additional tax, but favored retaining the existing carriage tax; *ibid.*, 648, 656. Ames was on the committee to formulate the new excise bill. *Ibid.*, 673, May 10, 1794. The bill passed May 17; *ibid.*, 700. Ames to Christopher Gore, Phila., May 2, 1794, Ames, *Works of Ames*, I, 142.

67. James Madison to Thomas Jefferson, Phila., May 11, 1794, Madison Papers, XVII, Lib. Cong.; Ames to Gore, May 2, 1794, Ames, *Works of Ames*, I, 142. At the same time Taylor wrote a memorandum to Madison concerning the conviction of King and Ellsworth that incompatibility between North and South made a dissolution of the Union desirable. Gaillard Hunt, ed., *Disunion Sentiment in Congress in 1794* (Washington, 1905).

From the Federalist standpoint the session had ended on a more promising note than it had begun. The irritations of the past months had largely subsided, and with the mission of John Jay in progress, there seemed to be a good chance of more harmonious relations with Britain. At the close of Congress Ames was glad to be able to plan his trip home. Reflecting a moment on the personal sacrifice a public man had to make, he commented that "the long absence I have passed has not reconciled me to the mode of life I am in, but the daily renewal of my interest in public affairs counteracts the chagrins that would devour me if I were unoccupied." Now with the public business behind him he could "fly, not on the wings of the wind ... but on the speed of the mail stage" and return to Dedham.[68]

68. Alexander Hamilton to John Jay, Phila., June 4, 1794, Lodge, ed., *Works of Hamilton*, X, 67; Ames to Dwight, Phila., June 3, 1794, Fisher Ames Papers, Dedham Hist. Soc.

Chapter XII

Clubs, Mobs, and French Influence

The interval of nearly five months between the first and second sessions of the Third Congress witnessed continuing and undiminished political strife.[1] Uncertainty over the negotiations of John Jay, mounting unrest in western Pennsylvania against the excise, intensified activities on the part of the Democratic societies, and the commencement of electioneering all served to keep politics simmering during the summer and autumn of 1794.

Ames was content to be removed temporarily from the drama of the national political scene and absorbed himself in family affairs and local activities. Shortly after the adjournment of Congress on June 9, he had traveled by stage to Springfield, where he met Frances, who had been visiting her family. Late in June the Ameses returned to Dedham in a hired conveyance, arriving at home on June 28, after having been caught in a violent thunderstorm en route. Little John Worthington had taken cold on the way, but recovered quickly without requiring any of the medicine prescribed by Dr. Nathaniel Ames. At nine months of age, the baby was at an interesting stage of development and had begun to imitate his mother, leading the fond father to express the hope that he was not becoming ominously forward.[2] Family correspondence reveals how devoted Ames was to both his wife and infant son.

1. The first session adjourned June 9, and the second session met on Nov. 3, 1794, *Annals*, IV, 784, 869.
2. *Ibid.*, 782; Ames to Thomas Dwight, Dedham, July 3, 1794, Ames, *Works of Ames*, I, 145.

Dedham, Ames found on his return, was growing in size and importance as a result of having become the county seat. The "squash town," as he called it, would soon have a new courthouse, designed by the famous Charles Bulfinch, which was to be erected near Ames's own land on High Street. Ames was proud of the growing community and hoped it could keep its recently acquired position as "shire town." When the courthouse was completed he suggested a civic plan to enhance the village by planting trees along the roads leading to Dedham, as well as around the common. If the people were made aware of the project, he thought many would help by going to the nearby woods and transplanting the trees.[3]

More than a year after the Ameses had settled in Dedham they began to build their own house. Ames had little experience in supervising construction and was reluctant to build at a fast pace, but he hoped that they could move in by the autumn of 1795. After Frances and he had visited the Gores and seen their "palace" in Waltham, he was spurred to go ahead with his own plans, as modest as they were by comparison. His house would not be "a smarter one" than the Gores, but he intended to make it a hospitable place. "To name it Springfield Hall is one step towards warming the house, and making it seem homeish, before we get into it," he wrote to his brother-in-law. "If I cannot see my friends there, I would not wish to live there myself." [4]

The house was to be built on the north side of High Street just a few rods from the old family tavern, where his mother had continued to live ever since his father's death. A short distance beyond, on the same side of the street, was Nathaniel's home. Fisher's land sloped gently from the road to the low meadows and the banks of the meandering Charles River. The area was both convenient and attractive for a residence. When the structure ultimately took shape it proved to be a stately one for a small community, with two stories and a large chimney at each end of the building. But Ames thought more of the comfort of living than of impressing his neighbors. Including a library and arranging the house to provide space for "as large a family as I may be blessed with" were of more concern to him than the exterior aspect of the house. It would be somewhat larger than he originally expected, he admitted, but he was certain it would be as plain and as cheap as he first contemplated.[5]

3. Ames to Dwight, July 3, 1794, Ames, *Works of Ames*, I, 145; Ames to Samuel Haven, Phila., Dec. 12, 1794, N. Paine Papers, Amer. Antiq. Soc.
4. Ames to Dwight [Dedham], July 24, 1794, Ames to Dwight, Boston, Sept. 3, 1794, Ames, *Works of Ames*, I, 146-47.
5. Ames used the land inherited from his father for his orchard, and the bottom land, although frequently flooded, to grow hay. Ames to Dwight, Dedham, Aug.

While the plans were maturing and the materials were being purchased, Ames was leading the active life of a country gentleman despite his remarks about being lazy. "To dig a cellar ... and to adjust
contracts, are jobs for which I am as ill qualified by inexperience as
indolence," he explained; yet he was anxious to make the necessary
preparations for the actual building of the house before he returned to
Congress. During the summer he had been busy improving his orchard,
grafting new stock onto his apple, pear, and plum trees, and within a
few years he hoped to have a variety of good fruit. It took his mind
away from politics, and he insisted that "as long as the Chronicle lets
my plums and pears alone, I will not attempt to rescue my character." [6]

Ames's happy family life and the opportunity to work on his own
place were a most pleasant contrast to the wranglings and contentions
of Congress. He had the leisure to read, to visit friends with Frances,
and to join his political circle in Boston for stimulating evenings of
discussion. On one occasion he recounted, "I played the fashionable
husband and stayed away from my wife last night. I dined at Jo. Barrell's palace and tho' sober (I hope) I could not finish some errands in
time to return." [7] His law work was progressing, though it was no more
burdensome than in the past. Sometime during the summer he opened
a small office on the corner of Court and High Streets, which henceforth became the center of his legal activities. He had no intention of
trailing the Supreme Court on its circuit to the various county sessions
and had to accept whatever local business there was. In August the
Court sat in Dedham and much to the delight of everyone, completed
its business in two and a half days. Ames argued one case before the
Court and reflected that he would be satisfied "to wear my law coat
again, especially if the pockets were properly lined." [8]

For the present he was glad to "live out of the vortex of politics"

24, 1795, Ames to Dwight, Sept. 3, 1794, *ibid.*, 147, 171. Description of the house
is from a water-color of Dedham *ca.* 1795 in the possession of the Dedham Hist.
Soc. Ames to Andrew Craigie, Dedham, Dec. 21, 1795, Emmett Collection, N.Y.
Pub. Lib. Ames to Dwight, Dedham, Sept. 11, 1794, Fisher Ames Papers, Dedham
Hist. Soc.

6. Ames to Dwight, Sept. 11, 1794, Fisher Ames Papers, Dedham Hist. Soc.
The letter is partially printed in Ames, *Works of Ames*, I, 149. Ames to Dwight,
Dedham, Aug. 8, 1794, *ibid.*, 147.

7. Ames to Dwight, Boston, July 24, 1794, Fisher Ames Papers, Dedham Hist.
Soc. The letter is partially printed in Ames, *Works of Ames*, I, 146.

8. "Dedham Village in 1795," *Dedham Hist. Register*, 14 (1903), 45; Ames to
Dwight, Sept. 11, 1794, Ames, *Works of Ames*, I, 150. In the September session of
the Norfolk Court of Common Pleas, Ames had five cases: Elias Bawn v. Benoin
Morse (a jury trial decided in favor of Ames's client), N. Carpenter v. S. Forrest,
Weld v. Murdock, L. Metcalf v. Morse, R. Ellis v. E. Gay (all cases were con-
tinued), Docket of the Court of Common Pleas, Clerk of the Court, Norfolk
County Supreme Judicial Court, Dedham, Mass.

and avoid the aggravations accompanying public life. Ames avowed that if he were still single and did not enjoy the congeniality of a wife and family, he might fear a defeat at the polls. In reality, loss of his congressional seat at this time would have shattered his spirit. Politics suddenly intruded through a particularly vindictive attack on him in the *Independent Chronicle*. He was incensed that the article dragged his father-in-law's name into the political controversy with insinuations that Colonel Worthington was a Tory on the eve of the Revolution. When Ames wrote to Dwight about the incident he was still seething. "Rascals, let him alone, and give me double beatings," he burst out.[9] To disturb an old man, giving him pain because of an election, seemed truly reprehensible to Ames.

Behind the renewed political agitation and the vocal enthusiasm of a large segment of the population for the French cause, Federalists in Boston were convinced they detected the baneful influence of the Democratic societies. Ever since the formation of a Republican society among the more radical German democrats of Philadelphia in April 1793, the idea of secret local organizations dedicated to a furtherance of democratic ideals and hostility to the opponents of the French Revolution had swept across the country. Coinciding with the emotional fervor of Genêt's mission to the United States, the Democratic societies had rapidly spread to both large and small towns so that by the end of 1794 thirty-five organizations were in existence.[10] In Boston the Democratic society, known as the Massachusetts Constitutional Society, had grown in influence to the point of creating lasting fears in the ranks of the Federalists. Men like Stephen Higginson and George Cabot were apprehensive lest these extremists gain a firm political hold on the electorate and jeopardize the Federalist party. Ames himself took a dark view of the activity of the society, equating it, as other Federalists did, with the revolutionary Jacobin clubs in Paris.[11]

After one meeting of this group held in Faneuil Hall in August 1794, Ames asserted that the gathering presaged a determination by the

9. Ames to Dwight, Aug. 8, 1794, Ames to Dwight, Dedham, July 3, 1794, Ames to Dwight, July 24, 1794, Ames, *Works of Ames*, I, 145-47; *Independent Chronicle* (Boston), July 21, 1794.

10. Eugene P. Link, *Democratic-Republican Societies, 1790-1800* (N.Y., 1942), 6-10, 13-15; William Miller, "First Fruits of Republican Organization: Political Aspects of the Congressional Election of 1794," *Pa. Mag. of Hist. and Biog.*, 63 (1939), 118-20; Cunningham, *Jeffersonian Republicans*, 62-66.

11. Link, *Democratic Societies*, 14, 22, 27, 107, 149; Link indicates that the Massachusetts society, composed of many former Whigs, played an important role as a liaison between other New England Democratic societies. Apparently it had some political significance. For the Federalist point of view, see Cabot to Theophilus Parsons, Brookline, Aug. 12, 1794, Lodge, ed., *Letters of Cabot*, 78-80; Stephen Higginson to Alexander Hamilton, Boston, July 26, 1793, July 12, 1794, Hamilton, ed., *Works of Hamilton*, V, 570-71, 603-4.

"rabble" to seize the local government from the hands of the yeoman. "Thus, Boston may play Paris," he forecast, "and rule the State." Expecting that the members would take a very active part in politics, Ames expressed his opinion that they would be "as busy as Macbeth's witches at the election." Although every right-thinking man detested such a society, it was dangerous in Ames's view to underestimate the strength of the organization. "They poison every spring; they whisper lies to every gale," he vividly wrote of the activities of the members. "They are everywhere, always acting like Old Nick and his imps. Such foes are to be feared as well as despised." [12]

Events outside of Massachusetts showed that Ames's misgivings were justified. In mid-summer the long-fermenting grievances of the western Pennsylvania farmers and frontiersmen against the national government burst forth. The headstrong resistance of armed farmers to the federal excise laws intimidated government officials and closed the courts. This situation evoked vivid memories for New Englanders of Shays' Rebellion with its threat to the men of property and position. Federalists were as alarmed as the President about the threat of the Whiskey Rebellion to the welfare of the republic. The Federalist *Columbian Centinel* unhesitatingly advocated the suppression of the insurrection at bayonet-point, asserting that "our country harbours within her bosom vipers who would overturn all order, government, and laws." [13]

Although the news from Pennsylvania was disquieting, Ames expressed confidence about the final outcome. "The Pittsburg rebellion cannot, I think, end badly for government, unless government flinches from its duty," he avowed. The insurrectionists had acted before they were "ready for more than intrigue and plotting." Inherent in his comments was the conviction that the troops, who had marched into the discontented area under the command of the President, would effectively assert the supremacy of the national laws while giving the federal government an opportunity to increase its strength. [14]

In the eyes of the Federalists the "Jacobins," through the machinations of the Democratic clubs, were directly responsible for the Whiskey Rebellion and the Republicans were not allowed to escape the blame. No amount of denial of complicity would convince the con-

---

12. Ames to Dwight, Aug. 8, Sept. 3, 1794, Ames, *Works of Ames*, I, 147-48.
13. Baldwin, *Whiskey Rebels*, 92-109; Miller, *Federalist Era*, 155-62; Freeman, *Washington*, VII, 186-89; Mitchell, *Alexander Hamilton*, II, 308-22; George Washington to Charles M. Thurston, Phila., Aug. 10, 1794, Fitzpatrick, ed., *Writings of Washington*, XXXIII, 464-66; *Columbian Centinel* (Boston), Aug. 9, 20, 1794.
14. Ames to Dwight, Sept. 3, 1794, Ames, *Works of Ames*, I, 148. Hamilton insisted that the show of strength on the part of the federal government increased its prestige. Miller, *Hamilton*, 411-12.

servatives that the uprising was not "the first *fruits* of the blessed *harvest* sown by the *Jacobin Societies.*" Federalists thus made every effort to turn the electorate against the Republicans by stressing that the societies aided and abetted the insurrection and, in the words of Ames, "were born in sin, the impure offspring of Genêt." Ames maintained that it was an opportune time to destroy the influence of the clubs by discrediting them in the public view so that "they shall have less than *no* influence." [15] This he felt should be done by articles in the press. Even though the influence of the Democratic societies was waning, he expected they would avidly support the two Republican congressmen, William Lyman and Henry Dearborn, in the coming election.

Excitement over the congressional election of 1794 rapidly gained momentum in September, and a month later Boston was in the grip of buffeting political winds as each party strove to gain the advantage over its rival. Interest and attention centered on Ames's campaign for re-election in Suffolk and Norfolk Counties and to a lesser degree on the claims of Samuel Dexter in Middlesex. Both were swept into an electioneering struggle far more intense than that of 1792. Increased activity of political parties and the international crisis of the preceding year had ended the apathy of Bostonians.[16]

The position of the Federalists in Massachusetts was not as secure as they might have wished in the autumn of 1794. They had not been able to overcome the legacy of personal following which Samuel Adams had inherited from Hancock, and in the gubernatorial election of 1794 they could not prevent Adams's victory. The Republican success in ousting two Boston Federalists from their seats in the General Court seemed to indicate a better state of organization under the encouragement of the Constitutional Society than in past elections.[17] In general, both parties were becoming more sophisticated politically. Early in the

15. *Independent Chronicle* (Boston), Aug. 18, 1794, referred to this Federalist comment as "an aristocratical lie." See also *ibid.*, Aug. 21, 25, 1794; Ames to Dwight, Sept. 11, 1794, Ames, *Works of Ames*, I, 150; Cunningham, *Jeffersonian Republicans*, 65-66; *Columbian Centinel* (Boston), Sept. 3, 10, 1794. By October the influence of the clubs appears to have been declining; see Jedidiah Morse to Oliver Wolcott, Charlestown, Oct. 15, 1794, Oliver Wolcott Papers, VIII, Conn. Hist. Soc.

16. The General Court had divided the state into eleven election districts, and Maine into three. Ames was the incumbent in the First Middle District comprising Boston and the towns of Norfolk County to the southwest of Boston. *Columbian Centinel* (Boston), July 12, 1794.

17. *Boston Gazette*, Apr. 14, 1794; Morse, *Federalist Party*, 142-44; John Adams to Abigail Adams, May 17, 1794, Charles F. Adams, ed., *Letters of John Adams, Addressed to His Wife*, 2 vols. (Boston, 1841), II, 160; Henry Jackson to Henry Knox, Boston, May 8, 1794, Knox Papers, XXXV, 99, Mass. Hist. Soc.; Goodman, *Democratic-Republicans*, 60-63.

congressional campaign, the Federalists met a strong challenge from
the Republicans, who had effectively concentrated their political support behind a single candidate and had vituperatively attacked Fisher
Ames, as well as the administration, in the press. In place of the frequently defeated Benjamin Austin, the Republicans turned to the popular patriot, Dr. Charles Jarvis. This physician-turned-politician had been
one of the leading Sons of Liberty in the 1760's and had held various
local offices since the Revolution. His public record and his amiable
personal traits made him a formidable contestant.[18]

The Republicans attempted to discredit Ames in the eyes of the
voters by reprinting parts of his speeches and remarks in Congress
against Madison's commercial resolutions. It was an effective move,
judging from the reaction of Jedidiah Morse, who wrote to Oliver
Wolcott, Jr., that "it is melancholy to find how much and how deeply
the mutilated speeches of Messrs. A and D [Ames and Dexter] published in the prostituted *Chronicle* have poisoned the minds of people.
... Their re-election, I am sorry to say is doubtful." Ames was por-
trayed as strongly pro-English in the Republican press, "more zealously
plead[ing] their cause in Congress than has been done by any of the
ministerial hirelings in the British House of Lords." [19]

Writers in the *Independent Chronicle* gave Ames no peaceful moment at the height of the electioneering. The Hamilton faction was
attacked as an "artful and unprincipled minority," and much was made
of Ames's reputed wealth derived from speculation, with imputations
that his sole interest in legislation was "to enlarge British imports which
would increase the value of his stocks." In contrast, Jarvis was upheld
as a paragon of public and private virtue who could "never descend to
become the organ or *sycophant* of a *treasury intrigue*." [20] Ames was
castigated for being a lawyer, for his opposition to France, for not supporting the carrying trade of American merchants, and as usual for his
aristocratic inclinations. Reminding the voters that he had once said,
"Democracy is a volcano, which conceals the fiery material of its own

18. Morse, *Federalist Party*, 148; for information on Charles Jarvis, see J. G.
Wilson and J. Fiske, eds., *Appleton's Cyclopaedia of American Biography*, III
(N.Y., 1888), 406; Josiah Quincy, "Dr. Ephraim Eliot's Account of the Physicians
of Boston," Mass. Hist. Soc., *Proceedings*, 7 (1864), 179; "Diary of Ezekiel Price,
1775-1776," *ibid.*, 185-262.
19. *Independent Chronicle* (Boston), Oct. 9, 16, 1794. The *Columbian Centinel*
(Boston), Oct. 25, 1794, defended Ames. Morse to Wolcott, Oct. 15, 1794, Oliver
Wolcott Papers, VIII, Conn. Hist. Soc.; *Boston Gazette*, Sept. 29, 1794.
20. *Independent Chronicle* (Boston), Oct. 20, 23, 30, 1794; the *Boston Gazette*,
Nov. 3, 1794, advocated avoiding "the Higginsonian, Hamiltonian, and Speculating
Parties, who to forward their base designs; would set up the D——l himself."

destruction," a critic suggested that only those who wanted a change in the form of government would cast their votes for the present incumbent.[21]

So persistent and abusive were the attacks on Fisher Ames that his friends made every effort to counteract the unfavorable impression his adversaries had created; but their writing was of necessity defensive and only occasionally hit hard at the Republicans. He was upheld as a representative who not only had consistently supported the President but had also helped prevent war and had promoted the welfare of the community. Under the title of "Mr. Ames's Vindication," the *Columbian Centinel* published a lengthy refutation of the strictures on his private and public conduct. "The venal *Chronicle* teem[s] with lying slander against Mr. Ames.... They have said he has supported the present Revenue system because he was a speculator in the funds and had made a great fortune in that way." Quite the contrary, his supporters maintained; he had invested his savings acquired before he went to Congress in government securities to have them in a safe and productive state. His support of the Treasury was not motivated by selfish interest but was proof of his interest in the prosperity of the nation.[22] The "Jacobin scribblers" were not in the least silenced, retorting that "it is rather curious to observe how the Hamiltonian party *winch* when anything is said against their idols." Both sides put their case bluntly on the eve of the election. The Republicans proclaimed loudly that "in chusing Mr. Ames we tacitly submit to the impositions of the British.... The votes of THIS DAY determines whether we are SLAVES to the British, or FREEMEN of America." "Do you wish for WAR, then oppose Mr. Ames," warned the Federalists in their final retaliation. "Are you fond of Jacobin Principles, then oppose Ames.... Do you wish to set the world in flames, then send a Jacobin." [23]

The world neither burst into flame, nor were the inhabitants enchained on November 3, 1794. Instead, a large number of citizens went to the polls between 11 A.M. and 1:30 P.M. and in good order cast their ballots. "We had a magnificent Election," wrote Jonathan Pierce to

21. *Independent Chronicle* (Boston), Oct. 20, 23, 1794; "Impartial Neutrality," *ibid.*, Oct. 23, criticized Ames for not being "a warm friend to the rights of man." "Anti-Manlius," *ibid.*, Sept. 29, 1794, attacked Gore, author of the *Manlius* articles, for being an "abettor of A——s [Ames]." "A Yeoman," *ibid.*, Oct. 27, 1794.
22. *Boston Gazette*, Sept. 29, 1794; "A Farmer," *ibid.*, Oct. 27, 1794, argued that Ames was opposed to a land tax and had prevented war. *Columbian Centinel* (Boston), Oct. 22, 25, 29, 1794.
23. *Independent Chronicle* (Boston), Oct. 23, Nov. 3, 1794; *Columbian Centinel* (Boston), Nov. 1, 1794.

Henry Knox, "so thronged for several hours that it was dangerous to attempt . . . to get into the Hall." [24] Pierce himself had been sick but had gone to the polls in a carriage in order not to lose his vote for Ames. By the end of the day it was obvious that Ames was moving decisively ahead of Jarvis. Nathaniel Appleton jubilantly informed Noah Webster that, "notwithstanding every vile, base, and scandalous effort of our aristocratic Jacobins, that at the close of the poll in *this* town, this day our friend Ames had 1627 votes while Dr. Jarvis had 1182." [25]

Ames had a sizable majority over Jarvis in most Suffolk County towns with the exception of Roxbury, where General William Heath's Antifederalist principles were influential. In Dedham ten "vile Jacobins" preferred the Republican candidate, but Ames did get seventy-two votes in his home town. The election fever did not subside quickly, however, for the Republicans immediately contended that he had won only because strangers had cast votes for him. By calculating the approximate number of ratable voters over sixteen years of age in Boston, the *Independent Chronicle* tried to prove that more votes were cast than there were legal voters. For a time there was a flurry of accusation and denial in the papers about the outcome; yet the charges either were too flimsy or could not be substantiated sufficiently to challenge the Federalist victory seriously. William Eustis, a moderate Federalist, recounted that when Benjamin Austin expounded to a friend of Eustis's that Ames had received the votes of Negroes, the friend had retorted, "D—n it . . . you have had 'em for these seven years . . . can't you spare 'em for once?" [26]

Even some of the closest political friends of Ames seemed to have had their doubts about his re-election, but according to Jedidiah Morse

24. *Independent Chronicle* (Boston), Nov. 6, 1794; Jonathan Pierce to Henry Knox, Boston, Nov. 3, 5, 1794, Knox Papers, XXXVI, 81, 84, Mass. Hist. Soc.

25. Nathaniel Appleton to Noah Webster, Boston, Nov. 3, 1794, Jeremy Belknap to Noah Webster, Boston, Dec. 9, 1794, Noah Webster Papers, N.Y. Pub. Lib.; Christopher Gore to Tobias Lear, Waltham, Nov. 3, 1794, Christopher Gore Papers, Lib. Cong.; John Adams to Abigail Adams, Nov. 15, 1794, Adams, ed., *Letters of John Adams*, II, 164; Joseph Jones to James Madison, Nov. 19, 1794, Madison Papers, XVII, Lib. Cong.

26. Abstract of Votes, Mass. Archives, Office of the Secretary of the Commonwealth, State House. Ames received 2,178 votes out of a total of 3,857. Unofficial tallies in the *Columbian Centinel* (Boston), Nov. 8, 1794, gave Ames 2,183 votes, Jarvis 1,664 votes. *Independent Chronicle* (Boston), Nov. 6, 10, 13, 17, 20, 27, 1794. The *Independent Chronicle* asserted 500 non-residents cast ballots for Ames and maintained that Ames was not legally elected. The *Columbian Centinel* (Boston), Nov. 8, 19, 1794, defended Ames. William Eustis to David Cobb, Boston, Nov. 5, 1794, David Cobb Papers, Mass. Hist. Soc.; Christopher Gore to Rufus King, Waltham, Nov. 6, 1794, King, ed., *Life of King*, I, 575-76. Gore wrote, "Many falsehoods told of Ames have been refuted. His character is deservedly high."

"their unusual ... exertions and influence ... have effected a most complete overthrow of the designs and expectations of the *Anarchists*." William Eustis thought that the "handsome majority for friend Ames must gratify every cockle of his heart." He hoped, however, that in the future Ames would be more responsive to the wishes of some of his constituents and hate the English somewhat more.[27]

Massachusetts Federalists, greatly pleased at Ames's re-election, tended in their jubilation to overlook the outcome of other contests within the state. Madison observed that the Republicans had gained in Massachusetts. "The two republican members have stood their ground; in spite of the most unexampled operations agst. them," he informed Jefferson. "Ames is said to owe his success to the votes of negroes and British sailors smuggled under a very lax mode of conducting the election there."[28] Other Republicans also considered the results symptomatic of an increasing trend away from Federalism. Sedgwick had received a bare majority of votes, and Dexter, of whom the Federalists had expected much, failed to win a majority over Joseph Varnum.[29] Equally serious was the fact that the Federalists had been unable to defeat William Lyman and Henry Dearborn in their districts. To the Federalists there was comfort, however, in the thought that the three stalwart leaders of Federalism in the House—Ames, Sedgwick, and William Smith of South Carolina—would be on hand to fend off the attacks of the "Jacobins" in the next Congress.[30]

27. Jedidiah Morse to Oliver Wolcott, Nov. 6, 1794, Oliver Wolcott Papers, VIII, Conn. Hist. Soc.; James Madison to Thomas Jefferson, Phila., Nov. 16, 1794, Madison Papers, XVII, Lib. Cong.; William Eustis to David Cobb, Boston, Nov. 16, 1794, David Cobb Papers, Mass. Hist. Soc.

28. James Madison to Thomas Jefferson, Phila., Dec. 21, 1794, Madison Papers, XVII, Lib. Cong. Madison indicated that the Democratic Society in New York influenced the election there and stated that "in Boston the subject is well understood, and handled in the Newspapers on the republican side."

29. *Columbian Centinel* (Boston), Nov. 8, 1794. The Dexter-Varnum contest was not determined until May 1795, Varnum winning by eleven votes. See *ibid.*, Apr. 11, May 23, 1795. Theodore Sedgwick to Ephraim Williams, Phila., Feb. 3, 1795, Sedgwick Papers, III, Mass. Hist. Soc. Sedgwick indicated Dexter was disgusted that Federalist support was largely given to Ames and that he himself was "left to be run down." On other election contests, see Thomas Dwight to Theodore Sedgwick, Nov. 29, 1794, Samuel Henshaw to Theodore Sedgwick, Dec. 21, 1794, *ibid.*, Vol. B.

30. John Adams to Abigail Adams, Nov. 15, 1794, Adams, ed., *Letters of John Adams*, II, 164; Fauchet to Commissioners of Foreign Relations, Phila., Nov. 15, 1794, F. J. Turner, ed., "Correspondence of the French Ministers to the United States," Amer. Hist. Assn., *Annual Report, 1903* (Washington, 1904), II, 471. Fauchet commented on the re-election of Ames and Smith. Washington was pleased about the Boston victory of the Federalists. Ames remarked, "The great man certainly was not indifferent—not because my *personal* weight was much but ... [because] his own system of negotiation was in trial." Ames to Christopher Gore, Phila., Nov. 18, 1794, Ames, *Works of Ames*, I, 152-53.

The election day in Massachusetts had coincided with the opening of the second session of the Third Congress, and once again Ames had not delayed his trip southward to await the outcome of the balloting. After leaving Frances and little John in Springfield, he accompanied his colleague Dwight Foster to Philadelphia, arriving in ample time to attend the first meeting. His insistence on being on hand for November 3 was in contrast to some of the senators and representatives who were two weeks late. While the Senate was awaiting a quorum, the House, too, marked time, and not until the President gave his address on the nineteenth did both houses turn to the work of the session.

President Washington, recently returned from suppressing the Whiskey Rebellion, utilized the occasion of his speech to Congress to accuse the Democratic societies of undermining federal laws by encouraging the insurgents. His outspoken condemnation angered Republicans, who felt the President had unjustly blamed members of these groups. After the address to Congress a heated battle developed in the House over the answer of the representatives to the President. Madison, the chairman of the committee preparing a reply, ignored the whole question of the clubs and the insurrection. He already had privately remarked that the President's statements were "the greatest error of his political life," and now, publicly, he wanted to show his party's displeasure.[31] The proposed reply to Washington was taken up by the committee of the whole on November 24. Quibbling over the wording of the draft set nerves on edge and led to a clash in which Jonathan Dayton accused Ames of making illiberal remarks. Ames arose, saying that the representative from New Jersey could not be referring to him. Dayton retorted, "I mean *that* gentleman, Mr. Speaker," pointing to Ames. Mr. Dayton then proceeded to deny vigorously that he was the victim of the "habits of jealousy" to which Mr. Ames had referred.[32]

Ames refrained from carrying the argument further and did not take part in the debate until both sides had exhausted their arguments regarding the Democratic societies. Then he fired a full broadside at the organizations. He attempted to induce the House to accept in its entirety an amendment attacking the clubs. A majority of representatives had voted in the committee of the whole to delete from the amendment

31. Ames to Dwight Foster, Dedham, Oct. 6, 1794, Washburn Collection, Mass. Hist. Soc.; *Annals*, IV, 870, Nov. 4, 1794. The House had a quorum, Nov. 4, 1794. Freeman, *Washington*, VII, 215-17, 219-21; Miller, *Hamilton*, 412-14; Mitchell, *Alexander Hamilton*, II, 325-28; *Annals*, IV, 791, Nov. 19, 1794; William Miller, "The Democratic Societies and the Whiskey Insurrection," *Pa. Mag. of Hist. and Biog.*, 62 (1938), 324-49; George Washington to John Jay, Phila., Nov. 1, 1794, Fitzpatrick, ed., *Writings of Washington*, XXXIV, 18; James Madison to James Monroe, Phila., Dec. 4, 1794, Madison Papers, XVII, Lib. Cong.
32. *Annals*, IV, 897, Nov. 24, 1794.

the words "self-created societies." Thus the proposal had been modified and emasculated. The vote of the members, Ames argued, did not reflect their true opinion regarding the Democratic societies; therefore, they should reconsider the question. Any other step would rekindle "the firebrands of sedition." The societies, he insisted, served no useful political purpose, despite Republican assertions. If they supplanted true representative government with their concepts of democracy, the results would be worse than sedition. Direct democracy on the Greek pattern had long ago been proven ineffective.[33]

In his speech Ames repeatedly emphasized the dangers inherent in the clubs and the urgent need for vigilance on the part of the government. History, he reminded his audience, presented numerous examples of such groups which vilified a government and then sought to control it. "The hypocrisy of the clubs will be unmasked," Ames asserted, "and the public scorn . . . will frown them into nothing." In several states the societies had attacked the system of laws, the government, and also the President; consequently, the criticisms Washington had leveled were entirely just in Ames's opinion. The choice was between aiding the destroyers of free government or its chief protectors. "The question is simply, will you support your Chief Magistrate? . . . This is the occasion," he urged.[34] Adopting the amendment *in toto* would be evidence of the support essential to the administration.

After an additional day of discussion, the Federalists were able to reverse the previous vote by a slim margin and retain the contested words. But ultimately the House vote went against the Federalists, and the condemnation of the clubs was eliminated before the reply was approved. The party furor over this issue served only as a goad to strife within the House. Madison understood better than many why his restrained draft of an answer had become the center of controversy. "This moderate course," he wrote to James Monroe, "would not satisfy those who hoped to draw a party advantage out of the President's popularity." [35] The objective of the Federalists, he explained, had been to connect the Democratic societies with the recent insurrection and the Republicans with both. The President was to be cast as head of the opposition, and he would be used to cover the establishment of a stand-

33. *Ibid.*, 920-24, Nov. 26, 1794.
34. *Ibid.*, 927, 931-32.
35. *Ibid.*, 943-45, Nov. 27, 1794. The original vote of the committee had been 47 nays, 45 yeas on the amendment approving the President's censure; the House vote was 47 yeas, 45 nays. A motion to limit the censure to the area of the insurrection passed, leading many Federalists to drop the entire amendment. Madison to Monroe, Dec. 4, 1794, Madison to Thomas Jefferson, Phila., Nov. 30, 1794, Madison Papers, XVII, Lib. Cong.; Brant, *Madison, Father of the Constitution*, 415-19.

ing army to enforce the laws. Ames, on his side of the political fence, saw the issues differently. "The private history [of the debates] deserves to be known," he wrote; "the faction in the House fomented the discontents without . . . the clubs are everywhere the echoes of the faction in Congress . . . the Speaker is a member . . . Madison and Parker are honorary members. Oh Shame! Where is thy sting!" The only way to combat the evil was to utilize all means to influence the public "as far as truth and decency allow" to support the government.[36]

In the opinion of some of his supporters, Ames's oration expressed precisely their apprehensions of the dangers inherent in the Democratic societies. William Plumer, a New Hampshire Federalist, highly approved the speech. "The pernicious consequence of these clubs he has thoroughly investigated and clearly demonstrated with all that inspiration that is so natural to him. I have a strong regard for him, tho' a stranger, and am gratified by his reelection."[37] Zephaniah Swift, a representative from Connecticut who heard Fisher Ames on this occasion, thought that the published version fell very much short of the original, especially with respect to "the energy of expression, and the wonderful brilliancy of metaphor, for which Ames has the most copious talents of any man I ever heard speak." Good Federalist that he was, Swift proclaimed Ames's speech the most eloquent one he had ever heard. Comparing Ames's oratory with Madison's, he could only deprecate the Virginian. Madison "had full time to collect his ideas [and] arrange his arguments . . . but I assure you he is a child in comparison with Ames. A hollow, feeble voice—an awkward, uninteresting manner . . . are his distinguishing traits. . . . He has no fire, no enthusiasm, no animation."[38]

Recent events, especially the intense election campaign and the western insurrection, had accentuated Ames's concern about the future of the nation. While there was a "pouting silence" in this session in contrast to the deafening clamor of the previous one, he was not deluded into thinking it was anything but an uneasy neutrality in which the vigilant slept upon their arms. Dispersing the insurgents had won the government support and increased prestige; yet it was clear to Ames that "faction is only baffled, not repenting, not changed."[39] Fortune had been kind, he felt. The discontented in the nation had not com-

36. Madison to Monroe, Dec. 4, 1794, Madison Papers, XVII, Lib. Cong.; Malone, *Jefferson and the Ordeal of Liberty*, 188-90; Ames to Dwight, Phila., Nov. 29, 1794, Ames, *Works of Ames*, I, 153-54.

37. William Plumer to Jeremiah Smith, Epping, Dec. 23, 1794, William Plumer Papers, I, Lib. Cong.

38. Zephaniah Swift to David Daggett, Phila., Dec. 13, 1794, Franklin B. Dexter, ed., "Selections From the Letters Received by David Daggett, 1786-1802," Amer. Antiq. Soc., *Proceedings*, 4 (1887), 374.

39. Ames to Dwight, Phila., Dec. 12, 1794, Ames, *Works of Ames*, I, 154,

bined extensively, but on another occasion the Union might be torn apart.

Exhorting the Massachusetts Federalists to rouse themselves and act against their rivals if the nation were to be preserved, Ames recommended that "mobocrats" be excluded from Congress. These men, rebellious in spirit, did not fear the "pit" of insurrection. "Will the people, seeing the pit open, approach it again by sending those to Congress who led them blindfold to its brink?" he asked.[40] New Englanders, who did not know the true situation outside of their own section, had to be stirred to "a revolutionary effort, a rising in mass, at the elections, to purify Congress from the sour leaven of antifederalism." Only by entrusting the government to the hands of the wise and the good could the dangers be avoided. "I stake my credit on it," Ames maintained. "I know but one cure—the real federalism of the body of the electors." The task, then, was to excite the public to a realization of the crisis, and this could be done only by molding public opinion through the work of the faithful and the medium of the press. "Our good citizens," he urged, "must consent to be more in earnest in their politics, or submit to be less secure in their rights and property."[41]

The House of Representatives, following the recommendations of the President to consider the reduction of the public debt, appointed Ames and four others to draw up a plan for its partial redemption. During the greater part of December, until the committee presented its proposals, the House was devoid of party strife, leading the representative from Boston to remark that business was accomplished with fewer difficulties than in any previous session. He had expected a storm, and although he preferred a peaceful meeting, he was not of a nature to flinch at the blast. Ames was determined to prevent the Republicans from obstructing the legislation which was designed to improve the financial position of the government.[42]

Shortly before the committee on the public debt presented its report, Ames sketched the essence of the plan for his friend Gore. Each year the redeemable part of the debt would be paid off, and the necessary sums would be raised by keeping in effect the duties and excises imposed at the last session of Congress. Undoubtedly the scheme would be opposed, he thought, and attempts made to substitute a land tax.

40. *Ibid.*, 155.
41. Ames to Gore, Phila., Dec. 17, 1794, Ames to Dwight, Dec. 12, 1794, *ibid.*, 155-56; George Cabot to Theophilus Parsons, Brookline, Aug. 12, 1794, Lodge, ed., *Letters of Cabot*, 78-80.
42. *Annals*, IV, 894, Nov. 21, 1794; Ames to Haven, Dec. 12, 1794, N. Paine Papers, Amer. Antiq. Soc.; Ames to Gore, Dec. 17, 1794, Ames, *Works of Ames*, I, 157.

"Keep your eye on the progress of this business," he warned Gore. The enemies of government aimed to reduce the income of the central government and to curtail the army. "No purse, no sword, on the part of authority," he exclaimed, "clubs, mobs, French influence, on the side of faction: A very intelligible arrangement." [43] Questions of finance inevitably stirred vigorous debates in the House and had, as well, the effect of rousing Ames to action. When Federalist representatives broached the need for continuing the temporary taxes if the public debt were to be reduced, the Republicans, as he expected, launched their protests. They had often maintained, with a considerable degree of fervor, that a public debt was an evil. Now, they opposed the payment of the debt, and Federalists were not inclined to overlook their inconsistency. [44]

The continued efforts of the Republicans to pose as the opponents of the debt, while countering every move to reduce it, led Ames on January 16, 1795, to make "a long speech and a loud one," which he hoped would show "*in puris naturalibus,* the loathness of the party to pay off the debt." His words were mild and conciliatory; yet like a persimmon, the surface sweetness concealed an underlying tartness. In this speech he did not resort to the analogies which so often made his important points lucid, but calmly stated the case for a permanent plan to reduce the debt. "It would seem to be a trite . . . inquiry," Ames began, "to ask whether Congress is . . . earnestly . . . reducing the Public Debt." All would agree, he asserted, that it was a basic objective; yet there was the threat that "speculative opinions and empty wishes" would hinder its accomplishment. [45] It was a matter of choosing between the evil of continuing the debt or the hostility which taxes always evoked. To make provision for a partial reduction of the debt by piecemeal appropriations was not the answer. He therefore hoped there would be no disagreement in determining to use "the whole strength of the revenues" every year until the debt was paid off. Rapidly Ames sketched the danger of losing the opportunity of reducing the financial obligations of the government. Too often European nations had ignored such opportunities and were like "the inhabitants of Italy [who] whistle unconcerned on the sides of Mount Etna while it vomits fire." [46] He himself believed strongly that a nation should sup-

43. Ames to Gore, Dec. 17, 1794, Ames, *Works of Ames,* I, 157.
44. *Annals,* IV, 1084-85, Jan. 14, 1795; Madison to Thomas Jefferson, Phila., Jan. 25, 1795, Madison Papers, XVIII, Lib. Cong.
45. Ames to Gore, Phila., Jan. 17, 1795, Ames, *Works of Ames,* I, 162. *Annals,* IV, 1104, Jan. 16, 1795.
46. *Annals,* IV, 1105.

port its public credit and use the years of peace and prosperity to free itself from debt.

The Republicans had unquestionably been guilty of misrepresentation and propaganda regarding the national debt, Ames asserted. For party reasons, they had accused New England members, heaping upon them the onus of being "patrons of a system of paper influence, of Treasury corruption, of certificate nobility." [47] Their statements about the Hamiltonian system and its supporters were still ringing in the ears of congressmen. Ames emphatically rejected the Republican assertion that his party wanted to preserve the debt for selfish motives. On the contrary, it had been their opponents who had persistently refused to reduce it. Now the opportunity had come to test their position. The result would show "in the teeth of calumny" that the eastern members continued to be strong advocates for a reduction. The retention of taxes was the deciding issue. If the other party were sincere and consistent they would either support the resolution or adopt other taxes. "No puny operation, no half-way measures will do." [48]

Step by step he refuted the various contentions against prolonging the tax laws, showing that the surplus funds of the government were not sufficient to afford a safe margin of operation for debt redemption, and likewise that the taxes were not injurious to manufactures. The object to be achieved was so great, Ames proclaimed, that Congress should not be deterred by difficulties ahead and should not abandon the plan. "It is worth some exertion and sacrifice. If we should effect it, any hopes of the destinies of our Government would brighten." [49]

Although Ames never indulged in self-commendation, he felt that speaking in plain terms to the Republicans had been effective. They were obviously annoyed that he had pointed out the extent to which they would depend on an unpopular direct tax on land to diminish the debt. New England, he hoped, would take note of their stand. As a result, the rival party was in an embarrassing position, Ames thought. "To reduce the debt they must help us. To oppose it they must disgrace themselves with the country." He expected the "Madisonians" in the House would keep up their clamor against the excises and in favor of the land tax, although they actually would do nothing to reduce the debt. "Read the inclosed speech of Madison," he suggested to Minot, "and see this doctrine avowed; although, having heard that it will ruin them among our Yankees, they try to wrap up the land tax in the

47. *Ibid.*, 1106.
48. *Ibid.*, 1106-7.
49. *Ibid.*, 1114.

hypocrisy of a tax on *property,* which, rendered into English, you will see reads *land tax.*" 50 By early February both Madison and Giles had shifted their ground in favor of an apportionment of taxes among the states to accomplish the objective. At the close of the debate only twenty-one members voted to reject the resolution favoring the application of funds derived from the increased excise levies for the reduction of the debt. With the aid of a committee composed, in part, of Ames, Fitzsimmons, and William L. Smith, the House then shaped a bill along Federalist lines.51

In the midst of Ames's speech on January 16, a message had come from Hamilton indicating that he had prepared a report on extinguishing the debt. Ames was elated that the opposition group was unprepared and could not forestall its presentation to the House. Yet the Republicans were not so easily deterred. Madison, who considered Hamilton's final report as Secretary of the Treasury "an arrogant valedictory," informed Jefferson in mid-February that some "remodifications" of the public debt proposed by Hamilton had been eliminated by the House. This congressional action incensed Hamilton, who had resigned his office as of the end of January. In a hot temper he wrote to Senator King, "The unnecessary and capricious and abominable assassinations respecting the unsubscribed debt... haunts me... and affects me more than I can express." 52

Despite the omission of certain essential ingredients of the Secretary's plan, Ames considered the completed act as "the finale, the crown of federal measures," which would place the control of revenue for debt reduction out of the reach of "future mobocrats." Yet Federalists had split ranks on the question, and some former advocates of a low rate of interest on public securities, the "three percent men" as Ames called them, were again active. Fortunately Sedgwick had remained loyal to the Hamiltonian principles, but James Hillhouse of Connecticut and Benjamin Goodhue of Massachusetts had argued strongly against a provision offering the non-subscribers to the debt better terms than the

50. Ames to [Thomas Dwight], Phila., Jan. 20, 1795, Fisher Ames Papers, Dedham Hist. Soc. Ames remarked on the inconsistency of the *Independent Chronicle*'s statements regarding the land tax and Madison's recent speech in which he "*stammered*" on the preference of land tax to excise." Ames to Gore, Jan. 17, 1795, Ames to George R. Minot, Phila., Jan. 20, 1795, Ames, *Works of Ames,* I, 162-65.

51. *Annals,* IV, 1203, 1205, Feb. 6, 1795.

52. Ames to Gore, Jan. 17, 1795, Ames to Gore, Phila., Feb. 24, 1795, Ames, *Works of Ames,* I, 162-67; Madison to Thomas Jefferson, Phila., Feb. 15, 1795, Madison Papers, XVIII, Lib. Cong.; Alexander Hamilton to Rufus King, Kingston, Feb. 21, 1795, Lodge, ed., *Works of Hamilton,* VIII, 337-38; Miller, *Hamilton,* 438-39.

current holders. Ames felt that it was entirely wrong to force the subscription of the remaining outstanding part of the debt at low rates of interest. "I have long seen," he commented, "that our measures are supported by prejudices, not less erroneous than those of their opposers." [53]

The House turned from the financial program to pending issues. Revision of the naturalization law of 1790 appeared to be essential in light of the concern, engendered by the political upheavals in Europe, that it was not strict enough to prevent the entry of undesirable foreigners. Madison presented a bill with only moderately strict provisions. Federalists looked askance at this, envisioning an unrestricted influx of revolutionaries from France. When William B. Giles recommended an amendment requiring a special oath of renunciation for members of the nobility, the Federalists, aware that he was playing the part of a committed democrat, quickly swung to the defense of Madison's proposal. In a fruitless debate, which Ames condemned, the House lost valuable days on the matter of titles.[54] The Massachusetts representative thought it would have been wiser to ignore the Giles motion, but hotheaded Dexter promptly countered it with an amendment of his own. Foreigners wishing to become citizens were to relinquish ownership of all the slaves they held. After this thrust it took all the efforts of moderates to calm the southerners. Ames felt constrained to remind his colleagues that the real issue was to make rules for citizenship in keeping with the nation's "tranquility and safety." [55] While he said nothing about Dexter's antislavery jibe, he cautioned against confusing the debate with abstract questions. He maintained that freedom of thought should apply to ex-nobles and that citizenship should not be denied to them because of their political heresies. There was no intention of establishing an order of nobility in the United States; this was only a "counterfeit alarm," which would revive political animosities. It was shameful to legislate on trifles, Ames concluded. But Republicans were unwilling to

53. Ames to Gore, Feb. 24, 1795, Ames, *Works of Ames*, I, 167; Christopher Gore to Alexander Hamilton, Boston, Apr. 20, 1795, Hamilton Papers, XXIII, Lib. Cong.; *Annals*, IV, 1237-40, Feb. 19, 1795.

54. Brant, *Madison, Father of the Constitution*, 420-21; *Annals*, IV, 968, 1030, Dec. 8, 31, 1794; F. G. Franklin, "The Legislative History of Naturalization in the United States, 1776-1795," Amer. Hist. Assn., *Annual Report, 1901* (Washington, 1902), I, 312-17; Theodore Sedgwick to Ephraim Williams, Phila., Dec. 12, 16, 24, 31, 1794, Jan. 1, 1795, Sedgwick to Henry Van Schaack, Dec. 23, 1794, Sedgwick Papers, III, Mass. Hist. Soc.

55. *Annals*, IV, 1039, 1048, Jan. 1, 2, 1795; Ames to Dwight, Phila., Jan. 7, 1795, Ames, *Works of Ames*, I, 160; "A Democrat," *Independent Chronicle* (Boston), Mar. 5, 1795. The writer commented, "In charity, I am willing to suppose that Messrs. Sedgwick, Ames, and Dexter...had no sinister views in their rash, impolitic opposition."

lose an opportunity to discomfit their rivals and insisted on a roll call vote, which they intimated would show who were the friends of nobility. Giles's motion was then triumphantly passed, as a party measure.[56]

Much to the annoyance of Ames, Congress continued its legislative progress at a lethargic pace. As usual he disliked the tendency he saw in the House to encroach on executive powers and to endeavor to handle all matters of government. The recent debates on titles of nobility had demonstrated that the House was "a collection of Secretaries of the Treasury," constantly ready to seize the reins in questions of "peace, war and treaty," yet neglecting responsibility for being a "popular check on the other branches" of the government.[57] Ames, looking beyond the minutiae of Congress Hall, found the weather outside invigorating. The cold of winter settled on Philadelphia in earnest by mid-January, followed by a succession of snow storms. So little business was going on that he thought the members earned their six dollars a day easily. "Is it not cold enough to drink flip and ginger'd cider?" he remarked. In the crisp air, reminiscent of Yankee winters, his spirits rose. Now he had somewhat greater hopes that the government would overcome the constant onslaught against it, even though there was no real decrease in party rancor. Yet he had confidence that the struggle would rally the Federalists, for he was convinced the spirit of defense would "rise in proportion to the violence of the attack," and then justice would be meted out to the "Catilines." [58]

Tempers flared perceptibly over the perennial question of organizing the militia. Ames took issue with the Republicans, who insisted on using the militia for frontier defense. Turning it loose against the Indians was "a system of slaughter, of desolation," Ames replied with vehemence. Republicans protested loudly at receiving a communication from the President on military affairs, which led Ames to make some remarks about the encroachment of the House on other branches of government. "The moment that this House is turned into a Convention," he declared, "there is an end to liberty." John Nicholas of Virginia took exception to his statements, and when Ames answered in a low tone, he replied, "The gentleman prevaricates." Instantly Ames's anger flared. "I prevaricate, sir?" he questioned. But within the moment, he let the matter drop. It was the same old controversy, as he saw it. The in-

56. *Annals*, IV, 1049, 1057-58, Jan. 2, 1795. The vote on Giles's amendment was 59 yeas, 32 nays. Ames voted nay. Madison to Thomas Jefferson, Jan. 11, 1795, Madison Papers, XVIII, Lib. Cong.; William B. Grove to James Hogg, Phila., Jan. 21, 1795, Henry M. Wagstaff, "Letters of William Barry Grove," ed. J. G. de R. Hamilton, *The James Sprunt Historical Publications*, 9, No. 2 (Chapel Hill, 1910), 53.
57. Ames to Gore, Phila., Jan. 10, 1795, Ames, *Works of Ames*, I, 161.
58. Ames to Dwight, Phila., Jan. 24, 1795, Fisher Ames Papers, Dedham Hist. Soc.; Ames to Minot, Phila., Jan. 20, 1795, Ames, *Works of Ames*, I, 164.

sistence upon economy, the constant attacks on the idea of a standing army, the preference for militia—all were evidence of Virginian influence in politics.[59]

Such clashes as the one with Nicholas subsided quickly, but the persistent attacks of the Republican newspapers in Boston were another matter. At the time of the election the preceding autumn, Ames had even been tempted to sue the editors of the *Independent Chronicle* for libel; now in February 1795 they carried their opposition beyond decent bounds. When certain "Democratic Addressors" in Vermont had circulated a scurrilous piece about the undue influence Mrs. Ames had had on her husband's politics, the *Independent Chronicle* had publicized the material. Ames was accused of being a blackguard, lacking in decency in his congressional speeches, which were full of "moon-governed flights of fancy." Cleverly the article mentioned his "elegant, amiable ... and accomplished wife," who had strong anti-Republican opinions, which she had absorbed from her Tory father. "Benedict Arnold had a wife, likewise strongly attached to the British Government," the writers continued.[60] Ames was violently angry at the unfair blow at his family and wrote heatedly to his brother-in-law when he first read the Vermont diatribe. "The newspapering a woman is an outrage I had hoped Hottentots would not commit. Is Vermont more enlightened than Whidah or Angola? Otherwise, I should think, they would not endure such abuse of types."

It was attacks of this nature which made him wonder why he endured being shot at "like a turkey the day before Thanksgiving" for the small salary of a congressman. There was some consolation in the fact that this outburst was only the product of the "despised clubbists," while there was evidence in Thanksgiving sermons and in the President's birthday celebration of a public swing to Federalism. He could not, however, say as much for Congress. "No public body exists with ... stronger propensities to mischief. We are Frenchmen, democrats, *antifeds;* every thing but Americans, and men of business." [61] The last few days of the session did not alter Ames's opinion, especially as noth-

59. *Annals*, IV, 1075-77, Jan. 12, 1795; Ames to Thomas Dwight, Phila., Feb. 3, 1795, Ames, *Works of Ames*, I, 166; Theodore Sedgwick to Ephraim Williams, Phila., Jan. 13, 1795, Sedgwick Papers, III, Mass. Hist. Soc.

60. Ames to Gore, Dedham, Nov. 18, 1794, Fisher Ames Papers, Dedham Hist. Soc.; *Independent Chronicle* (Boston), Feb. 26, 1795; "A Middlesex Farmer," *ibid.*, Mar. 16, 1795, approved the resolutions of the Chittenden, Vt., Society; *Columbian Centinel* (Boston), Feb. 28, 1795.

61. Ames to Dwight, Jan. 7, 1795, Ames to Gore, Jan. 10, Feb. 24, 1795, Ames to Dwight, Phila., Feb. 24, 28, 1795, Ames, *Works of Ames*, I, 160, 162, 168-69. On the influence of pro-Federalist sermons, see Jedidiah Morse to Oliver Wolcott, Cambridge, Dec. 17, 1794, Mar. 18, 1795, Oliver Wolcott Papers, VIII, Conn. Hist. Soc.

ing could be or was done to take steps to protect the nation from the
effects of the naval war raging in the Atlantic. The treaty with England
on which Federalists were banking so heavily had not yet arrived when
Congress adjourned on March 3, 1795, but Ames believed that "the
success of Mr. Jay ... [would] secure peace abroad, and kindle war
at home." [62]

Upon his return from Congress, Ames turned his attention to his
new house, which was yet to be built, and to a handful of local law
cases for the April term of the court of common pleas. In the spring
he caught a bad cold which nearly developed into a "lung fever," as
pneumonia was then termed. For several weeks he was gravely ill, and
when Frances returned from a visit to Springfield, she was shocked to
see him in such a weakened condition. According to Thomas Dwight,
who visited the Ameses at the end of May, Frances found her husband
"a mere ghost ... his eyes as big as saucers, staring at her ... and his
voice so weak as to render him unequal to conversation." [63] A few
weeks later he had recovered sufficiently to be able to walk over to his
own house from his mother's, where he had been staying, but he still
was excessively thin, weak, and subject to frequent relapses.

Ames did not regain his strength for a year, and after this period of
illness his health was permanently impaired. At times he appeared to be
as vigorous as before, but a change of weather or excessive physical
activity would cause a renewal of the symptoms of his sickness—a general weakness, loss of sleep, and failing appetite. While he was not an
invalid as a consequence of this siege in 1795, the recurrent debility had
a decided effect on his life thereafter. During his prolonged struggle
to regain his health, he had to face the hard fact that he might never
again be fit to carry on the burdens of public office.

The exact nature of his illness remains conjectural in the absence of
adequate contemporary medical diagnosis. There is reason to believe
he may have had a chronic respiratory ailment, possibly asthma, before
his illness, because he mentioned the difficulties he had in breathing
during a prolonged rainy spell and how much he preferred the crisp air
of autumn. After consulting his brother, Nathaniel, and Dr. William
Eustis, Ames himself was in a quandary about his sickness. "I am told
my case is nervous, bilious, a disease of the liver, atrophy ... as differ-

62. Ames to Dwight, Phila., Feb. 3, 1795, Ames, *Works of Ames*, I, 166; Henry
Tazewell to James Monroe, Phila., Mar. 9, 1795, James Monroe Papers, Lib. Cong.;
Freeman, *Washington*, VII, 237.
63. Docket of the Court of Common Pleas, Norfolk County, Supreme Judicial
Court, Dedham; Ames to Rufus King, Dedham, Nov. 5, 1795, Rufus King Papers,
Box 6, 1795-1796, N.-Y. Hist. Soc.; Thomas Dwight to Hannah Dwight, Boston,
June 2, 7, 17, 1795; Dwight-Howard Papers, Box I, Mass. Hist. Soc.

ent oracles are consulted," he commented. "I am forbidden and enjoined to take almost everything." [64] Both physicians who had attended him prescribed a variety of cures for him which were more in the nature of a tonic for a convalescent than a treatment of the causes of his illness. Thomas Dwight, who had seen Ames at various times after he was stricken, maintained that "his disorder has been principally on his lungs, which tho' now apparently sound are in my opinion far from being so in reality." As soon as he was strong enough, Ames began to ride horseback, taking five- or ten-mile jaunts along the country roads. "On my return," he wrote to his brother-in-law, "some glasses of wine renew the radical heat and moisture, to use the language of old fashion'd quackery." [65] A careful diet and limited activity enabled Ames to regain weight, but even so he was still thirty pounds under his usual weight of 175.

The long months of convalescence were discouraging to Ames; yet he hoped eventually to continue some political activity. His correspondence at this time reflected his concern about his health; he felt he had suddenly lost his vitality and had become an enfeebled, old man. Still, he strongly rejected any thought that he had become a hypochondriac. "The vapors," he explained, "are believed, tho' I think erroneously, a malady which a man makes for himself....I...ought to be solicitous to repel this opinion. I am in good spirits, not less happy than formerly and believe myself to be getting well." As determined as Ames might be to attend the Fourth Congress, he was forced to admit he would scarcely be worth his pay. Domestic concerns also confronted him in full measure. Frances was expecting her second child in the coming spring, and Fisher was extremely reluctant to leave her alone in Dedham. "Here am I ...," he wrote in September, "going to carry my musket in the wars of politics, leaving my wife to mope alone in my new house, under circumstances of uncommon discouragement. I will try my best not to go crazy as she approaches the period of her trial." [66]

There was much consolation to be found in his family life, Ames knew. His little son John was the pride of his parents and grandparents alike. As Ames recuperated, he was able to undertake various social ac-

64. Ames to Dwight, Phila., Jan. 7, 1795, Ames to Dwight, Dedham, Sept. 22, Oct. 3, 1795, Ames, *Works of Ames*, I, 159, 175-77; Samuel Eliot Morison, "Squire Ames and Dr. Ames," *New Eng. Qtly.*, 1 (1928), 18.
65. Thomas Dwight to Theodore Sedgwick, Boston, Jan. 23, 1796, Sedgwick Papers, Vol. B, Mass. Hist. Soc.; Ames to Dwight, Dedham, Nov. 11, 1795, Fisher Ames Papers, Dedham Hist. Soc.
66. Ames to Dwight, Nov. 11, 1795, Fisher Ames Papers, Dedham Hist. Soc.; Ames to Dwight, Dedham, Sept. 13, 1795, Ames, *Works of Ames*, I, 175.

tivities with Frances, going to hear an organ recital at the Episcopal Church or entertaining visitors like the Gores and the Cabots, who drove out from Boston to inquire after his health. Late in August, after much encouragement on the part of Thomas Dwight, the Ameses went to the coast at Newport, Rhode Island, hoping that the sea air would be invigorating. Unfortunately Ames did not benefit from the change and shortly after their return, he had another relapse.[67]

Building his new home absorbed his interest during the many weeks of enforced idleness, but the vexations typical of every such construction weighed upon him. The house had been "raised" on April 17, 1795, and by the autumn was nearing completion. The masons had delayed their plastering, then had disappeared from the job to avoid jury duty; consequently, the walls were still too damp in October to permit the Ameses to move in. At an inopportune time, when Ames had no cash, the workmen demanded immediate payment, and he had to borrow from a neighbor. The heaps of debris still surrounding the completed house reminded him of the scene in his college days when President Locke entered a student's room and, finding the furniture on the bed and ashes strewn on the floor, had exclaimed, "Oh, the abomination of desolation." [68]

Early in November the Ameses were comfortably established in the new house, and Fisher felt sufficiently recovered a few weeks later to invite thirty Dedham friends to a housewarming. Only tried and true Federalists were included. To invite a pronounced Republican, one of the "Jacobins," would have gone counter to his innermost political convictions. "It is some comfort," he explained, "that we found 30 respectables to invite—altho' it is a reproach that so much company has been unsocial." [69] After the supper party, when conversation turned to politics, Ames even allowed himself to scold against the Jacobins. But such a gathering took much of his vitality, and as a result he was ill for several days.

In a time of strong political convictions, a man's politics frequently governed his choice of friends and in the case of the Ames family,

---

67. Ames to Dwight, Dedham, Aug. 24, Dec. 20, 1795, Fisher Ames Papers, Dedham Hist. Soc.; Ames to Dwight, Dedham, Nov. 18, 1795, Ames, *Works of Ames,* I, 178.

68. Entry of Apr. 17, 1795, Edna F. Calder, ed., "Extracts From the Ames Diary," *Dedham Hist. Register,* 6 (1895), 134; Ames to Dwight, Aug. 24, 1795, Ames, *Works of Ames,* I, 171; Ames to Jeremiah Shuttleworth, Sept. 26, 1795, Nathaniel Ames Papers, Dedham Hist. Soc. The note from Fisher Ames requested $50. Ames to Dwight, Dedham, Nov. 18, 1795, Fisher Ames Papers, Dedham Hist. Soc.

69. Ames to Dwight, Dedham, Dec. 9, 1795, Fisher Ames Papers, Dedham Hist. Soc.

perpetuated a cleavage between Fisher and his brother, Nathaniel. Long years of differences over the disposition of the estate of Nathaniel Ames, Sr., as well as other family matters, were accentuated by the clashing temperaments of the brothers. Both Nathaniel and Fisher were strong-willed, emotional, intense, and often inflexible. Fisher Ames, well-educated, socially polished, a man of national reputation, was now a representative of the ruling class. His older brother, on the other hand, exemplified the native-born democrat. Somewhat rough-hewn, Nathaniel was more at home in the village life of Dedham, despite his two Harvard degrees, than in the higher social circles of Boston. He spent much of his time hobnobbing with friends in the local taverns, attending to his medical practice, or busily engaged in town affairs to the detriment of his farm and to the ire of his wife.[70]

Frequently provoked into outbursts against his fellow men, his relatives, and even his wife, Nathaniel seemed cantankerous. When his wife forbade him to visit Timothy Gay's tavern, he vented his anger in his diary. "Discovered worse malignity in my bosom friend, than I conceive it possible to dwell in human shape! She has made it necessary that I should avoid the only houses where I could associate with mankind." [71] It was not surprising that Nathaniel, having an irascible personality, would clash with his forceful, dogmatic brother. While evidence of affection between the two is limited, Fisher would call upon his brother whenever he needed medical care, and on occasion Nathaniel would lend Squire Ames a book.[72]

Nathaniel, older by sixteen years than Fisher, matured during the turbulent years before the Revolutionary War and was imbued with a Whig outlook which he never relinquished. In later years he supported the Hancock-Samuel Adams group, the heirs of the Whig tradition. To his conservative brother, this allegiance was tantamount to being a dangerous opponent of the government. During the 1790's, although Nathaniel served in the General Court for several terms, his political ambition did not extend beyond the local horizon. Whatever he may have thought about Fisher's role in the Federalist party at this time seems not to have been recorded. He did, however, look with jaundiced eye at the position lawyers, or "pettifoggers," as he invari-

70. Entries of Feb. 28, May 18, June 30, Aug. 3, Oct. 8, 1792, Sept. 24, 1793, Feb. 4, Mar. 31, June 2, 1794, Martha A. Smith and Edna F. Calder, eds., "Diary of Dr. Nathaniel Ames," *Dedham Hist. Register*, 6 (1895), 20, 22, 68, 70, 109, 110.
71. Entry of Apr. 3, 1792, *ibid.*, 21.
72. Entry of Oct. 1797, *ibid.*, 8 (1897), 28; Ames to Dwight, Dedham, Feb. 16, 1796, Fisher Ames Papers, Dedham Hist. Soc. Ames commented, "Little as I approve the Doctor's politics I am not yet so unfeeling as to rejoice in his unhappy illness."

ably called them, had acquired and the influence the upper class exerted on the government to the detriment of the "Sovereign" rights of the people.

It was but a natural evolution of Nathaniel's politics that in 1796 he emerged as a champion of Jeffersonian Republicanism.[73] Even after the French Revolution became a divisive factor in American politics, he did not immediately support the cause of France, for in January 1794, he criticized the French severely for executing Marie Antoinette so "inhumanly" and for having "no fixd principles of liberty." It was the events of the summer of 1795, when the Jay Treaty was ratified, which unleashed all of Nathaniel's hostility toward Britain, dormant since the Revolution, and made him a flaming opponent of the Federalists. At a period when Fisher was denouncing "the Jacobins" and hoping for the success of John Jay's negotiations, Dr. Ames was praising "the glorious success of the French republic against the British combin'd Powers" and proclaiming that France, "not the Justice or moderation of England or the Merits of our Envoy" had maintained peace.[74]

Both in politics and in their personal lives, the brothers were often antagonists; yet they never irreparably severed their ties. After the completion of Fisher's house, they were near neighbors with lands adjoining one another; still they lived worlds apart. To a degree they represented the dichotomy of New England politics and society of the period. In spite of their familial tie, they were ardent disciples of opposing philosophies. Nathaniel, inflamed in his youth by the provocative ideals of the Revolution, still regarded the common man as the principal figure in a renovated social structure. Fisher Ames, fearful of democratic excesses in an embryonic republic, combined the outlook of the old colonial aristocracy with the new spirit of business enterprise to arrive at a belief in political and social dominance by a business-minded upper class closely allied to a strong government. It seemed to Fisher Ames that Nathaniel exemplified the unfortunate effect of French influence on an apostle of rampant democracy.

73. Warren, *Jacobin and Junto*, 32-40; Ames to Dwight, Feb. 28, 1795, Ames, *Works of Ames*, I, 170; entries of Apr. 7, 1794, Dec. 7, 19, 24, 1796, May 10, 1797, Calder, ed., "Diary of Dr. Nathaniel Ames," *Dedham Hist. Register*, 6 (1895), 109, 117, 7 (1896), 27.

74. Entries of Jan. 15, 25, 1794, Mar. 31, 1795, Calder, ed., "Diary of Dr. Nathaniel Ames," *Dedham Hist. Register*, 5 (1894), 109; 6 (1895), 134.

Chapter XIII

Triumph and Retreat

Shortly after the adjournment of Congress in March 1795, the text of the treaty John Jay had negotiated in London arrived in Philadelphia, leading one Pennsylvanian, Alexander Dallas, to forecast that "political concussions" would revive "when the mystic tablets of the British Treaty shall be opened for public inspection." Even before the exact terms were revealed, it was evident that Fisher Ames had been right when he said, "Faction will sound the tocsin against the treaty." [1] Republicans were not willing to wait for official revelations, once they had fathomed the nature of the proposed agreement. Quickly they discovered, as John Beckley expressed it, "something rotten" in the treaty. To Madison it was convincing proof that the Federalist proponents of the treaty were "a British party . . . ready to sacrifice . . . the most sacred dictates of National honour." [2] Even Hamilton, who had so strongly promoted the rapprochement with Britain, could not wholeheartedly accept it. "I expect the treaty will labor," he had written. "It contains

1. Alexander Dallas to Jonathan Dayton, Phila., Apr. 13, 1795, Gratz Collection, American Miscellaneous Section, Hist. Soc. of Pa.; Freeman, *Washington*, VII, 237; Bemis, *Jay Treaty*, 252-69; A. L. Burt, *The United States, Great Britain and British North America* (New Haven, 1940), 141-65; Alexander de Conde, *Entangling Alliances, Politics and Diplomacy Under George Washington* (Durham, 1958); Ames to Dwight, Feb. 3, 1795, Ames, *Works of Ames*, I, 166.
2. John Beckley to James Monroe, Phila., June 1, 1795, Monroe Papers, N.Y. Pub Lib.; James Madison to Robert R. Livingston, Aug. 10, 1795, Madison Papers, XVIII, Lib. Cong.; Donald H. Stewart, *Jeffersonian Journalism, Newspaper Propaganda and the Development of the Democratic-Republican Party, 1789-1801* (Ann Arbor, 1951), 352, 355-56, 368, 370-85; *Independent Chronicle* (Boston), Jan. 8, Feb. 16, Apr. 9, 13, 23, 30, 1795.

many good things, but there is one ingredient in it which displeases me
—of a commercial complexion," he stated, referring to Article XII, limiting to seventy tons American vessels trading with the British West
Indies.[3] He also objected strongly to the provision of the treaty which
prevented American re-export of British West Indian products. Yet the
Federalists were determined to defend the treaty as essential to the
preservation of peace as well as to their own domestic program. The
resultant political battle was not only a test of party strength but also
a fundamental clash over the direction American foreign policy should
take.

In early June 1795, the Senate met in special session to debate secretly
the ratification of the agreement. Rumor after rumor spread in public
about the treaty and the impact it would have on the nation. The reaction was instantaneous as pent-up antagonism for Britain was unleashed. Mobs in Philadelphia burned Jay in effigy, denouncing his
work, and feelings ran equally high in Massachusetts, leading Nathaniel
Ames to comment that the treaty was "the highest insult on the feelings
of Americans of anything that has happened this long time." [4]

On June 24, the Senate advised the President to ratify the treaty
without the offensive twelfth article. Senator Stevens T. Mason of
Virginia no longer felt bound to keep the exact terms secret and di-
vulged them to the Philadelphia *Aurora*. Its editor, Benjamin F. Bache,
hurriedly carried the text to Boston, spreading firebrands of dissension
along the way. On one of Fisher Ames's infrequent trips into Boston,
early in July, he discovered that the town was in a highly inflammatory
state over the treaty with many prominent citizens so wrought up that

3. Alexander Hamilton to William Bradford, May (n.d.), 1795, Hamilton to
Rufus King, N.Y., June 11, 1795, Lodge, ed., *Works of Hamilton*, X, 98-101. Ham-
ilton wrote the *Camillus* articles defending Jay's treaty which appeared in the
New York *Argus* beginning July 22, 1795; Mitchell, *Alexander Hamilton*, II, 344-
45, 683-84; Oliver Wolcott to Oliver Wolcott, Sr., Phila., June 27, 1795, Gibbs,
Memoirs, I, 201; Ames to Jeremiah Smith, Dedham, Jan. 18, 1796, Ames, *Works of
Ames*, I, 183. Ames commented on the *Camillus* essays, "So much answer to so
little weight of objection is odds. He holds up the aegis against a wooden sword."
Charles, *Origins of Party System*, 103-4, 122.
4. Freeman, *Washington*, VII, 251; Brant, *Madison, Father of the Constitution*,
424-27; De Conde, *Entangling Alliances*, 111-14; Pierce Butler to James Madison,
Phila., June 12, 1795, Madison Papers, XVIII, Lib. Cong.; Alexander Hamilton to
Rufus King, N.Y., June 20, 1795, King, ed., *Life of King*, II, 14-15; Abigail Adams
to Mary Cranch, N.Y., June 25, 1795, Mitchell, ed., *Abigail Adams*, 85; Mercy
Warren to George Warren, July 1795, Mercy Warren Letterbook, Mass. Hist. Soc.;
Benjamin Goodhue to Thomas Fitzsimmons, Salem, July 16, 1795, Dreer Collection,
Fitzsimmons Papers, Hist. Soc. of Pa.; entry of June 6, 1795, Calder, ed., "Diary
of Dr. Nathaniel Ames," *Dedham Hist. Register*, 6 (1895), 134; *Independent Chron-
icle* (Boston), June 11, 18, 23, 1795; *Boston Gazette*, July 6, 1795; Ralston Hayden,
The Senate and Treaties: 1789-1817 (N.Y., 1920).

they were agitating for a town meeting to discuss means of protest. Such an attempt to judge Jay's actions without knowing the circumstances behind his decisions merely angered Ames. "I could neither repress my indignation, nor disguise my contempt for the blindness and gullibility of the rich men who so readily lend their strength to the party which is thirsting for the contents of their iron chests," Ames wrote indignantly to Oliver Wolcott. There were so many vociferous opponents of the treaty that few persons had the courage to counter the popular will; consequently he felt that it was pure folly to have a town meeting on the subject.[5]

As Ames contemplated the scene from his fireside in Dedham, he was alarmed by the "factious spirit" which was more and more evident. Tempestuous town meetings such as the one in Boston on July 10, irate citizens condemning the treaty as "ruinous and destructive," the Republican press filled with invective against the Federalist treaty, and a mob spirit seething beneath the surface—all afforded Ames proof of his opinion that "our federal ship is near foundering in a millpond." [6] Since the mood of the public was such that the treaty could not be discussed calmly, it seemed to Ames that the only course open to the Federalists was to encourage merchants and other men of property in New York and elsewhere to take a stand favoring the treaty. If this important segment of society were won over, it would have the effect of "a double brick wall" to stop the spread of flames from Boston. In addition, he proposed that the advocates of the treaty should write "temporate and masterly vindications" for the public press. Much depended on the firmness of the administration in keeping the support of the rural areas, which, fortunately, were still uninfluenced by the passions of the towns. The events of midsummer had intensified his conviction that the federal structure must be supported against the "disorganizers," and a

5. Freeman, *Washington*, VII, 256; Stephen Higginson to Timothy Pickering, Boston, July 14, 1795, J. F. Jameson, ed., "Letters of Higginson," Amer. Hist. Assn., *Annual Report, 1896* (Washington, 1897), I, 787-88. The text of the treaty was first published in the Boston *Columbian Centinel*, July 8, 1795. Ames to Oliver Wolcott, Dedham, July 9, 1795, Oliver Wolcott Papers, XVIII, Conn. Hist. Soc.; *Columbian Centinel* (Boston), July 8, 1795; *Independent Chronicle* (Boston), July 9, 1795; Christopher Gore to Tobias Lear, Boston, Oct. 18, 1795, Christopher Gore Papers, Lib. Cong.

6. Ames to Wolcott, July 9, 1795, Jedidiah Morse to Oliver Wolcott, Boston, July 21, 27, 1795, Oliver Wolcott Papers, VIII, Conn. Hist. Soc.; George Cabot to Rufus King, Brookline, July 25, 27, 1795, Lodge, ed., *Letters of Cabot*, 80-83; Stephen Higginson to Timothy Pickering, Boston, July 14, Aug. 13, 16, 1795, J. F. Jameson, ed., "Letters of Higginson," Amer. Hist. Assn., *Annual Report, 1896*, I, 787-93; John Beckley to DeWitt Clinton, Phila., July 24, 1795, DeWitt Clinton Papers, Columbia Univ.; *Independent Chronicle* (Boston), July 13, 15, 23, 1795; *Columbian Centinel* (Boston), July 15, 1795; Morse, *Federalist Party*, 151-54.

watch kept alert, for "these little whirlwinds of dry leaves portend a hurricane." [7]

When the news came that President Washington at last had signed the treaty, the heavy clouds lifted momentarily for Ames and the Federalists. "Now let the heathen rage," Ames exulted. "If the government dare act right, I still believe it can maintain it." Massachusetts and Connecticut could be depended on, so one could shout *"ca ira"* like the French. The treaty would go through despite the mobs. With more vehemence than he usually exhibited, Ames now advocated that the government come to grips with the demagogues who were inciting the lower classes "to a pitch of fanaticism." There was no need to shirk from the test, he insisted. "I see no objection to joining the issue tendered; for governments are oftenest lost by flinching from the trial." [8] If the government fell, it would prove how frail it really was, but at the moment Ames had faith its loyal adherents would preserve it.

In view of the approaching struggle with the foes of the government, he was extremely anxious to return to public life; yet it was obvious that he would not be able to attend the opening of the Fourth Congress in early December. Dr. Eustis had encouraged him to go to Philadelphia whenever he could ride twenty miles a day, but Jeremiah Smith, stopping at the Ameses on his way to Congress, reported that he did not expect his friend to be able to leave home before spring. Ames eagerly awaited word about the new session and the events transpiring in Philadelphia. To Dwight Foster he wrote, "I lie on the gridiron of impatience, as still as I can." Meanwhile he busied himself with trivial affairs at home.[9]

Removed from the main stream of political life, Ames was prone to draw a somber sketch of current affairs. To him the resumption of party disputes was a threatening thing, and all he could hope for was that moderate Republicans would keep the more hotheaded from going to extremes. Tallying the strength of each side as nearly as he could determine matters so early in the session, he counted fifty-six Republi-

7. Ames to Wolcott, July 9, 1795, Oliver Wolcott Papers, XVIII, Conn. Hist. Soc.; Ames to Thomas Dwight, Aug. 24, 1795, Ames, *Works of Ames,* I, 172.
8. Ames to Dwight, Aug. 24, 1795; Ames to Dwight, Dedham, Sept. 13, 1795, Ames, *Works of Ames,* I, 172, 174; Ames to Wolcott, Sept. 2, 1795, Gibbs, *Memoirs,* I, 230; George Cabot to Oliver Wolcott, Brookline, Aug. 24, 1795, Lodge, ed., *Letters of Cabot,* 86. The President signed the treaty with Britain, Aug. 18; Freeman, *Washington,* VII, 291. Marshall Smelser, "The Jacobin Phrenzy: Federalism and the Menace of Liberty, Equality, and Fraternity," *The Review of Politics,* 13 (1951), 457-82.
9. Ames to Dwight, Dec. 9, 1795, Fisher Ames Papers, Dedham Hist. Soc.; Ames to Dwight Foster, Dedham, Dec. 10, 1795, Ames, *Works of Ames,* I, 180; Jeremiah Smith to John Smith, Dec. 12, 1795, Morison, *Life of Smith,* 82-83.

cans out of a total House membership of 105, which placed his own party in a minority position. Although the treaty was ratified by the executive and the Senate, Madison had already signified his intention of killing it by refusing to appropriate funds with which to execute it. Thus there was little to hope for from a Congress so infused with the "spirit of folly or jacobinism," Ames maintained. Individuals could do little, he asserted grimly. "When a house is divided against itself, it cannot be held up by main strength." [10]

Fallen snow in December and January had accumulated sufficiently so that Ames could risk starting out toward Philadelphia in a sleigh. A lumbering coach would have taxed his frail constitution far too much. Both Dr. Eustis and Dr. Ames had permitted him to go but, perhaps with true Republican foresight, had exacted a promise from him to refrain from making speeches in Congress. By easy stages he traveled to New York via Springfield, expecting, as he jestingly commented, that John Jay, now Governor of New York, would honor him with a mounted escort. With tongue-in-cheek, Ames remarked that if Jay refused to provide an escort, he could get "understrappers" like Hamilton to defend his treaty. Doggedly determined, sick much of the time en route, Ames pushed on, arriving in Philadelphia on February 9.[11]

In the interval of Ames's absence, the House of Representatives had only stirred up a momentary conflict over the answer to the President's address. Always an initial test of party strength in each session, the response of the House at this time delighted Federalists because of its conciliatory tone. Such calm within Congress when the treaty issue was still a center of furor did not deceive Ames, who was the more convinced that "faction is preparing its mines, and getting all ready for an explosion." The House was obviously marking time until the treaty was received from the President. Meanwhile, the members attended to necessary legislation, engaged in skirmishes, but avoided a debate over the treaty. All parties were "preparing for the onset," as Uriah Tracy expressed it, which might shake the government to its foundations.[12]

10. Ames to Dwight, Dedham, Dec. 30, 1795, Ames, *Works of Ames*, I, 180-81. Brant, *Madison, Father of the Constitution*, 432-34. John Beckley to DeWitt Clinton, Phila., Sept. 13, 1795, DeWitt Clinton Papers, Columbia Univ.

11. Ames to Dwight Foster, Dedham, Jan. 4, 1796, Ames to Jeremiah Smith, Mamaroneck, Feb. 3, 1796, Ames to Dwight, Phila., Feb. 11, 16, 1796, Ames, *Works of Ames*, I, 182-86; Thomas Dwight to Theodore Sedgwick, Boston, Jan. 23, 1796, Sedgwick Papers, Vol. B, Mass. Hist. Soc.; Thomas Dwight to Hannah Dwight, Boston, Jan. 22, Feb. 4, 1796, Dwight-Howard Papers, Mass. Hist. Soc.; *Annals*, V, 307, Feb. 9, 1796.

12. Ames to Dwight, Feb. 11, 1796, Ames, *Works of Ames*, I, 186; Uriah Tracy to Jeremiah Wadsworth, Phila., Feb. 3, 1796, Jonathan Trumbull to Jeremiah Wadsworth, Phila., Jan. 23, 1796, Jonathan Trumbull Papers, Conn. Hist. Soc.

Public opinion had gradually become less hostile during the early winter months, in part because of the active campaign of the Federalists to win support for the treaty. Madison was quite perturbed by the fact that "the name of the President is everywhere used with the most wonderful success by the Treaty partizans in subduing the popular objections to that instrument. No where has this policy been exerted with so much effect as in New England." [13] Before the Republicans could demand a copy of the treaty from the executive, Washington took advantage of the auspicious developments and transmitted the much-delayed text to the House on March 1, 1796. Commenting on the event to William B. Giles, Jefferson wrote, "I congratulate you on the arrival of Mr. Ames and the British treaty. The newspapers had said they would arrive together." [14] Unspoken was his hearty dislike for both.

On the day after receiving the treaty the House began its great debate on appropriating funds to put it into effect. When Edward Livingston of New York precipitously introduced a resolution calling for all the papers relating to the treaty negotiations, his objective was almost obscured as each side endeavored to prove whether or not the House had any constitutional right to share in the treaty-making power through its power over appropriations. The Federalist position, expounded largely by William Vans Murray of Maryland, William L. Smith, and Theodore Sedgwick, was that the President and Senate alone had the power and that the House had no authority to interfere. In the words of Smith the "House had no more right to send to the PRESIDENT for the papers in question than the printer of a newspaper had." [15] Albert Gallatin of Pennsylvania contended, in contrast, that the House could legitimately demand papers which were essential to a full understanding of the treaty in all its ramifications. In support of Livingston's motion, Madison declared that in a government limited by

13. James Madison to Edmund Pendleton, Phila., Feb. 7, 1796, Madison Papers, XIX, Lib. Cong.; Ames to Dwight, Feb. 16, 1796, Ames, *Works of Ames*, I, 186; Theodore Sedgwick to Ephraim Williams, Phila., Feb. 13, 1796, Sedgwick Papers, III, Mass. Hist. Soc.; Peleg Coffin, Jr., to Dwight Foster, Boston, Jan. 25, 1796, Dwight Foster Papers, Chamberlain Collection, Boston Pub. Lib.

14. Thomas Jefferson to William B. Giles, Monticello, Mar. 19, 1796, Ford, ed., *Writings of Jefferson*, VII, 65; Freeman, *Washington*, VII, 347; *Annals*, V, 394, Mar. 1, 1796.

15. *Annals*, V, 400-401, 438-44, Mar. 2, 8, 1796; White, *Federalists*, 63-64; Mitchell, *Alexander Hamilton*, II, 347-48; Peter C. Brown, "Executive Papers: the President and the Congress," New York State Bar Association, *Bulletin*, 20 (1948), 166-76; Westal W. Willoughby, *The Constitutional Law of the United States*, 2 vols. (N.Y., 1910), I, 480-83; Edward S. Corwin, *National Supremacy: Treaty Power vs. State Power* (N.Y., 1913), 59-98. S. B. Crandall, *Treaties, Their Making and Enforcement* (N.Y., 1904), 54-128.

constitutional checks and balances, it was erroneous to interpret the treaty-making power in such a way as to give the president and the Senate exclusive rights and to prevent the House from participating. His construction of the Constitution was a mere spinning of cobwebs, said Ames privately. "Conscience made him a coward," for Madison had not quite dared to expound a bold creed of anarchy. According to Ames, Giles, who likewise defended the Republican position, had no such scruples as his fellow Virginian and "certainly less sense." [16]

When the reverberations of the intense debate reached distant Monticello, Jefferson remarked, "All America is a tip-toe to see what the House of Representatives will decide on it." Ames, sitting in the midst of the contending forces, closed his mind to the incessant "sophisms and rant against the treaty" and hoped that the President would refuse to yield to the demands of the House. If he did refuse, Ames reasoned, it would be possible to carry the treaty into effect, as the Republicans would be in the awkward position of attacking Washington's "character, powers, and doings: all our strength against part of theirs." [17] By a substantial majority of sixty-one to thirty-eight, the Republicans carried Livingston's resolution in the committee of the whole, despite valiant efforts of the Federalists to sway the House. The resolution was then taken up by the House, where it passed sixty-two to thirty-seven. Searching for advice on the thorny question of whether the House actually had the power to demand diplomatic documents, Washington turned to members of his cabinet for advice before deciding on a course of action. He also consulted with Alexander Hamilton, who having retired from public life, was living in New York City. With mounting tension congressmen and the public awaited the President's decision. When an answer reached Congress Hall, the representatives learned that Washington had vehemently denied the House's right to the treaty papers. Ames observed that the Republicans "seemed wild on its being read." [18] Federalists were elated and breathed freely again. "It is just

16. *Annals*, V, 465, 477-95, Mar. 9, 10, 1796; Ames to Christopher Gore, Phila., Mar. 11, 1796, Ames, *Works of Ames*, I, 189. At this time Ames thought that Giles merely wanted to establish the precedent that the House could sanction or refuse treaties incorporating legislative powers of Congress. Thereafter he expected Giles would allow the treaty to pass. John S. Adams, ed., *An Autobiographical Sketch by John Marshall* ... (Ann Arbor, 1937), 20.

17. Thomas Jefferson to James Monroe, Monticello, Mar. 21, 1796, Ford, ed., *Writings of Jefferson*, VII, 67; Ames to Dwight, Phila., Mar. 9, 1796, Ames to Gore, Mar. 11, 1796, Ames, *Works of Ames*, I, 187-89.

18. *Annals*, V, 759; Freeman, *Washington*, VII, 350-54; Madison to Thomas Jefferson, Phila., Apr. 4, 1796, Madison Papers, XIX, Lib. Cong. Madison asserted in regard to Washington's answer, "There is little doubt in my mind that the message came from N.Y. [Hamilton]." Ames to George R. Minot, Phila., Apr. 2, 1796, Ames, *Works of Ames*, I, 191; Cunningham, *Jeffersonian Republicans*, 82-83.

such an one as we wished," wrote Jonathan Trumbull, referring to the President's message. "Our old *Friend* has in this instance come out with all the dignity, firmness and Independence, which could have been desired. It is illy relished by the Disorganizers." [19]

It was galling to Ames to be a silent listener instead of a gladiator. The tempo and stress of the recent debates had made him well aware of his own helplessness in a critical period. "Never was a time when I so much desired the full use of my faculties. . . . To be silent, neutral, useless, is a situation not to be envied," he wrote with feeling to Thomas Dwight. "I am like an old gun, that is spiked . . . and yet am carted off, . . . to balk the enemy of a trophy. My political life is ended, and I am the survivor of myself, or rather a troubled ghost of a politician, that am condemned to haunt the field of battle where I fell." In spite of his depressed mood he was confident that the opponents would be defeated, but before that could be accomplished "the conflict will light up a fierce war." [20]

Beneath Federalist jubilation over the President's stand were uncertainties and anxieties that the Republicans would yet succeed in preventing the treaty from going into effect. The opposition, for all of the wishful thinking of some Federalists, was not yet broken, and it was clear to Ames that the strength of his party in the House could not be stretched into a majority. The Federalists were obviously on quicksand with only a slight chance of victory unless Republican leaders deserted their position. Republicans persistently talked in exaggerated terms about the dangers to liberty and the trend toward monarchy. They gathered in caucus, planned their tactics on the floor of the House, and took steps to hold onto any waverers. When the Republicans succeeded in referring the President's message to a committee of the whole House in order to reply to the executive, Ames interpreted their move as "a manifesto or declaration of war against the other two branches." [21] The committee and then the House proceeded to approve two resolutions spelling out the constitutional right of the representatives to deliberate on a treaty. The way was open for a full-scale debate on the merits of appropriating money to carry the treaty into effect.

Federalist prospects darkened considerably during the second week

19. Jonathan Trumbull to Jeremiah Wadsworth, Phila., Apr. 2, 1796, Jonathan Trumbull Papers, Conn. Hist. Soc.; Madison to Jefferson, Apr. 4, 1796, Madison Papers, XIX, Lib. Cong.
20. Ames to Dwight, Mar. 9, 1796, Ames, *Works of Ames*, I, 187-88.
21. Ames to Minot, Apr. 2, 1796, Ames to Gore, Mar. 11, 1796, Ames, *Works of Ames*, I, 190-91; Jonathan Trumbull to Jeremiah Wadsworth, Phila., Apr. 2, 1796, Jonathan Trumbull Papers, Conn. Hist. Soc.; Henry Tazewell to John Ambler, Phila., Apr. 4, 1796, Tazewell Papers, Lib. Cong.; *Boston Gazette*, Apr. 18, 1796; *Independent Chronicle* (Boston), Apr. 21, 1796; *Annals*, V, 771, Apr. 6, 1796.

of April. Speeches of Republican members, especially one of Madison's, indicated anew their determination to defeat the treaty. Chauncey Goodrich, a Federalist representative from Connecticut, candidly acknowledged, "We still continue in a state of disgust and anxiety." [22] Federalist tactics were in great need of revision inasmuch as the effect of the President's stand had already faded. In desperation Theodore Sedgwick proposed combining the appropriations for the Jay Treaty with those of three other pending treaties—Pinckney's treaty with Spain, the treaty with Algiers, and Anthony Wayne's pact with the Ohio Indians. The Federalist plan was vitiated when Gallatin induced the committee to take up each treaty separately. Again the Republican majority prevailed. With a growing sense of frustration, the Federalists threatened to block the progress of other legislation if they could not accomplish their objectives. "Here, we dance upon the edge of the pit," commented Ames in bitterness, "it is but a little way to the bottom. . . . Reject the treaty. . . . There will be no adjournment, if no treaty—no motion to the wheels of government. The mill will be stopped, if the *antis* refuse to grind this treaty grist." [23]

Ames wrote Hamilton telling him of the Republican caucus decision to refuse appropriations. The former Secretary of the Treasury then provided the Federalists with a plan which he was convinced would be more effectual in defeating the enemy than the previous "wrong and impolitic" steps. By capturing and molding the public mind and utilizing the great prestige of the President, the treaty might be saved. Let the President issue a strong protest, Hamilton counseled, if the treaty be refused. Have senators express agreement with the President's course, and encourage merchants to send approving petitions and resolutions, while holding the House in session until the funds are granted. At the same time, Federalist representatives in the House, he assumed, would battle tenaciously to hold the pro-treaty votes as well as to convince the doubting and undermine the opponents.[24]

Two of the most exciting weeks the House had known began on April 14. The resolution for carrying the treaty into effect came before the committee of the whole, opening a torrent of frenzied, impassioned oratory. Representative after representative gained the floor to expound his convictions about the treaty. Seldom had there been such feverish efforts in the House to contest the arguments of the opposing side.

22. *Annals*, V, 772-82, Apr. 6, 1796; Chauncey Goodrich to Oliver Wolcott, Sr., Phila., Apr. 9, 1796, Gibbs, *Memoirs*, I, 325.
23. *Annals*, V, 940, 965-66, 969, Apr. 13, 14, 1796; Ames to Dwight, Phila., Apr. 18, 1796, Ames, *Works of Ames*, I, 192.
24. Alexander Hamilton to Rufus King, N.Y., Apr. 15, 1796, King., ed., *Life of King*, II, 59-60. The letter from Ames, mentioned by Hamilton, is not extant.

Anticipating the clash of issues, Jonathan Trumbull commented, "The Devil seems to be renewing his reign with encreased violence." [25]

Both sides attempted diversionary tactics as the debate over the merits of the treaty commenced. Samuel Maclay, a Pennsylvania Republican, introduced resolutions condemning the treaty. Federalist William Vans Murray urged that the nation needed acts and not speeches, but his plea for an immediate decision was lost in the wave of discussion which followed. Madison led the Republican attack by criticizing the treaty on all fronts. In every respect, he found it was deficient—in its relation to the Treaty of Peace, to the law of nations, and to Anglo-American commerce. A refusal to accept it, he argued, "could give no cause, ... nor provocation for war," and it was highly unlikely Britain would threaten her best market. Samuel Lyman, the Massachusetts Federalist, undertook the difficult task of a reply to Madison's dissection of the treaty. He felt that the nation, lacking power, had made the best treaty it could. Did the result signify that the President had become a traitor or that the Senate had been corrupted with British gold? John Swanwick of Pennsylvania quickly responded, "To what purpose ... sound the alarm ... ? Do we charge bribery and corruption? No Sir." Then he too combed the treaty for flaws. John Nicholas of Virginia followed on April 16 by condemning Jay for yielding to British extortions. Zephaniah Swift of Connecticut retaliated, trying to stem the Republican tide by maintaining that the adjustment of disputes had prevented war.[26]

The onslaught upon the treaty gained momentum during the first week of debate, and after Madison's keen analysis on Friday the sixteenth, Tench Coxe had decided doubts that the appropriations would be made for the treaty. Giles continued the momentum of the Republican attack, scrutinizing and weighing each clause, then pronouncing that "this torch of discord" endangered the position of the United States and must be defeated. Ames, surfeited with Republican diatribes, took refuge from Giles's speech in a committee room and spent the hour enjoying his correspondence from his family, leaving his colleagues to answer the Virginian. Staunch Goodhue, veteran of years of political combat, rallied the Federalists. His prediction that war would follow if the treaty were rejected and that the House would bear the responsibility earned him an outburst from John Heath.

---

25. *Annals*, V, 969-1292, Apr. 14-30, 1796; Jonathan Trumbull to Jeremiah Wadsworth, Phila., Apr. 13, 1796, Jonathan Trumbull Papers, Conn. Hist. Soc.
26. *Annals*, V, 969-71, 973, 987-91, 1006, 1018, Apr. 14, 15, 16, 1796; Brant, *Madison, Father of the Constitution*, 436-38.

"Good God! I am lost in astonishment!" the Virginia colonel replied. "Is there a man within these walls so dead to all the dearest interests of his country . . . as to plunge . . . [it] into a wanton and unnecessary war?" [27]

In spite of their aggressive attack, the strength of the Republicans was waning by April 23. The resolute defense of Federalist speakers like James Hillhouse of Connecticut and Abiel Foster of New Hampshire had had an effect on the hesitant members, and the campaign of Federalists outside Congress to persuade the business community to petition in favor of the treaty already was having an influence. According to Hamilton, petitions signed by alarmed merchants and prominent bankers had the effect of turning "the current . . . in our favor" in New York.[28] In staccato sentences Ames commented, "This city [Philadelphia] is right. . . . Alarms are contagious. I do not despair." [29] But the Republican orators remained formidable antagonists. Albert Gallatin, whose Gallic incisiveness laid bare the negative aspects of the treaty, carried the assault directly to the Federalists. Did they contend the government would be dissolved in the case of a postponement? "This idea was too absurd . . . ," he remonstrated. "By whom . . . was the Government to be dissolved? The gentlemen must answer, 'by themselves,' or they must declare they meant nothing but to alarm." [30] At such a critical juncture a powerful speaker like Gallatin could damage the Federalist cause. A Jupiter was needed who could hurl thunderbolts and confound the enemy. Federalists turned to Ames. Could this frail man preserve the day for Federalism and ensure a victory which some Federalists still expected? Nothing had been heard from him week after week. William Plumer anxiously inquired from New Hampshire, "Is Ames sick? . . . I hope he will be able to attend and . . . make a display

27. Tench Coxe to William Constable, Phila., Apr. 20, 1796, Constable-Pierrepont Papers, N.Y. Pub. Lib.; Ames to Dwight, Phila., Apr. 18, 1796, Fisher Ames Papers, Dedham Hist. Soc.; *Annals*, V, 1052-59, 1064, Apr. 18, 19, 1796.
28. Alexander Hamilton to Rufus King, Apr. 23, 1796, King, ed., *Life of King*, II, 61; Madison to Thomas Jefferson, Phila., Apr. 18, 23, 1796, Madison Papers, XIX, Lib. Cong. Madison acknowledged that the Republican majority had dwindled to eight or nine. John Beckley to DeWitt Clinton, Phila., Apr. 11, 1796, DeWitt Clinton Papers, Columbia Univ.; "The Crisis," extra edition of the *Columbian Centinel* (Boston), Apr. 28, 1796; *Massachusetts Mercury* (Boston), Apr. 29, 1796; *Annals*, V, 1077-94, 1172-75, Apr. 19, 26, 1796; Noble Cunningham, "John Beckley: An Early American Party Manager," *Wm. and Mary Qtly.*, 3d Ser., 13 (1956), 40-52.
29. Ames to Dwight, Apr. 18, 1796, Ames, *Works of Ames*, I, 192; Theodore Sedgwick to Ephraim Williams, Phila., Mar. 26, 30, Apr. 16, 20, 1796, Sedgwick Papers, III, Mass. Hist. Soc.
30. *Annals*, V, 1200, Apr. 26, 1796.

of that eloquence and intelligence so rare in this country." [31] Who was there in the House but this brilliant spokesman of Federalism, the orator who had mesmerized his audience so often in the past?

On Thursday, April 28, while yet another attack on Jay's Treaty was underway, it became known in the corridors of Congress Hall that Fisher Ames would finally speak. The information drew dignitaries magnetically to the House chamber where the galleries were already well filled by spectators anticipating a vote on the treaty that day. Vice President Adams hurried from the Senate to be joined in the House by Supreme Court Justice James Iredell.[32] Representatives themselves hastily reclaimed their seats, attracted by the prospect of hearing the speech. As the subdued murmurings of the audience died down, Fisher Ames arose. "Mr. Chairman," he began in a low voice. "I entertain the hope, perhaps a rash one, that my strength will hold me out to speak a few minutes." These arresting words commanded instant attention, particularly since Ames's pale, serious face and obvious feebleness reinforced his sincerity. Standing by his desk, this slight, fastidiously groomed man had in a moment evoked a sympathy for himself which increased the impact of his message on his listeners. According to John Adams, the impression that Ames made was unforgettable.[33]

For more than an hour, the Massachusetts Federalist gave a display of oratory which remained unsurpassed in his generation and which revealed more than any other of his speeches his splendid command of the language and his ability to infuse vitality into his subject. Above all, it showed the tough inner fibre of the man in overcoming his physical handicaps. Jeremiah Mason, who heard Ames speak, recalled in his reminiscences: "It was a most masterful display. . . . After the House had been . . . tired almost to death with discussions by the most talented men in the nation, . . . he revived and excited the highest state of feeling." [34]

Ames made a twofold defense of Jay's Treaty, first showing that the opposition unjustly endeavored to rouse a "jealous and repulsive fear for the rights of the House," then revealing the dire consequences of a

31. William Plumer to Jeremiah Smith, Apr. 12, 1796, William Plumer Papers, I, 290, Lib. Cong.
32. *Annals*, V, 1228-38, Apr. 28, 1796; "Fisher Ames," *Port Folio*, 3d Ser., 1 (1813), 11. John Adams to Abigail Adams, Phila., Apr. 30, 1796, Adams Papers, Microfilm Reel 381, Mass. Hist. Soc.; George Cabot to Caleb Strong, Phila., Apr. 27, 1796, Lodge, ed., *Letters of Cabot*, 95.
33. *Annals*, V, 1239, Apr. 28, 1796; "Fisher Ames," *Port Folio*, 3d Ser., 1 (1813), 11; Adams to Abigail Adams, Apr. 30, 1796, Adams Papers, Microfilm Reel 381, Mass. Hist. Soc.
34. Gilbert J. Clark, *Memoir, Autobiography and Correspondence of Jeremiah Mason* (privately printed, 1873), 35.

broken treaty. In his judgment the decision on the treaty rested far more on "the temper and manner" with which the members considered it than on "the development of any profound political principles." It was only pretense to deny that prejudice and heated feeling did not influence the debate; objectivity did not exist "while the peal to rally every passion of man is continually ringing in our ears." Man was not above his emotions, he averred. "The hazard of great interests cannot fail to agitate strong passions; we are not disinterested, it is impossible we should be dispassionate." [35] Having acknowledged the power of emotions, Ames proceeded to make an emotional appeal to his audience.

The opponents of the treaty, he remarked, claimed that they were fighting a plot "to nullify this assembly, and to make it a cypher in the Government." In addition they accused the President and Senate of "a scheme of coercion and terror, to force the Treaty down our throats." It was impossible to reason away such false assertions. "They are higher than a Chinese wall in truth's way." To have *esprit de corps* in the legislature and maintain its prerogatives was worthy of praise, but to deny appropriations because of exaggerated fears of encroachment was groundless. If these jealousies could not be allayed, he stated dramatically, he did not wish to have a further hearing of his ideas. An open mind was essential to judge the treaty wisely. [36]

Ames deftly revealed the inconsistencies in the Republican position that the treaty, though formally ratified, was still a mere proposition to be considered by the House. Hardly a month previous, the House had acknowledged that the treaty power rested exclusively in the executive and the Senate; yet now, he stated scornfully, "we pretend that the acts . . . are not valid until we have concurred in them." It was too "monstrous" an opinion to warrant further discussion. [37] Yet the House insisted on judging the expediency of a treaty, a doctrine which gave it a share in the treaty-making power, despite all allegations to the contrary.

Bluntly Ames asked, "Shall we break the Treaty?" If not, then the only alternative was to carry it out. "The Treaty is bad, fatally bad, is the cry. . . . If we listen to the clamor of party intemperance, the evils are of a number not to be counted, and of a nature not to be borne." Yet he was convinced that in an over-all sense it was not so bad, and its rejection was in no way warranted. With scant concern for the detailed arguments of the Republicans, he asserted that the treaty "by

35. *Annals*, V, 1239, Apr. 28, 1796.
36. *Ibid.*, 1240-41.
37. *Ibid.*, 1242. The reference was to Blount's resolution presented to the committee of the whole, Apr. 1, 1796. *Ibid.*, 771.

its stipulations for the posts, for indemnity and for a due observance of our neutral rights has justly raised the character of the nation." The public as a whole acquiesced in the treaty, Ames asserted; consequently, the government would be unable to justify the deed of rejection. Only one branch of the legislature proposed to reject it, not the entire nation. Those who now opposed the treaty were victims of lingering hatreds toward Britain, which had been accentuated artificially during the crisis of 1794. This group could not accept any treaty with Britain based on an idea of amity, insisting that "no Treaty should be made with the enemy of France." It was wrong, Ames proclaimed, for Americans to become attached to either Britain or France. Any subservience to a foreign nation, he held in contempt. "It is enough to be Americans. That character comprehends our duties and ought to engross our attachments." [38]

Reverting to his previous argument about the merits of the treaty, he observed that there was little to fear from its terms. In contrast, a rejection would have serious consequences. "There is nothing before us in that event but confusion and dishonor." The results of such a step were limitless, and he urged the members to reflect on the dangers "before we resolve to leap into the abyss." National honor would be jeopardized by the course the opponents were advocating. To maintain that we could refuse to carry out a treaty because of "our own sovereign will and pleasure" was a "shameless" doctrine which would "baffle the casuistry of a Papal council to vindicate." If Britain was bound by the agreement, he pointed out, the United States was also to a like degree. "It cannot be a Treaty, and yet no Treaty; a bargain, and yet no promise." Not even Algiers, where treaties might be had for money, would disown a ratified treaty, he added scornfully. "A Government whose origin is right ... [cannot] upon solemn debate make its option to be faithless—can dare to act what despots dare not avow." [39]

Ames had commenced his speech obviously weak in strength and in voice. In his enthusiasm he ignored his disability and reached the climax of his speech in a burst of forceful oratory. Even after a lapse of sixteen years, this speech remained vivid in the memory of one spectator, who wrote in the *Port Folio* that Ames had "addressed himself to every faculty of the mind. . . . Argument, remonstrance, entreaty, persuasion, terror, and warning fell now like the music and now like the thunder of heaven from his lips. . . . He threw a spell over the senses, rendering them insensible to every thing but himself." [40]

38. *Ibid.*, 1244-45, 1249-50.
39. *Ibid.*, 1251-56.
40. "Fisher Ames," *Port Folio*, 3d Ser., 1 (1813), 12; Morison, *Life of Smith*, 97.

Striking out repeatedly at his adversaries, Ames continued to put heavy stress on the serious effect their course would have on the nation. Redress of commercial spoliations would founder without the treaty. Would the answer of the "fierce champions" of justice be " 'Petitioners, go home and starve; we cannot satisfy your wrongs and our resentments?' " Retention of the Northwest posts by Britain was a certainty without the treaty. An Indian war would follow. Could western representatives assure the continuity of peace? "No, sir," he replied, "it will not be peace, but a sword; it will be no better than a lure to draw victims within the reach of the tomahawk." The horrible results of a misguided refusal stood graphically before him. "By rejecting the posts, we light the savage fires—we bind the victims. . . . The voice of humanity . . . exclaims that while one hand is held up to reject this Treaty, the other grasps a tomahawk. . . . I can fancy that I listen to the yells of savage vengeance, and the shrieks of torture. Already they seem to sigh in the West wind; already they mingle with every echo from the mountains." [41]

Abruptly and effectively, Ames turned from pathos to succinct summation. "The arguments I am urging would then come to a point," he said. "To use force, is war. To talk of Treaty again, is too absurd. Posts and redress must come from voluntary good will, Treaty, or war." Drawing all the strands of his speech together, he reiterated the grim consequences of rejection. "On the sea coast, vast losses uncompensated. On the frontier, Indian war. . . . Everywhere discontent . . . national discord and abasement. . . . Will our Government be able to temper and restrain the turbulence of such a crisis?" He hurled questions *seriatim* at the Republicans, hammering away steadily in his attempt to show the only choice that remained open to the nation. "Let us not hesitate, then, to agree to the appropriation. . . . Thus we shall save the faith of our nation, secure its peace, and diffuse the spirit of confidence and enterprise that will augment its prosperity." Ames ended his momentous speech on a personal note. "There is, I believe, no member who will not think his chance to be a witness of the consequences greater than mine. If, however, the vote should pass to reject . . . even I, slender and almost broken as my hold upon life is, may outlive the Government and Constitution." [42]

As Ames sat down, exhausted by the intensity of his labors, there were mingled cries of "the question" and "committee rise." Republican Abraham Venable of Virginia urged postponement of the final vote for an additional day. His plea prevailed with the support of seventy mem-

41. *Annals*, V, 1257-60.
42. *Ibid.*, 1260-63.

272 Fisher Ames

bers.[43] That the Federalists did not press strongly for an immediate decision on the treaty does not reflect on Ames's oration. It was to their advantage to postpone the final vote until the trend of public opinion, now veering to their side, was conclusive. Although the anti-treaty majority was definitely shrinking before April 28, it is reasonable to assume that Ames's speech had a strong influence on the final outcome. His dramatic appearance before the House at this time marked a peak in his public career. The combination of a long-deferred desire to enter the treaty controversy and a physical debility of a serious nature apparently caused him to express himself in an exceptionally melodramatic and emotional form. This, instead of having the effect of being merely histrionic, captured the imagination of many who heard him. For Fisher Ames the speech on the British treaty proved to be one of his final opportunities in Congress for eloquence.

Justice Iredell and John Adams, sitting together in the gallery, were greatly moved by the scene. "Our feelings beat in unison," Adams wrote to his wife. " 'My God, how great he is,' says Iredel, 'how great he has been.' He has been noble said I. After some time Iredel breaks out, 'Bless my stars I never heard anything so great since I was born!' "[44] Jeremiah Smith, with a close friend's predilection to praise, remarked that Ames's speech was the "most eloquent" he had ever heard, and Dr. Joseph Priestley, who had listened to Pitt, Burke, and Fox in England, stated that this was "the most bewitching piece of parliamentary oratory he had listened to."[45] Immediately after Ames finished, Smith and Samuel Dexter wrote out the speech with his help, but all agreed the printed version could not compare with the flashing spoken words. "I tell him," commented Smith, "that he ought to have died in the fifth act; that he never will have an occasion so glorious, having lost this he will now be obliged to make his exit like other men."[46]

43. *Ibid.*, 1263; Morison, *Life of Smith*, 97; William O. Lynch, *Fifty Years of Party Warfare* (Indianapolis, 1931), 57n; Charles, *Origins of Party System*, 115. Charles suggests that Sedgwick's pressure on Republicans caused them to change their votes. Jeremiah Mason, who was present during the speech, noted that "one of the opposition ... moved an adjournment, saying that under such feelings, the House was incompetent to act wisely or safely." Reminiscences of Mason quoted in Clark, *Memoir of Jeremiah Mason*, 35.

44. Adams to Abigail Adams, Apr. 30, 1796, Adams Papers, Microfilm Reel 381, Mass. Hist. Soc.

45. Jeremiah Smith to John Smith, Phila., Apr. 29, 1796, Jeremiah Smith to John Smith, n.d., Morison, *Life of Smith*, 96-97. Smith stated that Ames "spoke without premeditation." Harriot W. Warner, ed., *Autobiography of Charles Caldwell, M.D.* (Phila., 1855), 114.

46. Smith to John Smith, Apr. 29, 1796, Morison, *Life of Smith*, 96; Reminiscences of Jeremiah Smith quoted in *ibid.*, 97; Ames's speech was published by John

Not all comments were so laudatory. As usual the *Independent Chronicle* seized the chance to attack a Federalist by scathingly remarking that Ames "let loose his imagination ... and his mind enfeebled by disease, shrunk from the mighty monster which Great Britain presented to his affrighted view." [47] Benjamin Austin, Ames's old political antagonist, wrote sarcastically about the treaty debate, "The most curious part of the farce was the *sublime* speech of Mr. Ames.... He rose ... under all the infirmities of a man in the last stages of dissolution, [and] introduced his observations as the dying legacy of a departing patriot." [48] Albert Gallatin, just achieving prominence as a Republican leader during Ames's last year in Congress, was in a better position to appreciate his political foe's greatness. He commented, "The most brilliant and eloquent speech was undoubtedly that of Mr. Ames; but it was delivered in reference to the expediency of making the appropriations, and treated but incidentally of the constitutional question. I may here say that though there were, during my six years of Congressional service, many clever men in the Federal party in the House (Griswold, Bayard, Harper, Otis, Smith of South Carolina, Dana, Tracy, Hillhouse, Sitgreaves, etc.) I met with but two superior men. Ames ... and John Marshall." [49]

On the twenty-ninth, petitions favoring the treaty came in increasing volume. Republicans avoided answering Ames's speech, and a long-standing foe of the treaty, Speaker of the House Jonathan Dayton, not only extolled Ames but also stated to the House that he would cast his vote for the treaty. Gabriel Christie of Maryland changed his stand likewise, contending his constituents wanted the treaty passed. The

---

Fenno in pamphlet form, *The Speech of Mr. Ames, in the House of Representatives of the United States ... on Thursday, April 28, 1796 ...* (Phila., 1796). A second edition was published in Boston, printed by Jonathan & J. N. Russell, without publication date. Jeremiah Smith sent a copy to Joseph Dennie on May 22, 1796, Joseph Dennie Papers, Harvard Univ.; Gore in London gave the speech to Pitt and Lord Grenville, and promised to send a copy to "E.B." (Edmund Burke), Christopher Gore to Ames, London, July 26, 1796, Ames, *Works of Ames,* I, 200. Daniel Webster in 1802 found a copy of the speech in the Fryeburg, Maine, library and memorized it; Autobiography of Webster, Fletcher Webster, ed., *The Private Correspondence of Daniel Webster,* 2 vols. (Boston, 1857), I, 14.

47. *Independent Chronicle* (Boston), May 12, 1796. B. F. Bache, editor of the Philadelphia *Aurora,* acknowledged Ames's eloquence but criticized his "astonishing inconsistencies," *Aurora* (Phila.), Apr. 29, 1796; William C. Rives, *History of the Life and Times of James Madison,* 3 vols. (Boston, 1859-68), III, 563; Duke de La Rochefoucault-Liancourt, *Travels Through the United States of North America ... ,* 2 vols. (London, 1799), II, 148.

48. Benjamin Austin, *Constitutional Republicanism in Opposition to Fallacious Federalism; As Published ... in the Independent Chronicle under the Signature of Old-South* (Boston, 1803), 183-85.

49. Henry Adams, *The Life of Albert Gallatin* (Phila., 1880), 155.

resolutions to appropriate funds for the treaty were put to the vote in the committee. Forty-nine voted yea and forty-nine were opposed. Chairman Frederick Muhlenberg, risking his political future, cast the deciding affirmative vote.[50] Fortunately for the Federalists, Joseph B. Varnum of Massachusetts, and several other convinced opponents were absent. The treaty still could be lost in the House, and the tension remained unrelieved. Republican attempts to attach a condemnatory amendment to the appropriation bill roused the ire of Federalists, who refused to swallow such a bitter draught. Ames and the other treaty advocates gained enough support to reject it, fifty to forty-nine. Then, a few minutes later, in the deciding vote on the main question, the treaty was upheld fifty-one to forty-eight. The great debate was over. The agreement with England stood, though the repercussions would still be heard and affect party politics for a long time to come. The Federalists had influenced the decision by emphasizing war as an alternative to the treaty, by waging the campaign for public petitions, and by bringing pressure on vacillating representatives. But nothing had the dramatic effect nor gave such meaning to the Federalist cause as Fisher Ames's speech.[51]

When the treaty appropriation bill finally was sent to the Senate on May 4 it was "a Day of Universal and perpetual Peace" to John Adams; and Ames, reflecting on the events a while later, could see "nothing but blue sky" after the issue was settled.[52] In Dedham, Nathaniel commented tersely and bitterly, "The Treaty fish swallowed Tail foremost! by Congress."[53] The *Boston Gazette* expressed its view with sarcastic verse:

> Joy to the world, the fiat's past
> The treaty's ratified
> The final question ta'en at last
> And Congress has complied.

50. *Annals*, V, 1264, 1276, 1280, Apr. 29, 1796; Freeman, *Washington*, VII, 375; Brant, *Madison, Father of the Constitution*, 438-39; Miller, *Hamilton*, 433.
51. *Annals*, V, 1282, 1291, Apr. 30, 1796; Madison to Thomas Jefferson, Phila., May 9, 22, 1796, Madison Papers, XVII, XIX, Lib. Cong.; John Clopton to ?, Phila., May 1, 8, 1796, John Clopton Papers, Duke University, Durham, N.C.; Cunningham, *Jeffersonian Republicans*, 83-84; Cunningham indicates that the Republican ranks were entirely shattered. John Adams to Abigail Adams, Apr. 30, 1796, Adams Papers, Microfilm Reel 381, Mass. Hist. Soc. Adams remarked about Varnum: "Our Varnum who is as cross a Goat as any from Virginia...was out of the Way."
52. Adams to Abigail Adams, Phila., May 5, 1796, Adams Papers, Microfilm Reel 381, Mass. Hist. Soc.; Ames to Gore, Phila., July 30, 1796, Ames, *Works of Ames*, I, 196; *Independent Chronicle* (Boston), May 12, 1796.
53. Entry of May 2, 1796, Calder, ed., "Diary of Dr. Nathaniel Ames," *Dedham Hist. Register*, 7 (1896), 78.

> Ye tories now lift up your heads,
> And raise your triumphs high
> The whigs to quick destruction tread,
> Till their remembrance die.[54]

Even months after Ames's oration, the *Independent Chronicle* was unwilling to forget his role, contending that he had made "little short of a declaration of the surrender of our sovereignty and independence and that we must hereafter depend on the mercy of [Britain]." [55]

Surprisingly Ames had not been adversely affected by the strain of his speech. "My speech has not killed, most persons say it will cure, as I am decidedly better for some days than I was before I made that attempt." [56] He was more concerned at his wife's reaction when she read in the newspapers that he had been speaking. Since she was in the last stages of her pregnancy, he did not want her to be alarmed on his account. Frances already suspected that his letters were not entirely truthful about his health, so he hoped his friends Dwight Foster and Jeremiah Smith would mention that he was well. In the remaining month of the session Ames took only a minimal part in congressional activity, and instead of pondering over the fate of the nation, he cracked jokes in the committee room.[57]

54. *Boston Gazette,* May 9, 1796.
55. "Mercator," *Independent Chronicle* (Boston), July 18, 1796.
56. Ames to Dwight, Phila., May 9, 1796, Fisher Ames Papers, Dedham Hist. Soc.
57. Ames to Dwight Foster, Phila., Apr. 29, [1796], Ames to Dwight, Phila., May 19, 1796, Ames, *Works of Ames,* I, 192-93.

Chapter XIV

An Ebb of Influence

Shortly after the end of the congressional session, Fisher Ames made the decision not to be a candidate for a fifth term in the House of Representatives. The pattern of his illness, with occasional relapses, made him unwilling to consider another two-year term in office. Meantime, he expected to continue to take his seat in the House, if possible until the end of the Fourth Congress in March 1797.[1]

When Philadelphia friends, Mr. and Mrs. George Rundle, invited Ames to join them on a trip to "the Federal City," Mt. Vernon, and northern Virginia, in June 1796, he was uncertain about accepting. He wanted to visit the upper South both for reasons of health and sociability. His concern for Frances, however, made him particularly anxious to return home in time for the birth of their second child. Even though the excursion promised to be a pleasant and "healthgiving" one, he initially refused the invitation, as he would not only be delayed in seeing his family but also would lose the opportunity of an early voyage to Boston on board a coasting vessel. When he received the happy news of the birth, on May 17, of a son, Nathaniel, his immediate return seemed less urgent. He then decided to leave Philadelphia as soon as Congress adjourned and spend three weeks in travel.[2]

1. Ames to Thomas Dwight, Phila., May 30, 1796, Ames to Christopher Gore, Phila., July 30, 1796, Ames, *Works of Ames*, I, 195-97.
2. Ames to Dwight, Phila., May 9, 1796; Fisher Ames Account Book, Fisher Ames Papers, Dedham Hist. Soc. Ames to Dwight, May 30, 1796, Ames, *Works of Ames*, I, 195. Nathaniel was baptized, Oct. 2, 1796, Church Records, First Church in Dedham, Dedham Hist. Soc.; Jeremiah Smith to Samuel Smith, May 1796, Morison, *Life of Smith*, 99-101.

President Washington, having learned of the proposed trip, dispatched a letter to his manager at Mt. Vernon, William Pearce, asking him to "have a few Bottles of Porter there and some wine for particular company ... among these Mr. Aimes will, I expect, be one ... and is one I wish to be well treated while he stays." On the eve of Ames's departure, Washington sent him a note enclosing some letters he wanted carried southward. "Not meaning by doing so," the President wrote, "to avoid the pleasure of seeing you before you set out—and then, as now, to wish you an agreeable journey and the perfect restoration of your health." The President invited him for dinner on June 2 if he had not yet departed.[3]

Much to the relief of Ames, the first session ended harmoniously with "no windows broken" by the congressional "mob." He looked forward to the recess. Still, he regretted that with the Virginia trip, a brief stop in New York, and a return to legal business in Dedham and Boston, he would have so little time to spend on the domestic scene. Contemplating his position, Ames rejoiced that his "state of vagabondism" would soon be over. Ill health may have delayed his departure from Philadelphia, since the first extant letter on the trip was written at Martinsburg, Virginia, early in July.[4]

Physicians and friends had encouraged him to drink the waters at Berkeley Springs, and this resort near the upper Potomac River was his next stop. Unfortunately, his week's stay at the Springs did not have the beneficial effect that he hoped for, as he suffered a fainting spell which left him severely weakened. When he recovered sufficiently, he continued to Winchester, then returned via Martinsburg, Hagerstown, Maryland, and across southeastern Pennsylvania, arriving in Philadelphia at the very end of July. On his return, the capital was sweltering in mid-summer heat; consequently, he left almost immediately for Massachusetts. Despite his precarious health, the tour had been interesting and enjoyable to Ames. His companions, members of the Rundle family, looked back on it with real pleasure and hoped for another journey which would include him. Supreme Court Justice William Cushing,

3. George Washington to William Pearce, Phila., May 29, 1796, Fitzpatrick, ed., *Writings of Washington*, XXXV, 71; George Washington to Fisher Ames, Phila., May 31, 1796, photostat copy, Fisher Ames Papers, Dedham Hist. Soc.
4. Ames to Dwight, May 9, 1796, Fisher Ames Papers, Dedham Hist. Soc.; Ames to Dwight, May 30, 1796, Ames, *Works of Ames*, I, 195; Thomas Twining, *Travels in America 100 Years Ago, Being Notes and Reminiscences of* ... (N.Y., 1894), 162. Twining mentions that Ames was kept away from a large dinner party "by a sudden illness that alarmed his friends." Ames to Oliver Wolcott, Martinsburg, Va., July 5, 1796, Gibbs, *Memoirs*, I, 372-73. Ames accompanied the Rundles at least for the first part of his trip, George Rundle to Fisher Ames, Phila., Oct. 25, 1796, Fisher Ames Papers, Dedham Hist. Soc.

who saw Ames during his brief stay in Philadelphia, thought he was "much recovered in his health and appearance." [5]

After seeing many farms of the Virginians and listening to the political conversations in taverns on his trip, Fisher Ames remarked that the residents were nearly as bad politicians as farmers. Quickly moderating the severity of his judgment, he added that all the gentlemen with whom he had had contact reprobated their Republican congressmen and were attempting to elect Federalists in their stead. In the Northern Neck of Virginia he had discerned far more correct thinking with respect to the government and the Constitution than in the other parts of the state. "Bankrupts and rogues did not come near me," he admitted, "but the other sort who did seem to think as the Yankees do." [6]

Ames was both surprised and reassured that some Virginians strongly supported Federalist principles, leading him to urge his party to give them encouragement. An initial, though short-lived, move toward undermining the Virginia Republicans was already in progress during the early summer months. After Patrick Henry had let it be known that his Antifederalism had long since subsided, Hamilton suggested that Virginia Federalists endeavor to induce the Revolutionary hero to become vice-presidential candidate. While Ames was in the state, he sought to fathom Republican strength, and he corroborated the opinions of other Federalists that Henry would gain more votes than Jefferson. There was strong reason to expect that Jefferson would lose four of the state's electoral votes, he contended, because Virginia was "infinitely nearer right and more impressible" than he had expected. [7] Several months later his political conversations while in Virginia were unexpectedly thrust into the presidential campaign, drawing him into the maelstrom of the election. His comments regarding Patrick Henry as a potential Federalist candidate were quoted and misquoted for political purposes. In October 1796 the *Independent Chronicle* reprinted part of an address given by Levin Powell, a Federalist elector from Virginia, who contended that Ames stated New Englanders considered John Adams too greatly attached to the British and that they would prefer Patrick Henry. This politically embarrassing statement had appeared first in the *Gazette of the United States*, and its accuracy had been denied by "Civis," a correspondent for the Massachusetts Federalists. [8]

5. Ames to Oliver Wolcott, Hagerstown, Md., July 25, 1796, Gibbs, *Memoirs*, I, 373; Ames to Gore, July 30, 1796, Ames, *Works of Ames*, I, 195; William Cushing to Charles Cushing, Aug. 1, 1796, Cushing Papers, Mass. Hist. Soc.
6. Ames to Wolcott, July 25, 1796, Gibbs, *Memoirs*, I, 373.
7. *Ibid.*; Ames to Jeremiah Smith, Sept. 4, 1796, Ames, *Works of Ames*, I, 198-99.
8. *Gazette of the United States* (Phila.), Sept. 15, Oct. 6, 1796; *Independent Chronicle* (Boston), Oct. 24, 1796.

Federalists in Boston were girding themselves for the oncoming election battles. To find a replacement for Fisher Ames was a formidable task; yet by the summer of 1796 the party had chosen Harrison Gray Otis as the new candidate for the House of Representatives. Otis's selection followed soon after his vigorous defense of Federalism and the Jay Treaty in Boston town meeting. This youthful lawyer had risen quickly in the esteem of prominent Federalists. Ames was apparently not very close to him, but at the time of the election campaign he showed some understanding of Otis's character. To Gore he wrote in confidence that "his talents will distinguish him, and I hope he will be careful to wait patiently in Congress till they do; but he is ardent and ambitious." [9]

Upon hearing of Ames's prospective resignation, Christopher Gore wrote with dismay from London, where he was on a diplomatic mission. "When you are absent, who is to play your part in the House, and guide in the tempestuous element which will ever reign in a place where so many and so various views direct the members?" [10] In reply, Ames deprecated his friend's comments and at the same time evaluated his own abilities clearly, yet far too modestly. "As to my absence from the House, the loss will be nothing as to leading. I never had any talent in *that* way, and I have not been the dupe of such a false belief." There were but few individuals who were skilled in the art of directing others. Among them he included Hamilton, King, and Ellsworth. Without these men in leadership positions, the House would be "like sheep without a shepherd." "I never was more than shepherd's dog," he said in all sincerity, "and my friends have been too civil sometimes, in their praise of my barking, when the thieves and wolves were coming. My vanity (God knows I have enough) is laying no traps for an answer of praise; but I know, and you know, that if sometimes I can talk with some effect, I am good for nothing else." [11]

In this election, for the first time in eight years, Ames was essentially an onlooker. He was, however, immensely concerned about the outcome of the contest. Early in the campaign he had intimated that deciding "who shall be President and Vice ... will put an end to the armed neutrality of parties." Until President Washington made public

9. Samuel Eliot Morison, *The Life and Letters of Harrison Gray Otis, Federalist, 1765-1848*, 2 vols. (Boston, 1913), I, 52-57; Ames to Gore, Dedham, Oct. 5, 1796, Ames, *Works of Ames*, I, 202; Stephen Higginson to Timothy Pickering, Boston, May 11, 1797, Pickering Papers, XXI, Mass. Hist. Soc. Higginson wrote, "I am sorry that at this critical moment we have lost the Aid of Strong, Cabot and Ames etc., their weight in the Scale might have proved decisive. Mr. Otis who succeeds Ames will not be his equal in any view."
10. Gore to Ames, London, July 26, 1796, Ames, *Works of Ames*, I, 200.
11. Ames to Gore, Oct. 5, 1796, *ibid.*, 203.

his determination to retire, both parties made covert plans, and there was little evidence of the intense partisanship which emerged later. Then in September, Washington's Farewell Address acted "as a signal, like dropping a hat, for the party racers to start." As Ames anticipated, once the tempo of the election increased, "money . . . will be spent, some virtue and more tranquility lost." [12]

Both parties had begun to consider their presidential nominees in the early spring of 1796, and both had difficulty in choosing candidates. On May 19, Ames observed that "Mr. Adams will be our man, and Jefferson theirs. The second is yet on both sides somewhat doubtful." [13] In essence Ames was correct; yet his statement gave no hint of the developing dissension among the Federalists over the candidates the party would back. While John Adams was a logical choice of the Federalists for the presidency, he did not command unanimous endorsement within the party. Hamilton had long been at odds with the Vice President and was at best only moderately favorable to Adams's assumption that he had a natural right to be Washington's successor. Serious reservations about Adams's political strength against the Republicans led Hamilton and his closest associates to engage in political maneuvers which produced uncertainty and disagreement within the ranks of the Federalists. Influenced by Hamilton, party leaders chose Thomas Pinckney of South Carolina for the vice-presidency, ostensibly to strengthen their cause in the South. Under the existing election procedures, electors did not differentiate between presidential and vice-presidential candidates when balloting. Consequently it was possible for the Hamiltonians to further Pinckney's candidacy for the vice-presidency while privately encouraging Federalist leaders to support him for the presidency.[14]

The scheme of Hamilton, apparently as much a flexible plan to meet the vagaries of the election as a plot to defeat Adams, ultimately ran into the brisk winds of New England opposition. Ames himself did not take part in the anti-Adams move, and during the summer and early autumn months he continually expressed confidence that Adams would

12. Ames to Dwight, Phila., May 19, 1796, *ibid.*, 193; Ames to Wolcott, Dedham, Sept. 26, 1796, Gibbs, *Memoirs*, I, 384; John Beckley to James Madison, Phila., June 20, Oct. 15, 1796, Madison Papers, N.Y. Pub. Lib.; John Beckley to William Irvine, Phila., Sept. 15, Oct. 4, 17, 1796, William Irvine Papers, XIII, Hist. Soc. of Pa.; Cunningham, *Jeffersonian Republicans*, 89-94.
13. Ames to Dwight, May 19, 1796, Ames, *Works of Ames*, I, 193; William Smith to Rufus King, Charleston, July 23, 1796, King, ed., *Life of King*, II, 66.
14. Manning J. Dauer, *The Adams Federalists* (Baltimore, 1953), 92-103; Stephen Kurtz, *The Presidency of John Adams: The Collapse of Federalism, 1795-1800* (Phila., 1957), 99-113, 141-44; Freeman, *Washington*, VII, 411-12, 418-19, 424-26; Malone, *Jefferson and the Ordeal of Liberty*, 273-94; Miller, *Hamilton*, 435-50; Cunningham, *Jeffersonian Republicans*, 94-101.

be elected. According to the Massachusetts congressman, southern electors would be encouraged to vote for John Adams inasmuch as the eastern states were expected to "vote fairly for him and Pinckney." [15] The purpose of such a distribution of votes would be to assure solid support of these men. Ames does not seem to have shared the hope of some Hamilton followers that an equal vote in the East might give Pinckney the presidency because of southern reluctance to cast votes for Adams. In early December when the presidential votes were being counted, as each state held its meeting of electors, Ames was more and more convinced that the election would be very close. At this point, he estimated fifty-eight votes were certain for Adams and another twelve might go to him, giving him a bare majority of seventy. "Accident, whim, intrigue, not to say corruption, may change or prevent a vote or two," he forecast.[16]

The overriding fear of Ames, as with most Federalists, was that Jefferson would become president. Some New Englanders, including George Cabot, had been willing to back Adams if he had a chance of winning, but were quite ready to abandon him for Pinckney to block Jefferson. There is no indication that Ames took a similar position. He considered the possibility that the Republicans might ally with Pinckney to avoid defeat and that the South Carolinian might obtain more votes than Adams. Dismayed at such a prospect, Ames remarked, "That would be a subject of incalculable consequences." Pinckney, he sensed, was "a good man," but he believed that "even a good President, thus made by luck or sheer dexterity of play, would stand badly with parties and with the country." [17]

Not until mid-December was Adams assured of a majority of electoral votes with Jefferson almost certain to become the next vice president. This situation, in which a firm friend of France would obtain great influence in the new administration, seemed disastrous to Ames. In the past months there had been alarming evidence of French influence in American affairs when the foreign minister, Pierre Adet, blatantly attempted to affect the outcome of the election in Pennsylvania.

15. Ames to Dwight, Dedham, Oct. 25, 1796, Ames, *Works of Ames*, I, 204; Robert Troup to Rufus King, N.Y., Nov. 16, 1796, King, ed., *Life of King*, II, 110. Troup wrote, "we have Mr. Pinckney completely in our power if our Eastern friends do not refuse him some of their votes, under an idea that . . . they may injure Mr. Adams." Kurtz, *Presidency of Adams*, 150-51.

16. Ames to Gore, Phila., Dec. 3, 1796, Ames, *Works of Ames*, I, 205; Henry Van Schaack to Theodore Sedgwick, Jan. 2, 1797, Sedgwick Papers, Vol. C, Mass. Hist. Soc.; Aaron Burr to William Eustis, N.Y., Dec. 18, 1796, Aaron Burr Papers, Mass. Hist. Soc.; *Columbian Centinel* (Boston), Jan. 4, 18, 1797.

17. Ames to Gore, Dec. 3, 1796, Ames, *Works of Ames*, I, 206; Madison to Thomas Jefferson, Phila., Dec. 5, 1796, Madison Papers, XIX, Lib. Cong.

France would be made even bolder in her intrigues with Jefferson in office and with some Americans ready to pacify her. If the Virginian were to accept the vice-presidency "party will have a head, responsible for nothing, yet deranging and undermining every thing, and France would have a new magazine of disorganizing influence. An astute politician could use the position to gain power rivaling that of the chief executive. "Two Presidents, like two suns in the meridian, would meet and jostle for four years, and then Vice would be first," he prognosticated direly.[18] For that reason Pinckney, as a loyal Federalist, was distinctly preferable to Jefferson in the vice-presidency. Apropos of the current state of politics, Ames commented, "I own I am ready to croak when I observe the gathering of the vapors in our horizon." [19]

When the outcome of the contest was finally clear, Adams had become president and Jefferson the new vice president. With Adams's presidency resting on a slim three-vote lead over Jefferson, it was obvious that the Republican party was gaining in popular appeal and that the Federalists could only maintain their strength in the future under adverse circumstances. Nevertheless, there was some reassurance among Massachusetts Federalists in the fact that the Republicans had not enlarged their delegation to Congress. In the struggle for seats in the House, Otis was the victor in the all-important First Middle District; Stephen Bullock replaced George Leonard in the Third Southern District; two Republican incumbents, William Lyman and Henry Dearborn, were defeated, and seven Federalist representatives were reelected in other districts. A total of eleven members of the party would represent Massachusetts again in the House, as opposed to a group of three Republicans, of whom one was only nominally loyal to his party. Nationally, however, a strong contingent of Republicans had been elected to Congress.[20]

18. Ames to Gore, Dec. 3, 17, 1796, Ames, *Works of Ames*, I, 207, 211; Rufus King to General Pinckney, London, Jan. 14, 1797, Alexander Hamilton to King, Feb. 15, 1797, King, ed., *Life of King*, II, 129, 148; Arthur B. Darling, *Our Rising Empire, 1763-1803* (New Haven, 1940), 243-48.

19. Ames to Gore, Dec. 3, 1796, Ames to Dwight, Phila., Jan. 5, 1797, Ames, *Works of Ames*, I, 205, 213; Robert Troup to Rufus King, N.Y., Jan. 28, 1797, King, ed., *Life of King*, II, 135. Troup, closely allied with Hamilton, blamed New England for Pinckney's defeat and Jefferson's success. Henry Tazewell to John Ambler, Phila., Dec. 18, 1796, Tazewell Papers, Lib. Cong.; Benjamin Goodhue to Caleb Strong, Phila., Dec. 24, 1796, Caleb Strong Papers, Forbes Library, Northampton, Mass.

20. Ames to Gore, Dec. 3, 1796, Ames, *Works of Ames*, I, 205; Cunningham, *Jeffersonian Republicans*, 113-14; Dauer, *Adams Federalists*, 105-11. Nathaniel Ames reacted to the election, "The Prigarchy straining every nerve to carry the election;" entry of Nov. 4, 1796, Calder, ed., "Diary of Dr. Nathaniel Ames," *Dedham Hist. Register*, 7 (1896), 116. Otis received 1,713 votes while James Bowdoin was given 1,293; Abstract of Votes, Mass. Archives, Office of the Secretary of the Commonwealth, State House.

The effect of the Republican press on the election had annoyed Fisher Ames, and during the political furor he had tried to counter the "pestiferous" influence of the *Independent Chronicle* on the plain people by writing short newspaper articles. "I have proclaimed open war against all this," he related to Oliver Wolcott, "but a rower against the stream soon grows weak and weary." Passion and prejudice prevailed, while sound judgment among people was declining, he found. In a town meeting in Dedham, the current trend had been particularly evident when the Federalists were routed on an issue by "a word about liberty and putting bridles in the people's mouth." [21] At another lively town meeting Ames found his carefully reasoned speech completely demolished by the brash remark of a laborer, one Kingsley, who said, "Mr. Moderator, my brother Ames's eloquence reminds me of nothing but the shining of a fire-fly which was just light enough to show its own insignificance." Such incidents led him to observe sarcastically that *"vox populi* is, you know, always *vox sapientiae."* [22]

On his return from Virginia and for several months thereafter, Ames's health greatly improved. In spite of the long trip and the heat of summer, he had gained back several pounds and felt that he would be well enough to complete his term in Congress. His decision to retire, he recognized, had been a wise one inasmuch as he did not have the strength for the sustained political contests in Congress. "The fervors of the next two years, especially if our politics should go wrong," he admitted, "would destroy me." Ames hoped he would be *"in statu quo ante* 1795" when he returned to private life so that he could earn his livelihood with his legal work and busy himself with his farm. Neither the fees from his practice nor the yield from his shares of Bank stock would give him a substantial income, but he would have the "wherewithal to keep the pot boiling." [23]

He was quite content in the domestic setting. His stay in Dedham, on this occasion shorter than usual, was especially pleasant as he took up the threads of his personal life and enjoyed his little sons. He was still a public figure, however, for in September 1796 the Trustees of the College of New Jersey granted him an honorary doctor of laws degree, no doubt in recognition of his role in the Jay Treaty issue. Court week

21. Ames to Wolcott, Dedham, Nov. 14, 1796, Gibbs, *Memoirs,* I, 393; entry of Oct. 16, 1796, Calder, ed., *Dedham Hist. Register,* 7 (1896), 116. Ames occasionally contributed short, anonymous articles to the Dedham, Boston, and Philadelphia papers, no manuscript drafts of which survive.

22. E. S. Thomas, Reminiscences of Sixty-Five Years, typescript, Dedham Hist. Soc.; Ames to Dwight, Oct. 25, 1796, Ames, *Works of Ames,* I, 204.

23. Ames to Smith, Sept. 4, 1796, Ames to Dwight, Dedham, Aug. 22, 1796, Ames to Gore, Oct. 5, Dec. 3, 1796, Ames, *Works of Ames,* I, 197-99, 203, 207; Ames to Wolcott, Sept. 26, 1796, Gibbs, *Memoirs,* I, 384; Ames to Dwight, Dedham, Dec. 9, 1795, Fisher Ames Papers, Dedham Hist. Soc.

kept him occupied with clients clamoring for his legal advice, leading him to say, "Whether anybody will be hanged this term, I know not, but if justice is done, some persons will have to pay forty shillings." [24] Attending to improvements on his farm, arranging to lease additional land from the Episcopal church, and building a stone wall around his house were tasks Ames very much wanted to complete before his departure for Congress. Early in November he wrote to Dwight Foster that he planned to travel to Philadelphia with Jeremiah Smith and Chauncey Goodrich, and invited him to accompany them, promising his friend that "neither the driver nor the passengers would be demos." [25]

The second session of the Fourth Congress convened in December amid the uncertainties of an as yet unresolved presidential election. It was not, however, as quiescent a session as he first expected. He was immediately chosen chairman of the committee to answer the President's opening address, an honor frequently given to Madison. Sensing that the references of Washington to the influence of France in American politics would rouse Republican antipathy, Ames drafted the answer "as inoffensively as it could be, to avoid party points." His phrases eulogizing Washington's "wise, firm and patriotic administration" provoked Giles to say that he did not regret the President's retirement since he was "one of those who do not think so much of the President as some others do." Federalists prevented the House from returning the answer to the committee for further consideration, but could not stave off amendments designed to conciliate France. Ames thereupon undertook a spirited defense of the administration's policies, stressing that if the nation were on the verge of war, as the Republicans insisted, it was essential to support the government. "I would say ... in this time of danger ... we are neither Frenchmen nor Englishmen, but we are Americans." Such comments as Giles had made were inappropriate. Was this to be a respectful answer or an insult? [26]

When Republicans accused Ames of encouraging a war with France

24. Minutes of the Trustees, Sept. 25, 1796, Archives, Princeton University, Princeton, N.J. The College of New Jersey later became Princeton University. On the same occasion William L. Smith of S.C. was also awarded an honorary LL.D.; Rogers, *Evolution of a Federalist*, 288; Ames to Dwight, Aug. 22, 1796, Ames, *Works of Ames*, I, 197-98; Ames to John Adams, Dedham, Aug. 20, 1796, Etting Collection, Hist. Soc. of Pa.

25. Ames to Dwight, Oct. 25, 1796, Ames, *Works of Ames*, I, 204; Lease from the Episcopal Church to Fisher Ames, Sept, 24, 1796, Miscellaneous Manuscripts, N.Y. State Lib.; Ames to Dwight Foster, Dedham, Nov. 7, 1796, Slack Collection, Marietta College Lib.

26. *Annals*, VI, 1589, 1598, 1600, 1612-16, 1629, Dec. 5, 8, 14, 1796; Ames to Gore, Dec. 3, 17, 1796, Ames, *Works of Ames*, I, 207-11; Madison to Thomas Jefferson, Phila., Dec. 10, 1796, Madison Papers, XIX, Lib. Cong.

and forgetting the "war-whoop and the hatchet" of his speech in the previous session, he ignored their personal thrusts, emphasizing instead that the Federalists had always urged a strong defensive force for the nation while advocating a peaceful settlement of international issues. "Did this look as if they wished to truckle to Great Britain?" he asked.[27] He was so concerned about the continuing opposition to the administration that he asserted the public should settle the issue by choosing finally between those who supported the government and those who wished to tear it down. If the French were about to declare war over the British treaty, it was not because of administration politics, but because of agitation and intrigues by American citizens in France. "What auxiliaries they may have here," he would not attempt to point out. Giles's gross attacks on the administration were not supported by such Republicans as Madison and Gallatin, and Ames's resolute defense was largely responsible for splitting the ranks of the Republicans on this issue. Only a handful voted with Giles against the draft of the answer to the President. "Their defeat," Ames elatedly wrote, "will help to sink that exotic folly [the Republican party] faster than it was going before." [28] When Republican newspapers deliberately distorted his statements, giving him parting blows, it was but further proof to him that "*si populus vult decipi decipiatur.*" Yet in the face of popular opposition he would not change his convictions about foreign policy, which were best expressed, he felt, by Washington's Farewell Address. "I do not wish to see *Political* connexions with either [Britain or France]," Ames declared, "and I cannot but hope we are fast getting cured of our morbid propensity to engage with so excessive and pernicious a zeal as we have done in their quarrels." [29]

The relationship of France to the United States constituted only one of the problems which confronted Congress and increased Fisher Ames's disillusionment over the trend of government. In a lengthy letter to Alexander Hamilton, he analyzed affairs of state and at the same time revealed his own emotionalism. Republicans, he related, were demanding that an envoy be sent to France to aid Charles C. Pinckney, who had recently replaced the strongly pro-French James Monroe as foreign minister. Because the Federalists had supported Jay's mission to England, it was awkward for them to resist a mission to France. The Massachusetts representative suspected, however, that the Republicans would attempt "to ground some new delusive connection" with France

27. *Annals*, VI, 1632, 1644, Dec. 14, 15, 1796.

28. *Ibid.*, 1645, 1667-68, Dec. 15, 1796; Ames to Gore, Dec. 17, 1796, Ames, *Works of Ames*, I, 211.

29. Ames to [Samuel Haven], Phila., Feb. 4, 1797, Fisher Ames Papers, Dedham Hist. Soc.

on the pretext of solving the outstanding Franco-American difficulties. He consequently raised the question whether negotiations, if they took place, should not include the abrogation of the clause in the French treaty of 1778 by which the United States guaranteed the protection of the French West Indies.[30]

Financial affairs could no less be ignored than foreign relations. Ames was cognizant of the growing deficit in operating the federal government, but was reluctant to resort to a tax on land values, he explained to Hamilton, until other expedients had been attempted. A general tightening of the collection of taxes was essential; internal revenues should be extended; and the public should be informed of the need for the new direct tax. By imposing the land tax gradually, Congress could avert public opposition. The Republicans only supported it for political purposes, he assured Hamilton, aiming to "sharpen popular feelings—augment clamors against the debt, bank, etc.—enfeeble and discredit the other species of revenue." [31]

Ames's hope for an intelligent resolution of congressional problems was being extinguished. He viewed the scene about him with discouragement, remarking that "our proceedings smell of anarchy. We rest our hopes on foolish fanatical grounds . . . on human nature being different from what it is." Ames was certain "our whole system is little removed from simple democracy. What we call *the Gov't* is a phantom, as long as the Democrats prevail in the House." In practice he felt that governmental efficiency had been reduced to a minimum while "the proneness of a popular body to usurpation" was approaching a maximum. It was obvious that "sooner or later individuals and public bodies will act out their principles. Ours are I fear essentially more democratic than republican which latter are alone fit for our country." [32] The degree of Ames's pessimism at this time cannot be disassociated from the state of his health and its effect on his outlook.

In the closing days of the session, Ames rarely took part in the discussions. "I attend little in the house and am very little fit for attention of mind even less for exertion of body," he explained. His enthusiasm for public life had faded, and a certain ennui enveloped him, causing him to lose some interest in congressional affairs on the eve of retirement. He had expected to find in the organization of his party "all the combination and energy" necessary to reinforce the government. The

30. Ames to Hamilton, Phila., Jan. 26, 1797, Hamilton Papers, Lib. Cong. Kurtz, *Adams Federalists*, 206, considers the letter as an indictment of Hamilton and states that it "must have stung Hamilton as no letter on record did." It is difficult to agree with this interpretation.
31. Ames to Hamilton, Jan. 26, 1797, Hamilton Papers, Lib. Cong.
32. *Ibid.*

current proceedings demonstrated how ephemeral party strength was. Not only did Ames lack the stamina to resist the rising opposition, but above all to rally his own party and prevent complete defeat. "I am pretty well weaned from Congress," he said, adding, "I think I shall not die of a broken heart because I am not a Congressman all my days." [33]

The whole atmosphere of Congress was changing. Ames's own role as spokesman and defender of the Federalist faith was being assumed by William L. Smith of Charleston. But without Hamilton in the administration, Ames found there was no directive force in the House, "no leader, no *point de ralliement.*" Many of the men Ames most respected in Congress no longer took their former parts in the drama. George Cabot and Caleb Strong had resigned from the Senate, while Rufus King was serving as foreign minister in England. Oliver Ellsworth had also left to become Chief Justice of the United States. Even Madison had decided to retire and rarely spoke on public issues. In reflecting on the situation, John Adams commented acidly, "It seems the Mode of becoming great is to retire. Madison I suppose after a Retirement of a few years is to be President or Vice President. Mr. Cabot I suppose, after aggrandizing his Character in the shade, a few years is to be some great Thing too; and Mr. Ames, etc. etc. etc. It is marvellous how political plants grow in the shade." [34]

With Congress on the verge of adjourning, economy-minded Republicans, under the lead of Gallatin, attempted to stop appropriations for the completion of three frigates of the Navy. Ames was angered by the Republican recourse to the same obstinate tactics as in the Jay Treaty issue, and he lectured the House about the power of appropriation, which he contended was "not only a weapon but a shield" to be used cautiously and lawfully and not as a means of usurping authority. Republicans bristled; Venable condemned his "phillippic"; Nicholas criticized Ames for denouncing the House, and attempting to enlarge the executive power. The Massachusetts representative retorted that the opponents were endeavoring to claim extreme privileges. "Nothing was said about the public good, all was self," he remarked with asperity. Did they think "that they enjoyed the powers committed to them ... as barons of empire?" He was not charging the House, he insisted, with

33. Ames to Dwight, Phila., Jan. 5, 17, 1797, Fisher Ames Papers, Dedham Hist. Soc.; Ames to Gore, Phila., Jan. 27, 1797, Ames, *Works of Ames*, I, 214. Ames was able to attend an occasional evening theatre performance without serious aftereffects.

34. *Annals*, VI, 1517, 1626, Dec. 5, 21, 1796; Brant, *Madison, Father of the Constitution*, 444-45; Ames to Rufus King, Phila., May 30, 1796, King, ed., *Life of King*, II, 62; Jeremiah Smith to Samuel Smith, Phila., Mar. 5, 1796, Morison, *Life of Smith*, 91; John Adams to Abigail Adams, Phila., Jan. 14, 1797, Adams Papers, Microfilm Reel 383, Mass. Hist. Soc.

"breaking down the other branches of Government," but he asserted that the discretion in regard to appropriations had to "be regulated by duty." [35]

With these words on March 2, 1797, the public career of Fisher Ames as a representative from Massachusetts ended. His final days in Congress were devoid of more than a few flashes of his oratorical brilliance, and his remarks had more than a little of the contentious spirit he had so long avoided. But his exit was, as Jeremiah Smith had expected, like that of other men. Avoiding the hectic, concluding session on the night of March 3, he missed hearing Washington's last message to the House in which the President wished the members "a happy return to their families and friends." [36]

Ames's retirement from public life, just a month before his thirty-ninth birthday, was a blow to an exceptional man for whom the congressional scene had once been so stimulating. On his return to Dedham his activities for a time were circumscribed by his continued lack of strength. By riding horseback along the country roads each morning and evening, and otherwise leading a carefully planned life, he strove to regain his health. Doggedly persistent, he continued to exercise, frequently returning to his home worn out from the activity. Often too much exertion would bring on fainting spells, attacks of indigestion, or heavy colds, from which his recovery was invariably slow. "My life is of no more use to the world, my family except," he commented, "than the moss to the trees . . . it sucks out a very little of the sap, and that sustains a stunted and barren vegetation." [37]

While Ames tried to accept the changed pattern of his life with equanimity and even with jesting, he found it difficult to be less active in public affairs. He was not looking for sympathy from his friends, but he did not conceal the state of his health from them. Quite naturally he wanted to be remembered by his former colleagues, and in the period immediately after his retirement he could not tell whether he would yet accomplish anything which would stir people to speak of him. He would have to leave it to Federalists in Congress to save the nation. "Some of you," he remarked, "must watch and pray, and others must fight, if need be." [38]

Ames's desire to return to private life was not without qualification.

35. *Annals,* VI, 2339-47, Mar. 2, 1797.

36. *Ibid.,* 2368, Mar 3, 1797. The House of Representatives adjourned *sine die* at 11 p.m. Ames to [S. Haven], Phila., Mar. 4, 1797, Fisher Ames Papers, Dedham Hist. Soc.

37. Ames to Dwight Foster, Dedham, June 24, 1797, Ames, *Works of Ames,* I, 215; Ames to Foster, Dedham, Dec. 7, 1797, Miscellaneous Papers, N.Y. Pub. Lib.

38. Ames to Foster, June 24, 1797, Ames, *Works of Ames,* I, 215.

In one sense, he was surfeited with governmental disputes and wanted merely to be a country squire with family, books, and agricultural activities to absorb his interest. In another sense, he craved the turmoil and even the tension of the House where he had participated in the drama of government. It was impossible to satisfy these two drives simultaneously; of necessity, therefore, retirement could be only a restless compromise for Fisher Ames.

In January 1798, President Adams appointed Ames to a three-member mission to negotiate a treaty of peace with the Cherokee Indians in Tennessee.[39] George Cabot urged him to accept in the hope that a southern trip would be advantageous to his health. For a time Ames seriously thought of going, but when he learned that the monetary allowance was only eight dollars a day and traveling expenses, he remarked, "I am not clear that in point of emolument it would not be as well to be indian as commissioner." The long absence from his law work and his family, with only a modicum of recompense, finally induced him to decline the offer. To Secretary of War James McHenry he wrote that his health was not robust enough to endure the privations of a trip to the frontier and that the loss of fees from his legal business precluded his acceptance of the post.[40]

With two young sons to bring up and a large household establishment, Ames could not neglect his profession. He found that he had to devote much energy and attention to his work, leading him to comment that he would have to overcome his laziness. "I shall attend the courts more and take fees when offered. Sometimes *earn* them if clients are surly and insist upon it." As in the past most of his work consisted of routine cases of debt, trespass, and the administration of estates. Frequently the petty aspects of legal business were annoying to him, and

39. James McHenry to Fisher Ames, Phila., Feb. 1798, Fisher Ames Papers, Dedham Hist. Soc. McHenry wrote officially that the President had appointed Ames, Bushrod Washington of Va., and Alfred Moore of N.C. as commissioners. Ames had known unofficially about the appointment in January, Ames to John Worthington, Dedham, Jan. 27, 1798, Chamberlain Collection, Boston Pub. Lib. Thomas Dwight to Hannah Dwight, Boston, Jan. 31, 1798, Dwight-Howard Papers, Box 1, Mass. Hist. Soc. Nathaniel Ames reacted to the appointment: "What a fine thing to be a Federal man or Hedghog, ie. to black our Saviours the French, and praise our Enemies, the English!!!" Memoranda, 1798, Calder, ed., "Diary of Dr. Nathaniel Ames," *Dedham Hist. Register*, 9 (1898), 63; *Independent Chronicle* (Boston), Jan. 25, 1798.

40. Ames to John Worthington, Dedham, Feb. 3, 1798, Norcross Collection, Mass. Hist. Soc.; Ames to James McHenry, Secretary of War, Dedham, Feb. 18, 1798, Ames to Jeremiah Smith, Boston, Mar. 13, 1798, Ames, *Works of Ames*, I, 219, 223. Earlier in 1797 Ames was nominated as the fifth member of a commission on prewar debts, one of the Jay Treaty commissions. The appointment, however, went to a British merchant who was chosen by lot. Bradford Perkins, *The First Rapprochement, England and the United States, 1795-1805* (Phila., 1955), 117.

he heartily disliked having to "demand payment for boluses and pills to the last generation." Especially during the sessions of the court of common pleas, or the Supreme Judicial Court, the importunities of clients weighed heavily on him. At one court term Ames was overwhelmed "with Applications to stakes and stones and plots of land in ejectment" which exhausted him. Even more exasperating to one for whom the law had limited appeal was the necessity to spend hours "bawling to a jury" or to present a case to the court when a cantankerous judge presided.[41]

Ames's work, however, was not entirely devoted to mundane problems. As one of the more prominent lawyers in eastern Massachusetts, he was sought out as a consultant in intricate cases. Such a case was that of William Bingham, the Philadelphia entrepreneur and land speculator, who relied on the efforts of Ames and John Davis to extricate him from various law suits growing out of claims to the cargo of a ship seized as a prize during the Revolutionary War. Among others who retained the services of Ames were two leading New York speculators, William Payne and William Constable.[42]

From time to time the Dedham lawyer was engaged in criminal trials. When five "respectable citizens" of Nantucket were indicted in 1797 for allegedly robbing the local bank of $20,000, the case attracted much attention in Boston. At the trial in September, Ames as defense counsel won an acquittal for four of the men after arguing many hours before the jury. Randal Rice, who had been declared guilty, was remanded to jail for future sentencing when he could not raise $60,000 bail. More than a year later the former congressman was able to obtain a pardon for him from the court over the strenuous objections of Samuel Dexter. At the conclusion of the case Ames commented with feeling that Rice

41. Docket of the Court of Common Pleas, Clerk of the Court, Norfolk County Supreme Judicial Court, Dedham, Mass. Ames had seven cases in the April term, 1797, and nineteen cases in the September term, several of which were continued to subsequent sessions. Ames to Gore, Dedham, Oct. 9, 1799 [1797], *Works of Ames*, I, 255-56. Ames to Smith, Boston, Mar. 13, 1798, *ibid.*, 222; Ames to Dwight, Dedham, Dec. 22, 1799, Fisher Ames Papers, Dedham Hist. Soc.; *Columbian Centinel* (Boston), Oct. 21, 1797; Thomas, Reminiscences of Sixty-Five Years, Dedham Hist. Soc.

42. William Payne to William Constable, Boston, Mar. 13, 30, Apr. 27, 1798, Constable-Pierrepont Papers, N.Y. Pub. Lib. On the activities of Ames in the Revolutionary War prize case of Cabot et al. *v.* Bingham, see John W. Davis to William Bingham, Boston, Apr. 2, Sept. 28, 1799, William Lewis to Ames, Phila., May 6, 1800, Bingham Papers, Hist. Soc. of Pa.; Ames to William Bingham, Dedham, Apr. 14, June 21, Nov. 23, 1800, Ames to C. W. Hare, Dedham, Oct. 15, 1801, C. W. Hare to Ames, Phila., Mar. 5, 1802, Fisher Ames Papers, Dedham Hist. Soc.

"now enjoys the air of the wide world," although he probably had used up most of his property in the process.[43]

Neither legal responsibilities nor impaired health could permanently submerge Ames's inherent concern with government. After the first months of John Adams's administration had passed, he was decidedly more hopeful than he had been during his final days in Congress. He was confident that both the Senate and the presidency were in good hands; the judiciary and the executive departments were also "sound and true." Outside of the government the people were receptive and would respond to leadership. "I really think public opinion mends," he commented, "and that the immediate evil of anarchical sentiments has grown less." The House of Representatives, in contrast, was a more uncertain factor, for party strength was evenly balanced and both sides claimed the allegiance of uncommitted members. It was to Ames "an ill prognostic . . . that its dispositions are so dubious." [44]

This was an advantageous moment to adopt vigorous policies increasing the revenue and bracing the government. Instead, the measures proposed were "puny," and as a consequence, there could be little expectation of successful negotiation with France. The reluctance of Congress to support Federalist principles was indicative of a recurring and unrealistic fear of executive power which was "as lively as if the President were a king." Yet political safeguards and the whole temperament of the age would stand against usurpations of power. Ames wondered whether under the circumstances the Senate would not be proclaimed a useless institution and the presidency a dangerous office. The Republican foes of executive authority were "just such friends to liberty as they would be to the Bank if they forbid guards, locks, and keys for the safety of their vault." [45]

Since Adams's inauguration Franco-American relations had steadily deteriorated. The Directory in France had considered the ratification of Jay's Treaty evidence of American determination to violate the treaty of alliance of 1778 and had reacted with hostility to President Adams's public statements respecting relations with France. Regarding the United States virtually as an enemy, the French government attempted

43. Ames to John Worthington, Dedham, Sept. 24, 1797, Autograph Collection, Harvard Univ.; Ames to Gore, Oct. 9, 1799 [1797], Ames, *Works of Ames*, I, 255-56; Ames to Dwight, Dedham, Dec. 22, 1798, Fisher Ames Papers, Dedham Hist. Soc.; *Columbian Centinel* (Boston), Sept. 9, 16, 1797; *Independent Chronicle* (Boston), Sept. 14, 1797.

44. Ames to Benjamin Goodhue, Dedham, June 24, 1797, Benjamin Goodhue Manuscripts, N.Y. Soc. Lib.

45. *Ibid.*; Ames to Dwight Foster, Dedham, Feb. 18, 1798, Ames, *Works of Ames*, I, 218; Hamilton to King, Feb. 15, 1797, King, ed., *Life of King*, II, 148.

to curb American neutral trade. By a series of decrees in 1797 and 1798, France sought to prescribe the rights of neutrals and to forbid neutral vessels to carry English goods or to call at English ports. American ships were thereupon captured, confiscated, and harassed in large numbers in an effort to force the United States to conduct its commerce on French terms. Caught between the rivalries of Britain and France, the United States had to resist the annihilation of its limited prestige. In the eyes of one member of Congress, the position of the United States was critical: "Thus between Sylla and Caribdis we want a pilot of dexterity." [46] To Federalists like Hamilton and Ames, it appeared that the country might well drift on the rocks unless they guided the new helmsman.

Just before leaving Philadelphia in March 1797, Ames had called on the President to convey to him his concern about the crisis with France. Urging Adams to send a commission of three men to France to solve primary differences, he had unintentionally affronted the President. Twelve years later Adams referred waspishly to Ames's role in promoting negotiations with France by accusing him of merely being Hamilton's agent. "Mr. Ames was no doubt one of Mr. Hamilton's privy council when he *resolved* to send a new commission of three. Mr. Ames, with much gravity and solemnity, advised me to institute a new commission to France. . . . I had rolled all these things in my own mind long before." He had already considered sending Madison, Hamilton, Cabot, and Ames himself, Adams revealed, but had had more important business to attend to than "to communicate all these reflections to Mr. Ames." [47]

New England Federalists were divided over the President's ultimate decision to send special envoys to France. Oliver Wolcott, Adams's Secretary of the Treasury, was adamantly opposed to the idea and had argued persuasively that efforts to reach an agreement would indicate a fear of France and might encourage her adherents within the United States. Wolcott felt that he had countered Ames's proposals to the President respecting the mission. "By means of my most sincere and urgent expostulations—nay supplications, it was postponed," he explained to

46. Henry Tazewell to John Ambler, Phila., Jan. 16, 1797, Tazewell Papers, Lib. Cong.; Darling, *Our Rising Empire*, 226-62.

47. Letter XIII, "Correspondence Originally Published in the *Boston Patriot*," Adams, ed., *Works of Adams*, IX, 283-84. William Vans Murray stated regarding the possible successor of Monroe as Minister to France, "I had hoped that Ames would have been the man, if a move took place and was yet aware of the obstacle in his seat." Murray to James McHenry, Aug. 29, 1796, Bernard C. Steiner, *Life and Correspondence of James McHenry* (Cleveland, 1907), 189.

Hamilton.[48] Subsequently Ames acknowledged the validity of Wolcott's position, but insisted that settling the disagreement by diplomatic negotiation presented fewer difficulties than other plans. French depredations on American commerce fully justified war; yet he speculated that neither Congress nor the public would support such a move. "Perhaps a majority prefer peace with outrage, rapine, insult, dishonour, and the interdiction of the ocean, to a war with France." Acquiescence after the numerous French insults was wrong; a mere embargo on American commerce was no better; in contrast, a policy of unity and forcefulness might be successful. Only by supporting negotiation would it be possible to secure the adherence of "weak and trimming" congressmen to defense measures. "I see no such evident dishonour or mischief in it, as the best and wisest of my friends seem to do," Ames remarked. As long as diplomacy was backed up by military preparation, "to negotiate again is not servile or mean." It was imperative that the public be made to understand that the solution to the impasse was dependent on the action of the French—"peace, if they are just and friendly; war, if insolent and rapacious." [49]

Fisher Ames's arguments did not immediately win over George Cabot, who insisted that the refusal of the Directory to receive Charles C. Pinckney as minister to France had "shut the door of negotiation." Thus in the former senator's opinion, it was inexpedient to send commissioners. The French, so adept at intrigue, might out-maneuver the Americans, giving the "French party" in America a new stature. Far more would be gained, Cabot contended, by arousing the nation, though not inflaming it, and preparing the people to accept added taxes, arming of merchant vessels, and the completion of the naval frigates. In discussing the matter with Cabot, Ames upheld the project of sending envoys "chiefly upon the ground, that without it, the government could do nothing; and with it, might be brought to prepare for an ultimate efficient defense." [50] Cabot had lingering doubts which were finally dispelled by President Adams's vigorous address to Congress in May 1797. Secretary Wolcott and the other members of the President's cabinet, taking their cue from Hamilton, dropped their objections to the mission. Adams, who had his own ideas about possible nominees, did not accept Ames's suggestion of George Cabot as one of

48. Oliver Wolcott to Alexander Hamilton, Phila., Mar. 31, 1797, Gibbs, *Memoirs*, I, 485-86.
49. Ames to Wolcott, Dedham, Apr. 24, 1797, *ibid.*, 497-99.
50. George Cabot to Oliver Wolcott, Brookline, Apr. 10, May 15, 1797, George Cabot to Jeremiah Smith, Brookline, Apr. 17, 1797, George Cabot, Circular Letter, Apr. 6, 1797, Lodge, ed., *Letters of Cabot*, 126-32, 137.

the envoys. He proposed to the Senate the names of John Marshall, Francis Dana, and Charles C. Pinckney. When Dana declined, Elbridge Gerry was appointed in his place, much to the dismay of the Federalists, who did not consider him politically reliable.[51]

In the spring of 1797 the paramount question in the nation was whether there would be war with France. News of increasing French captures of neutral American vessels intensified the resentment engendered by Pinckney's treatment in France, and the nation appeared to hover on the edge of war. The New York *Argus* remarked, "What an awful crisis does this make in the affairs of the country?" Other Republican newspapers loudly defended the French, ignoring their infringements of American neutrality, and endeavored to place the entire blame for the imbroglio on pro-British Federalists, who had imposed Jay's Treaty on the nation. Endeavoring to implant in the public mind the evil consequences of Federalist diplomacy, the *Independent Chronicle* proclaimed, "The British Treaty, illegitimately begotten . . . and fostered by the worst means, will be to you an inexhaustible source of calamity." [52]

Ames himself was blamed for his efforts in behalf of the treaty with England and for conspiring to bring on hostilities with France. Under the pseudonym of "A Republican," a critic implied that Hamilton and a few British agents, including Fisher Ames, had made the United States subservient to British influence. Ames's frequent public assertions that Federalists adhered to no foreign nation evoked a bitter reply. "Talk no more . . . ye Treaty advocates of being Americans. . . . If we are Americans let us be uniform in character both as it respects ENGLAND and FRANCE. But how can . . . 'the bold and loud Mr. Ames' . . . presume now to reprobate a foreign influence when the *fear of Britain* was the sole argument of his . . . speeches?" [53]

Ames did not attempt to answer such strictures, but they intensified his conviction that "the Jacobins had the people so long that they filled all the weak heads." The discontented in society were always prone to attack the government and were unable to discern in this case that France was the source of their troubles. A consequence of their igno-

51. George Cabot to Oliver Wolcott, Brookline, May 24, 1797, Gibbs, *Memoirs*, I, 536; Dauer, *Adams Federalists*, 124-27, 130; Darling, *Our Rising Empire*, 276-81; *Columbian Centinel* (Boston), June 7, 10, 1797; *Independent Chronicle* (Boston), June 29, 1797.

52. New York *Argus* reprinted in the Boston *Independent Chronicle*, Mar. 20, 1797; *Independent Chronicle* (Boston), June 22, July 20, Aug. 7, 1797.

53. *Independent Chronicle* (Boston), Aug. 3, 1797. Ames's private correspondence indicates that while he admired England, he was not willing for the United States to be subservient to her or to any other European nation. Ames to Gore, Dedham, Oct. 5, 1796, Nov. 10, 1799, Ames, *Works of Ames*, I, 200-201, 267-68.

rance was that "France is feared as if her cut-throats could fraternize us, and loved by the multitude as if they were not cut-throats." Ames therefore took the stand that the Federalists must "undeceive the misinformed part of the citizens in respect to the conduct of the Gov't towards France." [54] To accomplish a task of such magnitude demanded a concerted effort on the part of the Federalists, decisive leadership from the President, and supporting action from Congress. So overwhelming was the evidence of French penetration in American affairs that Ames was rapidly abandoning his former advocacy of peace and neutrality for the United States. His own role in the crisis, he jestingly said, would be that of a fifer while his friends carried their muskets.[55]

When the second session of the Fifth Congress met in the late autumn of 1797, Ames wrote to Sedgwick, "I am half willing that you should have a storm as usual in Congress . . . I . . . begin to hunger and thirst for the trial." [56] Even if Congress had been tardy in reacting to French affronts, he still hoped that the members would eventually respond to public demand. He ceaselessly encouraged his Federalist colleagues to promote spirited nationalistic policies. The Republican success in obstructing the proposal to arm commercial vessels and the evident unwillingness of many congressmen to pass other defense measures greatly perturbed Ames. "Congress is so divided," he informed Gore, "and faction has so debased and alienated the *amor patriae*, I almost despair of any right measures." [57] In the face of French aggrandizement, American vessels should retaliate, and the courts should condemn French ships infringing on American rights. Only by such actions would France be induced to end her current tactics. Intermittently during the winter of 1798, unofficial news from Europe indicated that the mission to France was doomed to failure. None of the three American envoys had been received officially. Marshall and Pinckney were actually being snubbed, while Gerry appeared to be favorably regarded by French diplomats. When President Adams received the first official dispatches from his envoys in March 1798, he immediately encouraged Congress to increase defenses in case of war. Late in the month, the chief executive recalled Marshall, Gerry, and Pinckney with the stipulation that only if they had been properly received and were now in-

54. Ames to Wolcott, Dedham, Mar. 24, 1797, Gibbs, *Memoirs*, I, 477.
55. Ames to Wolcott, Apr. 24, 1797, *ibid.*, 499.
56. Ames to Theodore Sedgwick, Dedham, Dec. 14, 1797, Sedgwick Papers, Vol. C, Mass. Hist. Soc.; Ames to Wolcott, Dedham, Jan. 27, 1798, Oliver Wolcott Papers, XVIII, Conn. Hist. Soc.
57. Ames to Gore, Dedham, Feb. 25, 1798, Ames, *Works of Ames*, I, 221; Ames to Theodore Foster, Dec. 19, 1797, Theodore Foster Papers, Rhode Island Historical Society, Providence, R.I.; Dauer, *Adams Federalists*, 137-38; Raymond Walters, *Albert Gallatin, Jeffersonian Financier and Diplomat* (N.Y., 1957), 105-6.

volved in official discussions should they remain. Subsequently, Pinckney and Marshall returned to the United States, and Gerry, encouraged by the French, stayed on as an unofficial American representative.[58]

Pressured by the Republicans to reveal the contents of the dispatches, which had obviously spurred him to action, Adams transmitted them to Congress on April 3. These documents revealed that agents of Talleyrand had demanded a loan for France and a bribe of $250,000 to facilitate negotiations. The agents were unnamed; they were simply designated as X, Y, and Z. The affair "really electrified all classes," according to Ames, and even Republican leaders privately admitted their indignation at Talleyrand's effrontery. In the effusion of national resentment and a surging demand for military preparedness, the Republicans were temporarily silenced, and the Federalists basked in the warmth of popular approval and anti-French sentiment. In Boston Ames analyzed Republican reaction to the dispatches, "The Jacobins were confounded, and the trimmers dropt off from the party like windfalls from an apple-tree in September, the worst of the fruit—vapid in cider and soon vinegar." [59]

Ames realistically sensed that the Republicans would soon recommence their attacks on the government. "The late communications have only smothered their rage," he observed; the flames would soon rise again if an indolent Congress failed to lead the nation.[60] In a moment of despondency, before word reached Dedham that the House was enlarging the military forces, he bitterly excoriated the nation. "Government is paralized by faction, the nation by avarice; like two dead bodies they must lie and putrify side by side, till the French tiger comes to devour them." The very system of government gave "anarchy . . . a vote" [61] by permitting opposition to vital measures before they became laws. Yet Ames did not imply that the government should be altered in the crisis. All who cherished Federalist principles, he avowed, must unite to preserve it. In the winter months the Republican press in Boston continually lashed at the high Federalists. Ames, Otis, and others were accused of attempting to precipitate war "by their own writings

58. Ames to Gore, Feb. 25, 1798, Ames, *Works of Ames,* I, 222; William Vans Murray to John Quincy Adams, The Hague, Nov. 4, 1797, Jan. 15, Mar. 3, 1798, William Vans Murray to Timothy Pickering, The Hague, Mar. 18, Apr. 3, 13, 17, 1798, Worthington C. Ford, ed., "Letters of William Vans Murray to John Quincy Adams, 1797-1803," Amer. Hist. Assn., *Annual Report, 1912* (Washington, 1914), 366, 370, 381, 391, 393-96; Darling, *Our Rising Empire,* 281-93.

59. Ames to Gore, July 28, Dec. 18, 1798, Ames, *Works of Ames,* I, 238, 245-46; Thomas Jefferson to Madison, Phila., Mar. 21, 1798, Madison Papers, XX, Lib. Cong.; Kurtz, *Presidency of Adams,* 298-301; Miller, *Federalist Era,* 210-12.

60. Ames to H. G. Otis, Dedham, Apr. 23, 1798, Ames, *Works of Ames,* I, 225.

61. Ames to Wolcott, Dedham, Apr. 22, 1798, Gibbs, *Memoirs,* II, 47.

and the exertions of the Hamiltonian Clubs and Presses regularly planted through these States and manured." [62] The thrust at Ames was not misdirected. More and more he upheld aggressive policies for the nation, finally encouraging the government to carry on a limited war. "It is too late to preach peace, and to say we do not think of war," he wrote to Harrison G. Otis; "a defensive war must be waged, whether it is formally proclaimed or not. That, or submission is before us." He observed that "passive virtues are little better than treachery. Zeal is now better than logic." [63]

To Secretary of State Timothy Pickering, by far the most extreme anti-Gallican in the administration, Fisher Ames expounded his concept of national policy. "All, *all* we can do is little enough," but immediate acts would stop the French. Further military forces and increases in revenue were necessary; abrogation of the French alliance and granting the executive power to embargo trade with the French West Indies were also essential goals; and finally the passage of a sedition act would strengthen the hand of the government. Halfway measures were insufficient to prevent the revival of "Jacobinism." Only "a full state of *war*, waged but not *declared*, and limited cautiously to the existence of their vile acts" would be a tenable solution.[64] Wage an undeclared war on the high seas and forbid communication with the French on the basis of self-preservation, Ames counseled. Then France might be brought to terms, her plotting in the United States ended, yet the nation not be divided. Severing all connections with the French would have the beneficial political effect of making the Republicans "obnoxious" before the next election. "As I dread the art of France, even after detection," he explained, "I wish to have our political thraldom legislatively terminated." [65]

62. *Independent Chronicle* (Boston), Feb. 5, June 5, 1798; Jefferson to Madison, Mar. 21, 1798, Madison Papers, XX, Lib. Cong. Jefferson suggested that extremists might be contemplating "a separation of the union, which has been so much the topic to the Eastward of late."

63. Ames to Otis, Apr. 23, 1798, Ames, *Works of Ames*, I, 225; Ames to Wolcott, Apr. 22, 1798, Gibbs, *Memoirs*, II, 47; Stephen Higginson to Timothy Pickering, Boston, June 9, 1798, Pickering Papers, XXII, Mass. Hist. Soc.

64. Ames to Timothy Pickering, Dedham, July 10, 1798, Ames, *Works of Ames*, I, 233; Ames to Wolcott, Dedham, June 8, 1798, Gibbs, *Memoirs*, II, 51-52; Ames's correspondence with the Secretary of State began during the crisis with France. A firm friendship developed between the two men, leading to an interesting interchange of ideas on foreign policies, domestic politics, and agriculture. Henry J. Ford, "Timothy Pickering, Secretary of State," in Samuel F. Bemis, ed., *The American Secretaries of State and Their Diplomacy* (N.Y., 1927–), II, 163-244.

65. Ames to Wolcott, Dedham, June 8, 1798, Gibbs, *Memoirs*, II, 52. Ames was only peripherally concerned with the controversy regarding the choice of a second in command to Gen. Washington in the newly augmented army. He did support Hamilton for the appointment and approved the efforts of Cabot to induce

In his own community Ames tried to undermine the strong local influence of the Republicans by stirring popular enthusiasm for the Federalist cause with a patriotic Fourth of July dinner. Sixty guests, predominantly "respectable" men, or Federalists, gathered to hear an oration, various patriotic songs, and to join in drinking numerous Federalist toasts. At the gathering nearly all of the guests signed a laudatory address to President Adams which was probably written by Ames. Ten days after the document was sent to Adams, he wrote his thanks for this public testament in support of his policies. In compelling language he expressed his opinion that Americans had been deluded by France for nearly a generation and that now there no longer was an alternative between war and submitting to France.[66]

The response of the participants at the dinner was most gratifying to Ames, who now felt that the political regeneration of Dedham had begun. His recent experience intensified a long-held belief that even though the people were often incorrect in their political principles, "they receive strong impressions of political truth very readily." [67] Nathaniel Ames did not share his brother's enthusiasm, reacting emphatically against the dinner and its sponsors. "I told them I chose to consider yet if the Gag bill etc. is cram'd down our jaws as well as Stamp Act etc.: direct taxes," he wrote in the pages of his pocket diary. "4 July— by squeezing teazing greasing the Fed band obtain the signature of a few deluded people to a flattering address to J. Adams president—they soon repent!" Nathaniel remained enraged for several days at the Federalist "frolic," commenting that "tools of F.A. work hard to get signers to an adress." [68]

Federalist fears about the safety of the nation ran deep and were not to be diverted by the intense patriotic fervor which had spread through the nation in mid-1798. An alarming international situation in

---

Henry Knox to withdraw his claims. George Cabot to Timothy Pickering, Brookline, Oct. 6, 1798, Lodge, ed., *Letters of Cabot*, 170-71; Miller, *Hamilton*, 475-78.

66. Ames to Timothy Pickering, Dedham, July (n.d), 1798, Ames, *Works of Ames*, I, 231; Ames to Wolcott, Dedham, July 6, 1798, Gibbs, *Memoirs*, II, 69. Ames sent the address to Secretary Pickering for transmittal to the President. Warren, *Jacobin and Junto*, 79; John Adams to the Inhabitants of Dedham and Other Towns in the County of Norfolk, Mass., Adams, ed., *Works of Adams*, IX, 209-10.

67. Ames to Gore, July 28, 1798, Ames, *Works of Ames*, I, 237-38.

68. Diary of Nathaniel Ames, June 30, July 4, 5, 1798, Nathaniel Ames Papers, Dedham Hist. Soc. Nathaniel Ames considered the Alien and Sedition Acts as the culmination of Federalist attempts to undermine all the liberties of the Revolutionary era. "It is amazing to see the apathy of the People under worse usurpation than that which once excited them to war," Memoranda, 1798, Calder, ed., "Diary of Dr. Nathaniel Ames," *Dedham Hist. Register*, 9 (1898), 63.

which France seemed to be at the point of subjugating both the Continent and Britain made the future of American independence highly problematical. French influence appeared omnipresent in the domestic scene; French agitation was rampant in the newspapers; French sympathizers were bold and numerous; French ideas were seductive and pernicious. The French problem in the United States illuminated the real problem for the Federalists: namely, the continuing growth of the Republican party and the possibility of their own party's demise.

Fisher Ames persisted in his view that an opposition party could only have detrimental effects on the government. For him Federalism, properly adhered to, assured the perpetuation of the Constitution and the new republic. He was convinced that if the present form of government was to be protected from extreme democracy and anarchy, the Federalists must do it. The Republicans were equated in his mind with current French aggression. "The struggle with our Jacobins is like the good Christian's with the evil one," he declared.[69] Articulate resistance to the Republicans tended to maintain Ames's prestige in his party; yet he was frustrated when he noted the limited degree to which he could influence ineffectual Federalists and the general public by his opinions. Efforts of Ames and the arch Federalists to arouse Congress were rewarded, however, when in June and July 1798 both Houses finally passed restrictive legislation which was designed to curb the influx of aliens and control the outpourings of the Republican press. In quick succession President Adams, reflecting the pugnacious and vindictive mood of Congress, approved a new naturalization law, "An Act concerning Aliens," "An Act respecting Alien Enemies," and a sedition act.[70]

In Massachusetts the Sedition Act was rigorously upheld, and of the four cases commenced in the federal circuit court, two directly involved Fisher Ames and the townspeople of Dedham. Ebullient Republicans in the town had been stirred by a clever itinerant workingman, David Brown, to erect a liberty pole, reminiscent of the Revolutionary period. Attached to the pole was a sign declaring, "No Stamp Act, No Sedition, No Alien Bills...downfall to the Tyrants of America." [71]

69. Ames to Gore, Dec. 18, 1798, Ames, *Works of Ames*, I, 245.
70. Peters, ed., *U.S. Statutes at Large*, I, 566-97. James M. Smith, *Freedom's Fetters, The Alien and Sedition Laws and American Civil Liberties* (Ithaca, N.Y., 1956), 22-155; John C. Miller, *Crisis in Freedom, The Alien and Sedition Acts* (Boston, 1952), 3-85.
71. *Independent Chronicle* (Boston), Nov. 12, 1798; Smith, *Freedom's Fetters*, 260; Frank M. Anderson, "The Enforcement of the Alien and Sedition Laws," Amer. Hist. Assn., *Annual Report, 1912* (Washington, 1914), 122.

Fisher Ames was thoroughly alarmed at the swift resurgence of Jacobin spirit. "What are we to do?" he inquired of Jeremiah Smith. "The Devil of sedition is immortal, and we, the saints, have an endless struggle to maintain with him." The fulminations of Brown, who publicly accused Ames of acquiring a large fortune through his friendship with Gore, did not disturb Ames as much as the poisoning of people's minds in Dedham. The township had not been politically redeemed as he had anticipated it might be earlier in the year, and in comparison with other counties, Norfolk seemed deficient in Americanism. He observed that there were men dreaming of democracy, such as a deacon in his church who said he would always vote "for the liberties of the people," and such as Nathaniel, who was "a political Quixote." [72]

Convinced that the Republicans were sending "runners everywhere to blow the trumpet of sedition," Ames was in no mood to give them quarter. "I am clear . . . the more the General Court can be made to hunt the Demos out of office the better—not a bone should those curs have to growl over." Only the loyal Federalists could be trusted and "the government must display its power *in terrorem*, or if that be neglected or delayed, in earnest." Since the public was so easily misled and was prone to engage in foolish activities like that of the liberty pole, the insult to government must not be overlooked and the instigators must be taught a lesson.[73]

After a fracas with the Republicans, the Dedham Federalists cut down the liberty pole and the federal marshal moved swiftly to arrest those who had originally set it up. Benjamin Fairbanks, a prominent citizen of Dedham, was seized for his part in the incident, and several months later David Brown was apprehended on a warrant charging him with seditious utterances. At Fairbanks's trial in the federal circuit court, Ames's sympathy was evoked when the defendant acknowledged that he was "sick of his folly." Ames had not been willing to defend Fairbanks in court, but did plead for leniency toward him. Observing that his acts were the result of a "warm and irritable temperament," he placed the blame on Brown, whom he called a "wandering apostle of sedition." Fairbanks was released with a minimal jail sentence and fine. No mercy, however, was to be shown to Brown, and Ames's denunciation of him may have been a factor in convincing Judge Samuel Chase

72. Ames to Jeremiah Smith, Boston, Nov. 22, 1798, Ames, *Works of Ames*, I, 240; Ames to Dwight, Dedham, Nov. 12, 1798, Fisher Ames Papers, Dedham Hist. Soc.

73. Ames to Dwight, Dedham, Dec. 7, 1798, Fisher Ames Papers, Dedham Hist. Soc. The sentence quoted is omitted from the letter published in Ames, *Works of Ames*, I, 243-45. Ames to Gore, Dedham, Dec. 18, 1798, *ibid.*, I, 247.

to make an example of the culprit, for he was sentenced to a year and a half in prison and heavily fined.[74]

Nathaniel Ames also became enmeshed in the case against Brown. In June 1799, he was twice summoned to testify in the circuit court, but chose not to appear. He noted that "I was not legally sum'd and had not time to attend." Nathaniel's anger over this incident was aggravated later when Judge Cushing refused to admit a redress and insulted him further by referring him to Fisher Ames for counsel. Dr. Ames bemoaned such injustice and reflected that "Civil War [is] threatening all over U.S." [75] His discontent was as great as his brother's, but the sources were infinitely different.

74. *Independent Chronicle* (Boston), June 20, 1799; Smith, *Freedom's Fetters*, 265-66; Anderson, "Enforcement of Alien and Sedition Laws," Amer. Hist. Assn., *Annual Report, 1912*, 123-25; Miller, *Crisis in Freedom*, 114-20.
75. Entries of June 7, 8, Oct. 22, Nov. 13, 1798, Calder, ed., "Diary of Dr. Nathaniel Ames," *Dedham Hist. Register*, 9 (1898), 112, 10 (1899), 26-27. In "Memoranda for 1798," Nathaniel Ames remarked, "Benjamin Fairbanks ... taken by ... the Marshal of the High fed Court ... in pompous array of tyrant power seiz'd on suspicion carried out of his own County to answer to charges solely within the jurisdiction of his own state laws." *Ibid.*, 10 (1899), 27.

Chapter XV

The Bane of Politics

Harsh equinoctial storms and snow in the fall and winter of 1798-99 appeared to be a fitting accompaniment to the unabating tumult of politics. Two long winters passed before the political tempest reached its peak in the election of 1800. With the triumph of the Republicans, it became clear that the persistent efforts of Fisher Ames and others to avert the decline of Federalism on a national scale had been unsuccessful. Only when Ames's closest associates gave up an attempt to salvage the Federalist party, did his own efforts become half-hearted. Annoyed at their resignation, he continued to have rapport with these extreme conservatives.

Throughout this period Fisher Ames's health fluctuated, and his spirits reflected the degree of his vigor at a particular time. Amid the vexatious aspects of his life, Frances and their children provided him with a vital sense of balance. From the clamors in law office and court house, he turned to the congenial milieu of his home. Here he could enjoy his family and the many friends who came out from Boston or stopped on their way to and from Congress. The retired congressman took particular delight in the development and activities of his children. On one occasion when John W. Ames was visiting his grandparents in Springfield, Ames revealed his affection for the boy, now almost four, by admitting that he and Frances were pleased to have an account of all of his childish "prattle." He himself was concerned that he had not devoted sufficient attention to "his early impressions" and could offer only the excuse that it was Frances's task. Apologetically he compared their own son to his cousins, John and Mary Dwight. "Poor John, however I fear has need of some excuses for himself," Fisher wrote. "He is yet a dunce at his book." [1] Trips to western Massachusetts were exciting for young John, but were quite difficult for the Ameses, as it was necessary to hire a chaise and take along much equipment for the baby, Nat. In February 1798, however, Frances took the hundred-mile journey to spend a month with her parents, leaving Fisher in a "solitary state," deeply involved in his law work. While his family was away, he wrote his congratulations to Jeremiah Smith on the recent birth of the Smith's first child. "I salute my daughter-in-law, whose merits and accomplishments are so rare and excellent." John Ames, he admitted, had already "cast his eyes on a young lady" in Springfield, but he offered his second son as a likely suitor for the Smith baby.[2]

In October 1798 Fisher Ames left Frances, who was then expecting their third child, long enough to travel with Thomas Dwight and "Sophy" Worthington to Lebanon Springs in the western Berkshires. Ames's primary objective was to try the efficacy of the spa waters with the hope that they would aid his recurrent digestive troubles. From Lebanon he made several side trips, first to Albany on October 15th and then to Stockbridge, where he may have called on the Sedgwicks. Later he went with his friends to the Shaker settlement, where they attended divine services and saw the Shaker dance. This experience was described by Thomas Dwight, who concluded that the Shakers, as a sect, were "poor deluded fools" deserving pity.[3]

By the first of March 1799, the birth of the Ames baby was imminent. In a letter to Colonel Worthington, Ames related that Frances was in good health and excellent spirits; still "the suspence at this crisis is mingled with much anxiety." On the same day, Mrs. Ames gave birth to a baby girl, who was soon christened Hannah. Fisher had wanted to add Hopkins to her name in memory of Frances's mother, but his wife insisted "that three names was less proper for girls than boys." [4] Nat, who now conversed endlessly "like a Frenchman," was delighted with his sister. His older brother endeavored to keep up with him by

1. Ames to John Worthington, Dedham, Sept. 24, 1797, Autograph Collection, Harvard Univ.
2. Ames to Christopher Gore, Feb. 25, 1798, Ames to Jeremiah Smith, Boston, Mar. 13, 1798, Ames, *Works of Ames*, I, 220, 223.
3. Ames to Thomas Dwight, Dedham, Sept. 25, 1798, Fisher Ames Papers, Dedham Hist. Soc.; Thomas Dwight to Hannah Dwight, Lebanon Springs, Oct. 17, 1798, Dwight-Howard Papers, Mass. Hist. Soc.
4. Thomas Dwight to Hannah Dwight, Boston, Feb. 13, 1799, Dwight-Howard Papers, Mass. Hist. Soc.; Ames to John Worthington, Dedham, Mar. 1, 1799, Gratz Collection, "First Congress," Hist. Soc. of Pa.; Account Book, Fisher Ames Papers, Dedham Hist. Soc.; Ames to Dwight, Dedham, Mar. 8, 1799, *ibid.*

showing some interest in the baby, too. Their father observed that Hannah was growing "fat as a pig" and was as quiet as a well-fed one. Hannah proved to be an only daughter, though the family continued to grow until there were six sons. William was born on October 3, 1800, Jeremiah Fisher on October 9, 1802, and Seth on April 19, 1805. The youngest child, Richard, was born in Dedham on June 16, 1807.[5]

Surrounded by ebullient children, Fisher Ames was by turns concerned and amused, yet invariably indulgent. In writing to Colonel Dwight a few weeks after the birth of William, he reported, "I am well again, except that the child William is a terrible bedfellow and squalls so jacobinically towards day break that I am done over as if I had been out half the night at a tavern. He is a good boy except when he is *very* bad." Several years later when his fifth child, Jeremiah, had just taken his first steps alone, Ames commented that he himself enjoyed the occasion as much as Mrs. Randolph delighted in the congressional speeches of her husband.[6]

As the children grew older, their Springfield cousins were invited to visit them from time to time in the house on High Street. Mary Dwight, who entered Mrs. Newton's boarding school at Medford when she was eleven, was a welcome guest during her vacations. Ames took a particular interest in Mary, keeping Thomas Dwight informed of both her health and educational progress. John, her brother, was likewise warmly received when he came to Dedham. His disposition, according to Ames, was "a gift of nature of more worth than any of fortunes." During an extended visit in the summer and autumn of 1802, he, John, and Nat Ames spent a memorable day touring Boston. After visiting the museum, they climbed to the top of the new state capitol, explored the Long Wharf, and watched the drawing of a lottery at the old State House. Before they left for Dedham, they "loaded themselves with organs, mummies, [and] trumpets" at the toy stores.[7]

The health of the Ames children caused their parents real anxiety. Exposed as they were to the various diseases of childhood, their father commented, "After all, I must place my trust for their safety in God's good providence." When at eight years of age Nat developed a severe

5. Ames to John Worthington, Dedham, Dec. 22, 1798, Miscellaneous Manuscripts, N.-Y. Hist. Soc.; Ames to Dwight, Mar. 8, 1799, Fisher Ames Papers, Dedham Hist. Soc.; Ames to Worthington, Dedham, Mar. 30, 1799, Chamberlain Collection, Boston Pub. Lib.; Account Book, Fisher Ames Papers, Dedham Hist. Soc.; Ames to Dwight, Boston, Mar. 4, 1800, *ibid.*

6. Ames to Dwight, Dedham, Dec. 27, 1800, Jan. 15, 1804, Fisher Ames Papers, Dedham Hist. Soc.

7. Ames to Dwight, Dedham, Oct. 20, 1802, July 9, Aug. 9, Dec. 15, 1803, *ibid.*; Thomas Dwight to Hannah Dwight, Boston, Aug. 6, 1802, Dwight-Howard Papers, Mass. Hist. Soc.

infection in his leg, Ames turned to his brother for medical advice. Although the boy was delirious and suffering pain, and then passed through a lengthy period of recuperation, Dr. Ames was not unduly solicitous. Thomas Dwight concluded that Fisher Ames "shews more than a christian charity in employing him at all, sooner would I apply for medical aid to one of the aborigines." [8] Gradually Nat recovered, though months after his siege the knee remained swollen.

Although his mother and physician brother lived so near, Ames was actually closer to members of Frances's family in Springfield. Culturally and politically, he had allied himself with the Worthingtons and the Dwights. Deborah Ames, although still sprightly, could be both demanding and irritable, leading Thomas Dwight to comment that he had heard she was "a drum" at Fisher's ear. Dr. Ames, with his abrasive personality, was often at odds with his brother. The intensity of feeling, which was characteristic of Mrs. Ames and her sons, led to uncompromising attitudes and to misunderstanding. Despite any disagreements, however, Fisher Ames, in a political letter written toward the end of his life, could obliquely refer to Nathaniel as "a man of so much real worth." [9]

Ames was saddened by the physical and mental decline of Frances's father at the end of the century. In 1800, when John Worthington was in his eighty-first year, he died after being disabled for several months. Fisher, who had always respected his father-in-law's political sagacity and business acumen, also had a high regard for his character. "It inspired an awe that was uncommon. *Sic transit gloria mundi*," he reflected near the close of Worthington's life.[10] When the Colonel's estate was distributed according to the terms of his will, Frances shared equally with her sisters. As a part of her inheritance she received more than 128 acres of land in Springfield valued at $2,777.64. By 1803, after various parcels of land were sold, she had realized over $5,000.[11] It was this increment to the Ameses' capital which, with the profits from

8. Ames to Dwight, Dedham, Aug. 15, 1800, Ames, *Works of Ames*, I, 279; Ames to Dwight, Dedham, Nov. 27, Dec. 9, 1804, May 19, Nov. 29, 1805, Fisher Ames Papers, Dedham Hist. Soc. Ames to Dwight, Jan. 10, 1805, Manuscript Collection, University of Virginia, Charlottesville, Va.; Thomas Dwight to Hannah Dwight, Washington, Dec. 13, 1804, Dwight-Howard Papers, Mass. Hist. Soc.

9. Thomas Dwight to Hannah Dwight, June 17, 1795, Dwight-Howard Papers, Mass. Hist. Soc.; Thomas, Reminiscences of Sixty-Five Years, Dedham Hist. Soc.; Ames to [Josiah Quincy], Dedham, Mar. 19, 1806, Ames Family Papers, Leland Stanford University, Palo Alto, Calif.

10. Ames to Dwight, Dedham, Jan. 6, 1800, Fisher Ames Papers, Dedham Hist. Soc.; Thomas Dwight to Theodore Sedgwick, Apr. 26, 1800, Sedgwick Papers, Vol. C, Mass. Hist. Soc.

11. "Lands and Estate of John Worthington," Box 1, Dwight-Howard Papers, Mass. Hist. Soc.; Account Book, Fisher Ames Papers, Dedham Hist. Soc.

Fisher's farm and business investments, enabled the family to live comfortably though never affluently.

Ames's farming activities, avidly pursued once he was living permanently in Dedham, were those of a scientific farmer seeking to develop a profitable source of income. Not a man to make an ostentatious display with a country estate, Fisher Ames conceived of his enterprise as one which he himself could supervise. He placed his hopes "and those of my children on the *terra firma* of a highly improved farm," less likely to be influenced by the vagaries of politics than capital invested in funded stock.[12] Inherent in his scheme was the idea of security even if the Republicans prostrated the government and abolished the national debt.

Since Boston was a scant ten miles away, Ames endeavored to produce meat, butter, and vegetables for marketing there, and at various times he experimented with raising watermelons, cucumbers, and silver skin onions. After a busy summer of growing vegetables, he remarked that his market wagon had "*done well for the country*, as the french used to say." He slowly built up his land and stock, acquiring additional acres from time to time and attempting to improve the quality of his cattle. By 1801 he was also raising pigs, keeping them penned in his barn in a way which he hoped his friend Timothy Pickering might approve. When food prices were high, Ames made a profit from the sale of a drove of some thirty pigs even after they had consumed quantities of expensive corn. In answer to an inquiry on farming from Colonel Pickering, he explained that his main purpose in raising hogs was the production of a by-product, manure, "the sinews of good husbandry." Initially, he had kept careful records, showing the pattern of expense and the limited profits in the sale of swine. Now, he no longer endeavored to keep accurate accounts of such farm ventures, discouraged primarily by hired hands who "thought it sufficient to have fat hogs without troubling their heads to make a book."[13]

Establishing a model dairy was Fisher Ames's chief interest, and his discussions of the breeding and the care of cattle with Gore and Pickering show how imaginative yet practical his scientific ideas were. He experimented with different grasses for his cows and in addition fed them grain, carrots, pumpkins, and fodder corn. Thus he was able to increase milk production so that each cow gave a minimum of "a common Hingham pail of 10 wine quarts full at night." Ames an-

12. Ames to Dwight, Dedham, Dec. 7, 1801, Ames, *Works of Ames*, I, 296; Ames to Dwight, Dedham, Feb. 6, 1804, Fisher Ames Papers, Dedham Hist. Soc.
13. Ames to Dwight, Dedham, Aug. 10, Sept. 12, Dec. [10], 1804, Fisher Ames Papers, Dedham Hist. Soc.; Ames to Timothy Pickering, Dedham, Oct. 26, 1805, Pickering Papers, XXVII, Mass. Hist. Soc.

nounced proudly that one cow actually gave sixteen quarts. Frances
was as involved in managing the dairy as was Fisher and knew all the
cows "by name, sight and reputation." [14]

As an addition to his dairy, Ames devised an icehouse in which to
keep butter pure and unspoiled before sending it to market. Bostonians,
however, were so inured to rancid butter that he had doubts they would
pay the six cents more a pound he wanted to charge. By packing the
butter boxes in ice and protecting them with straw and flannel bags,
he could provide enough refrigeration to sell superior butter to his
customers. His attempt to construct an efficient icehouse was unsuccessful initially, but constant experimentation led to a solution of the
excessive melting of the ice. The use of straw under the icehouse floor
permitted him to keep the ice through a hot summer; consequently he
had the building and an addition filled with sixty-eight loads of ice in
midwinter from the Charles River. "If I can sell half a dozen pounds
of ice for a pound [of] loaf sugar I shall not lose my labour," he remarked.[15]

Dedham had long been an area ideal for fruit growing, and the
Ameses had a flourishing orchard. In his effort to produce superior
fruit, Squire Ames would request cions of pear and apple trees from
friends in other parts of the country. When Pickering sent him seeds
from southern France, Ames responded that it was fortunate they came
from the aristocratic part as seeds from democratic soil would not grow
in his garden. Musing on his attempts at farming, Ames commented,
"Cattle and fruit trees are my themes, in prose. Poetry, if I had any,
I would devote to my pigsty and politics—two scurvy subjects, that
should be coupled together." [16]

Before Ames had become involved in developing his farm, he had
been searching for investment opportunities. While still a member of
Congress, he had become interested in the India trade through Benjamin
Goodhue and had established business contacts with William Gray, Jr.,
a leading merchant and shipowner of Salem. Through Gray's agency,
Ames invested $1500 of his capital, sending a box of silver dollars with
Captain John Bickford on board the brig *William and Henry* bound

14. *Ibid.;* Ames to Gore, Dedham, Jan. 11, 1799, Nov. 4, 1802, Ames, *Works of Ames,* I, 249-50, 303-8; Ames to Dwight, Dedham, Apr. 17, 1800, Fisher Ames Papers, Mass. Hist. Soc.

15. Ames to Dwight, Dedham, Jan. 26, Aug. 10, 1804, Jan. 27, Feb. 6, 19, 1805, Fisher Ames Papers, Dedham Hist. Soc.; Ames to Pickering, Dedham, Apr. 28, 1804, Pickering Papers, XXVII, Mass. Hist. Soc.

16. Ames to Pickering, Dedham, Mar. 12, 1799, Ames to Gore, Dedham, Nov. 7, 1802, Ames, *Works of Ames,* I, 253, 303-4. Ames wrote in an amusing vein that his cows enjoyed orchard grass in defiance of the Royal Society's statement that it was unfit for the consumption of cattle.

for Calcutta in December 1794. There were risks of wind and weather, British and French privateers, and uncertain market conditions. But Gray had assured him that they were not excessive as the vessel was one of the safest afloat and was making a direct voyage to India and return.[17]

A little more than two years later the vessel came into New York harbor, bringing in its cargo the goods purchased with Ames's funds, six bales of Bengal cottons and a box of bandanna handkerchiefs. When the consignment was sold, Ames realized $717.86 profit after all freight charges, duties, and the commissions had been deducted. He was so pleased with the results of this "adventure" that he left both capital and profits, totaling $2217.86 with Gray until another opportunity for an investment arose. To this sum he first added $1600 in April 1796, and after selling eight shares of his stock in the Bank of the United States, he transferred the major part of his proceeds, $4069.20, to Gray. Colonel Worthington, who in the last years of his life joined forces with Ames in foreign trade, contributed $5000, making a total of nearly $13,000 invested in this family enterprise.[18] In acknowledging Fisher Ames's frequent help in transacting the business, Worthington had assured him that his participation with his son-in-law was primarily for "the benefit and happiness of my children." [19]

Dividing the capital, Gray shipped $1600 on a second voyage of the *William and Henry* and $2000 on the *Elizabeth*. On another of his ves-

17. Morison, "India Ventures," Amer. Antiq. Soc., *Proceedings*, New Ser., 37 (1927), 14-16; "Summary or General Memorand, India Ventures," Fisher Ames Papers, Dedham Hist. Soc. Gray's *William and Henry*, a vessel of 166 tn., was replaced by a ship of 256 tn., built in 1796, James D. Phillips, "Salem Merchants and Their Vessels," Essex Institute *Hist. Collections*, 80 (1944), 264; James D. Phillips, "East India Voyages of Salem Vessels Before 1800," *ibid.*, 79 (1943), 233; Edward Gray, *William Gray of Salem, Merchant* (Boston and N.Y., 1914), 13; Kenneth W. Porter, *The Jacksons and the Lees, Two Generations of Massachusetts Merchants, 1765-1844*, 2 vols. (Cambridge, 1937), I, 27-39; see also James D. Phillips, *Salem and the Indies* (Boston, 1947).

18. Morison, "India Ventures," Amer. Antiq. Soc., *Proceedings*, New Ser., 37 (1927), 16. Ames sold his eight shares of Bank stock at $520 each for $4160 minus the brokerage commission realizing $4149.60; Richard Rundle to Ames, Phila., Sept. 26, 1796, Ames to William Gray, Jr., Dedham, Mar. 19, 1799, Fisher Ames Papers, Dedham Hist. Soc.; Transfer of 8 shares, Documents, Aug. 31, 1796, Chamberlain Collection, Boston Pub. Lib.; William Gray, Jr., to Ames, Salem, Dec. 21, 1796, Autograph Collection, Hist. Soc. of Pa. Ames's profits for the first adventure were actually less than they appear to be. An insurance premium of $188.75, paid by Ames in a separate transaction, did not affect the balance of $2217.86 which was left with Gray for re-investment.

19. John Worthington to Ames, Springfield, Sept. (n.d.), 1796, Mar. 5, 1799, "Summary or General Memorand, India Ventures," Fisher Ames Papers, Dedham Hist. Soc.; Ames to Worthington, Dedham, Mar. 30, 1799, Chamberlain Collection, Boston Pub. Lib.

sels engaged in the Bengal trade, the *Betsey*, he sent three thousand "Spanish mill'd dollars" for Ames's account and another separate venture of $2000 for John Worthington. Early in 1797 he forwarded the remainder of the capital on his ship *John*. When Ames inquired about the advisability of further investment, Gray cautioned him against it, explaining that it was too hazardous to "put property a Float" as long as the French continued their depredations on American commerce. Ames was convinced, however, that the India trade, even with the dangers and the consequent high insurance rates, offered him the best means of investing his capital. In January 1798 he received reassuring news from Gray that the *Elizabeth* under command of Captain Sage had arrived safely in New York. Ames's four ventures, when finally settled, proved to be remunerative for him, bringing in $4185.12 net profits, but he was nevertheless disappointed that his return on the *John* had been much less profitable than his other transactions.[20] He recognized, however, that this adventure yielded as much as if his capital were invested in government securities.

In 1798 Ames and Worthington were still engaged in the India trade, but influenced by the declining market for Bengal cottons, they now broadened their commercial ventures to include China. Gray shipped $5000 for the Colonel on the *Elizabeth* bound for Canton in April 1798; later he sold $2000 of the investment, as Worthington did not want to risk so much on any single voyage. To Worthington's sum of $3000, the Salem merchant added $5000 in Ames's name. Gray wrote his Dedham client that the *Elizabeth*'s incoming cargo was considered "good property" which could sell at 25 per cent profit before the vessel reached port. "It is fortunate for you that I shipped so large a sum for your account," he observed.[21]

Since Ames had invested heavily in various India voyages, he was especially anxious that this adventure in the *Elizabeth* should turn out well, explaining that "her arrival would be truly fortunate for me ... tho I should be placed many thousands below *affluence* I should be so near to a *competence* ... as with frugality to abate the most uncomfortable exertions in my professions." Ames's profits in this instance cannot be exactly computed, but in July 1801 William Gray transferred to the branch of the Bank of the United States $4023.02, the sum real-

20. "Summary or General Memorand, India Ventures," William Gray, Jr. to Ames, Salem, May 16, Nov. 24, 1797, Ames to William Gray, Dedham, Dec. 16, 1797, Mar. 19, 1799, Fisher Ames Papers, Dedham Hist. Soc.; Ames to John Worthington, Dedham, Feb. 3, 1798, Norcross Collection, Mass. Hist. Soc.; Morison, "India Ventures," Amer. Antiq. Soc., *Proceedings*, New Ser., 37 (1927), 17-18.

21. William Gray, Jr., to Ames, Salem, Feb. 15, Mar. 12, 1799, Fisher Ames Papers, Dedham Hist. Soc.

ized in the voyages of the *Elizabeth* and the *Ulysses*.[22] Fisher Ames respected Gray and trusted his business judgment, although he could not subscribe to his strongly commercial outlook which placed profits above the nation's welfare. At times Gray took the initiative in shipping funds for Ames, making advances on his own, but Ames apparently rarely borrowed money to carry on his business activities. When he did, it was with considerable reluctance and he took care to insure the venture fully.[23]

In the years after 1800, Ames's investments, like those of the Salem merchants themselves, became extensive and diversified. While he continued to conduct part of his overseas ventures through the agency of William Gray, he also invested through Joseph Lee, Jr., a staunch Federalist merchant of Boston, and his brother, Nathaniel Cabot Lee.[24] Over a period of twelve months he invested $2000 with Joseph Lee "in Mr. Prebbles Ship to Manilla," $4000 in Lee's *Regulus*, another $4000 in the *Perseverance*, $3000 in the ship *Cyrus*, $2000 in the *Thomas Russell*, and $1000 in the brig *Joseph*. In July 1801 one of Gray's vessels, the *Laurel*, returned to Salem from Manila with a very rich cargo, including indigo, consigned to Ames. Later the dye was sold for $5125.62, yielding him a profit of $1417.08. Ames was not deterred by the growing competition in the India trade, nor by the high insurance rates and the inevitable premiums for silver dollars. Thomas Dwight shared his interest in ventures to China, and sometimes the brothers-in-law jointly invested in a trading voyage. Through Timothy Williams, they sent $5000 on the ship *Eliza* in 1802, purchasing 9,735 pieces of Nankeen cloth which ultimately sold for $8891.11. After impost duties, commissions, and freight charges of 30 per cent of the profits had been deducted, a profit of over $2000 remained.[25]

Through his contacts with Goodhue, Fisher Ames in 1800 branched out into marine insurance, underwriting policies issued in the office of James King in Salem. At the time, the business of insuring vessels and their cargoes was in a transitional stage. Insurance charges, based on

22. Ames to Gray, Mar. 19, 1799, and Account Book, Fisher Ames Papers, Dedham Hist. Soc.

23. Ames to Benjamin Goodhue, Dedham, Feb. 18, 1799, Benjamin Goodhue Manuscripts, N.Y. Soc. Lib.; Ames to John Worthington, Dedham, Mar. 30, 1799, Chamberlain Collection, Boston Pub. Lib.

24. Account Book, Fisher Ames Papers, Dedham Hist. Soc.; Porter, *Jacksons and Lees*, I, 9-10, 473-74, 498, 535.

25. Account Book, Fisher Ames Papers, Dedham Hist. Soc.; Phillips, *Salem and the Indies*, 246; Porter, *Jacksons and Lees*, I, 516. Another example of Ames's investments with Joseph Lee, Jr., was a venture of $5000 in the brig *Caravan* which sailed from Calcutta, arriving in Boston in Oct. 1803. She carried a cargo valued at 100,000 sicca rupees consisting of cottons and "gruff goods" such as goat hides, twine, and gunny sacks. Ames's proceeds were $6493.37; *ibid.*, 538; Account Book, Fisher Ames Papers, Dedham Hist. Soc.

marine risks, were almost casually computed and varied with the particular agent, whether merchant or ship captain.[26] Approaching this new venture with caution, Ames instructed Benjamin Goodhue not to commit more than $500 for him through King on any single ship. "I have some habits and like most other men rather more maxims of . . . prudence," he explained, "and I have sometimes a little flinched from the purpose of trusting it to fortune in her worst temper to strip me." [27] It was a wise move to distribute the risks, for the underwriters were quickly faced with many claims for vessels captured by marauding British and French privateers in the West Indies. In his first six months of insurance investment, Ames had to remit $217 to Goodhue for various claims and then pay $404.70 as his share of the policy on J. Orne's schooner *Whim*, which was taken prize.[28] These experiences convinced him that the premiums for the West Indies had been too low to compensate for "the nest of pirate's in the Islands"; consequently he preferred to underwrite vessels bound for India or Europe.[29] Scattered in Ames's business correspondence after 1800 are references to numerous policies such as "Ship Eliza Thos. Brown to India and home @ 17 $400," indicating his continued participation in this commercial activity. But insurance companies with more sophisticated methods were gradually making inroads into the business of such single agents as King. Exaggerated hazards which limited opportunities ultimately influenced Ames to curtail his investments. In 1806 he wrote to Goodhue, "I see I was too late in the business. When every brook had sands of gold, you and I were at Congress helping to make a statute book." Ames had decided to withdraw from further underwriting and requested his friend to settle outstanding policies. This Goodhue did, crediting him with $906.27.[30]

Another business enterprise of particular importance to the former congressman was the Norfolk and Bristol Turnpike. His persistent concern for the growth and improvement of Dedham was evidenced by his efforts to have better mail service instituted, a stage line established, and the town highways reconstructed. Ames was one of the moving forces behind the formation of the turnpike corporation, chartered by the state in March 1802 to build an improved road between

26. Phillips, *Salem and the Indies*, 217-18.
27. Ames to Goodhue, Dedham, Sept. 13, 1800, Benjamin Goodhue Manuscripts, N.Y. Soc. Lib.
28. Goodhue to Ames, Salem, Dec. 20, 1800, Mar. 20, 1801, Fisher Ames Papers, Dedham Hist. Soc.
29. Ames to Goodhue, Dedham, Mar. 23, 1801, Benjamin Goodhue Manuscripts, N.Y. Soc. Lib.
30. Goodhue to Ames, Mar. 20, 1801, Account Book, Goodhue to Ames, Salem, June 25, 1806, Fisher Ames Papers, Dedham Hist. Soc.; Ames to Goodhue, Dedham, July 30, 1806, Benjamin Goodhue Manuscripts, N.Y. Soc. Lib.

Dedham and the Rhode Island boundary at Pawtucket.[31] At the first meeting of the incorporators held in Attleborough on March 30, 1802, Fisher Ames was chosen president. He had declined the post of treasurer, which he felt was troublesome, although, as he humorously remarked, "A percent would have stuck in my fingers." Ames caught some of the enthusiasm sweeping New England at the turn of the century for this new mode of improving communication and travel and was certain that Dedham, as well as investors in the enterprise, would benefit greatly from a well-constructed road on the important route between Boston and Providence. Turnpikes radiating from Boston, he had long been convinced, would regain much of the commerce of the city and would "restore to the South End rum-and-molasses shops the Jonathans who used to have their sweet communion with them." [32] Ames himself subscribed to forty shares in the company, ultimately investing $8000 after he had paid all of the assessments. As president of the corporation he was very anxious to have control of the turnpike remain in the seaboard areas, among investors who would have a personal interest in furthering the enterprise. Consequently he actively promoted the sale of shares to such business acquaintances in Salem as Benjamin Goodhue, William Gray, Jr., Simon Forrester, and James King. Many of the details of the "Turnpike business" were handled by the clerk of the company, James Richardson, a young Dedham lawyer who had studied law in Fisher Ames's office.[33]

By the summer of 1803, construction was far advanced on the new road, and Ames, after traveling it on horseback, was certain that it would be "super excellent." He watched its progress avidly, weighing its success as winter came on and snows fell, at times as "deep as a man's knee." [34] All of the toll gates had been erected by December 1804, but the turnpike was not completed until 1806, and two years later there still was much to be done to perfect it. In a statement on the finances of the road which Ames prepared in 1807, the company had incurred expenses of $228,797.78 while its capital was only $192,553, and in the years of its operation $16,195.28 had been collected in tolls. The heavy traffic on the Roxbury extension between Dedham and Boston was very

31. Ames to Dwight, Dedham, Apr. 16, 1802, Fisher Ames Papers, Dedham Hist. Soc.; Frederick J. Wood, *The Turnpikes of New England* (Boston, 1919), 87-88.
32. *Ibid.*; Ames to Gore, Boston, Mar. 5, 1800, Ames, *Works of Ames*, I, 277.
33. List of Shareholders, Aug. 9, 1802, Folder dated 1802, Report of 1807, in hand of Fisher Ames, concerning the Norfolk and Bristol Turnpike, Goodhue to Ames, Salem, Sept. 6, 1802, Norfolk and Bristol Turnpike Papers, Dedham Hist. Soc.; Ames to Goodhue, Dedham, May 29, June 10, Aug. 14, Sept. 17, 1802, Benjamin Goodhue Manuscripts, N.Y. Soc. Lib.; Ames to William Gray, Jr., Aug. 10, 1802, Fisher Ames Papers, Dedham Hist. Soc.
34. Ames to Dwight, Dedham, July 9, 1803, Jan. 27, Feb. 29, 1804, Fisher Ames Papers, Dedham Hist. Soc.

promising for the future, the president maintained in the report, but privately he explained that most of the hundred teams which daily passed through Dedham still used the old road to avoid toll charges. Until the last months of his life he remained actively concerned with affairs of the Norfolk and Bristol Turnpike, urging the constant improvement of the right-of-way and promoting the appointment of directors who could "shovel gravel or oversee those who are hired to do it." [35]

Despite the demands of his business ventures, Ames found time for social gatherings, for books, and for an occasional trip to the theatre. It was not unusual for visitors to be "dinnered" in the High Street house, where the gracious Mrs. Ames presided over a kitchen equipped with an oven that yielded "a good crop of hot apple pies." [36] Over their Madeira wine such friends as Rutledge of South Carolina, Gore, King, Cabot, and Judge Benson talked with their distinguished host. Urbane and witty, Fisher Ames continued to be a vivid conversationalist whatever his mood. But he could listen, as well as talk, and respond to the views of those with whom he conversed. After seeing a performance of *The Robbers*, he enjoyed a discussion of the merits of the play with his servant, Leonard Parsons, who had driven him to Boston and also attended. He observed that Leonard was much less critical than he had been of the production.[37] With the passage of time books claimed more of Ames's attention than the law. He acknowledged, "My declamation is not of the bar sort.... I hate the sort of application that needs drudgery. Impulses command me; I cannot command them." Since his methods of creating income had proven sufficiently successful by 1802, he felt that he no longer had to "work hard at the bar." [38]

Ames increasingly felt himself to be "a man of straw," for he was losing the battle with ill health. His malady affected him in such various ways that the physicians he consulted could not definitely diagnose it.

35. Ames to Dwight, Dedham, Dec. 9, 1804, *ibid.*; Ames to I. P. Davis, Dedham, Feb. 27, 1808, Manuscript Collection, Boston Pub. Lib.; Report of 1807, Norfolk and Bristol Turnpike Papers, Dedham Hist. Soc.

36. Ames to Dwight, Dedham, Dec. 7, 1798, Ames, *Works of Ames*, I, 243; Christopher Gore to Rufus King, Boston, Apr. 12, 1804, Rufus King Papers, Box 10, N.-Y. Hist. Soc. On one occasion in 1798, Ames invited thirty to forty persons for a fishing party and a dinner served in a grove of trees on the banks of the Charles River; Thomas, Reminiscences of Sixty-Five Years, Dedham Hist. Soc.

37. Ames to Dwight, Dedham, Dec. 22, 1798, Feb. 13, 1804, Fisher Ames Papers, Dedham Hist. Soc.

38. Ames to Gore, Dedham, Dec. 14, 1802, Ames, *Works of Ames*, I, 311. Gore sent Ames from London the collected works of Suetonius, Herodotus, and Demosthenes. Several anecdotes were related regarding Ames's interests in books and his entertaining comments about various authors whose works he had read; Daniel White to Theophilus Parsons, Salem, Sept. 15, 1858, Parsons, *Memoir of Parsons*, 448; James S. Loring, *The Hundred Boston Orators* (Boston, 1853), 293.

Most often he was the victim of severe and prolonged colds settling in his lungs and making him hoarse and miserable. He continued to have digestive problems, which diminished his appetite, and to be subject to exhaustion resulting from insomnia. On the advice of his doctors, he undertook rigorous exercise, walking and riding for long periods of time. Because of his limited strength, however, this exertion would on occasion help to bring on the fainting spells, which were a constant threat. In analyzing his condition Ames observed, "Some believe my fainting fits proceeded from muscular not mental irritability." He constantly sought to regain his health by experimenting with food, with drink, and with hot baths. Though he would gain weight, he would invariably lose it again. When a friend urged him to consult a physician in Beverley and consider a voyage to Calcutta for his health, Fisher Ames responded, "It is not necessary I should live—but while I do, it is necessary that I should live at home with my family." [39]

No matter in what direction his family needs and his own interests led him, he could not avoid an intense discouragement over political developments. He was often disconsolate, and a cloud of pessimism enveloped him. His own sense of doom could not be easily separated from his foreboding about the future of the republic. More than any other event of Adams's administration, the decision of the President to resume negotiations with France was a shattering one for Ames and most of the high Federalists. To their consternation Adams had ignored the objections of several cabinet members and also of party leaders in nominating William Vans Murray in February 1799 as minister plenipotentiary to France. Anger, resentment, and mortification were rampant among Ames's circle of friends as they contemplated the effect a reorientation of American foreign policy would have on the party and its objectives. All condemned "the flinching retrograde step," the retired congressman observed.[40] A peace with France Ames regarded as an un-

39. Ames to Dwight, Dedham, Apr. 17, 1800, July 9, Sept. 26, 1803, Dec. 9, 1804, *ibid.;* Ames to Gore, Boston, Dec. 14, 1802, Oct. 3, 1803, Ames to Dwight, Dedham, Oct. 31, 1803, Ames, *Works of Ames,* I, 311, 322, 330-31. Ames wrote, "My constitution is like that of federalism, too feeble for a full allowance even of water-gruel, and like that, all the doctor I have is a Jacobin"; Ames to Dwight, Dedham, Jan. 15, 1804, *ibid.,* 337.

40. Miller, *Hamilton,* 493-504; Darling, *Our Rising Empire,* 337-47; Kurtz, *Presidency of Adams,* 282, 347-51. Dauer, *Adams Federalists,* 230-33; Ames to Worthington, Mar. 1, 1799, Gratz Collection, Hist. Soc. of Pa.; Stephen Higginson to Timothy Pickering, Boston, Jan. 1, Mar. 3, 1799, Pickering Papers, XXIV, Mass. Hist. Soc. Higginson, speaking for the arch Federalists, remarked, "We have been much disappointed in the P's communications. We are afraid he has committed himself too far respecting ... the terms on which he would negotiate." The Federalists still advocated participation in the European war so as to be parties to the peace.

mitigated evil since it would "chill the public fervor" and undermine popular support of the Federalist program. By his unexpected move the President appeared to be wooing the French while encouraging the Republicans at home. Ending the state of hostility with France inevitably would remove the *raison d'être* for the enlarged army and navy and also preclude the further extension of federal powers.[41]

Like many of his friends, Ames was at a loss to account for the President's conduct; yet he had an underlying appreciation of Adams's intelligence and personal rectitude which acted as a brake on his reaction. To members of his own family, the former representative was less restrained. "My respect and attachment to his character will not permit me to vent my vexation . . . with much freedom to any except to a few discreet friends," he explained. Just as Ames feared, the political prospects of the Federalists dimmed rapidly and the Republicans "raise[d] their fallen crests upon the news" of the resumption of negotiations. Existing tensions between the President's supporters and the Hamiltonian wing of the Federalist party were now reaching the breaking point, but Ames continued to hope that the most serious divisive effects on the party could be avoided. Therefore he counseled against open attack on Adams, however much he warranted censure and criticism. In analyzing the President's principal weaknesses, he remarked, "No man, his friends say, has more invincible prejudices than Mr. Adams, nor acts more suddenly from their impulse. His being a great, and good man does not exempt him from the force of this objection." [42]

Even after the initial surprise at John Adams's diplomatic move had faded, Fisher Ames could not reconcile himself to a rapprochement with France and maintained that sending a mission was unwise and indefensible. Distrusting the wiles of French diplomacy, he expected that a treaty, full of blandishment, would "paralise our energies." Only by opposing France in an open war was there a possibility of diminishing her inordinate power and curbing her ambitions. Yet the chance of Americans waging such a war was slight, as "building great ships and spending millions is not to our Dutch taste." [43]

Prior to the state election in the spring of 1799, Ames saw "clouds and thick darkness in our horizon" as the Republicans pursued "their

41. Ames to Dwight, Boston, Feb. 27, 1799, Ames, *Works of Ames*, I, 252-53; Alexander Hamilton to James McHenry, N.Y., June 27, 1799, Hamilton Papers, Special Collections, Columbia Univ.

42. Ames to John Worthington, Dedham, Mar. 1, 1799, Gratz Collection, Hist. Soc. of Pa.; Ames to Dwight, Feb. 27, 1799, Ames, *Works of Ames*, I, 253.

43. Ames to Timothy Pickering, Dedham, Mar. 12, Oct. 19, 1799, Ames, *Works of Ames*, I, 253, 257-58; George Cabot to Gov. Trumbull, Brookline, Sept. 20, 1799, Dreer Collection, Hist. Soc. of Pa.; Ames to Rufus King, Dedham, June 12, 1799, Rufus King Papers, XLI, N.-Y. Hist. Soc.

work of sedition and electioneering and seemed sure of getting the State Gov'ts into their hands to play them like batteries on the U.S. Gov't." Spurred by evidence that the President's party was dispirited and divided, they seized the opportunity to hammer at the weaknesses of the Federalist position. This onslaught simply emphasized the need, which Ames discerned, for a forceful defense of Federalism in the press. In his opinion "the sword of public opinion" could be an invaluable weapon for the present government's use. Separated as he was from the national scene, he endeavored to bolster his party's forces by writing two articles which appeared successively in the *Boston Gazette* during April 1799.[44] At intervals in the years that followed, Fisher Ames submitted various essays for the use of Boston newspapers.

He wrote the articles entitled "Laocoon" in brisk, scholarly language, revealing, as he invariably did, his knowledge of governments and important figures of antiquity. Above all, he revealed his own oppressive and persistent fear that American republican government would ultimately be strangled. Ames attempted to reach readers who had public concern but were passive, as well as those "trimming" Federalists whose loyalty was equivocal. He observed that too often the Federalists were exhausted by exertion and that "their spirit, after flaming brightly, soon sleeps in its embers; but the jacobins, like salamanders can breathe only fire." In consistently referring to the opponents of Federalism as "jacobins," Fisher Ames made perfectly clear that this group, which was under French influence, included all of those who opposed the contemporary government. He held that parties inevitably existed in free governments, but that it was necessary "to sustain an everlasting conflict with faction; a foe destined to be the companion of liberty, and, at last, its assassin." [45]

The writer vigorously defended John Adams and his principles of government. His critics, Ames noted, were victims of a mania, "hatred of the government," and their influence was felt at "every threshing-floor, every husking, every party at work on a houseframe or raising a building," even at funerals. Ames pointed out that the opposition everywhere behaved "more like an armed force beating up for recruits, than a sect of political disputants." [46] Actual resistance to laws, he foresaw, would probably result if their candidates were elected in New England. There was no question in his mind but that "the jacobins" had created elaborate machinery to seize control in the "violent crisis"

44. Ames to King, June 12, 1799, King Papers, XLI, N.-Y. Hist. Soc.; "Laocoon, No. I," Ames, *Works of Ames*, II, 115.
45. "Laocoon, No. I," Ames, *Works of Ames*, II, 110-12.
46. *Ibid.*, 115.

which was developing. He was determined to guard the "Hesperian fruit" of republican liberty, to reveal the imminent perils, and to prevent the triumph of Federalist opponents at the polls. As was so often true of Ames's writings, the "Laocoon" articles had both vivid and violent passages. The Dedham essayist genuinely believed that the government was in jeopardy, but he also thought that the public could be awakened only by dramatizing the dangers. To him it was "proper to paint the probable evils strongly," even though there was usually hope that they might be averted.[47]

The victory of the incumbent, Governor Increase Sumner, over the Republican candidate, General William Heath, was heartening to Federalists. With a staunch party member in the governor's chair and a General Court which had not gone over to the enemy, "old Masstts stands firm," Ames exulted. Nevertheless, he, together with other extreme Federalists, was apprehensive that the Republicans would win in the next year's election, thereby sweeping Thomas Jefferson into the presidency. In John Adams's foreign policy he saw the seeds of discord, both within and without his party. It seemed probable to him that Great Britain's aggravation over American diplomacy would result in war, that union within the United States would be weakened, and finally that commercial capital in the North would "melt away" to the relief of "Jefferson and other patriots." He could not be optimistic about the state of affairs. "Our system never could stand alone, and scarcely with holding up, and if the men who hold the property and respect the principles that will protect it, are compelled to even a passive silence ... the Jacobins will ... get possession of the public authority."[48]

Ames's annoyance with Adams mounted as he watched his party being torn apart. "Shallow duplicity that plays the fool in attempting to play cunning—levity that tampers with a nation's fate, false pride that sees rivals in ministers ... with so much sense you wonder the man is so weak—with such weakness you wonder he is so honest." However much he criticized Adams, Fisher Ames still had faith that he would reconsider his acts and allow his "real virtue and discernment" to prevail. Even if he were temporarily won over to the Republican view, his principles as well as his traits of character would soon make him "intractable" to the opposing party. He might be induced to return to

47. "Laocoon, No. II," *ibid.*, 128; Ames to Timothy Pickering, Dedham, Nov. 5, 1799, *ibid.*, I, 261.

48. Ames to King, June 12, 1799, Rufus King Papers, XLI, N.-Y. Hist. Soc.; Ames to Pickering, Nov. 5, 1799, Ames, *Works of Ames*, I, 261-63; Sumner received 24,073 votes; William Heath 7709 votes. Abstract of Votes, Mass. Archives, Office of the Secretary of the Commonwealth, State House.

the Federalists; therefore for the present "he must be spared, and not driven quite over to the foe." [49] Subsequently Ames, anxious to avoid a war with Great Britain, decided that Adams need not be completely protected from party opposition. He suggested that for the benefit of other nations, ardent Federalists in the House of Representatives should disclose their resistance to the President's foreign policy.

Ames was not alone in viewing national affairs with considerable pessimism. Confronted with a change in the tide of popular support and a loss of control over the executive, the extreme Federalists alternately heaped coals on Adams and the Republicans. None overlooked the fact that 1800 would be a crucial election year. With Federalist strength in the South very slim at best and the party "palsied," as Theodore Sedgwick aptly expressed it, it would prove difficult to avoid political defeat. Among the New England Federalist leaders, Pickering was so affronted by the President's moves that he insisted Adams could reunite the party only by publicly announcing his retirement from office. Cabot, obviously searching for a glimmer of light in the darkness, proclaimed that he still had faith in the future destiny of the nation. "If we are to have an inundation of democratic evil, we shall have better dikes afterwards," he maintained.[50]

Secretary of the Treasury Oliver Wolcott, Jr., who kept Ames informed by letter of the administration's course, analyzed party prospects and in so doing reflected growing dismay. Ames agreed wholeheartedly with Wolcott's evaluation, responding with his own appraisal of the dilemma in which the nation found itself. "Your observations," he wrote, "furnish the materials for a book which I have no fancy to write, as the reader would consign it to ... the hangman to burn." The essential difficulty, according to Ames, lay in the fact that the government was republican and public opinion, in contrast, basically democratic. Such a disparity could not continue, he declared; the two forces had to be equalized. Even that part of the public which read and thought was amenable to "false notions of liberty," and public opinion had been too strongly influenced by Virginia leaders who typically were susceptible to "silly principles." Jefferson, in Ames's view, had

49. Ames to Dwight, Oct. 20, 1799, Fisher Ames Papers, Dedham Hist. Soc.; Ames to Pickering, Dedham, Oct. 19, Nov. 5, 1799, Ames, *Works of Ames,* I, 258, 261.

50. Ames to Pickering, Dedham, Nov. 23, 1799, Ames, *Works of Ames,* I, 272; Theodore Sedgwick to Rufus King, Phila., Dec. 12, 1799, King, ed., *Life of King,* III, 154; Timothy Pickering to George Cabot, Trenton, Oct. 22, 1799, Cabot to Pickering, Brookline, Oct. 31, 1799, Oliver Wolcott to Cabot, Phila., Nov. 4, 1799, Lodge, ed., *Letters of Cabot,* 248-49, 257; Robert Troup to King, Nov. 6, 1799, King, ed., *Life of King,* III, 142; Cabot to Timothy Pickering, Brookline, Dec. 16, 1799, Gibbs, *Memoirs,* II, 312.

adhered to these principles when he "wrote some such stuff about the will of majorities, as a New Englander would lose his rank among men of sense to avow." A feeble government, plagued by "organized factions," should take the steps necessary to defend itself against an armed clash. Ames concluded, "On the whole the prospect is dismal, and perhaps human wisdom is too short-sighted to provide resources against danger." [51]

In the midst of party turmoil, news came from Mt. Vernon in December 1799 that Washington was dead. To the Federalists this event signified the loss of a powerful bastion against the rising army of Republicans. The nation expressed its sorrow by a prolonged period of mourning in which numerous civic tributes to his memory were offered. Federalists, endeavoring to capitalize on his death, claimed Washington as the true head of their party, and the Boston leaders immediately proposed that their chief spokesman, Fisher Ames, should have the honor of giving a commemorative oration. Political feeling and local pride, however, influenced the decision to choose Judge George R. Minot of Boston, whose Federalism was more moderate than that of Ames. "We had no idea of going to Dedham, and giving the inhabitants a triumph in saying, that we were indebted to them for an orator," commented a participant in the Boston town meeting. The General Court, still strongly Federalist, soon invited Ames to give an oration before both houses of the legislature. Initially he was quite reluctant to interrupt the legal work in which he was engaged at the time. Convinced that he would disappoint his friends who expected an inspired performance, he remarked, "I am intriguing to parry this malicious blow of the fates." [52] At last he accepted the invitation, won over by the persistence of his political acquaintances.

Old South Meeting House was "stuffed and packed like apples in a basket" on February 8 as an audience of General Court members, Boston citizens, and their wives, crowded into the hall to hear Ames give an oration once more. Clashing cymbals and a choir made the building resound with music. After Dr. Thacher's prayer restored a contem-

---

51. Oliver Wolcott to Ames, Phila., Dec. 29, 1799, Ames to Wolcott, Dedham, Jan. 12, 1800, Gibbs, *Memoirs*, II, 313-32.

52. Freeman, *Washington*, VII, 625; *Columbian Centinel* (Boston), Jan. 1, 11, 18, 1800; A. M. Walters to William S. Shaw, [Boston], Jan. 2, 1800, J. B. Felt, *Memorials of William Smith Shaw* (Boston, 1852), 87-88; Stephen Higginson to Timothy Pickering, Boston, Jan. 12, 1800, Pickering Papers, XXVI, Mass. Hist. Soc. Higginson remarked that Minot's speech was "admired by most, though it must wound One at least." *Independent Chronicle* (Boston), Jan. 2, 13, 1800; Ames to Dwight, Boston, Jan. 6, 1800, Ames, *Works of Ames*, I, 273; George Cabot to Oliver Wolcott, Brookline, Jan. 16, 1800, Gibbs, *Memoirs*, II, 321; *Columbian Centinel* (Boston), Jan. 22, 1800.

plative mood, the speaker held forth for an hour to the pleasure of the Federalists, who "unboundedly applauded" his efforts. Ames was confronted with a difficult task. Whatever he might say about Washington, already deified in the minds of many, would be inadequate. "To interest people after their impressions had all grown flat, and to play tricks with pathos, when they had buried their grief was not to be done," he later commented.[53] Wisely he avoided excessive eulogy of the nation's hero; unwisely he permitted himself to become extremely partisan, incorporating his own political outlook in his oration and castigating the Republicans.

Washington, as Ames delineated the General, was "firm in adversity, cool in action, undaunted," a man of patriotic devotion whose talent for sound leadership had been sustaining during crucial years. He shared with the nation in "the singular glory of having conducted a civil war with mildness, and a revolution with order." To Ames, Washington's transcendent achievement had not been his military leadership, which had excited "the wonder of mankind," but his statesmanship. Great generals had frequently arisen in times of crisis, riding the whirlwind to "direct the storm." Far more rare in history was a chief magistrate of Washington's stature. When "the peace of America hung by a thread, and factions were already sharpening their weapons to cut it," it was Washington who had had "commanding power over the popular passions." Even though he had twice rescued the nation, first in war and then in the precarious years of the Confederation, Washington had been subjected to vituperative attacks while President. The French and their sympathizers within the United States constantly were striving to overturn the government by fomenting internal rebellion or usurping the powers of government. By issuing the neutrality proclamation Washington "arrested the intrigues of France and the passions of his countrymen, on the very edge of the precipice of war." [54] Like Leonidas at Thermopylae, he had defended a nation's independence.

To many who heard the oration, the performance was "very brilliant"; and as the *Independent Chronicle* noted, "by the silence and attention with which it was received, it appeared to make a favorable impression upon the audience." Men of Federalist persuasion were jubi-

53. Thomas Dwight to Hannah Dwight, Boston, Feb. 7, 9, 1800, Dwight-Howard Papers, Mass. Hist. Soc. Dwight indicated that Mrs. Ames was unable to attend the oration. Eliza Southgate to Octavia Southgate, Boston, Feb. 7, 1800, *A Girl's Life Eighty Years Ago, Selections from the Letters of Eliza Southgate Bowne* (N.Y., 1888), 22; *Columbian Centinel* (Boston), Feb. 12, 1800; *Independent Chronicle* (Boston), Feb. 10, 1800; Ames to J. W. Fenno, Dedham, Feb. (n.d.), 1800, Ames, *Works of Ames*, I, 276.
54. "Eulogy on Washington," Ames, *Works of Ames*, II, 73-76, 84-85.

lant that Ames had struck a blow at the Jacobins and had been "as severe upon French politicks as our language would admit him to be." [55] When the Dedham Federalist sent Colonel Pickering printed copies of the eulogy, the Secretary of State acknowledged the difficulties of Ames's task, commending him for having "justly sought the proofs of excellence in the assemblage of his [Washington's] virtues." Pickering, always rather hostile in his evaluation of the former President, could not refrain from observing that there were, after all, no "brilliant acts" in Washington's life on which an orator could expatiate to the delight of his audience.[56]

Federalists in general could not consider the oration critically because of their enthusiasm for the message it contained. It was a speech which in lucidity of style and in careful organization displayed Ames's skill as writer and orator. But the eulogist failed to present a penetrating analysis of Washington's character. Instead of revealing a man whom he himself had known in the formative years of the government, Ames followed convention and spoke in impersonal generalities. His own sense of crisis in government and party was so overpowering that Washington came forth from the oration the personification not only of national virtue and honor but, more important, of Federalism.

Fisher Ames's former political rival, Benjamin Austin, severely criticized the eulogy in a series of articles printed in the *Independent Chronicle* under the pseudonym of "Old South." Derisively he asserted that the orator had been indifferent to those traits which had endeared Washington to all who had "the feeling of '75" and further had deprecated his military achievements. Austin asked rhetorically whether "such a pointed sarcasm" could actually be presented before the members of the General Court.[57] The accusations of "Old South" against Ames, whom he identified as "a practitioner of law," led to a spirited newspaper controversy in which "New South" in turn maintained that Austin "garbled and mutilated" parts of the speech, altering the meaning of Ames's statements.[58]

Political interest remained at a high pitch with the approach of the

55. *Independent Chronicle* (Boston), Feb. 10, 1800; Dwight to Hannah Dwight, Feb. 9, 1800, Dwight-Howard Papers, Mass. Hist. Soc.

56. Timothy Pickering to Ames, Phila., Mar. 17, 1800, Pickering Papers, XIII, Mass. Hist. Soc. Regarding his speech, Ames commented, "My oration was composed in the midst of the hurry of a law court." Ames to Pickering, Dedham, Feb. 22, 1800, *ibid.*, XXVI. The Rev. William Bentley, a Salem Republican, criticized the speech in part because "it is not in an equal style nor is all its imagery happy," *The Diary of William Bentley, D.D.*, 4 vols. (Salem, 1905-14), II, 330.

57. "Old South," *Independent Chronicle* (Boston), Mar. 10, 1800.

58. "New South," *Independent Chronicle* (Boston), Mar. 13, 17, 1800; "A Few Candid Remarks on New South," *ibid.*, Apr. 7, 1800.

state election in the spring of 1800. At the time of his oration on Washington, Ames unexpectedly became the center of political speculation
when his name was proposed in the Dedham *Columbian Minerva* as a
candidate for the governorship. It was embarrassing as he had always
been on friendly terms with Caleb Strong, the nominee of the Federalist party caucus. In Ames's opinion the party's candidate was a person
of great worth who genuinely merited the post, and he could only
interpret the recent suggestion of his own name as an attempt of the
Republicans "to disaffect the people" from Strong.[59]

Intense electioneering on behalf of Elbridge Gerry, now an avowed
Republican, seriously threatened Federalist control of the governorship
and the General Court. This activity underscored Ames's warning of
the previous autumn that "the *rabies canina* of Jacobinism has gradually spread, of late years, from the cities, where it was confined to docks
and mob, to the country." [60] If the Republicans prevailed in the General Court, Massachusetts might well have a Republican slate of electors
in the coming presidential election. The danger led Ames to exhort his
friends to arouse the public. "*All* the strength of the upper counties
must be called out en masse," he urged. "We are poor miserable sin-
ners, you know, in Norfolk and there is no health in us. . . . Do you try
to save the Commonwealth." [61]

The tension in Dedham itself was reflected in a public encounter between Fisher and Nathaniel Ames. Passing along the street, the retired
congressman discovered Dr. Ames haranguing a group of excited
townspeople in his usual colorful and vituperative language. Nathaniel
berated the government as a "hotch potch an usurpation, a tyranny, a
monster" that should be vehemently resisted. Before leaving the gathering, Fisher Ames, with good humor and determination, attempted to
counteract Nathaniel's words by defending the government under the
Federalists. Inwardly he felt that his brother had "a perfect *furor politi-
cus,*" but that he was far, far less "malignant at heart" than many Jacobins running for office.[62]

On going out of his house in the evening of the same day, Squire
Ames found Nathaniel again "spouting" to a large group in the street.
When Fisher Ames replied a second time to the Doctor's political com-

59. Dedham *Columbian Minerva* quoted in *Columbian Centinel* (Boston), Feb.
8, 1800; Ames to Dwight, Boston, Mar. 4, 1800, Fisher Ames Papers, Dedham Hist.
Soc.; Ames to Gore, Boston, Mar. 5, 1800, Ames, Works of Ames, I, 277-78. Ames
remarked that some Bostonians objected to Caleb Strong since he "lives a hundred
miles from salt water" and because his wife "wears blue stockings." *Columbian
Centinel* (Boston), Feb. 19, 22, 1800; Morse, *Federalist Party*, 178.
60. Ames to Gore [Dedham], Nov. 10, 1799, Ames, *Works of Ames*, I, 265.
61. Ames to Dwight, Mar. 4, 1800, Fisher Ames Papers, Dedham Hist. Soc.
62. Ames to Dwight, Apr. 17, 1800, *ibid.*

plaints, he felt that Republican partisans in the audience readily perceived that Nathaniel had not done their case justice. During the two public exchanges, there was no sign of disagreement between these apostles of opposing parties except on the political level. There were repercussions of the meetings, however, for after breakfast the following morning Fisher Ames twice fainted and was forced to remain on his back for several hours to avoid a recurrence of the attack. Even so, he did not attribute his condition to the political struggle of the previous day.[63]

The weak victory of the Massachusetts Federalists in the state election of 1800 enabled the party to keep the governorship, even though tenuously, and to continue its majority in the General Court. Such a balance in the Court virtually guaranteed the choice of Federalist electors in the November presidential contest.[64] Uppermost in the minds of party adherents within the state, as in the minds of Federalists everywhere, was the need to keep the Republicans from winning the presidency and control of Congress. Yet the extreme Federalists had either to swallow their intense resentment of Adams and back him for re-election or else risk further party dissension if they deposed him as a candidate. Despite their aversion to returning the President to office, they were confronted with the fact that many rank-and-file members and moderates within the party were his loyal supporters.

Early in the campaign Ames assumed that Adams would be "supported by all the Feds," but renewed political maneuvering on the part of Alexander Hamilton altered the picture. In the state election in New York, the Republicans had achieved a decisive legislative victory, increasing Hamilton's concern for his party. He now revived the plan of 1796 to have a presidential ticket which included John Adams and Pinckney, this time Charles C. Pinckney. His hope was that the political tide would sweep Pinckney, rather than Adams, into the presidency. Through the instrumentality of Theodore Sedgwick, the former Secretary of the Treasury influenced Federalist congressmen in Philadelphia to agree in caucus to support both Adams and Pinckney equally. At the same time Hamilton expected South Carolina Federalist electors to withhold sufficient votes from the President to ensure a victory for

63. *Ibid.* Nathaniel Ames merely commented about the election, "Votes for Govr. Gerry, most here and most towns round Boston." Entry of Apr. 7, 1800, Calder, ed., "Diary of Dr. Nathaniel Ames," *Dedham Hist. Register*, 10 (1899), 65; Stephen Higginson to Timothy Pickering, Boston, Apr. 16, 1800, Pickering Papers, XXVI, Mass. Hist. Soc.

64. Caleb Strong polled 19,630 votes, 100 more than the majority necessary for a choice, while Elbridge Gerry polled 16,050 votes; Abstract of Votes, Mass. Archives, Office of the Secretary of the Commonwealth, State House; Morse, *Federalist Party*, 178-80.

Pinckney. When rumors reached Ames that Adams was currently wooing the Republicans, the Dedham Federalist observed, "Never was there a more singular and mysterious state of parties. The plot of an old Spanish play is not more complicated with underplot. I scarcely trust myself with the attempt to unfold it." [65]

In the late spring Ames made a trip to Hartford, where he consulted with several important Connecticut Federalists, among them Uriah Tracy, regarding an appropriate course of action. His presence in Hartford at a time when the Connecticut leaders were meeting together may have been as accidental as a friend of Oliver Wolcott suggested, but his trips to this community were at best infrequent. The conversations he had there reinforced his conviction that loyalty to Adams might cause electors in Massachusetts to favor him and prevent the "unanimous vote for Adams and Gen. Pinckney." Only in joint support of the party's candidates could Ames and his circle of political friends see a chance of continuing Federalist control of the national government. They were willing to accept the President's candidacy for reasons of political expediency. Ames believed at the time that Pinckney's and Jefferson's chances of winning the presidency were actually better than Adams's, and that therefore, the South Carolinian deserved the party's support "at the risk, which every one I converse with suggests, of excluding Mr. A." But he regarded any public declarations against Adams as unwise, foreseeing a complete split in the body of Federalist voters if the President were rejected by his party. He, as well as Cabot, had long been aware of Adams's foibles and serious shortcomings; nevertheless, he advised that "instead of analyzing the measures of the man . . . you must sound the tocsin about Jefferson." By publicizing "the dreadful evils to be apprehended from a Jacobin President," the electorate might be swayed.[66]

There was little assurance during the summer and fall of 1800 that the plans of the high Federalists "to save the declining cause" in Massachusetts could be carried out.[67] Adams and his followers resented the scheme to equalize votes for the President and Pinckney. The extreme

65. Ames to Gore, Boston, Mar. 5, 1800, Ames, *Works of Ames*, I, 278; Ames to King, Boston, July 15, 1800, Rufus King Papers, XXXI, N.-Y. Hist. Soc.; Miller, *Hamilton*, 513-16.
66. Ames to Chauncey Goodrich, Dedham, June 12, 1800, Ames to Oliver Wolcott, Dedham, June 12, 1800, Richard Stockton to Oliver Wolcott, Princeton, June 27, 1800, Gibbs, *Memoirs*, II, 366-68, 374-75. In his letter to Goodrich Ames stated, "I scorn, as much as my friends do, duplicity, or timidity in politics; yet, while I avow my opinions and expectations as much as any enquirer has a right to know them, I think myself bound to exercise that discreet reserve [without which] we might divide the votes, and mar the success of good measures."
67. George Cabot to Oliver Wolcott, Brookline, June 14, 1800, *ibid.*, 370.

group did not alter its course but endeavored to counter the pro-Adams faction, ensure the choice of electors favoring both men, and prevent the Republicans from making gains among the voters. As Ames explained to Federalist leaders outside of the state, "due care will be taken to get men of sound, independent patriotism for electors"; yet he acknowledged the possibility that they would support Adams but not vote equally for the candidates, according to the agreement. In spite of the cautions exercised by Ames and his colleagues not to strain party bonds, they were frequently accused of dissimulation with respect to their professed support of Adams. Under the pseudonym of "Detector," a writer in the *Independent Chronicle* gleefully charged Representative Robert Goodloe Harper of South Carolina with letting "the cat out of the bag" that the "truly Anti-Federal party" wanted General Pinckney to win more electoral votes than Adams.[68]

In the bitterness of the intra-party feud, the political plan of the high Federalists caused the President to retaliate and dismiss from his cabinet Secretaries Pickering and McHenry. He had become convinced that these men were loyal to Hamilton as leader of the party, rather than to him. According to Christopher Gore, "Pickering, Hamilton and Higginson he seems to hate without any modification. Cabot and Ames are not behind in his estimation ... altho' his hatred is not so extreme against them." [69]

John Adams now referred to the arch Federalists of Massachusetts as the Essex Junto, a term of opprobrium often used by the Republicans. This term, a familiar one in Massachusetts politics, had vague origins in the pre-Revolutionary struggle against the royal governors. More recently it had been applied by John Hancock to a group of similar-thinking conservative political leaders, mostly from Essex County, whose strong influence had greatly shaped affairs within the state. In the last years of the eighteenth century the Essex Junto, though amorphous, took shape in the public mind as an organization of the most conservative Federalists. The title came into wide usage, being essentially an epithet antithetical to *Jacobin.* Among those who supposedly were members of the Junto were Fisher Ames, George Cabot, Timothy Pickering, Stephen Higginson, Theophilus Parsons, John Lowell, Jr., Benjamin Goodhue, and Josiah Quincy.[70]

68. Ames to Goodrich, June 12, 1800, *ibid.,* 367; Ames to Rufus King, n. pl., Sept. 24, 1800, King, ed., *Life of King,* III, 304; *Independent Chronicle* (Boston), May 29, 1800.
69. Christopher Gore to Rufus King, Boston, May 5, 1800, King, ed., *Life of King,* III, 232.
70. Timothy Pickering to G. H. Rose, Washington, Mar. 22, 1808, Pickering Papers, XIV, Mass. Hist. Soc.; Henry Adams, *History of the United States of*

The fever of the election continued to rise. Federalist representatives in the General Court defeated a resolution to retain the old district method of choosing electors and by their action prevented any electoral votes from being given to Jefferson. Using its influence, the so-called Junto committed the party members in the Court to support both Federalist candidates; yet it was not altogether certain whether these legislators would adhere to such a plan, as "it seems to be expected that the ferment of the people [will] awe the Genl. Court in Nov. next to choose Electors who will vote for Mr A and *throw away* the votes for the other candidate." [71]

Disquieting information regarding political affairs in New England led General Hamilton to make a trip through Connecticut, Rhode Island, and Massachusetts, ostensibly to review troops from regiments being disbanded. Politics, however, took precedence over military matters. Passing through Dedham on June 24, he very likely stopped to see Fisher Ames, who later commented, "Gen H. came this way and spoke in most companies without reserve.... he is the most frank of men." In contrast, Nathaniel noted the visit in his diary, "A. Hamilton, the high Adulterer run after a tiptoe thro' Dedham." [72] The conclusions the former Secretary drew from his conversations with Massachusetts Federalists did not put him in a sanguine frame of mind and led him to the politically fatal decision to reveal publicly "the facts which denote unfitness in Mr. Adams." [73]

When word reached Fisher Ames that Hamilton was determined to

America, 9 vols. (N.Y., 1891-98), I, 88-89; Miller, *Federalist Era*, 261-62; Charles R. Brown, *The Northern Confederacy According to the Plans of the "Essex Junto," 1796-1814* (Princeton, 1915), 7-10; David H. Fischer, "The Myth of the Essex Junto," *Wm. and Mary Qtly.*, 3d Ser., 21 (1964), 195, 203, 221, 226. Typical newspaper attacks on the Junto are in the *Independent Chronicle* (Boston), May 8, 12, Aug. 25, 1800. There is a long defense of the high Federalists with biographical sketches of leading individuals in the *Columbian Centinel* (Boston), July 2, 16, 1800. Harrison G. Otis, Nathan Dane, Samuel Dexter, although sometimes listed as members of the Junto, were moderate Federalists and Adams's supporters in the election of 1800.
71. Ames to King, July 15, 1800, Rufus King Papers, XXXI, N.-Y. Hist. Soc.; John Rutledge to Alexander Hamilton, July 17, 1800, Hamilton Papers, LXXVIII, Lib. Cong. Rutledge reported that Dexter, Otis, Cushing, and Gerry were attempting to have Pinckney dropped from the Federalist ticket but that they would be "outwitted by the Gov., Messrs. Ames, Sedgwick, Cabot, Goodhue and their friends." Ames to King, Aug. 19, 26, 1800, King, ed., *Life of King*, III, 295-97.
72. Ames to King, July 15, 1800, Rufus King Papers, XXXI, N.-Y. Hist. Soc.; R. Troup to King, N.Y., Aug. 9, 1800, King, ed., *Life of King*, III, 290; Mitchell, *Alexander Hamilton*, II, 470; entry of June 24, 1800, Calder, ed., "Diary of Dr. Nathaniel Ames," *Dedham Hist. Register*, 10 (1899), 80.
73. Alexander Hamilton to Oliver Wolcott, N.Y., July 1, 1800, Gibbs, *Memoirs*, II, 376.

publish a tract exposing the President, he hastily wrote urging the General to avoid an open party battle. The Massachusetts Federalist could see no way to prevent Mr. Jefferson's election. "The question is not," he said, "how we shall fight, but how we and all federalists shall fall, that we may fall, like Antaeus, the stronger for our fall." [74] Hamilton could not be dissuaded from his decision, and the critical essay actually appeared. Subsequently, Ames in writing to Hamilton voiced his negative reaction to the publication of the essay. Commenting on the Federalist position after the election, Fisher Ames analyzed the effect of the General's pamphlet, "though I think it one of your best written performances, there existed more unlucky momentary causes to make it unacceptable to federal men, than anything you ever wrote." Friends of Mr. Adams regarded it as "insidious, unfair, and deeply, rancorously hostile." [75]

Despite the frantic attempts of some Federalists to prevent disaster, contention finally weakened the party and helped to bring on a national defeat. Federalism, however, continued to predominate within the state of Massachusetts, even though its strength was much reduced. In mid-November 1800, Ames attended a meeting of the General Court where electors known to be committed to the Philadelphia agreement were chosen. These men cast their votes equally for Adams and Pinckney on December 3. The outcome of the congressional election was uncertain initially, but it later became clear that Federalists had won eight of the fourteen seats to which the state was entitled in the House of Representatives.[76]

The presidential electors in other New England states, with the exception of Rhode Island, equalized their votes between Pinckney and John Adams. But New York was utterly lost to the Federalists when its electoral college supported Jefferson and Burr. Another pivotal state, Pennsylvania, divided its presidential votes between Federalist and Re-

74. Ames to Hamilton, Dedham, Aug. 26, 1800, Hamilton Papers, LXXVIII, Lib. Cong.; George Cabot to Hamilton, Brookline, Aug. 21, 1800, Lodge, ed., *Letters of Cabot*, 286. Cabot indicated that he and Ames agreed that Hamilton's move was an unwise one.
75. *Letter from Alexander Hamilton, Concerning the Public Conduct and Character of John Adams, Esq., President of the United States* (N.Y., 1800); Ames to Hamilton, n.d., Ames, *Works of Ames*, I, 284-85. Cabot wrote to Hamilton after the election that "some very worthy and sensible men say you have exhibited the same *vanity* in your book which you charge as a dangerous quality and great weakness in Mr. Adams"; George Cabot to Hamilton, Brookline, Nov. 29, 1800, Lodge, ed., *Letters of Cabot*, 300.
76. Benjamin Goodhue to Hamilton [Salem], Nov. 15, 1800, Hamilton Papers, LXXVIII, Lib. Cong. Ames as a member of the Governor's Council since 1798 had an excellent opportunity to keep in touch with developments in the General Court.

publican candidates.[77] As Ames had foreseen early in the campaign, it was South Carolina whose votes were decisive. He believed that if the party won in South Carolina, enough votes might be garnered to bring about a national victory. Through his contacts with John Rutledge, Jr., he had attempted to bolster the southern Federalists and to build a political alliance between Massachusetts and South Carolina. When electors in South Carolina voted for Jefferson and Burr, the Republican triumph was assured, and Ames's hopes for cooperation between the two states came to nothing.[78]

The election plunged Republicans into the presidency and vice-presidency, but which office would be filled by Jefferson and which by Burr remained uncertain since each candidate had received seventy-three electoral votes. In accordance with the Constitution, the House of Representatives was expected to choose between the two. The stalemate caused Federalists to hope that they could still wield enough power to deprive Jefferson of the presidency. Burr might be won over by throwing Federalist support to him. Fisher Ames, on being informed of developments, dismissed as "bravado" any attempt to block Jefferson's accession to the presidency. Before the question was decided in Congress, he wavered between Jefferson and Burr, trying to decide which would be the lesser of two evils. To the Speaker of the House, Theodore Sedgwick, he confessed that he fluctuated on the issue and was "not ripe for a decision between the two Jacobin chiefs." Jefferson had proven himself easily deceived and unworthy of the name of statesman; yet Burr was ambitious and untrustworthy. Nevertheless, for several weeks Ames favored the New York politician, believing that he

77. Cunningham, *Jeffersonian Republicans*, 229-31; Dauer, *Adams Federalists*, 257; *Columbian Centinel* (Boston), May 21, June 25, Nov. 5, Dec. 24, 1800; Ames to King, n.p., Sept. 24, 1800, Rufus King Papers, XXXI, N.-Y. Hist. Soc.; Ames to Theodore Sedgwick, Dedham, Dec. 1, 1800, Sedgwick Papers, Vol. D, Mass. Hist. Soc.; James Madison to James Monroe [Nov. 10, 1800], Madison to Thomas Jefferson, Orange, Dec. 20, 1800, Jan. 10, 1801, Madison Papers, XXI, XXII, Lib. Cong.; J. B. Varnum to William Eustis, Washington, Nov. 21, 1800, William Eustis Papers, Lib. Cong.; Theodore Sedgwick to Caleb Strong, Washington, Dec. 16, 1800, Caleb Strong Papers, Forbes Library, Northampton, Mass.

78. Ames to Dwight, Aug. 15, 1800, Ames to Gore, n.p., Dec. 29, 1800, Ames, *Works of Ames*, I, 279, 287; Ames to King, Sept. 24, 1800, Rufus King Papers, XXXI, N.-Y. Hist. Soc.; Ames to John Rutledge, Jr., Dedham, Oct. 16, Dec. 15, 1800, George Cabot to John Rutledge, Jr., Brookline, Oct. 22, 1800, John Rutledge Papers, Box 1, Southern Historical Collection, University of North Carolina, Chapel Hill, N.C. Ames, in his letter of Dec. 15, expressed his conviction that even though Federalist strength had been "impaired and dissipated" it might still be revived. He commented, "If for four years we can prevent an explosion by a Jacobin rebellion and keep the true friends of the country vigilant and firm we may do well afterwards." Cunningham, *Jeffersonian Republicans*, 231-38; Rogers, *Evolution of a Federalist*, 343-44, 348-52.

might accept Federalist support on terms favorable to the party. In the final analysis, Fisher Ames's "doubts and perplexities" led him to conclude that only Federalists "on the spot" in the national capital were qualified to make the wisest choice. After a series of ballots, representatives in the House decided the issue on February 18, 1801, when Jefferson was finally elected president, leaving the vice-presidency to Burr.[79]

Ames looked upon domination by the Republicans with genuine dread. Soon after the election he wrote, "While evils are in prospect, it is right to aggravate their magnitude and our apprehensions; after they are arrived to make the best of them. Bad is the best." [80]

79. Ames to Dwight, Dedham, Jan. 1, 1801, Ames to Gore, Dec. 29, 1800, Ames, *Works of Ames*, I, 288-90; Ames to Theodore Sedgwick, Dedham, Dec. 31, 1800, Jan. 7, 23, 26, 1801, Sedgwick Papers, Vol. D, Mass. Hist. Soc. Nathaniel Ames remarked, "Here ends the 18th Century. The 19th begins with a fine clear morning wind at S.W.; and the political horizon affords as fine a prospect under Jefferson's administration . . . with the irresistible propagation of the Rights of Man"; entry of Dec. 31, 1800, Calder, ed., "Diary of Dr. Nathaniel Ames," *Dedham Hist. Register*, 11 (1900), 17; Miller, *Hamilton*, 524-25; Cunningham, *Jeffersonian Republicans*, 239-41.

80. Ames to Gore, Dec. 29, 1800, Ames, *Works of Ames*, I, 286.

Chapter XVI

Fisher Ames: Party Symbol

In the final years of his life, Fisher Ames lived in the political wake of the election of 1800. Politics were inescapable both on a national and local level. Even Dedham's old First Church became the center of a dispute, which seems to have had subtle political rather than merely doctrinal origins.

As an active member of the Congregational church, Ames took an interest in the choice of a new minister to succeed his elderly friend, the Reverend Jason Haven. After forty-six years in his pastorate, Mr. Haven was to retire, much to the relief of Dr. Nathaniel Ames and others, who often regarded his sermons as tiresome and vindictive. The controversy which developed in 1802 split the parish and resulted in the withdrawal of a segment of the congregation. Ostensibly, the parishioners disagreed over the stipulations in the contract for a new minister. Beneath the surface of the clash, however, lay fears on both sides that a minister might be appointed whose political faith would not be theirs.[1]

Under the leadership of Fisher Ames the parish decided to invite a young theologian, the Reverend Joshua Bates, to become its pastor. Ames and a number of members wanted to offer Bates the usual lifetime contract, while the opposition group, supported by Dr. Ames, wanted him only on a trial basis. In an explosive parish meeting on December 30, the two factions vehemently disagreed over the precise terms of the contract. When the document was at last approved, it gave

1. Warren, *Jacobin and Junto*, 288-89.

Joshua Bates the right to serve as minister indefinitely. Dr. Ames, infuriated by the contract and its approval, withdrew from the First Church and joined the local Episcopal church. After attending the decisive meeting, he concluded that Fisher wished "to shut me out of the meeting so as to enjoy my pew," and that "he cram'd the Priest down their throats tail foremost." [2]

Nathaniel Ames continued to simmer as he repeatedly recalled his "excommunication" from the First Church. Months after the fracas, he displayed in his diary lingering aggravation over the part his famous brother had played in the dispute. With customary subjectivity, Dr. Ames wrote about an incident which occurred when he was spreading manure on his fields. "F. Ames came and stormed at my presumption to my men, in buying dung without his leave, when I did not know he arrogated all the dung as well as religion in Dedham. After turning me out of the House of God, I expected he would allow me to grovel in dung." [3]

As might have been assumed, the Reverend Mr. Bates proved to be strongly Federalist in his political outlook, and he soon antagonized the many Republicans in his parish. But Frances and Fisher Ames maintained their membership in the First Church in Dedham for several years despite persistent conflict among those in the congregation. Ultimately, in January 1808, Ames wrote a formal letter to Joshua Bates, requesting that their connection with the Church be dissolved, as they would henceforth attend St. Paul's Episcopal Church. He assured the Reverend Mr. Bates, however, that he would "continue to cherish the sentiments of esteem and respectful attachment to which your merit as a man and a minister so justly entitle you." [4] In making this move, Fisher Ames escaped from a politically charged situation into one which proved more satisfying to him. The fact that his brother had preceded him to St. Paul's did not discourage him from joining.

The Dedham Congregational church, divided by factional problems, was a microcosm of the larger world. Ames saw this world as one

2. Diary of Nathaniel Ames, Dec. 30, 1802, Feb. 10, 1803, Nathaniel Ames Papers, Dedham Hist. Soc.; Ames to the Rev. Joshua Bates, Dedham, Apr. 26, 1802, Fisher Ames Papers, Dedham Hist. Soc.; Ames to the Rev. Joshua Bates, Dedham, Dec. 12, 1802, Gratz Collection, Hist. Soc. of Pa. Nathaniel Ames was also highly critical of the Episcopalian minister, the Rev. William Montague; entry of Dec. 20, 1804, Calder, ed., "Diary of Dr. Nathaniel Ames," *Dedham Hist. Register*, 13 (1902), 52-53; "Records of the First Parish in Dedham, New England, 1763-1807," in custody of Deacons of the First Church, Dedham Hist. Soc.

3. Diary of Nathaniel Ames, Dec. 6, 1803, Nathaniel Ames Papers, Dedham Hist. Soc.

4. Diary of Nathaniel Ames, Mar. 1805, *ibid.;* Ames to the Rev. Joshua Bates, Dedham, Jan. 21, 1808, "Memoir of Fisher Ames," *The Diocesan Register*, 243-47.

where differences and animosities were increasing, rather than subsiding. Soon after the election of 1800, he had been spurred to resume his efforts to reach the people by writing articles for the press. His continued emphasis on newspapers as a party instrument seemed logical, as he noted that the extensive and effective use of the press by the Republicans had greatly enlarged public support of them. Too often, he felt, the Federalists had ignored the efficacy of this medium. He insisted that in a nation where public opinion was "sovereign" and where contending political groups struggled to influence it, leaders of his party should actively encourage the growth of the Federalist press.[5]

Following the Federalist defeat, Ames considered his party in a dubious position, its members divided, dispirited, and susceptible to the blandishments of the new president. "Popular confidence grows like Jonah's gourd in a night," he remarked with concern. Few in the party seemed to understand that there was "danger of the utter dissolution of the federal phalanx." Unfortunately, all too many were blindly confident and trusted "in the *sinless* perfection of a democracy." By arousing the party spirit, Fisher Ames thought it might be possible "to stay the contagion of Jacobinism" and place the Federalists in a position to resume control of the government in future.[6]

Envisioning a national newspaper comparable in stature to the *London Gazette*, Ames and several of his Boston friends were willing to support the *New England Palladium*, which had the potential of becoming the outlet they had in mind for the Federalist party. In order to reach their goal, the new editor, Warren Dutton, would have to be encouraged, the paper's circulation increased, and "partizans...engaged in every quarter to press it."[7] Initially "literary help" was even more essential, and Ames had hopes that Rufus King and John Lowell, Jr., would aid the paper by contributing political essays. The Dedham

5. Ames to Timothy Pickering, Mar. 12, 1799, Ames, *Works of Ames*, I, 254; Robinson, *Jeffersonian Democracy*, 68-69.

6. Ames to Oliver Wolcott, Dedham, Mar. 18, 1801, Oliver Wolcott Papers, XVIII, Conn. Hist. Soc.; Ames to Theodore Dwight, Dedham, Mar. 19, 1801, Ames, *Works of Ames*, I, 293; Ames to Rufus King, Boston, Oct. 27, 1801, King, ed., *Life of King*, IV, 2-4. Ames took the position that "despair ought not to be confessed—still less circulated. . . . We must openly and zealously and with all our skill labor to prevent it." Cabot remarked about Ames's letter, "You will see by it that he adheres to the good old maxim of *never despairing of the Commonwealth* yet . . . his faith is not only without evidence but in fact against it." George Cabot to King, Nov. 6, 1801, *ibid.*, 12.

7. Ames to John Rutledge, Dedham, July 30, 1801, John Rutledge Papers, Southern Historical Collection, Univ. of N. C.; Ames to Wolcott, Mar. 18, 1801, Oliver Wolcott Papers, XVIII, Conn. Hist. Soc.; Robert Edson Lee, "Timothy Dwight and the Boston *Palladium*," *New Eng. Qtly.*, 25 (1962), 229-39. Lee gives President Timothy Dwight of Yale credit for establishing the *Palladium* as a Federalist organ.

Federalist also asked Oliver Wolcott, Jr., if "the mighty Trumbull" could not be enticed to take up "the club of Hercules in Satire" as he had in the past when he had written "McFingal" and other poems. Ames was willing to write briefer articles and essays, but he professed laziness in literary matters and feared that he would "set the readers yawning." [8]

If the paper was to acquire prestige, the editor would have to avoid sensational accounts as well as the "turgid bombast" so prevalent in newspapers. Ames found the numerous "accounts of murders, suicides ... or monstrous births" in the popular press appalling, and he later deplored in the columns of the *Palladium* the propensity to cater to the lowest tastes of the public. The paper he wanted to develop would have to have, in contrast, a light approach which would arouse the interest of the general reader. It would analyze public affairs, presenting ideas on important questions clearly and forthrightly, "in the manner that will confound and disarm jacobin liars." To give it appeal, cultural topics, book reviews, and agricultural subjects would all have a place in the newspaper. Thus the *Palladium* would be "well-bred," reflecting Federalist journalism at its best. "It should whip Jacobins as a gentleman would a chimney-sweeper, at arm's length, and keeping aloof from his soot." Summing up the canons of Federalist policy, Ames declared, "We must use, but honestly, and without lying, an engine that wit and good sense would make powerful and safe." [9]

Fisher Ames's attempt to develop an outstanding newspaper of national dimensions met with little response from his fellow Federalists. Even so, the *Palladium* became a leading local newspaper under its new aegis. The corps of able political writers which he had visualized as a mainstay of the enterprise did not become a reality, and much of the burden of keeping the paper supplied with political material fell on Ames himself. From time to time George Cabot sent his articles to the *Palladium*, but he lacked his friend's faith that public opinion could be won over or that the "rich and wise and good" would unite to carry on the necessary efforts. Ames was dismayed to find that the party members were so reluctant to commit themselves to the project. "They sometimes yield to, but oftener stare at my zeal," he commented, "and oftener still, laugh at my means." Unlike these individuals who readily abandoned hope for Federalism, he believed that the cause of good

8. Ames to Theodore Dwight, Mar. 19, 1801, Ames to Thomas Dwight, Dedham, Jan. 1, 1801, Ames, *Works of Ames*, I, 290, 295.

9. Ames to John Ward Fenno, Dedham, Feb. 1800, *ibid.*, 274; "Monstrous Relations in Newspapers," *Palladium* (Boston), Oct. 1801; "Hercules," Ames, *Works of Ames*, II, 406-9. Ames to Jeremiah Smith, Boston, Dec. 14, 1802, Ames to Theodore Dwight, Mar. 19, 1801, *ibid.*, I, 315, 294.

government was not irretrievably lost. If the French nobles and priests
had not run away at the outset of the Revolution, he reasoned, and
instead had exerted themselves through the press to expose "democratic
folly and villainy," the worst aspects of the upheaval in France would
have been averted.[10]

Relentlessly the spokesman of the Federalists carried on an unceasing
war against the Republicans, their ideals and aims. The numerous essays
in which he waged this war were for the most part published in the
New England Palladium and the Boston *Repertory*.[11] These essays revealed the ramifications of Ames's later political position and his gifts
as a polished writer who stood far ahead of most journalists of his
period. He wrote with characteristic clarity, drawing on his wide vo-
cabulary and extensive knowledge of Latin to choose the right, the
imaginative word in the proper place. To prove a point, he would
sometimes depict a hypothetical scene in harsh colors. Yet his articles
were tightly written, unmarred by circumlocution, one segment of
logic carefully built upon another. They had a distinctive quality unlike those of his contemporaries; they were passionate but not pompous.
Although raised to a scholarly level, Fisher Ames's essays were both
epigrammatic and quotable in the tradition of his father's more mundane almanac writings. Inevitably they disclosed his dogmatic and prejudiced belief that the nation's constitutional government could not
survive. Intrinsic to the articles was a hope that disaster could be warded
off, but the hope was obscured by melancholy prognostications.

Ames wished to attract as many readers as possible, but the audience
which he was most anxious to reach was a select one. On the supposi-
tion that intelligent men confronted with "truth and argument" could
see their error in supporting the Republicans, he consciously addressed
his essays to the educated. In his attitude toward the people as a whole,

10. Ames to Oliver Wolcott, Dedham, Dec. 2, 1802, Oliver Wolcott Papers,
XVIII, Conn. Hist. Soc.; Ames to Christopher Gore, Dec. 14, 1802, Ames, *Works
of Ames*, I, 312; Lee, "Dwight and the *Palladium*," *New Eng. Qtly.*, 25 (1962), 232.
11. The first identifiable essay of Ames printed in the *Palladium* was "Falkland,
No. I," in Feb. 1801; the last was "Monitor" in Apr. 1804. Ames's essays submitted
to the *Repertory* was printed between July 1804 and Mar. 1808. A few articles
were printed in the Boston *Gazette* and in the *Monthly Review and Boston
Anthology*. Morison, "Squire Ames and Dr. Ames," *New Eng. Qtly.*, 1 (1928),
21-23, 28-29. Elisha P. Douglass, "Fisher Ames, Spokesman For New England
Federalism," American Philosophical Society, *Proceedings*, 103 (1959), 712-13.
"Original Biographical and Critical Sketch of Fisher Ames," *Analectic Magazine*,
3 (1814), 326-29. The writer commented on Ames as an author, "He has nothing
tame, nothing languid, nothing tedious. Every sentence bears the strong stamp of
an original mind. All is impressive, animated, fascinating." *Ibid.*, 326. See also
"Review of Works of Fisher Ames," *Brownson's Quarterly Review*, 3d Ser., 2
(1854), 502-14.

he was ambivalent, for though he saw much latent good in them, he could not trust their judgment. On the one hand, he found the public full of "good sense and honest zeal"; on the other, he observed, "Our mistake is in supposing men better than they are. They are bad and act their bad character out." [12] Whatever misgivings he had about the populace in general, he never quite relinquished the belief that it was susceptible to the "correct" ideas of the reasoning, thinking segment of society.

The retired congressman chose to write on such varied topics as Republican policies, American political principles, the tyranny of Napoleonic France, similarities between Rome and France, and the comparative military capabilities of France and England. Whether he wrote about domestic issues or current affairs in Europe, there was a basic constant in his essays: the transcendent threat to the nation of Republicans allied with and dominated by revolutionary France. But his writing during this period was not wholly confined to political subjects. Had the fate of the nation not been such a consuming worry to him, he might have turned more frequently in other directions. Articles which he wrote on "The Institutions of Lycurgus," "School Books," and "American Literature" reveal his incisive literary style.[13]

In his Falkland essays, published in 1801, Ames emphasized the effect Jefferson's political victory would have on the nation, sketching the dismal results for all to ponder. It was eminently clear that the writer had no illusions about the Republicans, as he expressed his conviction that the American experiment in republicanism was now being abandoned while the "artificers of ruin" systematically planned to destroy commerce, capital, and the nation's military force. Only the "steady good sense of New England" now was an armor against the "wild theories" of the "political sophists" who were acquiring power.[14]

Jefferson himself was a subject for irony and ridicule, although the writer attacked him as a theorist rather than on a personal level. The Virginian "like most men of genius, ... [had] been carried away by systems" and having lost sight of reality, sailed "in his balloon into clouds and thick vapors." His fallacious philosophy was one in which "man rises from the mire ... shakes off the sleep of ignorance and the

12. Ames to Pickering, Oct. 19, 1799, Ames, *Works of Ames*, I, 258. Ames to Richard Peters, Dedham, Dec. 14, 1806, Richard Peters Papers, X, Hist. Soc. of Pa.
13. "Hints and Conjectures Concerning the Institutions of Lycurgus," Ames, *Works of Ames*, II, 410-28; "American Literature," *ibid.*, 428-42; "School Books," *ibid.*, 405-6. The editors of the 1809 edition of Ames's works mention that in the final period of his life he "could scarcely speak of his children ... without expressing his deep apprehensions of their future servitude to the French." *Works of Fisher Ames* (Boston, 1809), 374.
14. "Falkland, No. I," "Falkland, No. II," Ames, *Works of Ames*, II, 129-33.

fetters of the law ... [and becomes] a gorgeous new being, invested with perfectibility, a saint in purity." [15] The President's foreign policy, based on visionary concepts, seemed as unrealistic to the Dedham Federalist as his view of man. In one series of essays, Ames severely castigated Jefferson for guarding national security with an inadequate militia force, and promoting friendship with the contemporary "Attila," Bonaparte. "The man," he contended, "whose chief merit is grounded on his having penned the declaration of independence, has done more than any other man living to undo it." Privately the journalist revealed his opinion of Jefferson's fundamental problem as chief executive: "Mr. Jeff. only takes care of his popularity, which forbids him to govern at all." [16]

As polemical writings, Ames's six essays on "Equality" were among his best. By placing the democratic interpretation of equality in juxtaposition to his own, he attempted to show that the reasoning behind the one was specious, and behind the other logical. The "democratic articles of faith," containing some truth, bore the appearance of truth. Of these "sacred" maxims, none had excited men more than that which pronounced them free and equal. According to the essayist, this doctrine had been "threadbare in America" even before Thomas Paine came to the colonies and stirred the public imagination with his writings. The upheaval in France had spread the creed around the world. A desire for equality in democratic terms brought revolution and hope for "regenerated liberty." Restless peoples, hungering for power, strove to make their "passions sovereign." But the path toward equality had led directly to a despot, in France at least, and liberty was nonexistent.[17]

To Fisher Ames equality did not mean social destruction and levelling, but the protection of the individual within society. While democratic philosophers talked of equal rights, he suspected that they were thinking of equal property as well. He believed that equality should not be interpreted to mean "that all men have an equal right to all things, but, that to whatever they have a right, it is as much to be protected and provided for as the right of any persons in society." Ames continued, "All cannot be rich, but all have a right to make the attempt; and when some have fully succeeded, and others partially, and others not at all, the several states in which they then find themselves become their condition in life; and whatever the rights of that condition

15. "Falkland, No. II," *ibid.*, 134-35.
16. "Dangerous Power of France, No. I," *ibid.*, 293, printed in the Boston *Palladium*, May, 1806; "Dangerous Power of France, No. IV," *ibid.*, 320; Ames to Josiah Quincy, Dedham, Dec. 11, 1806, Ames Family Papers, Stanford Univ.
17. "Equality, No. I," "Equality, No. IV," Ames, *Works of Ames*, II, 207-18.

may be, they are to be faithfully secured by the laws and government." [18]

Woven into the fabric of the "Equality" articles was Ames's belief that the American people, though living under a republican government, courted democracy. If they allowed the Constitution to be altered by democratic sympathizers, the nation might well follow France into despotism. In an essay published in the *Monthly Anthology and Boston Review* in 1805, he elaborated on the evils of democracy per se. To him the word automatically denoted a violent form of government; he could not conceive of it in a milder state, free of mob domination. A democracy allowed the people to be "the depositaries of political power." [19] Unfortunately, men as a whole were too easily flattered by demagogues, too emotional, too unthinking, to be capable of governing en masse. With opinions of the majority constantly veering, the "temple of the publick liberty has no better foundation than the shifting sands of the desert." Fisher Ames considered that a republic such as the United States differed from a democracy more than did a democracy from a despotism. Even so, republics had a strong inclination to alter and to destroy. The founding fathers endeavored to counteract this inclination by a careful distribution of governmental power. But the democratic theories of Jefferson's administration were gaining, and the judiciary was already "prostrate." In Ames's mind, disaster loomed ahead. "We are sliding down into the mire of a democracy, which pollutes the morals of the citizens before it swallows up their liberties." [20]

A recurring newspaper theme for Ames was the hegemony of France in Europe. His abhorrence of the revolutionary tactics of the French had not diminished an iota through the years, and in his many essays on the state of European affairs, he reiterated his firm conviction that the France of Napoleon had not changed at all from that of the Jacobin period. A nation where "the sword is the only utensil" constituted an ever-present threat to America and Europe.[21] The road to safety was

18. "Equality, No. II," *ibid.*, 210-11.
19. Ames, "For the Anthology," *Monthly Anthology and Boston Review*, 2 (1805), 564. Also reprinted in Lewis P. Simpson, ed., *The Federalist Literary Mind: Selections from the Monthly Anthology and Boston Review, 1803-1811* (Baton Rouge, 1962), 51-54. The journal of the Anthology Society indicates that the members, probably not Federalists, reacted unfavorably to the essay. "The Society thought it a poor thing, but as Mr. Ames was the author and as we had solicited his assistance, it was voted to be accepted"; *ibid.*, 54.
20. Ames, "For the Anthology," *Monthly Anthology and Boston Review*, 2 (1805), 565-66.
21. "Phocion, No. VI," Ames, *Works of Ames*, II, 170. French power and influence is discussed in such essays as "Foreign Politics, Nos. I-IV," and "Equality,

"thorny and perilous," he reminded his countrymen, and security could be found only by arming the nation. An inordinately avaricious and ambitious France had not relinquished her desire to dominate over the United States. In America the French created emotional fervor in order to "obstruct . . . then subvert and revolutionize the government," acting through the Republican party and press.[22]

The French Revolution, as Ames analyzed its import, had established a new tyranny and brought about the resurgence of Roman militarism.[23] France had "sublimated all the passions to fury and extravagance," casting aside the old cultural values. "Justice has fallen on its own sword," he wrote, "and liberty, after being sold to Ishmaelites, is stripped of its bloody garments to disguise its robbers." [24] The French, in quest of the same glory sought by the Romans, were overpowering Europe. Reliance on coalitions against Napoleon had proven illusory, and the smaller European states, finding no security in the balance of power, had been annihilated by France. In 1805, Fisher Ames warned that England's naval might stood as the only bulwark against the enslavement of Americans. Whether England would continue to resist was "a question of life or death to American independence, and the awful decision is near." [25]

Federalists in New England acclaimed the Dedham essayist for his brilliant productions; yet his discouragement grew because so few were willing to give him the support he felt essential to achieve his larger goal of a cohesive, well-organized political minority awaiting a return to power when circumstances were favorable. After two years of intense effort to enlighten the public, he became convinced that his labors had not succeeded in establishing a cadre of active party members who could exert a determining influence on the rank and file. At a time when he himself was plagued by extreme ill health, he bitterly reflected on his failure, condemning himself for being "fool enough" to believe "that the mighty men could be induced to do great things." The tidal currents against Federalism were too strong to overcome alone, and he

---

No. VI." Ames cogently discussed the bases of French military power in "The Combined Powers and France," and in "Dangerous Power of France, No. II." French political power is discussed in "The Duration of French Despotism." *Ibid.*, 192-204, 223-28, 278-84, 293-99, 336-44.

22. "Dangerous Power of France, No. II," "Phocion, No. VI," *ibid.*, 294-95, 169, 173.

23. "New Romans, No. I," "The Duration of French Despotism," *ibid.*, 173-76, 337-41.

24. "Phocion, No. VI," *ibid.*, 171.

25. "History Is Philosophy Teaching by Example," "Reflections on the War in Europe," "Balance of Europe," "On the Prospect of a New Coalition Against France," "The Dangerous Power of France, Nos. I and II," *ibid.*, 228-30, 265-66, 231-37, 274-78, 293, 300.

made up his mind to abandon his journalistic efforts. "Why should I become scribbler or bully on the federal side?" he asked. "Why should I consume my marrow with the fires of that zeal that seems ridiculous to my friends?" [26] Ames repeatedly questioned the value of the plan to sway the public through the press. Yet his hope revived, and he continued to write sporadically for the newspapers until the last weeks of his life. He saw clearly that the *New England Palladium* was not to achieve commanding importance as the mouthpiece of Federalism. In 1803 its editor resigned, and in the following year Ames supported the development of another paper to be known as the Boston *Repertory*.[27]

To Fisher Ames and the extreme Federalists it seemed that President Jefferson and the Republicans could do no right. The foundations of the American government were disintegrating under the weight of Republican acts: the removal of Federalists from office, the reduction of the armed forces, the repeal of the Judiciary Act, the impeachment of certain Federalist judges, and the purchase of Louisiana.[28] Since the early 1790's, the Massachusetts statesman had foreseen a national crisis; now he regarded it as imminent. He was unable to shake off his aggravation with those members of his own party who could not be forced to recognize serious dangers, and those who were certain that all was lost. The real tragedy, as he saw it, was "Federalism takes opium; Jacobinism gunpowder and rum." Under the circumstances, he would let the world go its own way and accept the fact that he was "an outside passenger in the journey of the political folks." [29] As often as he renounced the world, however, his restless concern drove him to return to the political struggle, for he could not remain aloof when the government he prized was at stake.

With the approach of another presidential election in 1804, the alarm of Federalists in Congress was comparable to that of Ames. They feared that their own party's strength would soon be permanently smothered

26. Ames to Oliver Wolcott, Dedham, Mar. 9, 1803, Oliver Wolcott Papers, XVIII, Conn. Hist. Soc.

27. Ames to Isaac P. Davis, Dedham, Jan. 6, 1804, Fisher Ames Papers, Dedham Hist. Soc.; Lee, "Dwight and the *Palladium*," *New Eng. Qtly.*, 25 (1962), 237.

28. Ames to Thomas Dwight, Dedham, Apr. 16, 1802, Oct. 26, 1803, Ames to Smith, Dec. 14, 1802, Ames to Dwight Foster, Dedham, Feb. 6, 1803, Ames to Gore [Dedham], Oct. 3, 1803, Ames, *Works of Ames*, I, 297-98, 313-14, 317-18, 322-27; Manasseh Cutler to Dr. Torrey, Washington, Feb. 27, Apr. 7, 1802, Mar. 3, 1804, Cutler and Cutler, eds., *Life of Manasseh Cutler*, II, 87, 100, 104; Alexander Hamilton to Rufus King, N.Y., June 3, 1802, Lodge, ed., *Works of Hamilton*, X, 437; John Quincy Adams to King, Boston, Oct. 8, 1802, Ford, ed., *Writings of John Q. Adams*, III, 8-9.

29. Ames to Thomas Dwight, Dedham, Feb. 29, 1804, Fisher Ames Papers, Dedham Hist. Soc.; Ames to Foster, Feb. 6, 1803, Ames, *Works of Ames*, I, 318; Ames to Wolcott, Dec. 2, 1802, Oliver Wolcott Papers, XVIII, Conn. Hist. Soc.; Ames to Gore, Oct. 3, 1803, Ames, *Works of Ames*, I, 323.

by rising Republican power. In the midst of congressional tensions, a plan to escape Republican domination through secession was proposed by a group of prominent ultra-Federalists from New England. The separation of a state or a segment of the nation was by no means an original suggestion. In a government yet to be tested, it had been contemplated and sometimes threatened by leaders in various sections. Congressmen, acquainted with this device in legislative debates, were not inclined to regard it as traitorous.[30]

In private conversations during the winter of 1803-4, a small clique broached the subject of secession to trusted congressional associates. This group, dominated by Timothy Pickering, included two New Hampshire members of Congress, William Plumer and Samuel Hunt, as well as Senator Uriah Tracy and Representative Roger Griswold from Connecticut.[31] Pickering and Tracy had long been convinced that decisive steps must be taken to eliminate Virginia's political domination and now were ready to move boldly. Writing to such close friends as George Cabot and Rufus King, Pickering attempted to get the support of other influential Federalists. In a letter to Cabot, the senator discussed Republican oppression, adding, "I do not believe in the practicability of a long continued union. A Northern confederacy would unite congenial characters, and present a fairer prospect of public happiness; while the Southern States ... might be left 'to manage their own affairs in their own way.' " Under the lead of Massachusetts the New England states, he expected, would readily join a "Northern League," ultimately to include New York, New Jersey, and even the British provinces of Canada and Nova Scotia. He insisted that the plan of separation could be carried out "without spilling one drop of blood." Pickering's provocative letter was obviously designed to elicit the reaction not only of George Cabot, but also of the notorious Essex Junto as well.[32]

30. Adams, *History of the United States*, II, 60; John Quincy Adams to Messrs. H. G. Otis, Israel Thorndike, T. H. Perkins, *et al.*, Washington, Dec. 30, 1828, Henry Adams, ed., *Documents Relating to New England Federalism, 1800-1815* (Boston, 1877), 47, 52-53, 56-58; "Appeal to the Citizens of the United States," *ibid.*, 73, 77-79; James Hillhouse to Hon. James Gould, New Haven, Apr. 8, 1829, *ibid.*, 100; Memorandum of William Plumer, May 11, 1829, *ibid.*, 106; Morison, *Otis*, I, 262-67; Lynn W. Turner, *William Plumer of New Hampshire, 1759-1850* (Chapel Hill, 1962), 133-39; Brown, *Northern Confederacy*, 31-33.

31. Adams, *History of the United States*, II, 61-62; Brown, *Northern Confederacy*, 35-36. As early as 1797, Uriah Tracy promoted the separation of the northern states; Uriah Tracy to Theodore Sedgwick, Mar. 29, 1797, Sedgwick Papers, Vol. C, Mass. Hist. Soc.; Uriah Tracy to Alexander Hamilton, Mar. 29, 1797, Pickering Papers, Memoranda, II, Mass. Hist. Soc.; Hervey Prentiss, *Timothy Pickering as the Leader of New England Federalism* (Salem, 1934), 26-27.

32. Timothy Pickering to George Cabot, Washington, Jan. 29, 1804, Pickering to Rufus King, Washington, Mar. 4, 1804, Pickering to Richard Peters, Washington, Dec. 24, 1803, Pickering Papers, Vol. XIV, Mass. Hist. Soc.

On February 14, as Cabot was writing in answer to Pickering's letter, Fisher Ames was admitted to his study. Having been confined to Dedham for some weeks by his health, he now had an opportunity to discuss political problems with his Boston friend. According to Cabot, the frail visitor read Senator Pickering's letter "with pleasure and a mingled emotion of anger which it was impossible wholly to repress." He also read Cabot's reply and agreed in essence with the stand he had taken. Cabot had indicated that he regarded Pickering's analysis of the nation's plight as an extremely accurate one, but that he felt a separation would not eliminate existing evils *"because the source of them is in the political theories of our country and in ourselves."* [33] He was dismayed by the virulent spread of democracy, even though he believed that "no government can be relied on that has not a material portion of the democratic mixture in its composition." [34] In the present situation Cabot was convinced that secession was "impracticable" since the people as a whole would not support such a move. He could, however, conceive of it in the future if the Union in crisis could not remain an entity. Then a confederacy would be the natural outgrowth of unavoidable circumstances.

When Fisher Ames later wrote to Timothy Pickering on the problems of his Dedham farm, he confirmed his own opposition to any precipitous action which would split the Union. Clearly he did not belong to the school of "mutual friends" who felt that nothing could save the government now. Yet he insisted to Pickering, "Nothing is to be done rashly, but mature counsels and united efforts are necessary in the most forlorn case. For though we may not do much to save ourselves, the vicissitudes of political fortune may do everything—and we ought to be ready when she smiles." [35] These rather enigmatical statements might imply that Ames approved the basic objectives of the disunion scheme, but was proposing delay until an auspicious time. An examination of the limited evidence, however, indicates that he did not agree with the secessionists that the fundamental problem of Jacobinism in New England would be eliminated by a confederacy. In his opinion political purity could not be maintained because democratic

33. George Cabot to Timothy Pickering, [Boston], Feb. 14, 1804, *ibid.*, XXVII; Turner, *Plumer*, 139-42.
34. Cabot to Pickering, Feb. 14, 1804, Pickering to Theodore Lyman, Washington, Mar. 14, 1804, Pickering Papers, XIV, XXVII, Mass. Hist. Soc. Pickering mentioned that Cabot had given his letter to Parsons, Higginson, and Ames, and commented, "They think the measure premature, while they deplore the existing evils and our future prospects." Stephen Higginson to Pickering, Boston, Mar. 17, 1804, *ibid.*, XXVII.
35. Ames to Pickering, Apr. 28, 1804, *ibid.*, XXVII; *Repertory* (Boston), Aug. 31, 1804.

misconceptions were too widespread. Even though Ames was unduly
apprehensive about the country's future, his faith in republican government in the Federalist mold was fanatic and unshakable. By encouraging Federalists to entrench in individual state governments, he sought
to perpetuate his party rather than destroy national unity. Undoubtedly
he could have been brought to support a regional confederacy only if
the Union had been *in extremis*.[36]

Undaunted by the negative reaction of some Federalists, Pickering
attempted to insure the success of the plot by intriguing with Aaron
Burr to wrest control of the Federalist party in New York from Hamilton and elect the Vice President governor of the state. The Federalist
defeat in the election and Hamilton's subsequent death led to the sub-
sidence of disunion talk.[37] Nevertheless among New England Federalists the secession threat was not extinguished until a decade later in the
fiasco of the Hartford Convention. But long before this event took
place the Embargo of 1807 had tested the bonds of union again. Concerned at the end of his life with the embargo's effects, Ames spoke
emphatically on the need to preserve the Union. In old age Isaac P.
Davis recalled that when he and Cabot had visited Ames for the last
time in Dedham, the statesman had declared, "Rather than that the
Union should be endangered, every sacrifice ... should be made—every
evil submitted to. *For his own part ... he would stand by the ship to the
last—he would pump so long as a single plank could be kept above
water.*" [38]

Fisher Ames's prestige had not faded away in the years since his
retirement from Congress. Among the honors which came to him was
his election to the presidency of Harvard College in December 1805.
After having been officially notified that the Corporation of the College had acted and that his appointment would be final when the Board
of Overseers confirmed it, he hesitated, pondered, and finally declined
the offer early in 1806. To Professor Eliphalet Pearson he wrote explaining that his delicate health precluded the assumption of responsibilities which would utterly alter his habits of life.[39] Thomas Dwight

36. Ames to Gore, Boston, Dec. 13, 1802, Ames to Thomas Dwight, Dedham,
Nov. 29, 1803, Ames, *Works of Ames*, I, 310, 336.
37. Brown, *Northern Confederacy*, 39-44; Mitchell, *Alexander Hamilton*, II,
518-27. Hamilton took a forceful stand against any secession project just before
his death. Alexander Hamilton to Theodore Sedgwick, N.Y., July 10, 1804,
Miscellaneous Personal Letters, Lib. Cong.; Pickering to Lyman, Mar. 14, 1804,
Pickering Papers, XIV, Mass. Hist. Soc.
38. Isaac P. Davis to Theodore Dwight, Apr. 1, 1829, Fisher Ames Papers,
Dedham Hist. Soc.; Brown, *Northern Confederacy*, 46-52.
39. Ames to Eliphalet Pearson, Dedham, Jan. 6, 1806, Ames, *Works of Ames*,
I, 346-48. A draft of the letter is in the Ames Family Papers, Stanford Univ.
Morison, *Three Centuries of Harvard*, 190.

was to learn the particulars of the decision. Ames quipped, "Sir, I was elected President—not of the United States; and do you know why I did not accept? I had no inclination for it. The health I have, would have been used up at Cambridge in a year." Besides, Frances had withheld her approval of an acceptance, remarking facetiously that she was unwilling to learn Greek, but that if her husband insisted on going, he could take the intellectual Hannah Adams. Having settled the issue negatively, he felt "like a truck or stage horse, who is once more allowed to roll in the dirt without his harness." [40]

Ultimately all of Ames's business affairs and interests were restricted by the state of his health. The vigor of his mind contrasted with his malaise. For a man by nature dynamic rather than passive, his position was infuriating. No matter whether he curtailed his legal practice, his farming enterprises, or his social encounters, he was a helpless victim. His attitudes, exposed to fireside introspection, took on a darker hue. The sardonic humor and refreshing wit, characteristic of his resilient spirit in earlier years, were much more frequently transmuted into stark reflections on man's fallibility and on political corruption.[41]

At every hand, events of the day contributed to his pessimism. The violent death of Alexander Hamilton in the summer of 1804 had "sorely wounded" Ames, causing him to comment in his eulogy of the former Secretary of the Treasury, "We are left to endless labors and unavailing regrets." [42] Jefferson's re-election and succeeding Republican acts tended to prove that the Federalists, without strong leadership and solidarity, were an ineffectual minority, lacking public support. Once Ames had suggested that in spite of jeopardy, the country might "like

40. Ames to Thomas Dwight, Dedham, Feb. 1, 1806, Ames to Josiah Quincy, Dedham, Mar. 19, 1806, Ames, *Works of Ames*, I, 355, 372; Jeremiah Smith to the Rev. Mr. Buckminster, Exeter, Dec. 14, 1805, Chamberlain Collection, Boston Pub. Lib. Smith expressed his pleasure at the election of his friend, Ames, to the presidency, contending that it should have been of the United States. William Bentley indicated that Ames was chosen after the Federalist members of the Corporation had refused to elect the senior professor, Eliphalet Pearson. Entry of Mar. 16, 1806, *The Diary of William Bentley, D.D.*, III, 219. Timothy Pickering to Ames, Washington, Feb. 19, 1806, Pickering Papers, XXXVIII, Mass. Hist. Soc.

41. Ames to C. W. Hare, Dedham, Mar. 14, 1804, Gratz Collection, Hist. Soc. of Pa. Regardless of his health, legal cases were sometimes referred to Ames because of his prominence as a Federalist. In 1806 he was one of four Federalist lawyers retained as counsel for Thomas O. Selfridge in his sensational trial for the murder of Charles Austin, the son of Benjamin Austin. Warren, *Jacobin and Junto*, 196, 199.

42. Ames to Thomas Dwight, Dedham, Aug. 6, 1804, Autograph Collection, Harvard Univ.; "A Sketch of the Character of Alexander Hamilton," Ames, *Works of Ames*, II, 263. Ames's memorial to Hamilton was printed in the *Repertory* (Boston), Aug. 7, 1804, and also in pamphlet form by John Park in Boston; Mitchell, *Alexander Hamilton*, II, 542-43. Mitchell regards the essay as the "most thoughtful" and "perceptive" of the eulogies on Hamilton.

a wounded snake, drag... [its] slow length along for twenty years, and time will in that period have more to do in fixing our future destiny than our administration." Now that the people had clearly condoned Republican action, the government's fate seemed obvious. The former congressman concluded that liberty "is gone, never to return. To mitigate a tyranny is all that is left for our hopes." [43] It was the democratic spectre that haunted him. He had never wanted "to strip the people of all power—for then slavery would ensue," but to him democracy was a plague. Only in the environment of republican government could he find satisfaction.[44]

In Fisher Ames's eyes, not only the judiciary, but also the Constitution was under mortal assault. Unsound policies of economy and of military preparation were being promoted. A heavy reliance on gunboats for protection put the United States in an absurd position, "scarcely a match for the Mamelukes." [45] The Republicans, their relations with Britain based on false premises and old prejudices, were taking steps that would lead to war. Although Ames acknowledged that Britain probably was in the wrong in confiscating American shipping for violations of the Rule of 1756, he considered Republican moves to confiscate British debts and pass nonintercourse laws as clumsy retaliatory diplomatic weapons. France, he contended, still constituted the most serious danger, for if England fell to her, the United States would soon follow. "We are prostrate already," he insisted, "and of all men on earth the fittest to be slaves." His disillusionment was complete when he wrote, "Indeed I consider the whole civilized world as metal thrown back into the furnace, to be melted over again." [46]

Regardless of his dolorous analyses and prophecies, Fisher Ames constantly fought in the only way now possible for him, in correspondence and conversation, for the cause of Federalism. Behind his resistance to

43. Ames to Thomas Dwight, Dedham, Nov. 29, 1803, Nov. 29, 1805, Ames, *Works of Ames*, I, 333-36, 341.

44. Ames to Pickering, Dedham, Mar. 10, 1806, Pickering Papers, XXVII, Mass. Hist. Soc.

45. Ames to Josiah Quincy, Dedham, Feb. 12, 1806, Ames Family Papers, Stanford Univ.

46. Ames to Pickering, Dedham, Feb. 14, 1806, Ames, *Works of Ames*, I, 366. In this letter Ames assessed the relative military strength of Russia and Britain in contrast to France. The letters of Senator Pickering to Ames dealt extensively with U.S. foreign policy. Pickering to Ames, Washington, Dec. 28, 29, 1805, Feb. 1, 2, 19, Mar. 11, 21, Apr. 1, 2, 7, 1806, Pickering Papers, XIV, XXXVIII, Mass. Hist. Soc. Cabot remarked to Pickering in a letter on European affairs, "I have lately read *your gloomy* letter to Ames, and *his desponding* answer. It was a *melancholy* pleasure *to me....* Would to Heaven all the men whom I esteem thought as correctly!" Cabot to Pickering, Boston, Feb. 17, 1806, Lodge, ed., *Letters of Cabot*, 352; Adams, *History of the United States*, II, 44-45, 96-97; Perkins, *First Rapprochement*, 176-181.

Republican rule obviously lay the hope that the popular trend could yet be averted. Ames's interest in politics continued to blaze while his physical strength ebbed away. At the end of 1807, his role was little more than that of a semi-invalid. With tongue in cheek, he questioned his *raison d'être* and " 'whether bare being, without life or existence, is better than not to be, or not?' " The future of his family was a source of persistent anxiety to him, especially as he contemplated the Jeffersonian universe in which he found himself.[47]

For some time Ames had been anxious to assure his children of an excellent education. Arrangements were finally made for John Worthington Ames, now called Worthington, to enroll at the academy in Deerfield, some 150 miles from Dedham. Late in January 1808, Leonard was assigned to drive him to his Uncle Dwight's in Springfield, from which place he could proceed by hired pung to Deerfield. With reluctance Fisher Ames saw his eldest leave home at fourteen.[48]

To supplement his son's education, he encouraged him to write frequent letters to Frances and himself, and above all to keep the *"private journal"* recommended by Dr. Johnson. Worthington responded to his father's suggestion, and the result was an interchange of lively, revealing letters. In an initial note, Fisher Ames described with what pleasure his wife and he had received their son's first letter. He assured him, "Our love will not fail you," and added, "O may kind heaven grant you health." After Worthington's departure, he had had "a sick week" with a cough, which seemed "to give Doctor Ames some fears." Subsequently he wrote, "I relish a letter from you, my dear boy, more than my dinner. This indeed is no great praise as you know what a poor appetite I have." [49]

Worthington endeavored to describe life at Deerfield in detail for his ailing father. By late winter he commented, "The wild ducks begin to come here very thick. I have not been out after them yet nor do I intend to let them interfere with my studies." A resolution to put studies first seemed to be the *sine qua non* of a situation where there were many diversions. With fellow students, he took part in a sleighing

47. Ames to Pickering, Dedham, Nov. 6, 1807, Ames, *Works of Ames*, I, 398; Ames to Josiah Quincy, Dedham, Dec. 31, 1807, Miscellaneous Collection, Lib. Cong.; George Cabot to Pickering, [Boston], Mar. 9, 1808, Pickering to Cabot, Washington, Mar. 17, 1808, Lodge, ed., *Letters of Cabot*, 380-388.

48. Ames to Thomas Dwight, Dedham, Feb. 29, 1804, Jan. 30, 1808, Ames to John W. Ames, Dedham, Feb. 15, 1808, Fisher Ames Papers, Dedham Hist. Soc.; Ames to Dwight, Nov. 29, 1805, Ames, *Works of Ames*, I, 341. Ames's two older boys attended school in Cambridge for a time while Hannah went to a boarding school in Medford with her cousin, Mary Dwight.

49. *Ibid.*; Ames to John W. Ames, Feb. 15, 27, 1808, Fisher Ames Papers, Dedham Hist. Soc.

party, a ball, and a trip to Shelburne, where he watched the local Baptists making maple sugar. The visit to the maple sugar camp heightened Worthington's disdain for this particular group of Baptists, who practiced their religion with wild enthusiasm, even cutting holes in the ice in mid-winter "to dip their prosilites." He looked upon them as a "contemptible set" having "stupid and ridiculous" tenets.[50] His father, after learning of his critical views, could not refrain from observing, "I make no doubt the Baptists are ignorant enthusiasts, but they are no doubt sincere. Their ignorance I suppose they could not help, but God will accept sincerity. Their forms make them no better perhaps no worse, and if their religion makes them better men, it does much good. Be careful how you shew scorn and contempt for these poor people, and indeed for anybody as long as you live. In the course of our lives we can hardly avoid making too many enemies, and contempt is bitterly remembered when real injuries are forgotten." And he added, "I charge you read your Bible often always study it on Sundays." [51]

As a part of his academic program, Worthington was enrolled in a public speaking class which met every other Saturday. He confessed that his efforts were not very satisfying since his voice, as his family knew, was now "more like a crow's than any thing else." His remarks elicited advice on public speaking from Fisher Ames. "Of all things, avoid empty noise and affectation. A good speaker, unless ignorant and affected, seldom fails to command the preference over his equals in sense and knowledge, who may happen to mumble and snuffle, and repeat their words. Learn to speak right off whatever you have to say." [52]

Father and son continued to exchange letters, discussing a variety of topics. Worthington thought his own messages "rubbish" and humorously suggested that they be bound in book form with "flaming characters Ames's Letters" on the cover. In a serious vein, he assured his father that he was willing to remain at Deerfield until August, since he recognized that it created a "sad breach" in his studies when they were interrupted. His Greek had almost "been lost in the fog" during the week he had spent en route to the Academy.[53]

Ames did not live to see his son return. In April he wrote that his health was improved and that he hoped to be able to ride out as soon as there was spring sunshine. Meantime old friends still sought his stim-

50. John W. Ames to Ames, Deerfield, Mar. 14, 28, 1808, *ibid.*
51. Ames to John W. Ames, Dedham, Apr. 9, 1808, *ibid.*
52. John W. Ames to Ames, Mar. 28, 1808, Ames to John W. Ames, Apr. 9, 1808, *ibid.*
53. John W. Ames to Ames, Deerfield, Apr. 30, 1808, *ibid.*

ulating company in the High Street house. After calling upon him, Christopher Gore reported that he was definitely failing. George Cabot viewed the situation as very serious, though he remembered that Ames had come out of a similar decline the previous year. In Washington, Timothy Pickering bemoaned the fact that he would probably never see him again. On his part, Fisher Ames, regardless of his condition, could enjoy with his Federalist visitors the gains which the party made in the state election that April.[54]

On June 10, Ames wrote Thomas Dwight, "I am sick." In the midst of a final illness he was thinking of Worthington and wondered if his brother-in-law would talk to John Williams at the Deerfield Academy to discover his honest opinion of the boy and his progress. Ames's other children were not far from his thoughts. The youngest, Richard, had recently rejoined the family after staying at his nurse's for some weeks. Although Frances was distracted by domestic activity and concern for her husband, she did not fail him but assumed ever greater responsibility.[55] It was she whom Fisher Ames named as "sole executor" when he made his will on June 22, 1808. By this time Mrs. Ames had already written Worthington urging him to return home immediately because of his father's condition.[56] When Dr. Eustis drove out from Boston on the twenty-fourth, he found Ames a mere skeleton. But he had not lost his hold on his friends, for Dr. Eustis commented that "he was very amiable and interesting—more so now than ever." [57]

At the end of June, Ames could no longer rise from his bed. Thomas Dwight, realizing that he could not live, came to Dedham to be with

54. Ames to J. W. Ames, Apr. 9, 1808, *ibid.;* Cabot to Pickering, Mar. 9, 1808, Pickering to Cabot, Washington, Mar. 16, 1808, Lodge, ed., *Letters of Cabot,* 380, 388; Adams, *History of the United States,* IV, 242. While the Federalist candidate for governor, Christopher Gore, lost to the Republican, James Sullivan, it was only by a small margin, and the Federalists regained control of the legislature. Gore to Rufus King, Boston, Apr. 8, 1808, King, ed., *Life of King,* V, 91. Abstract of Votes, Mass. Archives, Office of the Secretary of the Commonwealth, State House; Goodman, *Democratic-Republicans,* 196-98.

55. Ames to Thomas Dwight, Dedham, June 10, 1808, Ames to John W. Ames, Apr. 9, 1808, Fisher Ames Papers, Dedham Hist. Soc.; Thomas Dwight to Hannah Dwight, n.p., June 17, 1808, Dwight-Howard Papers, Mass. Hist. Soc.

56. Isaac P. Davis to Theodore Dwight, n.p., Apr. 1, 1829, Fisher Ames Papers, Dedham Hist. Soc.; Will of Fisher Ames, Registry of Probate, Norfolk County Court House, Dedham, Mass. Ames left $500 to each of his children at age 21. To his wife he gave the Ames "dwelling house" and certain lots of land for her lifetime. He also gave her other lands, which she had the right to sell, and the remainder of his personal estate. Frances was named executrix; Notice of Appointment as Executrix of the Last Will of Fisher Ames, *Norfolk Repository* (Dedham), Aug. 16, 1808.

57. William Eustis to Henry Dearborn, Boston, June 24, 1808, Miscellaneous Bound Vol. Dated 1808, Mass. Hist. Soc.

him and with his family. Fisher Ames talked calmly and objectively with Dwight about death. He took the position that it was "a weakness becoming him neither as a Christian or a man to repine at an approaching event which there was no possibility of avoiding or escaping—that holding fast the Christian faith he should die with resignation to his maker's will." On Friday, July 1, Ames sank into a delirium, his mind clouded except at rare intervals. When he did emerge slightly from mental confusion, he struggled vainly to speak, but he could command neither thought nor speech. The only intelligible sentence he uttered, with great effort, was, "Oh that I could hold out until Worthington arrives." [58] Frances's urgent letter to their son had obviously not reached him, for he did not come. Leonard, therefore, departed hastily by chaise on Saturday morning with the hope that he would meet him en route. Otherwise, he would have to travel the whole distance to Deerfield.

Fisher Ames lived another day. But his strength had dwindled, and at sunrise on Monday, July 4, he died quietly "without a single struggle, a single groan." Death had come to Congress's great orator on a significant day; thirty-two years had passed since the Declaration of Independence had been officially approved. Nathaniel Ames wrote in his diary, "My only brother, left, died of a lingering atrophy." In the town records, it was briefly noted that death was due to "consumption." [59]

Frances Ames made the necessary arrangements for her husband's funeral to take place among family and friends in Dedham. Prominent Federalists, however, took the position that the people should have an opportunity to pay tribute to so eminent a leader of the party in a public funeral in Boston. At a special meeting held on the floor of the State House at nine o'clock on Tuesday morning, it was resolved that "the family of Mr. Ames be respectfully requested to permit his *Remains* to be brought" to the capital for a funeral service. A "Committee of Arrangements," made up of twelve staunch Federalists, was appointed to carry out this resolution, to invite Samuel Dexter to give an oration, and to plan all other details. On the same morning, a servant of George Cabot was dispatched to Dedham with a letter requesting Fisher Ames's widow to grant permission for a public ceremony. Influenced by the wishes of her husband's closest friends, she agreed to the

58. Thomas Dwight to Edmund Dwight, Dedham, 7 A.M., July 4, 1808, Autograph Collection, Harvard Univ.

59. *Ibid.;* Diary of Nathaniel Ames, July 4, 1808, Nathaniel Ames Papers, Dedham Hist. Soc.; *Norfolk Repository* (Dedham), July 5, 1808; Hill, ed., *Records of Dedham,* II, 111.

proposal and canceled the Dedham service. Though the funeral would be in Boston, actual burial would be in the Old Village Cemetery at Dedham.[60]

Many Federalists looked upon Ames's passing not only with keen regret, but also with foreboding. Behind their fear lay the suspicion that Fisher Ames and the party shared the same destiny. They regarded a public funeral as a possible *point de ralliement* for Federalism. Nathaniel detected the fine hand of the Junto in the elaborate plans being made. His disgust was intensified when George Cabot himself called and tried to entice him, as Dr. Ames put it, "into a sanction of ridiculous pomp of pretended apotheosis." While visiting the elderly Mrs. Ames later, Mr. Cabot commented that Nathaniel should certainly be present at her son's funeral. But all was to no avail, for Dr. Ames refused to participate in a ceremony which he considered a political farce. Certain other relatives also refused to attend.[61]

Despite this opposition, plans for the public ceremony were not altered. The body of Fisher Ames, placed "in a superbly trim'd mahogany coffin," was taken by coach on Tuesday night to the Boston residence of Christopher Gore. There it remained until the next day, July 6, when Frances Ames and her children were brought from Dedham for the funeral. The committee in charge had planned a formal procession, and participants gathered for the five o'clock service near the Gore mansion on Park Street.[62] A broadside issued for the occasion specified the "Order of Procession." Behind the leading deputy marshal marched the junior and the senior classes of Harvard University, the tutors and professors, the clergy of the area, the president of the University, the head marshal, the Committee of Arrangements, and the officiating clergyman. At this point in the procession came the pallbearers with Ames's coffin—Harrison G. Otis, Christopher Gore, Edward H. Robbins, George Cabot, Theophilus Parsons, and Timothy Pickering. Among other distinguished mourners forming the cortege were relations, neighbors, the governor, the lieutenant governor, the Council, Massachusetts state officials, judges of the Supreme Judicial Court, judges of the United States Circuit Court, judges of the common pleas and municipal courts, Members of Congress, "Gentlemen of the Bar,"

60. Diary of Nathaniel Ames, July 4, 5, 1808, Nathaniel Ames Papers, Dedham Hist. Soc.; *Palladium* (Boston), July 8, 1808; *Repertory* (Boston), July 8, 1808; *Columbian Centinel* (Boston), July 6, 1808.

61. Diary of Nathaniel Ames, July 5, 1808, Nathaniel Ames Papers, Dedham Hist. Soc.

62. *Ibid.*; *Columbian Centinel* (Boston), July 9, 1808; *Repertory* (Boston), July 8, 1808.

members of the Academy of Arts and Sciences, members of the Massachusetts Historical, the Agricultural, and the Humane Societies. At the end of the slow-moving line marched "Strangers and Citizens." [63]

Huge numbers of Bostonians watched silently as the procession, reportedly made up of 1,000 people, advanced through Winter and Marlborough Streets, Cornhill, Court and Tremont Streets to King's Chapel. "In testimony of respect" the ships in Boston Harbor hoisted their bright flags half-mast, and shopkeepers along the route voluntarily closed their doors to business. Upon the arrival of the procession, the Chapel immediately filled to capacity. Ames's coffin was borne to the chancel and placed in front of the altar. The Reverend Mr. Montague, Rector of St. Paul's Church in Dedham, conducted the service with the assistance of the Reverend Samuel Gardiner of King's Chapel. A choir with organ accompaniment sang the "sentimental and pathetick Stanzas" of an ode to Ames written especially for the ceremony by Mr. Gardiner.[64]

Samuel Dexter then gave the funeral oration. In the tradition of the time, it was a eulogy marked by grandiloquence and praise. But even though the deceased statesman was already a political symbol, the speaker did not emphasize his political position. Instead, Dexter reviewed in some detail Ames's life and public career, attempting to show the nature of his brilliance. He observed that "the richness and vividness of his fancy, the fertility of his invention, the abundance of his thoughts were as remarkable as the justness and strength of his understanding." Samuel Dexter saw in Ames qualities which drew people to him. "When he rose, in a short time, from small beginnings to eminence and fame, he never lost that simplicity of character, that purity of mind ... that endeared him to all." At the conclusion of the speech the funeral service came to an end.[65]

Soon after, Dr. Ames petulantly recorded in his diary, "Dogget gone with the herse to bring back the putrid corpse." It was unclear whether

63. *Arrangement For the Funeral Procession at the Funeral of Fisher Ames, Boston, July 6, 1808*, Broadside, Mass. Hist. Soc.

64. *Ibid.; Columbian Centinel* (Boston), July 9, 1808; *Repertory* (Boston), July 8, 1808; Evert A. Duyckinck, *Cyclopaedia of American Literature*, 2 vols. (N.Y., 1855), I, 557-58. The final stanza of the ode was:

These gifts were thine immortal AMES
Of motive pure, of life sublime!
Their loss our flowing sorrow claims;
Their praise survives the wrecks of time.

65. *Repertory* (Boston), July 8, 1808; *Columbian Centinel* (Boston), July 9, 1808; "Veracity," *Independent Chronicle* (Boston), July 18, 1808. "Veracity" described Dexter's oration as "cold and dull," and indelicate.

Nathaniel could not forgive the Federalists for their "mummery" over his brother's body or whether he could not forgive Fisher for his devotion to Federalism. In his evaluation of the Boston ceremony, however, Nathaniel Ames was only one of many Republicans who concluded that "nothing is deemed too sacred or too tender to be pressed into [the] vile service" of the Federalists. At least one Federalist was also critical. John Adams commented, "The aristocratical tricks, the *coup de theatre*, played off in the funerals of Washington, Hamilton and Ames are all in concert with the lives and histories written and to be written, all calculated like drums and trumpets and fifes in an army to drown the unpopularity of Speculations, banks, paper-money and mushroom fortunes. You see through these masks and veils and cloaks but the people are dazzled and blinded by them and so will posterity be." [66]

Fisher Ames's life had ended, but the legend of his life had just begun. Within a few months, George Cabot and other close friends arranged for the publication of his essays and selected letters. The obvious purpose of the project was to keep Ames and his political philosophy alive in the minds of the people and to keep Federalism alive as well.[67] Federalists welcomed the appearance of the volume, while Republicans greeted it with hostile criticism. In a biting review, John Quincy Adams dismissed the *Works of Fisher Ames* as the product of a writer diseased both in body and mind.[68] As the era of Federalism gradually ended and Jeffersonian democracy took its place, his-

66. Diary of Nathaniel Ames, July 5, 1808, Nathaniel Ames Papers, Dedham Hist. Soc.; *The Democrat* (Boston), July 9, 1808. In contrast, the *Newburyport Herald* printed a glowing tribute to Ames comparing him to Quintilian, Cicero, Chatham, and Burke, reprinted in the *Palladium* (Boston), July 12, 1808; *Norfolk Repository* (Dedham), July 12, 1808. John Adams to Benjamin Rush, Quincy, July 25, 1808, Adams Papers, Microfilm Reel 118, Mass. Hist. Soc.
67. Lodge, ed., *Letters of Cabot*, 370; Oliver Wolcott to George Cabot, N.Y., Sept. (n.d.), 1808, Cabot to Wolcott, Boston, Nov. 27, 1808, Jan. 3, 31, Mar. 10, Apr. 10, 1809, Oliver Wolcott Papers, XXI, XVIII, Conn. Hist. Soc.; *Repertory* (Boston), Aug. 9, Oct. 25, 1808; Andrew Peabody, *Harvard Reminiscences* (Boston, 1888), 15.
68. [John Quincy Adams], *American Principles, A Review of Works of Fisher Ames, Compiled by a Number of His Friends* (Boston, 1809). The review was first published in the Boston *Patriot*, Apr.-June, 1809. Samuel F. Bemis, *John Quincy Adams and the Foundations of American Foreign Policy* (N.Y., 1949), 152-53. Richard Rush to John Adams, Phila., Jan. 5, 1811, Gratz Collection, Hist. Soc. of Pa. Rush commented about John Q. Adams's essay: "The just censure, mixed with the poignant satire, which it inflicts upon a set of opinions so hostile to every thing American, is combined with a masterly defence of the principles of our government and the character of our country." John Lowell, *Remarks on the Hon. John Q. Adams' Review of Mr. Ames's Works, with some Strictures on the Views of the Author* (Boston, 1809).

torians increasingly looked upon Ames as a self-appointed prophet, wringing his hands and wailing behind the fortifications of a besieged city. He was now the personification not only of arch-Federalism, but also of a malignant conservatism.[69] This picture of him, while having an element of validity, was inaccurate. It resembled the man, but was actually a caricature.

In death, Ames moved into the center of ever greater controversy. The decision of high Federalists to publish his papers, among them informal and spontaneous letters, simply contributed to a one-sided view of him. He was a man who could not be perceived in a glance. His scintillating mind, his wit, and his unusual verbal skill had elicited envy; his dogmatism, his determination, his emotionalism had elicited opposition. In human relationships he often displayed gentle sensitivity. He had a penchant for making friends and keeping them, though he by no means maintained all of his friendships as his political attitudes narrowed his outlook. With a warm personality, and with social grace and ease, Ames made men feel privileged to be numbered among those who knew him well. He rarely relinquished a fundamental courtesy even with political opponents. His view of the common man's limitations did not affect his amiable association with yeoman-farmer neighbors and other Dedham townspeople. Fisher Ames's own origins had, after all, been far from aristocratic. He was one of the many his father referred to in the maxim, "All Men are by Nature equal, But differ greatly in the sequel." [70]

Federalism offered the orator a creed in which he could believe. Inevitably his political faith was tinctured by his individualism. In his impressionable early years educational foundations were laid on the bedrock of the classics, giving him insight into the Greek and Roman governments with their strengths and weaknesses. Out of his studies both then and later grew his respect for republican government. At the beginning of his career he observed the course and effect of Shays' Rebellion in Massachusetts. The struggle convinced him of the danger

69. Adams, *History of the United States*, I, 88. Vernon L. Parrington, *Main Currents in American Thought*, II: *The Romantic Revolution in America* (N.Y., 1939), 279-88; Brant, *Madison, Father of the Constitution*, 263-67; Schachner, *Founding Fathers* (N.Y., 1954), 35-36; Shaw Livermore, *The Twilight of Federalism: The Disintegration of the Federalist Party, 1815-1830* (Princeton, 1962), 8. Livermore categorically refers to Ames's "Rasputin-like effect upon his colleagues." Douglass, "Fisher Ames," Amer. Philos. Soc., *Proceedings*, 103 (1959), 695, 713-15.

70. Parsons, *Memoir of Parsons*, 115. Theophilus Parsons, Jr., remarked, "No man in this community ever won so much public admiration, and at the same time, the warm affection of so wide a circle of friends." Sullivan, *Familiar Letters*, 58. William Sullivan regarded Ames as a person "of most amiable disposition, and most sincerely beloved by his friends." *Diary of Bentley*, III, 370-71. Ames, *Almanack for 1762*, Briggs, *Essays of Nathaniel Ames*, 327.

latent in emasculated government where the general public dominated. He quickly became a fervent disciple of a strong, centralized republic, with administration in the hands of the intelligent few. In the development of the new government under Washington, he could begin to see the realization of his ideal. The concept in his mind, however, was a rigid, static one, unalterable even under variable circumstances. Ames was an incurable idealist with an inflexible ideal of government. Faction in his system could have only detrimental effects. As political parties evolved and his own health declined, his spirits sank. Had he been less idealistic in his own terms, he would have been less discouraged.

As a statesman, Fisher Ames was atypical, for his temperament was in many respects an artistic one. A high-strung individual, in days of health he could be ebullient, and in days of illness, utterly disconsolate. The perpetual minutiae of legal work bored and annoyed him. In Congress the combination of law and oratory, and principally oratory, brought him genuine satisfaction. He was challenged by the issues at stake. There was in his make-up a sense of the dramatic, of the interplay between actor and audience. The theatrical effect of his speeches was heightened by his intellectual magnetism. Iconoclasm, an essential ingredient of his oratory and prose, was clearly a device to shock the listener into action. In struggling to reach the public through his essays Ames, without the feeling of audience response, was frustrated. It has been implied that he could have made a real contribution to literature had he devoted himself to writing.[71] He disliked, however, a regimen in which he would be forced to remain at his desk, writing, polishing, improving without the stimulus of people. Much of his brilliance lay in his verbal spontaneity, which brought his speeches to life and made his conversations fascinating.

The malady which drove Ames from Congress and ultimately resulted in his death at fifty has left a cloud of mystery about him. Confusing medical diagnoses and inadequate medical records helped to create this mystery. The illness of a person with such arbitrary and controversial political views has invited psychological interpretations of its causes.[72] Obviously, Fisher Ames's physical and mental health were interrelated. The cycle of his impaired health, however, began after his attack of pneumonia in 1795. From that time until his death thirteen years later, a primary source of his ailment seemed to be weakened lungs, implying a tubercular condition. Undoubtedly, during this pe-

71. Morison, "Squire Ames and Doctor Ames," *New Eng. Qtly.*, 1 (1928), 28-29; William Tudor, *Letters on the Eastern States* (Boston, 1821), 53.
72. Douglass, "Fisher Ames," Amer. Philos. Soc., *Proceedings*, 103 (1959), 695. Douglass maintains that Ames was a victim of "hysteria."

riod Ames's characteristic emotionalism had a detrimental effect on recovery. Likewise, however, the attempts of physicians to devise remedies to counteract his decline may have actually promoted it. The remedies, indicative of limited contemporary medical knowledge, were often inappropriate or ineffectual.

The fact that Ames's anxiety for the nation increased under the impact of prolonged illness was not surprising. He did not become suddenly erratic and irrational; he maintained a consistent position. The fears which he had experienced from the beginning of his public career merely became more exaggerated and extreme. While the disasters he dreaded did not materialize, the American government in its evolution moved away from his idealized concept. The rule of the patrician, whom he admired, waned with the rise of the majority to political power.

Ames's strenuous efforts to rescue the Federalist party were futile. Averse to a party system, he was an inept politician. Public opinion had little influence on the ideas to which he clung with great zeal. Never fully able to understand and sympathize with the aspirations of the lower classes, he misjudged the direction and import of the American democratic movement. In many ways the government was still fragile and untried; he could not envision its democratic destiny. New England tended to limit his vision of the larger world. No matter how he struggled to avoid regionalism, he was an inveterate Yankee.

Fisher Ames was instrumental in establishing the government under the Constitution. His tenacity of purpose, so valuable in the initial stages of governmental development, became a tragic flaw when it prevented pragmatic insight. He brought to the Federalist party a vivid intelligence which helped to make it strong and helped to make it weak.

A Note on the Sources

Toward the end of his life Fisher Ames remarked to Richard Peters, "Though a ready scribbler, I am no author—I shall never rise to the honor of being bound in calf or sheepskin." His attitude about the value of his writings is reflected in the fact that Ames rarely kept copies of anything he wrote. Apparently he did not even keep a diary noting his activities, as did his brother, Nathaniel. While a number of Ames's letters to friends have been preserved in manuscript collections, many are no longer extant. Correspondence between Ames and his intimate friend George Cabot is conspicuously missing. To a large degree family correspondence has also disappeared. Fortunately, however, some revealing letters remain from Ames to his brother-in-law, Thomas Dwight, and between Ames and his eldest son, John Worthington Ames. But a biographer of Ames is inevitably confronted with limited source materials in comparison to the voluminous records available concerning a number of the orator's contemporaries in public life.

The 1809 edition of the *Works of Fisher Ames,* edited by George Cabot and others, consists largely of Ames's essays, but includes fourteen of his letters as well as three of his speeches. The book is prefaced by a eulogistic sketch of Ames prepared by John Kirkland, later president of Harvard. A new edition of the *Works of Fisher Ames,* edited by Ames's son Seth, appeared in two volumes in 1854. The most important addition was 196 letters. In general, the editor deleted personal references but the intrinsic value of the letters was not destroyed. Pelham W. Ames edited the *Speeches of Fisher Ames in Congress, 1789-1796* (Boston, 1871), including only the longer formal speeches of his grandfather in the House of Representatives. Ames's analytical speech on biennial

elections in the Massachusetts Ratifying Convention was published in
The American Museum, 3 (1788), 358-62. A group of interesting letters
from Ames to William Tudor in 1789-91 appeared in a "Memoir of the
Hon. William Tudor," Massachusetts Historical Society, *Collections,*
2d Ser., 8 (1819), 285-325.

Fisher Ames was the subject of various articles published during the
nineteenth century. In many instances the influences of Kirkland's interpretation of him is obvious. None of the articles contributes significantly to an understanding of the man. Perhaps the most informative
is "Fisher Ames," *Port Folio,* 3d Ser., 1 (1813), 2-21, while the most
objective is a "Biographical and Critical Sketch of Fisher Ames,"
Analectic Magazine, 3 (1814), 304-33. Ames's rector, the Reverend
William Montague, wrote a "Memoir of Fisher Ames" for the *Diocesan
Register and the New England Calendar for 1812* (Dedham, 1811),
in an attempt to characterize the orator and explain his conversion to
Episcopalianism. Among other articles which appeared were: "Essays
of Fisher Ames," *Quarterly Review,* 53 (1835), 548-73; "Fisher Ames,"
Christian Examiner, 57 (1854), 78-94; James B. Thayer, "Fisher Ames,"
in *American Statesmen* (New York, 1860), 285-86; Mellen Chamberlain, "Fisher Ames," *Harvard Graduates' Magazine,* 4 (1895), 23-33.

Ames was first viewed in historical perspective by Samuel Eliot Mor-
ison, who published several articles in the late 1920's about the Dedham
Federalist. In addition to a biographical sketch in the *Dictionary of
American Biography,* Morison wrote "Squire Ames and Doctor Ames,"
New England Quarterly, 1 (1928), 5-31, and "The India Ventures of
Fisher Ames, 1794-1804," American Antiquarian Society, *Proceedings,*
New Ser., 37 (1927), 14-23. More recently, Elisha P. Douglass examined
the nature of Ames's political theories in an article, "Fisher Ames,
Spokesman for New England Federalism," American Philosophical So-
ciety, *Proceedings,* 103 (1959), 693-715.

Manuscript collections were essential to a full-scale biography of
Ames. Of primary importance were the holdings of the Dedham Historical Society, Dedham, Massachusetts. The Fisher Ames Papers, which are
the largest single collection of the statesman's writings, include letters
from Ames, fragments of his newspaper essays and speeches, some legal
papers, as well as business accounts and correspondence relating to his
ventures in the India trade. Seth Ames drew heavily on this source in
his edition of the *Works of Fisher Ames,* though many of Ames's letters
still remain unpublished. The Nathaniel Ames Papers consist of a set
of the Ames *Almanack,* 1725-1775, scattered letters of Nathaniel, Sr.,
papers concerning his litigation, and the manuscript diary of Nathaniel,
Jr., for the period 1758-1822. Related collections are the Shuttleworth
Family Papers, the Jonathan Avery Account Book, and the Norfolk
and Bristol Turnpike Company Papers. The Church Records of the
First Church of Dedham, in the custody of the Board of Deacons, are
also housed in the Dedham Historical Society. These records were

sources of additional information. Other pertinent papers found in Dedham were the Records of the Court of Common Pleas for Norfolk County, Office of the Clerk of the Court, Supreme Judicial Court, Norfolk County Court House.

Four manuscript collections contributed greatly to my evaluation of Ames's influence in Congress and in the Federalist party. The Theodore Sedgwick Papers in the Massachusetts Historical Society, Boston, revealed details of Federalist policies on the state and national levels. For the purposes of this study the Sedgwick collection was most valuable in the period 1785-1800. The Timothy Pickering Papers, also in the Massachusetts Historical Society, were particularly informative for the period after 1796. On the one hand the firm friendship between Pickering and Ames was made evident; on the other, fragmentation of the party was made equally clear. Aside from disclosing much about early American finance and Connecticut politics, the voluminous Oliver Wolcott Papers in the Connecticut Historical Society, Hartford, spelled out the political principles of such New England Federalists as Ames. The Rufus King Papers in the New-York Historical Society, New York City, include letters to and from King which indicated the reaction of Massachusetts Federalists to Fisher Ames's growing prominence in the Federalist party. Much material from the Wolcott Papers has appeared in George Gibbs, ed., *Memoirs of the Administrations of Washington and John Adams* (New York, 1846), and from the King Papers in Charles R. King, ed., *The Life and Correspondence of Rufus King* (New York, 1894-1900). But many important items in these collections have not been published.

Some business and legal activities of Fisher Ames were seen through documents and letters in the Andrew Craigie Papers, American Antiquarian Society, Worcester, Massachusetts, the William Constable Papers, New York Public Library, and the William Bingham Papers, Historical Society of Pennsylvania, Philadelphia. A noteworthy, though little used collection, the Benjamin Goodhue Papers, New York Society Library, New York City, contains letters from Ames, dealing with his business investments and politics in the 1790's. In the manuscript legal records located in the Office of the Clerk, Supreme Judicial Court, Suffolk County Court House, Boston, there are significant documents relating both to Nathaniel Ames, Sr., and to Fisher Ames. The indexes to the Suffolk Files, 1629-1799, and the Minute Books of the court sessions were helpful in tracing particular legal cases. The papers relevant to these cases were found in the Court Files for the Several Counties. Information about certain of Ames's financial transactions was obtained from the volumes pertaining to the Massachusetts subscription to the United States loan of 1790 in the Fiscal Records Section, Old Treasury Records, National Archives, Washington.

Other collections which enlarged the scope of this book deserve special mention. They were discovered in widely separated locations.

Ames's vivid letters to George R. Minot, describing the congressional scene, are in the Massachusetts Historical Society. Letters from Ames to Josiah Quincy, accounts and bills of the Ames family, and genealogical data are filed as "Ames Family Papers" at the Stanford University Library, Palo Alto, California. Many of the letters to Minot and Quincy were published in the Seth Ames edition of the *Works of Fisher Ames*. Interesting Ames material was also found in the Autograph Collection, Houghton Library of the Harvard College Library, Cambridge, and in the Miscellaneous Personal Papers as well as in the Alexander Hamilton Papers, both located in the Manuscript Division, Library of Congress, Washington. While many libraries have only a few Ames letters among their holdings, the total amount from such sources is substantial. Scattered items are in the following libraries: Chicago Historical Society, Chicago, Duke University Library, Durham, North Carolina, Haverford College Library, Haverford, Pennsylvania, Marietta College Library, Marietta, Ohio, Pierpont Morgan Library, New York City, New York State Library, Albany, University of North Carolina Library, Chapel Hill, Historical Society of Pennsylvania, Philadelphia, Rhode Island Historical Society, Providence, Yale University Library, New Haven, and the University of Virginia Library, Charlottesville.

Of the many original papers consulted in an attempt to understand Ames's times, certain sources were especially fruitful. Economic and political phases of contemporary life in Massachusetts were brought out in the Papers of Henry Knox, David Cobb, and Harrison Gray Otis. In the Warren Family Papers, Mercy Otis Warren's sprightly letters displayed an aristocrat's resistance to the Federalists in her analysis of current affairs; all are in the Massachusetts Historical Society. The George Thatcher Papers, Boston Public Library, the Loring Andrews Letters, Houghton Library of the Harvard College Library, and the Papers of William Eustis and Elbridge Gerry, Library of Congress, extended the picture of Massachusetts Federalism. Still other collections were rewarding in the areas of national politics, congressional activity, and American foreign relations. Particularly helpful were the Gouverneur Morris Papers, Columbia University, New York City, the Jeremiah Wadsworth Papers, Connecticut Historical Society, the William Plumer Papers, Library of Congress, and the Papers of George Clymer, Thomas Fitzsimmons, and Jasper Yeates, Historical Society of Pennsylvania. The Papers of James Madison, Harry Innes, Henry Tazewell, and Levin Powell in the Library of Congress disclosed southern reactions toward national events in the period 1789-1800.

Additional documentary records, both published and unpublished, provided details fundamental to an interpretation of events. The Harvard University Archives in Cambridge, Massachusetts, contain the Records of Harvard College, the Faculty Records, and the Records of the Board of Overseers. Pertinent volumes of these records shed light on the college, its faculty, and the student body during Ames's years at Harvard. Filed in the Massachusetts Archives, State Capitol, Boston, the manuscript Journal of the House of Representatives supplied facts about the Massachusetts General Court during the late 1780's. Both the Abstracts of Votes for Governor and the Abstracts of Votes for Federal Representatives, also in the Massachusetts Archives, provided data on elections. The records of the Massachusetts Ratifying Convention of 1788 appear in *Debates, Resolutions and Other Proceedings of the Convention* (Boston, 1788), and also in Jonathan Elliot, ed., *The Debates in the ... State Conventions on the ... Federal Constitution* (Philadelphia, 1836-59). Judge Theophilus Parsons's journal during the convention is printed in B. K. Peirce and C. Hale, eds., *Debates and Proceedings in the Convention of the Commonwealth of Massachusetts ... 1788* (Boston, 1856). Reports of the debates in Congress were of uneven quality and at times were far from verbatim. In spite of many deficiencies, the *Debates and Proceedings in the Congress of the United States*, edited by Joseph Gales (Washington, 1834-1856), were indispensable. This compilation, known as the *Annals*, was supplemented by reference to the printed *Journal of the House of Representatives of the United States* (Washington, 1826), *Journal of the Senate of the United States, Being the First Session of the Second Congress ... 1791-1792* (Philadelphia, 1792), the *Journal of the Senate of the United States* (Washington, 1820), and to newspapers such as John Fenno's *Gazette of the United States* (New York and Philadelphia), which carried transcriptions of many of the debates in Congress.

The newspapers of Ames's day, often vitriolic and polemical, focused principally on political issues. Among the numerous Boston newspapers in the late eighteenth and early nineteenth centuries, three were especially influential. The *Columbian Centinel*, though stanchly Federalist, in Ames's view did not always give the party adequate support because its editor, Benjamin Russell, preferred "a joke to an argument." The *Boston Gazette*, founded in 1719, remained a vital force in the community until it ceased publication in 1798. Politically it leaned to the Democratic Republicans although occasionally it supported the Federalist party. The *Independent Chronicle*, the "lying Chronicle" to Federalists, was vehemently pro-Jeffersonian and pro-French. In Philadelphia, Philip Freneau challenged Federalist papers with the brisk *National Gazette* for a brief period, 1791-93. At a later time Benjamin F. Bache's Philadelphia *Aurora* subjected the Federalists to scathing attacks. The *Gazette of the United States* (New York and Philadelphia) was staid journalistically and expressed the official Federalist position. Some other newspapers which were utilized as sources of fact and opinion were the *Herald of Freedom* (Boston), the *Massachusetts Mercury* (Boston) and its successor, the *New England Palladium* (Boston), the *Repertory* (Boston), the *Columbian Minerva* and the *Norfolk Repository*, both of Dedham.

For this book the standard editions of the writings of such leading public figures as John Adams, Alexander Hamilton, Thomas Jefferson, James Madison, and George Washington were used. In cases where these editions were not comprehensive, the original manuscripts or microfilm copies were consulted. Published letters of other, less prominent individuals were also useful. Examples of these collections are: J. F. Jameson, ed., "Letters of Stephen Higginson, 1783-1804," American Historical Association, *Annual Report for 1896* (Washington, 1897), I; Joseph M. Beatty, "The Letters of Judge Henry Wynkoop, Representative From Pennsylvania to the First Congress of the United States," *Pennsylvania Magazine of History and Biography*, 38 (1914), 39-64, 183-205; and Lyman H. Butterfield, ed., *The Letters of Benjamin Rush* (Princeton, 1951).

Diaries and journals should not be overlooked in this discussion of sources. The incisive diary kept by Dr. Nathaniel Ames revealed his own personality and his relationship to his brilliant brother, as well as elements of village life in eastern Massachusetts. It has been partially published in the volumes of the *Dedham Historical Register*. Charles Warren in his *Jacobin and Junto* (Cambridge, Mass., 1931) also used the diary as the basis for his book. *In toto* published extracts do not constitute a definitive edition of Dr. Ames's daybook. Vital to any analysis of congressional business between 1789 and 1792 is the Journal of William Maclay. The volumes in the Manuscript Division, Library of Congress, are preferable to the published editions. Several diaries, frequently with terse entries, made obvious the milieu in which Ames lived. The Diary of the Reverend Jason Haven, American Antiquarian Society, dealt with Dedham affairs between 1769 and 1796 and Samuel Chandler's Diary, Harvard University Archives, sketched college life at Harvard in the early 1770's. The *Diary and Autobiography of John Adams*, edited by Lyman H. Butterfield (Cambridge, Mass., 1961), supplied essential information on the state of the legal profession and the study of law on the eve of the American Revolution. Other diaries and journals of importance were Nathaniel Cutting, "Extracts from a Journal of a Gentleman Visiting Boston in 1792," Massachusetts Historical Society, *Proceedings*, 12 (1873), 60-67; Franklin B. Dexter, ed., *Extracts from the Itineraries . . . of Ezra Stiles . . . with a Selection from his Correspondence* (New Haven, 1916), and John F. Whiting, ed., "Diary of John Whiting of Dedham, Mass., June 1743-May 1784," *New England Historical and Genealogical Register*, 63 (1909), 185-92, 261-65.

Limitations of space preclude naming the many historians and biographers whose works, whether books or articles, were examined in preparing this biography. Footnote citations acknowledge my debt to a number of these scholars; yet I am also indebted to others not mentioned.

Index